Writer's Companion

Carlos J Cortés & Renée Miller

ISBN:0987811207
ISBN-13:9780987811202

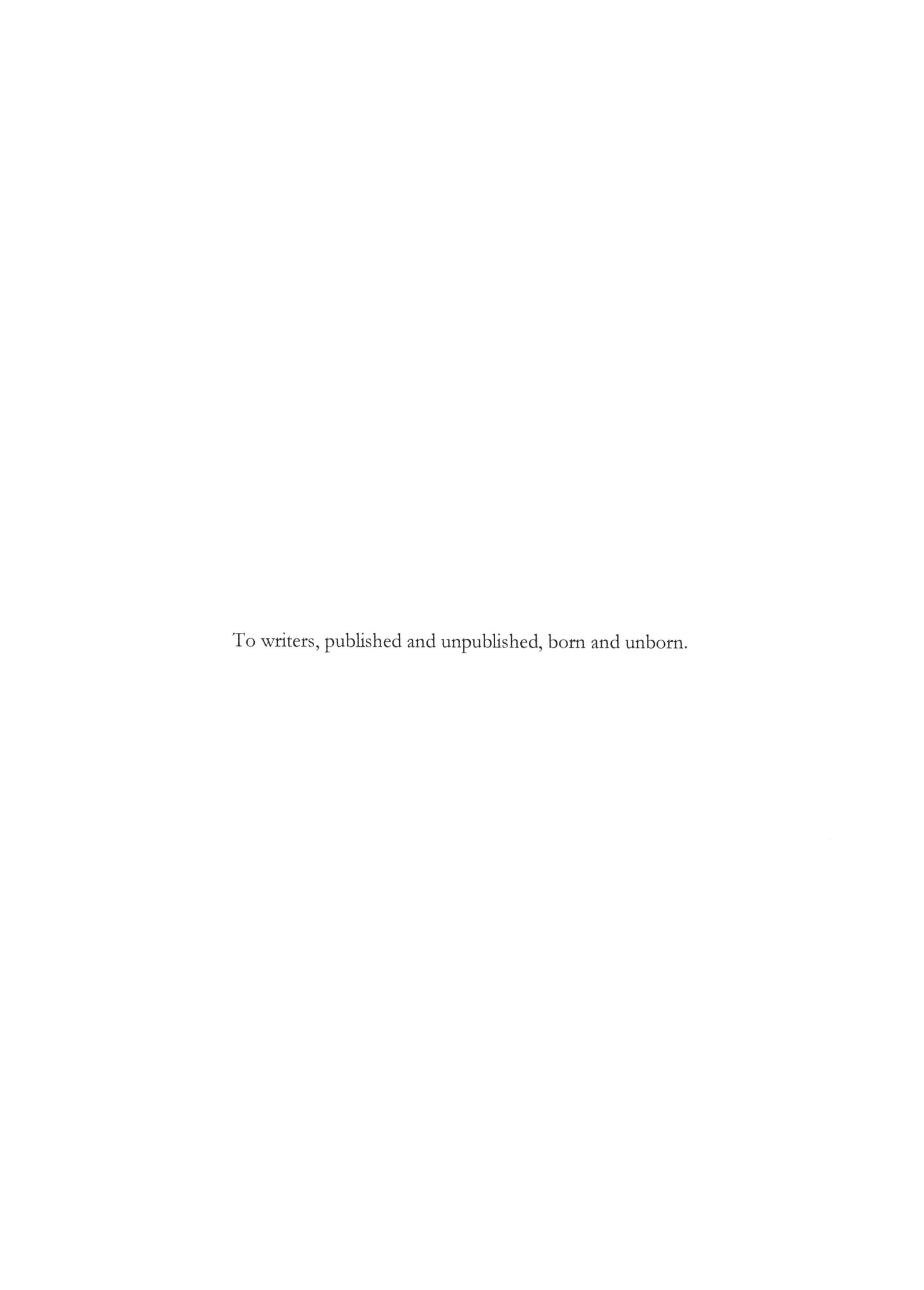

To writers, published and unpublished, born and unborn.

PREFACE

Prefaces must have a reason. They are not an author's self-absorbed ramblings about the awesomeness of his or her mad skills. This preface has several reasons that answer time-honored questions. Why this book? Why now? Why these authors?

Let's get the first question out of the way. Why this book?

Everything has a beginning. Ideas are no exception. The concept for this book began with a wistful breath held in a clenched fist, and that breath set the dice in motion. The idea crystallized during a transatlantic telephone conversation between Renée (the long) and Carlos (the short).

Though spanning two continents—and separated by an ocean—our shared bookshelf of creative writing texts grew and grew to ridiculous extent. Our repository was magnificent, chockablock with scores of books on characterization, POV, pace, dialogue, etc. The problem wasn't a paucity of information, but too much of it spread over so many volumes that finding anything was a nightmare. Does our dilemma ring a bell?

So in answer to the first question: Writer's Companion sprang from despair.

After our fortuitous exchange, we made discreet inquiries among our friends at various writer haunts and learned that we weren't unique in our frustration. Many writers shared a similar complaint: fragmented information forces writers to own tens of books, each touching only a narrow subject or technique. Of course, there's the Internet and millions of pages dealing with every possible theme, but the problem remains. The information is scattered all over the place, the very nature of which is sometimes contradictory and often structured in ways designed to confuse rather than enlighten. Thus, we set out to compile everything a creative writer needs to write well into a single reference volume.

But these are practical reasons to justify contents. Our primary goal, the ethos of this book, is to help other writers succeed.

Times are a-changing. As the Publishing Industry groans under a mighty shake up, new markets crop up like weeds and the tried and tested policies don't work anymore. Publishers, who used to dedicate large portions of their budget and time to polish manuscripts, have had to cut expenses to the bone by paring down their once abundant rosters of copy editors. As a result, manuscripts need to be print-ready to have any chance of publication, which in turn demands from the writer considerable technical skills.

In a market awash with millions of poorly written—and horribly edited—manuscripts seeking a place to roost, agents and publishers have closed ranks to a point where a writer must have not only superhuman abilities but also be willing to run a vicious gauntlet to have a reasonable chance of publishing traditionally.

With this book, we seek to give other writers the tools, weapons, and skills to negotiate the Caudine Forks[1] of the Publishing Industry. And survive with a smile at the end.

Why now? Besides the exponential growth of the Internet, globalized commerce, new consumer rights, and trading laws have fueled an unprecedented thirst for professional writing services. Though the volume of printed media remains unchanged, calls for content have soared, and with them, the need for creative writers. In turn, the market demands resources and tools to simplify the writing process while adding value and punch to prose. Writer's Companion fulfills these needs.

In a competitive society where clear and accurate information can mark the difference between success and failure, creative writers are in ever-increasing demand, and will continue to be in the near future. At least that's the overwhelming consensus of experts the world over.

At this point, our readers may frown. "Hang on a minute... this book is about writing fiction, novels, and stuff. No?" Yes. But the underlying concepts of fiction writing are equally applicable to all walks of creative writing. There are mechanical differences between writing news copy, contents for an Internet e-zine, or an article about Blue Tits[2], but the core techniques—the basics—are the same.

Why these authors? Because over the past ten years we've done little else except learning the hard way everything contained in this book. We've attended courses, endured many rejections, and between us published several novels and short stories, composed hundreds of articles, edited and reviewed thousands of manuscripts, and sold millions of words to paying markets.

Above all, we are mongrel writers, and that alone gives us the moral right to compile this book. We wanted to put together a book that would be useful to us and our harassed kin: other mongrel writers. In our opinion, a book on writing penned by one of the household names who monopolize the NYT Bestsellers List wouldn't be of much use to us. These thoroughbreds learned the craft (those who did) a long time ago and are used to being fussed over, groomed, vaccinated, deloused, and taken for walkies by agents, publishers, and editors. We, however, are there, on the street, under railway bridges, in mole-infested and unheated garages, and in vacant lots, burning the midnight oil in the company of other mongrel scribes because writing is our passion. We don't wear a tag or belong to any posh kennel club, but we have never forgotten our origins, or how to enjoy a good scratch.

Barcelona (Spain) and Tweed (Ontario; Canada) September 2011

Carlos J Cortés & Renée Miller

---

[1] The Caudine Forks is a narrow mountain pass in Italy, where the Samnites defeated the Romans in 321 BCE. So far, this snippet of history is not extraordinary; one can't hope to win every battle. But this particular defeat was unique. History books hint at the Samnites "forcing the Romans to pass under the yoke," but don't elaborate. The Romans, without weapons or clothes, were encouraged to negotiate their way to freedom through the yoke—a spear held horizontally between two warriors at waist height—whereupon the Samnites sodomized them.

[2] We mean *cyanistes caeruleus*, of course.

ACKNOWLEDGMENTS

Once we had the first draft of the Companion in our hands we realized that, like our works of fiction, this book wasn't even close to being publishable. We needed other sets of eyes that could rip our baby to pieces. We attempted it ourselves, but no writer can edit his or her own work effectively. Besides, this project had two writers—two passionate writers...

Who would want to pore over countless articles on the craft of writing, grammar, or punctuation? Who would care to spend valuable time offering suggestions, pointing out typos, and arguing over the little details we never thought might be arguable?

We fattened the coffers of Skype owners across the ocean, plotting, scheming, and despairing of ever getting this book polished enough to publish. We discussed who had enough knowledge to decipher our ramblings and who might be willing to try. When we hit the bottle (it was half-hidden in the sand), a most accommodating genie made the customary offer and we grabbed it. Soon, we were surrounded by mongrel writers of such boundless talent and enthusiasm that it was only a matter of time before our work became their work. Without these people, who we're lucky enough to call friends, the Companion would still be a draft that only the bravest of souls would dare attempt to read.

Michael Keyton, with his acerbic English wit kept our spirits high (distance prevented him from keeping us high on spirits), while Paul Mitton, the Welsh ogre, kept us on our toes endlessly tweaking our wandering prose. Wendy Swore often honored her surname and worked overtime posing endless questions and demanding answers that tested our ingenuity. Down Under, Deb Cawley lost her house in a hurricane, but found a spot among the rubble to continue writing, and reviewing thousands of pages; showing without telling the meaning of courage. Luis Cano ranted, complained, bitched, and designed the cover and much more. Through our trials, we were often scourged by Rita and T. J. Webb who wrote, read, beta-tested, and fought through their alligator-infested backyard to meet our deadlines.

Of course, all self-respecting slaves need a driver, and Donna Johnson loves to wield her whip disguised as a red pen. Our collective backs are raw, but we're used to pain, else we wouldn't be writers.

Thank you all, for sharing both your talent and your time to make our shared dream possible.

In addition, our heartfelt thanks to the 1400 members of On Fiction Writing, all of whom provided the inspiration for The Writer's Companion.

"Appreciation is a wonderful thing. It makes what is excellent in others belong to us as well." - Voltaire

CONTENTS

1 THE NUTS & BOLTS

We learn to write at an early age. As a follow-up to expressing ourselves with sounds, we add to our communication capabilities by setting strings of symbols on paper. Then, by the time we reach puberty, most of us can scribble the sensations stored in our minds.

In this sense, to communicate ideas and convey information, every literate person is a writer. Ask a boy to write about his birthday party, and he might come up with:

> "I had lots of presents a big gun from granpa but mom was angry and my friend has a mouse and we ~~eat~~ ate cake with soda an we went to the cinema and dad got popcorn and candy."

The young man shows promise. We understand that Mom blew a fuse when Grandpa unveiled an AK47 replica, but otherwise the boy had a whale of a time. Likewise, if we were to ask a high school student to comment about inefficient governments, he might write:

> "In our country, the school system is as deficient as the sanitation, while the army, bureaucracy, police, and intelligence agencies grow out of all proportion."

The sentence is clear, well structured, and concise: without flab. It conveys precise information: Governments don't provide quality services to their citizens and use the money instead to expand their power.

We would class the student's sentence as good writing. But good writing is not creative writing.

Among our reader friends, a few have university degrees in language or literature. They write well. Without syntactic or spelling mistakes, they structure correct sentences to convey complex thoughts and concepts. But none of them would ever consider writing a novel or short story. Why? Because being a good writer is a precondition, the starting point to *learn* creative writing.

Creative writing is damn hard. In the U.S. alone, there are literary agents, editors, and English professors by the thousands. It should be a sobering thought for anybody reading this book to enumerate (with the fingers of one hand) how many have written a passable piece of fiction.

Here in the Companion, the Nuts & Bolts chapter contains the basic elements of inner structure and technique to transmute common language into fiction prose. From the structural framework of the most common forms of fiction, we explore the skeleton that sustains and gives form to the different parts of a novel—the first step in our journey to bridge the chasm that separates common writing from fiction writing.

The imaginary high school student, who could have written the sentence we discussed in the opening example, used the language to relay information and state ideas. But a creative writer would have added an intangible to paint images and sensations in the reader's mind. One of the finest craftsmen of the pen ever, expressed the same idea with a magical choice of words:

> "While the small feeding bottle of our education is nearly dry, and sanitation sucks its own thumbs in despair, the military organization, the magisterial offices, the police, the Criminal Investigation Department, the secret spy system, attain to an abnormal girth in their waists, occupying every inch of our country."[3]

---

[3] Rabindranath Tagore, Nationalism.

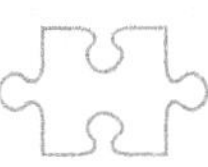 1.1 FRAMEWORK / ELEMENTS

 1.1.1 PROSE

Prose is simply the language we use to communicate in both speech and writing. It has a loose structure and is the usual form we use in fiction, newspapers, magazines, film, television, broadcasting, and most other communications. "Prose" comes from the Latin word *prosa*, which means "straightforward."

Verse is the only other form of written or spoken language available to humans. Unlike prose, verse has a formal structure, usually of meter and/or rhyme. Elements of prose and verse combine in prose poetry and free verse, where the writer relaxes or omits the metrical structure and versification rules. Hence, poetry is systematic and formulaic, whereas prose mirrors speech.

In writing, we can only express ourselves in prose or poetry, a point exemplified in this conversation between Monsieur Jourdain and an anonymous philosophy master in *Le Bourgeois Gentilhomme* by Moliére:

> Monsieur Jourdain: ...I'm in love with a lady of great quality, and I wish that you would help me write something to her in a little note that I will let fall at her feet.
> Philosophy Master: Very well.
> Monsieur Jourdain: That will be gallant, yes?
> Philosophy Master: Without doubt. Is it verse that you wish to write her?
> Monsieur Jourdain: No, no. No verse.
> Philosophy Master: Do you want only prose?
> Monsieur Jourdain: No, I don't want either prose or verse.
> Philosophy Master: It must be one or the other.
> Monsieur Jourdain: Why?
> Philosophy Master: Because, sir, there is no other way to express oneself than with prose or verse.
> Monsieur Jourdain: There is nothing but prose or verse?
> Philosophy Master: No, sir, everything that is not prose is verse, and everything that is not verse is prose.
> Monsieur Jourdain: And when one speaks, what is that then?
> Philosophy Master: Prose.

The levels of prose are difficult to define because their boundaries nebulous. Most of us write informal prose. Literary prose aspires to create art with language, character studies, and representations of reality.

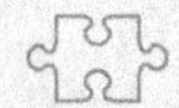

1.1.2 NARRATIVE

The word "narrative" derives from the Latin verb *narrare*, to recount, and comprises the unique set of tools of the storyteller. With these, the writer can organize a story to relate a sequence of fictional or non-fictional events.

The soul of narration is the mode, or the set of communication methods encompassing not only how the story is described or expressed but also the identity of the narrator.

Stories have been with us since the dawn of time, and the storyteller was the first educator and entertainer. Every ancient culture, be it Indian, Chinese, Egyptian, or Greek used storytelling to transmit lessons, legends, exploits, and memories.

Imagine a cave with a large hearth hemmed with stones, a roaring fire, dancing shadows on the walls, a varied group of listeners, and the voice of the storyteller.

> "When night arrived, Auk curled under an overhang. 'Mountain gods be merciful and show me a spring, for without water I will surely die.' Hungry, thirsty, and exhausted, Auk wrapped his bear pelt around him and fell asleep."

After delivering Auk's lines in a querulous voice, our master storyteller alters his countenance, changes his stance, puffs up his chest, casts a fierce glance at the audience, and bangs his staff on the ground.

> "'Who is this?' Tabor, god of the mountain, flew from the heights and roared at Auk's sleeping form."

In his narrative performance, our storyteller has used every tool of the trade to convey the plot to his audience: tense, point-of-view, structure, and voice. Our prehistoric storyteller and modern writers have the same narrative tools at their disposal—these and no others.

The narrative tense reveals the sense of time in a story, whether the events happened in the past, belong to the present, or will take place in the future.

The narrative point of view (POV) determines the perspective from which the story is told, perhaps that of an independent narrator, an all-seeing perspective, or a character or characters within the story.

The narrative structure controls the order in which the narrator lays down the events.

The narrative voice shapes how the narrator conveys the story and how the audience receives it.

In fiction writing, narrative is storytelling that communicates to the reader. The narrator can be a character created by the writer for the sole purpose of telling the story. He can be a non-participant, an omniscient voice that relates only to the reader. Most modern fiction, however, relies on the characters to narrate the story, hence the importance of tight viewpoint control.

1.1.3 MODE

Fiction is prose with distinct forms of expression, each with different purposes and conventions. These forms of expression are called "delivery modes."

Experts disagree about the numbers of delivery modes and the role of each, and to date there's no consensus. Some schools list action, exposition, description, dialogue, summary, and transition; others prefer action, summary, dialogue, feelings/thoughts, and background; others still advocate action, dialogue, thoughts, summary, scene, and description.

We agree with the first list since thoughts are an integral part of dialogue, while we can include background in exposition or description. Thus, we have chosen the delivery modes:

Action

Exposition

Description

Dialogue

Summary

Transition.

 ### 1.1.3.1 ACTION

Action is the description of events as they happen, chronologically, in a linear fashion, or with actions presented through flashbacks or flash forwards in a non-linear form. The action follows the story and one of its roles is to immerse readers in the plot. Some writers rely heavily on action as the main technique to carry a story through (Clive Cussler). Some favor characterization and description (Albert Camus). Still others blend action and description in their work (John Le Carré).

 ### 1.1.3.2 EXPOSITION

A writer uses exposition to convey facts, establish place, add color, and relate past events.

Stories are fragments of reality, limited in time and location, which seldom take place in a vacuum. Often, a writer needs to introduce background information, history, or the character's routine for the story to make sense.

Naturally, the amount of exposition is relative to genre and place. A writer considering a story set in Antarctica needs to acquaint urban readers with the difficulties of surviving the most inhospitable place on earth. The more unusual the setting (unusual to the target reader) the more exposition the writer needs in order to paint the scenes. Science fiction, fantasy, and works dealing with unusual social conditions, groups, or environments require well-developed exposition.

Since too much exposition at one time slows story pacing, dosing it out and embedding parts of it in with other modes creates one of the most challenging tasks a writer must face. The section "Exposition," in pages 116-118, explores a number of techniques for this judicious dosing.

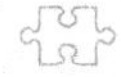 ### 1.1.3.3 DESCRIPTION

Description is often confused with exposition. While exposition deals in facts, history, and events, description is the mode for transmitting mental images of the story. It engages the reader's senses with choice and arrangement of words, bringing scenes to life.

As an example of the difference:

Exposition: Bernini's Cesar in Drag, a monumental marble statue brought at great expense from Carrara in Tuscany, Italy—a city bathed by the Carrione River, some 62 miles west-northwest of Florence—commanded a central position in the cemetery.

One would expect that Bernini's authorship of the statue and the excruciating geographical detail surrounding Carrara, would be crucial to the story. Otherwise, readers may be annoyed.

Description: The cemetery looked bleak and dark, as any cemetery should at midnight.

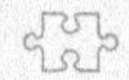 **1.1.3.4 DIALOGUE**

To exchange information between characters and to express thoughts, writers use dialogue delivery modes. Dialogue can portray conversation between two or more characters or it can be used to reveal introspection, also referred to as internal dialogue, to give the reader insight into the unexpressed thoughts or feelings of the characters.

> "Are you willing?"
> "Need you ask?"
> "Able?"
> "You bet..."
> "The fence needs mending."

In most works of fiction, dialogue plays a critical role in plot and characterization. Writers will agree it's a difficult mode to master. Though we use dialogue everyday in our exchanges, writing it is another matter. What we would actually say or think has little to do with the way our characters should express themselves.

> *Dialogue, contrary to popular view, is not a recording of actual speech; it is a semblance of speech, an invented language of exchanges that builds in tempo or content toward climaxes.*[4]

Summary

To summarize is to condense the story. This delivery mode skips people, details, places, and events that are irrelevant to the main plot. It condenses timelines, connects diverse parts of the story, and skims over points that, although important to the tale, only need a brief mention.

A writer working on the story of an Irish immigrant, might need to dedicate several chapters to the ocean crossing, and several more on the harrowing passage of third class passengers through Ellis Island, but only if these issues are germane to the story. Otherwise, a paragraph of summary, opening in Cork and closing in New York, would suffice.

Transition

A story revealed on a chronological continuum would be mind numbing. Imagine writing a story framed within a week and describing every minute of these seven days. No doubt, there would be key events interspersed to shape the plot, but most of the time characters would be waiting, eating, sleeping, taking a shower, or dressing. While these instances may compose the backdrop of plot points,

---

[4] Sol Stein

the writer will need to skip over most of them. For this, transitions do the work. These are words, phrases, sentences, paragraphs, and punctuation that mark changes in time, storyline, location, or POV, to skip over the mundane and get on with the story.

To handle transition, the writer uses section and chapter breaks, dialogue, flashes, summary, and introspection, among other resources. Transition also links, or paves the way, for a new paragraph, new setting, or new chapter so that even great leaps in time or place make sense.

In the excerpt that follows, the writer needed to prepare the set for a transition, a flashback, a technique we'll review on pages 125 to 126.

> Jolene stood at the sagging screen door. Shaking her head she sighed and turned. She'd spoiled the girl, and now it would be difficult to make her see that sometimes in life you had to take a few lumps. Not everyone had the opportunity to live a life full of fine things. Some would pay more than Rowan had to. Far more. The pain in her chest distracted her for a moment. Taking short breaths until it passed, she lay down on the lumpy couch.
> By early afternoon, the heat would make breathing harder and she would need her strength when Rosaline's man arrived and she had to drag her daughter back. Perhaps she should have arranged for him to take her when Henri finished. No matter. Rowan could only have run to one place, and Jolene was not afraid to go after her, black magic or no.
> Closing her eyes, she wandered back in time. Where had she gone wrong? At what point did she lose control?[5]

Transition is an important delivery mode neglected by many writers, until they discover that pace, tension, and story flow, all depend on the use of transitional elements.

---

[5] Renée Miller, Bayou Baby

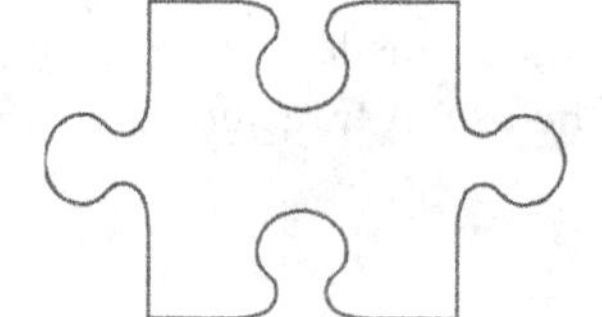

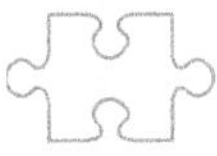# 1.2 FRAMEWORK / THE NOVEL

Every novel is a structure with layers, like an onion.

There's a conceptual plan for the story, with actors peopling a series of events:

> The villain captures a damsel. Enters the lovesick hero who kills the villain and elopes with the damsel into the sunset.

We have a protagonist (the damsel or the hero) an antagonist (the villain) a conflict (which is vital!), a climax (or outcome of the conflict), and a resolution.

The second layer is organizational. We need to marshal the events into chunks we'll call scenes, further arranged into larger bites we'll call chapters.

The next layer is technical and comprises scores of issues: characterization, setting, plot, pace, POV, atmosphere, etc.

The final layer is the law. There are rules to obey, conventions to follow, usages to hone, and formats to respect.

But we've left out the most important layer, the one that supersedes the others in importance. How must a novel *work* to succeed? What do readers *demand* from a novel? Notice that genre, plot, contents, and characterization are secondary at this point, for the primary essential is the intangible capacity to satisfy a reader.

Perhaps we can use an example from Carlos's childhood. He recalls that when he was young tables were different.

How can that be? A table is a table: a round, oval, or square flat board on legs.

Yes, a table is a table, but its use changes with time which, in turn, alters its shape, and even its soul. The writer penning these lines remembers that in his infancy tables were *exclusively* round.

They had a round top, four legs, and another flat board attached to the legs three or four inches above the floor. This second board had an eighteen-inch round hole in its middle. A thick cloth was draped over the top of the table, and it dangled all the way to the floor. A brazier of burning charcoal fitted in the hole. The family sat around the table and arranged the cloth so the legs would benefit from the brazier's warmth. Tables *needed* to be round; else, those sitting at it wouldn't have equal access to the brazier.

The use of the table was also different. We had no television, central heating, or even much food. We had a radio. So, the family sat at an empty table to keep their legs warm, listen to the radio, and forget their rumbling stomachs.

Fiction writing has shared the changes of that table remembered from childhood. Books are still rectangular, with numbered pages, chapter divisions, and lines of letters printed in them. There the similarities stop. Novel structure and its very soul are not the same. Whether we view the changes as evolution or involution depends on the way we understand the world we live in.

The table changed because its users changed, as a consequence of social pressures. People no longer gather around a table unless it's laden with food. Although, in many households the table is only used on special occasions, its owners preferring a tray on the couch or standing around the new kitchen's totem: the fridge.

We're not suggesting that cinema and TV stole the table's soul, but it certainly recast the way we read.

A fiction book is a commodity. As such, it's governed by the same forces that shape other market products: purpose, fashion, and usability.

Our first concern is to determine what the reader expects. We're not referring to contents—which we'll discuss later—but usability. Failing to take usability into account results in books nobody wants to read.

"But my novel is fantastic; the plot is awesome and the writing... move over Virginia Woolf!" a disgruntled writer might cry after the umpteenth rejection. This may be, but perhaps the novel's framework and conceptual structure doesn't fulfill the reader's expectation of what a fiction work *should* be. Our writer will rave about literary merits and characterization and a devilishly clever storyline while the manuscript gathers dust.

We propose a simple experiment. Imagine a novel about shape-shifters, the Roman Empire, or the antics of a platypus named Daisy. The plot is unimportant but the genre is. Browse through a film library or check what's available on cable, or rent a film from a supplier. The film must be of the same genre as that of your intended novel.

Settle down before the screen with a handy clock. Check the time and start the film. Don't bother about color, setting, décor, the heroine's legs, or the hero's abs. Concentrate on the moment when the action starts. Analyze the moment conflict sets in, the moment the film hooks you. It may be an explosion, a passionate glance, burned toast, or an alien bursting from an egg and fastening to a spaceman's helmet. Glance at the clock.

If the film was any good, the minute hand will have moved fewer than ten times. Ten minutes. That's the time a scriptwriter has to hook his audience.

Next, imagine discovering a film where the conflict doesn't set in for twenty minutes. Again, settle before the TV but gather a few friends and family. Instead of watching the screen, analyze the body language of those watching. Observe fidgeting, pouting mouths, furrowing foreheads or, (horror of horrors!) drooping eyelids. Glance at the clock.

Restlessness and danger signs of disinterest will have set in around the ten-minute mark.

Films and TV have changed the way we assimilate narrative. In bygone times, before readers watched TV and traveled wide, a writer spent thousands of words outlining setting, background, and atmosphere to immerse the reader in a given world. Now, thirty-seconds of imagery will convey the same effect.

Characterization remains unchanged. The reader needs time to learn what makes someone tick, to understand her goals, her motivations, and the conflicts she's likely to face because of personality. However, it is unnecessary to provide the painstaking description of unblemished skin or the silk petticoat with tucks at the waist, ruffles, and a dainty appliqué of Rosaline on an organza bustier that a film can accomplish in a single image. Description should reveal character and not exist for its own sake.

We live in a world that *expects* instant gratification, instant communication, and instant thrills. In a couple of hours, films deliver a barrage of images and sounds painstakingly engineered to keep the viewer's gaze riveted on the screen. Unfortunately, readers *expect* to gather a similar experience from a book. The medium is different but the writer must telescope time and configure the prose to sustain the reader's immersion. In many ways, holding a reader is far harder to accomplish than keeping a movie watcher seated before a screen. A writer must conjure images from words without the benefit of film and projection equipment. Simple words must sustain the same level of interest to compete. Furthermore, the writer knows (or must know) that the reader will stop somewhere, perhaps at the end of a chapter, to go to sleep, do the next chore, or get off the bus for work. He may not return to the novel for a day or a week. When this happens, the writer must hook his reader *again*.

The first layer of our onion structure addresses the shape of the novel's cardiogram, its crests, valleys and spikes, its rhythm and beat. We can no longer start with a flat reading, or else the patient may never recover.

In 2005, Noah Lukeman, a literary agent with a towering reputation, wrote *The First Five Pages: A Writer's Guide to Staying Out of the Rejection Pile*. The title says it all: Five pages is all we have to ensnare our reader, though we must confess Mr. Lukeman is an inveterate optimist when it comes to the astringent evaluation process of manuscripts from unknown writers. Often, the first five paragraphs, or sentences, or even clauses, will send a manuscript to the trash can.

Before we begin structuring our new project, before we condense a nebulous concept into the sentence that will start it all, and before creating the characters that will bring our plot to life, we must think of the outer onion layer. We must acknowledge that the reader expects immersion from the moment he opens the book, and structure the manuscript accordingly—from page one.

Novel structure pre-planning

Our first task is to set the tone of the story: solemn or animated, comic or tragic. This must occur in the first paragraph.

The reader *wants* to know the identity of the narrator. Who is telling the story? Who is talking? In whose head does she find herself? Unless we are writing in cinematic POV, we have the first couple of paragraphs in which to plant the POV and give the reader perspective.

The reader *needs* a platform: Where are we? What season? Who are these people? We have ten, perhaps twenty lines to establish the background.

Readers (and agents and editors) want to know what's at stake right away. Opening a novel with exposition is risky. It can be done, as many successful writers can confirm, but they probably knew what they were doing or relied on an adoring fan base to accept it. We must root plot and conflict within the first five pages.

> "But I need to establish lots of background leading up to the first moments of overt conflict!"

Perhaps, but a novel—and to qualify as such—must have a certain length, usually eighty thousand words or more. There's plenty of space for exposition and detail. We can fill in the background later, perhaps with a flashback in chapter two or, better yet, dosing it out over the following chapters.

Wherever we turn, the bellhops of exception carry on about some writer who does things differently, or they'll denounce a novel that starts with twenty pages of exposition and sells zillions. There are flukes, and there's no good reason to imitate them, for the real world is more pragmatic and cruel. The blurb on the jacket promises a payoff, and the reader expects to cash it in from the first page. That's reality.

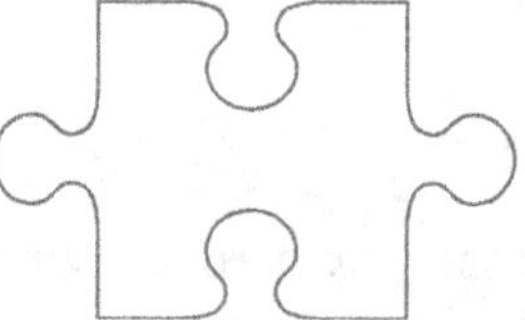

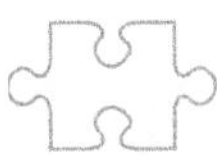

1.3 FRAMEWORK / OTHER FORMATS

Besides the novel, there are many additional fiction narrative formats. The most salient formats include: Novella, Novelette, Short Story, Flash Fiction, and New Sudden Fictions.

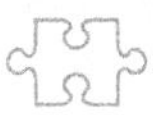

1.3.1 NOVELLA

A novella is prose fiction that is longer than a long story but shorter than a short novel. Its length ranges from 20,000 to 50,000 words. Word count, however, doesn't define the novella. The essence of the novella is the concentrated unity of purpose and design. Character, incident, theme, and language all focus on a single issue, often of a serious nature or of universal significance.

The events of the novella turn around a single incident, problem, or issue, without subplots or parallel actions. A limited number of principal characters, perhaps only one or two, populate the story, and the events often take place in one location.

Artistically, the novella is often unified by powerful symbols.

Examples of this genre include Henry James's *The Turn of the Screw* (1897), Thomas Mann's *Death in Venice* (1912), Herman Melville's *Billy Budd* (1856), and Joseph Conrad's *Heart of Darkness* (1902).

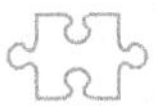

1.3.2 NOVELETTE

The novelette, like the true short story, features originality of theme and ingenuity of invention, but it's not restricted to the short story word count.

It shares the same structural characteristics as the novella—character, incident, theme, plot, and setting. The distinction between a novelette and a novella is word count. A novelette ranges from 7,500 to 20,000 words.

Examples of this genre are: Robert Louis Stevenson's *The Strange Case of Dr. Jekyll and Mr. Hyde* (1886), Henry James' *Daisy Miller* (1878), and Friedrich de la Motte Fouqué's *Undine* (1876).

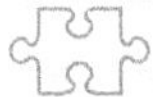

1.3.3 SHORT STORY

A short story is a work of prose, often in narrative format of limited extension.

Stating what separates a short story from longer fictional formats is problematic. A classic definition of a short story is that one should be able to read it in one sitting, although short story definitions based upon length differ. Since the short story format includes a wide range of genres and styles, the actual length is determined by the individual writer's preference (or the story's actual needs in terms of story arc), and the submission guidelines relevant to the target market. In contemporary usage, the term "short story" most often refers to a work of fiction from 1,000 to 7,500 words long.

Similar to the requirements of longer works, the five key elements that go into every great short story are character, setting, conflict, plot, and theme.

Some of the world's best examples of the short story are from nineteenth-century American writers: Washington Irving, Nathaniel Hawthorne, Edgar Allan Poe, Herman Melville, Mark Twain, and Stephen Crane. Turn-of-the-century writers O. Henry and Jack London also provided a foundation of superb story writing. Twentieth-century short story writers who have excelled in their craft have learned much from their predecessors.

1.3.4 FLASH FICTION

Flash fiction is a short work of prose, the accepted word count ranging mostly from 500-1000 words and containing all the classic story elements: protagonist, conflict, obstacles or complications, and resolution. The limited word count often forces some of these elements to remain unwritten, that is, hinted at or implied in the story line.

Very short fiction has been with us since antiquity, as reflected in Aesop and Phaedrus's fables.

Contemporary writers, such as Chekhov, Lovecraft, and Hemingway have bequeathed us splendid examples of this difficult form.

1.3.5 NEW SUDDEN FICTIONS

Termed New Sudden Fictions or Very Short Stories, are pieces of prose running from a couple of lines to a couple of pages. At fewer than five-hundred words, these works demand the painstaking attention to detail common in poetry. These narratives are different, not only because of their lack of space to fully develop a plot and characterization, but because they evoke a single idea or moment and have a reversal, often comic, in which the initial circumstances of the plot are transposed at the end.

Other terms, in addition to the older "short-short story" are flashfic, shortfic, ficlet, microfiction, drabble (exactly 100 words excluding its title), 69er (exactly 69 words excluding the title), or nanofiction (exactly 55 words). To qualify, these must be complete stories, with at least one character and a discernible plot. A six-word short-short allegedly penned by Ernest Hemingway is:

"For sale: baby shoes, never worn."

Though some elements are only implied, it has character, setting, conflict, plot, theme, beginning, middle, and end.

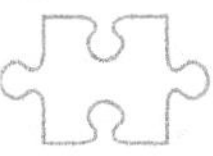# 1.4 STRUCTURE

This section discusses the plotting and structural tools to lay the framework of a genre fiction work. The extent to which a writer uses these is a matter of what works for him and the type of story he writes. Some character-driven novels need little or no outlining.

The question of whether to structure or not to structure has promoted rivers of ink and heated exchanges between the writers who structure, those who start with a blank page, and the great majority who do a little of each.

> *"Know the story—as much of the story as you can possibly know, if not the whole story—before you commit yourself to the first paragraph. Know the story—the whole story, if possible—before you fall in love with your first sentence, not to mention your first chapter."*[6]

Most problems in fiction writing stem from lack of structure. Floundering middle sections and dead ends, unworkable or silly or disjointed plots, writer's block and scores of other problems often are the result of poor planning—or no planning.

No sane scriptwriter would dream of settling down to write before diagramming the script. Novelists, likewise, have plans in some form or other. Written stories serve the same customers as films and TV—viewers and readers expect similar deliveries.

In real life, writers use structure for practical reasons: planning saves time and hundreds of pages of wasted words. A professional writer *can't afford* to suffer a block. To spend weeks or months writing without knowing where a story is going or how it will end is too frightening to contemplate. Diagramming key scenes or events of a story is a surefire way to see if the plot works.

Writers unwilling to invest time and effort to prepare a plan complain about the required complexity of a formal structure, when nothing could be further from the truth. A blueprint for a full novel might consist of a few lines scribbled on a scrap of paper, a page of notes, a synopsis, a spreadsheet, or a painstaking chapter and scene outline with character sheets. There are levels of structuring to suit every taste.[7]

Some authors swear by a story structure while others prefer to "wing it." This is understandable. The most technically demanding and difficult stages when writing a genre novel involve plotting the storyline and planning.

Writers are often eager to get to the actual writing and balk at doing the hard work first. We believe this is a myopic view.

---

[6] John Irving

[7] In *On Writing*, Stephen King, (who professes being an "off the cuff" writer), details the genesis of *Misery*. After having jotted a line or two in a cocktail napkin, he couldn't sleep. So he sought a quiet place and produced sixteen pages in longhand with the gist of the story. Perhaps we're using different words, but to us it reads very much like outlining.

Building a house is a monumental endeavor, perhaps the largest undertaking and investment of our lives. Men and machines enter the stage to lay down the concrete foundations. Once they finish, they cover up, cart away the excavated soil, disappear, and leave us with the sinking feeling of having paid a pile of cash while the lot looks as empty as before: no house.

Yet, we know that building a house without foundations and good drainage would be lunacy. Why any writer would insist on tackling stories without a foundation is beyond comprehension. And before the enraged voices of the cognoscenti cry from the wilderness, please, do not cite writers who eschew structures and produce technically perfect plots. They cheat. They work out the pattern in their minds and follow it up from there.

We would never suggest the layout must be on paper (though it helps) or a computer (though it's handy but risky if the data is not backed onto external devices). One can work out a novel outline and commit it to memory, and tweak it while riding a bus or mowing the backyard's jungle. We advocate a comprehensive structure, but the means of storage is up to the writer.

Some writers don't like plans; they cringe at the thought of knowing the full story beforehand. We would contend that writers *should know* the story beforehand. The great gurus of writing counsel to never write a single word without knowing the beginning, the end, and the plot points. Otherwise, what would one write about? Whatever comes to mind?

These writers complain that writing to a pattern is mechanical and hampers creativity. However, this need not be the case. A plot structure can have many levels, from loose to exhaustive, and nothing must be set in stone.

The writer can always alter it by introducing plot points; promoting secondary characters; or adding, removing, or altering scenes at will—and still retain full control of the plot. Even if the writer changes substantial parts of the story, a framework still helps because it's easier to get a clear picture of an entire novel if backed by good notes.

To write a story within a frame can be as creative as writing without it, but far more productive. For the professional, production is the key to success. Without a clear story line, good writing can often be wasted; sometimes paragraphs, passages, or even entire chapters must be discarded when they don't further the plot. Thus, we switch the creative plot building to a point before the actual writing. The writer plots the novel from beginning to end and expands each idea, concept, and scene during the writing phase.

By working to a layout, the writer can ensure that each key event or clue leads toward the ending. Without a good idea of where events will happen in the manuscript, the writer runs the risk of hitting dead ends, middle of the story blues, or the dreaded writer's block. These horrors can make the craft of writing unnecessarily hard.

With careful scaffolding, everything should contribute to the outcome of the novel, ensuring that the writing takes the writer closer to completion, saving steps, hardship, and frustration. Time building the structure is well spent.

But, how long? How complex? How comprehensive should a structure be?

Only the individual writer can answer these questions. There's no set length or level of complexity. Some writers will need one single page listing the opening, plot points, and ending. Others will want to add subplots and characters. Some will choose a scene structure and others will work from a synopsis.

In every case, a good structure should:

1. Contain a bird's-eye view of the plot.

2. Break the manuscript down into manageable chunks.

3. Keep track of the story beat.

Besides the unique idiosyncrasies of each writer, the genre also dictates the level of a novel's layout. Literary work may not require a detailed storyline, but for most commercial fiction, a structure is helpful.

Before committing the first sentence to paper, a writer should have an idea about the beginning, pivotal plot points of the story, and the end. Whether composed in the mind, on a screen, or on reams of paper is a matter of approach and personal preference.

Opening. A king sponsors a ball to find a wife for his son.

Plot point one. Girl's fairy godmother delivers a beautiful gown and glass slippers.

Midpoint or reversal. Girl and prince dance and fall in love.

Plot point two. The clock strikes twelve, and the girl loses a slipper.

Climax. Prince arrives with slipper. Sisters scorn the girl and try the slipper. Girl tries the slipper. It fits!

Ending. Girl and prince gallop into the sunset.

This is a full six-point structure in seventy-five words, and it provides the framework a writer needs to produce Cinderella.

In the next few pages we will explore in detail the structural tools for novels, though some aspects of these can be applied to plays, film scripts, and other fiction formats.

 **1.4.1 THREE-ACT STRUCTURE**

Aristotle defined structure and its principles in his Poetics. According to his definition, the classic linear plot has a beginning, middle, and ending. This inner structure is the underlying backbone that keeps the story moving forward. In diagram form, this structure is represented by a pyramid.

The beginning or Act One is critical. It gives readers a first glimpse into the story and often determines whether or not a prospective reader will buy the book. This act should introduce the characters and conflicts while setting the tone and mood for the rest of the story. Setting is important and if the fictional world differs from the real one, it should be detailed here. This should be a short act, limited to one-quarter or less of the novel's length.

The middle or Act Two usually begins with a complication, a point in the story where things go from bad to worse. Of the three, this act is most often overlooked. Many stories slow down toward the middle, perhaps because the writer didn't introduce enough complications. Traditionally, during this act, the hero's first plan will founder. In writing parlance, this is called the story midpoint and should cause a great change in the characters. This is the point where relationships fail, where the hero is captured, or the car runs out of gas. The key is that by the end of Act Two it should appear impossible for the protagonist to succeed. The climax, or high point of emotional intensity, follows, providing the moment of resolution.

The ending or Act Three is the wrap-up. The adventurer reaches the summit, the warrior fights his final battle, or the lovers find each other.

While the Three-Act Structure is a helpful organizing tool, it is not easy to use, in particular for those writers who don't know enough of their story before they start. A simple test to see if this is the right structure for a given story is for the writer to determine if he could write the ending first, knowing who the characters have become. From this point, the writer can plot backward to explain how the character got there, or became who he is.

No matter how much a writer may like or identify with the protagonist, the antagonist and the problems move the story forward. This is the key to the Three-Act Structure.

Act One: Create a problem for the main character.

Act Two: Make it worse or seemingly impossible to solve.

Act Three: Allow the character to discover the answer.

Follow these three steps and any story becomes interesting.

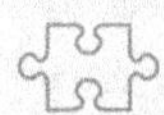

1.4.2 SIX-ACT STRUCTURE

The classic linear plot of beginning, middle, and ending, as evolved for novel writing, has six key scenes or points. 1. Opening; 2. Plot point one; 3. Midpoint or reversal; 4. Plot point two; 5. Climax; 6. Ending.

1. Opening. This is the character introduction and the set-up of conflict, setting, and background. Needless to say, it should start with fireworks and not with exposition or 'Once upon a time....' In *Alien*, this is the interval up to the moment where the crablike creature attaches to the astronaut's helmet.

2. Plot point one. This event concludes the beginning of the story and sets the rest of the plot in motion. Rather than the introduction of conflict, (it should have been introduced in 1) it's an event which moves the conflict forward. The opening of the story leads up to Plot Point 1, which carries the story into the midpoint or reversal. In *Alien*, this is the moment where the creature bursts from the wretched technician's belly.

3. Midpoint or reversal. Understanding the importance of this key element will help writers prevent a boring, foundering story middle—the dreaded middle-of-the-book blues.

The midpoint is the scene or event that transforms the characters or causes a big change. This event should anchor the scenes both leading up to the midpoint and away from it. In a mystery, it could be an overlooked angle. In a thriller, a disaster that may thwart the expected plot continuation. In a romance, the couple may break up. In *Alien*, this is the scene when they realize the thing will kill them all.

4. Plot point two. Just as plot point one closes the opening, plot point two closes the midpoint and readies the stage for the climax. This is the scene to wind up the action, twisting the strands of the story even further so they can be unwound in the ending. In *Alien*, this is the scene where Ripley manages to reach the escape pod.

5. Climax. The climax of a story is the high point of emotional intensity. It is the moment of payoff or resolution. In *Alien*, the climax is the moment the alien is sucked out into space.

6. Ending. The ending is the final scene of the story. At this point, everything has come to a logical conclusion. An ideal ending scene should convey a final image that remains in the reader's mind after he has closed the book. In *Alien* this is the instant when Ripley settles down in the hibernation capsule.

This six-point structure is the most useful tool to lay down a plot, but there's a caveat. As explained in the opening of this chapter, the writer must know the opening, the plot points, and the end before writing a word. These points hold up the structure.

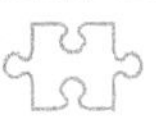

1.4.3 PROBLEM SOLUTION

Rather than a plotting tool, Problem-Solution is a device to use with any structure.

The natural structure of a problem has two parts:

1. The action that created the problem or inciting action.

2. The action that will resolve the problem or principle action.

The driving force of the inciting action is the threat, be that a terrorist, a frying pan on fire, an alien invasion, or Fido falling down a hole. The incident incites the action. Any of these can be the cause of the problem.

The anti-threat is the driving force of the principle action. The hero faces the threat and solves the problem.

If there's resistance, either of these actions will require assistance from the components of the classic structures (Three-Act or Monomyth). With enough resistance, there will be complications, a crisis, the need for action to resolve the crisis, and a resolution.

The classic structures are already built around the problem-solving principle action that encounters resistance, namely: conflict, complications, crises or turning points, climax, and resolution. It follows that plot development requires dividing the problem-solving action into scenes, units of action.

This is the natural structure of any problem-solving action—real or fictitious—that encounters resistance.

1.4.4 ORGANIC STRUCTURE

Although it has developed myriad variations, the organic structure is the oldest among the modern structural tools.

The organic structure became the indispensable working tool of scriptwriters. When producing a spec-script, the writer needed to break the play into scenes and set the scenes on cards to obtain an overview of the full work.

Later, the writer would tackle each scene, in whatever order he liked, or write the story linearly. Though much has changed in the scriptwriting industry, the scene-card core concept remains untouched. Nowadays, many scripts are the work of a team and not an individual writer. This is important in series, soap operas, and follow-ups. Senior writers craft the story arc and secondary writers churn out scenes or episodes while adhering to the outlines. Of course, this requires a detailed scene structure.

The organic structure replicates the human mind in the development of an idea. It starts with a concept, which can be boiled down to a single sentence.

> "An intelligent amoeba from the ocean's depths decides to get rid of an annoying species: humanity." Frank Schätzing's *The Swarm*.

> "A tycoon bankrolls the reproduction of dinosaurs from the DNA of amber-encapsulated mosquitoes." Michael Crichton's *Jurassic Park*.

> "A man awakens to discover he's turned into a monstrous insect." Franz Kafka's *The Metamorphosis*.

From the idea, blurb, or concept, the writer composes a synopsis: a few lines or a page. With the synopsis, the writer plots the opening, plot points, midpoint, climax and ending.

From these, already divided into sections, acts, segments, or structural elements, the writer produces scenes. These are the chunks forming the backbone of the story.

Once the scenes are on cards, a spreadsheet or a list, it's simple to shuffle the scenes around, delete, and add complications, plot points, subplots, or any other device to flesh out the story. Thus, the organic structure can be remodeled at any time and may be viewed as growing a plant from seed.

In the sections dealing with chapter and scene structure, you will find details about classing and rating scenes to ascertain tempo, tension, and story flow.

1.4.5 THE MONOMYTH

Before you skip these pages, please consider that even before humans invented the alphabet, storytellers built their stories, narrations, and plays around the conceptual steps outlined below.

From books of religious significance like *The New Testament* or the trials of Buddha and Mohammed to fantasies like *Lord of the Ring;* science fiction like *Star Wars, The Matrix, Ender's Game,* and *Avatar;* cartoons like *The Lion King;* and adventures like *Indiana Jones,* there's a solid thread that can be traced back to the mythic steps.

Homer, Shakespeare, Chaucer and Milton used these stages—however intuitively—and so have Conrad, King, and Lehane. Superman? Dr. Jekyll? Mary Poppins? Odysseus? Shapeshifters? Ben-Hur? The Sound of Music? The mythic steps are all there.

In *The Writer's Journey: Mythic Structure for Writers,* Christopher Vogler posits that most stories can be reduced to well-defined narrative structures and character archetypes. Vogler's work stems from the writings of mythologist Joseph Campbell.

In his search for a unifying theory, Campbell's seminal work *The Hero with a Thousand Faces* shone a blinding light on Jung and Freud's debate over the collective unconscious. He believed the world religions, rituals, deities, heroes, and legends to be "masks" of the same concept. Most authorities agree.

Regardless of genre or theme, plots can be boiled down to a series of structural phases, necessarily recurring, like a finite series of nails on a board. The writer threads the storyline using the available pegs in no fixed order, and sometimes wrapping the tale several times around a particular nail and skipping others. But a careful study of the base structure, the character's roles, and the underlying forces that pull a plot in one direction or another, will reveal that the stages are limited. There's nothing new under the sun. Mythos is our heritage of dreams and the stuff from which we craft fiction.

Scriptwriters have followed these steps or stages for decades, to structure not only mythological or legendary screenplays, but also many other genres. Likewise, writers have used these steps or variations of the same since time immemorial, sometimes unawares. Halfway through creating the Star Wars structure, George Lucas came across Campbell's work and was dumbfounded to discover he'd followed the mythic structural steps without knowing them.

We are not suggesting writers should approach plots from a mythic-step perspective, but rather that they can use them as guide posts, in particular when drawing a blank (one of those instances when we stare at an empty screen and don't know what to do next). In studying *mythos* from a conceptual standpoint, the writer will discover similar patterns in his own work. This will expose where the story wants to go next.

The following authors have each arranged the steps differently, according to their views or interpretation of mythos.

The Campbell & Vogler's Mythic 12-step lists the stages thus:

1. Ordinary World

2. Call to Adventure

3. Refusal of the Call

4. Meeting with the Mentor

5. Crossing the First Threshold

6. Tests, Allies, Enemies

7. Approach to the Inmost Cave

8. Ordeal

9. Reward

10. The Road Back

11. Resurrection

12. Return with the Elixir

Phil Cousineau, in *The Hero's Journey*, lists eight steps:

1. The Call to Adventure

2. The Road of Trials

3. The Vision Quest

4. The Meeting with the Goddess

5. The Boon

6. The Magic Flight

7. The Return Threshold

8. The Master of Two Worlds

David Adams Leeming, in Mythology: The Voyage of the Hero, suggests another eight-step formulation:

1. Miraculous conception and birth

2. Initiation of the hero-child

3. Withdrawal from family or community for meditation and preparation

4. Trial and Quest

5. Death

6. Descent into the underworld

7. Resurrection and rebirth

8. Ascension, apotheosis, and atonement

We find Campbell's *Seventeen Stages of the Monomyth,* from his 1949 masterpiece *The Hero with a Thousand Faces,* to be unsurpassed, and we've used his concepts to illustrate this structural tool.

The heroic Monomyth—also known as the Hero's Journey—describes the common stages of a hero's trials and adventures found in many stories. The terms and description of each step may sound fantastic or mythological. They are. But these are only labels. "Hero" is also a label we may attach to men, women, children, animals, or even constructs. Hitler and Bugs Bunny are heroes in this loose definition, even if their humanity is absent.

We'll call our hero Gladys. She's twenty-five and a mousy, shy, primary-school teacher, much prettier than she thinks, with a gorgeous mind and lousy luck with men. No pets or live-ins, only a lemon geranium struggling to survive on the window ledge of her tenement flat.

The Monomyth is structured in three acts, books, or phases: Departure, Initiation, and Return. Each of these acts is subdivided into five or six steps.

1.4.5.1 ACT ONE, DEPARTURE

Step One: Call to Adventure

This step, also termed separation, is the moment of change. Gladys awakens from a life of drudgery, from a mundane situation of normality or despair, to pursue a calling. Perhaps she suspects there's a world beyond her hometown.

The Call to Adventure is a point in Gladys's life when she first notices things are about to change. It's a turn away from the well-trodden path and into the unknown. We all remember turning points. They are the decisions, moves, and choices that have changed our lives.

The moment of call may present itself at any time, as Campbell notes:

> *"The adventure may begin as a mere blunder... or still again, one may be only casually strolling when some passing phenomenon catches the wandering eye and lures one away from the frequented paths of man."*

Something happens, either from external agencies or from something rising within, and Gladys must face change. Her job stinks. Josh left two months ago, taking with him her dreams of normalcy and her I-Pad. The postman delivered a postcard from La Havana into her letterbox, when it should have gone to number 345 instead of 543. A lawyer phones her. Uncle Tom died in the Andes and left her in his will a key to a bank's safe deposit box. Whatever the call, Gladys heeds it and heads off into the unknown.

In some instances a herald will appear. The herald, a harbinger of change, might be a friend or acquaintance who provides directions, acts as a sounding board, or causes Gladys to re-examine her concept of life. The herald might even join Gladys to act as a guide or companion.

Step Two: Refusal of the Call

Of course, there are crossroads where we cling to our familiar path, fearful of taking the wrong turn, perhaps to live with a burden many of us will carry to the grave: what if?

In Refusal of the Call, Gladys rejects the initial pull. She fears change. Gladys may resolve to justify her refusal from a sense of duty, from inadequacy, insecurity, or any of the rationalizations we adduce to retain our current circumstances. Humans are adept at self-delusion and reticent to move beyond the status quo.

There can be other variations of this stage. Another character might warn of the dangers ahead or sow uncertainty in Gladys's mind. A real event, such as an illness or disgrace might dampen the original impulse. But this stage is an interlude and could open intriguing plot possibilities. In Campbell's words:

> *"Refusal of the summons converts the adventure into its negative. Walled in boredom, hard work, or 'culture,' the subject loses the power of significant affirmative action and becomes a victim to be saved."*

This "need of salvation" could be the prompt the herald requires to step forward. Motive moves our characters and the herald also needs its fair share of motivation to read true. Nothing weakens a plot more than characters acting without stimulus. For example, on her way to the grocery store for coffee and sugar, Gladys delivers by hand the wrongly addressed postcard and meets the recipient, an ageing Jewish trapeze artist. Zvi befriends her. He warns her about her sudden wanderlust. Gladys returns to her flat *sans* coffee or sugar.

Gladys will eventually go on her journey. A supernatural power may come into play, or an event will force Gladys to move. The little handwritten diary in dear Uncle Tom's safe-deposit box, next to a key tagged with "33 Willow Lane, Topeka," causes her to reconsider.

By one means or another, Gladys overcomes her doubts and marches ahead into uncharted lands.

Step Three: Supernatural Aid

This step has been referred to in other compilations as "Meeting with the Mentor." Like every other one, the title is a loose metaphor to be interpreted even more loosely. The term "supernatural" is often understood as describing something belonging to a different realm or dimension, when nothing could be further from the truth. Supernatural is everything we can't explain through our understanding of natural law.

Thus, "supernatural" aid may come as a source of courage and wisdom Gladys summons from within. "Aid" may mean training, equipment, or advice. In the classical explanation there's a guide, a magical helper or mentor who will present the heroine with amulets, talismans, or artifacts that will aid in the quest.

Magic is required to plunge Gladys into the unknown. As in "Refusal of the Call," Gladys's natural inertia and Zvi's counsel both suggest staying put, where she would suffer predictability as payment for security.

As Gladys travels on her journey, she may meet with a messenger or a god/goddess who gives her weapons or magical powers. Of course, there is a great deal of variety in this apparent formula. The god might pose as a gas-station attendant and the magic manifest itself as a snatch of song.

In our plot, Gladys takes a day off and drives her rattletrap Volkswagen down a country road outside Atlanta in to organize her thoughts. Soon, the car starts making strange noises. At an old gas station on a secondary road, a kind old man points out that besides gas, Gladys's heap of metal and rust needs oil and water. As she fumbles in the car's glove compartment, Gladys discovers a card signed by Zvi with an address in La Havana and a U.S. telephone number. Outside her car, the old man tops the tank while singing Ludo's "I found God in a catalytic converter in Topeka on a Monday night."

Magic.

Zvi, the herald, guessed she would set off and has given Gladys a talisman. The god points out the way: Topeka. After her initial Refusal of the Call, Gladys heeds it, with the inestimable help of a little magic.

● Step Four: Crossing the First Threshold

Nearing the end of Act One, Gladys commits to leaving the familiar and enters a new region or condition with unfamiliar rules and values. A portal or threshold marks the transition into a different realm. There must be danger as well as opportunity. This threshold is the point of no return; Gladys must cross an imaginary gate, the line separating the home comforts and the predictable from a new world fraught with mystery and danger.

So Gladys reaches Topeka to find that the address on the tag of the key she found at Uncle Tom's safe-deposit box—a residential trailer-park—no longer exists. In its place there's an unkempt public park frequented by the local bliss-dispensers and their clients. Feeling a little silly, she reaches for Zvi's card and keys the number. A local number. How did Zvi know she would end up in Topeka? Coincidence? On the other end of the line, a soothing female voice tells her to come to a house by the local synagogue after eight.

Sometimes a gatekeeper guards the threshold, a man or beast the hero must defeat.

Campbell writes:

> *"With the personifications of his destiny to guide and aid him, the hero goes forward in his adventure until he comes to the 'threshold guardian' at the entrance to the zone of magnified power."*

Like everything else in the Monomyth, "gatekeeper" is a concept not to be taken too literally. Cerberus, the three-headed dog, guarded the gates of Hades. But any student of mythology knows that if faced with such a beast, Gladys would only have to wait for Heracles to finish his labors and clear the road.

Having determined the trailer's address on the key fob is no more, Gladys can return home defeated—even before starting her adventure—or pluck enough courage to attend the mysterious date. The given address is a cathouse. The Madame takes Gladys to a room where an ageing rabbi sits shelling peanuts with gnarled hands. Unknown to her he's the gatekeeper.

He likes what he sees. The rabbi tells Gladys the story of the trailer-park owner: a Nazi war criminal. One day he disappeared. The local bank sold the trailers to recover an unpaid loan. The trailers ended up in Cuba.

When Gladys was a little girl, Uncle Tom would compose riddles, and give her a coin if she guessed the correct answer. The little book Gladys recovered from Uncle Tom's safe deposit is packed with riddles she has never seen before. The first riddle is fiendish, "FARTED IN HITLER." Gladys guesses it's an anagram but she's shocked to discover its meaning: "FIND THE TRAILER."

At the threshold, Gladys must decide. Should she cross over? In this instance, the gatekeeper, besides testing her worth, will help with money and a companion: Ben is a trusted friend of the rabbi—early thirties, tall, athletic, and debonair, if unimpaired by a high IQ.

Step Five: Belly of the Whale

The decision made, and having crossed the threshold, Gladys finds herself alone. Nothing is familiar anymore. Ahead lies the unknown.

It's important to notice that the herald, and every other step in these stages, is interchangeable and repeatable, as is the order of the stages. In *Avatar*, for instance, James Cameron recreates each of the seventeen Monomyth themes, though not in their original order.

In this instance, Zvi was the herald in Step Two. Now Ben, her companion, replays the herald's role.

Ben goes to arrange false passports. They will cross into Mexico from where a bunch of friendly gunrunners will spirit them into Cuba in a creaky single-engine Cessna. In the darkness of a room in the synagogue's basement, Gladys faces herself. There, she must test her resolution to emerge from the "Belly of the Whale," as a new person.

Both the *Bible* and the *Qur'an* recount Jonah's trial: three days in the belly of a fish. When the whale vomits Jonah out, he emerges renewed, ready for Nineveh to prophesy doom to its inhabitants.

In taking this step, the heroine shows her willingness to undergo a metamorphosis. She could still leave, but her choice is a mirage; she burned her ships by accepting. At this stage, her job and tenement flat must appear remote, even though only a few hours separate the old life from the new. Having crossed the threshold—and fallen into an unknown abyss—she awaits rebirth or release from her purgatorial state. This is a recurring theme in much fiction, the protagonist's inner fight between mediocrity and a chance at significance. In a soul-wrenching stage of reckoning and self-doubt, everything is tenuous and surreal. The new world is strange—a world of hookers, peanut-wolfing rabbis, gunrunners, disappearing Nazi criminals, peripatetic trailers and dishy assistants. A foreign world, an alien planet in Topeka.

Nothing can be the same after Gladys's endless night. In the morning, when Ben knocks on the door, Gladys will be reborn. After pinching her cheeks to add a touch of color, she will step into the light.

1.4.5.2 ACT TWO, INITIATION

Step One: The Road of Trials

Initiation: Having crossed over into the new realm and escaped "The Belly of the Whale," Gladys enters "The Road of Trials," a series of challenges to test her resolve. Like everything else in life—of which fiction writing is but a reflection—a decision only serves to determine the traveling direction. The toil and the test are through uncharted land, encountering wild beasts on two, four, or countless legs.

Initiation is the ordeal a character must undergo to begin his transformation through inner growth. At this stage, our Gladys must evolve and conquer personal limitations to develop her unrealized potential.

Without the city's protective cloak, Gladys moves through an alien world with no laws to protect her from wrong decisions.

Crossing a border under a false identity, consorting with gunrunners and riding a spluttering flying machine scant inches over the waves, are trials. But most importantly, this stage explores Gladys's discovery: the sobering realization that she has entered a parallel world where survival is no longer reinforced by the state, its agencies, or handouts. Gladys is alone with only her wits to survive, and she must learn fast.

Ben's help is inestimable, but he doesn't control the new environment. A fine companion and assistant, he tags along and contributes the contrasting point of view Gladys needs to test her interpretation of people and situations. Gladys must develop her self-reliance to remain a leader.

Campbell stresses the pivotal nature of this stage:

> *"This is a favorite phase of the myth-adventure. It has produced a world literature of miraculous tests and ordeals."*

Here, the writer should strive to retain the respective roles of characters undiluted. The helper is just that, an assistant. His role is to nurture Gladys's development and growth as a hero. He should ease her passage through the trials by sharing her burden, not by solving the problems. Otherwise, the roles could easily be reversed.

● Step Two: The Meeting with the Goddess

The Road of Trials leads to "The Meeting with the Goddess." This is an encounter with the Queen of the World who can be seen as representing the Earth Mother or source of life. She can embody beauty and unrevealed mystery but—and this is important—she unifies good and evil.

Although Campbell symbolizes this step as a meeting with a goddess, the concept does not have to be represented by a woman:

> *"And when the adventurer, in this context, is not a youth but a maid, she is the one who, by her qualities, her beauty, or her yearning, is fit to become the consort of an immortal."*

In La Havana, Gladys meets Juan. She doesn't know what's hit her. Her knees buckle before Juan, the leader of the Cuban underworld—widower, late forties, suave, charismatic... and devilishly attractive.

It's love at first sight. This is the point where Gladys glimpses the kind of love poets write about—all-powerful and all-encompassing—the unconditional love that a fortunate infant may receive from its mother.

This moment can be written in many ways; the character meets his soul mate, or discovers his own repressed sexuality, or encounters a pure ideal personified in another man or woman.

Juan is reluctant to help. It will be dicey. The U.S. Army uses the trailers as storage space in Guantanamo; easy to get into but hell to get out of in one piece. During their conversations, Juan ogles Gladys.

To bring fullness to Gladys's character, it is important that she perceives a chance of emotional success, a hint or implication of what award awaits her when she finishes the quest. Thus Juan, as a prize, must appear remote but not impossible.

● Step Three: Woman as Temptress

In myth, "woman" is a metaphor for the physical or material temptations of life. The source of such temptation does not necessarily have to be represented by a woman. Gladys's trials have prepared her to recognize the richness of life that Juan offers.

As Ben puts together a team to hit Guantanamo and search Trailer 33, Juan becomes transfigured, in Gladys's mind, as a fine man destined to live in a parallel world. After a night of passion, she no longer cares much about her quest and prefers selfish pleasures to adventure. In the Odyssey, the hero faces a similar plight; he would rather stay with Circe than brave the seas.

The ease with which the hero falls into temptation is significant, and Gladys must soar beyond her complacency. In real terms, these steps are a continuation of The Road of Trials. Gladys will encounter the negative side of Juan and overcome her egoistic desires. This process will be a major milestone in her character development.

Temptation mirrors The Refusal of the Call. The hero seeks excuses to give up. Even though her life has changed, she craves normalcy and security. She thinks she might stay in La Havana with Juan and let Ben travel to Guantanamo to risk his neck.

Failing to illustrate this continuous inner battle between a thirst for adventure (change) and the natural temptation to stop playing and cash the winnings, results in cardboard characters. One of the recurring errors writers make in character development is to paint protagonists so strong, committed, and free of doubt, they appear inhuman to the reader. As character traits, doubt and weakness are as important as self-assurance and courage.

● Step Four: Atonement with the Father

In myth, the hero may encounter a fatherly figure responsible for guiding him through the journey. This representation—the pivotal point of the journey—echoes the trauma of transition from childhood into adulthood. The previous steps have brought Gladys to this place, and the following ones will move her out of it. Although this phase is symbolized by an encounter with a male entity, it does not have to be a male, just someone with power.

As Gladys recovers from an eventful night, sunbathing by a pool, the Cuban Army hits Juan's state. The soldiers kill him (along with a few hundred of his lieutenants), arrest Gladys, and throw her into a dungeon.

For the transformation to take place, the hero must die, so that the new self can come into being. Sometimes this "dying" is literal, and the hero's journey is at an end, though it may continue in another realm. More often, the hero dies a figurative death to be reborn as a new person. In more than one way, this stage shares echoes with Belly of the Whale.

Gladys realizes she has betrayed Uncle Tom, the rabbi, and Ben. Alone in a roach-infested cell, the air alive with the cries of other inmates, she breaks down.

Enters the rabbi from Topeka. He tears a strip of her skin and offers salvation—he has influence with the Castro clan—as long as she continues her quest.

According to the Monomyth, the father can be someone who feels threatened by the hero, a malevolent figure, or it can be someone who helps the hero in his journey. Just as the mother may be portrayed as good and evil, the father can represent ambivalence as a positive and negative force.

Gladys reconciles with the father. In the process, she understands him, the greatness of the quest, and herself. Thus, she is released from the situation through reconciliation, forgiveness, and mercy.

● Step Five: Apotheosis

A hero's apotheosis is his realization of the purpose of life and himself. With an expanded consciousness, he views the world in a different way than when he started his journey. At this point the hero often becomes a selfless person who cares for others before himself.

To apotheosize is to deify. Gladys hasn't suffered a physical death but she's nevertheless reborn on a higher plane. In James Clavell's unforgettable *Shogun*, the *gaijin* reaches a point where his only honorable recourse is *seppuku*, or ritual disembowelment. A samurai stills his hand when the Tanto knife grazes the skin of his belly. What follows is his apotheosis. After the event, the air tastes different and even the flowers display renewed colors; he feels reborn.

Gladys has gone with Ben and his cronies, staged a masquerade, and recovered a sealed package from Trailer 33. It was a heroic deed fraught with danger, but she has floated through it because she's a different person. The new Gladys is stronger. She is whole. She has happened.

To confuse this with grit or bravado would be a mistake. In *On Writing*, Stephen King recounts the accident that left him a mangled heap of flesh and broken bones by a roadside. He recovered, and his fellow writers and millions of readers rejoiced. But he wasn't the same man. Oh, he still lived in the same house and had the same family and friends, but his plane of existence was forever changed.

When a character dies a metaphorical death, the hero's transformation invokes a realization of the essence of life and ultimate purpose. Once more, we move through the Hero's Journey by change, the single element capable of moving a story forward.

● Step Six: The Ultimate Boon

The ultimate boon is achieving the goal of the quest. It is what Gladys went on the journey to get. All the previous steps have served to purify and prepare the hero to share the boon with humankind, whether it is an elixir of immortality, true love, the meaning of life, or a book full of long strings of numbers and notes.

The book contains the numbered bank accounts—one number shy—where Nazi criminals deposited billions. Next to the codes are riddles she must decipher to identify the bank names and missing number.

But this step goes much further. In many novel plots, this would be the end. The detail, to our view, demonstrates the vastness of the Monomyth's scope. We could shuffle most of these steps—as many scriptwriters and writers have done—and create a twist anywhere. The resulting plot would be different. What follows in the next act could be omitted in some cases. In others, the steps could be interspersed earlier, or rearranged, as James Cameron did in *Avatar*.

Gladys has left her old life behind and found change, a new persona, and the treasure. The End.

The wonder of this plotting tool is the interchangeable nature of its steps. In *The Odyssey*, Homer plays through all the steps, in different order, and revisits a few several times.

In our plot, though Gladys has found the treasure, she must still solve the riddles and return. She can try to go back to her old life, but a complete return would be impossible. The school would be there, as would her apartment, friends, family, and acquaintances, but she is a different person.

1.4.5.3 ACT THREE, RETURN

Step One: Refusal of the Return

After eating manna, drinking ambrosia, and chatting with the gods, why return to this valley of disenchantment and aridity?

The quest over, the hero generally sets off for home to bring the knowledge of his adventure to others. In some cases, the hero does not wish to flee the newfound world or circumstance—this is Refusal of the Return.

Travelers have experienced this strange phenomenon often enough. Juanmi, one of the rare people we call brother, is a sailor. A real sailor. Make that a real crazy sailor. He eschews going out in the absence of force-four winds. Juanmi once spoke of a French sailor who finished a solo round-the-world sail in a bucket. As he reached the point where he should change tack and head home to a hero's welcome, family, friends, and the bright lights, he paused and thought it over. Then he carried on south and said to hell with it all.

Of course, in most practical plotting applications, the writer can find ways to hand over the treasure to a Government representative or other agency who could, in turn, deliver the good news. This plot remedy has been used countless times by genre writers.

Gladys likes La Havana, its shapes, colors, and smells. She is welcome to stay and Don Antonio—Juan's successor—is making eyes at her. The temptation—another plot driver—is strong. For another option, she could head for the family farm in a hollow with views of the bluffs and valley of the Illinois River. But she has still to figure out the riddles, and Uncle Tom's correspondence, which may contain overlooked hints, is at her apartment in Atlanta.

Campbell sums it up:

> *"The full round, the norm of the Monomyth, requires that the hero shall now begin the labor of bringing the runes of wisdom, the Golden Fleece, or his sleeping princess, back into the kingdom of humanity."*

Step Two: The Magic Flight

We reach this step if the hero agrees to return home after completing his quest. There are numerous instances in story and play where the hero chooses to remain in the god's realm and forgo human miseries. Once the hero has decided to return there are two possible scenarios: flight or rescue.

If the treasure was obtained through conflict or without consent, The Magic Flight will become a race full of obstacles, the hero pursued by the angered force. It makes sense that returning from the journey can be as adventurous and dangerous as it was to go on it.

A protector or assistant, to help overcome the perils the hero might face on the return, may accompany the hero.

Campbell remarks that:

> *"...if the hero's wish to return to the world has been resented by the gods or demons, then the last stage of the mythological round becomes a lively, often comical, pursuit."*

Gladys sets off by boarding another single-engine flying machine, carrying with her the notebook rescued from Trailer 33 at Guantanamo, and chaperoned by a morose Ben. When they land on a barren field in Mexico, a welcome party awaits. A group of armed men kills the pilot and seizes Gladys and Ben. Before passing out, Gladys recognizes Zvi, the Atlanta grocer.

● Step Three: Rescue from Without

In the classical Monomyth, the force that has been robbed of the treasure may be angered indeed, and prove difficult to dodge. This scenario requires the outside world to pull the hero back from the adventure. This is the Rescue from Without.

Campbell writes:

> *"The hero may have to be brought back from his supernatural adventure by assistance from without. That is to say, the world may have to come and get him."*

Zvi can be charming. He claims to be working for Mossad, the Israeli cousin of the CIA. He sets Gladys up in a nice house and promises a percentage of the bounty, a sort of finder's fee, and a pretty residence in the land of milk and honey.

Though Gladys suspects something is amiss and Ben is incommunicado, she settles down to work and thus once again turns into a reluctant hero unwilling to take on the burdens of the world. Of course, she may be rescued from her state of helplessness and bliss. By a combination of overriding reasons or circumstances, someone or something may facilitate her return.

One night, a shadowy figure enters her room. Gladys awakens to find Ben metamorphosed into a ninja-like warrior. He is the *real* Mossad agent and Zvi is none other than Kurt Freiherr von Richthofen, the Nazi criminal and direct descendant of the Red Baron.

Just as the hero may need guides and assistants to set out on the quest, often he must have rescuers to bring him back. Sometimes the hero doesn't realize that it is time to return or remember that others need the boon.

● Step Four: The Crossing of the Return Threshold

Thresholds and gates are trials the hero must negotiate to cross over. In other phases of The Hero's Journey the thresholds identify with change, the hero must endure yet another trial, to perish or rise above the difficulty. The narrative now brings the hero full cycle; his destiny is to depart from the world he has discovered.

In the late stages of the Monomyth, Campbell writes:

> *"The first problem of the returning hero is to accept as real, after an experience of the soul-satisfying vision of fulfillment, the passing joys and sorrows, banalities and noisy obscenities of life."*

The Crossing of the Return Threshold is a harrowing race through the Mexican desert, hounded by relentless pursuers. If caught, Gladys and Ben will face death.

To return, the hero must retain the wisdom gained on the quest and then figure out how to share it with the rest of the world. This can be difficult. Gladys now retreats into a world of doubt, overwhelmed by her own frailty. Exhausted beyond endurance, frightened, hungry and wounded, she doesn't want to carry on; nothing seems worth this struggle and pain. She wants to be in control of her life once more. As they flee from their hunters, she collapses. She gives up.

Gladys may have to defeat another gatekeeper, and relive the harrowing process of crossing the threshold the first time. But the Monomyth roles are interchangeable. The hero's assistants and rescuers can be the agents responsible for saving the master. The supernatural guide, incarnated in good old Ben, saves the day. He scoops the comatose Gladys into his muscular arms and with her on his shoulder, Ben gallops across the Mexican tundra toward salvation.

⦿ Step Five: Master of Two Worlds

On return, the hero must resolve duality: divine and human, known and unknown, yin and yang, real and imagined, dream and reality. To understand the myth, the hero must realize the two kingdoms are one. The unknown is another dimension of the world we know. To explore that dimension is the quest of the hero. By crossing this final threshold, the hero understands that the apparent separation does not exist. When this happens, the hero becomes the Master of Two Worlds.

As they near the border crossing, all hell breaks loose. The Rabbi from Topeka—in reality he's a Mossad colonel and Ben's handler—leading a band of Tohono O'odham[8] bravos pounce on their pursuers. The Native Americans kill a few baddies, round up the others, capture Zvi, and send him off to Tel Aviv for reckoning.

Gladys rises like a Phoenix from the ashes of her old self. In Topeka she rests, pampered by a grateful Mossad. Healers tend to her body and spirit, supervised by a solicitous Ben.

In myth, a transcendental hero like Jesus or Buddha represents this step. For a human hero, it may mean achieving a balance between the material and spiritual. The person has become comfortable and competent in both the inner and outer worlds.

When she's recovered, Gladys sets out to unravel the riddles, helped by Uncle Tom.

It turns out that Uncle Tom didn't die in the Andes. As an undercover DEA agent, he'd been kept prisoner by a Mexican cartel. The Mossad just exchanged him for a truckload of dope and the rest of Zvi's helpers.

⦿ Step Six: Freedom to Live

The riddle solved, the Israelis bang on Swiss bankers' doors to recover the Nazi plunder. Our hero achieves a Freedom to Live. This step signifies the ability to pass freely between realms. Of course, this implies that the hero has become familiar with her existence. She is transfigured. Gladys has become a presence perpetually renewing herself, understanding perfected knowledge is imperishable.

Free from the fear of death, Gladys is unencumbered by personal limitations. This high plateau is the freedom to live. This stage, recreated in countless fiction works, brings with it a sensation of serenity and completion to a narrative end, with the hero at peace with himself. The hero understands that the present is the only reality, as the future has not happened, and the past only lives in memories. This is sometimes referred to as living in the moment, neither anticipating the future nor regretting the past. For we can't change the past; it's gone. The present we cannot change either, as any change would have to manifest outside the present. We can only change, or attempt to change, the future.

In a succinct sentence, Campbell sums the essence of the voyage.

> *"The hero is the champion of things becoming, not of things become, because he is."*

The new Gladys looks at the novel world around her to discover a fresh depth and a roguish twinkle in Ben's eyes., and hey, his IQ isn't as borderline as it first seemed.... To be continued.

---

[8] Group of Native Americans who reside primarily in the Sonoran Desert of the southeastern Arizona and northwest Mexico.

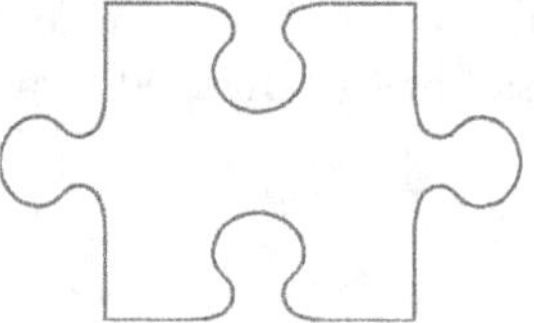

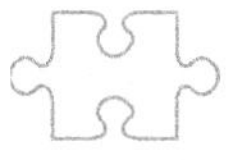

1.5 STRUCTURE / PARTS

Writing consists of words. In turn, words can be arranged into phrases, sentences, and paragraphs. The basic unit of writing is the word, not unlike the dollar in the US currency system. We have the humble one-dollar bill and larger denominations.

Dry-stone-walling is an art form, as one can appreciate after examining a well-built one. In some parts of the world, dry walls have withstood the passage of centuries. For those frowning, a dry wall is made from stones without mortar or any other binding agent. The craftsman piles rocks, one on top of the other, until he reaches the desired height. He then starts another section, seamlessly stitching it to the previous one.

Those who dream to build a wonderful wall often set about it with a pile of stones, enthusiasm, and little thought. After all, nothing but stones goes into a wall, and to a careless observer, every stone is the same. Of course, if we try to build a wall by merrily piling up stones, chances are the arrangement will soon crash down. The mason's art is in the structure. He positions each stone with great care to perform a different function. Stones can be ties, supports, fillers, anchors, cappers, etc. The elements of fiction share the structural diversity of stones when we create the walls some uninitiated refer to as manuscripts.

In this section, we will explore the definition and inner structure of each component of a novel, the shape of individual stones with which to build our wall.

A preface, prologue, introduction, or foreword may be used as foundation, although if the ground is firm, these won't be necessary.

In the different sections of this Companion we will dedicate much space to the scene, because the basic unit of *fiction writing* is not the word, sentence, or paragraph—it's the scene. These are the stones to build our wall. Their shape and arrangement will determine if our efforts produce a beautiful wall built to last, or a crumbling heap of rock.

Later we will explore the larger units, such as chapters, parts, and books—all constructed from scenes—to finish with capping stones, if necessary, and shaped as epilogues.

1.5.1 PROLOGUE

Contrary to popular belief, agents and/or editors don't hate necessary prologues. Here, as in every other aspect of fiction writing, the keyword is <u>necessary.</u>

A prologue is not a device to buttress weak opening chapters or to set a more global picture than can be accomplished in the first pages. It should not be a mere segue into the story itself, nor needs to be directly connected to the present story. If it is, it's a chapter. Likewise, the prologue is not about mood-setting: The place to set the mood is in the story.

Inexperienced writers use a prologue to provide factual background of how a given civilization, war, or event came into being, thus confusing the prologue with a <u>foreword</u> or a <u>preface.</u> Check the relevant sections for details.

There's a sure-fire test to determine if a prologue is necessary:

If "Prologue" can be replaced with "Chapter 1," or the prologue's contents can be dosed our within the opening chapters—and entire plot still makes sense—chances are it's not necessary.

A prologue is an introduction to a story. Its role is to establish setting, provide background details and other miscellaneous essential information *impossible* to convey any other way, and which the reader <u>must have</u> before reaching chapter one. Often, a prologue narrates events that happened before the story begins.

Set in the POV of a major character—though "major" is not a rule—the prologue's voice should fit in with the genre and storyline of the main text. In some instances, the prologue could be in the voice of a non-physical entity or comprise the reminiscences of an old man, to give a couple of examples. If the POV character doesn't appear later in the story, his or her presence must be justified on the timeline.

Clive Cussler exploited the prologue's role with a classic formula, which other writers have successfully copied:

Prologue: 814 BCE Carthage, the Mediterranean Sea

Chapter 1: Present Day

In this setup, chances are the prologue will explain the origins of an artifact, necessary to understand the main text of the story.

There are other instances where a prologue may be unavoidable, such as in a sequel that has been a long time coming out and where the reader needs to be acquainted with the story so far. In historical fiction, the writer may need to orient the reader in an unfamiliar period. Likewise, in fantasy or sci-fi, a prologue may equip the reader with the otherwise bizarre assumptions held by the inhabitants of the world they're about to enter. One more reason to have a prologue may be to show the perspective of the antagonist. If the story has been written in first person, the reader may not see what the bad guy plans until the end of the book. A prologue showing how evil the antagonist is can heighten the intensity of the book. Danger lurks around the corner. The reader knows it and the POV does not.

1.5.1.1 PROLOGUE DEVELOPMENT

Experts concur that the prologue should be written last, when the writer determines that the reader needs critical background before tackling the story. This should be done only if it is necessary, and executed with a flair matching the content of the novel.

The usual format is that of short story, with a beginning middle and end. The only difference would be that the conflicts are left unresolved.

Good prologues have a strong hook at the beginning to intrigue the reader. Their contents should stand out from the rest of the novel, perhaps set in a different period or setting from the novel itself.

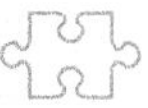

1.5.2 FOREWORD

The foreword consists of a piece of writing set at the beginning of a book or other piece of literature and before the main text.

Most forewords are devices for non-fiction works and are often written by someone other than the author, such as an expert in the field or the writer of a similar book. Many a times, it introduces the reader to the author, as well as the book itself. On the other hand, in the foreword the writer may explain how he came to write the book.

As marketing tools, forewords help authors by putting a stamp of approval on their work. They are an opening statement by a published writer or an authority that gives the book added credibility.

A foreword does not provide the reader with any extra information about the book's subject. Also, a foreword to later editions of a work often explains what has been changed.

1.5.2.1 FOREWORD DEVELOPMENT

Forewords are also often written after the book is complete, copyedited and ready for publication. The format is a short piece, one to two pages in length, split into three sections: opening, middle, and closing.

The opening contains personal touches explaining how the author of the foreword knows the author of the book.

The middle is the place for real-world examples to illustrate the theme—and show the reader that the author of the book is credible on the subject matter. This is also the place to highlight that the book solves a problem or offers a unique point of view.

In the closing, the author reminds readers why he has written the foreword, why it matters. This also coaxes the reader to buy the book because the expert—the foreword writer—is telling them that the book is a worthy read. A common technique is to echo an idea from the first paragraph in the final one.

Unlike prefaces or prologues, forewords are always signed with name and title.

1.5.3 PREFACE

The preface is an introduction (short) written before the body of the book by the work's writer, to provide the reader with significant information, background, or explanatory remarks about its contents.

The term "preface" can also mean any preliminary or introductory statement to cover the story of how the book came into being, or how the idea for the book developed.

In *Mahdi*, Carlos J. Cortes faced the problem of acquainting the readers with the meaning of an unfamiliar title.

> "Although the *Qur'an* doesn't mention the Mahdi, the 'Guided One' is a well-known figure in Islamic cultures. According to tradition, the Mahdi will appear at the end of time to combat unbelievers and the forces of evil. Islamic scholars have posited the Mahdi is a myth. Yet,

most Muslims throughout history have accepted the idea of an eschatological deliverer known as the Mahdi."

Prefaces are often followed by thanks and acknowledgments to people who were helpful to the author during the time of writing.

 ### 1.5.3.1 PREFACE DEVELOPMENT

A preface should feature background, preliminary, or historical content, the book's scope, and/or the intentions of the author, by answering one or more of the following questions: Why this book? Why now? What is the context? Who is this person? Why this author?

This is the space to explain how the writer acquired the information or provide a framework for what's to follow, or deliver, in brief, the main argument or point of view about the subject.

If there are conclusions to be made, viewpoints, or caveats, it's advisable to express them with more detail in a postscript.

 ### 1.5.4 SCENE

As discussed in the opening to this section, the scene is the building block of fiction writing. Rather than tackling a gargantuan task—often spanning hundreds of pages, or even several books in sagas and sequels—most writers concentrate on one scene at a time, a manageable piece of prose that is subject to the unforgiving rules of structure.

Beginning writers have many doubts about scenes, most of them legitimate. Let's open with a few:

Q. What is a scene?

A. A unit of action or event in a set environment and with a set number of characters.

Q. How long is a scene?

A. As long as necessary, from one or two lines to many pages.

Q. How many characters in a scene?

A. As few as possible.

Q. How many scenes in a novel-length manuscript?

A. How long is a piece of string? Banter aside, between 150 and 300 on average.

Q. Do scenes have structure?

A. They do, and the rest of this section will attempt to answer this question more fully.

Q. What is a good scene?

A. One that moves the plot forward.

Q. And a bad scene?

A. Filler.

A brick wall is made from bricks. We know this sounds trite, but great truths are. Height, breadth, length, color, design, and embellishments (such as coping pieces) are physical characteristics and features of a wall. But the unit of reference, the element craftsmen use to build walls, is the brick.

Often, when we appraise a brick wall, we ignore the bricks. Instead, our eye takes in its features, and abstract sensations like strength or security. And yet, regardless of its scope, the builder started his wall with a single brick, followed by another, and another....

Good writers write scenes; scenes are the units of fiction writing as bricks are units of masonry.

We have concluded that a significant difference between professional writers and hobbyists is their understanding of the scene's role in fiction.

Though we'll cover the finer points of scene structure in the following sections, we must stress a single detail before we go any further: every scene must have a goal.

Before writing a single word, answer the question: what's this scene's role?

If the answers are to describe, to set the scene, to explain or (horror of horrors) because I like it, the scene should never be written. Of course, description, setting, color, explanation, and backstory belong in scenes, but only if the scene has the definite goal to advance the plot.

Imagine we have a story with the following plot:

Mary awakens, showers, eats breakfast, drives to the office, and plunges into a pile of manuscripts awaiting rejection.

How many scenes are necessary to cover these events? There can be a single scene or a score, and the answer will depend on what is "necessary."

<u>Mary awakens.</u> Nothing unusual here, everybody does. No scene.

<u>Mary showers.</u> So? No scene.

<u>Mary eats breakfast.</u> A healthy habit but no scene.

<u>Mary drives to the office.</u> Don't we all? No scene.

<u>Mary plunges into a pile of manuscripts awaiting rejection.</u> This is better. Her work must be connected with publishing, she's not the boss (the manuscripts would have been pruned by someone else), and the material awaiting her tender mercies is ghastly. This gives the reader more information about Mary than anything else thus far.

At this point, we hope the manuscript sorting *has a bearing to the story or advances it*. Otherwise, there's no reason for it. "But I need to get Mary behind her desk! I can't make her materialize out of thin air!" the writer cries.

It's easy. Stitch these events into the opening of the next "real" scene:

> Mary runs into the office cursing the traffic, runs the fingers of one hand through her still-damp hair and stifles a belch. "Damn corn-flakes," before sitting behind her desk to stare cross-eyed at a pile of manuscripts.

Of course, the story (not the writer) may need each of those scenes. Let's return to the point when the alarm clock goes off.

<u>Mary awakens.</u> "What the...?" Throws the comforter aside. Her legs are covered in two-inch black hairs. Ear-splitting scream. This *definitely* needs a scene. We would love to write it.

<u>Mary showers.</u> A strawberry blonde, she's aghast. Hers legs resemble fringed rodeo chaps. She tries plucking, shaving, and trimming with the garden shears to no avail. Nice scene.

<u>Mary eats breakfast.</u> She doesn't, really. Between bouts of cursing, tears, and trying to encase her leg's exuberance into the largest pants she can find all she managed was a cup of coffee. But great scene material.

<u>Mary drives to the office.</u> The hair continues to grow, spilling out her trouser bottoms. She almost kills herself when her tresses foul the brake pedal. A hair-raising scene.[9]

<u>Mary plunges into a pile of manuscripts awaiting rejection.</u> A title catches her eye. 'Mary's Wild Legs.'

Is a scene *absolutely* necessary? No? Delete, tear, destroy or, better still (and much less work) don't write it.

Scenes are like takes on a film. From a static or moving camera, the director follows the action until the characters move away. Perhaps a second unit takes over for continuity but, if the action moves to a different environment, the scene is over.

It's no coincidence that most novel-writing and structuring software uses scenes as the basic building blocks. Scenes are moved into chapters later in the writing process.

Once the writer has plotted the novel, however loosely, the resulting events or plot points will be written as scenes. Depending on the level of structure chosen by the writer, the number of set scenes at this point may be only a handful. This doesn't represent a problem because the plot will often provide automatic scenes. If the mad shaman is after the heroine at A and she must flee to B, a scene or two may be required to explain how she managed a trip to Vienna with furry legs and without a cent (the shaman stole her purse).

Every scene in a work of fiction must advance the plot and/or deepen characterization. In other words: stories are written in scenes, not in exposition. A scene must be conceived with a purpose (the goal) and contain conflicts or resolutions that tell us something new about the plot or the characters.

If it doesn't accomplish its goals, then the scene has no reason to be in a novel. It's filler.

A scene, singly or in pairs (more about this in the Scene Development section), is a unit of prose. As such, it requires the same internal divisions. A book has a beginning, middle, and end, and so does every scene. Just as we construct chapter ends with cliffhangers, to keep the reader turning pages, the end of a scene should coax the reader into reading the next paragraph or chapter.

A scene has two levels of structure: Macro-structure and Micro-structure.

Think of a car. The <u>Macro-structure</u> in a scene comprises essentials like bodywork, wheels, and engine, and every car has these. A scene's <u>Micro-structure</u> deals with the elements without which the major components won't work, like paint, air, or gas. Bodywork without paint doesn't shine; it's a rust bucket. Tires without air are flat, and an engine without gas doesn't run.

 **1.5.4.1 SCENE DEVELOPMENT**

The traditional-structure school proposes that a scene must have an opening, middle, and end.

The <u>opening</u> poses a question or introduces a goal. The <u>middle</u> is where the tension grows as the writer works conflict in. The <u>end</u> should build to a conclusion.

This is fine but limited. What if the scene ends on a cliffhanger? Do we start the next scene with another goal?

This problem is solved in the Micro-structure with three possible choices of scene models:

    A. Resolved

    B. Unresolved

---

[9] As TJ Webb—one of our much-abused beta-readers—remarked: "Pun at the end is horrible punishment."

C. Reactive

These three patterns (there are no more) offer the writer two possible choices A or B + C

An example is the easiest way to analyze scene models. Our POV is Mary, a young woman, and the setting is a bathroom with pink tiles.

Opening

Mary has missed two periods. She enters the bathroom, washes her hands, and winks at her reflection in the mirror.

Middle

After removing a stick from its foil wrapper she squats, does her bit, places the stick—window up—on the counter, and waits.

End

A few bars of "It's a long, long way to Tipperary" later, she peers at the stick. The face in the mirror glows. Positive!

This is a resolved scene, but the reason for its classification has nothing to do with the result of the test but with the POV's expectations. The scene could also be resolved had the test been negative.

Imagine Mary enters the bathroom looking gloomy. She doesn't sing. She peers at the stick and her face lights up. Negative! In the first scene, Mary expected a positive result. In the second, she expected the opposite. In both instances, the scene is resolved for the main POV.

We don't know what Mary will do next. Will she dance, call Peter, call Mom and Aunty Gladys or friends... The next scene can be resolved or unresolved, but never reactive. There's nothing to react to since Mary has achieved the scene's goal.

Let's revisit the last two sentences in our scene, but change two words and the punctuation.

"The face in the mirror sags. Negative."

Now the scene is unresolved. The POV's expectations have floundered. This leaves an issue up in the air. The next scene in Mary's POV must register her reaction, perhaps making an appointment to visit her doctor.

The different classes of scenes have dissimilar inner structures:

The resolved scene has a three-part pattern: goal, conflict, and achievement.

The unresolved scene has a three-part pattern: goal, conflict, and failure.

The reactive scene has a three-part pattern: reaction, impasse, and decision.[10]

Though writers use many other patterns, when boiled down to essentials they fit into one of the three types described above.

---

[10] Obviously, the reactive scene has a goal: to address the problem that caused the failure in the previous scene.

Before we analyze the diverse patterns, it's important to note that resolved scenes must be used with caution and often sparingly. The reason is psychological. When things keep turning out according to the POV's expectations, tension slacks. This is not bad—if planned—as long as the writer is aware of the danger.

🧩 1.5.4.2 RESOLVED SCENE

Goal: These are the POV's expectations and the drive behind the scene.

The POV enters an elevator, intending to ride the car to the thirtieth floor, where Don Julio awaits to pay him for a successful killing.

This is the goal, which must be explicit and unambiguous. Unless the reader knows the goal, it's impossible to ratchet the tension.

Conflict

These are the obstacles thrown in the POV's way to derail his purpose. Without conflict there's no scene and the reader's interest will flag.

The POV enters an elevator, pushes a button, and rides without a hitch up to the thirtieth floor.

These actions beg the question: what's the use of this scene? Perhaps the writer has a fixation with elevators, but that's no reason for the scene and it should be nixed. We repeat: no conflict, no scene. Let's rewrite:

Half way up, the elevator shudders before stopping. The lights go off.

This is conflict. Of course, we can push the conflict as high as we want by adding other passengers riding the elevator, say a Buddhist monk, two guys built like linebackers, and a little old lady on crutches.

Achievement

The resolved pattern demands that the POV character achieves his aim. In this instance, the lights return, the car moves once again, and our hero makes it to the thirtieth floor.

We mentioned earlier that resolved scenes should be handled with care. If the hero succeeds at the end of a scene, the reader feels no compunction to turn the page and find out what happens next. Although readers are not writers, they have an uncanny subliminal sense for plot. After the scene in the elevator ends in victory for the hero, the reader will suspect something happened inside the car while the lights were off. Why? Because otherwise the scene doesn't make any sense and it shouldn't be there.

This is one of the most difficult issues for a new writer to understand: since every word, phrase, sentence, paragraph, and scene must have *a reason*. If the reader (or agent or editor) can't find any, they will get upset (make that "mad"). Readers will not invest in books riddled with bits the writer *liked* or penned for the hell of it.

A resolved scene is an end in itself; the POV has won. Unless handled with finesse, these scenes can be boring, and after a while, predictable.

 1.5.4.3 UNRESOLVED SCENE

Goal: The POV's expectations and the drive behind the scene don't change.

The POV enters an elevator, intending to ride the car to the thirtieth floor where Don Julio awaits, to pay him for a successful hit.

● Conflict

To thwart his purpose we've stopped the elevator and added passengers.

The POV enters a crowded elevator. A Buddhist monk, two guys built like linebackers, and a little old lady on crutches shuffle to make room. He checks that the thirtieth floor is not lit up and presses the button. Halfway up, the elevator shudders before stopping. The lights go off.

The passengers are not "color" or "background." If the writer intended transparency, he would have written "other passengers shifted to make room." Any reader will zero on the description of the passengers and mull (however subliminally) that *there must be a reason* why the writer chose *these* characters and not transparent others. We can imagine the reader sliding toward the edge of his seat.

A feeble emergency light illuminates the car. The hulks reach for their pieces. The hero ducks and freezes when the little old lady beats them to the draw. When she's finished, both men are dead. Then her gun seeks him. With a deafening shriek and a flap of saffron robes, the Buddhist monk leaps high into the air and kicks the little old lady's head. A sickening crunch and she collapses in a flurry of crutches. The monk bows and cradles his hands into a stirrup for the hero to reach the service hatch.

Though this plot is a farce, it doesn't take much imagination to assume the reader won't leave the scene at this point. What, with the Buddhist monk peering at the hero's climbing figure from a car strewn with corpses and hardware? No way.

● Failure

The unresolved pattern demands that the POV character fails to achieve his goal.

The hero climbs the elevator cables, his gaze on a service opening with a door ten feet over his head. When he draws level, he leaps, and his foot misses its mark. With lightning reflexes his fingers catch the lower edge of the opening. A whine, lights, and the elevator starts moving again in the wrong direction: up.

Our hero's plans are in disarray. Not only did he not make it to the thirtieth floor and Don Julio, but he's hanging on for his life while an elevator barrels in his direction.

An unresolved scene implies a sequel, a continuation, a reactive scene to have another shot at the goal.

The reactive scene doesn't need to be at the turn of the page. The writer may have cunningly structured his plot to keep the reader on edge and shift to another scene, perhaps in the monk's or Don Julio's POV. Of course, these unresolved scenes must also be handled with care. Distance is important lest the reader forgets our hero's predicament. If not right away, the reactive scene must follow at a reasonable distance.

 **1.5.4.4 REACTIVE SCENE**

The purpose of a reactive scene is to follow and tidy up an unresolved one. If the hero sought a goal and encountered a setback, he shouldn't try anything new until the problem at hand has been solved, or replaced with a new problem.

What if the reactive scene doesn't resolve its goal? Can there be reactive-positive and reactive-negative scenes? One could envisage a scene where the hero fails many times to achieve his goal. No?

No. A reactive scene's goal is to react to a failure. A novel may consist of many scenes trying to reach the goal outlined on page one, but each will have its own goal (or mini-goal in the large scheme of things) or react to an unachieved goal.

The reactive scene has three parts: <u>reaction</u>, <u>impasse,</u> and <u>resolution,</u> and each is critical for its overall success.

Reaction

A reaction is the emotional follow-through to a failure. If disaster strikes—following the initial rush of adrenaline—the character struggles, off-balance, until he gathers his wits. POV characters must react to failure and adjust to change, submit to a new ball-game. This is a boon for any writer, the opportunity to add deep characterization because character surfaces in extreme moments. In the end, the POV needs to take stock and look for options and their alternatives.

The car races upward, threatening to crush him. The hero flexes his muscles and pulls himself up, squeezing into the narrow ledge as the elevator trundles past.

Of course, the best scenes are those where the POV has no escape, no options left. These tax the writer because there must be an option, however hidden, and it must be a clever or imaginative one the hero might have overlooked—or a reckless one born of despair.

Impasse

After a good old failure, there aren't any good choices. If there are, it wasn't much of a disaster. The POV must be in a bind with no good obvious alternatives. In our silly plot, the hero is as we would colloquially describe: shafted.

Fighting for balance on a ten-inch ledge, his fingers explore the door. It's unlocked. As the hero steps through the door, he halts. The opening is an access communicating two elevator shafts. As he compares the two voids, elevators dash past in both directions at breakneck speed. One must still carry the corpses.

Now what? The reader will wonder what can happen next because the hero's choices are one shaft or the next. Not good. The reader will turn the page.

Decision

To decide is to make a choice. Here, the POV must work through his choices, however illusory or wild these may be. As he sifts through the options, he will take the one that offers the greatest chance of success. Even if it means choosing a harrowing one, the choice must be reasoned. Otherwise, the reader will get the impression the POV has been lucky, and that's a sign of careless writing. Intelligent readers believe in probabilities, not luck. The reader must respect the POV's decision and perhaps nod in agreement. "Yup, I would have done the same." Or cringe in awe at the POV's choice, an avenue so crazy—despite a slim chance of success —the reader had not considered it.

The elevator he escaped now stops. The corpses must have been discovered. (How the monk got away is another matter.)When the elevator in the new shaft halts on the floor below, the hero makes a split-second decision and jumps. He crashes through its roof, and lands next to another little old lady. This time, the hero doesn't take any chances. He picks himself from the floor, socks the lady, presses all the buttons, and as soon as the car stops on the next floor, he bolts toward the fire escape.

In this scene, the character has not resolved any goal. Rather, he has simply reacted to his failed attempt in the previous scene.

What happens now? Who knows? The hero may reach the fire escape. There, the writer will concoct another scene with a new goal, perhaps to get away from the building in one piece. The reader will follow to find out the next goal of the POV.

The important mechanism to understand is the interrelation of scenes and their inner structure with reference to the story. A novel is a sequence with a few resolved and many unresolved scenes. These are followed by reactive scenes that, in turn, open the door to another scene.

The magic of plotting a novel in scenes is this action-reaction continuum; one scene leads to another until the cycle breaks at THE END.

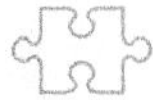 ### 1.5.5 CHAPTER

A chapter is like a word, a phrase, a sentence, or a paragraph. It's a logical division of thought into a grouping with similarity or a binding concept.

In general terms, a chapter may contain a scene, or group of scenes, which perform a specific function within the novel, and it's built around events that occur and belong together.

Like novels and scenes, chapters need an inner structure consisting of beginning or opening, middle, and end. Like everything else in fiction writing, a chapter should pull its weight and contribute to forwarding the plot. Since a novel is a sequence of steps toward a goal, a chapter should include, at least, one of those steps.

The building blocks of a fiction work are the scenes. Chapters are sections of such work made from the same elements. The number of scenes in a chapter will depend on the portion of the plot the chapter contains.

A chapter consisting of a single scene with different POVs requires breaking into sections for each POV change. The usual way to signal this is by placing a single pound sign (#)[11] centered on a line without extra spacing before or after. This practice is not universal and some editors prefer an asterisk (*) or a series of these, also centered on the page. On the formatting sections (pages 405-408) we've listed a number of alternatives.

Chapters are important pacing and rhythm elements in a novel. They may confine incidents or interactions and bring them to momentary or permanent resolution. A chapter can bridge two otherwise separated parts of a story and be used as a transition tool. As such, they can contain the event of hours, days, or years.

---

[11] Hash sign in the UK and some other English-speaking countries.

Each chapter is, or should be, a mini-story which affords benefits to the reader—a sense of progress, of advance through the plot and closure. But chapter divisions also entail costs. After reaching one, the reader may set down the book, interrupt the onward flow, and detach from the story.

Chapter openings, length, inner structure, type of closing, and other technicalities are the most subjective issues in fiction writing, which we will analyze in the next section.

 **1.5.5.1 CHAPTER DEVELOPMENT**

So far we've determined that a chapter, with few exceptions, should be a self-contained segment of the plot and leave the reader with a feeling of having completed a stage of the storyline. But, like scenes, chapters have components: openings, length, contents, ends, and sometimes titles. In this section we'll analyze these capital elements.

Chapter Titles

Q. Should we use chapter titles or not?

A. In literature, nothing should ever be done for the hell of it, but backed by solid reasoning.

Q: Does a chapter need a title?

A: It depends whether the title adds value to the chapter or not.

Titles *may* add two types of value: illustrative and aesthetic.

Illustrative chapter titles (POV and/or location and/or date and/or time)

We're reading a novel where the narrative is linear but the action shifts between three different places. Knowing where we are at the start of the chapter is helpful, and no doubt relieves the author of the tedium of setting the scene each time.

Timbuktu

Kampuchea

Berlin

If the plot covers a few days, it may be helpful to open the chapters with the day and perhaps the time:

a. Monday, 06:45

b. Monday, 6:45 a.m.[12]

The first time notation (a)—twenty-four hour, military time, or astronomical time—is perhaps more apt for action and techno-tales, while the second style is more common for other settings. Historical, fantasy, SF, and other genres demand great care when using time/date titles. Though astronomers and clock makers used the 24-hour notation for a long time, its common use dates only to the 20th century.

---

[12] Never 06:45 AM

In twelve-hour notation (b) we use the abbreviations a.m. (ante-meridian) and p.m. (post-meridian). Typography depends on house style.[13] To avoid confusion, the correct designation for 12p.m. is 12 noon or <u>noon</u> and for 12a.m., 12 midnight or <u>midnight</u>.

Some writers use extensive titles, such as Charles Brokaw in *The Atlantic Code*:

> Kom Al-Dikka, Alexandria, Egypt, 16 August 2009

Writers must question everything—a concept we'll repeat like a mantra throughout this manual. Are there chapters set in other *Alexandria* locations? Even if the answer is affirmative, is Kom Al-Dikka necessary? We can pose the same question of the other elements in the illustrative title.

Unless the area, region, country, and/or date are *capital* to understand the chapter or they *add* something of value to the reading experience, titles are unnecessary. And reminding the reader that Alexandria is in Egypt may cause offence. Yes, we know there's an Alexandria in Virginia but, to our knowledge, there are no archeological digs or Roman circuses in the vicinity.

Other times, writers may use illustrative titles to set the scene, not just in time, but within a strange world. In doing so it's possible to append color and atmosphere to the title, thus limiting exposition within the main text.

For example, Donna Johnson's *True Daughter* opens the first chapter with:

> Evening of the Joining Sun, Elder Phase of the Sap Moon, Spenara
> 967th Cignarian Cycle in the reign of Shadal Orna Mandel
> Nuya'ama Village

● Aesthetic Chapter Titles (Title or title + epigraph)

When used well, chapter titles can make the reading experience richer, more nuanced, more complex in texture and meaning, or even add subtle ambivalence to the events that follow (or precede) them. A good title can capture a mood in a few words and improve the reading experience.

Conversely, writers may upset readers with titles designed to show off—and in doing so puzzle the reader or imply he or she is an ignoramus.

In *The Labyrinth Key*, Howard V. Hendrix titles a chapter: "GÖDELIAN LOVE KNOT"

We wonder how many readers have ever heard of Gödel or his theorem and know enough Elementary Number Theory to even understand the chapter title.

Epigraphs and/or teasers—such as a quote pertinent to the upcoming events—can foreshadow, add layers of structure or satirical counterpoints by reference to other texts, etc.

In *True Daughter*, Donna Johnson titles the last chapter "MOTHER SPIDER WRAPS HER PREY." In the final section of the chapter, just above her complex date notation, she appends a quote from the literature of the world that speaks to theme:

> "Every Apprentice meets a Master as the path unfolds. It is the Master who searches for that truth-ready soul, struggles to obtain it, and forges the path ahead that leads to Awareness and then Oneness, while the Apprentice must merely follow. When the Apprentice is ready, the Master will come. These connections, we have learned, are the ties that bind."—Slvaian Tortean, chapter 3 "Masters"

---

[13] For punctuation and usage check a.m. / p.m. on page 356.

John Fowles begins each chapter of *The French Lieutenant's Woman,* with an epigraph. Chapter One's example he borrowed from *The Riddle* by Thomas Hardy:

> "Stretching eyes west/Over the sea,/Wind foul or fair,/Always stood she/Prospect impressed;/Solely out there/Did her gaze rest,/Never elsewhere/Seemed charm to be."

As the chapters progress, it becomes clear that this quotation offers a fair description of the heroine.

But titles can be dangerous. If they give too much away, titles may ruin the reading experience by clueing the reader into what is going to happen.

Chapter Openings

Chapter openings and closers are critical to make a storyline work. Before analyzing form and content, a writer must never assume a reader will devour a book at one sitting. Instead, hours, days, or weeks may lapse between the end of one chapter and the beginning of another. It's unreasonable to expect a reader will flick back page after page to determine what's going on. Hence, establishing the POV is critical, soon followed by an idea of setting to refresh the reader's memory.

There are no set ways to start a chapter, but there are several things to avoid, or at least, use with care items such as exposition, bland sentences, and repeated subject-verb starts.

> He was nearing the end of his one-year tour. He had flatly refused to extend. He loathed the country...[14]

> He awoke in the darkness, shivering and remembering the past. He could feel warmth against his back and,[sic] groaning he rolled over, hand reaching out to stroke soft fur. There was a noise...[15]

> He locked the rest room door. There was an ancient toilet and equally ancient marble sink basin, and it smelled pleasantly of cleaning liquid. He pulled out...[16]

These are boring and soon echo. Chapter openings are ideal places to show variety of composition:

> Neither her disproportionate response to Melik, nor her frigid response to Brue, were isolated episodes in Annabel's new existence.[17]

> "That nigger going down the street," said Dr. Hasselbacher standing in the Wonder Bar, "he reminds me of you, Mr. Wormold."[18]

> Night fell as the airport taxi rattled along the six miles of coastal road into Beirut.[19]

---

[14] Frederick Forsyth, Avenger.

[15] Andy Remic, Spiral.

[16] Robert Ludlum, The Sigma Protocol.

[17] John Le Carre, A Most Wanted Man

[18] Graham Greene, Our Man in Havana

[19] Thomas Harris, Black Sunday

> Manuel and his wife were poor, and when they first looked for an apartment in Paris, they found only two dark rooms below the street level, giving onto a small stifling courtyard.[20]

> "My hair!" commanded the young officer as he sat before the dressing table in the small vaulted room of the Hotel Fontenoy.[21]

Each of these openings, ranging from thriller to historical and erotica genres open chapters with subtle compositions designed to whet the reader's appetite. After these sentences, the reader shifts buttocks to a comfortable position and settles down to enjoy the writer's promise of a fine story.

Chapter openings beg design and ingenuity to showcase talent. Dialogue, intriguing atmosphere, sensitive description, or colorful character introductions are but a few of the devices a writer may use to set the tone.

In contrast, check these openings:

> Martha flicked through a few channels on the TV and decided she might have a nap before doing the laundry.

> The group of men parted and two men attired totally in combat fatigues and sky [sic] masks, their gleaming dark eyes peering out of their wrapped visages, attacked.

> Kate opened her eyes and stared fixedly at the ceiling of her room and the fawn molding against the pristine white of the stippled ceiling.

We've picked these at random from the scores of first chapters submitted for consideration to a long-suffering agent. Having read these opening lines, no amount of buttock shifting will afford solace to a weary reader.

Chapter Length

Let's open by declaring that there's no rule regarding how long a chapter is supposed to be. Some chapters can be scores of pages long and others just a few, or even contain a single paragraph.

When deciding how long a chapter *should* be, the writer needs to decide which scene or scenes belong in the chapter. Anything that does not further the story, including information dumps, lengthy scene setting, or unnecessary back story should be deleted.

Is there an exact answer?

No, but a few years back, *Writer's Digest* suggested a formula for successful novels of 2,500 to 3,000 words with three to four scenes to a chapter.

If this provokes a frown, we're thinking like writers. This answer is subjective. Writers craft novels targeting a particular readership (or they should). How long does a reader read? The answers can be as varied as chapter lengths, but intermittent bursts of thirty minutes or so seems to be a good average. And half an hour is what it takes to read a 3,000-word chapter. Of course reading speeds vary, not only between readers but also as a function of the chosen genre; literary fiction demands slower paces. Constructing chapter endings with cliffhangers and unresolved plot points is a writer's device to coax readers into dedicating another thirty minutes to the novel.

---

[20] Anaïs Nin, Little Birds.

[21] Lajos Zilahy, Century in Scarlet.

Another reason to determine chapter length is to maximize drama and suspense. Often, we find knowledgeable writers shortening chapters, say to two or three pages, at pivotal areas in the book.

Using this concept, chapters lengthen or shorten according to what manner of scene—or how many scenes—comprise each chapter. A lengthier emotional dialogue chapter, sort of the calm after the tempest, may follow a short action-packed chapter. Short descriptive internal dialogue chapters may follow longer intense chapters. In other words, by varying the flow and pacing of the narrative, the rhythm changes.

Resuming: Books without rhythmic variation, full of too-fast or too-slow chapters, cool the reader's interest. We need the spice of life; we need variety. Action and climax chapters tend to be shorter than other chapters in the book.

Chapter Ends

Following from the previous section, the story, action, and characters, not an arbitrary word count, should dictate when a chapter ends.

Chapters should end at the crucial moment and with a question that will not be answered until a later chapter. In other words: a chapter end shouldn't be an ending.

Inexperienced writers close chapters with the completion of an action, when the trick would be to stop a little shorter. For example, in a scene where the hero climbs up a tree to escape a grizzly, the chapter should end when the branch from where the hero offers a stiff middle finger to the enraged animal breaks with a sickening crunch. To wait until the bear has had his dinner is overkill. If the scene needs the hero crashing down before the grizzly, then the chapter could end when the hero remembers the counsel of a lumberjack and plays dead to fool the animal. Would the bear fall for the ruse or have his dinner anyway?

If a maiden gallops down the stairs—to escape a fate worse than death at the hands of rowdy intruders—the chapter should end when she trips and falls.

The next chapter could then begin with her regaining consciousness and checking she's in one piece under the solicitous eyes of a debonair police officer who made it to the scene just in time. If this happened in the same chapter, it would give the reader no incentive to read on and find out what happens next. The chapter ends best where the action stops at a crucial point: a "cliffhanger."

Other chapter-end devices are stunning revelations, interrupted conversations, discoveries, items gone missing, and any unresolved development.

 **1.5.6 PART**

"Part," "volume," and "book" are broader divisions of a novel, often crafted from a number of chapters. These impose an even deeper split and greater cost, but imply a much stronger shift in time, place, or viewpoint.

These great story divisions beg self-completeness. Unlike chapters, parts require ends with finality, not unfinished actions or cliffhangers. The reason is the intrinsic role of a "part." It is intended to signal that a major block of the story is over.

Boris Pasternak's *Dr. Zhivago* is split into two parts, Eugene O'Neill's *Long Day's Journey into Night* into four, Margaret Mitchell's *Gone with the Wind* into five, Mario Puzo's *The Godfather* into nine and Leo Tolstoy's *War and Peace* into fifteen.

Novels spanning different periods benefit from a "part" division. A number of books built around the Holocaust follow the harrowing stories of families through three well-defined moments: before Hitler came to power, during the war, and in the aftermath once the allies won and set out to clean the bilges.

Other internal structures may follow a family saga through different generations or the genesis of a wondrous object.

Large literary works often require even more complex divisional structures. An example that comes to mind is Fyodor Dostoyevsky's *The Brothers Karamazov*. This monumental work is split into twelve books, further arranged into four parts and a three-chapter epilogue.

Of course, part division can also be used for effect as a ticking-clock device. To use this technique well, requires a great deal of ingenuity from the writer. Take the story of a boy who discovers a box containing six pebbles, each engraved with a rune. The novel may be divided into six parts, each opening with one of the runes. If cleverly executed, the effect on the overall novel structure can be rewarding to the reader.

In Jurassic Park, Michael Crichton used such a device. He started with a simple geometric drawing on page nine, a diagram he terms "Iteration One." Later, on pages 29, 81, 179, 269, 315, and 365, these iterations—seven images that divide the seven sections of the book—grow more complex.

 **1.5.7 EPILOGUE**

Also called an afterword, the epilogue is a short section following the last chapter that reveals consequences, what happens to the characters after the main story is over.

In certain genres, like romance, epilogues are common. The writer goes on to give additional information about the main characters to satisfy reader's expectation that they will live happily ever after. Often, the writer shows the protagonist married and with children. In suspense or thriller genres, it can narrate the outcome of previous events or how the villain served twenty years hard labor.

Epilogues aren't always about the future lives of the characters. Sometimes, they cover days or even follow where the story left. In this sense, epilogues can wrap up story questions that the writer has not answered after completing the main story arc.

Epilogues, like prologues, can be powerful tools to give the story closure, but—there's always a *but* in fiction writing—most stories don't need epilogues.

Like an unnecessary prologue, the epilogue can be a tacked-on tidbit that wouldn't be necessary if the writer had taken his time to improve the scenes that came before. Often, epilogues don't deserve the name and consist of explanations of events that happened at the end of the book or unfortunate ruses to tie up plot strings. Also, flip epilogues, or attempts at setting up the next book with cliffhangers should be avoided. Pushing readers into buying the next book may have the opposite effect.

Epilogues can frustrate readers to the point of ruining a good novel. To have an engaging book ruined by a trivial, unbelievable, or lousy epilogue is a tragedy. This is not as unusual as it might first appear. Like writers (most of them, anyway), readers are also human beings. As such, they understand the world in different ways, nurse their own pet peeves, and fantasize about dissimilar outcomes. The writer must analyze the plot and determine if the end is clear, a real end, but with possible alternative continuations.

The story is finished, but we hope some characters have survived. One reader may root for a particular character, or imagine his or her future will follow a given line. To have the hero survive overwhelming odds only to succumb to swine flu six weeks after THE END demands the writer be tied to a stake, forced to read the offending piece aloud, and then shot.

An epilogue can make a book memorable... or ruin it. That a few lines can make or break a story lovingly built to its resolution over hundreds of pages and tens of thousands of words should give a writer pause to determine whether the story needs an epilogue or not.

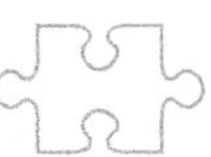

1.6 STRUCTURE / WORKING

The following sections structure a mainstream novel, and the process would have been similar with any fiction genre. Here, the chosen concept is developed from a single word to a synopsis:

A. Concept structure

B. Basic plot structure

C. Section structure

D. Chapter structure

E. Scene structure

F. Synopsis

Writers must determine where to stop. Some will have enough structure with A, while others will carry on to D or even to F. As long as it performs its intended task there's no right or wrong in terms of detail or length. It can never be said too often:

Time spent on the structure is like putting money in the bank.

1.6.1 CONCEPT STRUCTURE

A concept is the most basic stage of an idea, the seed from which a towering tree will grow, or the twinkle in the groom's eye when roving the future mommy's blushing face.

A novel is a story, a tale, a play grown from the germ of an idea. Concepts expand into full-fledged sagas, but our present concern is not how to develop a concept, but the nature of the concept itself.

We don't know the genesis of successful novels, but a few blockbusters come to mind and it's easy to fantasize about their origins.

Michael, a man of pale skin the insects find irresistible, scratches a lump in his arm where mosquitoes have fed to their proboscis's content and peers at a piece of amber in a trader's tray. Inside the amber, there's a large mosquito. The trader blesses his cousin's knack with polyester resins, dyes, and insects, while he pitches the tourist.

> "The insect, in this rare piece of fossilized genuine amber, flittered about in the epoch of the dinosaurs."

The man stops scratching. He smiles and walks away from the shop with a concept that will make him a millionaire: Mosquitoes bite. Mosquitoes in the Cretaceous period would bite Cretaceous creatures. In theory, it's possible to grow an individual from a single strand of DNA. Blood contains DNA. Mosquitoes suck blood. Dinosaurs had blood: *Jurassic Park*.

Peter dozes under an umbrella on a crowded beach, while the wife and kids squeeze through the seething mob to reach the sea and wet their feet. Wouldn't it be nice if the beach was deserted? A joyous giggle and the man opens one eye. A few feet away, a toddler sits on a towel and hammers a mound of sand with a rubber fish. The man closes his eyes, makes a wry movement with his mouth and the toy shark on the toddler's hand projects against the screen of his closed eyelids. He jerks alert: *Jaws*.

These are raw concepts, and turning them into full-fledged stories requires vast amounts of work, talent, and ingenuity. However, even the most convoluted ideas have a starting point: a concept.

One of the writers co-authoring this manual has a repository of ideas stored in a database. To produce a novel, this writer browses through the file, selects a notion suitable for a given market and settles down to expand it into a full structure. To illustrate the structure-development process we picked one of these ideas: Hermaphrodite.

After choosing the concept, we set about to develop it on different levels in the following sections.

 **1.6.1.1 CONCEPT STRUCTURE DEVELOPMENT**

We have the working concept of a hermaphrodite. In biology, a hermaphrodite is an animal or plant that has reproductive organs associated with both male and female sexes.

A number of animals, like snails and slugs, and a few fish are *true* hermaphrodites.

Why stress *true*? Well, the idea we want to develop involves mammals like us. In humans, we find the pseudo-hermaphrodite, a person with the physical traits of one sex and the genetic instructions of the other. There are people with both sets of external sexual organs, like vagina and penis, but they cannot impregnate themselves because it's impossible to have both ovaries and testes. These organs always develop into one or the other. Hence, *true* hermaphroditic humans do not exist.

Once we have the kernel of our idea, we store it away. If this seems contradictory, consider that although an idea may be the theme of a story, the plot can take any shape and go in any direction. We could fashion a romance, a horror tale, a mystery/thriller, or an adventure. In each instance, we would develop the idea along a different path. Though the concept would be the same, the novel would be different.

Since we are professional writers, our concept must adjust to the first two articles of genre-fiction law:

 **1. The theme should be original and unique** 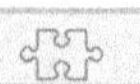

This is the litmus test of a concept. In genre fiction, most ideas have been exploited to exhaustion. This is the reason agents and editors demand a blurb or mini-synopsis to accompany a query; they want to read about the concept—before rejecting it—because they've seen the same plot a zillion times before. Then, unless the writer has a unique voice, the manuscript will be impossible to sell.

Dear agent, my novel is about:

Goblins, unicorns, and sleeping princesses

True love and happily ever after

Confused vampires

Intergalactic empires

A serial killer more beastly than the last one

Templars, Freemasons, and the Holy Grail

The list is endless.

So we examine our ideas with as much objectivity as we can muster. We've never heard of stories involving a true hermaphrodite, so the concept looks original and unique.

2. The theme should have mass-market appeal

This means genre. At the time of writing this Companion, fantasy is overcrowded with a million manuscripts seeking a place to roost, and the same is true of romance, vampires, and interstellar conflict. A hermaphrodite serial killer has possibilities, and the same can be said of hermaphrodite Templars, Freemasons, and Ayatollahs. But even before we start, there's a problem looming on the horizon: true hermaphroditic humans do not exist. We could make an exception and create one, but the biological problems would be enormous.

Why humans? Why not aliens? When we think of aliens, we identify the creature as male or female. Why? What about if the members of a given extraterrestrial species couldn't comprehend the distinction between male and female? They wouldn't use gender pronouns and each individual would be a self-contained family nucleus.

Aliens, however, reek of SF, and from what we hear; the genre is chockablock with unsold manuscripts. Mass-market appeal? Fine, let's make an adventure-thriller-SF-fantasy-romance-historical-horror-novel. A little of each, shake well, and we have a winner with broadest market appeal.

With our concept safely tucked away, we gather cheese, crackers, and a bottle of fermented grape juice. Bottled in 1980 it must be well past its sell-by date. It isn't.

We have an alien, but interstellar travel is dicey to say the least. Why would an alien choose Earth? He/she/it (this will be difficult, let's have him masculine) could be here from time immemorial, hiding somewhere. This is good because we could have an adventurer (say John) looking for him. And we have history too. But, why would John try to find an alien? This doesn't work. John finds the alien when he's looking for something else. Better. John may fall in love with the alien so we have the romance angle covered. Horror? Imagine John's face when he unpacks the goodies. Not good, this is weak; John could be bisexual and hit the jackpot. We have everything but the horror and thrilling bits. No problem, we'll throw in one cliffhanger after another and have John running and escaping by the seat of his pants from horrors galore.

The grape juice a memory, let's recap.

1. John sets off looking for the treasure (must determine what, where, why him, his reasons, his goal and his backstory).

2. After a harrowing ordeal, John finds whatever, and the alien (must determine the difficulties, ordeals, trials and the nature of the treasure).

3. Alien guards the treasure from time immemorial and tells John his story (must characterize the alien and determine why him, why on Earth, why is he guarding the treasure).

At this point, we discover a huge flaw in our budding plot. If the alien and John fall in love, they must be friends first (it makes sense). Where's the antagonist? We need extra grape juice to oil rusty neurons.

> 4. Someone else is after the treasure. (We need a powerful organization, unethical, prone to botch things up, and ruthless. Easy: any government will do.)

This is stroke of genius and saves the day.

> 5. The government hits the place where the alien keeps the treasure (must determine how, with what means, why, and their goal).

> 6. The alien arranges the escape of his paramour and sacrifices himself, taking the antagonist thugs with him (must determine why sacrifice after all this time, what means he has to wipe out the enemy, what happens to John).

To end here is weak, too many loose ends. Above all, why would the alien commit suicide? Love is a powerful reason, but it's been done far too many times. After a third bottle of grape juice, we find a solution.

> 7. The alien needed John to alter or add something to him. At the story's end, he's not dead, but hidden again. Now that the alien is complete, he can pull off his master plan (must determine what's happened, what John has given him, and what his master plan is).

Not bad for a single sitting. We have an idea slowly developing into a concept.

The important aspect of this silly scene is to portray the gestation of an idea. So far, we don't know how to start the novel, or how to end it. We don't know where to locate the action. We don't know the goals, plot points, or anything else for that matter. We know one of the characters is an alien hermaphrodite.

In real life, the writer would mull over the seven points we've outlined to develop his concept over a period of days or months, jotting down notes or exploring possibilities. He or she may not need anything else in terms of structure to start writing, but for a plot of the complexity we envisage, going on what we have would be dangerous. We would become stuck after only a few pages.

This concept we'll expand into a basic plot. Later we'll break it into sections, rustle up a chapter outline, continue with a scene structure and then, write the synopsis.

1.6.2 BASIC PLOT STRUCTURE

A structure in rough draft is termed a basic plot, and consists of the first logical addition after outlining the concept. The aim of a basic plot is to outline the events that must take place in the novel in steps or broad strokes.

We are not looking for detail, characterization, or precision—but plot. We don't need to worry about names, features, color, or background—just plot. Why stress plot, plot, plot like a mantra? Because at this stage, structure *means* plot.

Spaceship. A transmission from a nearby planet. The crew goes to investigate. The signal source is a derelict alien spacecraft. Inside they discover a chamber with eggs. John, a crew member, looks closer. A creature attaches itself to his face. Back at the ship, the crew attempts to remove the creature from John's face. Soon the creature detaches on its own and dies. The crew resumes their trip.

John recovers, then a thing bursts from his chest, killing him and escaping into the ship. The crew attempts to locate and capture it. Soon they discover the thing is huge and vicious. It starts killing the crew. When Mark is the only one left, he manages to initiate the ship's self-destruct sequence and narrowly escapes in a shuttle as the ship explodes.

As Mark prepares to enter stasis, he discovers that the thing is aboard the shuttle but manages to eject it into space.

Does it read familiar? In a basic plot of *Alien*, we need no description of anything, only events. Later we'll add precision: Mark will become Ripley, there will be a cat and an android and the mother of all badass creatures.

In the following pages, we will focus on plot.

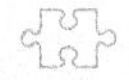 **1.6.2.1 BASIC PLOT STRUCTURE DEVELOPMENT**

The first item we need is setting. Where is the treasure? If we can decide on a location, it may give us an idea of the treasure's nature itself. If our alien has been hiding for a long time, cities are out of the question. We are left with the oceans and uninhabited or sparsely-inhabited land.

Aliens living in the ocean's depths have been portrayed before. Besides, we would face a plot where the action would take place in submarines or deep-sea stations, which has also been done to exhaustion.

On land we have deserts, jungles, and mountains. Deserts don't look too promising, and mountains would mean caves. We could try Antarctica, but that has been already done. The ideal thing would be something that adventurers have been seeking for centuries and never found, despite countless references to it. A lost city would do.

Problem is there are many lost lands, from the legendary Atlantis to scores of others whose remains have been found or have forever disappeared in cataclysms.

A writer should write about what he or she knows; this is the counsel of countless experts. Hence, if a real writer considered developing our plot he would choose an environment he's more familiar with. In our team, one of the writers has had enough jungle experience to last a lifetime, so we sought a lost city in a jungle.

Ciudad Blanca, or White City, in Honduras is as weird as they come: People have been looking for hundreds of years, and many claim to have seen its buildings but nobody has ever found it. From 1526, when Hernan Cortes first recorded it, there have been scores of expeditions involving adventurers, governments and even the CIA. All came back empty-handed. Wonderful.

This highlights another issue of plot building. A writer should seek untried concepts, unexplored avenues, or original themes. There's nothing new under the sun, but the writer must root for different angles or unique aspects for the plot to stand out.

Hernan Cortes heard the tale of a white gleaming city in the Honduran Mosquitia (or Mosquito Forest), the most impenetrable forest on the planet, and even in the twenty-first century, largely unexplored. But "city" can mean a large structure. However improbable, it could have been an alien craft. The craft crashes and there are reports of a huge white structure in the jungle. The survivors realize they can't repair the thing, so they scheme to cover or bury it. Thus, the "city" disappears.

Adventurers have sought Ciudad Blanca because sixteenth century reports tell of gold by the truckload. So, we have a goal for any adventurer: gold. And a twist in the plot when whomever thinks he is onto the prize finds a lovesick hermaphrodite.

Let's recap and lay another layer of structure.

1. Satellites detect magnetic anomalies in Honduras, consistent with low-grade ore. The Mosquitia is impossible. Scientists disregard the find. A rich villain thinks the anomaly is not mineral but Ciudad Blanca.

2. Villain puts together a bunch of muscle. Since he's pushing seventy, his son will lead. Off they go kitted out with high-tech gadgets. Every day they report. When they near the spot, communications cease.

3. Two years later: Villain hears our hero giving a talk about jungle flora. Our hero has no formal training but an encyclopedic knowledge of the Mosquitia. He treks through the forest and lives off the land. Hero is a widower. He wants to rebuild his life and that of his kids (4) but his new sweetheart has contracted a rare illness. Villain finds out, and concocts the story of wanting his son's remains brought home. He will give a sack of cash to Hero, enough to pay the best hospital for his woman.

4. When Villain marshals another team of mercenaries, Hero decrees no gadgets, or bulky equipment.

5. As the group nears the area where the first group disappeared, the mercenaries vanish one after the other until Hero is alone. He stumbles into a big cat, fights, and manages a pyrrhic victory; before dying itself, the cat mauls him to within an inch of his life.

6. Hero recovers in a strange place tended to by IT, a strange woman.

7. Hero is alive because he didn't wear any electronic device, even his watch is wind-up (as befits that of any sensible person venturing into a rainforest). He meets several other women, much older, all that remains from the ITS, a race from another world.

8. Hero tries to escape. IT nabs him and locks him up deep within their complex. There he will learn the saga of the ITS. The flesh is weak and IT is most accommodating, though full of surprises.

9. A deranged Villain has had enough. Months have gone by. He bribes half the Honduran Army to find out once and for all what's happened *and* find that damned Ciudad Blanca.

10. When the ITS sense an army is on its way, they go for broke. IT shows Hero a network of caves to get the hell out. The army deforests the area and when Villain arrives in a chopper, IT blows the place to smithereens.

11. Hero returns to his village with a pocketful of diamonds to get his woman on her feet and the kiddos to University.

12. IT is not dead, but hiding deep and very much pregnant. Hero's ministrations have returned her fertility. Now she will kidnap the local talent, use them as breeders and rebuild the ITS.

This is a basic plot, with more holes than a Gruyere cheese (some Swiss cheeses have no holes), full of inconsistencies, problems, and details requiring much research. There's no characterization, setting, atmosphere, subplots, or any of the myriad issues required of a full-fledged structure. But these 450 words, or one single-spaced page, have the bones of a 450-page novel.

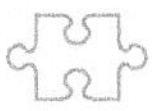

1.6.3 SECTION STRUCTURE

In this chapter's opening pages, we cited three important aspects of a good structure. The second point was to break the manuscript down into manageable chunks.

The story concept is like the drawing of a new airliner. No matter how beautiful and impressive its rendering, it's empty. A member of the public will gape at sinuous aerodynamic lines, size, color, and overall aesthetic beauty. An engineer will cringe when he thinks about the gargantuan task of building the thing.

The same is true of fiction writing. We start with a concept, which can be awe-inspiring. The concept will grow from a basic single-word idea into a nebulous skeleton that gradually acquires focus and resolution. This is what we've done so far with our crazy plot.

No man or woman can build a modern aircraft from scratch, and no writer can write a book all at once. Some writers have phenomenal memories and can structure a novel in their heads, but the process is the same whether we plot on a piece of paper, on a screen, or in our brain.

When an aircraft dream matures from concept to design, the chief designer breaks down the job into sections: airframe, avionics, and power plant. Later, each of these major sections breaks down into many subsections and each subsection into a myriad of specific design jobs. One designer, or a team of them, will design the device to flush the toilets, and a different designer, or team, will tackle the struts for the landing gear.

Breaking a plot into sections is a rewarding experience. After thrashing about wild ideas, there comes a point when these concepts crystallize into physical containers, like the drawers on a chest.

In the following section we'll explore the first major plot division.

1.6.3.1 SECTION STRUCTURE DEVELOPMENT

On the loose structure, we had twelve loose points, which we will now double. The plot remains the same but, henceforth, in blocks with a semblance of order.

<u>First Section:</u> We ground down the premise.

1. Discovery of something odd in the Honduran Mosquitia.

2. Villain organizes a party led by his son.

3. The explorers disappear.

The section should be almost a prologue. Exposition must be reduced to a minimum and the plot should move forward swiftly.

<u>Second section:</u> We introduce the hero and lay down the challenge.

4. Two years later. Villain hears a Miskito Indian (Hero) giving a talk.

5. Villain recruits Hero.

6. Villain organizes a second party.

7. Hero lays down the law.

8. Second party hacks into La Mosquitia.

9. Second party disappears.

In this part, we enter into the real plot. We can blend in the backstory of the project and characterize the hero and the antagonist. We'll hike the tension with a secondary character reporting to Villain behind Hero's back and a few jungle scenes, to end when Hero is half-dead.

<u>Third section:</u> We introduce the treasure, the alien community, and the dilemma.

10. Hero recovers in a strange place tended to by IT.

11. Hero meets several other ITS.

12. Hero tries to escape.

13. IT nabs him and locks him up deep within their complex.

14. Hero learns the saga of the ITS.

15. IT and Hero develop a strange relationship.

This is the novel's core section and the most fun to write. The alien's characterization will be a challenge and will require much ingenuity to describe the environment and the particular biology of the ITS. Also, this will be the section needing the most research.

<u>Fourth section:</u> We stage the climax.

16. A deranged Villain has had enough.

17. Villain bribes the Honduran Army to find out what's happened and locate Ciudad Blanca.

18. The ITS sense an army is on its way and gather to decide what to do.

19. IT shows Hero a network of caves to escape.

20. The army deforests the area and Villain arrives in a chopper.

21. IT blows the place.

This is a frantic section, with many short ticking-clock scenes, and it is the place to explore cinematic POV and fast shifts between the players to build the tension.

<u>Fifth section:</u> We tie up loose ends and explain everything.

22. News reports on a small meteoroid impact in La Mosquitia (to cover up the Honduran Army's fiasco).

23. Hero returns to his village.

24. IT is not dead, but hiding deep and very much pregnant.

Rather than an epilogue, we should craft this as the real ending of the novel. When the reader is about to relax thinking that the tale is over, we will spring a different reality. The real nature of the ITS will leave the reader gasping.

At this point, it's important to realize that nothing is static. Our twenty-four notes are not plot points. Far from it. They are like Post-It notes on a board. In the real world, we would spend weeks, perhaps months developing each section, gathering the research, discovering flaws, and attempting to remedy them. Of course, before we set to write down this plot, we had a good idea of the overall structure down to the smallest details.

But its genesis and development followed the process we've outlined. Structuring is not a matter of sitting down before a computer and striking keys, but a mental exercise; the writer adds details at odd moments. To memorize the sections and subsections is easy. Take item 22.

News reports on a small meteoroid impact in La Mosquitia.

With this in mind, the writer could work out the structure of that scene when having a drink with friends, if the program on the TV suddenly blanks out and a somber-looking anchor delivers news of a natural disaster. This is the purpose of structuring: to break down a plot into smaller parts and develop them in isolation.

Some writers start at point one, and that's shortsighted. In this instance, we would start the story at point three and weave points one and two into the second section. We can only accomplish this because we already know what comes after points one, two, and three.

Once we break down the plot further, add detail, names, and events, the easiest thing in the world will be to shift elements about to suit the overall beat of the story.

 **1.6.4 CHAPTER STRUCTURE**

An observant writer makes a good writer. The best novels read as if written by a skillful "Peeping Tom," a guy or a gal with an uncanny sense of body language, acute ear, roving eyes, and analytical brain.

Imagine jotting down items on a shopping list, ready for the weekly adventure at the supermarket. The list is unlikely to include:

A bottle of Tabasco sauce (red) to spice Buster's Bloody Mary (as if he needed spicing; at this rate he'll be the end of me).

A jar of French mustard (but without the stupid little seeds that get stuck between my teeth and defy flossing, so I have to resort to toothpicks and then my gums bleed).

Most likely, the scribbles will read:

Tabasco

Mustard

Florid prose is unnecessary to buy groceries. Buster's (or Mary's) commendable interests and hatred of mustard seeds are understood.

Outlining a novel is the process of listing reminders and keeping it as simple as possible. Of course, the writer can add detail to his heart's content, though it's a risky proposition at this early stage. Why? Because things will be changed around, bits will added, and sections will be deleted. Having to ditch pages of hard-worked text is more traumatic than deleting a single sentence.

Many writers feel it is harder to write an outline than the novel itself, and they might be right. Outlining has little to do with writing and much to do with an intense mental exercise. Rather than releasing pent up talent on pages of narrative and dialogue, an outline is a sequence of still images; instead of words and sentences the writer must list events.

The good news is once events are listed, fleshing them out is much easier. Freed from having to keep the intricacies of plot at the forefront of her thoughts, the writer can concentrate on writing.

1.6.4.1 CHAPTER STRUCTURE DEVELOPMENT

The chapter outline is an intermediate step favored by many writers and eschewed by others—with good reason. Chapters are capital divisions of a fiction work. Their contents, openings, closings, and inner structure are far too important to be determined at this stage.

A chapter structure is little more than a collection of tentative scene ideas, the building blocks which we'll structure in the next section.

Since the main trait of a good structure is its flexibility, we shouldn't be overly concerned about the final chapter shape; we can always move scenes about, change contents and eventually shape the chapters to do their job.

The structure of a full-length novel would be cumbersome, therefore we've outlined what will be the book's first part: from the conceptual presentation to the second plot point.

We have chosen to open the novel with a fast sequence of scenes split between three locations: Villain's study, the jungle, and the explorer's base camp by the river.

> Chapter One: Two years earlier. Introduce Villain at study, Villain's son in jungle, Henchman by river. Villain at study when link lost. Henchman downriver discovers almost empty pipante.

The first chapter is complex and difficult to write. We want to show Villain in his element, in control and surrounded by his wealth and power, as a contrast to the harrowing progress through virgin jungle. When we plotted the scenes, we realized that Villain would be removed from the action most of the time. This would be unreasonable. Therefore, we summoned another player: The Henchman. This guy, Villain's trusted retainer, is his link to the action and the keeper of the base camp in this first chapter. Later, he will accompany the explorers and show how nasty he can be. Originally, we brought him in so he could make a discovery at the closing of chapter one: the first plot point that will (hopefully) coerce the reader into the story.

Please, note that Henchman didn't exist when we first thought of the plot. This point of technique merits further explanation. Rather than starting with a gaggle of people, it's often more sensible to limit the cast to hero, antagonist, and perhaps, one or two key characters. Instead of building characters— and finding something for them to do—this technique follows a contrary approach: The writer creates scenes and plot-points. These, in turn, will demand secondary characters to pull them off. Concisely: the plot dictates the need for additional characters, not the writer.

Since chapter one must be fast, we had no room for much backstory or exposition, besides what little we could weave into the character's inner dialogue. Therefore, we planned to dose out the exposition over the rest of part one.

> Chapter Two: Now, introduce Hero on his way to meet Villain. Flashback conference day before. Villain greets hero and makes its pitch. Enters Henchman. Hero lays down the law to accept. Villain agrees.

Sages threaten fire and brimstone if the protagonist doesn't open chapter one. This is nonsense. Chapter one opens with a whirlwind of a story, and the protagonist doesn't belong there. In addition, we've shaped the first chapter to bring the reader up to speed with the story, planning to open chapter two in the protagonist's POV. In "Perfect Circle," Carlos introduces the protagonist in chapter three.

Had we opened the second chapter at the lecture hall where Hero delivers his talk, we would have succumbed to showiness and plain mind-numbing information about the Mosquitia. This would have been bad technique. Instead, we chose Hero lost in the winding roads of a secluded urbanization, trying to find his bearings and thinking back to the previous day's events. Later we'll meet the antagonist and his lackey and close the scene on a troubled Hero's POV, that of a man who feels he has just sold his soul to the Devil.

Chapter Three: Hero leads in jungle. Henchman reports to Villain. Man disappears.

Here we have the opportunity to describe the jungle along with Hero's introspection. Characters lose their patina of civilization when things get dicey; man's basest instincts and flaws surface when the chips are down. We plan to paint the crumbling resolve of men facing the horror of an environment in perpetual darkness and close the chapter when one of the men disappears.

Chapter Four: Hero and Henchman are the only ones left. Flashback to the loss of three more men. Henchman forces Hero to continue. Henchman disappears.

Though it was tempting to continue hacking through jungle and losing people à la Agatha Christie *And Then There Was None,* we plotted a change of scene where Hero and Henchman are the only two survivors. We can write a few lines of internal dialogue in Hero's POV to cover how the other men vanished. The idea behind this chapter is to characterize Henchman as a bastard and Hero as a pragmatic man, with knowledge of the environment the other lacks.

When Hero proposes to cut their losses and get the hell out, Henchman will pull a gun on him and force Hero to continue. As conditions worsen, we'll hike tension to a cliffhanger where Henchman will disappear.

Chapter Five: Frantic Villain tries to make contact with his men. Hero finds Henchman dead. Hero turns around. Dusk. Hero climbs a tree. Cat there first. Hero half-dead.

To close the first part, we open the chapter with Villain at the end of his tether. The explorers have ceased transmission. His base camp keeper can't do a thing but wait. The Villain faces his second failed attempt and we can characterize him further. To wrap up the first part we have Hero find Henchman murdered in a particularly nasty way. To continue the quest would be lunacy. Hero beats a hasty retreat and removes to a tree to spend the night, in the process disturbing a local cat. We close with a badly mauled Hero plummeting thirty feet to the forest floor.

The snippets above are just reminders, or the gist of what happens in each chapter. There are no details or even names. For that, we need a scene structure.

From a technical standpoint, the plot has dictated the structure development. The core of the story resides on the IT, their nature and the reason they've been hiding for centuries in the Mosquitia. To narrate this tale, our problem all along has been to structure a series of events and drive the actors toward our chosen stage: one point in la Mosquitia Forest. This we've done in the five-chapter first part; a mini-novel in itself with beginning middle and end.

With the first part, we've placed Hero in the exact location we needed him to launch the second part.

But there's a future problem. Once we have told the IT's story, and to craft a climactic end to the novel, we need an external agent to intervene. This is the reason we've disposed of Henchman, leaving the antagonist primed to do something rash.

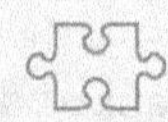 **1.6.5 SCENE STRUCTURE**

A scene layout is the most comprehensive and detailed form of structure, with its own set of advantages and disadvantages.

The advantages of constructing a structure of the project and having the full plot detailed will eliminate becoming stuck, blocked, or just frustrated. Empty areas, lulls, unresolved subplots, and parts requiring more tension will leap out. Many writers, eager to get on with the writing, despair at having to structure a plot. They have an idea for a story and a random assortment of mental images, but how should they arrange these fragments into a coherent plot?

The disadvantages can be condensed in one word: time. A scene-by-scene structure is time consuming or, to be exact, claims the time a writer will spend plotting throughout the novel at the beginning and in one lump sum.

Other technical issues are worth mentioning. In a flexible structure, the writer can switch scenes around, add new ones, fill in the gaps and take out what doesn't work. We can try new ideas without having to spend hours writing pages of the story. We may discover that to spring a subplot halfway into the novel we need "seeding." Seeding consists of dropping hints or inserting a line of inner dialogue with the germ of an idea or event in preparation for the subplot.

A novel we recently edited opened in a church service attended by a motley crowd. Much later in the manuscript, the hero discovers he's being stalked. Though the subplot worked, it didn't have the potency it deserved. We suggested to the writer mixing another character among the church's patrons, perhaps a serious man on a rear pew. When the heroine pans over the faces in the hall, she does a double take at the stranger's face but thinking nothing of it. In the original version, an event causes a commotion in the church and the chapter fizzled to an uneventful end. In the revised work, the heroine glances back to discover the man is no longer there. By peppering two or three similar sightings (real or imagined) through the manuscript, we rattled up the tension. Soon, the silent character on the rear pew became a subliminal menace.

To add the church's twist in a fully structured project would have taken five minutes, instead of having to rewrite vast tracts of text.

 **1.6.5.1 SCENE STRUCTURE DEVELOPMENT**

We now have our budding plot layout and our alien hermaphrodite waiting in the Mosquito Forest. Now it's time to rig the décor, bring in the characters, set them on the stage, and get them to play.

Before we start, we need to flesh our characters. Not much, just enough to get going. In section 6.1, the reader will find examples of character files, also available for downloading from WWW. ofwcompanion.com.[22]

For Chapter One of our novel we've picked the intervening actors:

---

22 Character files, like structures, can be simple or comprehensive. We have included two sample template files. One (Section 6.1.2, pages 434 and 435) contains the basics of character building. Two (Section 6.1.3, pages 436 and 437) provides a deeper layer. By using as many or as few sections as are comfortable, each writer can adapt this tool to the way he or she writes.

Sandor Gulyás, 79. Millionaire industrialist (abattoirs). Emigrated from Hungary in 1944. Small fry war criminal. Struck a deal with the U.S. State Department. 5'10", thin, aristocratic, sparse white hair. Cast-iron health. Lifelong fascination with Mesoamerican cultures.

Miska Gulyás, 46 Sandor's son. Law graduate. Worked on and off at his father's empire. Sportsman. Ocean racing. Three divorces. Father threatened disinheritance if he didn't lead the Mosquito party. 6' athletic build. Port wine mark on cheek. Addicted to cocaine.

Stanley O'Conner, 42. Sandor's right-hand man. Gay. Dishonorably discharged from British SAS. 5' 8", overweight.

Kurt, 45, East German Ex-Stasi, keep-fit fanatic. Gay. Stanley's companion. Chief of security at Gulyás Enterprises. 6'1" Long ponytail.

Francisco (Bosco), 38, Ex-Marine Corporal. Mexican. Hates any reference to his clown namesake. Security employee Gulyás Enterprises.

Matthew. 32 Ex-Marine. Security employee Gulyás Enterprises.

Henry. Ex-Marine. Security employee Gulyás Enterprises.

A few comments on character description. Sandor's character file is five pages long. The secondary characters (Miska, Stanley and Francisco) occupy less than half a page. Those of Kurt, Matthew and Henry are only a couple of lines long. The level of character detail should be proportional to the character's importance and exposure. It's a waste of time to collect details (or even surnames) for characters whose life will be short.

It's a good idea to open a file for each character in the story, and add detail as needed while writing the rough draft. Later, on rewrite, these files can be vital to check continuity and further characterize the players.

Likewise, scene files are a good format to keep the scene basics and add details, notes, and reminders (like calls for researching a given issue or checking a factual point).

Let's recap what we have for Chapter One:

Two years earlier. Introduce Villain at study, Villain's son in jungle, Henchman by river. Villain at study when link lost. Henchman downriver discovers *almost* empty *pipante*.

As we've mentioned before, this is a complex multimodal chapter with three settings: a room in a mansion, the jungle, and a river hut.

To structure a scene we need to imagine the settings. A room is a room, more or less ornate with antique furniture and modern communications equipment. This leaves the river hut and the jungle.

In the Mosquito, there are navigable rivers and the locals use motorized canoes that go by the name of *pipante* (a long pirogue with a small outboard motor at one end.) We chose a large river and a small tributary disappearing into thick jungle. Our party would have traveled to the tributary's mouth where they would set up a base camp in a hut. This is consistent with the local geography and custom. Usually there are huts at the junction between rivers and tributaries. We can think of them as a last chance of contact before proceeding through narrower waterways.

Why a base camp? Communications.

Forests, often misnamed jungles, are the most complex ecosystems on Earth. Imagine a bunch of umbrellas held high. Those would be the tall trees forming the top canopy. They get most of the sunlight and the animals living there seldom venture down.

Since the top canopy is not very thick, some sun passes through. Now imagine another layer of umbrellas farther down. This would be the secondary canopy. Under this layer, let's place another set of umbrellas farther down, (a tertiary canopy) and so on up to five layers. In many places, no light ever reaches the ground of the forest. Traveling on foot is a nightmare of darkness or, at best, a misty twilight which is soon swallowed by more darkness in conditions of one-hundred percent humidity and stifling heat, like a womb. This is our third setting.

Satellite communication from the heart of a jungle is impossible, but certain low frequencies travel a few miles. Since the tributary mouth is only ten miles away from the party's destination, it makes sense to have someone there with a low-frequency receiver and a satellite phone to reach the rest of the world. In virgin forest one mile a day is excellent progress.

This level of inquiry precedes writing a scene set in any unusual environment. In Fantasy and Sci-Fi, it's termed world-building, and the concept is the same whether the novel is set on Mars or in medieval Europe, ancient Greece, or the Kingdom of Never-Never. Unless the setting is right—and the writer feels comfortable in familiar surroundings, however imaginary—the scene will read manufactured or downright false.

In this chapter, we'll use another advanced technique called "parallel scenes." It works like this:

We have one man in a room, one man in a hut and a group of men in thick jungle. These are the main scenes. Then, there's another section when the hut man is outside and by the river.

Our problem is that the three main scenes run concurrently and we may want (we do) to switch between them. Imagine one TV set and three films running on three separate channels. With a flick of the remote, we select them in sequence. Of course, when we return to the first, the time we've spent on the other two will have lapsed.

We have the points for chapter one, but we don't need to respect their order, and we may add, delete, or shift events to other parts of the book. In this instance, we're sticking to the original point outline, but we'll reorganize their sequence and open the chapter at the Mosquito.

We are prefacing each scene with the setting and the POV.

Chapter One

Scene 1. Forest. Cinematic. Dawn. Five cocoons hang a few feet from the ground. Darkness. Forest awakening noises. Something moves under the farthest cocoon.
Third person limited. Miska flicks on a light. Almost six. Unzips hammock. Forest normal. Slurping sound. Miska reaches for weapon. He shakes the nearest cocoon. Henry. Slurping ceases. Kurt rouses Francisco and Matthew. They edge the clearing. Movement. Something slithers from under Henry's hammock. Kurt raises his machete. Miska steadies his hand. Henry's intestines.

Scene 2. Study. Third person limited. Sandor assesses the situation. Stanley relays Miska's muddled report. The team has lost a man. No animal. Hammock sliced open. A scalpel-sharp knife. Sandor doesn't believe it. Six-line backstory. They're almost there. They must push on.

Scene 3. Hut. Third person limited. Stanley replays Miska's story. Something wrong. The man is probably as high as a kite. Six-line backstory. He fears for Kurt. Checks clock. Two hours until the next transmission.

Scene 4. Forest. Third person limited. Another night over. Miska has set two-men, four-hour watches. He's tired. Takes a snort. Francisco awakens the other two. Miska reports to

Stanley. No news. They push on. Six-line backstory. Ahead of the line Matthew falls. He sinks to his chest in a narrow hole. Kurt and Francisco reach for his arms. Something tears at Matthew's legs. A whistle. A screaming Matthew sinks, trailing his dislocated arms behind. Kurt lobs a grenade in the hole. War council. Kurt and Francisco vote to abort and return with more men. Miska reports. Stanley agrees. They set back.

Scene 5. Study. Third person limited. Sandor exhausted. He changes transmissions to every hour. Six-line backstory. Next transmission. Miska and the two survivors race toward the tributary and their canoe. Sandor demands Stanley to round a group of locals and try again as soon as his son returns.

Scene 6. Forest. Third person limited. Miska, Kurt, and Francisco reach sight of the inlet where their canoe awaits. A whistle. Francisco falls over, legs severed above the knee. Miska and Kurt fire their automatic weapons and run. A whistle. Kurt's head topples over. Miska backpedals toward canoe. Runs out of ammo. Then he sees her. Beautiful.

Scene 7. Hut. Third person limited. Another hour and no report. Six-line backstory. Stanley tries the radio again. Outside, forty locals ready their *pipantes*. A shaman chants. The gods are angry.

Scene 8. Study. Third person limited. Sandor stares at sat-phone. Equipment faulty. Miska should be close to the river. Six-line backstory. Locals must have set traps to prevent strangers from discovering the treasure, so they are at the right spot. Miska must return at once. Sandor pours a drink, stands, and barefooted dances on the rug. He senses victory. Almost there.

Scene 9. River Cinematic. Noises hushed. Shaman's lament. Waning light. A canoe inches back down the tributary.

Scene 10. Third person limited. Stanley steps outside. One man maneuvers a long branch to draw an empty *pipante* closer to the bank. The explorer team's craft. Silent crowd. Shaman points his stick to a floppy mask on its prow. Stanley draws near. A port wine mark. No mask, but what's left of Miska's face. Man reaches for trailing mooring rope to secure craft. Rope heavy. Tied to its end is Kurt's ponytail and his head, already nibbled at by fish.

We've chosen an unusual first chapter to show that, in fiction writing, nothing is set in stone. Our first chapter is long, about five-thousand words and it doesn't introduce the protagonist.

Each of the scenes we have designed to accomplish a goal, and draw the plot forward.

The scene description is about five-hundred words, or one-tenth of the text. We can't vouch for others, but for us, writing the chapter from this scene structure would be a breeze, without lulls or writer's blocks. Furthermore, since we have a clear idea of future events we have added detail as we worked. From the port wine mark to the ponytail in the character's description to Sandor's callousness, to the whistling sound, the shaman's presence, and the emotional relationship between Stanley and Kurt, every detail, however minute, has a purpose.

Drawing from experience, producing a scene structure with this level of detail—for a full-length novel—would entail forty hours, including character files.

Research would consume another forty hours. Two hundred hours would see the first draft complete and half of that again would take care of the rewrite. Total, say four hundred hours; ten weeks at full tilt, twenty at half-time, and forty for a couple of hours a day. Considering that bestselling authors usually produce one book every two years or so, this isn't bad going.

1.6.6 SYNOPSIS STRUCTURE

We plotted our unlikely tale by listing a mixed bag of events, plot points, and twists to guide us through the writing.

1. Discovery of something odd in the Honduran Mosquitia.

2. Villain organizes a party led by his son.

3. The explorers disappear.

4. Two years later. Villain hears a Miskito Indian (Hero) giving a talk.

5. Villain recruits Hero.

6. Villain organizes a second party.

7. Hero lays down the law.

8. Second party hacks into La Mosquitia.

9. Second party disappears.

10. Hero recovers in a strange place tended to by IT.

11. Hero meets several other ITS.

12. Hero tries to escape.

13. IT nabs him and locks him up deep within their complex.

14. Hero learns the saga of the ITS.

15. IT and Hero develop a strange relationship.

16. A deranged Villain has had enough.

17. Villain bribes the Honduran Army to find out what's happened in Ciudad Blanca.

18. The ITS sense an army is on its way and gather to decide what to do.

19. IT shows Hero a network of caves to escape.

20. The army deforests the area and Villain arrives in a chopper.

21. IT blows the place.

22. News reports on a small meteoroid impact in La Mosquitia. (To cover up the Honduran Army's fiasco)

23. Hero returns to his village.

24. IT is not dead, but hiding deep and very much pregnant.

Perhaps (most likely) events will change; some characters might be promoted; other characters will be demoted, replaced, or shelved; and new plot points may crop all over the manuscript. This is normal because a structure is never cast in stone. Rather, it serves as a changeable guide.

Our manuscript finished, we're ready to prepare a synopsis by condensing four-hundred pages into three or four.

If we were to start from zero, the task would be daunting (it still is), but we have our list, character files, and the notes we've collected on details, events, and other bits and pieces we scribbled on scraps of paper to use in the synopsis.

On pages 400 and 425 of this book, we review the technique of synopsis composition, detailing what should go in, and more importantly, what shouldn't. We also analyze its format, length, composition, voice, and style. Here we are concerned with structure.

After much debate, we've settled on a medium-length synopsis of some 1,500 words, or six double-spaced pages, in an unusual format that includes a foreword and an epilogue.

 **1.6.6.1 SYNOPSIS STRUCTURE DEVELOPMENT**

After drafting the original synopsis, we realized a little background was needed to ground the tale. Rather than weaving the details into the text, we chose to include a short foreword, 160 words with the historical background of the Ciudad Blanca.

AUTHOR'S FOREWORD
In 1526, Hernan Cortes first mentioned the fabulous lost city of Honduras Mosquito Forest, one of the most impenetrable places on earth.
Over the centuries, rumors ebbed and flowed; explorers and adventurers funded expeditions to find it, and some thought they had. In recent years—after a vast undertaking by venture capital using SAR image enhancement techniques—the Honduran Government claimed to have found the scattered city remains.
But archaeologists remain skeptical of these claims. Every time the White City is found, events conspire to conceal its location before its existence is verified.
Local Indian groups have a different version of the lost city. Their legends cite the Ciudad Blanca, the white city created from lightning and thunder by the god Wata. Other writings and engravings show Ciudad Blanca as the origin of the human deity called Quetzalcoatl by the Toltecs and Kukulkan by the Mayas. This man-god and his disciples came from the stars. From a race of white-skinned people.

Historians are aware of legend's fiendish nature. Tucked among tales passed through ages, lurk bits of fact, however improbable. The trick is to separate truth from fabrication, an often impossible task. The foreword details are historical, and we've used them to our benefit by distorting, adding, and changing at will, as befits the storyteller's tradition. Wata and Quetzalcoatl we have appropriated to add a little "what if?" to our tale.

As we wrote, we used *Ciudad Blanca* to name the manuscript. Now we need a title and *The Hive* seemed appropriate; it doesn't give much away but fits nicely with the core concept of the story.

<u>THE HIVE</u>

Scientists charting Earth's magnetic lines discover an anomaly in Honduras. The readings are consistent with low-grade ore deposits. Since the point is in La Mosquitia, the most impenetrable forest on Earth, they file the discovery away.

Sandor Gulyás, a wealthy ageing industrialist from Chicago, suspects the anomaly may be the fabled Ciudad Blanca, the White City. He recruits a group of jungle-trained mercenaries led by Miska, Sandor's son, and an ex-Marine colonel to explore the point where the magnetic glitch occurs. Sandor stays in Chicago and follows the group's movements beamed from cameras in their headgear. After difficult progress, electrical and electronic devices stop functioning. Their link with the outside world gone, the group disappears. Later, the base camp's keeper will discover the team's scattered remains; body parts excised with surgical precision.

Months later, Sandor attends a lecture on primitive people's survival techniques by Fabian Andras, a Miskito Indian. Impressed, Sandor demands Fabian's curriculum. Though lacking formal training, Fabian is a walking encyclopedia on the Mosquitia. Ten years earlier, when Fabian was thirty and tired beyond endurance, he miscalculated when navigating upriver. His canoe caught in an eddy. He survived, but his wife didn't. After ten years of self-recrimination—during which he tended to his four children—he fell in love with a young woman from the same village. Only she has contracted a rare disease requiring expensive treatment at the Mayo Clinic. Sandor offers to finance an expedition to recover his son's remains, cover the clinic costs, and still leave a small fortune for Fabian. Fabian agrees to lead a team.

When Sandor asks Fabian to wear helmets with cameras, he refuses. Fabian hates gadgets. On his expeditions, he's never used electronics or firearms, but tools and weapons he can repair, craft, and replace from nature. At the end, he consents to carry a limited number of rifles, one GPS, and satellite phones.

Once in the field, the group reports to Sandor twice a day. Three weeks into the Mosquito Forest, their electronic equipment dies.

Fabian pushes on. One by one, the members of his team disappear. Alone, Fabian tries to retrace his steps, keeping high on the trees at night. There he encounters a jaguar. He kills it, but the great cat mauls him badly. He passes out.

He recovers consciousness in a white windowless room.

After a while, a strange creature enters. It looks human but there's a feeling of wrongness about it; hairless, white skin, muscular, athletic, angular face, masculine and yet beautiful and feminine. Its name is Kokine.

During the months of his convalescence, Fabian meets Kokine's aged and wizened family, Jaro, Poyta, Oitapi, and Margarola, their mother. The five creatures are the sole survivors of the Wata. Fabian learns that the Wata age slower, and have average life spans of 180 Earth years. They achieve sexual maturity at age forty and remain fertile for eighty years. Kokine, Fabian's guardian, is the youngest at eighty-six; the others range between 120 and 150 years old. Margarola is two hundred. The Wata share an uncanny similarity, but what really excites Fabian is their power of extra–sensory perception and a bizarre detail: the Wata never lie.

One night, Kokine joins him in his cell and they make love. Afterward, Fabian is unsure about wanting to repeat the experience—in particular after he discovers the Wata's origins.

The Wata inhabit a cluster of twelve planets in the quadrant of Proxima Centauri. To scout for habitable planets, Wata leaders sent ships to different points of the galaxy. The Wata spaceships, self-sufficient colonies capable of traveling hundreds of years, were heavily armed and equipped with terra-forming technology. Their weapons could depopulate vast areas to adapt the fauna to their particular biology.

While probes gathered information, their spaceships would remain in orbit. Eighty-five years after their departure, in the proximity of Earth, disaster struck. In 371 CE, after an explosion in the craft's drives, the Wata spaceship crash-landed in the Mosquito Forest. From two hundred and eleven crew members, only forty-two survived: twelve males, twenty females, and ten gymale.

Communications gone, along with most of their equipment, they couldn't return home. Their weapons and machines were destroyed.

The Wata have three sexes: gymale, male, and female. Gymales share the characteristics and reproductive organs of both male and female. On their native planets, gymales can adopt a female role and carry the offspring of a male or another gymale. As males, they can fertilize other gymale and the females of the species. In addition, gymales are capable of self-fertilization, but the product is a clone unable to reproduce.

The Wata used the remains of their ship to erect a containment building on the surface, a vast metallic structure that shone white under the sun. To protect their sensitive skins from the sun's radiation, they built a colony underground in a network of natural caves. They could surface only between dusk and dawn. Though they tried to reproduce, the difference in gravity made fecundation impossible but for a few self-fertilizing gymales. Males and females died of old age until only gymales remained.

Through the centuries, the Wata gymales attempted to couple without success with the men and women of neighboring tribes. Eventually, they abandoned the practice and accepted their unavoidable extinction. They dismantled the surface buildings and retreated deeper into the network of caves. Margarola is the last of the fertile gymales. Her clones are unable to self-fertilize. They are the last of a race.

When Fabian asks what happened to previous expeditions, he learns that Kokine killed them, using Wata technology to destroy their electronic equipment.

Why spare him?

Unlike the warriors, he didn't carry offensive weapons. The Wata respect tribesmen and identify offensive weapons with firearms or devices causing magnetic fields.

Fabian is dazzled. Fertile or not, the Wata reached Earth to conquer the planet. Had a biological fluke not prevented it, the Wata would have destroyed humanity, perhaps keeping a few tribesmen in remote areas as a source of genetic variety. After stealing a star map engraved in a strange metal and several small objects, he escapes in broad daylight. At night, Kokine captures him. Labeled a dangerous thief, Margarola orders his disposal. Kokine drives Fabian away from their complex and into an area of the caves with many individual penlike cells. Every few days Kokine brings him food and water but doesn't communicate anymore. Fabian realizes that learning the Wata story was a poisoned gift. They will never set him free. Yet, he can't understand why Kokine disobeyed Margarola and kept him alive.

Meanwhile, a frustrated Sandor offers millions to the Honduran government if they will send in the army. The press carries bogus rumors planted by Sandor about a drug cartel having a clandestine lab in the spot where the other expeditions disappeared.

The Honduran army defoliates a large swathe of the forest before sending in troops and heavy equipment.

Even though the Wata destroy the advancing army's electronic equipment, it's obvious they can't withstand their push. Rather than risking capture, Margarola activates the colony's demolition system. An explosion destroys their complex and obliterates the Honduran army.

In the cave pens, the explosive shock has created fissures. Fabian rummages through the debris for glow balls that impart dim lighting to the corridors. Then, he sets off deep into the caves to find water and a way out. Many days later, half-crazed from hunger and exhaustion, Fabian surfaces on the mountains north of Bonanza, almost twenty miles away from the legendary Ciudad Blanca that will now never be discovered.

This is the rough synopsis we will later polish by removing extraneous details and tightening the prose to half its present length. But there are a few loose ends, and loose ends beg tidying, hence an epilogue.

<u>Epilogue</u>

At the Mosquito, there's peace after the cataclysm. The news desks have been busy with vague stories about a small meteoroid crashing in the jungle, a ruse fabricated by the Honduran Government to cover up the real events.

Deep in the cave network, Kokine has survived, and life stirs in its belly. The unnoticed genetic change, caused by a surge of radiation in 1945, has turned Kokine receptive to human fecundation. Not only will it give birth to Fabian's baby but can now inseminate women.

Mother Margarola, Jaro, Poyta, and Oitapi sacrificed their scant remaining lives so Kokine could remain hidden. Kokine will rebuild a nest in the caves, harvest young women from the local tribes, and impregnate them. They will give birth to fecund Wata, strong Wata. Then it will be a matter of time and geometric progression. Kokine couldn't kill Fabian, not the father of the new Wata. Kokine wishes Fabian a long and eventful life, but regrets having misled him. The Wata never lie, unless the survival of their species is at stake. They didn't destroy their machines, or their weapons.[23]

It occurred to us that we could use the Trinity tests of the Manhattan Project as the event that triggered the Wata's genetic change.

---

[23] Carlos J Cortes, The Hive

Careful comparison of our original notes and the synopsis contents will highlight the many changes in the structure and development of the tale, down to several subplots, the ending, and plot mechanics. Had we actually written the book, the changes would have been substantial, perhaps altering the plot even more. This is an important detail to highlight. Structures, no matter how detailed, don't impair the writer's creativity. Quite the contrary. They serve as a springboard to greater creative freedom.

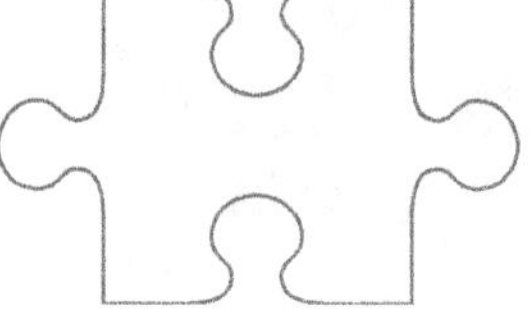

2 THE CRAFT OF WRITING

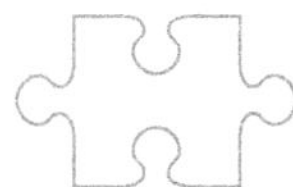

As writers, we're often asked how we write or where we come up with ideas for our stories. Probably the most frustrating response we receive—after we fumble around trying to explain just how we write—is the assumption that anyone can write if he or she has the time.

Well, yes, everyone can write, but not everyone can write *well*. If it were as easy as picking up the proverbial pen and letting our imaginations fly, we'd have a million bestsellers and everyone would stand in line to publish. Writing takes a pinch of natural talent mixed with a generous dollop of skill and hard work. Skill is acquired and improved upon with practice. How? We start at the beginning by understanding the basics.

There are five basic elements to writing fiction: Character, Plot, Setting, POV and Conflict.

The scope of these terms can be intimidating, but once we understand what each element is, and how it functions in the framework of our story, we're on our way to not only writing, but also writing well.

Let's look at the elements in a little more depth.

In journalism, reporters must ask six questions to get the full story, and the same is true in fiction. Before beginning to write a news item, a journalist must ask and answer <u>who</u>, <u>what</u>, <u>when</u>, <u>where</u>, <u>how</u>, and <u>why</u>. How does this process relate to the elements of fiction? Who is the tale about? The character is <u>who</u>. What is it about? The plot is the <u>what.</u> When is it happening and where? The setting is <u>when</u> and <u>where</u>. How are we telling this particular account? The POV is <u>how</u>. Why are we writing it? The conflict is the <u>why</u>. With these nuts and bolts we create a full story.

While we can define these elements, it's difficult to place a level of importance on each one or advise a writer on how much focus he should dedicate to one as opposed to another. Writing fiction is an art, not an exact science, so to determine whether each element should be present in equal parts or that he should include so much of this and not so much of that is both arid and pointless. If we're writing a plot-driven story, then our plot—or <u>what</u> is happening—will dominate the story. If it is character driven, then <u>who</u> is doing <u>what</u> will drive the story more than <u>how</u> or <u>when</u> they are doing it.

These elements, in whatever measure a writer decides is right for his story, combine to create theme. Theme isn't an element of fiction writing but the result or effect of the story as a whole. The theme is the main idea, or what the writer wants the reader to remember. It is a statement. For example, the theme cannot be love. Love is a topic. But the theme can be that love is a battlefield. Stereotypical perhaps, but it illustrates the point, even if this particular theme has been done to death.

Understanding the basics of fiction will set a writer on the right track to writing well. We'll explain each element in more detail in the following sections.

In <u>The elements of Fiction,</u> we explore:

> Character
>
> Plot
>
> Setting
>
> Theme
>
> Style
>
> Pace

In <u>Technique,</u> we review:

> Point of view
>
> Characterization
>
> Dialogue
>
> Exposition
>
> Narrative
>
> Storytelling

Finally, under <u>Data,</u> we analyze:

> Research
>
> Plagiarism

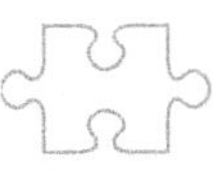

2.1 ELEMENTS OF FICTION

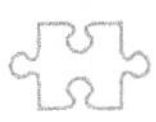

2.1.1 CHARACTER

Characters are the people or <u>actors</u> in a novel. What makes characters flat, rounded, major or minor depends on how a writer depicts them and what roles they are given in the events of the story. Characters are central to the plot, sometimes even more important. Because characters are defined by how they think, feel, and behave, they can't be separated from the action. The plot—how the story moves and flows—depends on how the characters respond to events.

When creating well-rounded, believable characters, the writer should know them well. This helps to avoid inconsistent or "false" characters. When writing a character, a writer should feel as though he's writing about himself, a friend, or family member—in the sense of portraying that character consistently.

Let's put it more simply: a character's traits, actions, beliefs, and dialogue should make sense for who the character is. If these aspects don't add up, then the writer has created an unbelievable character. Characters may do crazy things or lack in common sense, but the writer and the reader must understand why the characters do the things they do. Weak characterization can spoil even the most brilliant and complex plots, so it's important to understand the process of creating characters and what role each type plays. There's an old adage: a strong protagonist is only as great as the characters surrounding him. Flat characters, no matter what their role in the plot, pull the reader from the story, and we want to grab the reader and hang on until the final page.

In fiction writing there are several kinds of characters slotted into different categories.

Major characters directly influence the resolution of the plot. Their actions affect the development and the conflicts within the story. More simply, the plot focuses around principal characters, which include the main character, protagonist, hero, and antagonist.

Stories also have secondary or minor characters. Minor characters complement the major characters and help move the plot forward but, in general, secondary characters do not affect the resolution of conflict. These characters include sidekicks and obstacle characters.

Every writer has heard the terms "dynamic" and "flat" in terms of characterization. Major characters tend to be dynamic, or three-dimensional. They are *real* and the reader can visualize and remember them. Minor characters are often flat. The story has little to do with them, so the writer doesn't develop these characters as much as a hero or a villain. However, that doesn't mean that minor characters must always be flat. Some of the most memorable characters in literature have been sidekicks.

How should the writer achieve a brilliant cast of characters? We will answer that question and look at characterization and types of characters in more detail in later sections.

 **2.1.2 PLOT**

Plot is the <u>what</u> of a story, or the series of events that gives a story meaning. Plot is not story, but perhaps it's the most important element because without plot we have nothing. So how does plot work? What does a solid plot need? First, we'll establish that our plot must have a beginning, middle, and an end. A plot needs structure.

A plot should begin with action, or a hook, and this action must build in intensity and complexity as the character encounters conflicts that—hopefully—tangle him further into the problem or issue he faces. The conflict builds with subplots that serve to intensify the action or drama, until we reach the climax of the story, where the drama reaches *fever pitch*. The climax then leads to the resolution. In writing circles, we often hear the term "story arc." As indicated, the plot should resemble an arc. We begin, inch upward to the high point of the story, and then come back down to the resolution.

As we mentioned, every plot must have certain elements, all of which combine to make a story arc. These elements are: introduction (and hook), conflict, subplots, climax, and resolution (denouement).

2.1.2.1 INTRODUCTION

Every piece of writing, be it an article, essay, or a story needs an introduction. In terms of story, the introduction is the beginning of our plot. It lays out the big question as well as introduces the story's main character(s). Readers aren't about patience anymore, and we don't have pages and pages to put in back story, build character, or set the tone. We have one page. If we're lucky, a potential reader may skim two or three, but only if we're lucky.

The introduction presents characters, setting, and the central conflict. Our protagonists, or the main issue—sometimes both—should be introduced within these first pages. (In The Hive, the goal is set in the first two-hundred words). A writer can't leave readers to ponder why they're reading. We must tell them in the first pages what makes our novel worth committing to.

How we begin a novel is one of the most important elements of plot. Of course, the rest is important too, because we don't want them getting off the line once we hook them. However, many stories are judged on the opening pages, as often readers will pick up a book and read the first lines when deciding whether or not to buy it.

Let's look at the first pages of *Shutter Island*, by Dennis Lehane: In the opening of the prologue, written by the character Doctor Lester Sheehan, Lehane sets up at least a dozen questions. His writing is clean, he gives the facts with just enough detail to grab the reader, and he establishes the mystery. Granted, Lehane sets up *Shutter Island* slower than the average mystery. This is because this particular plot is complicated and twisting with many conflicts popping up throughout.

We might choose to begin with action or dialogue, a popular method with many writers because it gets right to the point of the story in the first lines. However the modern writer chooses to begin, he must avoid backstory, overly long character descriptions, internal dialogue that leads nowhere, and grand descriptions of setting. (This was not so in the classics but has changed to reflect modern sensibilities and experiences). A writer must find the voice and the tone of the story from the first words and hold onto it throughout.

Once we have established a hook, the introduction needs to expand and include conflict and rising action.

 **2.1.2.2 CONFLICT**

Conflict creates plot by supplying a reason or point to our story. Our characters must want something, and whether or not they know this is irrelevant. They must also overcome challenges to change and grow. Conflict creates rising action, a major component of plot. Rising action consists of a series of obstacles or problems that lead to a climax. Our story develops interest with the introduction of conflict, which can be separated into two types: internal and external.

External conflicts depict a character fighting with outside forces and can be categorized into three types:

Man vs. man is conflict that pits one person against another.

Man vs. nature is a conflict with forces of nature such as natural disasters, disease, or animals.

Man vs. society conflict is often used to show the insignificance of humanity in the grand scheme of things or to highlight man's survival instinct and our strong will to live. Conflicts that depict man versus society explore our values, morals and customs, often challenging the norm. In this type of plot, the character's convictions may lead to his demise, or he may bring others around to understanding another point of view.

Internal conflicts depict a character battling an internal or psychological issue. Plots that use man vs. self may reveal an internal conflict that tests a character's values or actions. Does he give in to temptation? Does he conquer an addiction and rise above his weakness? Does he find that some ideal he's held for a long while is wrong or working against him, and how does he react to that? Does he strive to achieve the most from himself or settle for something less? Does he even bother to struggle?

In real life more than one kind of conflict will take place at the same time. In Dennis Lehane's *Shutter Island*, the conflict begins as man vs. man. Teddy searches for a missing woman, but the hospital's psychiatric administration, the doctors, the warden, even the police on the island, all seem to work against his finding out how this woman escaped a locked room. Later in the story, a storm brews and traps Teddy—who planned to leave the following day—on the island. This injects a little bit of man vs. nature into the story. Soon—we don't want to give away the secrets of this magnificent plot so we'll be vague—Teddy finds himself in a man vs. himself conflict. Who is he? Why is he there? What is going on? All of these questions are internal. By this point, Teddy doesn't know which end is up or how he'll even figure it out.

No matter which kind of conflicts we use or how many, they create suspense and interest, making the reader want to turn the page. Building suspense creates intensity and is called <u>rising action</u>. The conflicts we place in the way of the protagonist should push him and the reader forward until our conflict reaches a turning point where opposing forces meet and the conflict becomes most intense, often called the point of crisis in our story. The crisis will occur before or at the same time as the climax. In *Shutter Island*, the crisis or turning point occurs when Teddy reaches a lighthouse where a doctor waits for him with a story that sends Teddy's world spiraling out of control. And this is where our story reaches its climax.

2.1.2.3 CLIMAX

The climax is the result of the conflict and rising action. It is the resolution of the story's crisis. The climax of a story should be the high point for the reader. It's the moment of the highest interest and most intense emotion. When a story reaches its climax, the reader should be attempting to guess how it will turn out. Perhaps he almost has it, but if we've plotted well, the ending shouldn't be clear. This uncertainty keeps the reader turning the pages.

Some writers might think of all those whodunits where the culprit is revealed in the climax. Isn't that giving away the ending before the ending? No. Finding the culprit does not resolve the plot. How we build our climax, and plot our story's ending, will depend on a few things.

If we've plotted well, we can reveal "whodunit" without answering the main question. How did he do it? This is a staple of many mystery novels. The question isn't so much who as it is how or why. In another genre, let's say romance, the hero and heroine might come together in the climax. Whether they've come together many times before is up to the writer but, this time, they realize the depth of emotion they feel for each other. What makes this the climax? It's the intense, emotional point in the story where no matter what has happened or will happen, they strive to preserve that love. The falling action will reveal just how they do this.

In our previous example, *Shutter Island*, by Dennis Lehane, the climax occurs when Teddy, the protagonist, makes it to the lighthouse. He's fought real and imagined enemies, headaches, hurricanes, and time to get to the place he believes holds the answers he's looking for. He runs up the stairs, his life in jeopardy chased by an unseen assailant. He hears sounds, bumps, finds empty rooms, until he comes upon the good doctor waiting for him in a room at the top. This is where the reader believes Teddy will get all the answers and has an idea of what will happen next. But Lehane is a crafty one and uses the falling action, or the events right after the climax, to twist the plot and clues left along the way into an ending that no one suspects.

No matter how we build to our climax, it should pull all the plot points together. The reader must wonder how the protagonist can resolve his main conflict. How will he survive, decide, or get past whatever it is in his path? Hints, clues, or suggestions are present, but they don't tell the reader what will happen—not yet. All is revealed when the action falls, after the climax, as we work toward the story's resolution.

2.1.2.4 RESOLUTION

The resolution or denouement, which all stories contain, concludes the action. This is the ending of the story. We have seen many a cliffhanger ending ruin a superb plot. Questions (at least major ones) are answered, mysteries unraveled, and the protagonist can resolve his main conflict or goal in such a way that is satisfying to the reader.

Resolution should not take a long time. We want the intensity and emotion of the climax to resonate with our reader through the closing so those feelings are part of the ending of the story.

When we reach the resolution, there should be little left to explain to the reader. If there is, we might want to go back to the climax and see where we went wrong. The plot's themes, climax, and events leading to the ending should be conveyed so that at the end everything ties together and makes sense. Of course, some things can be left unexplained at the resolution, but only those things that make sense to the character and the story without leaving it unfinished. These should be minor things, not major plot points, or conflicts. Perhaps we have a subplot, a minor issue like a character's fear of cake. This doesn't have to be explained with the story's main point. A line at the end to tie that loose end is okay. And we're eager to discover what could possibly inspire an irrational fear of something as wonderful as cake.

In Dennis Lehane's *Shutter Island*, the resolution is short and to the point. After the climax, where Teddy finally admits his reality, everything falls into place in the reader's mind. The questions, the intrigue, and the seemingly obvious villains are explained in a harrowing account of why Teddy is really on Shutter Island. Lehane could have resolved it without the subplots. He might have taken the easy way out and plotted in such a way that the questions and answers were obvious, making Teddy the stereotypical hero, saving the day and taking down the villain. But Lehane is not a lazy writer, and chose the ending most likely to leave the reader saying "Damn! I did not see that coming." More work for the writer, but well worth it. Endings will make or break a story. A writer must take care in how to construct the events leading up to it and how to resolve them. The last page is what echoes in the reader's mind.

2.1.2.5 SUB-PLOTS

Sub-plots are the mini-stories woven into our main plot and can involve main characters or they can involve a minor character.

If we've written a rich, intriguing, solid plot, one that carries the entire story and keeps the reader dangling on that line, then we don't have to use subplots. It's much easier to write a story without them anyway. There's no backtracking, no fading away from the main story, no blending... but that can be boring.

Subplots can add a depth to our story that we can't get any other way. They add layers and give more satisfaction to our readers. It's worth the extra effort to get a "wow, that was amazing," from a reader.

Another *bonus* of subplots is how they can round out secondary characters. Many writers use flat characters to fill the spaces, but if they made them special, made them stand out a little, the entire story would be enhanced.

It's a myth that subplots make more work. Let's debunk that right now. We have to keep one storyline going for 80,000 or more words. That's a long time to maintain the reader's interest in just one storyline. That's a lot of thinking, writing, back flipping, head standing, etc. It's tough to make a single idea interesting enough to persuade someone to hang on for 300 pages.

Now, if we spread that amount of words over a couple of related story lines, *voila!* Instant interest. Subplots help to build tension, in particular if the subplots are twisted into the main plot, which we recommend. Sometimes a subplot can fill the reader in on a little bit of back story that otherwise would weigh down the rest of the plot.

The subplot might run one of two ways. The first possible way is <u>parallel</u> and uses characters that know each other (which keeps the subplots related but independent). Perhaps the story contains two friends, and one is the main character. The other is the typical sidekick, someone who is supportive, caring, and always there. But on the side, the friend is a stripper turning tricks just to keep food in her kids' mouths, and she is being blackmailed by another friend who is jealous of the relationship between her and the protagonist. Oh my! Fed up with her secrets, tired of lying and hating herself for what she's done, the friend confesses her other life to the protagonist who—surprise!—is sympathetic and offers the friend a place to stay so she can get out of the life she so hates. Separate story, separate resolution, tied only by the relationship between the friends. Granted, this is a poor plot as related, but a good writer could make it work. When done right, parallel plots, like the one outlined above, can be tools to show growth in our protagonist, to enhance our story and the emotional attachment of the reader to the characters. Done poorly, it will feel clichéd and lazy. At their worst, such a subplot can detract from the main plot.

If we choose an <u>interwoven subplot</u>, then we must construct one that affects the outcome of the main story. Let's review our *friend* example. If we changed the plot so that the friend's secret life affected the protagonist's story and its outcome, we'd have an interwoven plot. Let's turn jealous blackmailer into the protagonist's emotionally abusive, philandering husband—from whom the protagonist just can't seem to break away to pursue her dream of being a wandering poet in Tibet. If the friend knows he's cheating, she must tell. She has tried, but the protagonist wants proof. After all, this is her soul mate. So to tell her how she knows, and convince the protagonist that this man is holding her back—preventing her from becoming the person she is meant to be—the friend has to confess her life as a stripper-prostitute. This will affect the story and its resolution by becoming an interwoven subplot.

Let's continue using Lehane's *Shutter Island* as an example because there are so many excellent subplots in this novel. What originally seems to be part of the main plot—the woman's disappearance from the hospital—at the end turns into a subplot. The main plot, Teddy's reality versus his perceived reality takes over at the climax. The hospital's plot against him—to force him to stay on the island and to keep him from discovering the missing woman—is another interwoven subplot. His partner goes missing, and Teddy presumes him dead or worse—in the lighthouse. Another subplot. Then there's Teddy's seeing his dead wife in dreams. She's guiding him in his search for the woman and urging him to find the woman no matter what the cost. She warns him away from this person and that. All these things, which appear to be conflicts or obstacles to Teddy's finding the answer to the mystery turn out to be subplots interwoven into the rest of the story. The doctors have their story, Teddy's wife, the missing woman, and his partner each have their own story too, and every one is linked to Teddy's story. We are being vague because those who haven't read this book will not appreciate our giving it all away. Our point is, at the end, every subplot from the partner, the doctors, the patients, Teddy's dreams, to his dead wife, etc., all come together and create such an obvious ending that the reader is left wondering how he didn't see it.

The goal when writing subplots, whether interwoven or parallel, is to give the reader a surprising and satisfying conclusion. It must all make sense at the end.

2.1.3 SETTING

Imagine the empty stage at a film studio. It's a vast hangar-like building with bare concrete walls and floor. Such an uninspiring void will metamorphose into a set when production takes over. Crews of scenographers, carpenters, painters, electricians, and specialists will recreate a scene of seventh century Venice, complete with canals, gondolas, and gondoliers. This is setting, or as fantasy and science fiction writers refer to it: world building.

But setting is critical in any genre, not only in science fiction and fantasy. Fiction plots are plays where characters will interpret their roles and deliver their lines in a set or scenario.

To write a scene, writers must take four unavoidable steps:

A. Decide what's to happen. (plot)

B. Create the environment. (setting)

C. Choose the performers. (characters)

D. Write

Though some rules are flexible—to accommodate the individual preferences of writers—the steps preparatory to writing a scene are not.

"But I don't do any of that, and I write scenes," cry the proponents of improvisation. Perhaps some writers don't follow these steps consciously, but somehow they work out the details in their minds. Without them, coherent prose would be impossible.

Plot implies a setting for events to unfold and players to perform. Therefore, actions contained in the storyline dictate the setting where the performance will take place. In turn, plot and setting will affect the story's characters.

Whether the action takes place on an imaginary world or in present day Topeka, setting is crucial. It plays a vital role in the credibility of any story and will determine the reactions and behaviors of the characters.

Let's imagine the hero must travel. He packs, drives to the LA airport, boards his flight, and disembarks at New York. If the scene is set in the 50s, it will bear no resemblance to the same action set in the 70s, 90s, or last month. A writer needs to understand how characters fit into a given period and the changing physical world around them.

"Ah, but my novel is set in an imaginary village, so I don't need to worry about setting."

We beg to differ. Every scene needs setting.

We have a fantasy plot. We are in a closed kingdom: an island. The level of technology is Medieval. The queen gathers her ministers to deliver bad news. Where? In a castle. How many people? Six (three men and three women).

This simple scene is fraught with problems for a conscientious writer. Somewhere, the creator of this image will have to acquaint readers with the environment: the walls, floor, windows, and lighting of the room. Do the windows have glass windowpanes? Did they have flat glass sheets in the Middle Ages? Lighting? Oil lamps? Torches? The characters will be clothed (we guess) and their dress will have texture and color. Color? Which color? Porcelain dishes? Forks and knives?

A careless writer will get on with the story, let his imagination run and write away. A serious writer will describe his setting beforehand and address possible pitfalls. The color of the clothing is problematic. Which natural local colors were available in the Middle Ages? Being on an island, we are in a closed world and there can be no imports. Many of the colors we take for granted can only be made with complex chemistry at modern laboratories. Does the imaginary word have such an industry? Fine clothes? Not unless the world knows silk (otherwise it's down to wool or linen homespun). The list is endless.

Is there no way out? It's called research and planning. Unfortunately, cinema and TV are not good examples. What may work on the screen seldom does on the printed page without special effects to cover it up. Without research and planning, a writer must limit setting to familiar places, current times, and current props, such as cars, appliances, apparel, etc., the writer knows well.

Write what you know is the best advice.

"And if I don't know?" Then the writer must research, read about it, and if possible, experience firsthand the proposed setting. After the hero's arrest, the heroine has been summoned to the local police station. To set this scene, many writers would rely on the images they remember from films or TV shows. But this practice is dangerous. Film and TV stages are just that: sets. They may bear no resemblance to the real thing. It would take one hour to visit the local police station with one excuse or another and take a few notes.

When taking notes for a setting, the important details are the tiny ones, not the overall picture. In a working copy *Spider's Web: Labyrinth*, Donna Johnson prepared the setting for a ceremony where young women would endure branding as part of the ritual. She described it thus:

> The maidens placed one arm against the sheaf adorning their pot. For the next few breaths, there was an occasional hiss, the sound of clay burning flesh. Then came splashes and sighs, hugs and laughter. There would be much fuzzy leaf burn salve to apply before Soupra.

Donna refuses to explain actions in detail, but her prose conveys the hints and prompts a reader needs to flesh the scene in his mind. In the previous passage, she needed Mullein, *verbascum thapsus*,[24] an unusual and striking plant known for its medicinal properties since Roman times. She slipped such a gem in the last sentence, in the unobtrusive *fuzzy leaf burn salve*. To craft these four words needs much research, an intimate knowledge of medicinal plants, or both.

To prepare the setting, the level of documentation is proportional to the location, timeline, and other plot demands. If the setting is a room, it pays to jot a line or two about furniture and other features. If the scene involves several players, a simple square drawn on a piece of paper with dots representing each player can help visualize the setting. More complex environments, like the control room of a nuclear power station, a particular airport's arrival lounge, or a mature garden, will benefit from photographs or a visit to the real environment. A trick, much exploited by pros, is to draft the overall setting and later focus on one or two details, like a piece of equipment, a vending machine, or a particular flowering plant. These details add realism and depth to settings.

2.1.4 THEME

Theme is the soul of fiction; its quality can give a story universal appeal. Theme is the abstract concept behind a story. Idea and plot are physical entities, which can be reduced to a few lines of text. A synopsis is a good example. In a synopsis, the writer condenses storyline and plot points in a few sentences. If well executed, a synopsis conveys what the story is about.

Like other abstract notions, theme can better be explained with an example. Let's analyze Crichton's *Jurassic Park*, a work with such broad projection that most readers will be acquainted with it.

> Idea. The blueprint for any living thing resides in its DNA. Blood cells have DNA. Mosquitoes are blood suckers. In sudden death, a mosquito will have in its stomach the blood of its latest victim. Amber is a fossil. Some mosquitoes are trapped in amber.

---

[24] Never use uppercase in Latin names or quotes. The Latin language has no uppercase letters.

Plot. A rich man bankrolls a process to recover DNA from fossil mosquitoes. This way, he harvests the DNA of extinct species. With genetic engineering, he manages to reproduce extinct animals. He then buys an island to create the mother of all theme parks where dinosaurs are the star attraction. Things start to go wrong and the visitors must run for their lives. At the end, a few manage to escape and leave the island.

Theme. The dinosaur's biological relationship to modern-day birds and the theory of chaos: Man can't harness nature.

In the same vein, the theme in *Star Wars* is good vs. evil.

Theme is implied in a work and is seldom, if ever, pronounced outright but hinted at with subtlety through the plot. Nabokov's *Lolita* is a literary masterpiece, however problematic its contents have proven to be for many readers. The plot has been deemed a pornographic rendition of a man's infatuation with a young girl and its theme is clear: There's no fool like an old fool.

The writer's interpretation of feelings and emotions, his expression of truth, causes an unforgettable impact on the reader. Theme is the reason why some novels become universal. In Mario Puzo's *The Godfather*, the theme is law vs. justice and the many faces of power. The man on the street lives under the delusion that judges impart justice, when the reality is they interpret and apply the law, just or not.

Blending theme into a story can be accomplished in several ways, though it's essential to have a theme to begin with. Most works of genre fiction have no theme. To flesh out a theme, the writer will often use the actions of protagonist and antagonist to illustrate contrast: good vs. evil, wisdom vs. ignorance, love vs. hate, cowardice vs. heroism, etc.

Other techniques consist of writing around a theme, but without touching it. This highlights the importance of showing vs. telling.

With the benefit of insight, we examine classics like Jules Verne's *20,000 Leagues under the Sea* and find his science wanting. Verne was no scientist, and much of his production fits better into the fantasy genre rather than science fiction.

Yet, *20,000 Leagues under the Sea* is a dangerous book because of its theme: If you can't right wrongs—real or imagined—by conventional means, there's always terrorism.

2.1.5 STYLE

We can often identify our favorite authors by reading just a few pages of their works. What we recognize is the writer's style. Prose has a rhythm, a music to it that is unique to each writer.

Writing style is made up of the different techniques or strategies chosen by the writer to address elements like plot, characterization, and structure. Style is in the rhythm of the language we use, figures of speech, how we punctuate our story and characterization.

All writing has style, whether fiction or nonfiction. Sometimes, the framework or guidelines will restrict the expression. For example, a scholar would avoid figures of speech and use precise definitions and descriptions in her writing. It would be informative and formal. A journalist would use exact words and shorter sentences so any reader can understand the message conveyed in the writing. However, unlike the scholar, the journalist would relax the formality somewhat to appeal to a broader audience. We writers tailor our style to the situation based on the goal of what we're writing, be it informing or entertaining.

Fiction writers have a little more freedom than academics and journalists to arrange words, sentences, and techniques in many different ways to create a writing style. Often these arrangements are determined by what is popular at the time. At present, many writers adopt a loose, clean prose style, while many years ago the writing was more formal and dense with description tinted rather purple. For example:

> Mr. Bennet was so odd a mixture of quick parts, sarcastic humour, reserve, and caprice, that the experience of three-and-twenty years had been insufficient to make his wife understand his character. HER mind was less difficult to develop. She was a woman of mean understanding, little information, and uncertain temper. When she was discontented, she fancied herself nervous.[25]

> Borg and Blomkvist had known each other for fifteen years. They had worked together as cub reporters for the financial section of a morning paper. Maybe it was a question of chemistry, but the foundation had been laid there for a lifelong enmity.[26]

The difference between Austen and Larsson is more than just genre. After reading a handful of books published at the same time as *Pride and Prejudice*, we see similar elements in the writing style. The same is true of Larsson. Listening to the music of each passage, we notice another difference. While Austen's writing isn't the most florid example of writing at that time, it still has a rhythm far different from most fiction written today.

Every writer should read his own work to determine how he structures his writing. Does he favor longer words and sentences or uses short ones? Does he use curse words or slang or does he avoid them? Is she more prone to using active verbs or passive? Does he follows grammar rules or bend them just a little? What about narrative patterns? How does she mix action and dialogue? Does he lean toward elaborate description or summarize setting into a single line?

These choices combine to create a writing style. How do we develop such a thing? We read. Then read some more. We read poor and great writers. We read popular writers and the obscure—fiction and nonfiction. We analyze what we like and what we don't. Why does this appeal to us, while that other doesn't? Some writers worry that reading other work will influence their style—or they'll copy someone else's. Our answer to that concern is that we cannot copy style. Sure, we can imitate and write like an author that we enjoy. Often critiques include comments that say a piece has a Lovecraftian feel or that it seems influenced by a popular author's style. This is okay. We have influences because we learn to write through reading other writers. It seeps in to what we write. But each writer's voice is still unique.

2.1.6 PACE

Pace is one of the five pillars of fiction writing, the others being story, narrative voice, characterization, and description. Elsewhere, experts, gurus, cognoscenti, and other pests swear that: Pace is the amount of time readers spend in each part of a story. Pace has nothing to do with reading time or speed.

---

[25] Jane Austen, Pride and Prejudice.

[26] Stieg Larsson, The Girl with the Dragon Tattoo.

Rather, pace is about events or the lack of them. For a reader, pace is the rate at which plot items develop. In other words: There isn't one tidy little definition to explain pace, but we'll try: Pace is the artistic sensitivity with which the author tunes the reader's experience.

If the writer scratches his head here, we've failed. Why? Despite a belief held dear by many bad writers, the reader is seldom at fault when he "doesn't get it."

Let's try another explanation: Pace is the ratio between story and exposition.

When something happens in every sentence, a reader will gasp at the intensity of the tale and its supposed "speed." However, when something happens followed by five lines of description until something happens again—followed by more lines of whatever, except plot—the pace slows.

In workshops, we've read countless reviews where the critics complained, *"nothing happens in the next four pages"* or *"there's no action!"* Does this sound familiar?

Pacing is about action—about events. If the actress said to the bishop, "I need action," we would doubt she meant a glowing description of the Aubusson tapestries—or a flashback to His Excellency's childhood tadpole-hunting. Rather, she would be asking for *something* to happen.

Instead of murky conceptual musings about the nature of pace, we will address its mechanics and control. After all, that's what a writer needs.

Fiction writing, as stated earlier, consists of story, voice, characterization, description, and pace.

<u>Story</u> is a concatenated series of events we term plot.

<u>Narrative voice</u> is the writer's choice of vocabulary and syntax to convey the plot.

<u>Description</u> is the information a reader needs to follow the other elements of plot.

<u>Characterization</u> is the nature, ethos, description, and makeup of the people in the plot.

We can reduce every book to two elements: story and exposition. Reading speed and pace have little to do with extension. A complex story may occupy many hundreds of pages, while we can write a simple one in a few lines.

Story (A) consists of plot, dialogue, description, and backstory.

The plot has no fluff. Dialogue, description, and backstory might contain exposition or not.

Exposition (B) consists of color, description, and information.

As we described earlier, pace is the ratio between story and exposition. Therefore, pace is the ratio of A to B. If we rate as neutral a scene containing 50% story and 50% exposition, any passage with more of the latter would be slow. More story would mean a faster pace. The greater disparity between these elements, the more effect on pace.

Fast pace means a fast read? We wouldn't say so; most of the time we read at the same speed. We term "fast reads" these stories where the writer has tuned the pace in such a way that the reader *carries on reading*. Pace is about the number of events and their spatial distribution within a scene or chapter.

 **2.1.6.1 PACE CONTROL**

We won't attempt to explain how to pace a novel to perfection for a number of reasons:

Every scene needs different pacing as a function of its relative location within the story or plot moment.

Different genres benefit from different pacing structures.

Only the writer can determine how to pace a story.

Some writers maintain that the perfect pace or intensity of a scene depends on the scene itself, which is misleading advice. If this were so, the reader would move faster through the boring parts (if there are any) and linger, spending more time on the exciting bits. Yes, we know readers skip blocks of exposition, but that's skimming, not reading. Shouldn't the heart pounding moments be quick and with fewer words—to make the reader feel as though he's rushing through the scene? Not really. On the contrary, writers often use more words in action scenes than, say, a scene where the protagonist gets dressed or makes dinner.

Tuning pace is an art, akin to playing an instrument. Only the writer can decide how to pace his narrative and deliver a wholesome reading experience to the readers. Like a musician, the writer can work his prose, heightening or toning down the pace, by adjusting the ratio of plot and exposition.

To highlight this technique, we've used the following example and underscored the words and passages relevant to plot:

> The gathering was underway.
>
> Throughout the afternoon and well into the night, in eerie silence, thousands of dark-robed figures poured into the bowl court, a never-ending stream of creatures with tormented faces, lips blue from the bitter cold, sunken, sallow cheeks and set grimaces of pain.
>
> As cottonwoods rippled by a gentle wind, the crowd swayed and the sweet rustle of cloth sighed faintly in the arena, intermingled with the subdued whispers of bare feet on cold stone.
>
> The bowl filled. Ninety-six thousand souls stood next to one another, in the structure that the elders designed centuries ago, a compound ellipsoid shape carved out of solid rock. The amazing gritty shell amplified sounds from one edge to the other, without echo or reverberation, a wondrous acoustic design of awesome simplicity.
>
> Al-Khouri stood in the center of the basin. He ached at the sight of the suffering faces, and he understood their awareness and yearnings. He shared with them the universal feeling, the great equalizer that allowed any being to understand how others felt, regardless of species or nature. Hunger. Al-Khouri was hungry. He was as famished as they were, with a deep-seated, aged, profound, and all-encompassing ravenousness. He shared the lost despair of his brothers. Their land was barren, inhospitable, cold, and sterile, as it had been for a long time, as it would always be. [27]

The excerpt is 229 words long, from which fewer than sixty—those underscored—are plot. That's twenty-five percent plot and seventy-five percent exposition, or the hallmark of slow pace. But slow pace is not a sin, only a mode. At this point, the writer might want the pace slow to gather speed later. Sedate narrative with a large ratio of exposition to plot has its place in fiction writing, a counterpoint to other pages with heightened pace. What matters is that the writer *knows* the passage is slow and *how* to speed it, if he so desires.

---

[27] Carlos J Cortes, The Gathering

The underlined sections above belong to the plot. Of course, we need description, color and information, but for this example we'll do away with these. We have:

> The gathering was underway. Thousands of dark robed figures poured into the bowl court in the structure that the elders designed centuries ago. Al-Khouri stood in the center of the basin. Al-Khouri was hungry. As famished as they were. Their land was barren, as it had been for a long time, as it would always be.

If we rewrite to tidy it up, we would have:

> The gathering was underway.
> Thousands of dark robed figures poured into the bowl court, a structure the elders designed centuries ago. Al-Khouri stood in the center of the basin. He was as famished as they were. Their land was barren as it had been for a long time, as it would always be.

Fifty-four words of plot. Now the excerpt is almost 100% story—and fast. The writer can determine if he wants to slow it down or keep it moving. He can add as many words as he wants to slow it down or make it neutral.

Writers can control pace by dosing out the ratio of plot to exposition or description. To do so, a writer must learn to separate the prose components and adjust them at will.

Besides the ratio of story within a scene or chapter, writers use other tools to control pace. Sequencing, how we transition through scenes, rising and falling action, will affect the pace of a novel. In the following sections we'll discuss those and how an error in these areas can undo much hard work.

2.1.6.2 SEQUENCING

As writers, we approach plotting with a handful of nails (plot points), a hammer (writing or recording means), a length of string (plot or story line), and a pencil or marker (pace).

Then we face a blank white wall.

The first task is to determine our canvas size. Height doesn't matter, as long as we can reach; Renée can write on the ceiling while Carlos must struggle to reach the edge of the table. We write in pages with a set height. With our marker, let's draw three parallel lines. The top one represents 100%, the middle one 50%, and the lower line 0%.

100% ───

50% ───

0% ───

The length of the lines in our imaginary wall will depend on the work's extension, such as a few feet for a short story or miles long for a saga. But we have to start somewhere, usually at the beginning. There we set our first nail or event.

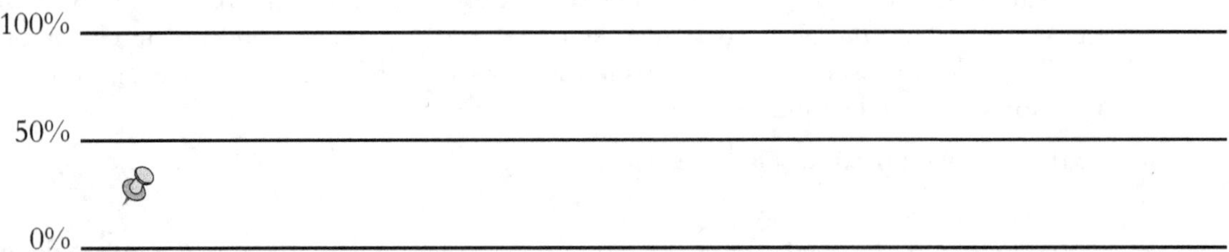

The height of our first event is critical. If we start too high up, we have less room to hike up tension; too low and the story may stall.

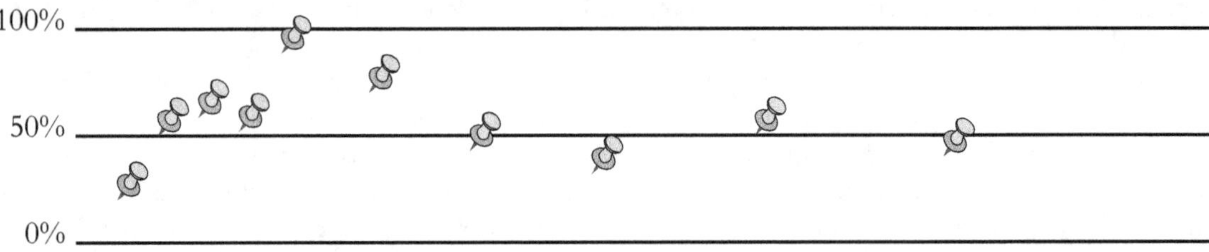

Next, we nail down the first ten events. The vertical distance is the tension and the horizontal separation between events represents our pace. After event number five, pace slackens and the events separate. The type of event determines tension (height), while pace dictates their nearness.

With our length of string, we join the nails on the wall and the result is the storyline following the sequence of events.

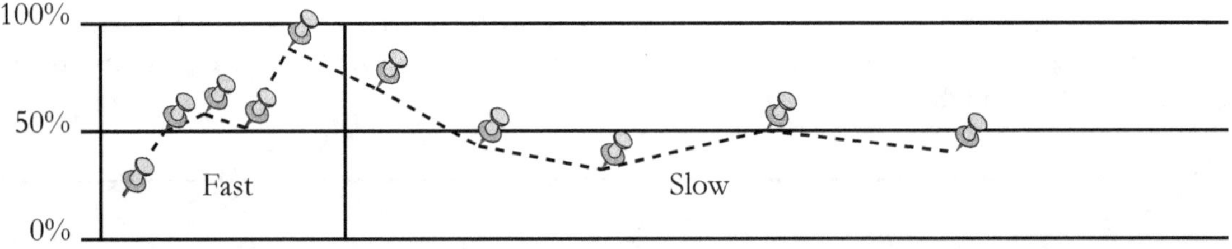

Here we must stop, address the path our storyline follows and ask hard questions.

Is every event necessary?

Do events follow a linear sequence?

Are transitions smooth from event to event?

Does the ratio of events increases with tension?

Are there missing events in the plotline (holes in the story that might baffle the reader)?

Are the problems presented in the story resolved?

Fine, a shrewd writer may point out, but a high conflict point may need careful and lengthy detail, which would slow pace.

To address this, we joined our nails by threading the string through them, but at certain points, we wrapped the line several times around the same nail and compressed the action.

Consider the slow motion playbacks in most televised sports. Let's use Sidney Crosby's gold medal goal in the 2010 Olympics in Vancouver, British Columbia. (That's in Canada). The goal happened fast but, when he scored, the world (or at least North America) let out a breath, some in rapture and others in anguish. That couple of seconds was the most intense and exciting part of the game. Yet, the sense of exhilaration didn't reach the viewers until the broadcasters showed the goal in slow motion replay. We saw every pass, the attempts to block Crosby, the goalie trying to see amid the sea of bodies in front of him, the clock winding down with only seconds left and then, just before the buzzer, Crosby secured gold for Canada. In slow motion, the moment didn't feel any less intense than the original goal. Actually, the tension increased. This is because when he scored the goal it happened in the blink of an eye. The viewers didn't see much beyond the players celebrating afterward. In slow motion, we compress time and see the details. In fiction writing, the same principle applies. We spend far more time creating a faster pace, utilizing shorter sentences and paragraphs.

However, we can't maintain such a level of intensity for long periods—it would drive readers nuts. In our graphic, pace slows down after the fifth point. A breather. We up the pace for intense scenes where the stakes are high for the characters. The resulting graphic is the story beat.

The order of events within a story affects pace.

Elements of fiction writing have layers of complexity and pace is no exception. Macro pace—or how the sequence of events affects the story—is critical, but micro pace, which is word choice and syntax, can bring a well-designed sequence of events to a screeching halt.

Many writers slow down the pace of a novel with improper word sequencing in sentences. The most basic error is leaving out important information or wording the events so that things happen at the same time when they shouldn't. For example:

Mary reached into the pantry, grabbed a can of soup, and closed it.

The sentence is atrocious, but that's not the problem here. The sequence of events is wrong; this reads as if Mary closed the soup. We know what the writer meant, but this syntax flaw will slow the reader, forcing him to re-read and make sure he understands what happened. The sentence should read: Mary reached into the pantry, grabbed a can of soup, and closed the door.

So far, we have touched linear sequencing. If the writer chooses to arrange events in a non-linear way, matters become more complicated.

Let's consider a novel where time shifts backward and forward. Each time the story shifts in time, the reader slows down. One chapter could end with heart-pounding action, but when the next begins in a different period, a reader must shift his thinking mode as well. This slows the pace. This is also true of jumps forward in time. A story might begin in 1975, for example, and we remain chronologically accurate for, say, three years. Then we jump to 1989. If we hoped to maintain a steady pace, we've just ruined that flow. It's not wrong and can be a great tool in terms of pulling the reader back, but it does affect how the reader experiences the story.

If we think of sequencing a novel in terms of the alphabet, then event A starts the story, soon followed by B, C, and D. This should be easy on the reader's brain. Now, we move that sequence around going for a non-linear approach and we're asking a lot from readers. A sequence of C, A, B, F and K events is not easy to remember.

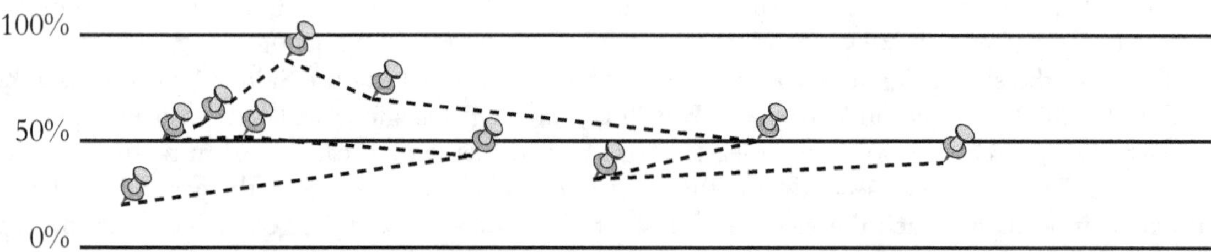

When we add backstory through flashbacks, we bump the storyline out of sequence. While flashbacks aren't wrong, too many factors may accumulate that will make it difficult for the reader to follow the story. If we complicate it further by jumping forward in time, the reading becomes arduous and the pace, difficult to control.

Before using flashbacks or flash-forwards, writers should think long and hard. Is there a way to accomplish the goal without doing so? If there is, keep the plot linear. Shifts in time and circumstance will slow a story to a halt. The reader must pause, confirm the time or setting has changed, and adjust before moving on. That's not good if we're hoping to keep them breathless.

We will discuss elsewhere how to handle flashbacks with flair. For now, our advice is to write linear plots, as in point A moves to point B, which moves to point C, and so on, until the writer understands what he's doing and why.

When learning piano, to use a familiar example, the budding musician will practice scales, arpeggios, and chords for years, while playing increasingly harder pieces. He or she will start with *Twinkle, Twinkle, Little Star*, major through the easy bits of *Für Elise* and other classical primers before attempting *Chopin's Studies* (devilishly hard). It never ceases to amaze us that a writer would choose to "play" the equivalent of Rachmaninoff—one needs hands like spades to hammer down some chords—when he barely knows musical notation.

Writers should only stray from sequential plot points with extreme care, keeping in mind what digressions expect from readers.

How should we create the right pacing in our novels? There's no *right* pacing, only a clear story line with highs and lows determined by the writer's craft and intention. Many factors can affect the pacing of a novel. But when it slows down, it should be because the writer wants it to. After much hard work, to accidentally pull a reader from the story is tragic.

2.1.6.3 TRANSITIONS

Anything that jolts the reader from the story, reminding him that he is reading, will slow the pace. Transitioning is critical to fine tune the pace of a novel. Measured and well-placed transitions keep the flow of the narrative smooth, even when we switch to another time, setting, or character.

Transitions are words, sentences, paragraphs, or punctuation used to indicate changes in time, location, POV character, mood, and (therefore) pace. How we transition will depend on what effect we hope to achieve. For example, we transition *between* scenes using different techniques than transitioning from the present into a flashback. Ideally, when writing these scenes the movement or change should be seamless, i.e., undetectable by the reader.

So, how is it done? A chapter break is a major transition. We can use the beginning of a new chapter to move to a different POV or setting. This is the easiest way to let the reader know something has changed. Scene breaks, often represented by either extra spaces between paragraphs, asterisks (***) or a pound sign (#) is another major transition.

Another method of transitioning—often used incorrectly—is a linking sentence or paragraph. These act as a bridge connecting one idea to another.

Let's look at an example. (There's a nonfiction transition sentence right there).

> Shelly screamed when Olivia bit into the spot Aedon had mauled earlier and pain flooded her body, soon replaced by a sickening pleasure that further weakened her legs and fueled a searing craving for yet more pain.
> The last image in Shelly's mind was of Aedon's eyes as he stared down at her in disappointment. She begged his forgiveness as darkness overtook her.
> "Your turn boys." Olivia dropped Shelly's inert body to the ground. "I like them kicking and screaming."
> The others fell upon Shelly until there was nothing but a bloodless husk lying on the cold earth. Then, the group moved away slowly swaying toward the house, whispering in melodious tones that sounded like song.
> When the sun chased away the night, the wolves had carried off chunks of their prize and Shelly's bones lay scattered through the woods.[28]

There are two transitions in this excerpt. We begin with Shelly, poor doomed soul, who is having a rough night. As Olivia and her "boys" drain the life from Shelly's body, we keep the scene going by moving into Olivia's POV. Our transition?

"The last image in Shelly's mind…."

This prepares the reader for the POV shift. Shelly is dying, so she will no longer have a POV.

The next transition is in the last two paragraphs.

"Your turn boys."

Olivia's opening remark begins the signal to the reader that the scene is shifting, leaving the last bit in omniscient POV, no longer third limited as it has been the entire scene.

The transition helped to slow the pace of the scene from heart pounding to a gradual closing, not an abrupt halt. Had we used a break to transition, this scene it wouldn't have worked. The transition is so fast, so brief, that a scene break would have jolted the reader. It would have shifted too suddenly.

On the other hand, had this scene ended with them carrying Shelley to the house, we'd have used a scene or chapter break because the reader would have been prepared for the shift. Of course, if the "boys" carried Shelly's body off, something must happen in a new location. The reader wouldn't be yanked from the scene but follow the plot to the new one.

Transitioning without slowing the pace requires that a writer learns these techniques and when and how to use them.

---

[28] Renée Miller, Ancient Blood

● Rising Action

Rising action consists of building the events and the action of a story to a fever pitch, right before the climax is revealed. The rising action should comprise at least the first two thirds of a novel, from the beginning to the climax.

When done well, the challenges or conflicts facing a character will pile up in stages, with the problems first being easy for the character to overcome. As the plot moves along, conflicts increase along with the tension. Problems become more complex and harder to resolve. We're moving through the rising action and toward the climax of the story, but each scene or challenge should include its own mini-climax. This will keep the action constant for the reader by raising questions and offering answers as rewards if they continue to read.

Let's look at a brief example of rising action.

A story begins with the protagonist coming home from work. He calls out for his wife but receives no answer.

> <u>Conflict number one:</u> Where is his wife? Why isn't she answering?

> He moves through the house. Here and there he spots signs of a struggle, such as a bloody handprint on the wall and an overturned picture on the mantle.

> <u>Conflict number two:</u> Something awful may have happened to his wife.

> He panics and searches the house frantically for her—or her body.

> <u>Resolution to the second conflict:</u> Relief floods through him when he realizes his wife isn't in the house.

> <u>Conflict number three rears its head:</u> But wait, if she's not dead, and she's not here, then what happened?

With each conflict, the tension hikes and the reader becomes more entrenched in the story. The writer gives the reader a solution now and then but then replaces it with a new conflict.

The rising action must build in intensity, forcing the reader to continue reading. When one issue is resolved, the reader can breathe, but we must remember the key is "rising." Therefore, we must replace one challenge with another. At the climax, all is revealed.

At the end of each scene, the reader should be aware that there is still more for the character to do. They may not get to it right away—we must give readers a breather now and then—but the reader *knows* that the resolution will come. Because he knows we must resolve it at some point, he will keep reading in a bid to figure out what it is. Rising action maintains the suspense and tension, and this is a key to pacing.

In our pace graphics with nails on the wall, the distance between the nails along the wall denoted the nearness of events. The height of the points represented the action: high nails = heightened intensity.

We want to keep readers turning pages even when we slow the pace. Rising action is the tool writers use to do this.

Falling Action

In falling action the events wind down and wrap up. This stage occurs after the climax and before the end of the story. It shows the results of the climax and suggests the plot's resolution.

For example, at the climax of our sample story, the protagonist finds his wife. She's fit and *very* alive. She's with another man. The resolution to most of his questions comes at this moment. But wait, what is she doing with this man? Why the blood? Who is he? Why is she smiling?

We will answer these questions in the falling action, leading to the end and the most important question: What the heck happened?

The pace doesn't have to slow much when we reach this point in the story. The reader will keep reading because he doesn't have all the answers yet. We should slow down only enough for the reader to assimilate what has happened at the climax.

Falling action is the moment of reversal, where the conflict between the protagonist and the antagonist unravels. The reader begins to see how the protagonist might win or lose. Yes, it should be possible for the protagonist to lose. A crucial element in the falling action of any story is a moment (or moments) of final suspense where the reader isn't quite sure what the outcome will be.

For example: The wife levels a gun on her distraught husband. Then she explains that she's part of ASS, a secret organization. The sect worships the donkey sun god and they need a sacrifice. His blood will do.

Wow, he knew his wife was unstable, but he never imagined this kind of crazy. Does she shoot him? Does he escape? Well, it turns out the "other man" is a mole. He infiltrated the organization to stop mass suicide. In the final moments, he trains his gun on the wife, and reveals all to the protagonist. She's the ASS's leader.

"Go on," a reader begs, "does he shoot her?"

Keep reading.

In other words, while the action slows down we still have to make it interesting. We need to give readers a little extra to keep them reading. It doesn't have to be as weird and twisted as the donkey sun-god plot, but the pace should move along fast enough that while the resolution approaches, the reader has reasons to keep turning the pages.

As the mole's finger depresses the trigger, the woman uses a remote concealed in her pocket. A hidden trap door opens and she drops away into safety, her cackling laughter drowned by the gun's blast.

Will her ASS surface elsewhere? Will she seek revenge? The reader needs to buy the next book to find out.

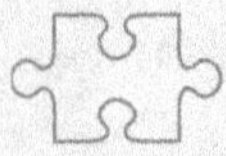

2.2 TECHNIQUE

Technique, when applied to fiction, refers to the devices we use to create a story. These are the rules of fiction writing that often frustrate and anger new writers. The rules of characterization, dialogue, narrative, exposition, and point of view (POV) are what make up writing technique. When creating setting, for example, we must try to provide readers with words that enable them to see, hear, touch, taste, and smell the world we've created. Part of creating great description is mastering the narrative technique.

A good writer understands and can use a variety of writing techniques with mastery. So what do these terms mean? Let's look at each.

POINT OF VIEW

Which is the right perspective for our novel? First, third, or omniscient; each has a set of rules that a writer should understand to employ and give the reader the best vantage point on a scene. Choosing which POV to use is a technique in itself. Sometimes writers will write something in one POV, first person for example, only to realize upon editing that third person limited reveals the story far better.

CHARACTERIZATION

Characterization should be mastered to create vivid and dynamic characters. Our protagonist, antagonist, and main character (if not performing one of the other two functions) can make or break a story. Developing the technique for creating these characters as well as secondary characters is critical to bringing a reader into the story.

DIALOGUE

Creating real, natural dialogue isn't a small task, in particular when it must be on target to best reveal character and story, but it is crucial for creating the dream world in which we want to immerse the reader. Tags, attributions, quotes, and language are just a few elements to create great dialogue. There are so many right and wrong ways to create good dialogue, that it's often difficult for even experienced writers to master.

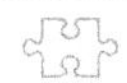 ## EXPOSITION AND NARRATIVE

Through exposition and narrative, the writer informs the reader or explains events or motivations within the story. These techniques are tough to master and often writers include too much of one or both, which can slow the action to a standstill. Exposition does nothing to move our plot forward. By contrast, narrative can be useful to add backstory or important facts—all of which must be crucial to what is happening at that point in the novel. Writers often struggle with these techniques and worry that removing too much of one or the other will leave the reader confused.

 ## STORYTELLING

The art of storytelling requires the use of several techniques. Writers must create gripping openers and tempting closers. We must master writing flashbacks and create place, atmosphere, and color in a way that best suits the story. We combine these elements to create vivid worlds and characters that drag the reader in and force her to hang on until the final page.

In fiction writing, each of these techniques involves a variety of skills. In the following sections, we'll discuss each in more depth.

 ## 2.2.1 POINT OF VIEW (POV)

Point of view (POV) is the perspective from which the writer tells the story. We can think of it as the point from which the camera sees things when filming a movie. Whose head are we in to see the events? Whose thoughts, emotions, and conflicts are we experiencing as we read? In most novels, the writer chooses to tell the story through the eyes of the hero, making her the viewpoint character. However, this is not always the case because it isn't always the best choice. POV is the most powerful tool the writer has, and because of this, it must be understood before tackling that bestseller.

It doesn't matter how well the writer constructs the prose, how intense the action is, or how much drama she inserts into the climax; if the POV is written so we're hopping uncontrolled from one head (or perspective) to the next, the story is ruined. POV control must be deliberate.

Let's begin by establishing whose POV we're in. This must be done at the beginning of every scene and chapter. It doesn't matter if the writer uses only one POV for the entire novel; it must be established at each new scene. We can't assume anything. He or she cannot know for certain that the writer won't shift to another character and will be lost until POV is established. Here's an example:

> Crickets sang from the beneath the bushes that lined the clearing. Their raspy music grated on the nerves of those trying to sleep in the tents nearby.
> Amelia pulled the blanket over her head and sighed. Her blonde hair peeked from a small opening she left at the top, just a curl or two. The scent of raspberry drifted around the tight confines of the tent to tease the noses of its occupants.
> Almost time. Once everyone succumbed to the Sandman, Amelia's time would arrive. Sad she had to die. He quite enjoyed the smell of raspberries.

Well, though the writing is iffy, the setting is nice. However, it's rather confusing. We like the opening to set the scene, then we're led to believe that perhaps Amelia is the POV character but then, wait, she's tucked into the blanket and can't see her own hair. Raspberries? Are we not in Amelia's mind? Maybe the others in the tent? What is going on? Oh, there, it's the killer's POV. Right? We think it is anyway.

Let's write it another way:

> Crickets sang from the beneath the bushes that lined the clearing. Their raspy music grated on the nerves of those trying to sleep in the tents nearby.
>
> Bobby rolled to his side, his gaze falling on his companion. Amelia pulled the blanket over her head and sighed. Her blonde hair peeked from a small opening she left at the top, just a curl or two. The scent of raspberry drifted around the small confines of the tent, teasing his nose.
>
> Almost time. Once everyone succumbed to the Sandman, Amelia's time would arrive. Sad she had to die. Bobby quite enjoyed the smell of raspberries.

Bobby is established as the POV character within the first two paragraphs. Ideally, we want to establish POV at once, so the reader doesn't struggle to get her bearings. This is the first rule of POV: Establish it early.

When a writer begins to write, she does so under the absolute constraint of POV. We cannot just sit down and write any way we feel is right. This is a mistake made by many new writers (and some not so new). We are hemmed in by the demands of POV and must adhere to them. Let's examine this more closely with Bobby and Amelia.

> Bobby felt around for the knife beneath his sleeping bag. Its point pierced the skin of his thumb, and though he winced, the stinging bite of the blade caused a tightening in his groin. He loved this part.
>
> He shifted closer to Amelia, running a finger over the edge of her blanket. Should he wake her first? He liked a bit of a struggle. Sleeping prey was no fun.
>
> Bobby didn't know that Amelia was already awake. She waited for him to make his move, her hand wrapped tightly around the small gun she secreted away in her bra before leaving the city. He lifted the blade and pulled the edge of her blanket down. Amelia's blue eyes blinked up at him and she smiled. Smiled? Bobby hesitated.
>
> Her hand moved and a loud pop echoed through the silent night, sending a ringing through his ears. Bobby's head felt strange but he couldn't examine it further. He fell, darkness taking over his thoughts. Amelia sat up and pushed his slumped form aside. Bobby didn't feel it.

Let's begin with the obvious error—head hopping. We began in Bobby's POV, switched to Amelia's, and then went back to Bobby's. No, no, no. POV demands we stay in one person's head throughout the scene. No jumping from one to the other. The reader can only see and experience what the POV character sees and experiences.

The second error? When the POV character loses consciousness, or dies as is the case here, the scene is over. The writer must begin a new scene to continue. Let's try this example written within the constraints of the POV we've chosen.

> Bobby felt around for the knife beneath his sleeping bag. Its point pierced the skin of his thumb, and though he winced, the stinging bite of the blade caused a tightening in his groin. He loved this part.

He shifted closer to Amelia, running a finger over the edge of her blanket. Should he wake her first? He liked a bit of a struggle. Sleeping prey was no fun.

He lifted the blade and pulled the edge of her blanket down. Amelia's blue eyes blinked up at him and she smiled. Smiled? Bobby hesitated.

Her hand moved and a loud pop echoed through the silent night, sending a ringing through his ears. Bobby's head felt strange. He fell, darkness taking over his thoughts.

#

Amelia sat up and nudged his slumped form. Bobby didn't move. She lifted her arm to speak into the microphone in her watch. "Got him."

We separated the ending, where Bobby dies, with a scene break (#) to indicate to the reader that the POV is about to change. We also eliminated the bit about Bobby not knowing about the gun. First, we're in his POV so, unlike in a movie, the reader cannot know these things. All will be clear when she pops up with the gun anyway. The reader can only discover things as the POV character discovers them. If the writer must shift to another POV, then she must begin a new scene.

How do we know what the other character is feeling then? We have to switch POVs? No, we don't. A good writer can show emotion, thought, and such through dialogue and facial expressions. One doesn't have to be inside a character's head to show these things. In the scene above, we know Amelia was ready for Bobby. Why? First, she had a gun. Second, she smiled. That says pretty much everything necessary to the reader and to Bobby. Slipping out of our POV character's head into another to show these things is lazy writing.

But what about those novels where we see the POV shift all the time? Isn't that head hopping? How did those writers get published?

Head hopping is seldom right. Chances are the novels where you've seen POVs switched in a scene have been written in third person omniscient and by writers who fully understand the rules of POV. These writers, like Nora Roberts or Stephen King, have been writing for a long time and they only bend the rules when they have a full knowledge of them. If we peruse these novels, we'll also notice something else. The writers only switch when necessary and never to showcase the other character's thoughts. These writers use dialogue and action first, as they should, because these are good writers.

The next problem the writer faces is to determine the POV. Whose perspective is best to show the scene? The writer must ask which character has the most to gain or lose in each scene. Which one has the major conflict? We should use this POV to write the scene. Why? Because the reader benefits most when identifying with the POV character. Unless it is a first person narrative told from a POV outside the story (narrator not involved in the events) then the writer must ask the same questions before writing each scene to ensure she writes from the most compelling viewpoint.

In the following sections, we'll examine the rules of POV closer as we look at first person, third person limited, omniscient, and cinematic POV.

2.2.1.1 OMNISCIENT POV

Omniscient means all-knowing. The omniscient point of view is often described as putting the author in the place of a god. Rather than being limited to a certain character's POV, the author describes the thoughts and feelings of all characters—with a camera held high above the story—capturing everything for the reader like in a movie. We are often able to see inside the mind of the protagonists, the villain, secondary characters, and even spectators.

Using third person pronouns such as he or she, his or her, the writer can jump into the head of any character. This is the least intimate POV. It doesn't allow the reader to bond with one character as the rest do, but when done well it can add an extra dimension to a story by showing what the motivations of each character might be rather than implying or relying on the POV character to figure them out.

Omniscient POV requires that each of the characters have a distinctive voice so that the reader is never at a loss as to whose head he is in. It is often difficult to manage because if the writer gives the wrong information—like telling the reader everything—the tension is lost. If the writer controls this tendency, only supplying the information needed and sprinkling it throughout, then he increases the tension. Confusing? Here's an example.

> "What have you done?" Billy placed his hand on the charred remains of his CD collection, grief clutching his heart, making the simple task of drawing a breath difficult.
> "I warned you." Mary smiled, pleased with herself. She'd warned him, hadn't she? If he wasn't careful, the next time she'd incinerate his Mustang and those wretched golf clubs. A woman had to establish control early, or she'd lose it completely. This time he forgot their anniversary, next time he might forget to come home and the next…. She wouldn't tolerate any of that.
> "I spent years collecting these. Do you realize how much money is here?" He turned to look at his wife, unable to comprehend why she'd do such a thing. He went fishing, as he did every Sunday. It's not as though he messed around on her, and he could if he wanted. He just went fishing.
> Tossing the lighter onto the melted pile of plastic, Mary walked away from her husband. Priorities, that's what he needed to learn.

Have we given too much information? The reader doesn't need everything spelled out, as is the temptation with omniscient POV. We should sprinkle the information throughout the text, rather than lumping it into one scene. Let's try to improve the scene.

> "What have you done?" Billy placed his hand on the charred remains of his CD collection, grief clutching his heart, making the simple task of drawing a breath difficult.
> Mary smiled. This time he forgot their anniversary, next time he might forget to come home and the next…. She wouldn't tolerate any of that. She'd incinerate his Mustang and those wretched golf clubs if she had to. "I warned you."
> "I spent years collecting these. Do you realize how much money is here?" He turned to look at his wife. It's not as though he messed around on her, and he could if he wanted. He just went fishing.
> Tossing the lighter onto the melted pile of plastic, Mary walked away from her husband. Priorities, that's what he needed to learn.

In the second version, we resisted the urge to show the reader every thought and motivation of the two characters. We didn't spell out every feeling, thought, or reason they had. We allowed readers to gather the information themselves. The first way isn't wrong, but we ruin the tension with too much internal thought; we're thinking for the reader. Omniscient is useful for allowing the reader to see much more than other POVs, but too much isn't good either. The second version still shows the scene well and without the *extra* stuff. This way, the reader can assume motivations through words and actions. The issue of controlling the husband is clear without stating it. His shock and inability to understand why she'd burn his CDs is clear as well. We need not state it. In writing omniscient POV, the writer has two options: true or limited. True omniscient POV is seldom used anymore, but limited is common.

Limited omniscient means that while we have a godlike perspective, we limit ourselves to being in one character's head at a time. It still allows us to switch characters as many times as necessary, even within a scene.

Another way to approach this concept is to consider true omniscient POV as a camera panning around the room at a party. The camera dips into anyone's head, and perhaps more than one person's at a time, by taking on the group's perspective collectively. Limited omniscient, on the other hand, is like passing a camera around the room with each person taking the camera and filming their own POV. For example:

<u>True Omniscient:</u>

> Bodies crushed together, the smell of sweat and liquor permeating the air. Bobby watched the brunette in the corner gyrating to the music. She knew he watched her but, as her mother advised, she played hard to get, only glancing his way now and then to make sure that she still held his gaze. Across the room, next to the long table laden with food and drinks, Marla scowled. Obviously Bobby Smith didn't know what the word date meant. She tipped her glass, draining the contents, which tasted like battery acid, and fumed. Jacob leaned on the bar and grinned when she turned, looking him over. He'd always liked Marla, but her infatuation with Bobby forced him to stay in the background. But Bobby just got caught. She'd be ripe for the picking in no time. Screw Bobby. It's not like he gave a shit anyway.

<u>Limited Omniscient:</u>

> Bodies crushed together, the smell of sweat and liquor permeated the air. Bobby watched the brunette in the corner gyrating to the music. Damn she was hot. Something tickled the hair on the back of his neck, and he turned his gaze to the far side of the room, meeting Marla's cool glare.
>
> Marla tipped her glass, draining the contents, which tasted much like battery acid, and fumed at the way he gawked at the slut by the stereo. Obviously, Bobby Smith didn't know what the word date meant. She turned, catching Jacob staring at her. He grinned. Jacob always seemed to be watching her. She considered him for a moment. Maybe a few more drinks, then Bobby could piss off.

In the first example, the camera transitions from one head to another. Although each POV is clear, it can become tricky and dizzying for the reader to know when a transition has occurred and whose POV they've switched to. The writer must ensure that each shift is smooth and clear. With limited omniscient, the head-hopping is made easier on the reader by putting us firmly in one head and then showing the transfer of POV by physical or visual contact. So we start the scene in Bobby's POV as he stares at the brunette. Then when we switch to Marla, we show his gaze moving to her, they make eye contact, and use that opportunity to switch to her viewpoint.

A more obvious way is to show one character's POV then have them touch another on the shoulder, or shake their hand, and use that to switch.

Omniscient, whether we use true or limited, is not an easy challenge for a writer. A reader's attention is limited, and often they expect immediate gratification. This means that we need to give them something that movies, television, and the Internet cannot. The intimate and personal involvement they get with a story is that *something*. As writers, we are allowing them to become part of another world.

If we use omniscient POV to tell a story, then we may take away from that intimacy, which is something that should be considered before choosing this form of narrative. Omniscient is seldom used for entire novels. So, another option is to begin this way to give readers a sense of time and place, and once that's established, move to third person to put the reader firmly into one character's head.

For example, the party scene could be shown from one POV, but open the same way. Let us imagine a camera shot of the room. First we see the girl by the stereo, then Marla at the table, then Jacob staring at her (Omniscient POV). Then, the camera moves to Bobby, who nurses his drink while watching the girl dancing. When he sneaks a glance at his date, he realizes he has been caught. From that point onward, we can stay in his POV for the rest of the scene. We want to know what happens with him, whether he will go for the "hot" girl or try to change things with his date, or even try to get Jacob out of the picture.

If a writer chooses to use omniscient POV for a story, it's important to remember these considerations. How intimate do we want the reader to be with the characters? Can we convey tension and immediacy while moving among several heads in a scene? Does it enhance the story to do so? Properly executed, omniscient POV can be very effective. *Anna Karenina* by Leo Tolstoy and *Under the Dome* by Stephen King are two examples of omniscient POV done well. We recommend reading novels like these to study how it's done. The reader feels connected to the characters and the story while never really becoming entrenched in one POV.

 ## 2.2.1.2 FIRST PERSON POV

First person POV is often mistaken as the easiest narrative to use. It requires a lot of skill to pull off this POV well. A writer can go wrong in many ways and turn what should be an intense read into a "telly," annoying, and hard-to-follow story.

Often that crafty letter "I" sneaks into first person narration unnoticed by the writer. Soon, every other sentence (at least) begins with that hateful little vowel. "I walked," "I said," "I picked," "I stabbed myself in the eyes so that I wouldn't have to see the wretched repetition anymore." But this is inexcusable. There are many alternatives to using "I" in first person narrative to open sentences.

> For example: I heard a noise outside my window.

> Could be: A scratching sound drew my glance to the window.

> Or: My gaze moved to the window, where something scratched the wall outside.

When reworded, the meaning is the same but the repetitive "I" is gone. Good. This habit is hard to break. We recommend that every writer who has penned a story in first person POV try a little experiment: go through the manuscript and circle every sentence that begins with "I." Circle it, underline it, and strike it out with a giant red "X." Writers should reconsider starting sentences with "I."

After stifling the penchant for using "I," a writer might want to explore how to handle what the narrator experiences in first person. Many writers give the reader information that cannot be possessed by the narrator. Writers should put themselves in the protagonist's shoes to make sure that they haven't slipped out of POV.

> Mary walks in through a door to an office. Dust motes drift lazily toward the floor, caught in the tiny shaft of light that the dark blinds allow where they don't quite fit the window. Mary walks toward the computer desk in front of the window. She checks out the screen saver. Mary's hand darts to her mouth as she appraises the nakedness of a handsome actor filling the computer screen. She blushes, wondering where the occupant of this room managed to get such an indecent picture of this hunk of a man. She could tell Mary of course, as she's standing in the closet to the left, where she heard Mary coming and waited for her to enter. She's planned this, hoped that Mary would come into her space and look at what she's displayed on the screen….

No, the mistake isn't the crappy setup or ridiculous premise. That was for amusement. As the POV character, Mary cannot know she blushed. Her cheeks may warm, she may feel scandalized and embarrassed by the man whose bits and pieces are exposed to anyone who might care to look. But Mary would not know she blushed because, unless there is a mirror present, she can't see her own face. Also, Mary can't know the room's occupant hides in the closet or any of her plans. Why? The POV is Mary's head, not the other woman. Only the information Mary has at each moment can be given. The other woman's presence can't be revealed until Mary becomes aware of her.

Another example:

> I set the last dish on the rack and grabbed the towel from the stove to begin drying. My eyes burned, so tired from the late night before with Adam. My lips still tingled from his kisses, and I blushed, thinking of the other places he kissed. If I didn't get some sleep soon, I'd drop right on the spot. I didn't see the man wielding the axe as he crept up behind me. I picked up a plate and swiped the towel over it, and he raised the axe preparing to strike. I turned just before it met my skull, and drove the knife I'd hidden under my shirt into his stomach. The axe clattered to the floor behind him.

In this passage, the POV couldn't know the axe murderer stood behind her. She said she didn't see him. Also, she couldn't prepare with a knife hidden in her shirt if she didn't see him or know she was in danger. That little bit of information should have been known to the reader as well. As the reader is in her POV, they would have been aware of her grabbing the knife.

Here is a better way to write such a scene:

> I set the last dish on the rack and grabbed the towel from the stove to begin drying. My gaze caught a large shadow in the hallway. So he was back. Moving my hand to the drawer in front of me, I slipped a large butcher knife out, stuffed it under my shirt, and resumed drying the dishes. My eyes burned, so tired from the night before when I waited for him to appear. If I didn't get some sleep soon, I'd drop right on the spot. In the window above the sink, I watched him creep up behind me, and averted my gaze so he wouldn't suspect I'd heard him. I heard his jacket rustle and spun around, plunging the knife into his gut. The axe clattered to the floor.

The scene is atrocious and telling, but it highlights the POV issue. The reader can't see what the POV narrator can't see but must see everything the POV sees. When writing first person, the most important rule to remember for perspective is to imagine ourselves as the narrators. This way we won't make the mistake of slipping out of the narrator's POV and including information that the narrator can't know.

First person can evoke a stronger emotional attachment with readers than other narratives. The reader connects with the protagonist from the beginning. It is her thoughts and feelings portrayed, and it's easier to bond with her for that reason.

When writing in first person, we're only in one point of view and that is the narrator telling the story. The advantages are that we get inside the character's head, and the reader gets to live the story with the protagonist, rather than just observing. First person creates an intimacy between the reader and the narrator that isn't easily achieved with other narrative modes. It has the potential to be very intense and compelling, but only if the writer can make the character interesting and believable. It's easier to stick to one POV and avoid head-hopping when writing first person. That's always a good thing. Most readers find head-hopping annoying.

The POV character colors everything the reader learns. We only get one side of the story. The narrator must be present during most scenes so the reader knows what the narrator knows. Writers need considerable skills to describe the narrator as well. Of course, this can be done through dialogue or comments from other characters. Good writers can show description in action and behavior. Often writers try the mirror trick, where the character observes his reflection and gives the reader a description. This is shoddy, weak, and unreliable; our appearance is never what we think it is.

Writers should avoid unreliable narrators, an easy mistake to make in first person. In other words, the writer shouldn't withhold from the reader information already known to the narrator. This has been done several times in stories where the narrator is a ghost. The reader only finds that out at the end. The ploy has often worked in such a story, but as it's been done to death (pun intended). Unless the writer is skilled—with a fantastic and original way to do this clichéd plot—it's best to avoid it.

In first person, many writers also make the mistake of describing what is going through other characters' minds and this is something she cannot know, unless she can read minds. Telepathic narrators have also been done *ad nauseam.*[29]

In this POV, writers also tend to show their narrators watching themselves from a distance. The narrator describes events as they happen but not why, or their protagonist's reactions. There is no involvement from the protagonist, no active participation in the story. That's telling.

Before a writer begins a manuscript, he should consider the limitations and demands of first-person POV. He should ponder whether its use would add the desired effect to the story.

 **2.2.1.3 SECOND PERSON POV**

Second person narrative is the least used when writing fiction. This POV is told from the "you are" perspective and is often written in present tense.

For example:

> This is not the type of place you would typically frequent. You are uncomfortable under the blinking lights, and the scent of desperation and booze makes your stomach queasy and your head ache. But that's okay, you'll get used to it. You pull up a chair and sit down, waiting for

---

[29] Using Latin or foreign expressions, when good alternatives exist in English, is bad writing. But we're human and weak. The expression we borrowed from the legal profession means "to the point of being sick."

your friend to arrive. He always drags you into messes like this, doesn't he? And you allow yourself to be manipulated every time because you love him. He is, after all, your brother.

Second person is popular in non-fiction genres such as self-help books, but there are some genres where second person narrative is more common. Interactive fiction like *choose your own adventure* books is perhaps the most popular. Children's fiction authors use this POV as well.

But we should add that just because a writer uses *you* and addresses the reader, it doesn't make it second person POV. Sometimes the writer creates a story in first person, while addressing someone else. The two look very similar, but there is a difference.

<u>First Person</u>: You know what I'm talking about, right? I love it when we agree.
<u>Second Person</u>: You know what he's talking about. He loves it when you agree with him.

<u>First Person</u>: You would love Canada, especially the moose. Have you ever seen a moose? I am enamored with them. They're possibly the most magnificent animals I've ever seen. You should visit someday, if only to catch a glimpse. You'll remember I recommended the poutine as well?
<u>Second Person</u>: You've often been told that Canada's best feature is the moose. Of course, you've never been but you plan to visit one day if only to catch a glimpse of those majestic creatures. You might try the poutine as well, it sounds interesting.

Writers, sometimes make the mistake of slipping out of second person and into first in this way. The easiest way to stay in second person, should a writer choose to use it, is to remember the task consists of projecting a story directly onto someone else. We describe what they're doing, seeing, feeling as though they are unable to.

Let's say Paul and Mike went out with friends a few nights ago. The tequila flowed, and by the end of the night, things were a bit hazy. Waking up late, Mike finds himself in a strange bed, a strange house, and when he looks outside and sees the cars driving on the other side of the road, he realizes he's not even in the same country anymore. If he were to call Paul up and ask what he did that night, how would Paul tell him the story? Paul would use "you" as he's relaying it, trying to show Mike the things he can't remember. It might go something like this:

You drank tequila shots with this hooker from that place on Second Street. Man, she was a big woman with large teeth and muscular shoulders. Her voice sounded a little deep, remember? She had a funny accent too, like she'd shoved marbles into her mouth or something. You danced all night with her and then, when they flashed the lights for last call, you and the hooker disappeared outside. She took you to some chapel on the edge of town. You know the kind, shifty-looking little man, a hundred dollars, and he marries you while still wearing his boxers and a tatty old robe.

So then you left, newly married to *Tony*, who seems eager to get to the airport for your honeymoon. You gave her your wallet, because you can't see straight enough to piss, let alone buy airline tickets and such. Now that *Tony* is your wife, she can do those things. So tickets purchased, you boarded a plane and flew to her home, in Germany. You've never been to Germany. You called a couple of friends to tell them you're okay, except that *Tony* turned out to be short for Anthony and you had to ditch him shortly after arriving. You found a motel and you crashed, but now you have no wallet and no way of getting home. So, there you are.

Aside from the corny setup, that is how we'd go about writing second person POV, by providing details to the protagonist as the narrator. Second person POV draws attention to itself, making it difficult for the reader to escape into the story. It also has the disadvantage of sounding corny and contrived, as you've seen in our example above.

This POV is difficult to execute well. Writers should consider other options before attempting it.

2.2.1.4 THIRD PERSON POV

In third person point of view, the narrator relates the action using the third-person pronouns he or she. Third person allows the writer more freedom in how the story is told, which is probably why most writers use this narrative mode.

Third person is classed into either *omniscient* or *limited*, although some writers have invented other forms by tweaking these to fit what they need for their story. Writers shouldn't attempt virtuoso performances until they've mastered the original forms first.

Omniscient third person

This mode allows the writer to relay events that happened to any character in the narrative. The writer can delve into a character's thoughts, mess around in their head for a while, and then jump out and into a different character's head. Omniscience allows the writer to show the thoughts of anything, from a dog to a human to a garden shovel. Although what a garden shovel could add to a story is debatable.

Shifting from the perspective of one character into another during the same scene can create problems. It's been done, but often by experienced writers who know the secrets to doing it without making the reader dizzy. We've explained omniscience in a previous section, so we won't repeat details and examples.

Limited third person

This mode shows a single character's thoughts and feelings. Different from first—not limited to the I point of view—it still limits the writer to a single character's thoughts and visuals. What the character sees and feels is what the reader must see and feel. The character doesn't narrate, and the writer can't turn the camera to another place or dive into anyone else's mind. This is the most common POV used by writers, and is often told in past tense. It can be the easiest for new writers to master if they're careful with passive voice, telling, and head-hopping. The author tells the story through the eyes of one character, and the POV doesn't often shift within any given scene. Of course, we can shift POV, but this is done by using chapters and scenes to move into the new POV and refraining from head-hopping. Switching POV within the same scene is possible, but difficult to do well. In Chapter One we can be in Joe's POV and in Chapter Two move on to Jill's. This way, the reader can follow the change without confusion.

The reader can only know what the POV character learns through overheard dialogue—both spoken and internal—and actions. The writer shouldn't cheat the reader by supplying these things from other characters. The same as in first person, if our POV character doesn't see, hear, feel, or experience it then neither he/she nor the reader can know about it, unless another character or the action supplies the information. For example:

> She paused before stepping onto the road. No one drove the streets at this time of night, but she still looked both ways before crossing, a habit ingrained from childhood. As she moved her foot to cross, her neck tingled. Someone followed her.

Okay, that's wrong. Why? Because unless she has superhuman abilities, or eyes in the back of her head, she wouldn't *know* someone was behind her. If we want this known to her and the reader, we must show it through action. Here's a better way:

> She paused before stepping onto the road. No one drove the streets at this time of night, but she still looked both ways before crossing, a habit ingrained in her from childhood. As she moved her foot to cross, her neck tingled. Were those footsteps behind her? The footsteps quickened and she turned, her heart pounding in her chest. About ten feet away, a lanky man walked toward her, wearing a hooded sweatshirt. Something about him seemed familiar, but with the hood pulled over his baseball cap she couldn't make out his features. She turned back and broke into a trot, instinct forcing her to move faster.[30]

The second version takes the scene further, showing the POV character seeing a man behind her, rather than feeling him, which is lazy. We could also correct the scene by changing it to say:

> ...she had the uncanny feeling someone was behind her, but she wouldn't turn to see. Lengthening her stride, she rushed across the road and to the safety of her house.

Of course, this way, the reader isn't sure someone is following her, but the urgency is still potent.

A sort of bastard child of the two forms of third person that has emerged recently in fiction is called third person objective. It differs from the other forms of narration by following multiple characters around like in omniscient mode, but it does not enter the thoughts of the characters. Think of it as a hidden camera following people in a documentary. There may be actions to hint at the thoughts of the characters, but there is no internal dialogue to know *for sure*. This way, multiple stories can be told at once.

With so many types of third person POV, it's easy for a beginning writer to become confused and think mixing them is okay. To clarify: in any POV—except omniscient—it is *never* okay to head-hop within a scene. Never.

Let the reader know whose head they're in right away. For example:

> Julie rolled over, pulling the blanket over her head to block out the sun's inconsiderate rays. Didn't the universe realize it was too early to be awake?

Is there any doubt here whose head we're in? If we were in another POV, we wouldn't know that the bright light of morning bothered Julie, unless she said so in dialogue. We could show through actions, the blanket over her head for example, but the rest of her thoughts couldn't be shown, and therefore, the reader wouldn't feel them with her.

When should we use third person? We must consider that third person allows the reader to see all the events that happen in the story. It allows the writer the opportunity to mislead the readers without cheating, or being an "unreliable narrator" and lying to them, which loses reader confidence.

---

[30] Renée Miller, Dirty Truths, rough draft.

Is third person right for our story? Do we have a large cast of characters who will play important roles within the story? Do we have more than one central character? Is it important that the reader relate to the good, the bad, and the ugly in our story? Yes? Then third person is the POV required. It is the most used and often easiest to master.

2.2.1.5 CINEMATIC POV

Cinematic POV, as the term implies, borrows techniques used in film and is used (sparingly) to begin a novel, chapter, or scene.

Cinematic POV is a tool, like dialogue or setting, and is not meant to be used throughout a novel. This POV is more for the reader's benefit, to set the story or scene so that the reader knows where they are.

It should be brief, one sentence to two short paragraphs at most, and focused. Like a camera panning across a scene.

Writers should not maintain this POV throughout the story, often shifting into third person after the first passage.

Cinematic is used in particular for opening scenes in complex surroundings. It allows the writer to float about omnisciently, giving the feel of a scene as the camera floats overhead. Once the scene is clear, the camera settles down on a character and his POV takes over. The difference between third person and cinematic is that with third person we create the scene through the head and perceptions of the POV character, and with cinematic, we use outside description to set the story or scene. We don't slide inside any heads to know what characters are thinking or feeling. For example:

> High above the wreckage, grey clouds rolled nonchalantly across the sky as the mountain shook. With the rumble of a beast in pain, the ground shuddered before a chill wind that blew through the trees, their foliage wilting and drifting through the thickened air. The earth split. Tearing crevasses belched sulphurous black smoke, rolling like a malignant plague, and scattering ashes in its wake before drifting downhill. The roar grew in intensity and volume until it drowned out the burning aircraft's racket. On the plains, water bellowed over the land, leveling out everything in its path until its momentum slowed to a hushed growl around the base of the mountain.
>
> #
>
> Rayne woke with a start, his eyes darting around the dark cavern that trapped him and his mind worked to understand what happened.[31]

This is a rather long passage for cinematic, but Renée is long-winded. After the cinematic paragraph, the POV moves into third person, Rayne's perspective, and it will continue that way. The use of cinematic in this scene serves to show what has happened to put Rayne into the dark cavern, as he cannot know and the information is crucial to the story.

Once we've established the setting using cinematic POV, we can proceed with the story.

---

[31] Renée Miller, False Prophet.

 ## 2.2.1.6 MULTIPLE POV

Multiple POV, unless done very well, is difficult to write without head-hopping. In this POV, several characters and the author (as narrator) can see, hear, and react within the story.

If a writer uses multiple POV, he should keep it limited to one viewpoint within a scene. Jumping from one character to another loses the focus of the story and such head-hopping is confusing and distracting. He risks pulling readers from the story and losing their attention. For example:

> Brian lowered his face, and Amy closed her eyes, waiting for the warmth of his lips against hers. Instead, his tongue tickled her jaw, trailing down her neck before she felt a slight pinch below her ear. Amy opened her eyes, startled.
> Smiling at her shock, Brian bit into the tender flesh of her neck. She tasted sweet, like an innocent. God, how he missed innocents. Wretched feminist movement.
> "Please," she whispered. "You're hurting me."
> Amy pushed, but Brian stood immovable as a stone wall. Panic rose in her chest and threatened to erupt in her throat. Was he drinking her—? Oh shit!
> Outside a shadow moved across the windows. She knew she'd find him with her. Damn him. Fingering a lock of black hair, she cursed and tossed it over her shoulder. Carly's mouth curved in a bitter smile, Brian always did have a weakness for blondes.

Is this multiple POV—from Amy to Brian to Amy to Carly—well executed?

No it isn't. That is head-hopping and that is what NOT to do in multiple POV. The scene should have been done more like this:

> Brian lowered his face, and Amy closed her eyes, waiting for the warmth of his lips against hers. Instead, his tongue tickled her jaw, trailing down her neck before she felt a slight pinch below her ear. Amy opened her eyes, startled.
> "Please," she whispered. "You're hurting me."
> His lips moved against her neck. "You taste sweet, like an innocent. I haven't had one of those since the feminist movement."
> A chuckle rumbled in his massive chest and Amy pushed, but Brian stood immovable as a stone wall. Panic rose in her chest and threatened to erupt in her throat. Was he drinking her—? *Oh shit!*
> (Scene break, or new chapter here).
> Carly sunk back into the shadows, furious at the scene played out in the window. She knew she'd find him with her. Damn him. Fingering a lock of black hair, she cursed and tossed it over her shoulder. Carly's mouth curved in a bitter smile. Brian always did have a weakness for blondes.

By sticking to Amy's POV in the first scene, we can still show Brian's thoughts in dialogue and maintain intensity. The first version loses that because the reader stumbles around trying to figure out who is thinking or talking and wondering when the writer will rip them out of that POV again. Then, because it's important to show that someone is watching, we switched scenes, indicating it with a break and moved into Carly's POV. It's clear, the tension is good, and the reader—most important—is not lost. But we cannot shift back and forth simply because we have that handy little scene break available.

We must try to stay in a single POV for an entire scene. Too much switching, scene break or not, is dizzying and not the correct way to do it.

Often, third person *alternating* is placed under the umbrella of multiple POV. In this POV, more than one character's viewpoint can be shown within a scene, but this should only be done if the writer has a good reason and never alternate between more than two characters. Romance writers often use multiple POV when writing scenes between the hero and heroine.

Writers be warned, though, this POV doesn't often work.

If a writer insists on using multiple POVs within a scene, it works best when all POVs are superficial and the transitions are subtly done. This requires considerable skill. If written deep into the character's POV, the result is scattered and we lose the effect we hoped to achieve. We wouldn't recommend it until a writer has first mastered all other POVs. Even then, it's difficult to pull off.

The advantage of using multiple POVs is that it leaves the writer free to move the story around and to shift time if he or she so chooses, making it less of a linear presentation than with other POVs. This can strengthen the story and add intrigue. An example would be a crime novel where we get to see not only the detective's POV but also the serial killer's and the victims' POVs.

The biggest disadvantage to using third person multiple is that stories may lose structure and credibility if the writer is not careful. With more than three or four POV characters, it's difficult to achieve one strong character the reader can identify with. Our advice would be to determine which POVs are essential to the story and remove the others.

2.2.2 CHARACTERIZATION

Characterization is the method writers use to develop the characters in their stories. To create and build characters, they use a variety of tools such as appearance, actions, thoughts, dialogue, and interaction with other characters. Mannerisms, for example, like chewing fingernails when nervous or twirling hair around a finger allow the reader to see the characters clearly. Physical characteristics like tattoos or a tacky comb-over also help to develop the character in the reader's mind.

The writer combines these small things to build a character that has dimension and believability. Each detail should be subtle and added over the course of the story, not dumped on the reader in one large description. We shouldn't bring a protagonist in and write:

> Wade was a big hunk of a man who wore tight jeans that showed off his tight ass to perfection. He worked for some bikers—a hit man and a dealer according to rumor—and also had a thing for Kristina, a much younger woman recently divorced from a man who knocked the crap out of her almost daily. Wade's dark blue eyes could seduce even the strongest of women. Adding to his dangerous aura, a tattoo of a python curled around his bicep. He was unhappily married to a woman out to destroy him.

This description is not characterization. It's telling the reader all about the character in one big dump. Good characterization feeds the reader details like this slowly, piece by piece. For example, let's observe the image formed from these lines.

> Each time their eyes met, the naked hunger in his gaze made her want to climb over the bar and drag him off somewhere private. Hell, she'd have probably settled for the alley outside.

> She'd lived long enough in denial and she couldn't fight anymore. Why would any sane woman fight Wade anyway?
> Leaning over the top of the computer, Kristina traced a finger across the python tattoo that coiled around his right arm.
> He shook his head. "You're asking for trouble, little girl."[32]

In this passage the writer depicts Wade as one sexy beast with his tattoo and his lecherous stares. Kristina seems like a horny teenager taking a walk on the wild side. However, Wade is a more complex character than that and Kristina, well she's horny, but definitely not a teenager. Later, the writer further develops both characters to portray another layer of their makeup.

> Cadence banged on her chair.
> Wade turned and picked her up, tossing her into the air to her slobbery delight. He glanced at Kristina, catching the wistful smile she quickly turned into a stern frown.
> "You'll have her puking," she warned.
> "She likes it." He lowered Cadence and bounced her on his hip just in case. Her tiny fingers traced the tattoo on his arm, a python that curved from his elbow to his shoulder, her mouth forming a tiny 'o'.
> "That's a python, a big strong snake," he laughed when she raised her eyes to his and gurgled. "Maybe I'll get you one someday." [33]

Add a baby and the tattoo doesn't seem so…dangerous. Wade's obvious affection for the infant adds likeability to his character. Kristina also doesn't seem quite so immature. She's a mother and a normal, healthy woman who has needs that extend beyond being a mom.

When building characters, we use mannerisms, speech, and actions to develop each into either major or minor characters that are either static (unchanging) or dynamic (changing). Our protagonist is a major character who should be dynamic. After all, the point of the story is to show the protagonist changing to resolve the conflicts. Static characters often play minor or secondary roles. They are necessary to the plot but, because the conflict and resolution doesn't affect them, they remain unchanged.

Wade and Kristina are dynamic, meaning they are changing and have many layers, like an onion. Layers of characterization help to develop the character in the reader's mind. How far do we go? Depends on the character's role in the story. There are a variety of character types that we'll use. Their roles will dictate how we choose to characterize them. In the next sections, we'll look at these character types a little further.

 ### 2.2.2.1 MAJOR CHARACTERS

Major characters are often the first characters that the reader encounters. The major characters dominate the story. Our protagonist, main character, and antagonist are major characters. Their actions affect the resolution of the plot, and their motivations or goals are the reason for the story. Major

---

32 Renée Miller, Dirty Truths.

33 Renée Miller, Dirty Truths.

characters are dynamic, meaning that they change and should have many layers. Let's look a bit more at each major character type.

Protagonist

The protagonist is the person the story is about, the character whose goals we are trying to meet. Many stories have two or more protagonists, but some writing experts advise that sticking to one protagonist is easier on writers and the reader. While we agree that there is sense in this, especially for beginning writers, we believe that with good characterization multiple protagonists can add depth and interest to a novel. However many protagonists we decide to use, we'll want to devote a significant amount of time to developing these characters, because the protagonist is who the reader relates to.

Main Character

The main character is the person whose POV we are telling the story through. The main character doesn't have to be the protagonist, although often it is. In "Interview with a Vampire," Anne Rice tells the story through Louis, who is the main character, but Lestat is the protagonist. Things happen to Louis, but the plot and its resolution revolves around Lestat's goals and actions. Things happen because of Lestat. The story hinges on what Lestat does. Louis plays a major role because as the main character it is his voice that sets the story's tone.

Antagonist

The antagonist is the person who works against the protagonist's goals. This might be a direct or indirect opposition, and the antagonist isn't always the "bad guy." For example, a villain-type character like Cinderella's wicked stepmother works directly against the story's protagonist. Her goals conflict with Cinderella's goals.

However, in a crime thriller, a serial killer isn't necessarily thwarting the protagonist detective directly. The killer likely murders because of his own goals, not because it annoys the protagonist or causes him problems. He may not be aware of the protagonist at all. Their goals are in opposition—the protagonist wants to stop the killer, the killer wants to keep murdering, but it isn't a direct or intentional opposition. Of course, the protagonist could very well be the killer, and the antagonist the detective. Despite our tendency to view the antagonist as the bad guy, this isn't always the role he plays.

2.2.2.2 SECONDARY CHARACTERS

Secondary, or minor, characters are less noticeable than our major characters. These characters know the protagonist and react to her. They comment on behavior or developments in the plot, and their actions can affect what happens. Though secondary characters are often static, this doesn't mean they don't have to be developed as well as the major characters, and they can be just as dynamic. Their actions keep the plot moving forward. An ex-wife meddling in a budding relationship might be a secondary character. A best friend, a boss, a sidekick, or parents also play secondary character roles.

Often, writers choose to give the secondary characters traits that provide contrast to the main character. This can range from appearance (tall vs. short) to personality (extraverted vs. introverted). Secondary characters can make or break a story, no matter how small their role, so it's always best to give them careful development. By giving our minor characters quirks or eccentricities, we make them memorable, but not enough so that they overpower the main character. We should limit the number of secondary characters and make sure each is necessary to the story. Readers try to keep track of all characters, and having dozens to remember as they pop in and out of the story is dizzying.

Subplot Characters

Having given much thought to the characterization in our novel, our major characters are planned and they are dynamic, memorable, and very real. Good stuff. Now, what about that less important, but interesting character over there? No, not the murdering thug—that one. The best friend, usually the most important secondary character.

She's held her friend's hand through some rough times and offered valuable advice—we think. She's got a story too, doesn't she? That story actually affects her decisions and actions in the main character's life. As a driving force, her story can enhance the main plot, so how do we breathe more life into her story without overshadowing the protagonist?

Let's give her a story. For example, let's give this best friend—we'll call her Charmaine—information about something the protagonist needs to know. The protagonist dates a guy who by all outward appearances is Prince Charming. But wait, Charmaine is addicted to a variety of pills. She doesn't tell her friend, the protagonist, because Charmaine knows the protagonist's mother had a serious drug issue, which led to the protagonist being left to raise her younger siblings. The best friend goes to her dealer; she's running low on her precious pills. As she's waiting in the hallway of the spacious home her drug dealer owns, Prince Charming emerges from a room upstairs—with a shapely blonde. Well, well, well. Prince Charming is tarnished now. But does best friend tell the protagonist? How does she explain what she's seen? What possible reason would she have for being in a drug/whore house other than that she's either buying drugs or selling her body? Interesting indeed.

This might be more of a subplot than we want to give. We have written it as an exaggerated example to show how, by giving subplots to secondary characters, we can add layers of depth and interest to a novel. Subplots help to increase the pace, or to slow it just enough for the reader to catch his breath. A little side story for a secondary character can also be used to provide information or backstory without weighing down the prose with exposition.

2.2.2.3 OTHER CHARACTERS

Background characters, or incidentals, include neighbors, acquaintances, waitresses, police officers, drunks at a bar, or any character that plays little more than a walk-on part in the story.

Incidental characters should be used as setting; they add color to the story, and are necessary, but they don't affect the outcome of the plot. In Charlaine Harris's *Sookie Stackhouse* novels, background characters are plentiful, but she manages to prevent them from becoming confusing. Jane, a local alcoholic, is a fixture at Merlotte's, the bar where Sookie works. Jane is a desperate case, dirty, aging, and carries a lot of baggage. This character is memorable, and yet she is an incidental. She doesn't affect the plot at all and could be taken out without changing what happens. However, she adds to the background, which is what these characters are meant to do. To add interest, we should endeavor to color stories with characters like Jane.

Harris also uses other insignificant characters from one novel to play a supporting role in later novels. Because she has given these characters quirks and added color to their original roles, the reader easily remembers them. This promotes instant recognition. We might not be writing a series, but small things like a quirky postman or a nosy neighbor, can add much to the setting and atmosphere.

🧩 2.2.3 DIALOGUE

We're going to go out on a limb and assume that writers are aware that dialogue must be wrapped in quotations ("Hello, John.") and that each new speaker has a new paragraph. These are basics which every writer learn early. What we want to discuss is how to write good dialogue beyond the basics.

Dialogue serves many functions in a story. It conveys, through the characters, what we need to know about the plot, shows us the characters' personalities and quirks, gives us a sense of time and place through the speech patterns and vocabulary used, and develops conflict. Written well, dialogue can enhance the plot. Written poorly, it can ruin the entire novel.

Writing good dialogue is difficult for most of us to master. New writers tend to forget that dialogue has to feel *real* and still be of consequence. It has to flow, and the reader must believe he is reading a conversation. Dialogue should move the story forward and provide the reader a break from the narrative. In other words, it shouldn't pull the reader out of the story, but enhance the story experience.

For example:

> "Hello, Mary. Did you get my telephone call?" June greeted her friend.
> "No, I did not, June. When did you call?" Mary asked.
> "I called this morning. I was wondering if you would help me with something," June replied.
> "What do you need help doing?" Mary queried.
> "I need to hide a body," June replied gravely.

Is this how real people talk? Not where we come from. First, we seldom address each other so formally by name. Second, we tend to use a lot of slang, omit words, etc. Last, those tags and attributions are atrocious. Here's the conversation, as it could be:

> "Hey, did you get my message?" June asked.
> "Shit, I've been so busy today I haven't checked my phone. When did you call?" Mary tossed her bags into the back of the van. She had ten minutes to get to school.
> "This morning. I hoped you could help me with something."
> "What?" Mary checked her watch.
> "A body."

We tend to use many contractions in natural dialogue (I've, haven't, goin', y'all) and profanity now and then (if we're honest), and most people do not refer to things using the proper name. We might say cash instead of money, phone instead of telephone, and often we leave parts of sentences hanging. Some of the most common mistakes include not only writing the speech too formally, as above, but also writing it exactly like real speech.

> "Uh…y'know, I like her an' all, but she's kinda none too bright. Ye ken?"

That's a bit much. We can build character, convey accents or dialect, and show personality, without making it so the reader has to decipher a foreign language.

> "I like her and all, but she sure ain't bright. Know what I mean?"

This is better. We're still showing the speaker's speech pattern, which leads us to believe that if this grammatically-challenged speaker thinks someone is dumb, that person must be more than just a few bricks short of a load.

To create the effect of dialect, we use rhythm, vocabulary, and description, without resorting to phonetic spelling. New writers will also write dialogue where the speaker relays a story in past tense, and this almost never happens. If we think about how we relate something to one of our friends, most often we would use present tense.

> "Then he tells me that someone stole the stars and put them in my eyes. What a line. I look at him and I say someone must have stolen his brain and put it in his pants."

Sometimes, dialogue shows interruptions, which are indicated with an em-dash.

> "No, you listen to me—"
> "I'm through listening to you." She raised the hammer.

We interrupt one another all the time, so having a character in a heated exchange with the wife—who is about to knock him over the head with his own sledge hammer—cut off mid-sentence is natural. He can't finish once he's unconscious, can he? Or perhaps the wife picks up the dialogue, interrupting him before he can spew more lies.

What about inner dialogue? We were just getting to that. Writers sometimes feel they have to put internal dialogue or indirect thoughts in quotes, as they would all other dialogue. No. If it isn't spoken aloud by the character, it does not have quotes. To show a character's exact inner thoughts, we use context, and failing that, italics. To paraphrase, we use regular font and leave off the quotes. For example:

> Why did she think she could raise any child, let alone someone else's bastard?
> *Because Carroll told you to.*[34]

In the first line, the internal dialogue is not the character's direct thoughts. The next line is, so it's in italics.

A good exercise is to either record or pay attention to dialogue from people around us. When we're on the phone, we can listen to the words used and the inflection in the voice. When in person, we can watch mannerisms, make note of slang, patterns of speech and such, and use these in our written dialogue.

Now, the words used are only half of the dialogue struggle. The speech is the easy part. We can figure that out quickly and write dialogue that is real and believable. But then, we screw it up with tags and attributions. In the next sections, we'll discuss how to use these properly.

 **2.2.3.1 ATTRIBUTIONS**

Attributions indicate who is speaking in an exchange. Attributions are the few words after the dialogue, telling the reader about who is saying what. Whether in our own writing or while reading another's, we've spotted dialogue with little or no attribution and gotten lost. "Talking head" syndrome is common in new writers. They figure if the quotes are around the dialogue then they've done their job.

---

[34] Renée Miller, *In the Bones.*

Dialogue must have attributions to help the reader follow the conversation. Too few and we're lost, but too many and we slow the pace of the story. We've seen (and used) the same tag written different ways to avoid repetition. Said, muttered, sneered, smiled, etc. are ways we try to add attributions, believing that as long as we don't use the same word too often, then we're okay. Often anything other than "said" is more distracting than using none at all.

Another mistake is to put adverbial attributions or tags at the end of a line of dialogue. Said angrily, replied slowly, and muttered incomprehensibly. These silly attributes don't help dialogue. They might identify the speaker, but they also clutter the prose and annoy readers. When we do this, we're telling the reader rather than showing

Stephen King had this to say about adverbial attribution in dialogue:

> "I can be a good sport about adverbs, though. Yes I can. With one exception: dialogue attribution. I insist that you use the adverb in dialogue attribution only in the rarest and most special of occasions ... and not even then, if you can avoid it." [35]

We bow to Mr. King. While adverbs have their place in a novel, that place is not in dialogue. The only time it's acceptable (and we hesitate to say this in case writers try to justify using them when they shouldn't) is when the reader would be confused without the adverbial tag. Often, we can rewrite dialogue so that the adverb is not needed.

Attributions should be minimal, but not non-existent. We need them to show who is speaking. To do so, we set them early in the dialogue to avoid "talking heads" and limit them to one every four or five lines (this is only a guideline, we can go six lines or three or ten if it is appropriate.) "Said" is an excellent attribution and invisible most times. We can slip in a "John said" and the reader won't notice as much as "John croaked." The reader is accustomed to seeing *said*, so it won't pull her as far out of the dialogue as another tag might. Using descriptors like muttered, yelled, cried, etc. can be distracting. The context of the situation in which the characters are speaking should enable any reader to accurately interpret how they're speaking.

We recommend breaking the monotony of attributions with action, to give the reader a visual of what is happening, while still giving proper attribution.

> "You look busy," Jack said.
> "I am busy," Maria replied.
> "I thought you'd moved. Jamie said you got a new job."
> "I did," Maria quipped.
> "Oh," John said.
> "Why did you come here?" Maria asked.

Now this is not great dialogue. Actually it's terrible. The attributions are there, but there are far too many. When we have only two characters in a scene, attributions are only needed to ground the reader and keep things clear. We use action in combination with attributions to identify who is speaking and to break up the monotony of said, asked, etc.

> "You look busy," Jack said.
> "I am busy." Maria folded a tattered blue sheet.
> "I thought you'd moved. Jamie said you got a new job."

---

[35] Stephen King, On Writing.

"I did."

"Oh."

"Why did you come here?"

In the revised exchange, we only used a single attribution, "Jack said." The rest of the dialogue is tagged with action or not at all, yet it is clear who is speaking each time. Combining attributions with tags is important to writing good dialogue.

2.2.3.2 TAGS

Tags are what we use to attribute dialogue and to show what is happening. Said, asked, replied, scolded, etc. are tags. We might also tag with actions like "John picked up the phone." Many writers believe that they need to get creative with tags to make the dialogue more interesting. This is incorrect. Tags are only necessary to identify a speaker or to show something happening within the scene. As we said before, it should move the story forward, not interrupt it.

Now that we've mentioned using attributions and tags, let's look at how some think that combining means to use attributions and tags at the same time.

"Hogwash," John said as he picked up the phone.

This is annoying for the reader. Why? The action identifies the speaker, so the attribution is unnecessary. It's a good idea to use a combination of attributions and tags but not together for a single line of dialogue. We are constantly moving as we speak, and so should our characters. But we shouldn't get crazy and include an action with every line of dialogue. The action tags should be treated the same way as attributions, only when necessary and only if they serve to move the story forward.

While we're on the subject of unnecessary tags, let's discuss further the tendency to *get creative* with them. Words like hissed, murmured, sneered, frowned, etc., serve little purpose other than making our dialogue read silly. Example:

"Come here," Joan hissed.

"Get lost," he laughed.

She hissed? Do we really hiss when we speak? Can we sneer a sentence? We can sneer, but talk and sneer at the same time? Just as we cannot laugh and talk, we can't sneer, hiss, growl, or frown a sentence either. We're either doing one or the other. Using a verb to describe the character's expression and then trying to disguise it as a dialogue tag is lazy. We just do not smile, grimace, laugh, or hiss our sentences. Is it necessary for the character to cry out or snarl? How will the reader interpret these tags? They highlight weaknesses in the writer. Why? Because, if the characters' words were strong enough, we don't need dramatic tags. Whenever a hero snarls and snorts, his dialogue weakens. Let's try those two lines again, the right way.

"Come here," Joan said.

He laughed. "Get lost."

He laughed first, and *then* told her to take a hike. Joan did not hiss because she doesn't need to. The information earlier in the scene should indicate that she is angry or grumpy, so the line "Come here." will be enough, and odds are, the reader is getting the right idea of her tone.

Tags are necessary to good dialogue. How many depends on the scene, the number of characters speaking and how we've written the story. In this area, as in many other areas of fiction writing, writers must remember to give the reader credit. Less is more.

2.2.4 EXPOSITION

Exposition and narrative are terms often used interchangeably because both are parts of inactive scenes. However, there is a difference between the two. We'll discuss narration later, first let's look at exposition. Here's an excerpt from a rough draft:

> Kristina's lawyer had lectured her on the threat Daniel posed, not only to Cadence, but to Kristina as well. He claimed he wouldn't tell her what to do but suggested she think about Cadence's future, growing up in a home of violence and anger. What would Daniel do when Cadence was old enough to disobey him?
>
> Shame rose like bile in her throat as she remembered her daughter lying so still in her crib that night. Daniel didn't look at the photos when they'd passed them to his attorney, he didn't need to. Instead, he'd stared at her, his mouth pressed into a firm line. He shook his head.

This is a lot of exposition for such a small chunk of text. It's telling the reader what happened in a previous meeting with Kristina's lawyer. This can be written without the exposition to give the reader the needed information, while still moving the story forward.

> "He could kill you the next time. He almost did that already, and he hasn't gotten better." He squeezed her hand.
>
> She looked away.
>
> "I'm not telling you what to do, dear, but if you were my daughter, I'd urge you to think about the future. What about your baby? What if she grows to be a difficult child? What will he do if she doesn't obey as her mother does?"
>
> Shame rose like bile in her throat as she remembered her daughter lying so still in her crib that night. Daniel didn't look at the photos when they'd passed them to his attorney, he didn't need to. Instead, he'd stared at her, his mouth pressed into a firm line. He shook his head.
>
> "No, I don't want that to happen to her, I don't think he—"
>
> "He would." [36]

Exposition doesn't contribute to moving the story along as we can see in the first example. It contains information the reader needs but as we said, it's inactive. While some exposition is necessary, it creates a distance between the reader and the characters. It tells, rather than shows, which reminds reader that they're reading. Does that mean exposition is bad? Not always. Sometimes we want the reader to pause for a moment. But no matter how fabulous a writer we are, exposition that goes on for too long without some action will lose the reader. In the examples above, the first version fills the reader in, and often this is a portion readers will skim over. Nothing happens, so why waste time

---

[36] Renée Miller, Dirty Truths.

reading it? They may miss an important piece of information because we've bored them with too much explanation and not enough action.

We must strive for balance between exposition and action, so it doesn't slow down the pace too much or for too long. Large blocks of exposition can slow the story to a halt, and this is when a reader sets down the book and finds another that can hold his attention. The idea is to let the reader experience the story rather than tell him about it. In the second example, the writer <u>showed</u> the reader what happened between Kristina and the lawyer through dialogue and action. There is still exposition, but it's sparse and the action is sprinkled in to keep the story moving forward.

But, if there is a lot of backstory that the reader must know, you need to use exposition, right?

Wrong. We can sprinkle information throughout the story to give the reader what he needs to know. Exposition in short bursts is okay, and often not noticed, but writing a huge chunk to explain something is like making the reader stop to learn what we forgot to include. It's jarring. If we must include exposition in the story, the best way to do so is to weave it into the action. In the next section we'll discuss how this is done.

 2.2.4.1 WEAVING

Sometimes exposition is unavoidable. The reader must know certain facts to understand what is happening, and we can't write the three hundred pages required to show it. Often in genres, such as science fiction or fantasy, writers create unique worlds, races, or technology, and the reader needs history or information to understand. Experienced writers will achieve this without using pages of exposition by weaving the details into the action.

Weaving exposition can be done in a variety of ways. What we'll do depends on the story and the information needed, as long as we don't dump the information in large chunks. Very few mistakes will turn a reader against a story faster than "info-dumps."

Let's look at techniques we might use to weave exposition into the action.

Let characters recall the information.

Using techniques like journal entries, dreams, or captain's logs, characters can recall important information without slowing the pace and dumping a chunk of information into the middle of the action. These are often only a sentence or two in length and feed necessary information to the reader. Captain Kirk's logs (*Star Trek*) are an example of weaving. These logs always began with "Captain's log, stardate…" and then crucial information was relayed to the reader within a couple of lines. This isn't a technique that is used often in a single manuscript, but it's an option if the writer has no other choice.

Show the POV character searching for information.

Writers often use this technique to provide technical information or history for the reader while keeping the pace moving along. The character may research something or find a note or a journal which contains the information. For example:

> Jack sorted through his wife's belongings, desperate for answers. The nightstand drawer resisted his pull. Locked. He yanked, breaking the flimsy lock. He closed his hand over a thin book and pulled it out. He fingered the worn cover. Carrie's journal. Should he read it? Her

life might depend on it. Jack opened the furry pink cover and flipped to the days before her disappearance.

July 31, 2005

Met with Carl. Promised to meet again on Saturday. Doctor called yesterday. Pregnant!

Jack's throat tightened. He blinked away the tears that threatened and turned the page.

August 5, 2005

Agreed on a price. Thought his baby would be worth more than $5000, but need the cash. Have to get the hell out of here.

August 7, 2005

Jack coming home tonight. Need to figure something out. Carl said he could be dealt with. Don't know what to do…meeting buyer tomorrow.

The remaining pages were blank. Of course, Carrie disappeared two days later—pregnant with his child. A child she never intended to tell him about.[37]

This excerpt contains some exposition, but it's sparse. The journal entries fill in blanks that Jack and the reader need to know. The wife was selling a baby, perhaps a motive for murder or a staged death. In a mystery or thriller, it's important to keep the pace moving, so adding little bits of information in this manner keeps the momentum of the plot, while providing the reader with important information that would otherwise require a full scene to show.

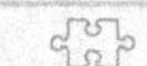 **Show the information in dialogue.** 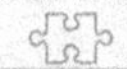

Another character can provide needed information to the POV character. However, we must ensure that the character has a believable reason for sharing this knowledge, and we can't let them vanish once they've given their little bit either. The information should be something integral to the plot, not some family history that will never be mentioned again or the history of a place the POV character is only passing through.

Use a protagonist or POV character's senses to describe a scene 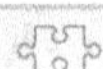

If we have to describe a new scene, particularly in fantasy or science fiction where the world may be a creation of the writer's imagination, we can rely on the character's five senses to show it to the reader, rather than giving him a straight description.

Shouts and thumps announced the crowd lining up outside the doors and the room suddenly went black. Just as quickly, red lights flashed to give the room an eerie glow. It reminded Gabriel of how things appeared in a blood haze. Grudgingly he admired Aedon's fondness for theater.

Everything took on a richness of color that captured the eye. Newcomers looked from one shade of red to another, seeing little else. At times, it could be dizzying and overwhelming for many humans. Just as Aedon intended.

Gabriel raised his gaze to the balcony wondering if Aedon watched the floor. From up there, through two-way mirrors, he could see the entire club in privacy. Gabriel felt his anger. It

---

[37] Renée Miller, The Auction.

burned at the back of his mind, sending sparks of heat down his neck, but he couldn't sense Aedon's eyes on him.[38]

Here, the POV character, Gabriel, is walking through the room, and the writer uses his senses to describe it to the reader. Action is woven in to keep the scene moving, but at the end of the scene—which is much longer than the example—the reader has a full picture of a vampire haunt called "The Bite."

Letting readers learn about setting as a by-product of the action or dialogue should be a writer's goal. We should only resort to telling if no other technique is available.

Occasionally, there is no way that the writer can weave the exposition into the action. This is fine, but if he must use exposition, he must strive to do so sparingly. A brief sentence (two at most) about an event or to describe the origins of a fantastical species never seen before is okay. If showing rather than telling would take far more time, then of course, the simplest route is often best, but we must use only enough exposition to move the story forward.

If a writer fears cutting out too much exposition and leaving the reader to scratch his head, we can attempt to put that worry to rest. Often, it's impossible to cut too much exposition. Yet, the story should never include writing that slows the momentum of the plot. Exposition in large amounts equals reading a dictionary or a history textbook. No fun at all. If the reader scratches his head, it's most likely that we've failed to flesh out the scene, and not that we've cut too much exposition. Telling is lazy, the easiest route to achieve a goal. Taking the time to include the necessary information is an essential element in the writer's craft. But this can be achieved by weaving it into the action—so that the reader understands the story without being pulled out of it by a lazy dump of information.

2.2.5 NARRATIVE

Narrative, in simple terms, is writing that tells a story. It is typically composed of information the reader needs to know to understand what is happening at the time in the story. While it is not technically active, unlike exposition, narrative can move the story forward. For example:

> They used to argue quietly, for the sake of the neighbors, but since the recession, many of the houses around them stood empty. They had nice paint and were pretty, but inside they held nothing. The houses were fake, like his family. [39]

In this excerpt, the writer explains an important bit of backstory and adds intensity to the scene with just a few lines of narrative. The family grapples through a recession, the parents argue but this is nothing new. This bit indicates they no longer hide the fighting. The POV character is struggling with his parents' carelessness and his own loneliness. This is all crucial to events that happen next, but to go into detail, showing the families moving away from the neighborhood, for example, would use far too much narrative.

There are times when background information is necessary for the reader to comprehend the significance of an event in the story. When this happens, narrative is often the best way to convey the

---

[38] Renée Miller, Ancient Blood.

[39] Wendy Swore, Firebug.

information. Now, to be clear, while narrative is sometimes useful, it can slow the forward progression of the plot and remind the reader that she is reading. For this reason, if we use too much, we'll risk losing the reader. Large chunks of narrative are hard to digest. If the narrative consists of information alone, the reader feels as though she is wading through a sludgy mire of boredom. She must wait for something active to happen… or she'll just skip the boring part.

As writers, our job is to create a dream world for the reader and maintain that *dreamlike* feeling throughout the novel. Sometimes it's impossible to do this without including important information. If we include backstory by writing scenes, dialogue, etc. to show the information, we might end up with two thousand pages and a novel that is tough to sell. This is where narrative is useful.

Renée's novel *Ancient Blood* has a large cast of characters and a relevant history for each. As a result, each character has different perceptions and motivations that the reader must know. The vampires in this story have a covenant that they follow. They have customs, beliefs, and a few myth-busting facts that must be included for the reader to understand the world they move about in. They also have old vendettas, loyalties, and agendas, which influence the protagonists. Narrative is used sparingly to relay bits of this information throughout the story and thus fill in the gaps for the reader. For example, Gabriel hates that the prince of the coven hunts humans in the woods behind their home, his setup sort of like the big game hunters who pay to hunt a stocked reserve of lions and tigers. Gabriel's motivation might be explained through dialogue, but it was much simpler to show through a small amount of narrative:

> Capturing one or two humans and dropping them in an alien dark wood was not a challenge—certainly not hunting, no matter what Aedon liked to call it. It was like shooting ducks in a barrel. They had no chance to escape. The poor bastards didn't even know what they were up against until it was too late.
>
> It had been different when he was younger. They would enter homes in the middle of the night while the occupants slept. In those days, people believed in what they called vampires and weren't unprepared. Many were eager to kill one of his kind and often killed innocent people for having the unfortunate luck of being pale skinned. [40]

If the writer chose to leave this narrative out, having Gabriel say simply that he preferred not to hunt humans with Aedon, prince of his coven, then it would feel as though the writer left something out. So she would have written pages of dialogue and action to show this hunting long ago compared to how the vamps hunt now, just to explain a simple motivation (pages that could be better used to show something active and more vital to the plot).

Narrative is also useful to transition from one time or place to another. We discuss transitions in more depth in another section, but simply put, transitions are like a bridge that fills the gap between scenes. The longer the transition, the more jolting it is for the reader. Writers use narrative to bridge the gap sometimes. Narrative might also be used when the writer wants to cue the reader that something other than what is being said or shown is meant.

Often, we use narrative to show that characters may say one thing but mean something else, or the character's perception of an event or person is different from the reality. We also use narrative to clue the reader in to the character's actual intent or their motivation as opposed to another character's

---

[40] Renée Miller, Ancient Blood.

perception of the same. The viewpoint and its depiction might be reliable or unreliable and this adds depth to the novel.

Narrative should reveal something new to the reader, and it must be necessary that the reader know the information to either understand what is happening in the story or to foreshadow something that will happen in the future. In other words, narrative must serve a purpose. If it doesn't, then it's just wasted prose that bogs the reader down. If we do that often in a novel, the reader will throw the book down and never pick it up to finish the story we worked so hard to write.

Narrative should never be inactive. It should be strong, compelling, and informative and push the story forward in some way. When we use unnecessary narrative, or convey irrelevant or redundant information, we are guilty of authorial intrusion. We'll discuss how to avoid this in the next section.

 ## 2.2.5.1 AUTHORIAL INTRUSION

Authorial intrusion (author intrusion) pulls the reader out of the story and reminds her that she is reading. Once upon a time, it was common for writers to insert their own comments or statements into a story. In the middle of a romantic scene, showing the protagonists finally coming together, for example, the writer might insert a little story about the statue they knock off the dresser in their exuberance. The reader is left to cool her heels while the author takes this little segue. Readers today don't tolerate such nonsense.

There are many ways writers intrude on the story, and sometimes the sin is not intentional. We might make a comment or observation that isn't what the reader would expect from the POV character. Perhaps dialogue seemed to be directed to the reader to explain backstory or as a way to insert the writer's personal view instead of being a natural part of the story. Sometimes the writer includes a detail about the characters or setting that isn't consistent with what was previously written. Factual errors and plot holes are also forms of authorial intrusion.

Let's look again at the example from page 105, as it matured from rough to first draft:

> The men crept around the house, unaware that Charlie waited in the shadows for them.

Of course they're unaware, or else they'd go to the shadows where Charlie is hiding, rather than go into the house. Right? Here's another example:

> Before stepping onto the road, Kristina paused. No one drove the streets at this time of night, but she still looked both ways before crossing, a habit ingrained from childhood. She didn't hear the footsteps behind her, but her neck tingled. Almost at the bridge, she lengthened her strides. No one in Laighton would be lurking in the shadows waiting to pounce on a lone woman at night. Hell, she'd walked alone in the dark for years and not once had she ever had a problem.
> Kristina turned around, sensing another presence, her heart pounding in her chest. About ten feet away a man, tall, lanky and donning a hooded sweatshirt, walked toward her.

So, she didn't hear the footsteps, but still turned around? This is annoying for readers. The writer has inserted information that isn't consistent with the setting or the character's POV. If she can't hear the footsteps—and we're in her POV—then the footsteps shouldn't be mentioned. Even better, let her hear the man behind her. It creates a more intense scene without the author intrusion to ruin it. Let's look at the scene without the intrusion:

> Before stepping onto the road, Kristina paused. No one drove the streets at this time of night but she still looked both ways before crossing, a habit ingrained from childhood. As she moved her foot to cross, her neck tingled. Were those footsteps behind her? Almost at the bridge, she lengthened her strides. No one in Laighton would be lurking in the shadows waiting to pounce on a lone woman at night. Hell, she'd walked alone in the dark for years and not once had she ever had a problem.
>
> The footsteps were real, and quickened. Kristina turned around, her heart pounding in her chest. About ten feet away a man, tall, lanky and donning a hooded sweatshirt, walked toward her. [41]

Novels aren't like movies. The reader cannot see or know what is happening off-screen because the characters can't see it. We must show the events as they would be seen through the POV we're using.

Using weak verbs or telling in narrative is another type of authorial intrusion. This is why we emphasize to "show" rather than "tell." Telling is one of the most obvious authorial intrusions. It reminds the reader that she is reading, pulling her away from the story.

Authorial Intrusion:

> He realized his choice had been made for him. He'd have to leave her.

No intrusion:

> He had to leave her.

Authorial Intrusion:

> Jack thought about Jenny with Ray and decided it was absurd. He believed Jenny definitely traded down if she chose Ray over him. Jack knew he was no Clive Owen, but thought he was a damn sight better than Ray.

No intrusion:

> Jenny with Ray? Absurd. Definitely trading down in Jenny's case. Jack may not be Clive Owen, but he was a damn sight better than Ray. [42]

To avoid author intrusion we must ensure that narrative adds something to the story, moving it forward. Narrative inserted for the sake of filling in a blank spot intrudes on the reader's experience. It reminds her that she isn't in the fictional world we've created. The reader should only know what the POV character knows and see only what the POV character sees. If we stay out of telling and keep the narrative active, we don't need to annoy the reader by inserting ourselves into the story.

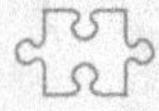 **2.2.6 STORYTELLING**

Storytelling conveys a sequence of events through words, images, or sounds. Stories or narratives have been shared for centuries as a form of entertainment, education and to instill cultural and moral values. Great storytellers master not only the basic elements of fiction, but the art of storytelling. This includes

---

[41] Renée Miller, Dirty Truths.

[42] Renée Miller, The Legend of Jackson Murphy.

creating brilliant openers and closers, the proper use of flashbacks, setting the right pace and creating atmosphere.

Primitive storytellers used words combined with gestures and expressions. As writers, we don't have the luxury of being physically there to tell the story and therefore we have to use a variety of techniques to keep the reader interested. This is why we call it an art; we must use the tools given to create a world in which the reader can become lost. Storytelling in its oldest form didn't need devices like hooks, cliffhangers, or color because the teller could create the suspense and intensity needed with voice, actions, and expressions.

In the following sections, we'll discuss openers, closers, cliffhangers, atmosphere, color, and setting the pace that best suits a story.

 **2.2.6.1 OPENERS**

As an exercise, walk around a bookstore and pay attention to people as they browse the shelf. Note how many prospective buyers open the book to read the first lines before buying the book or setting it back on the shelf. The opening lines of a book are crucial to dragging readers in:

It was a bright, cold day in April and the clocks were striking 13.[43]

You better not tell nobody but God. [44]

These first lines hold something intriguing or puzzling. This is what we want, to grab the reader's intention with that first line. Our first line is critical to convincing the reader she wants to share her time with us, as is the first paragraph, even the first scene. We want to bait the reader into finding out more about our characters and their story. While they might forgive a less than stellar hook line, they won't forgive weak openers throughout.

Opening lines of scenes and chapters are also important because they set the tone. Often writers forget that variety is needed, not just in sentences and paragraphs, but also in how we open a new scene or chapter. By opening each chapter or scene as though it's the first line of the entire story, we continue to hold the reader's interest. Scene openers:

That was the Thursday.

"Except," Brue muttered aloud.

Were they married? [45]

Chapter openers:

Dr. Cawley was thin to the point of emaciation.

They stood outside the room.

She comes down the hallway toward him. [46]

---

[43] George Orwell, 1984.

[44] Alice Walker, The Color Purple.

[45] John Le Carre, A Most Wanted Man.

[46] Dennis LeHane, Shutter Island.

These chapter and scene openings highlight a variety of techniques, such as, dialogue, color, exposition, thoughts, etc., and each sets a different tone. They also share something in common with the first lines of the entire book: They spark interest and questions. How we will write each opener will depend on the tone we want to set for that particular scene, and one opener shouldn't be similar to the one before or after. Readers must set the book down sometimes and it may be ages before they pick it up again. When they do, we must ensure that the scene or chapter where they left off drags them right back in.

2.2.6.2 CLOSERS

How we choose to close a chapter or scene is as important as how we begin. Ending in action or dialogue, leaving the reader with questions, will encourage readers to go on and read just one more page. As with opening lines, closers should also be varied.

These examples leave the reader anticipating what will happen next:

> "I take it that's the man in your life." [47]

> "What on earth do you know about unhappy?" [48]

> "I hope you enjoyed it, bitch," I said, and I turned as quick as I could and brought the brick down on Calvin's hand. [49]

Each is different, although the first two use interrupted dialogue as a closer, to instill in the reader the urge to turn the page and learn how the other character replied. The last also uses dialogue, but mixed with narrative to create a brilliant cliffhanger.

Scenes and chapters should end in a cliffhanger of sorts to make readers turn the page. If our reader is up until the wee hours because one last chapter just keeps turning into one more last chapter, we've done our job well.

A cliffhanger is a plot device in which the author leaves the character in a sort of dilemma or confronted with a shocking revelation. Cliffhangers are used to ensure the reader comes back to see how the events will play out and make a great tool for ending scenes and chapters.

But how can a writer create a cliffhanger that keeps the reader eager to turn that page? First and foremost, we must pace their delivery properly. Cliffhangers should follow a period of rising suspense before a slight easing of the tension to shoot back up again until the scene reaches its climax. The following scene or chapter should pick up at the moment we left off, but not necessarily resolve the climax right away. Instead, it could slowly bring the event to a close and then begin building toward the next cliffhanger. A cliffhanger interrupts the dialogue or the action at a critical moment to bait the reader into turning the page.

We recommend saving cliffhangers for chapter and scene endings alone and never for novel endings. We don't care if the novel is the first or tenth in a series. Readers deserve a satisfying ending. They've come along with us through emotionally wrenching, action packed, and captivating chapters.

---

[47] Ally Carter, Don't Judge a girl by Her Cover.

[48] Margaret Atwood, The Blind Assassin.

[49] Charlaine Harris, From Dead to Worse.

Do they deserve to be left wondering what happened to the characters or how the conflict was resolved? No, and they know it. If we leave our readers hanging like that at the novel end we risk losing them forever. The final line at the ending of the novel is possibly the most important. It's the one that lingers in the reader's mind.

Of course, different series use different treatments. In J.K. Rowling's *Harry Potter* series, Patricia Briggs' *Mercedes Thompson* series, Jim Butcher's *Dresden Files*, or Charlaine Harris's *Sookie Stackhouse* novels, there's a story arc that encompasses the entire series, but each book has its own adventure that is resolved in its closer.

2.2.6.3 FLASHBACKS

A flashback reveals something about the characters that the reader doesn't know. It's a narrative passage that takes the reader back in time before the story begins. Flashbacks are a delicate tool that should be handled with care. Writers should strive not to "tell" when writing a flashback and use them only when necessary. For example, we can use it to show the character moving into a behavior or situation that is contrary to what the reader has come to expect. But it has to be relevant to the story.

We advise avoiding flashbacks whenever possible. Not only does a flashback hinder the pace, it stops the story action by taking the reader back in time where events are finished. Going back in time can never have the immediacy of the present in the story. In addition, there is nothing worse than wasting five minutes reading something that has no relevance to the active progression of the story.

Of course, there are times when flashbacks enhance the story and can't be avoided. But if we do need to use them, we must try to limit the flashbacks to one or two per novel.

If a story is structured with consecutive scenes containing everything the reader needs to know, we begin with action and write the story sequentially until the end. We might, instead, structure a story that takes place in the present, but requires scenes from the protagonist's past to make sense, or needs a scene from a different country or continent last Thursday. We've determined that these scenes are necessary, and we can't do without them. This is where we'll need a flashback.

Flashbacks used well can make motives plausible, showing events in the past that compel a particular character to act a certain way. They fill in events and give crucial information that happened so long ago that we can't possibly show them any other way.

This is the only time we should use them: when there isn't any other way.

To minimize the impact of a flashback on the pace of a novel there are a few simple guidelines to note.

Flashbacks should always follow a strong scene, and should never be the first scene. It's best to insert a flashback well into the chapter, so that the reader has a solid pace going when she approaches it.

Mix the flashback into the present.

Don't flip from one flashback into another. We don't want readers scratching their heads and wondering how far back they have to go to get back to the real story.

Use transitions to orient the reader at the beginning of a flashback; otherwise, your poor reader treads water trying to figure out which end is up and what the heck is happening. Guide your reader in and out of the flash back using different verb tenses to signal the start and end of a flashback.

For example, we're telling the story in past tense, so we write the first few verbs of the flashback in past perfect (had taken, had said, had bought), and the rest in simple past tense (he slammed, they were, they came). This way, we orient our readers to the change in time during the first transitional lines. Once the reader knows it's a flashback, there is no need to maintain past perfect tense for the entire flashback, because it's awkward to write and to read. We switch to past perfect for the last few verbs before moving to the present to signal the end of the flashback.

● Opening a Flashback

Just weeks after leaving Garrett, Dana visited Opal expecting a cold reception. She wasn't disappointed.
Opal had launched into a lecture on what God expected Dana to do. "Marriage is forever. You don't just quit because you hit a rough patch; you do what you need to do to fix things." Opal's advice revealed much about the woman Dana thought she knew.

● Closing a Flashback

Dana had left it there. Arguing with Opal about her son was pointless.
Now, gazing at the early morning sunlight that filtered through the blinds to cast a striped pattern on the floor, she had to pack up again.[50]

In between this opening and closing, there is a page of dialogue, highlighting an event that happened in the past. Presenting this scene in the sequential course of the story wasn't an option. It spans four lives over forty years, so brevity whenever possible is crucial. The dialogue gives the flashback an active feel, while still showing what happened. The story is told in past tense, and the writer opens with past perfect (Opal had launched), switches back to past tense (Opal's advice revealed), and for a couple of verbs near the ending of the flashback, she moves to past perfect again (Dana had left), smoothly transitioning the flashback into the present scene.

What if your story is told in present tense? That's even easier. The present is in present tense, and the past should be in past tense. When the flashback ends, resume present tense.

Flashbacks are a great tool when used wisely, but.... Too many shifts in time result in bumps in the flow of a story. If we decide to use a flashback, we must be sure it's necessary and keep it brief. We should never stay in the past longer than we have to and bring the reader back into the current action as soon as possible.

⧉ 2.2.6.4 PLACE

The plot is killer, groundbreaking, absolutely amazing—and the characters—well they leap off the page and grab the reader by the throat. We've outdone ourselves. But wait, something is missing. It's not quite right. No matter how well a writer develops her characters and stories, without the right stage we have nothing but a bunch of actors running around saying profound things.

Place is the theater set, the world, the city, the haunted house, the village, the manor, the universe-- the stage where the players will play their parts.

The world we create must be consistent in rules and established norms and politics. No matter how crude or how sophisticated and modern the world is, it must have a framework for the reader to

---

[50] Renée Miller, I Do…and other Lies we Tell.

understand the motivations and abilities of the characters. Without this basic, sensible framework, the reader pulls away with each elaborate and improbable twist.

For example, the characters must have faults and weakness that balance out their strengths. How eager are we to read a story where the hero blasts through obstacles in a sentence or two? Don't we want to see him sweat just a little, to suffer for his cause, to struggle once or twice before he progresses? Rules shape fictional worlds.

Let's say you've set up a world of heavy detective work where the first two-thirds of the story is spent battling the Russian mafia in old-time Chicago. Then, in the moment where the big boss corners our hero sleuth on the rooftop, our hero steps off the roof, spreads his wings and flies.

Flies?

No. That's cheating. To have this huge twist work in the novel, we should have introduced the fact that flight is even possible early in the novel rather than throwing it in there at the climax. The reader will feel blindsided and betrayed if that ability shows up willy-nilly.

Now, for the part that seems contradictory: We must be surprising. While the setting must be consistent, it must also be compelling and unique to make it attractive to the reader. The consistency gives the reader a world she can identify with and understand, but the surprise elements promote interest. For example, we've created a quiet suburban neighborhood with soccer moms sunning in the backyard, balding business men coming in the front door as the pool boy leaps out the back window. Beneath the suburban normalcy lurks a dark presence that is bursting to be free. The eyes that glow just beyond the trees are watching, waiting to sink teeth into the soft tanned flesh of Bobbi-Jo Baker, the ex-homecoming queen and future werewolf mom. To succeed in such a fantastic idea, we must create a plausible framework that contains unfamiliar characters or stories within it.

In other words, place is the setting, the physical location where the plot occurs, and its place within the society of the writer's fictional world. It is the geography, inhabitants, streets, shops, social and economic structure, etc. The world or set.

2.2.6.5 ATMOSPHERE

Atmosphere is the description of the environment laced with the feelings, tension, relaxation, happiness, hate, or lust of the players. Atmosphere is key to writing a compelling story. Quite simply, it's the ambiance of the world in which the characters move about. To keep the reader immersed in this world, we must create an atmosphere for them to dive into.

Atmosphere is in the room the character is in, in the field in which he is lost, the car which she is driving. An example:

> Renée sits in her garage, plugging away at her latest work. She hears a scratching noise in the corner. She knows what is scratching over there and she's about to end this battle to take back her space once and for all. She grabs Logan's pellet gun to kill the wretched moles, when a different sound stops her before she steps across the dusty concrete to the pile of crap in the corner. She opens the door that connects the garage to the house and peeks inside. There's someone there. She looks around. The dogs are asleep, not that they'd be much good for anything but chewing and humping, so she's on her own. Renée steps inside the house, swapping the gun for a machine gun, hand grenades, and a flamethrower she's obtained through people she'd rather not discuss. With a deafening "Geronimo!" scream, she kicks the garage door open and starts firing.

Blood and gore plaster the walls. A "Happy Birthday!" streamer flutters down to land on a corpse. The stunned survivors stare in horror.

"Madre de Dios!" the Spaniard says, rubbing a shallow cut on his scalp and examining the bullet hole in the wall behind him.

Her business partner misses a trip across the River Styx by mere inches. Some of her less vertically-challenged friends are not so lucky.

This is atmosphere. The sounds, the space, the emotions. These create tension and emotion in the reader.

Let's look at the nuts and bolts of building the atmosphere up so that the reader becomes immersed in each scene. Atmosphere can be built over a few sentences or paragraphs by making use of the five senses. First, we should determine what type of feeling we want to evoke from the reader. Do we want her to feel fearful, lonely, happy, or aroused? Then we consider our options. By mixing and matching, we vary the way they're used in each scene so the reader becomes so immersed in the story that she'll have to be dragged from it.

We use touch by describing textures and surfaces. These can serve to conjure emotive from titillation to fear. Scent is a very powerful sense and can be used to draw the reader in, especially to memory. Often taste works well with smell, so if we use one, we should try to add a bit of the other (when appropriate) to give the reader a better feel for the atmosphere. Writers often have difficulty finding the right words for sound, but it can make the scene come alive, giving it the background noise of real life. We connect sound to many feelings, so using this sense is only logical. The most common sense to stimulate is sight, and this is for a very good reason. We can describe most things we see. But when building atmosphere, we need more than a blue shirt and tight jeans. We need to describe the visuals that aren't obvious to set the tone.

How do we use atmosphere to make that scene come alive? In the following example, we use the senses and just a brief line or two shaping the mood of the scene. Our goal is to make the ambiance of fear, disgust, and evil come alive.

> His fingers were rough and spidery, covering her whole hand. He tickled her palm, tracing the little lines scattered across it. "You know? I think you could be very special. Wouldn't you like to be special?" His voice sounded strange, not a whisper, but really quiet.
>
> "I don't know." Hayley just wanted to be out of the frigid garage. The smell of oil and wood gave her a headache. [51]

How about another example? Let's take a look at how Thomas Harris creates atmosphere:

> The windows of the Palazzo Capponi are dark now, behind their iron grates. The torch rings are empty. In that pane of crazed old glass is a bullet hole from the 1940s. Go closer. Rest your head against the cold iron as the policeman did and listen. Faintly you can hear a clavier. Bach's Goldberg Variations played, not perfectly, but exceedingly well, with an engaging understanding of the music. Played not perfectly, but exceedingly well; there is perhaps a slight stiffness in the left hand. If you believe you are beyond harm, will you go inside? Will you enter this palace so prominent in blood and glory, follow your face through the web-

---

[51] Renée Miller, I Do… and other Lies we Tell.

spanned dark, toward the exquisite chiming of the clavier? The alarms cannot see us. The wet policeman lurking in the doorway cannot see us. Come . . . [52]

Wow, we love that no matter how many times we read it. Harris combines sight, sound, and touch to bring a scene to life and to drag the reader in. This is how to create atmosphere.

We should strive to make a habit of observing different situations and experiences. Writers should write down what comes to mind while savoring a mouthful of Death by Chocolate ice cream. We might listen to the sound of the neighbor cutting his grass at dawn on a Sunday morning, make note of the colors in the room as we peel our eyes open and debate whether it's worth going at him with the pruning shears for waking us at such an ungodly hour. By observing with all senses, we use what is gleaned to create a vivid and tangible atmosphere to immerse our readers.

 **2.2.6.6 COLOR**

Color is more than just "the sky was an azure blue" or "the roses were red, like her lips." Color is the details, the tiny bits or observations that spice prose. In fiction writing, we can write prose that is vivid and alive with imagery by adding color to the story. This tends to be a difficult art to master; many authors unintentionally step past the imaginary color line into purple. Writing imagery that brings the story to life is a gift, a talent; but it's one that can be learned, no matter what we might have read elsewhere.

In the example we used earlier, Renée's epic garage-mole war, color is the feel of that gun in her hands, sweaty palms, and the tic, tic, tic, of the kitchen clock five times slower than her heartbeat, the snort of the dog happy in his dream of endless bones, and the itch on her bum that she can't scratch without dropping the hardware.

Let's look at some examples of color in prose:

> The grass sighed, caressing the worn moccasins with each step. Overhead, aspen leaves rustled and danced with the breeze, whispering secrets for one who would listen. Breathing peace deep into her spirit, Feather clutched her fringed shawl tighter and threaded the path. [53]

> Roosters sang their greetings to the sun. Outside the walls of the Spanish port town, the Atlantic Ocean shushed its endless lullaby, making more than one man stifle a yawn as they waited. [54]

These two examples add imagery and color to the story. The few lines used allow the reader not only to see the story, but taste it and touch it as well. Adding color is simple if the writer visualizes the scene first in his mind. In the first example, imagine the grass, a woman walking along in soft leather moccasins early in the morning. "The grass sighed" gives the reader many images and feelings, which is what our goal as a writers should be. By choosing precise and meaningful words to add color, we can evoke more than just one sense.

---

[52] Thomas Harris, Hannibal.

[53] Wendy Swore, Coyote Dreams.

[54] Henry Lara and Renée Miller, Por Amor.

But grass can't sigh. Yes, it can. Imagery is about using words we're used to hearing in other contexts to color a scene for the reader; using words to draw a picture. When we imagine a sigh, we think soft, light, and quiet. The grass is also soft, light, and quiet, as it caresses the woman's slippered feet. The ocean might not shush a lullaby in the traditional sense either, but the second example gives the reader an image of this moment in time, and lullaby is the perfect word to create this idea in the reader's mind. Now, not only can the reader see the scene, but she can also hear the gentle swell of the waves.

To color a story, the writer should be able to close her eyes and see the moment, smell the color around her, touch the objects in the scene, and taste the air around her characters. How does she do that? Practice. The writer takes a moment when she sees something that captures her interest.

She won't go for the obvious sunset just yet. She looks at that old man who keeps hitting on young women at the grocery store. No, she won't let him see her. Instead she spies from behind the safety of the vegetable soup. His gnarled hands, tanned and worn like the branches of that old oak tree her dad keeps threatening to cut down, the dirty fingernails, the way his hair reminds her of the dirty old mop gathering mold out in the garage. Now wait, he's turning. He smiles, baring corn yellow teeth, chipped and tarry at the gums. She looks at his eyes. His eyes, as he winks at that sweet young thing who only wants to take her bag of two percent milk and run, remind the writer of…what? Visualizing it is the secret to writing color into a story.

When the dog wants to snuggle up in bed, the writer notes the moldy honey smell that wafts from his ears, the silky smooth texture of the white hair under his chin, the weight of his dirty old body against hers. She'll save it, write it down, compare it to something, play with the imagery and file it away for later. Perhaps in the next story the writer will need to compare something to a dog to bring the reader into the scene. Or, maybe there's a reader who has never encountered a dog and she'll have to describe one to that reader.

We're sure writers have been to bars (those old enough to do so legally) perhaps a rough one or two. Rough bars are wonderful places to study color.

> Flannigan's was just as it sounded. Dark. Stinky. Full of noise and sprinkled with raunchy women. Ah, God love the Irish. That wasn't a racist thought either. Sure, generalizing maybe, but my mother's family is Irish and though all of them are loud—the women raunchy as shit—no one stank quite like Flannigan's. For that, I was thankful.[55]

And last, yes, we must drink in sunrises and sunsets. There is no greater inspiration for imagery and words than the sun making its fiery descent or stretching its early morning rays in a glorious golden yawn to greet us in the new day. But we don't stop at the sunset. We peer at the dew on the grass, the mud on a tire, the way a bird washes itself in the dust of a dried up puddle. We carry paper and pen everywhere and when something inspires us or catches our eye, we note the colors, the smells, the movements and write them down. We keep a file of the color that inspires us and use it in our stories. It works.

---

[55] Renée Miller, The Chosen

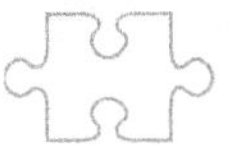

2.3 DATA

Fiction writers don't need to research, do they? Of course they do. All writers must do research. We've heard the crying and whining when writers have to look up something. They balk and even beg some unknown power to end their misery, but they do it.

For all of her complaining, the writer penning these lines spends several hours each day online or has her nose buried in a book, fact-checking and learning about things. Not only does she write fiction, but she is also a freelance writer and reporter. Part of a reporter's job is to research information and sources. When writing news or information articles, one wrong fact or a misquoted line or statement could lead to big trouble. Even the smallest detail in article writing needs to be checked, verified, and contrasted against opposing facts. While fiction writing doesn't require that we research every detail, we do need to be certain that anything we've included in our story is factual, and can be verified, because it has been thoroughly researched.

While research can be tedious and boring, the least amount of fun a fiction writer could have, it is necessary. Lazy writers avoid gathering data and checking their facts. Good writers embrace it, no matter how much they loathe it.

In this section we'll cover how and why we need to research data when writing fiction as well as what to do with the information once we have it.

2.3.1 RESEARCH

Write what you know. This is a simple concept and sound advice, but also very limiting for a writer. Sure, we learn things every day, encounter diverse people and cultures, adapt new ideas or methods for doing things, and visit different places. How much of that can we remember in minute detail? It is unlikely to retain every fact or every detail and recall it at will. This is why a writer must also be a decent (or better) researcher.

Some genres need more research than others. Historical, for example, requires extensive research to ensure details are correct. Fantasy might not require so much because world building is done in our heads, and although we'll need extensive notes, most (if not all) of the details about our "world" stems from us. However, fantasy is often rich in myth and legend that must be researched, and it is essential for even "possible" combinations of fantastic "facts" be both consistent and plausible enough not to draw attention and wreck the reader's suspension of disbelief. Plausibility makes research necessary. Science fiction, crime thrillers, and historical romances often require considerable investigation to depict even the smallest events.

For example, one of us is tackling a post apocalyptic novel that will be categorized as mainstream fiction. However, some elements require as much research as a hard science fiction novel would. In outlining, this writer had to determine how the world will end, where survivors will have to be to survive the determined event and what would be available to them in terms of food, water, and shelter. The outline written, extensive research quite easily came up with a meteor-induced tsunami and a location of Mount Kilimanjaro. In fact, this occurred so readily that it might be easy to think science fiction writers a bunch of whiners with all their talk of spending hours researching and planning. But then, the problem presented itself in a plane crash.

For the events to be accurate, this simple thing—a plane crashing into a mountain—had to be researched so that everything that happened, from impact to survivors to the condition of the plane, was accurate and possible. Turns out this is not a simple Google type of thing. How to write a plane crash when the writer has never experienced one or even been on a plane? Research.

Writers must investigate anything they haven't experienced firsthand or studied in depth. What kind of research? That depends on the novel, the subject, and how much detail we plan to include. In the case of our example, the plot opens on top of Mount Kilimanjaro and it moves later to the surrounding area. Of course, with that kind of devastation, major landmarks can be "destroyed," but a mountain? Nope. We must research the altitude, vegetation, paths up and down, possible crevasses and impassable areas to make sure that what we write is accurate.

With the information that must be recorded, sorted, and made available, organization becomes crucial. We will discuss this in the next section.

 **2.3.1.1 ORGANIZATION**

We've researched and done our job, covering everything we needed to know (and more that we didn't), and now we have a mess of notes and articles to help with writing a book. So, what's this rather thick document about, and how much of it do we need for the book? We don't remember. Without organizing our material, we're likely to forget information or struggle to remember why we included this bit or that. All writers have been there. Chaos is a terrible and confusing place.

We need a system to store information in such a way that we can search through to find what we need. A few organizational systems work well. Spreadsheets are useful for character and setting information or even plot points and research lists. These are sortable and can be indexed by subject, location, alphabetically, or in order of importance so that details are easily located and referenced. We've also used folders, both electronic and in paper. Each writer should try several methods and then mix and match to find what is right for him.

What kind of information should be stored in these systems? If we want to write a novel in which the Canadian Mounties and the Canadian legal system play a vital role, the easiest procedure would be to prepare an exhaustive list of everything we ignore: the origins of the famed police, their background, uniforms, creed, duties, etc. Then, if the novel is set in the wild north, we'll need files on terrain, towns, climate, fauna, flora, etc.

The information usually ignored is vital to writing a convincing novel. One tiny detail that we might think unimportant, such as a uniform, might be necessary to portray a character. Perhaps a scene where Mounties arrest a biker. The biker fights and the Mounties restrain him, grabbing handcuffs from—oh shoot. Where do Mounties keep their handcuffs? On their belt? Back pocket? Their coat extends down to their thighs, so the back pocket makes no sense. Do Mounties even carry handcuffs? Would they even be arresting a biker? Who handles biker related crimes in Canada? What the heck is a biker anyway and what do they do that's so illegal? Organized research can answer those questions and more.

Organizing our data to pull up a description of the officer's (or "member," as the Royal Canadian Mounted Police, or RCMP, are often called) uniform can save us hours of research in the middle of writing a novel. It also prepares us for unanticipated questions that can and most often will arise.

 ## 2.3.1.2 CREDIT

Depending on how we use our research, there might be details or information that requires crediting. Credits can be a footnote or, as is more common in fiction, an addenda at the back of the book that gives credit to where "facts" were acquired. Typically, writers crediting information in a work of fiction use MLA (Modern Language Association) style. Copies of MLA style guides can be downloaded free from any online library or from University sites. We can also pick up a print copy at our local library or from most bookstores.

MLA is very simple, and perhaps, the easiest way to cite sources if we've used several while writing a manuscript. With MLA style sourcing, we create an addendum (list at the back of the book) that cites our sources of information in alphabetical order by the author's name. If our source has no author, then the title is used. We never alphabetize sources using the articles a, an, or the, and always place the last name first and exactly as it appears. For example, if the name is P.J. Sampson PhD, then we'd list it as Sampson, P.J. PhD.

Most often, the type of credit given in fiction is when we use another's words, facts, or ideas in the story. A song, for example, or lines from a book already published. When we write an addendum to cite where these came from, we give the author's last name and the page(s) of the source where we found the quote. However, if we used the authors name in the text, then we don't have to do this, as we've already given them credit there.

It's always wise when using a work by another author or lyrics from a song to get permission before including them in a manuscript. We must still cite the source, but this also covers us legally if the owner of those words or ideas decides to take exception to them being used. Plus, it's just good manners.

Citing sources is not as difficult as it sounds, but we strongly recommend following the MLA style guide. Most often, we'll have one source or perhaps two, and fiction writers usually cite them in the acknowledgements page at the front of the book. This is fine too. The important thing when citing sources is that we give them proper credit due and that we never plagiarize someone else's words or ideas.

2.3.1.3 SOURCES

Sources are vital to research and writing. Though in fiction we do not need to list all of them, word for word citations should receive source credit. Plagiarism is a nasty—and dangerous—mistake.

In addition, the writer must ensure sources used are accurate. As we mentioned earlier in this section, one of this book's authors writes articles of the newspaper and online variety. Reliable sources are a must.

What about Wikipedia?

Although Wikipedia is often accurate, we can't always be certain. Unlike traditional encyclopedias, compiled by experts, thoroughly researched, backed by the reputation of a publishing house, and set in the permanence of paper, Wikipedia is always in flux. Anyone can add, delete, append, and tweak.

Eventually, the professionals staffing Wikipedia will spot gaffes and inaccuracies as reported by readers and set the articles straight. However, the information will be flawed in the meantime.

What sources are reliable? When writing a medical thriller (or a scene that requires medical information), medical texts from the library or a medical site like the Mayo Clinic constitute a good choice. Of course, we must ensure the site has credentials. The FDA or hospital websites are ideal. Even better would be information directly from a doctor or other medical practitioner. If the information is about law or crime, legal sites run by either government organizations or a proven lawyer's site, or law books from the library are good choices. Again, interviewing a lawyer is the best. It's surprising how eager professionals are to share.

Perhaps real life professionals aren't handy. That's fine. We can still find reliable sources. Ironically, Wikipedia is a good place to start. Article sources are listed at the end, and those sources qualify for good research sources.

So, here's a pop quiz. If we Google our topic and come up with five blogs, a retail site selling something related to our topic, and one listing for a government organization with a PDF file on a report written about the subject, which should a writer choose for information?

The last one.

Blogs are not reliable unless we know without a doubt that the person running the blog is an expert. Sites selling something will only highlight information most beneficial to them—but not necessarily provide the whole picture.

Sources with information given by an anonymous person are not reliable at all. Why? Imagine we print our book, only to find that the little page depicting a riveting game of high stakes poker (which we've never played so we studiously researched it and used that to write the scene) is a game of Crazy Eights. We did our research, but the information came from a site with no known author, and somewhere in the world, a fourteen year old is laughing maniacally at our gullibility.

Using a reliable source will save precious rewriting time, and spare the embarrassment of a significant mistake.

2.3.2 PLAGIARISM

Claiming another's ideas or words as our own is possibly the vilest and definitely the naughtiest thing a writer can do. Yes, we know that ideas are not copyrightable, but to steal an idea is a foul way to broadcast the writer's lack of imagination. The difference between stealing ideas or words is not in the deed—theft is theft—but in the consequences. Stealing ideas may earn the writer a rebuke from critics and readers, stealing words can send him to prison. The internet tends to make some people believe that all information is free and there for us to use as we please. This is not so. Using information we find and twisting it to read "in our words" doesn't absolve us from the responsibility of citing our sources. It's still plagiarism to use another person's words, however twisted, and claim it as our own. Even in fiction.

Sometimes it's confusing to know if something has been plagiarized or not, and we know it might be an unintentional thing now and then. Many new writers aren't aware that they cannot use slogans or lyrics or quote lines from movies or books without proper citations or (in some cases) permission from the copyright owner. They think that since everyone knows the lines or because they've only used a couple, then it really isn't plagiarizing. False. If we use even the smallest amount of someone else's work, we've got to give them credit somewhere. Place a credit within the text. Something like:

> Thomas stood, his gaze following the gentle sway of her generous backside. "Oh yes, Sir Mix A Lot, I do indeed like big butts, and I cannot lie," he muttered.

What? You aren't familiar with the poetic lyrics of the talented Sir Mix A Lot? The point is that to use a line like: "I like big butts and I cannot lie" without crediting the original, copyrighted singer of the song is plagiarism. To use the above line alone without citing the source would insinuate that we, the writers of the book, have thought that up all by ourselves. As we mentioned in previous sections, we don't have to include the credit in the text, but in an addendum to the back of the novel, citing the page and the line the quote is located on and giving Mr. Mix A Lot his credit.

We've found some simple ways to avoid accidental plagiarism, which is how lines and words might get recycled as ours. Never cut and paste any text into your own. We know writers don't mean to copy, and that they work better if they can see the words. We know it's easier to work ideas or thoughts when we have the text in front of us. That may be so, but the odds that we'll write what we see are extremely high. Often our brain refuses to see the idea any other way. Plus, we can easily forget to erase it.

Also when researching, we don't keep whole documents for reading later. We like to read the document, make very brief point remarks and keep only our notes for later reference. Unless we are quoting, that is. Then, we write the quote and its source into our research notes and nothing more than that.

In our research and endeavors to ensure that we never plagiarize and cite every source that we've used in this book, we've discovered a handy little tool online. Copyscape is a site where any writer can check text to ensure that he hasn't inadvertently plagiarized someone else's work. Copyscape's plagiarism checker can also search to find out if our own work has been copied anywhere online.

The bottom line is, no matter what we do, we must never use other writer's ideas as our own. We all work hard to create unique ideas and content, whether it is fiction or nonfiction, and there is no need for any of us to plagiarize one another.

As Wendy—our beloved fellow writer—deadpans in her sternest voice: "The deepest bowels of hell are reserved for murderers, lawyers, and plagiarists."

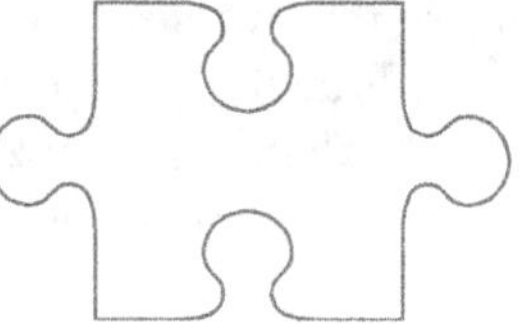

3 THE CRAFT OF REWRITING

A few words of caution: Nothing can improve a writer's craft more than the ability to stand back from the completed manuscript and address it as one would a momentous document, as a contract where each word, clause, sentence, article, caveat, and piece of punctuation could mark a life-or-death difference for the writer. Faced with such a document, any sane person (this includes writers, though many would disagree) would tackle the first sentence, analyze its components and ask questions:

What does it mean?

Is it clear?

Does it convey my intended meaning?

Can it be improved or strengthened?

Can it be shortened while keeping its meaning intact?

Is it interesting? Does it capture the reader's interest?

These questions are easy, mostly concerning grammar, syntax, voice, and style. But there's another inquiry, harrowing because to some writers it represents an admission of failure, though nothing can be farther from the truth. No writer can answer it until he or she addresses the manuscript with a single-mindedness bordering on hostility. The question is:

Is this necessary?

Contrary to popular belief, agents and editors don't read first-time-writer submissions, chapters, or manuscripts with an eye to justify their purchase. They read seeking the slightest excuse to reject the work.

This is not a behavioral quirk of publishing industry professionals, but common in our species. When faced with an imposition, we bow to the inevitable and seek reasons to justify our actions in a bid to escape the sensation of being an insignificant cog.

For established authors and bestsellers, this phenomenon works in their favor. "Mr. Smith, have a look at this." The editor will reach for the manuscript and note its author and title, *Mein Kampf,* before reading the thing looking for positive details to praise. Failing to do so may promote a middle-of-the-night visit by a bunch of thugs. This is the same attitude an editor displays when perusing a manuscript by a house writer whose previous releases have sold a gazillion copies. Since the editor cannot dump it, he or she must look for justification, however feeble, and even accept what could only be described as shoddy and amateurish.

As an example, consider Dan Brown's *The Da Vinci Code.* Seldom in history has there been a writer so capable of paying for the best copyedit in the business or to demand from his publishers the undivided attention of their star editor.

> "Almost inconceivably, the gun into which she was now staring was clutched in the pale hand of an enormous albino."

"Almost inconceivably?" How can something be "almost" inconceivable? How can anything be "almost" true or false, conceivable or inconceivable, material or immaterial? How can something be "almost" dark or light or tall or short or green or mauve? With few debatable exceptions, writers should exorcise "almost" from their writing. We refuse to believe that any editor worth his title would let that one pass, unless coerced.

The work of an unknown writer is a different matter. Novels (even good ones) are ten a penny in a saturated market. To attempt spotting a diamond in so much rough is a soul-destroying chore for agents and editors. In addition, this overabundance of worthless prose carries with it the insidious sting of probability: "Since only one in a thousand manuscripts is worth reading past its opening sentence, chances are this is trash." So the agent or editor grabs the first page with a close to absolute certainty he or she will find something to back the statistics. Subliminally, these professionals know the manuscript will be trash. Now they only need to prove it.

When it comes to editing or rewriting, a naïve writer will approach the manuscript with kindness and ill-conceived love for turns of phrase, pretty scenes and devilishly clever plot points. Other writers, the lazy or ignorant, will dispense with rewriting. After all, it would be an insult to their boundless talent. Only the determined writer will settle before a draft with open hostility, looking for sections to delete, sentences to destroy, words to change and chapters to ditch, as if his worst enemy had penned the thing. In many ways, it has. The writer's task is to remove excuses, kill any pretext to stop reading, ruthlessly deny justification to the men and women who will try to reject his work to a point where, defeated, they will bow before the fact: The manuscript merits publication.

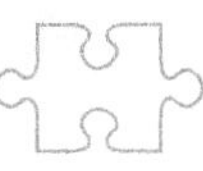

3.1 TECHNICAL FLAWS

3.1.1 TELLING

This article, one of the longest in the Companion, is an attempt to clarify an often debated—but little understood—flaw in fiction writing: the dreaded showing vs. telling.

Telling states facts and observations or summarizes action rather than allowing the reader to experience what the character experiences right along beside him. The giants of nineteenth century literature, including Chekhov, Dickens, Victor Hugo (and his contemporaries), relied on storytelling techniques to deliver their magnificent tales. In those times, omniscient POV was the standard. Writers were present in their works as the "all-knowing narrator." A godlike invisible being would float high above the scenes, reading characters' minds and telling the reader how everyone felt and understood existence. Some modern readers (even writers) find it hard to read these works, not from their extension and complexity but from the strangeness of omniscient storytelling.

Storytelling is a wonderful technique that has served writers through the ages. Imagine people gathered around a campfire while the narrator's voice paints enchanted realms and larger-than-life characters. The narrator would describe the hero's exterior, his leather cloak or feathered hat, and go on to details of his thoughts and innermost feelings. At times, the storyteller would reach for onomatopoeia to adorn his tale with *sssssss* for the sibilance of steel when leaving the scabbard.

Why writers used omniscient storytelling owes much to information, or the lack of it. For much of antiquity, a typical reader's world was limited to a few miles around his birthplace. Melville's *Moby Dick* presented albino whales and harpooners to readers who had never seen either, and at times when the oceans still harbored the monsters, mothers would threaten colicky children with.

The radio brought special effects into every home. Actors enthusiastically banged coconut halves to create an illusion of clip-clopping hooves and shook metal sheets to conjure a thunderstorm.

In 1979, The Buggles, a British group, released "Video Killed the Radio Star," a condemnation of how Cinema and TV changed the way we experience the world. Readers no longer had to imagine albino whales; they could see them.

It's important to realize how the information era has affected our reading habits and the way we write fiction. Though the revolution touched every aspect of fiction writing—such as structure, scenes, tension management through cliffhangers and interrupted action, POV, chapter and scene length, payoff, and scores of other issues—the deepest change has been in the reader's expectations.

Films changed the public's POV from omniscient to limited and tight. Rather than having a narrator dishing out a story, Cinema and TV immersed the spectator in the action. Suddenly a rhino charged across the screen and the heroine gasped. People were drawn in by actions and not the narrator's running commentary.

> The ground shuddered. Jackson shouldered his rifle, feet splayed. A small hill of piled rocks, barring the beast's advance, exploded when the rhino charged through it.
> Brenda held her breath, mesmerized by Jackson, who stood immobile like a bronze demigod, corded arms straining against the stock.
> He pulled the trigger, and the hammer struck an empty cartridge.
> She gasped, anguished the beast might gore the debonair hunter.

Of course, we have killed (on purpose) an otherwise passable scene or chapter ending. That *anguished the beast might gore the debonair hunter* is awful, unnecessary, and… telling.

Check the paragraphs above. The first describes the action from a narrator's vantage point. The narrator is a spectator describing what he sees. He's detached. He doesn't hint to any feeling or thought the players may have. He's an observer.

The second paragraph is looser. Here the narrator intrudes a little with "mesmerized by Jackson" because he's slipping into Brenda's mind. A thorough editor would recommend reworking to eliminate the slight POV slip.

The third paragraph is another detached observation.

Then, on the last paragraph, after "She gasped," follows a gross POV flaw. The writers intrude in the narrative by telling the reader Brenda's thoughts.

We know Brenda is anguished; she's gasping for breath. We know a rhino is like a freight train with a big horn in front. We know the hunter is nice looking; "corded arms" and "bronze demigod." Yum.

How do we fix it? In this instance it's simple. We delete the inane words and replace a comma with a period:

> She gasped.

And here we finish the chapter. The reader will likely turn the page to find out how Jackson manages to survive. Note that the reader *knows* Jackson will pull through; there are three-hundred pages left and Jackson must pull through to scoop Brenda into his lap, wrap his "corded arms" around her, and gallop away in the general direction of a sunset. (More about scene and chapter endings on pages 162 to 165).

The current publishing market demands pieces that immerse the readers in the story. Telling the reader how the characters see, feel, or experience their surrounds belongs in another era and not modern fiction. By getting inside the characters' heads, readers experience events from their POV. This is showing.

New writers often underestimate the reader's capacity to work out emotions by themselves. Instead of showing specific details for the reader to feel, they connect the dots and draw a conclusion. Or, to put it another way, rather than listing the emotions of the characters, the writer should use prose to convey these and draw the reader in.

> John could never forget how he felt after Gladys died. He was depressed and the house felt empty, as if it had lost its soul.

Telling the reader what the character feels is lazy and flat. Different readers will experience the predicament in different ways, if they step into John's shoes, because degree, intensity, and even the existence of feeling as a reaction to an event are not universal. Some readers will cringe, others will cry, and the few who were elated to be free from their Gladyses may even smile.

Instead of searching for ways to show by inference the character's turmoil, many writers attempt to disguise their imposition with heavy description and more details, thus increase the telling pressure.

If he still lived for another thousand long years, John could never ever forget how utterly and terribly alone he felt after Gladys's untimely demise. He was so thoroughly and awfully depressed; John couldn't help but think that he would surely die too. Days, weeks, and endless months went by, and it seemed as if everything, no matter how mundane, paltry or seemingly insignificant, reminded him of her. John eventually reached an agonizingly painful point in his wretchedness when he actually despaired of ever getting over his beloved Gladys's death.

<u>Don't tell the reader</u> John loved Gladys or that he hasn't come to terms with her death. <u>Don't tell the reader</u> that the house is empty or that John is depressed. <u>Use talent</u> and the power of prose to help the reader share John's experience.

John wandered through the house, touching a picture frame, moving an ashtray and disturbing the dust before shuffling over to the kitchen. When the water boiled, he prepared tea, strong tea. He would have added a sprig of mint, but there was nothing except dry earth and straw on the window ledge. John poured a second cup and stirred a spoonful of cream— just the way she liked it—before he remembered. Gladys had been dead for three months.

And here the reader pauses to assimilate the last sentence and how it turns an otherwise tame paragraph into a cry of anguish, perhaps glance at a loved one and repress a shudder. This is showing.

To tell the reader the events of a story or how a character feels may be good journalism and an acceptable method of presenting facts. However, fiction writing calls for magic. A writer must draw readers in with the illusion of being part of the story.

In the following pages, we will explore nine techniques a fiction writer can use to avoid "telling."

Tightening POV

Avoiding telling forms

Removing vagueness

Controlling sentence structure

Reviewing passive constructions

Reviewing linking verbs

Reviewing other weak constructions

Reviewing the use of "was"

Reviewing adverbs and intensifiers

 **3.1.1.1 TIGHTENING POV**

Writers who are part of a critique group or have had a beta reader or two will have heard the suggestion "Tighten the POV." What does that mean? If the writer isn't deep enough into a character's POV, then the writing will tell. In other words, a tight POV means readers experience what the characters experience as they experience it. They are not told about it. It's often subtle, but the words chosen make the difference between the reader becoming engaged and identifying with the character... or not.

Consider these sentences:

Kristina stepped away until she felt the playpen behind her.

Dan felt his anger subsiding, she knew she was wrong.

In these sentences, the POV is moving away from the character. The writer is telling the reader what is going on, how the characters feel, and this doesn't allow the reader to see and do things with the character. Words like "felt" are telling because they remind the reader that she is reading. To tighten POV, keep the actions with the characters. <u>Show</u> the reader what's happening.

Tightened:

Kristina stepped away until the playpen dug against her thighs.

Daniel's anger subsided; she knew she was wrong.[56]

To tighten POV, we look for telling words like watched, realized, felt, decided, thought, etc. and eliminate them, replacing them with active verbs that enable the reader to experience the scene with the character.

<u>Telling</u>: He realized that he was too late.

<u>Tightened</u>: He was too late.

<u>Telling</u>: Carol decided to leave before her husband got home. He'll kill me if he knows what I've done, she thought.

<u>Tightened</u>: He'll kill me. Carol left before her husband arrived home.

<u>Telling</u>: He watched the woman approach, and felt a strange tingle in his head.

<u>Tightened</u>: As the woman approached, a tingle tickled his brain.

We also tighten POV by looking at dialogue. In dialogue, action tags are always stronger and these can be used to show a character's emotions, rather than tell the reader about them. When rewriting, look at tags on every line of dialogue. If both a dialogue and action tag are used, keep the action tag and delete the dialogue tag. Remove vague action tags like "he smiled," "he nodded," "he laughed." If you keep them, add to them because they don't give enough information.

Telling: "Wait until we tell him," Julie said as she smiled.

Better, but vague: "Wait until we tell him." Julie clapped, an eager grin lighting her face.

Best: "Wait until we tell him." Julie clapped, and her face lit up.

"Said as" is the indicator that the writer is telling. The attribution alone would be enough but the best way is to use action only as we did in the last example.

Telling: "Don't you dare," she warned and picked up the gun to aim it at him.

Better: "Don't you dare," she warned, picking up the gun.

Best: "Don't you dare." She picked up the gun.

---

56 Renée Miller, Dirty Truths.

The first example here is wordy, and telling. We've used action, but we've also added an attribution and a bit of authorial intrusion with "to aim it at him." The second is better in that we've eliminated the intrusion, but it still tells with the attribution and action together. The last example is tight, in the character's POV, while active.

The deeper the writer delves into the minds and bodies of her characters, the more bonded the reader becomes to them. It's important to give the reader as many ways as possible to become one with the POV character. If the writer head hops, or changes POV too often, then this is not possible. A good rule of thumb is to stay in one POV for at least two pages. If the POV switches twice in one page, try to rewrite to keep it in a single POV instead.

Writers should remember that everything the character hears, smells, sees, touches, and thinks is reflected through POV. Even the reactions and feelings of the non-POV characters can be relayed. When these are conveyed correctly, the use of "he thought" or "he watched" becomes redundant.

3.1.1.2 TELLING FORMS

Telling forms are those constructions that pull the reader out of a character's POV and should be used deliberately or when there is no better choice. These include:

Linking verbs (conjugations of the infinitive "to be," such as "am," "is," "are," "was," "were," "seems," "becomes," "be," "been," "being"), which convey states of being rather than action;

Prepositional phrases, such as "to her," "at him," "for her," "by him," which are often implied, and therefore, weaken sentences when left at the end;

Helping or auxiliary verbs, such as "may," "could," "should," "would," "did," "must," "will," "shall," "might," "can," "could," "ought to," "used to," "need" that express time and mood;

Verb forms that imply action that continues, such as "started to" and "began;"

Progressive verb forms using "ing;"

Distancing verbs like "remember," "heard," "saw," "thought," "felt."

Each of these, to varying degrees, lends itself to sentence structures that tell at best and create a passive construction at worst. Often, telling forms can be eliminated to improve the clarity of the prose and reader connection to the character or action.

> Kristina paused, dismay <u>swept over her as she remembered</u> Wade <u>coming in</u> that night <u>with his hands</u> bloody and his shirt disheveled.

This sentence uses many telling forms. First, by using "remembered," the reader is distanced from the present. Then the writer uses the progressive verb "coming" combined with the prepositional phrase "with his hands" to drag the reader out of the moment. The reader knows she is reading because she must sort through the sentence to discern the meaning. Remove the worst telling forms to make the sentence show instead:

> Kristina paused, dismayed at the memory of Wade's bloodied hands and disheveled shirt.

Not only is the sentence more concise, containing fewer words, but the reader is also held in the scene, seeing things as they happen. The information is still there, but the unnecessary telling forms are gone. Let's look at a few more:

> Telling: She paused when she saw the light on the machine blinking.

> Showing: She paused at the blinking light on the answering machine.

Telling: The sound made her chest tighten.

Showing: Her chest tightened at the sound.

Telling: Kristina stood for a moment, staring at the machine, her body trembling.

Showing: Kristina stared at the machine, trembling.

Telling: Now, she felt as though she'd failed everyone: her friends, her family, Daniel, and Cadence. She felt worthless.

Showing: She'd failed everyone: her friends, her family, Daniel, and Cadence. I'm worthless.

Using internal dialogue, we make telling forms like "she felt" active. In the last example, "felt" is removed and the character's emotions are shown with stronger verbs that were already present in the sentence, though weak.

Telling: Hanging up the phone, John made his decision. He felt betrayed by her lies.

Showing: John hung up the phone. How dare she lie to me?

Telling: Carly couldn't go on this way. She felt cheap and dirty.

Showing: I can't go on this way. Shame, hot and painful, settled into Carly's heart.

Search for telling phrases that include these and similar words: "Saw," "heard," "felt," "moved," "watched," "thought," "knew," and "reached." Rewrite to show by removing these forms and using action:

Telling: He knew he had to go.

Showing: He had to go.

Telling: She heard the sound of a door closing and moved to the curtain to hide.

Showing: She slipped behind the curtain as the door closed.

Telling: She watched him approach and thought he looked angry.

Showing: Stepping back as he approached, she cringed as his glare pinned her to the spot.

Removing the telling forms creates active sentences in the examples above. In the last sentence, the showing is slightly different from the first two. This is because not only is it passive, it is vague.

 ### 3.1.1.3 REMOVING VAGUENESS

Direct writing makes clear writing. Vague constructions create a style that loses impact and focus. Sentences can be short and vague or meander and become difficult to follow. Active constructions and descriptive words remove the sense of "telling" and show.

Vague: She left angry.

This is a statement of fact that implies observation and removes the reader from the present of the story. What does angry look like? Is she stomping, snarling, or spitting? Show the reader what angry is.

Specific: She stomped from the room, kicking at the cat who dared to block her exit.

Another example:

Vague: He poured a glass of cheap wine.

Cheap to one person might be rather good to another. Cheap is a vague word in this sentence. What makes the wine cheap? Did it taste cheap? Bits of grape still floating around? Show the reader the wine is cheap.

Specific: Reaching into the cupboard, he hefted a dusty white box from the shelf and set it on the counter. Placing the wine glass beneath the plastic spout, he pushed the lever and watched the purple liquid gurgle out.

There, whatever is in the white box can only loosely be termed "wine."

Vague: She was pretty.

What makes her pretty? Does she have nice eyes? A firm butt? Pretty to one might not be pretty to another. While the writer imagines Angelina Jolie smiling down at the protagonist, a reader might picture Madonna, or Princess Diana, when pretty is all he has to work with. Show the reader a picture.

Remove adjectives that generalize. "Angry," "mad," "sad," "happy," "pretty," "ugly," "nice," etc. summarize, which is telling. Specific writing engages the reader. Naming emotions and summarizing descriptions isn't enough to create interest. To create a work that succeeds, writers must find a way to create the same feelings and images in the reader that we see and feel as we're writing.

Rather than weak nouns like "happiness," "kindness," "arrogance," and "courage," use concrete nouns. Show the characters being happy, kind, arrogant, and courageous. Also use the most vivid, active verbs possible, avoid linking verbs, and eliminate modifiers.

Telling: A girl was standing at the counter.

The sentence above is telling. Some writers would rewrite this and give into the temptation to go overboard in order to show the reader the scene:

Overdone: A beautiful, slim, tall, enchanting girl was standing at the long, dirty, overloaded counter.

This example is still telling, and now it contains too many modifiers. Modifiers galore will not make the picture any clearer for the reader. This just serves to clutter the prose and slow the pace. Often it leads to more confusion. Show the reader without overwhelming her:

Showing: A slim blond filed her nails through the chaos of the service desk.

This shows the reader the scene. The writer might go on to describe the desk briefly as well. Perhaps the girl turns and knocks over a pile of papers.

Telling summary: She felt sad.

Showing: His retreating form disappeared over the hill and an empty darkness filled her. Tears stung her eyes and blurred the now empty road.

Telling: A pain shot through his side.

Showing: Liquid fire ripped through his right side, and he crumpled to the ground.

Vague sentences can be short or long. If more than one modifier is used to describe something, chances are the sentence is telling more than it should. By using the most powerful, active verbs and the best modifier, writers eliminate the need for extra modifiers to describe a subject or an action.

🧩 3.1.1.4 SENTENCE STRUCTURE

Long sentences aren't a bad thing in fiction writing, but unclear sentences are. Some of the most beautiful and brilliant sentences ever written are more than five lines long. The trick is in the structure. To ensure the sentences haven't moved past brilliance into elaborate passages of telling, check comma placement in compound sentences. If a sentence contains two separate ideas, either divide the sentence into two or place a semicolon where the period should go.

> Loose: The smells of beer and stale cigarette smoke clung to the narrow space despite the fact that no one had smoked inside the Smuir for years.

> Tighter: The smells of beer and stale cigarette smoke clung to the narrow space, although no one had smoked in the Smuir for years.

> Tight: Though no one had smoked in the Smuir for years, stale cigarette and beer clung to the narrow space.

Let's look at a longer passage:

> Loose: Millicent's cold eyes <u>were staring</u> down at them and nearly bulged from their sockets. Audrey <u>looked</u> at the rope around her neck, which ran over the rafters. Her hands <u>were hanging</u> at her sides. They <u>weren't</u> limp like Audrey would have <u>thought</u> they <u>would be</u>. They curled into claws as though she <u>was clutching</u> at something.

Clutching at something? Something? Where do we begin? Note the passive verbs that pull this out of a tight POV? The sentences are crazy as well, and contain similar ideas which could be rewritten tighter to improve the flow. Let's try that again, removing the passive verbs and keeping the POV tight.

> Tight: Millicent's cold eyes bulged. A rope circled her neck and ran up over the rafters. Her hands hung at her sides, fingers curled into claws…as though clutching at vanishing hope.[57]

It's important that writers remember when constructing sentences that the typical structure of a scene is stimulus/response. We've repeated this over and over. We can't write one without the other. If the phone doesn't ring, why should the character answer? If the door doesn't make a sound as it opens, then the character would find no reason turn to see who entered.

The character cannot react to being shot by thinking first that there is someone shooting at him, then jumping to avoid the bullet, then thinking that his heart is racing.

Because of a circumstance or action, another action occurs—the reaction. Sentences need to relay information about the cause before the effect or result. For example:

> Response/stimulus: She jumped as the phone rang.

> Stimulus/response: When the phone rang, she jumped.

---

[57] Renée Miller, In the Bones.

Stimulus/response: The phone rang, and she jumped.

Response/stimulus: The children opened their books and quieted as the teacher entered the room.

Stimulus/response: As the teacher entered the room, the children opened their books and quieted.

Stimulus/response: The teacher entered the room; the children quieted and opened their books.

 **3.1.1.5 PASSIVE CONSTRUCTIONS**

Active writing produces vivid and tight scenes. In an active sentence, an object or subject receives the performed action. (The boy hit the ball). In passive sentences, the object becomes the subject, which creates the effect of the subject receiving the action. (The ball was hit by the boy). In other words, a passive construction places the subject of the sentence in the grammatical "objective" position after the verb. In our example, the boy acts. He "hits" the ball. The ball receives the action. Eliminating passive constructions means first identifying them, and there are a variety of techniques to use in our revision processes. The simplest is to rewrite in steps.

Look for conjugates of "to be" + a past participle (usually, but not always, ending in "-ed"). This combination identifies a passive construction.

Passive: The castle has been demolished by the giant.

Active: The giant demolished the castle.

See if the sentence describes an action. If so, identify the actor. In a passive construction, there is always an actor, an action, and a recipient, just like in an active construction, even if the actor is only implied. Is this noun at the front of the sentence (in the grammatical subject position) or at the end of the sentence (in the object position) or missing entirely? If the "acting" noun is not at the front of the sentence (before the verb) then the construction is passive.

Check if the sentence ends with "by...." Many passive sentences include the one who acts at the end of the sentence in a "by" phrase, as in the aforementioned "The ball was hit <u>by</u> the boy." The boy still acts on the ball, but to make the sentence active, "ball" and "boy" must trade places to "The boy hit the ball." "By" alone, however, isn't a conclusive sign of the passive voice. As an example, "I read the *OFW Writer's Companion* <u>by</u> Carlos J. Cortes and Renée Miller." This sentence is active with "I" as the subject, "read" as the verb, and "*Companion*" as the object.

Examples of passive constructions:

Passive: Her hair was pulled by Jacob.

Active: Jacob yanked her ponytail.

Passive: The boy was left alone by his parents.

Active: The boy's parents left him alone.

Passive: The knight was attacked in the castle. (Useful construction if we don't know who attacked the knight).

Active: The brigands attacked the knight in the castle.

Passive: Residents were surprised by the news.

Active: The news shocked residents.

Active writing is strong, clear, and concise. It catches the reader's attention.

 **3.1.1.6 LINKING VERBS**

Linking verbs are conjugations of the infinitive "to be," including "is," "am," "are," "was," and "were." While action verbs show actions that can be seen or performed, "linking verbs" (sometimes called copulas) express states of being and connect the subject of the sentence with information about it. For example, "Susan is pretty." "Is" links "Susan" (the subject) with "pretty" (the adjective that describes her).

While linking verbs are useful, they are telling constructions. In our example, for instance, showing the reader how Susan is pretty, what she looks like, or what she does that makes her pretty, will give the reader a chance to connect with both Susan and her observer. Expanding the sentence to show the image is one way to do this:

Being: She is pretty. (How is she pretty?)

Action: A wisp of sunlit hair blew across her delicate features.

Being: The dog was hungry. (How do we know?)

Action: The dog gulped the hamburger meat, never using his teeth.

Being: His teacher was cruel. (How was the teacher cruel?)

Action: His teacher thrilled in giving loads of homework. John caught the light in her beady eyes each time the students groaned. Mrs. Smith squealed in delight if a student broke into tears.

Sometimes the best option is to delete the sentence. If it doesn't change the meaning of a paragraph or section, that's a good choice. However, if rewriting alters the meaning of the sentence or paragraph or detracts from the clarity, another way to eliminate an unnecessary linking verb is to combine the sentences. The best method for combining depends on the sentence itself. A few possibilities include:

1. Combine two sentences to make a single compound sentence

Example: The morning air was frigid. Julie decided to stay inside.

Combined: The frigid morning air kept Julie inside.

2. Use a prepositional phrase to combine the sentences

Example: During the frigid morning, Julie stayed inside.

3. List items in a series

Example: Julie disliked cold, mornings, and going out on cold mornings.

4. Use a subordinating conjunction with a dependent clause

Example: Unless she wanted to freeze, Julie would stay inside.

5. Use a dependent clause beginning with a relative pronoun

Example: Julie woke early to a morning that brought frigid temperatures and stayed indoors.

6. Use participial phrases

Example: Staying indoors, Julie warded off the frigid temperature outside.

As for when to delete linking verbs, writers must evaluate each usage. Try the methods above for rewriting the sentence, and if nothing improves it, then the offending word can remain.

3.1.1.7 OTHER WEAK CONSTRUCTIONS

Using weak verbs to summarize action detracts from both the atmosphere and action of the writing. Replacing these with stronger, and in some cases, more interesting verbs enhances the experience of the sentence.

Often, we write prose using the past tense of the verb. For example, "walked" is the past tense of "walk." Search each sentence for the verb and determine its correct use; it may be weak, or past perfect ("had walked") when it doesn't introduce a flashback. We can replace blasé verbs to tighten the prose. In many cases, clarity increases as well.

> Weak: Carly stepped through the crush of bodies. She moved past Mary, who as usual tried to stay to the front of the crowd.

> Strong: Elbowing her way through the crush of bodies, Carly pushed in front of Mary. (Here, we learn more about Carly.)

> Weak: The boy had cringed at the idea of cleaning his room. (Takes us out of the immediate action.)

> Strong: Shouldering the garbage sack, the boy cringed as wrappers and banana peels squished into the bedroom carpet beneath his feet.

Constructions such as "seemed to," "tried to," and "began to" also weaken the prose. Delete them and go with the simple past tense of the verb to make the sentence active.

> Weak: Her scent seemed to envelope him.

> Strong: Her scent enveloped him.

> Weak: She tried to begin the report again.

> Strong: She wrote the report again.

> Weak: He began to run but the sound seemed to get closer.

> Strong: He ran, but the sound drew closer.

To find weak constructions, writers can search for words like those listed below and substitute a stronger, more visual verb to strengthen the action. Sometimes a word, such as "reached" in the example below, is not needed. The key is to make a replacement that doesn't overdo the intent. If the action is dramatic or emotional, show it with the verb. Verb choice conveys character, action, and pace. It can also be used to build suspense or create panic for the reader.

Move	Push	Reach
Bring	Pull	Went
Brought	Press	Came

Weak: She reached into the cupboard and pulled down a cup.

Strong: She took a cup from the cupboard.

Dramatic: She yanked a cup from the cupboard.

Weak: Julie reached the door and tried to push it open.

Strong: Julie opened the door.

Dramatic: Julie rammed her side against the door, but the lock jammed.

A search through the manuscript using Word's "find" feature will locate words that indicate weak constructions. Rewriting weak constructions to active ones will "show" action, senses, and emotion rather than "tell" about them. This draws the reader deeper into the character and enhances his experience of the story. In addition, look for progressive verbs, such as "walking," "talking," etc., combined with words like "was" and "were." Evaluate them. While the words do not always need striking, they often muddle the action or distance the reader from the character.

Distant: She was thinking about quitting her job.

Close: She considered quitting her job.

The progressive verb "thinking" is further weakened by the use of "was." Action verbs state the information concisely, giving the reader a clear mental image of the action performed. This enables the reader to become engaged in the story. "Considered" is an action verb that eliminates the need for "was."

When removing weak writing, also replace verb forms like "has" with verbs that convey the meaning of the sentence. Example:

Weak: She has friends over every Friday.

Strong: She hosts parties every Friday.

Watch for sentences that begin with "there are" or "there were." These two words add nothing and are often called "empty" because eliminating them changes nothing.

Weak: There are four dogs playing in the yard. (present progressive tense)

Strong: Four dogs played in the yard. (past tense)

Weak: There were cars sinking in the water. (past progressive tense)

Strong: Several cars sank. (Unless we're in a desert scene with quicksand or traveling through mud, sinking usually requires water). (past tense)

The next step is to drop the infinitives "to be" and "to have" and replace them with action verbs that describe the action.

Weak: He wants to have a birthday party.

Clear: He wants a birthday party.

Weak: She planned to be home by eight.

Clear: She planned to arrive home by eight.

Weak: Jack wanted to be single again.

Clear: Jack wanted a divorce.

Writers can use the simple present tense (she runs) and simple past tense (she ran) to avoid weak constructions. This replaces the present progressive (she is running) and past progressive (she was running) that weakens prose.

Writers can't eliminate the weak verbs in every sentence because, like linking verbs, they are often necessary. In small quantities, they tend to be invisible, much like "she said." However, it is important to be aware of how often we use weak verbs and weak constructions and identify what can be changed.

The caveat to all rules is in the case of "voice," which is a subtle blend of rhythm and feel. A dogmatic pruning of every "non-active" or weak construction can make for an exhausting read, and sometimes a choppy voice. In other words, once a writer is aware of and sensitive to the presence and uses of weak constructions and telling writing, she should have the confidence to "break" the rule when instinct dictates. Rules are meant to be used to enhance our skills not dogmatically followed.

3.1.1.8 ON "WAS"

Not only a linking verb, "was" is a sign of weak constructions. To detect and remove these, writers can highlight them in the manuscript. In the Edit menus of Word, use the Find and Replace option. Type "was" (for example) in the Find section and >was< in the replace section and click Replace All. Word highlights the chosen word, and gives a count of how many times "was" appears in the manuscript. Another option, which some writers find a distraction, is to do the same thing using the Autocorrect feature in the Tools menu to highlight as we write.

Some options for replacing "was" include:

1. Combine was + "ing" into one verb.

Was falling = fell

Was shouting = shouted

Was running = ran

Was crying = cried

Even better, if possible choose a stronger, more interesting verb like "dashed" or "plummeted" whenever possible.

> **2. Replace "was" + a modifier with another verb.**

She <u>was late</u> for dinner.

She missed dinner.

> **Change the sentence structure.**

There <u>was a sound</u> in the bushes.

She heard a sound in the bushes. (Use sparingly because "she heard" is a construction that can pull the reader out of empathy with the character.)

Charlie <u>was angry</u> at his mother.

Charlie's mother infuriated him.

> ### 3.1.1.9 ADVERBS AND INTENSIFIERS

Writers often use adverbs perhaps believing the change makes the verb actionable. Adverbs do have their place now and then, though they should be used with measure. Adverbs modify verbs, adjectives, and other adverbs and answer "how," "when," "where," and "to what extent" an action is performed. Likewise, an intensifier is a type of adverb that defines the intensity of an adjective or adverb. "Very" is the most used example, but "somewhat," "rather," and "quite" intensify as well. Intensifiers come before the adjective or adverb they modify. Overusing adverbs and their intensifiers signifies lazy writing to publishers.

Lazy: She glared at him arrogantly. (arrogantly answers how)

Better: She glared. (Show her arrogance through other actions.)

Lazy: The boy was quite impressed with his obvious brilliance. (quite is the intensifier)

Better: The boy considered himself brilliant.

Lazy: She eyed him rather suspiciously but didn't speak. (rather is the intensifier and suspiciously answers how)

Better: She glared, but remained silent.

Writers need not eliminate all adverbs or all intensifiers, but it's reasonable to expect that ninety-five percent of those most often used can be eliminated and alter the prose for the better. Replacing adverbs also means replacing verbs with stronger choices, eliminating unnecessary telling.

 **3.1.2 THOUGHTS**

Writing our character's thoughts is a great way to bring the reader deeper into the story. However, thoughts are often constructed to tell, rather than show.

John thought the girl was crazy.

She decided to act.

Mr. Smith wondered if he'd ever met a woman as beautiful as his mother in law.

The examples above convey thought by telling the reader and not showing her. This is easily fixed. Before we get into how to write thoughts, let's examine what we're talking about.

Characters' thoughts are either direct or indirect. Direct thoughts are similar to language, a character thinks a sentence or a comment, but quotes aren't used. Indirect thoughts occur when the narrator comments on the prose. This is an example of a direct thought. They are both correct.

She ran the fingers of one hand through her hair. Is he going bonkers?

She ran the fingers of one hand through her hair. *Is he going bonkers?*

Often, writers are advised to use italics to make a direct thought clear, but many editors, in contrast, frown on the use of italics. In the second example, we can show the thought without using italics. This method works when accompanied by a tight POV. It is clear she is wondering if the man is nuts.

She ran the fingers of one hand through her hair. He must be going bonkers.

This is an indirect thought. She isn't thinking it directly, but it implies she's thinking it. Italics are never needed in this case, because the thought is not direct. This is correct, but writers need to be aware of the effect. The construction is more telling and creates distance for the reader.

Now that we've established what types of thoughts we use in fiction writing, let's look at how to incorporate our characters' thoughts into the story. One of the biggest mistakes new writers make with thoughts is to head hop. We must be aware of whose POV we're in and maintain that relationship unless the shift is deliberate and appropriate. In short, we can't show the thoughts of a non-POV character.

Another mistake is to use too many thoughts, giving the reader a continuous feed of internal dialogue. Writing characters' thoughts should feel natural and not manufactured to fill space. Consider limiting thoughts to a maximum of four lines at a time and break these up with narrative and action. Thoughts, when used well, connect the reader with the character and add color to a story. To incorporate thoughts properly, writers use a combination of tags, italics, deep POV (close to the thoughts of the character), and the reactions or conclusions other characters draw. We'll look at how each of these tools is used.

3.1.2.1 TAGS TO SHOW THOUGHTS

Dialogue tags, as we explain in section 2.2.3, show the reader who is speaking or thinking. Using tags such as "he thought," "he wondered," or "he imagined," enables us to show who is doing the thinking, and they help show POV. Readers are accustomed to seeing quotes when a character speaks but, when he isn't speaking, we need to show that the prose is linked to him somehow. While we frown upon the use of tags like "he thought," they can be used if absolutely necessary and when written properly.

Don't: I wonder if she'll come home, he thought.

Don't: "I wonder if she'll come home." He thought.

Do: He wondered if she'd come home.

3.1.2.2 ITALICS TO SHOW THOUGHTS

As mentioned earlier, editors frown on the use of italics. However, italics do have their place and can be useful. Writers should use italics to emphasize important thoughts, although limiting how often they're used. Short and sweet gut reactions—or sudden realizations—are the best way to use italics to show thought. Large sections of internal dialogue written in italics are a bad idea. Too much text in italics is tiresome to read. Plus, the change reminds the reader she is reading. When we do use italics to show thoughts, we must remember that tags are not needed. The italics show the reader who is thinking and act as the tag.

Don't: She crept along the corridor, careful to avoid the sludge that pooled in the center. *Gross*, she thought.

Do: She crept along the corridor, careful to avoid the sludge that pooled in the center. *Gross*.

Don't: *He better have a damn good excuse for making me come out here. I could be reading my stories, but no, I'm out here searching for his sorry ass. Honestly, I don't know when he'll grow up.*

Do: He better have a damn good excuse for bringing her out. She could be reading her stories, but instead here she's outside searching for his sorry ass. *When will he grow up?*

In the last example, the italics aren't really necessary. They aren't wrong, but because the POV is deep and clear, the italics aren't needed for the reader to know who is thinking. However, they add emphasis at a critical point. Several lines of the first version become irritating, and readers don't appreciate being annoyed.

3.1.2.3 DEEP POV TO SHOW THOUGHTS

Deep POV, or a tight POV, is the best way to show thoughts in fiction writing. Deep POV provides a seamless integration of thoughts into narrative, and it feels natural for the reader. We are able to show thoughts without distracting with tags or italics, making the experience more enjoyable for the reader. Everything is experienced through the character's eyes, so both emotions and thoughts are clear.

For example:

Don't: She'd have to explain this, but how? Barbara pulled her neighbor from the pool and curled her nose. She wondered if she should just dispose of his body.

Do: She'd have to explain this, but how? Barbara pulled her neighbor from the pool and curled her nose. She could just get rid of the body.

In this example, the reader knows that she is looking at the world through Barbara's eyes. The opening sentence is deep in Barbara's POV. Barbara is obviously asking "but how?" Adding "she wondered" intrudes on the scene and pulls away from the character's POV. The tag isn't needed at all, as we see in the second example.

Deep POV also makes those important thoughts stand out when we do decide to use italics.

> She'd have to explain this, but how? Barbara pulled her neighbor from the pool and curled her nose. *Just get rid of the body.*

 ### 3.1.2.4 OTHER CHARACTER'S INTERPRETATION OF THOUGHTS

This is not the same as head hopping. We're talking about using other characters to highlight the POV character's internal dialogue. Unless dealing with a POV that reads minds, which can be confusing, the character can't know what the others are thinking. However, they can guess from facial expressions, tone of voice, and body language.

> Don't: Mark slammed the phone on the desk. She'd be wise to just leave the room.

> Do: She fingered the button of her blouse and shifted her feet. *I will not leave.*

This first example is wrong. We begin in Mark's POV, but still show the other character's thoughts. This is head hopping. The line of italics showing her thoughts can be deleted to stay in Mark's POV only. To show her thought, have the character speak it aloud, so that we stay in one POV while still allowing the reader to know what the other character is thinking.

> She fingered the button of her blouse and shifted her feet. "I will not leave."

Combining these tools can add intensity to a scene that one can't do on its own.

> After closing the cabinet, Dana stared at the woman in the mirror. Her face pale, eyes so sad, Dana ached for that woman. She wished she would disappear, but she remained there, accusingly staring back. "What have I done?" **(tag here is: she wished)**

> Suddenly Dana knew she'd made a mistake. She didn't want to die. The woman frowned. Dana hated that woman, hated how she ruined everything. Screaming, Dana hit her. Her face cracked. Overwhelmed with rage, fear, and regret, Dana hit the woman repeatedly, until her hand ached and blood covered the sink and the floor. **(Deep POV)**

> "Dana?" Ronny called from the hall.

> Now he'd be angry with her too. She was stupid, pathetic. **(Deep POV)**

> The door opened. Ronny swore and ran to her. He picked her up and examined her hands. "Dana, what have you done?"

> "I don't want to die. I'm sorry," she murmured, silently pleading with him to fix her.

> Ronny looked at the shattered mirror, the blood, and finally the empty bottles on the floor. His gaze, shocked, terrified turned to her. "Oh Jesus. What were you thinking?" he took her face in his hands. **(Other character's reaction)**

His face blurred. Dana's stomach rolled, and her world darkened. She felt herself lift off the floor, and Ronny shouting to Devon. *No, don't wake Devon.* Her brain felt heavy, foggy, and she couldn't keep her eyes open. A pain in her chest, her heart beat painfully within and so fast that she could barely take a breath. Dana stopped fighting it, allowing herself to drift away once more.[58] **(Italics)**

In this example, the emotions and the actions of the POV character (Dana) are intensified by the use of all four tools to show her direct and indirect thoughts. The reader can connect, and even with other characters running into the scene, she clearly sees that the thoughts are Dana's.

Thoughts blended into the narrative are the least intrusive way to convey what a character is thinking or feeling. However, sometimes emphasis is needed, and this alone can't achieve the intensity the writer wants. Using tags and italics along with character reactions is a great way to provide this, but use them sparingly.

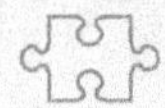 **3.1.3 OVERWRITING**

Another common issue among new writers is overwriting. To prove our writerly skills, we write extremely descriptive prose, but often this type of writing swallows the characters and plot. There is nothing that screams "I'm a newb!" quite as loudly as overwriting.

Most writers have overwritten in their rough drafts, and that's what rough drafts are for: getting it all out. The difference is that a good writer will learn to recognize overwriting and know that when rewriting these descriptions must be thinned out and pared down to best suit the story.

Although there are many ways a writer can overwrite a story, we'll look at the most common ways.

 **3.1.3.1 EMPHASIZING UNIMPORTANT ELEMENTS**

We'll begin with an example:

> The phone rang, startling her from her story about a knight sent to modern times to save a beautiful but unhappy woman from years of barren loneliness. It was a real page turner in her opinion. Kaitlyn folded the page and closed her book. She set it on the oak table, worn rough from years of use, and stood. Shuffling across the floor she stopped to pick up a piece of confetti left from the party she'd thrown in her mother's honor the night before. The phone continued to ring. She wondered who it might be, and took a few more steps to reach it. Her bare feet slapped against the tiled floor. Tile felt so cold in the mornings. She picked up the squalling instrument, pushed "talk" and held it to her ear.
> "Hello?" She asked, her voice rose in question.
> "Hey, it's Chad."

That is overwriting. What do we need from this scene? What is important to the plot?

> The phone rang.
> Kaitlyn picked it up.

"Hey, it's Chad."

Done.

The most important yet most difficult skill a writer learns is what is worth including and what isn't. This is not to say that description isn't essential, but its placement is also important. Consider our example:

> The phone rang.
> Katlyn picked it up. "Hey, it's Chad."
> His voice flooded her senses. A deep baritone coated in hot, melted chocolate. Kaitlyn's throat constricted, blocking a timely response.
> "Kate?"
> Her fingers tightened on the phone, and she drew a long, shaking breath. "Hi, I've missed you."

The description here brings us further into the character's POV, and while it's debatable whether all of it is needed, it is far more appropriate here than it is for the simple act of answering the phone. We want the reader to slow down in this passage, so that she can experience the moment as Kaitlyn does. We don't want the reader to slow down for the simple act of answering a phone.

Ultimately, the writer must practice recognizing the difference to learn how to decide what needs weight and what should be handled swiftly.

3.1.3.2 OVER-DESCRIBING CHARACTERS OR SETTING

Description is necessary, but we must try not to use pages, or even paragraphs, to describe a single thing.

> The glass, tall and slender with a small chip in the lip, tipped toward her, sending the frothy amber liquid over the bar in a narrow wave to her waiting lap.

Adding this much detail for an insignificant object serves no purpose other than to clutter the prose. Instead, use only the most necessary description to enable the reader to see what is happening. Give the reader something sensory to cling to and move into action.

> The glass tipped, spilling the frothy amber liquid over the bar and into her lap.

This is better, although we must decide if we really need to explain to the reader what the beer looks like.

> The glass tipped, sending the beer over the bar and into her lap.

This is okay, but we must consider, have we already told the reader it was beer in the glass? If in previous sentences, she ordered a beer, or even sipped the beer, we don't even need that.

> The glass tipped, sending its contents into her lap.

We've nixed "over the bar" as well, because the reader can safely assume that the beer didn't spill under the bar. A reader imagines, much as the writer does. When detail descriptions of height, eye color, the phase of the moon, and the exact pitch of the drunk singing "Old MacDonald" on the stage, we ruin the reader's enjoyment. Why? Because, part of the pleasure we find in reading is being able to form our own images. Providing too many details does all the work for the reader, leaving him bored and weighed down by every thing she has to remember. Give a quick glimpse of a character or setting that reveals just enough to allow the reader to imagine the scene.

3.1.3.3 CHARACTER DESCRIPTION

The crone threw her hood back, revealing her withered face.

Janice moved like a linebacker, with force and purpose.

The man blinked, and his puffy eyes struggled to focus.

In the above examples, we don't need to go into a detailed description of the crone's wrinkles, Janice's broad shoulders and aggressive personality, or how tired the man is because it's all there in a few words. Withered is a strong word, giving a perfect visual of a really old woman. The words "linebacker," "force," and "purpose" speak volumes about Janice. Puffy eyes give the impression of a weary demeanor, and making an impression is the goal.

Setting:

Saturday morning dawned bright and clear.

The door opened to a chaotic room full of books and papers.

The rain beats a steady staccato against the steel roof of the old porch.[59]

Setting is tempting to overdue because we have so many senses to choose from. Often a line or two is all we need, using one or two of the six senses to give the reader an image. More than that adds nothing. In the first example above, six words give the reader all she needs to move into the action. What time of day is it? It's morning. Weather? Sunny. What day? Saturday. We've established a lot in six words. The second example provides a visual clue to the place the character enters in the scene. In the last scene, we use sound to give the idea a sense of place. The next lines will be action, and another line of setting, but no more. Mixing the setting into the action provides the writer an opportunity to add more detailed descriptions without slowing the pace. The rain beating a staccato is active and descriptive at once. Then we get an idea of place with steel roof and old porch.

3.1.3.4 OVERUSE OF ADJECTIVES AND ADVERBS

It bears repeating that overusing adjectives and adverbs hints at a lazy writer. We use them only when necessary. Sometimes, we'll find a simple adjective replaces an overly descriptive phrase, and this is fine. But even better is to rewrite the phrase with strong noun and verb choices instead.

Don't: She quickly forced the stubborn lock in place and wiped her moist brow exhaustedly.

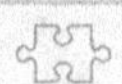 59 Renée Miller, Dirty Truths.

Do: She forced the lock in place and wiped her brow.

Don't: Mary liked the way his thin t-shirt barely covered his gloriously sculpted and tanned abs.

Do: Mary liked the way his t-shirt barely covered his abs.

Words which serve the sole function of holding up other words should only be used if you're trying to eliminate too many "which" or "who" clauses.

When it came time for him to leave, he reflected on the evening, <u>which</u> wasn't horrible in its entirety. The dinner, <u>which</u> was put on by a remarkably good cook, <u>whose</u> sole purpose in life must have been to cook a duck to its most tasty level of perfection, and the woman he loved seemed to be quite fond of him. However, the part in <u>which</u> he set the guest of honor's hair on fire could probably have been omitted and then it might have been an evening that he'd remember with fondness.

Or, we could write:

The evening wasn't wasted. Apart from setting the guest of honor's hair ablaze, he'd enjoyed himself.

The first is rich in adjectives, adverbs, and "which" and "who" clauses, making it impossible for the reader to digest on a single read. The only time we want the reader to read a passage twice is when she is basking in the brilliance of the prose and cannot resist that second read. The second sums it up.

Writers should be wary if we find that we have to support one necessary word with words like "which," "what," "that," "what," and "who." Eliminate them often and use the single word instead, even if it must be an adverb or an adjective.

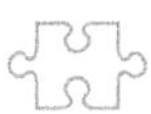 ### 3.1.4 PURPLE PROSE

Pulsating loins, glorious orbs, manroots, love clubs, flowering blooms upon porcelain cheeks—purple prose. Similar to overwriting, purple prose clutters the story and slows the reader down. Purple prose is full of metaphors, melodramatic language, clichés, and cartoonish imagery. Consider this passage:

He dragged her roughly against his rock-hard body. She felt his manroot pressed against the soft recess of her secret place.
"What did you say?" he queried, raising a chocolate brown brow.
"I said I hate you." She spat, bravely attempting to extract herself from his impossibly powerful grasp.
His gaze, now an azure blue, meandered down to the porcelain skin of her heaving bosom. Tears stung her eyes as she endured his loathsome scrutiny. Vile; he was the most vile, obstinate, arrogant creature she'd ever had the displeasure of laying eyes on.
"No you don't hate me at all." His generous lips curved into a derisive grin. "You want me, and you despise yourself for that fact."

Purple prose like the writing above, provides the reader with excessive description that is both tedious to digest and ultimately vague. Adverbs and adjectives are abundant in purple prose, as are euphemisms and hackneyed metaphors. The writer must ask if they tell the reader anything. The scene above could have been written with more clarity and more intensity if the purpleness is removed.

> He dragged her against him, pressing his hips into hers. "What did you say?"
> "I said I hate you." She struggled to free herself.
> His gaze raked her chest.
> Humiliated, she blinked away the tears that stung her eyes.
> He smiled. "No you don't hate me at all. You want me, and you despise yourself for it."

While there is still work to be done, this is much clearer and easier for the reader to digest. The words we removed changed nothing, and without them, the reader is free to imagine what she chooses, not what the writer forces upon her.

We've collected some favorite purple words and phrases commonly used by writers. To share a few:

"Framed by" hair/tresses/curls, etc.:

Her face, framed by delicate blond curls, lit up with joy.

Chestnut tresses framed her pale face.

The sunlight framed his chiseled features, making them sharper, more intimidating.

These have all been used so often that they've become cliché and boring. The reader sees this and often rolls her eyes, perhaps wondering if the writer ran out of creative juice. Try something stronger, less used, to create the image needed.

Her face lit with joy. (Not great, but this is what the writer says, without the curls).

The second example is not worth rewriting because it adds nothing to a character's description. We would strike it out.

The sunlight sharpened his already intimidating features. (This creates the same image for the reader, but without the cliché.)

Swelling bosoms or erupting manhood

Swelling bosoms? Is she going to be okay? Are they sprained or bruised? What has this woman been up to? Swelling bosoms do not create the image we want, and it only serves to clutter the prose and possibly lose the reader. Erupting manhood? Writing love scenes is difficult, let's not make them just as awkward to read with such ridiculous euphemisms.

Revealed by / set off by followed by a description of clothing / fashion

We've seen this often, when writers are trying to give a character description but go just a bit too far. Readers don't need to know the details down to the buttons and color of thread used. The reader doesn't even care about the brand most times. A blue t-shirt, black jeans, or a short skirt is often enough.

Julie entered the room, wearing a Donna Karan pencil skirt and jacket, set off by black hoop earrings that dangled to her shoulders and four inch heels on her tiny feet.

This unwieldy description can be tightened to:

> Julie's heels clicked on the floor as she entered the room. She bent to smooth the tight skirt that had risen to her thighs.

The reader only needs a couple of well placed words to create a picture. When we describe a character from head to toe, using cliché phrases, she isn't getting the opportunity to use her imagination.

Reflecting/reflected through anything that isn't actually reflective, as in "his gaze held reflections of past sorrows captured in his soul and unable to break free from the dark abyss of his heart," is purple prose. If it isn't a mirror, or a least shiny surface, it cannot reflect anything.

◉ Limpid pools

What exactly is a limpid pool? This description adds nothing.

◉ Euphemisms or metaphors used for anatomica descriptions

Anything that writers use to make a word less offensive should be rewritten. If we struggle to find a less obvious word or phrase because we are concerned about offending our readers, then perhaps we should reconsider eliminating the entire scene. Love cave, orbs, dagger (or its cousins sword, weapon, etc.), womanhood, manhood, mound, and anything like this only serves to give the scene a cartoonish feel, not the intense love scene we're hoping for. Yes, readers might be offended by certain words, but then, those same readers might be offended by any type of love scene. Purpling the scene won't make it better; rather, it will turn off readers who aren't easily offended. We believe that sex can be depicted without resorting to coarseness or purple prose:

> Pressure in her bladder brought her back to reality. She smiled and inched to the edge of the bed. Strong arms dragged her back. The hardness of his body pushed against hers and the stubble of his beard dug around her mouth.
>
> Nell squealed a protest, begged for mercy. *Don't listen to me, please don't.*
>
> He didn't.[60]

Purple prose is a telltale sign that we're showing too much. It achieves the opposite effect we're striving for. Rather than give the reader a clear image of the scene, it slows the pace. Showing never slows the pace.

Flowery writing isn't unnecessary or wrong. In small doses, description that gives a little more can add atmosphere and depth to a scene, but it should never force the reader to stop or slow down in order to digest it. The words used should be invisible, meaning the reader should understand them on sight, without having to puzzle through them.

If we struggle for the right words to describe something, we're apt to tread into purple territory. If it's a snake, call it a snake. If the snake is brown with black spots, then say so. Don't try to make the spots more interesting.

> The brown snake slipped beneath the sheets until its spotted tail disappeared.

This is all a reader needs, if it's needed at all. Another important lesson: Writers must first get the words out necessary to plot and characterization, and then use what is left to add setting and color. Because this leaves us with limited words, we're less likely to pack the prose and weigh it down.

---

[60] Carlos J Cortés, Mahdi.

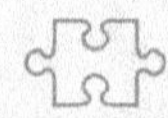 **3.1.5 CHAPTER AND SCENE**

At the end of a chapter or scene, comes the beginning of another. At each beginning, the writer must hook readers all over again. We've all heard how important the first lines of a novel are. We also know the first chapter is crucial. We agree the first pages are what spark interest in the readers, but writer's don't always recognize they must keep reader attention throughout the story.

Chapter and scene openers must grab the reader's attention at once. We have mere seconds to latch onto the reader and hang on. It doesn't matter that she's bought the book; we need to ensure she stays with us until the final page. The opening of each new scene must ground the reader in the scene right away. She needs to know when and where the chapter or scene takes place and who is involved. The opening paragraphs should anchor the reader in place and time.

Stories should open with a dramatic or interesting situation or character and jump into the action, dragging the reader into the moment. This creates immediacy from the outset. Also important is to ensure that chapter one opens in a different way from chapter two, and the first scene should begin differently than the second. Like sentences, as we discuss on page 173, writers should vary how to open every scene and chapter. Believe it or not, despite the brilliant stuff happening in between, if we begin each new scene with the same structure (John walked to the door/John flung the torch/John stretched) the reader will notice the echo and find it boring.

Just as our opening lines must hook readers, chapter and section endings must also grab them and propel them to the next chapter or section. Endings that work tempt readers to stay up that extra twenty minutes to read more.

In the following sections we'll discuss common mistakes writers should look for when rewriting openings and endings.

 **3.1.5.1 OPENINGS**

The first lines of a book are crucial to entice our reader to buy the book. The first lines of each chapter and each section or scene must persuade the reader to keep reading. Some of the ways to achieve this include: an unusual phrase; a unique voice; a compelling snippet of action or dialogue; or an active description of setting. Remember, we have about three seconds to convince the reader our story is worth reading. Let's use that time wisely.

- **Unusual Phrasing**

Among the periviggles of atmospheric Alpha Centuri, it's all about snarflagoging. [61]

Lucy ate her brain.

October 5th, the last day of the year.

Boiled snake does not taste like chicken.

---

[61] Donna Johnson, All about Snarflagoging.

These sentences might make a reader scratch her head, but they certainly draw attention. In some cases, these type openings make clever misdirections. In others, they are indicators we have left reality and entered the world of the story. Unusual phrases, statements that we wouldn't often hear in normal conversation or in everyday events, pull the reader in. To find out how Lucy ate her own brain or what a "periviggle" is and what it does when it's "snarflagoging," we must read on.

Action

He rode hard to escape his doom. [62]

Squeezing the trigger, Julie said goodbye.

His parents finally put a stop to his loafing ways.

Vandrygal bit the head off a rat and crunched the skull, ignoring the body's death throes. [63]

Dialogue

"She sees us as demons." [64]

"I feel bad that I'm leaving you like this," Amelia said. [65]

"Withdraw your tentacle, Spevot, and tell me what happened." [66]

Active Description

…and everywhere, rough concrete walls, damp—as if weeping with insufferable sadness. [67]

Hot metal crackles and sighs as it settles into the scorched earth, flames hiss over blistering surfaces as the fuel remaining in the aircraft's tanks burns out. [68]

Late spring and early fall, when birth becomes life and life succumbs to death and the renewing earth is irritated by the effort, there's a distinctive smell, much like fish, that often follows too much rain. [69]

Readers set books aside, often for weeks or months, usually stopping at a new chapter, section, or scene. It's crucial that we yank the reader right back in when she goes back to that scene.

A quick way to determine if we've done this is to read the first page of the new section and write down what we have learned about the setting and character. If we find fewer than ten things, we

---

[62] Henry Lara, The Knight and the Demon.

[63] Donna Johnson, True Daughter.

[64] Michael Keyton, Elizabeth's Head.

[65] Charlaine Harris, Dead in the Family.

[66] Donna Johnson, Alien Dead: Dogean Fellows Say News to Blame.

[67] Carlos J. Cortes, My Valentine.

[68] Renée Miller, False Prophet.

[69] Donna Johnson, Drowning of Worms.

rewrite because we don't have enough. If we can't answer where and what is happening and to whom, the reader can't either and this will pull her from the story. Then we ask: Is it interesting?

Give the reader something to puzzle out in the first lines. If we raise questions in each new section, the reader wants to keep reading to the end to find out how it is resolved. To do this, we use dialogue and/or a line or two of narrative. We try to combine setting and characterization with action and dialogue to keep the pace moving. We never place backstory or exposition in the opening lines. The first lines of a chapter or scene must be active. Action will hook the reader again, while brief narrative provides important information and grounds the reader in the moment. Exposition and backstory distance the reader from the moment and the character. If we find that our openers are telling the reader or filling in blanks in the plot, we need to rewrite to either show this in dialogue or scatter the information through the action of the scene.

Variety is important. When rewriting, after we've established that we have what we need in the opening lines to place the reader, we write the first sentence of each chapter and scene on a piece of paper. These we write in order without skipping any. Examine them, looking for echoes, repetition, and structure. For example:

> John pulled out his gun.

> Mary screamed.

> John gripped the buoy, trying to keep his gaze on the circling shark.

These are repetitive subject-verb constructions with limited modifiers, though the third example adds a little variety. The reader may not identify why these openings echo, but she will notice it. Let's look at some varied chapter openers:

> Though the sting had faded over the last hour, a red handprint still adorned the boy's cheek.

> Broken bricks and rocks made up the ring surrounding the makeshift fire pit at the back of the yard.

> The silver spoon clinked rhythmically against the coffee cup.[70]

The examples above are the first lines of the first three chapters of Wendy Swore's novel. Notice how the writer uses a different sentence structure to open each? Yes, we might have several scenes between one chapter and the next, but the variety of openings is crucial to avoid echoes. The same is true for each scene or section within that chapter.

In summary, the beginning of each scene or section poses a question, gives the reader conflict, and moves into the action. For example, the character enters a room to find a stranger standing by the window. Who is this stranger? Why is she standing in the…? Set the scene. It's dark, past midnight on a rainy evening. Cliché, but this opening contains the elements that lure the reader in. By the end of the scene, we'll have shown the character confronting conflict and resolving the mystery of this stranger. However, we must present another conflict at the end.

---

[70] Wendy Swore, Firebug.

 ### 3.1.5.2 ENDINGS

Endings in each chapter and scene are as important as our openers. Readers remember those books that kept them up into the wee hours of the morning or caused them to ignore the laundry piling up and the movie marathon on television.

While we must resolve at the end the question posed in the first lines of the scene, we must also pose another question in closing it. Writers can use a variety of methods to keep the reader turning the page.

We can choose to end in the middle of the action or dialogue to keep the reader turning the page. When used wisely, it is a superb tool.

> Do: Turns out, I was right to worry.[71]

> Don't: John died in his sleep.

> Do: Other times, I wanted to smack him. [72]

> Don't: Maria relented, knowing the next month would be the hardest.

Ending a chapter or scene at the height of the action keeps the reader turning the page. She wants to know what will happen, so she continues to read. As you can see above, endings can contain narrative or dialogue, either internal or external, but the important thing is that they should be active and showing, not telling. In the above examples, the first leaves an unspoken question. It's ominous, vague and makes the reader wonder what will happen next.

The second example is iffy. It resolves the scene without giving the reader any reason to rush to the next page. The third works because it interrupts the action, making the reader curious about the relationship between the characters. Why does he want to smack this nice boy?

In the last example we've given too much away. It might have been better at simply "Maria relented." If we've foreshadowed something obvious, we should rewrite to remove it. Perhaps we should end earlier in the action to add suspense and continue the next chapter opening with "Maria relented." Often, to repair sections and chapters that are not working, we need only to shift the endings around, either closing the scene earlier or later in the story.

Another way to close a section or chapter with a hook is to pose a direct question. Writers should be careful that this question doesn't give too much away, though. Lead up to the question with action, and using either internal or external dialogue, pose the question for the reader.

> Would he meet the monster this afternoon?

> If Carroll were in his shoes, he wouldn't trust any of them either, but then he knew things that Ryan Cassidy didn't.[73]

---

[71] Wendy Swore, Crop Circles.

[72] Jeanne Voelker, Unlocking William.

[73] Renée Miller, In the Bones.

Both endings pose a question, one directly and one indirectly. The reader is tempted to turn the page to find out about the monster and later to learn what it was this Carroll character knows that Ryan does not.

As with openers, writers must vary the endings of each scene and chapter so that no consecutive endings are structured alike. If we end with a question in one scene, the next should end perhaps in the middle of action, or with dialogue.

This doesn't mean every chapter should end with a nail-biting, stomach churning, can't-breath-because-the-suspense-is-just-too-much-cliffhanger ending. We should not leave every scene hanging like that, but we must make sure that when we don't use one, the ending still is riveting. A good method of doing this is to go through the manuscript and list whether the ending of each section is negative or positive for the protagonist.

We should alternate endings so that, for instance, scene one is positive and scene two is negative. For example, the endings we used above from Renée's novel show a positive and then a negative for the protagonist. These are from consecutive scenes. In the first, Ryan is excited that maybe he'll find answers to the mysterious monster his dead grandfather hints at in a letter. The second scene is in the antagonist's POV, and doesn't bode well for Ryan's future. This contrast helps to increase tension. Does it need to alternate all the way through? Of course not. But it's good to keep an even measure of both to ensure each ending differs from the last and the one that will follow. If we notice that for five consecutive scenes the endings are negative for the protagonist, we should rewrite to include positives in between.

Sometimes, a section or chapter ends with a bang, a long preparation to deliver a single item, a detail to instill a sense of wonder in the reader:

> Before his eyes flashed a strange recurring dream he'd experienced as a boy. It always started the same way. He stood by the sea, on a long stretch of sand gleaming under a silver moon. The moon dipped into the sea then surfaced as a golden sun in a dark sky. Small ripples formed like an echo, traveling over thickened water, changing sand into fluffy gold. A gentle breeze blew in from the sea, rousing tiny waves in groups of three, lapping the sand with froth and a murmur, almost a breath; oooh-eeh-aaah; oooh-eeh-aaah, oooh-eeh....
> "What do you want?"
> Yehudi eyed their untouched tea mugs. "A battalion of elite troops primed to seal the area within minutes." Though the Mossad was, in theory, solely concerned with intelligence operations outside Israeli soil, he knew Maccobi could reach for Army goods should the need arise.
> Maccobi held his gaze for a long time, then nodded once.
> In Yehudi's dream, a woman stood at the water's edge—between him and the dark sea—the sun casting a halo of golden mist around her as the wind billowed out her dress and teased her long floating hair. Yehudi never saw her face. He stood still, unable to reach her, willing her to turn so he could satisfy his craving to enjoy her face, to know her, while the wavelets continued to lick her feet in threes; oooh-eeh-aaah; oooh-eeh-aaah.
> Now, thirty years later, the dream had revisited his nights, only this time the woman turned to face him; she was Professor Onella Keating and the waves whispered her name.[74]

---

74 Carlos J Cortés, Mahdi.

The ending of a chapter or a scene must raise questions or paint images that are so intriguing or provocative the reader is compelled to turn that page.

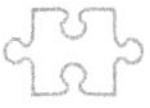 ### 3.1.6 DIALOGUE

Dialogue should serve a purpose. When well written, it moves the story forward and adds depth to our characters. It's pivotal to create intimacy between our readers and the story. In section 2.2.3 we cover the mechanics of good dialogue. Now let's discuss rewriting to eliminate common dialogue problems.

If dialogue doesn't provide information, add emotion to a scene, or move the story forward, then we have to ask if it's necessary. If it does none of these things, we cut it. Our goal when cutting dialogue is not to remove so much that we lose the "feel" of the character, but to remove anything that is no more than filler or fluff. When rewriting, begin by reading the dialogue aloud. Listen to each line to pick out the difference in each character's speech, and most importantly, to make sure the dialogue feels natural. Any area that has us stumbling is likely to trip up the reader as well and needs rewriting.

Next, we compare our dialogue to the narrative. There should be a balance between the two. When rewriting, we estimate how much of our novel is narrative and how much is dialogue. If there is more of one or the other, edit to bring them back in balance. But don't eliminate whole sentences and paragraphs for the sake of cutting. When rewriting to trim dialogue, we examine each line, searching for redundant words or thoughts. When we want to add dialogue, we find areas where the narrative is telling. Perhaps we could show the same information through dialogue. Often, rewriting to eliminate colloquialisms or descriptive words tightens dialogue enough to achieve the goal, but we must take care not to lose meaning or tone while doing so.

For example, we can remove dialogue prompts, or statements that are intended to elicit a response. In most cases these are not needed and can be removed without changing the meaning.

> "Did you see that?" he asked.
> "Yes."
> "Whoa, that's a big hotdog."
> "Sure is."

In the above, no matter what comes before, the first two lines of dialogue serve no purpose. They fill a space, and nothing else. If we rewrite to remove those, the scene has the same information while tightening the dialogue.

> "Whoa, that's a big hotdog."
> "It is."

Of course, there is much more to rewriting dialogue than what we've discussed here. In the following sections, we'll examine tags and attributions and how to rewrite them to tighten the prose.

 **3.1.6.1 TAGS**

The best is "said." Simple, perhaps boring, but preferable to chortled, moaned, growled, or laughed. Many writers feel the word is dull and replace it with what they believe to be a more exciting choice. Sometimes, a more interesting word is fine, but most times, it doesn't benefit the dialogue.

Readers accept invisible tags like "said" because they hardly notice them when reading. Words like whispered, shouted, cried, etc. draw the reader's attention from the dialogue to the tag, which yanks them from the story.

Dialogue tags such as these are often called "said bookisms." They give our prose an amateur feel; perhaps not to readers, but definitely to editors and other writers. While our readers might not realize these tags are a no-no, they'll still draw attention, in particular if the writer is fond of using them.

Said bookisms pull the reader away, distracting her and slowing down the story. Writers should avoid littering dialogue with phrases like murmured, shouted, whimpered, inquired, queried, or muttered. Use of these words illustrates that we have a solid relationship with our thesaurus but not a good grasp of fiction writing. If the dialogue is strong, we don't need more than "he said" or "she said." If it is not strong enough, or if it doesn't clearly show the tone, we must rewrite the dialogue, rather than adding "said bookisms" to give it a little boost.

Of course, we can use these tags occasionally. As with all things, moderation is key. We should think of them as decoration, like jewelry. We wouldn't wear ten earrings in one ear, or two rings on each finger, and expect to be elegant. Like jewelry, we use "said" to add to the finished product, and reserve it for special occasions. Characters do sometimes shout, and they might even mutter, but most will not do so all the time.

Before we move on, we'll acknowledge that many bestselling authors use outlandish tags all the time. It doesn't make it right, and it doesn't mean new writers will sell their work if they do the same. It means that many of these writers are good enough at the other stuff to get away with silly tags now and then. Writers should work at ensuring the dialogue is so strong that "said bookisms" aren't needed.

Silly or Melodramatic Tags

Tags that create a melodramatic or silly image for the reader should be avoided. When we use tags to add tone or color, such as "blazed," "hissed," or "shrieked," we should first make sure that it's physically possible for the character to do what we're describing.

> "So are you," he laughed.
> "I am not." She hissed.[75]
> "Go on," he muttered.

When we try to do these things while speaking, the difficulty becomes apparent. We cannot laugh a line of dialogue, nor can we hiss it. When we see dramatic tags like these, we first ask ourselves if the character can really say the line the way we've written, and if not, determine if we must remove the tag, change it to another tag like "said," or use action instead.

> He laughed. "So are you."
> "I am not."

---

[75] Because of the period here, it suggests she said her three words. Then for some unaccountable reason she hissed.

"Go on." He waved a hand, dismissing her.

Verbs used to describe an expression, such as "grimace," "sneer," "smile," "frown," and "grin," are not good dialogue tags. These are physical movements. We don't grimace our sentences, nor do we frown them. When rewriting, examine all dialogue tags, and if the tag contains an expression, we should rewrite. If the character must sneer, then the line should be written so it is possible.

Don't: "That's what your mother said," he sneered.

Do: He sneered. "That's what your mother said."

Here we have a subtle, yet important distinction. On the first line, the comma before the tag implies that the speaker sneered through the delivery of "That's what your mother said." On the second, he sneered and then delivered his line. In this last instance, the emphasis starts with the expression and then shows the language to back up its meaning.

Of course, we can delete it, trusting that the reader will get that the sneer is implied. The dialogue and character actions before these lines should be enough to signal the reader the sneer without our telling him about it. This is true for most tags where we've inserted an action rather than the description of speech.

The word "hissed" can be avoided because it's not possible to hiss and speak, except for cats and snakes. When rewriting, search for hiss and rewrite or delete every time. Editors will appreciate this little courtesy. (Even the reptilian kind).

3.1.6.2 ATTRIBUTIONS

In section 2.2.3.1 we discuss the use of attributions, which we use to indicate who is speaking and to add color to a scene. An attribution is a sentence or a group of sentences set before or after the dialogue line and in the same POV, used to signal who is speaking. In contrast to tags, we separate attributions from the dialogue with a period, never a comma.

A good rule for writers is to keep it simple when using dialogue attributions. As with tags, too much fluff when attributing dialogue will weigh it down and pull the reader away from the dialogue itself. When too flowery, the reader pauses to imagine this thing the character is doing as he speaks.

Another problem that keeps popping up when writing drafts is to use tags and attributions on the same dialogue line. If the identity of the speaker is clear, the tag isn't needed. For example:

> "Why can't you be more like your brother?" Maria said, and picked up the pile of socks jammed next to the hamper.
> "Why can't you be more like any other person on this planet?" Henry replied, and stomped from the room.
> "I don't know why I married you," she neared the window, muttering.
> He sighed. "I ask myself the same question every day," he said.

In all the examples above, the action combined with the attribution is overkill.

> "Why can't you be more like your brother?" Maria picked up the pile of socks jammed next to the hamper.
> "Why can't you be more like any other person on this planet?" Henry stomped from the room.

"I don't know why I married you." She neared the window.
He sighed. "I ask myself the same question every day."

Though attributions work like dialogue tags, they are less obtrusive and spice dialogue in ways that simple tags can't. If there is a choice, attributions are preferable. For example:

Boring: "I hate you," Maria said.

Exciting: "I hate you." Maria threw the ring in his face.

Showing her anger will keep the pace moving, rather than slowing the reader down—and it still attributes the speech to Maria.

When rewriting, we need only one attribution (or two) every four to five lines. We work on one page at a time and examine the dialogue. If we see four consecutive lines with attributions or tags, we look first to see if these are necessary. Is it clear who is speaking? If not, we examine the lines to detect the point where a reader might lose track of the speakers and insert one. If "said" is appropriate, we can use it, unless there's a way to append an attribution to add color, movement, or emotion.

3.1.6.3 DIALOGUE PUNCTUATION

Punctuating dialogue is straightforward, and follows the punctuation rules outlined on pages 277 to 320. In addition, there are some issues writers must keep in mind.

Punctuation of complete sentences goes inside the quotations. Always.

"What did he say?"
"Aaarghh!"
"Pardon?"
"That's what he said."

If what follows the dialogue line is a tag, we punctuate the dialogue with a comma.

"He fell," Lazar said.

If what follows the dialogue line is a non-speech attribute, description, or anything else, we punctuate the dialogue with a period.

"That's what he said." Cain looked crestfallen.
"María said you were nothing but trouble. She's the queen of understatements." Desmond drew one hand to his forehead, feeling faint.

If what follows a dialogue line ending with a question mark or exclamation point is a tag, or speech attribute, we use lowercase, unless what follows is a proper noun.

"And then?" he demanded.
"Aaarghh!" Cain grunted.

If we insert description, narrative, or attributions in a line of dialogue, the interrupted dialogue must be separately surrounded by quotation marks.

"That man stepped back toward the phone there." Lazar nodded to a narrow table on thin legs, like a ballerina on tiptoes. "Then he stopped, clutched his chest, said something, and fell."

If we write uninterrupted dialogue by the same speaker and insert a paragraph break, we should omit the closing quotation on the end of the line before the break.

> Surreal. Desmond swallowed. "So, after breaking in, instead of heading for the safe you stopped at the kitchen, drank a gallon of milk and raided the cookie tin. Then you climbed up here and scared the man to death.
>
> "María said you were nothing but trouble. She's the queen of understatements." Desmond drew one hand to his forehead, feeling faint. "Any cookies left?"

Altogether, these are the norms for correct dialogue punctuation. The excerpt from which we've drawn the examples is reproduced below.

> Crouched on the floor by the bed, a plump porcelain chamber pot decorated with colorful peonies sat next to a velvet slipper and a handsome foot attached to a leg and a sprawled plump form wrapped on a brocade housecoat. The body's outstretched hands still grasped a double-barreled gun.
>
> "What happened to him?" Desmond nodded to Gordon Tyler's corpse.
>
> "He fell," Lazar said.
>
> "I can see that," he whispered.
>
> "He was standing there with his gun."
>
> "What did you do?"
>
> Lazar and Cain lowered their heads.
>
> "Well?"
>
> Cain stretched both arms over his head. "We raised our hands."
>
> "And then?" he demanded.
>
> "That man stepped back toward the phone there." Lazar nodded to a narrow table on thin legs, like a ballerina on tiptoes. "Then he stopped, clutched his chest, said something, and fell."
>
> "What did he say?"
>
> "Aaarghh!" Cain grunted.
>
> "Pardon?"
>
> "That's what he said." Cain looked crestfallen.
>
> Surreal. Desmond swallowed. "So, after breaking in, instead of heading for the safe you stopped by the kitchen, drank a gallon of milk and raided the cookie tin. Then you climbed up here and scared the man to death.
>
> "María said you were nothing but trouble. She's the queen of understatement." Desmond drew one hand to his forehead, feeling faint. "Any cookies left?"[76]

---

[76] Carlos J Cortés, The Damn Book.

3.1.7 SYNTAX

Syntax is the order and relationship among the structural elements (sentences and paragraphs) in our writing. In essence, it is how we place our words. Syntax is often dependent upon our individual styles, but that doesn't mean there isn't a correct way to create sentences and put them into paragraphs that lend music to the rhythm of the prose.

Syntax isn't just about what we put in a sentence. It's also about which words we choose, the punctuation (or lack thereof), and how we put it all together. A well written sentence makes a huge difference for the reader. It can convey thoughts or messages far better than a poorly crafted line. Careful attention to syntax is the difference between writing that rambles and a crisp, memorable piece of prose.

We don't often think about syntax when writing the rough draft. This is fine, because we can fix it on rewrite. However, understanding what makes a good sentence, a good paragraph, and a good structure, means sentences are more likely to be well constructed the first go 'round, saving editing time later. The instinct for good syntax comes with practice. This means paying attention to these things when rewriting so that we don't make the same mistake with another draft later.

When rewriting, we read each sentence and consider the following:

Is the sentence clear?

Sometimes we imbue sentences with ambiguity, but this should be a conscious choice rather than an accident. When a message or an idea is clear in our minds, we may not realize what we've actually written is unclear for the reader—who can't see inside our heads. Often confusion is due to poor word choice or incorrect punctuation.

Medusa shifted her gaze to his, which petrified him.

Did Medusa turn him into stone, as is her tendency, or did we mean that he was scared that she looked his way? If the latter, the word choice is poor. It can mean too many things in this sentence. On rewrite, we must clarify what we mean.

Medusa shifted her gaze to his, which terrified him.

Medusa shifted her gaze to his, turning him into stone.

By saying what we mean, instead of using vague words, the sentence is clear to the reader.

Does the sentence have an echo?

In other words, have we inserted the same idea twice in the same sentence?

Bob was a big man, so he didn't need a ladder to reach the top shelf because he was so tall.

This sentence says the same thing three times. We've said he's a big man and indicated his height with the "didn't need a ladder" part of the sentence. Why add that he's tall?

Bob didn't need a ladder to reach the top shelf.

Enough said. Echoing ideas often occurs in a first draft because we overwrite to get the information out. When we read it back, it's important to look for thoughts that echo not only in sentences, but in paragraphs as well.

Writers use syntactical techniques to invoke a response in the reader. We want to create emotions such as fear, excitement or tension. Using short sentences or long, we manipulate the reader into feeling what we want her to feel. We dictate through punctuation when we want her to breathe, to slow down, or to read faster. The way that we build sentences and paragraphs influences the rhythm of the prose.

When rewriting for syntax, we look at more than just individual sentences. We have to look at the prose as a whole and how each part builds on the previous. In section 4.3 we discuss normal syntax order (subject, verb, object), but in the following sections, we'll look at rewriting to ensure we show variety in sentences and paragraphs.

3.1.7.1 VARIETY

Sentence Structure

Writing made from short sentences tends to be choppy, which can be annoying to read. Writing that contains mostly long, complex sentences tends to be boring and is often difficult to understand. Neither is a good choice.

Good writers use a variety of sentence lengths and types in their writing. We have four sentence types to choose from when building our prose or creating our rhythm. These are categorized by the clauses they contain. A clause, as defined in section 4.2, is a part of a sentence containing a subject and a predicate.

Simple sentences contain a single, independent clause 

She hated spiders.

The diner would close before dark.

Mary loves chocolate-covered cherries.

Compound sentences contain two independent clauses joined by a coordinating conjunction (and, or, but, so, etc) 

Each of these could be written in two separate sentences.

She hated spiders, and her husband adored them.

The diner must be closed before dark, or creatures of the night will eat the patrons for dinner.

Mary loves chocolate coated cherries, but her waistline does not.

 **Complex sentences contain an independent clause and a dependent clause** 

She hated spiders because of their ability to hide in the most inconvenient places.

The diner would be closed before dark, since the creatures roamed the streets at that time.

Although they do not love her, Mary loves chocolate-covered cherries.

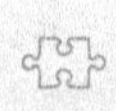 

Compound-complex sentences have two or more clauses. At least two of those clauses are independent and at least one is independent and at least one is dependent.

She hated spiders, and her husband adored them, which caused their marital problems.

The diner closed before dark, averting an attack, and the patrons lived safely through the night.

With a passion, Mary loved chocolate-covered cherries, but her waistline did not.

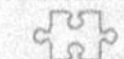 

Fragments contain a dependent clause alone.

Spiders!

Help.

Mmmm.

Because these don't contain a subject and a verb, they are fragments. Complete sentences must have at least one subject and one verb.

When rewriting, writers must identify problematic sentences. After spotting a cluster of shorter sentences, determine if they can be combined or added to by crafting a longer sentence to balance it out. For example:

John loved the winter. Snow meant skiing. Skiing meant girls. He loved girls more than winter. The slopes waited. He tossed his skis in the trunk. Where was Matt? Late as usual.

This paragraph doesn't create intensity with its short sentences. It's clunky and needs cleaning up. To rewrite, we must look at what's needed, and what might be combined to create variety.

John loved snow. It meant skiing, which meant girls, and John loved girls more than anything. He tossed his skis in the trunk. Where was Matt?

We've rewritten from several simple sentences and a fragment to a variety of sentence types. This balances the prose, and cleans it up. The fragment isn't needed, so we delete it.

 ### 3.1.7.2 RUN-ON-SENTENCES

A run-on sentence contains two or more sentences strung together without punctuation.

Despite his best intentions Joey managed to fail in all aspects of his life including but not limited to his career and his marriage and he believed that he would never succeed at anything because fate was against him though he claimed not to believe in such a thing.

There are several ideas in this example, necessitating separate sentences. Most times we can correct this with commas or a periods.

Despite his best intentions, Joey managed to fail in all aspects of his life including, but not limited to, his career and his marriage. Though he believed he would never succeed at anything because fate was against him, he also claimed not to believe in such a thing.

To find run-on sentences, read each sentence aloud. When we speak, we make natural pauses that mark the ends of sentences and clauses. If the punctuation in the writing doesn't match how we speak, we might have a run-on sentence. These can often be broken into two sentences, or corrected by punctuation as we've shown earlier.

 ### 3.1.7.3 SENTENCE FRAGMENTS

Fragments are unfinished sentences. Though these are frowned on in English class, they aren't always bad. Fragments are useful in dialogue, but in narrative we should keep them to a minimum. When rewriting, read the writing backwards, sentence by sentence, to detect the fragments. If we see a fragment, we can easily correct it by attaching the fragment to the sentence before it.

Fragment: He loved her hair in the moonlight. Because of the lustrous shine.

Better: He loved her hair in the moonlight, because of the lustrous shine.

Fragment: Mary shopped when angry. Which proved unhealthy for her bank account.

Better: Mary shopped when angry, which proved unhealthy for her bank account.

Fragment: She cried herself to sleep. Soaking the pillow with tears.

Better: She cried herself to sleep, soaking the pillow with tears.

Sometimes a fragment is fine and can be left, if it creates the effect we want. For example:

He loved her hair in the moonlight. So shiny.

Mary shopped when angry. Bad idea.

She cried herself to sleep. Poor girl.

Experienced writers with a full understanding of sentence structure can choose to use fragments now and then, but they must make sense and serve a purpose. If they look like a mistake, the writing loses credibility in the reader's eyes.

3.1.7.4 RAMBLING SENTENCES

Rambling sentences are easy to spot, and a common mistake (intentionally or unintentionally) made by writers. These sentences are made up of many clauses and connected by a conjunction such as "and" or "so."

She rolled over and slammed a fist on the alarm clock, and pulled the blanket over her head because she did not want to get up, so this would make her very late for work, which would not go over well with her boss.

We should remove rambling sentences, if only to ensure the reader won't pass out from reading such longwinded passages. Look for sentences that contain three or more conjunctions (and, so, but) and read these aloud. If we run out of breath, we've written a rambling sentence and should rewrite. Rambling sentences are not the same as run-on sentences. Rambling sentences aren't technically wrong; they are simply irritating for the reader. A better, more balanced sentence structure would be:

She rolled over and slammed the alarm clock, pulling the blanket over her head. This would make her late for work, which would not go over well with her boss.

If your sentence stretches over many lines of writing, you may have a rambling sentence and risk a run-on sentence. Once we've cleaned up the problems, we can look to sentence length to create variety and add rhythm to the prose.

Sentence lengths must be varied to match the tone and the emotion in each scene, but not with incorrect structures. Each sentence must lead naturally into the next, creating coherent ideas. We don't set out to annoy the reader with our run-ons and our rambles, but often, when trying to vary sentence length, we sacrifice clarity. We should read the writing out loud, paying attention to how we've punctuated it while listening closely. If it sounds awkward or unclear, the reader will have the same experience.

3.1.7.5 PARAGRAPHS

Paragraphs, like sentences, must vary in structure and length. One of the most common errors in fiction writing is failure to vary paragraph length. Writers either combine what should be several paragraphs into one long, dizzying block of text or create many short paragraphs with a choppy, stilted effect.

A paragraph typically contains four to five related sentences that deal with a single idea. Of course, that is a guide, and writers should strive for paragraphs that extend beyond five lines as well as ones that are shorter. Writers may have amazing or brilliant ideas, but if they are presented in a disorganized way, the greatness is lost.

Creating paragraph variety is simple. First, examine each page. Don't read it, just look at the page as a whole. When readers see large blocks of text, their instinct is to either skip it or close the book. If we're lucky, they'll give it a go, but that doesn't happen often. We recommend going through each page of prose looking for balance. For example a page that contains one large block of text isn't balanced. This should be broken into at least one medium and one short paragraph. A page that contains five lines, two lines, eight lines, and four lines, is a fairly balanced page. To the eye it looks varied.

However, there is much more to paragraph variety than just the number of sentences we've created. What about the types of sentences? We must also examine each sentence within the paragraph.

> Maria hated dogs. She loathed the beasts. One of the filthy mongrels licked her face once, and she'd kicked it. The owner had much to say later.

Feel the harsh choppiness of the simple sentences? This paragraph begins with two simple sentences, followed by a compound sentence, and ends with another simple sentence. It's not varied. Sure we've got a compound sentence mixed in there, but it still doesn't read smoothly. It jostles. There are four sentences, so we could vary this using four different sentence types, or delete the unnecessary bits. The second simple sentence isn't needed. With it removed, the paragraph shows more balance.

One technique for creating sentence variety is called the diamond paragraph. Using simple, compound, complex and compound-complex sentences in each paragraph creates a diamond shape when the sentences are listed. It works like this:

> Julie hated her boss. (simple) The man behaved like a pig, and his booming voice irritated her. (compound) Although his replacement was a jerk, she couldn't imagine a worse boss, or

one as attractive. (compound-complex) His appearance didn't make up for his attitude, not in her opinion. (complex). Things would be simpler without him. (simple).

The paragraph above creates a diamond in the sentences we've used. How? Let's list the sentence types and we'll see:

Simple

Compound

Compound-Complex

Complex

Simple

When rewriting for paragraph structure, list the types of sentences used within each. Do we have significantly more of one or another? Rewrite to vary them. The diamond pattern doesn't have to happen in each paragraph, but in longer passages of five or more sentences, it creates a varied piece of prose that is pleasing for the reader. Careful use of sentence and paragraph variety creates a smooth and flowing story.

 **3.1.8 VOCABULARY**

As writers, we must choose words that accomplish several tasks. A single word can convey many meanings (a metaphor, for example), evoke all five senses, play off the meanings of other words in surrounding sentences, and allude to a host of other bits of information. Being able to select a single word to do these things distinguishes a good writer from a lazy one.

We should choose the right word for the right novel, for the right plot, and the right scene, paragraph, and sentence. We'd never hear a five year old (unless he was a genius) speak in a formal way without contractions.

"Might I have an Oreo cookie along with a glass of that delicious milk, Mother?"
"Sure, Jack."
"Last night, I had a nightmare that terrified me. I would like it if you would leave the bathroom light on henceforth."

Does that sound like a five-year-old kid asking for milk and cookies or discussing a nightmare? The words we choose make a difference in the overall impression of the story or scene.

"Can I have some Oreos and milk?"
"Sure, Jack."
"Can you leave the light on tonight? I had a scary dream last night."

A five year old can speak well, but simply. Kids don't often waste a lot of time finding the perfect words, so these words fit the scene more than terrified, delicious, and henceforth.

It's also necessary to know when to use slang or profanity when the scene calls for it. Some writers overuse both of these; some never use slang. Both choices can hurt a scene. While we agree profanity can often be safely left out, well placed slang can add a lot of color and interest to a character or a scene.

177

"That is a magnificent woman."
"Yes."

Well, this says nothing about the characters. What if we need more color? We use more colorful words that suit the character.

"Well, damn, that gal is built like a brick shithouse."
"Built like a what?"
Charlie glanced at his companion. "Don't you get plain English?"
"I might, when you start speaking it."

The second example, while using profanity that may not be appropriate for all audiences, contains slang often heard in Renée's neck of the woods. It creates an image of the character speaking that the first example does not. When writing scenes, we often use characters that aren't part of the main plot. To give the reader a good image of who and what they are, we don't have the luxury of using pages and pages to build their characters. This is when the words we choose become critical.

Writers should also consider the intended audience for their material when choosing words. When writing literature, the language might be more convoluted than when writing commercial fiction (not always, but in general). Writing a romance will often mean more words that reflect emotion than we'd use when writing a science fiction novel. We want to choose words sometimes that are forceful, but words that preach a message to the reader.

We should avoid unusual words that force the reader to search a dictionary to find their meanings. These don't give the impression of an intelligent writer with a huge vocabulary. Often, unusual or obscure words are annoying for the reader. Use these words only when there is no other alternative.

"From his pocket he drew a netsuke. This one was old. Albert caressed the little ivory figure that traditional Japanese tucked under the sash of their kimonos."[77]

In using "netsuke," an unusual word, we've added a description. This is not because the reader is dumb, but because we know that some people wouldn't have heard of such a thing before. The description is smooth, fitting into the action. It doesn't talk down to the reader, but explains the strange word.

In the following sections we'll discuss weak forms in our writing. Verbs, nouns, adjectives, and adverbs all have weak forms which are best avoided. We will also look at "look" and "see" words and how to avoid those as well.

 **3.1.8.1 WEAK FORMS**

Substitute "damn" every time you're inclined to write "very;" your editor will delete it and the writing will be just as it should be. Mark Twain

We writers litter our manuscripts with weak forms of verbs and adjectives. By avoiding weak forms, we strengthen the prose. When rewriting, writers should search for certain words to remove outright.

Words to remove include, but are not limited to: "very," "about," "usually," "strange," "beautiful," "handsome," "slowly," "suddenly," "tall," "short," "big," "little," "fat," "thin," "dark," and "light." Removing these will not lose meaning and will tighten the prose in most cases. For example:

---

[77] Carlos J Cortes, Oiran.

Shelly usually felt calm in most situations, but suddenly dark fear overwhelmed her now. Standing on the short ledge she looked down into the little lake. Why did she come here? The handsome stranger behind her counted down very slowly. In ten, nine, eight…she'd jump.

Delete the useless words rather than substitute or elaborate. When we read the prose after doing this, we can see a marked difference.

Shelly felt calm in most situations, but fear overwhelmed her. Standing on the ledge she looked down into the lake. Why did she come here? The stranger behind her counted down. In ten, nine, eight…she'd jump.

The words we've removed had only clutter the prose, nothing more.

Weak Verbs

The difference between a weak verb and a strong one is in how the past tense of the verb forms. Weak verbs (regular verbs) form the past tense by adding ed, d, or t, to the present tense form of the verb. For example, called, walked, and moved are weak. Strong verbs (irregular verbs) form the past tense in a variety of ways, but typically by changing the vowel of the present tense form. For example, gave and stuck are strong verbs.

Irregular verbs are strong because they don't rely on an added ending to form the past tense. Weak verbs must add the "ed" or "d" ending.

In cases where the word we need cannot be expressed with an irregular verb, we look to specific and vivid verbs rather than generalities. For instance, walk, laugh, run, sat, jump, and move are examples of weak verbs. Consider the many synonyms for each of these and the many images that each synonym evokes.

She laughed.

What if she chortled, tittered, sniggered, giggled, cackled or snickered? Every one of these other verbs is stronger than laughed, because each gives a distinct image.

She walked.

She might saunter, limp, swagger, creep, or skip instead.

She ran.

Let's have her bolt, jog, sprint, or gallop, and we'll show much more about her and the scene.

She sat.

Did she just sit, or did she sink, settle, or slouch?

She moved.

Move can be deleted because it offers nothing specific. How did she move? Did she run, leap, fall or slink along the floor? Or perhaps she's moving to a new house, city, or country. We can't be sure with a vague "moved." Find something that shows more than just an indistinct action.

She jumped.

We see her leaping, bounding, or hopping instead.

When rewriting, search for weak verbs and try to replace them with strong verbs. For example:

Weak: Joel walked to the window.
Strong: Joel limped to the window.

Weak: The hairy beast jumped into his lap.
Strong: The hairy beast bounded into the room and onto his lap.

Weak: She ran away.
Strong: She bolted.

Weak Adjectives

As a writer, language is our medium for painting the worlds we've created for our reader. Imagine doing so with only a box of primary colors. This is the dull effect that weak adjectives create. We think we're painting the scene, but some adjectives are so bland, so generic, that they add nothing at all.

"Interesting," "lovely," "beautiful," "bad," "good," "large," "little," "long," "new," "old," "short," "small," "unique," and "black" are just a few empty adjectives that litter our prose, doing nothing except take up space. Sometimes we can leave them, but often, more descriptive choices are needed. Consider the many synonyms for happy: "content," "joyful," "ecstatic," "blissful," "pleased," "merry," "thrilled" and "jubilant;" not to mention "paradisial," "halcyon," "riant," or "felicitous," if one wants to ruin most readers' experience. Any one of these might show more than happy would because these synonyms give the reader an idea of just how happy the character is.

Sometimes a specific adverb or adjective in the right place strengthens or clarifies an image. Many writers, however, in a misguided attempt to make their fiction writing descriptive, overuse these words.

The <u>fragrant liquid</u> tickled her nose, and she sighed <u>happily</u>.

This can be shown with more precise language. Fragrant? What kind of fragrance? Happily? We can do better than that.

The scent of chamomile tickled her nose, and she smiled.

We could expand more still but we've shown what we wanted to without the weak forms. The second example gives us more information. We want adjectives to describe; if they add nothing, they're useless. Many times, strong nouns and verbs will show what the adjective is describing instead.

Weak Nouns

Precise nouns enhance our writing, because they provide the reader with much more than the dictionary meaning. People, places, and things have distinct names in most cases, so we can use those to add description without the clutter of adverbs. For example:

Weak: He gave her a bouquet of brightly colored flowers for their anniversary.
Precise: He gave her a rainbow of roses for their anniversary.

Weak: John gazed at the plane they'd chartered for him.
Precise: John gazed at the crop-duster they'd chartered for him.

Weak: Popping a candy in her mouth, June smiled.
Precise: Popping a gumdrop in her mouth, June smiled.

The precise nouns in these examples give a visual image for the reader, and might also hint at time of year. Certain flowers for example, are hard to find in colder months. A bouquet of roses implies a larger amount of money spent than a bouquet of tulips. In the second example, we don't get an idea of what the plane looks like without going into a long description. "Crop duster" gives more of a visual. It also makes the reader wonder why on earth they'd charter such a plane for this man. Perhaps he works for a company with tight purse strings, or maybe he's in a rural area where the plane is all that's available.

We can read through our manuscript and upgrade weak nouns like "anger," "hate," "body," "death," "end," "face," "girl," "head," "kiss," "life," "love," "man," "time," "way," "woman," and "boy," replacing them with precise nouns that show a clear image.

Empty Adverbs

Empty adverbs have earned a bad rap for all adverbs. Examples of adverbs that add nothing to the prose include, but may not be limited to:

> Actually, totally, absolutely, completely, continually, constantly, continuously, literally, really, unfortunately, ironically, incredibly, hopefully, finally, usually, fairly, considerably

Yes, some writers litter their prose with these and sell zillions, but that's a sign of the times. These writers published despite their careless writing, not because of it. Had circumstances varied by a tiny constraint at the beginning of their careers, luck in particular, the work of these writers would have never seen the light of day.

> About three things I was absolutely positive: first, Edward was a vampire. Second, there was a part of him—and I didn't know how dominant that part might be—that thirsted for my blood. And third, I was unconditionally and irrevocably in love with him.[78]

The prose on the above paragraph was rejected by twelve agents. But for a fluke, it would have been rejected by any other. In our opinion, writers should strive for success on the basis of talent and excellence, not luck.

These and words like them might seem to give more emphasis to a word, but the reverse is true. They take away from the prose, sucking the meaning out of it.

The only area where empty adverbs are appropriate is in dialogue. This is because we do use these in speech. But we must be careful, too many and our characters sound dated. If that's not the goal, writers should limit adverbs in dialogue as well.

On most occasions, we can delete empty adverbs and change nothing else. If we've used a poor choice to modify or strengthen a weak noun or a weak verb, we pick a stronger word instead to do the job instead of combining the two. All of the words we've listed above can be deleted right off when rewriting. Look at the beginning of every sentence to make certain an empty adverb hasn't popped up there.

> Weak: Actually, I've come to see you.
> Strong: I've come to see you.

> Weak: Hopefully he'd meet the strange women again.
> Strong: He hoped to meet the strange women again.

---

[78] Stephenie Meyer, Twilight.

Weak: She literally laughed in his face.
Strong: She laughed in his face.

Some adverbs introduce redundancy, which is not wanted in fiction writing. For example:

She scrubbed her hands vigorously.

Scrubbed implies the intensity on its own. "Vigorously" is redundant.

The sirens blared loudly.

Blared means at a high volume, so "loudly" is redundant.

Mary yawned tiredly.

If she yawns, it is implied that she is tired. The adverb is redundant again here.
Adverbs may also contradict the meaning of the verb or adjective they modify. For example:

She felt slightly sick.

She's either sick or she isn't.

He held a fairly unique statue.

Unique doesn't have degrees. Something is either unique or it isn't. It can't be very unique or fairly unique, just unique by itself.

3.1.8.2 OTHER WEAK FORMS TO LOOK FOR

"Had been" and "could," in particular with any verb ending in "ing" at close quarters, should be inspected and perhaps rewritten to show. These constructions lead to telling.

Lucy had been crying all day.
Better: Lucy cried all day.

Mel could hear music.
Better: Mel heard music.

Traveling down the road, she saw a man approach.
Better: A man approached.

Walking toward her, Michael could see that she'd been crying.
Better: As he approached, she wiped red-rimmed eyes.

Other weak forms we should watch for when rewriting include "after," "all," "and," "another," "before," "went," "but," "down," "however," "just," "only," "that," "up," and "with."

Writers must also search for overuse of the verb "was" and its variations, and rewrite to remove it. For example:

He *was sitting* on the porch while Celia <u>was sleeping</u> on the couch inside.

We want to create a sense of immediate action in our writing, so we need to change "was sitting" and "was sleeping" to an active verb form.

He sat on the porch while Celia slept on the couch inside.

In rewriting this sentence, we've eliminated unnecessary words. Weak forms add extra words to our sentences, which we don't want. Extra words can add up, slowing down the pace and stealing space for more important words like those used to develop plot, scenes, and characters. If we expand our vocabulary beyond vague descriptors and master the use of precise nouns and verbs, we'll avoid using empty adjectives and other intrusive modifiers.

3.1.8.3 "LOOK" AND "EYE" WORDS

"Flashing," "lighting," "darkening," "burning," "lingering," and "dropping" to the floor. Eyes can be busy, can't they? While "gazes" can do a few things, "eyes" are rather boring. New writers overuse words that describe looking or eye movements and impossible actions because they think it adds color or imagery to a scene. Rather, it's an inaccurate distraction.

Among new writers it's not uncommon to find an eye reference in every paragraph, because the tendency is to describe visually, rather than make use of other senses to provide setting. We visualize our stories and play them as movies in our heads, so instinctively we reach for sight words. While facial expressions show much, the looks passed between characters reveal almost nothing to the reader.

He looked at her.

As the writer, we see the look, but the reader cannot. To correct, the writer might plug in one of the other sight words, believing it makes things more clear.

He watched her.

He leered at her.

He stared at her.

He glared at her.

Now is it clear? No, still we see very little. So the writer digs deeper and describes what the eyes are doing.

His eyes blazed.

He looked at her, his eyes full of hatred.

His eyes burned.

His eyes darkened.

Now the writer has created clichés that in no way represent what eyes really do. This doesn't clarify the expression because, unless we're showing a scene where his eyes are dry and we're in his POV, we can't know his eyes burn as a result. They can't burn when looking at someone else. They also can't drop, or the character is in big trouble. It is the face around the eyes that holds the expression. Telling the reader his eyes are full of hatred is a lazy way to tell her how the character feels.

While a couple of these are handy now and then, as a gaze or a brief glance can mean a lot in a particular scene, having these eye movements every paragraph, even every other paragraph, diminishes the effect of such moments. It becomes comical and reads amateurish at best.

When rewriting, we search out "eye" words to see how many time the eyes have been acting crazy and doing all sorts of impossible things. For example:

Look Words

Glance, ogle, gaze, study, see, survey, peek, leer, notice, watch, stare, scan, glare, and eyeball.

Eye Words

Flash, burn, linger, travel, darken, brighten, drop, bulge, roam, and blink.

These words should be removed, and the sentence or moment must be rewritten to show the emotion instead of making the eyes tell the reader about it. Writers must examine each line. When we see "eye" and "look" words, we try to make our eyes do the action we're describing them doing. If it is physically impossible, remove it. Use another way to show the emotion or expression. For example:

> Don't: He ogled her.
> Do: He enjoyed the way her bottom jiggled with each step.

> Don't: Her eyes flashed.
> Do: Pressing her lips into a thin line, she ripped the key from his hand.

In the first example, we show what we mean by ogle. We determine what is happening within the scene and use that to show that he's ogling her. In the second, her flashing eyes indicate anger, but eyes cannot flash. On rewrite, we show her anger through action instead.

When we find an eye or look reference, including raised and furrowed eyebrows, we try to find a better way to reveal the thoughts and emotions of the characters without using the eyes. Gestures and dialogue reveal far more and can be infinitely more powerful than a burning stare.

We must end this section with a health warning: Too much "activity" may injure the health of your novel. We've edited works that used the variety rule to excess. Nobody ever just laughed. They chortled or tittererd, sniggered, and snickered. And when we consider these are often tags or attributes to dialogue, if overused they can distract from the meaning and irritate. To an extent "weak verbs" have similar strengths to the *invisible* "said." The inexperienced writer may be tempted to insert an inappropriate "laugh word" to a character and ruin it. Conan the Barbarian wouldn't "snigger" or "titter." Writing is an art, and measure a virtue. We shouldn't go overboard on "strong" verbs, nouns, or adjectives, but we should gauge their effect on the overall musicality of sentences and paragraphs.

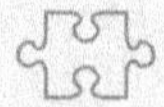 **3.1.9 GENERAL EDITING**

First drafts contain many errors, but the simplest ones are often overlooked. We've eliminated the telling, removed icky adverbs, and tightened our POV. We've done all the fun stuff that is required when editing. What could we have forgotten?

We suggest that, after editing for the obvious things, writers go through the manuscript once again and ask the following questions:

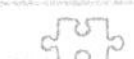

Is the writing simple and straightforward?

This means that we say what we want to in the most direct and clear way possible. We avoid long words when shorter ones are available and we don't clutter the prose with adjectives, adverbs, and metaphors. It's tempting to weigh the narrative down with elaborate descriptions, but good writers resist this urge and remove what isn't necessary.

Have we overused expressions and cliché words?

If the writing contains babies being thrown out with the bathwater, reaping and sowing, needles in haystacks or clichés along the same vein, we delete them. We want the prose to be unique and distinct, and clichés do not do this. Search for the most commonly used clichés such as:

He saw the writing on the wall.

Don't cry over spilled milk.

Better late than never.

Thinking outside of the box.

At the end of the day...

The bottom line is...

Rocket science

Easy as 123 or pie.[79]

Smart as a whip or dumb as a stump.

Sharp as a tack.

Like taking candy from a baby.[80]

Love/hate makes the world go round.

Selling/Going like hotcakes.

In the nick of time.

When life gives you lemons...

What goes up must come down.

The sharpest knife in the drawer/handiest tool in the shed/brightest bulb.

Everything but the kitchen sink.

Used with flair, a cliché phrase or two may be just the right addition. We can use them for effect in characterization or dialogue, but we should avoid clichés that are not well chosen.

---

[79] This cliché is wrong, wrong, wrong. Pie is not easy. Perhaps we get the filling right, but making the perfect crust is very difficult. We've tried and failed every time.

[80] This is also quite meaningless, because if ever we have the opportunity to try to take a sucker or a piece of chocolate from a baby, we'll discover it is not such an easy task.

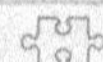 

Is the tense consistent?

Check the tense throughout the story. Make sure verbs agree with the tense chosen. For example:

Present tense: She creeps along the wall. Her fingers touched the chipped masonry.

"Touched" isn't a present tense verb. We should have used "touch" here instead.

Past tense: She crept along the wall. Her fingers touch the chipped masonry.

Here, "touch" should be "touched." It reads simple, but often these mistakes are overlooked because we see on the page what we know we should see in our minds, in particular after several revisions. While we're at it, we should endeavor to check that the tense we've chosen makes sense to our story. In other words, could the story be better if written in past tense instead of present (or vice versa)?

 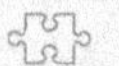

Are there any echoes?

Sometimes writers repeat a word or a phrase because we want to create a certain effect. When rewriting, we should check how often we do this, and determine if it really does do what we want it to. It's easily overdone and when we've used this too often in a single manuscript, it loses effectiveness.

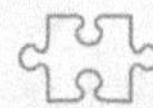

3.1.10 OTHER ERRORS

3.1.10.1 STYLE

Style errors are overlooked because, hey, it's style. That's personal and unique isn't it?

Style is how writers use words and sentences. It's also the tense we choose to write in and the POV. What makes a good style versus a bad style? This is subjective, but we can try to write so that our style of writing suits the story. The least obtrusive writing is the best writing. The reader must stay interested in <u>what</u> is being said, not <u>how</u> it is being said. Common style errors include:

Incorrect Tone

The level of formality in our tone will depend on the characters and type of story we are telling. Informal is personal, simple, and active. Sentences are shorter than with a formal tone. We use contractions and slang occasionally, but we still pay attention to proper grammar and punctuation. A formal tone is more impersonal, and reserved for academic papers and research articles. Formal writing uses more passive voice, and writers using this tone use a more complex vocabulary and longer sentences. For example, a scene depicting a courtroom hearing would require a formal tone while a scene depicting teenagers hanging at the mall would be informal.

Too Much Passive Voice

Eliminate passive voice in fiction unless it is necessary. We check the manuscript to ensure all sentences are active. For example:

Passive: The man was hit by the ball.

Active: The ball hit the man.

Passive: Joanie was meeting her friends at the mall.
Active: Joanie met her friends at the mall.

Passive: The gun has been hidden by the culprit.
Active: The culprit hid the gun.

Passive: Her hair was brushed.
Active: She brushed her hair.

Unclear Words or Sentences

Use simple and concise words and sentences. No matter what our tone, be it formal or informal, writers should use clear sentences and words so that the reader is neither struggling to keep up nor bored to tears. When a short, familiar word is available, we use it. When we can state something in four words rather than ten, we should. Sometimes, writers use phrases like "the fact that," "in regards to," or "because of." If we see these in our prose, we know we've written something convoluted.

Wordy: She fell because of his shoes lying in the hall.
Better: She fell over his shoes.

Wordy: Due to the fact that Joe's mother hated dogs, he'd never had a pet.
Better: Joe's mother wouldn't allow pets.

Wordy: Her call was in regards to his behavior the night before.
Better: She called to discuss his behavior.

Empty Modifiers

We don't need words like "very," "quite," or "fairly" because they add nothing to the prose besides clutter, which is annoying for the reader. This is a style error made by many writers who believe the words give the reader a better image of what they're describing. When words like these pop up in our prose, we rewrite, using a stronger modifier. For example, instead of "very big" try "huge" or "massive." In most cases, we can delete the empty modifiers and lose nothing.

Improper Word Usage

Readers notice when writers use confusing words, and use them wrong. In section 4.5.1 we list commonly confused words and the correct usage. If we are unsure of a word's usage or meaning, we must either delete it or find out the proper way to use it. This includes synonyms. The thesaurus is not always a writer's best friend. Using the thesaurus to find ten ways to say the same word, is not clever unless we understand the word we're using. For example:

Her lustrous brown eyes sparkled.

We agree this sentence is overwritten, but let's just play along. Lustrous has several synonyms which include "shiny," "glossy," "gleaming," "radiant," "shimmering," "glistening," and "effulgent." In this case, let's say we used lustrous already to describe her hair, so we need another word to describe her brown eyes. Some writers might look at this list and think that "effulgent" surely won't be a common word, so why not use that? First, the reader might not have heard it. Even if she has, the problem is that "effulgent" reeks of showing off. Have we ever used the word in our lives until this point? How can we know we're using it in the right context?

We don't use "effulgent" for these reasons. If we're struggling to find a synonym for a certain word, we should reconsider using it. Maybe there's another way to show what we're trying to show in that particular sentence. In this case, why not just remove "lustrous?" Does it change anything? No.

Wrong POV

When we look at the POV we've chosen, we look at both the POV of the story (first, third, or omniscient) and the characters we've chosen to tell the story. Are they best suited to the story we're writing? We want the story to grab the reader at once, and the wrong POV can affect how easily the reader can slip into the world we've created. For example:

First Person:

> I walked to the car, my keys ready, and I heard her call. Good God, could the woman not just leave me alone? I turned, waiting for her to emerge from the shadows. She always hid in the shadows, creepy witch.

Third Person Limited/John's POV:

> John held his keys, ready to get in his car. Behind him Gertrude called. Good God, the woman never left him alone. He turned, searching the shadows. Gertrude always hid in the shadows.

Third Person Limited/Gertrude's POV:

> John emerged from his house, keys in his hand, and strode to his car. He lifted his hand to the lock, and Gertrude called to him. His shoulders slumped and he turned. She covered her mouth to suppress a giggle. He made it too easy.

Which shows the story better? Hard to tell in such brief examples, but it depends on the story. Who is the protagonist? If it is John, does including a scene in Gertrude's POV furthers the plot and moves the story forward? We want to use the POV that is going to do something for the story.

Style is personal for each writer and manifests as a unique voice in our work. What we must ensure when rewriting is that the style we're using isn't clunky or telling (as in not engaging for the reader) and that it produces a smooth well paced story easy for the reader to follow.

3.1.10.2 NAMES

We sometimes forget that the names we choose for our characters can affect the story. While character names aren't as critical as components—like plot—we shouldn't just pull them out of a hat without consideration. Avoid trying to be cute or clever because, in most cases, it has the opposite effect. For example, family names that sound the same but are spelled differently are not recommended. These create confusion for the reader. Naming a woman Jeanne and her husband Jean, is a definite no-no. When rewriting, we should examine the names we've chosen and look for a few common errors.

Names that don't match the setting

Hayley or Porche don't fit in a story written in 17th century Scotland. These names weren't used in that country at that time, so our story would lack accuracy. When naming our characters, we must consider the time and the place of the story. Writers who base their stories in modern times don't face this problem as often as historical writers do, but nationality, time period, and culture should weigh when choosing names for our novels.

Difficult to Pronounce

Readers often mention that names they find hard to pronounce are annoying. Indeed, try to read a book with a name like Srinivasan (See-reen-ee-vaza) for the protagonist. Every time the reader sees this name, she stops, tries to pronounce it, and this pulls her from the story. Even if the reader chooses to ignore it, each time she reads it, the annoyance flares again. We want the names to be memorable, but not for the wrong reasons. If the story is set in a foreign country or another time where we must use uncommon names, we should try to write the pronunciation somewhere in the story. Perhaps someone calls the character by the wrong name, and he corrects them. Another option is to use the full name once, and quickly incorporate a nickname for the remainder of the story, which is a lot of work for a simple name when we can choose one the reader can pronounce.

Rhyming Names

Bill, his wife Jill, and their children Dill, Phil, and Will are the central characters in a novel. The reader sees this and sighs. Not another cute and clever little writer bent on naming the characters so that they all rhyme—even if it is realistic at times. We don't want the reader rolling her eyes at our naming attempts. She can't read if her eyes are busy rolling.

Try to avoid using names that rhyme. First, it creates an echo in the prose. Second, the reader may be forced to pause and reread to ensure she's thinking of the right character. In the interest of clarity, writers should use names that sound different from other characters. The reader can keep track instead of pausing to find out. Using different names also eliminates the possibility that the writer will mistakenly write Dill instead of Bill in a love scene with Jill, which would create an entirely different story.

Common Names

It's good advice to stick to common names for characters. Common names tend to blend into the story much like using "said" as a dialogue tag. Such names become invisible for the reader. For a protagonist, this isn't a problem because "Bob Smith" is in nearly every scene. No chance of the reader forgetting Bob Smith. But for secondary characters, like Bob's mother-in-law, we want something a bit more memorable, especially if she floats in and out of the story. Perhaps her name is Zena or Roberta, names the reader easily links to her. If we have characters that appear in scene two, and then disappear until scene forty or fifty, we should give those characters more memorable names so the reader doesn't have to wonder where the heck they came from.

Wrong Meaning

Sometimes writers choose names for characters that are opposite to their personality in meaning. Consider the name Belle. We see images of beauty and youth with that name. The name itself means beautiful and it's often used to refer to an attractive woman. "Belle of the ball" or "Southern Belle" come to mind when we see it. Suppose we give an old hag the name. She's got a wart on her nose and three teeth scattered in her gaping mouth. While this is sometimes clever, writers must remember the odd pairing of a name like Belle with a character like this will cause the reader to pause each time it's used in reference to ugliness.

Recycling Names

We've all recycled names before, and in most, cases it's okay. However, if a writer recycles the same name in each story it will be noticed. When naming, we should ensure that our protagonists always have a different name from the previous protagonists. If our works are published, someone (several someones) will note that our male lead is always named Jake, Jacob, or Jack. We may think the reader will find it quirky and fun, but it's more likely the reader will see a lazy writer who can't be bothered to come up with original names.

Names that begin or end with the same letter or sound

For the starring roles, writers should use names that are different in pronunciation and spelling. Consider a cast named Rick, Roger, Randy, and Rosie. Although the writer might not see it, the "R" appearing so often becomes confusing for the reader, and we end up with the same problem we had with rhyming names. Alternately, look at how each character's name ends. Jason and Jackson are easily confused, as are Carrie and Mary. Avoid repeating vowel sounds as well. In Janie, Bailey, Cory, Lori, Murphy, the long "e" sound echoes and can be annoying for a reader. We want the characters to stand out as individuals, and any similarity in names leads to their blending in the reader's mind.

What is the perfect name? There isn't one. What we name our characters depends on the character and the story we're telling. Although naming might seem the most trivial part of writing our novel, errors can affect the entire story. We recommend getting one of those handy little books of baby's names. Many of these books separate names by gender and origin and include meanings for each. They also include information on the most popular or common names by time period. Several websites also list the same information with a larger database. This means you can simply enter the information you're looking for, such as girl's names common in the 1960's, and a list of names will appear.

When we've selected the names, checked that they are all unique, no rhymes, echoes, or weird spellings, we ensure that we've picked a name and stuck with it. For example, Renée has a terrible tendency in first drafts to call her characters by several names. In her novel *In the Bones*, the villain, Carroll Albert, is referred to as Carroll, Albert, and the Reeve. This is littered through the rough draft like she'd forgotten his name. Writers don't need to use synonyms to substitute character names. It's not clever, it doesn't eliminate echoes, and it makes things more confusing for the reader. For example:

> She hugged her knees to her chest, unable to move from her spot on the floor in front of her counter. The memory of what the Reeve would do if he thought she might not be loyal had haunted her dreams for many years, long after her parents died and she could have left.

Audrey snorted, blinking away the tears that threatened to spill. Like she could have left, despite what she'd told Ryan. She was tied to this place as much as anyone else. She might not have taken money from Albert, but she turned her head to everyone who had, and the things Carroll asked them to do in payment for his generosity.

Who are we talking about? In this passage Carroll is described three ways: the Reeve, Carroll, and Albert. Rewritten, it reads much better.

> She hugged her knees to her chest, unable to move from her spot on the floor in front of her counter. The memory of what Carroll Albert would do if he thought his spouse might not be loyal had haunted her dreams for many years, long after her parents died and she could have left.
> Audrey snorted, blinking away the tears that threatened to spill. Like she could have left, despite what she'd told Ryan. She was tied to this place as much as anyone else. She might not have taken money from Carroll, but she turned her head to everyone who had, and the things he asked them to do in payment for his generosity.[81]

Unless we're using the name three times in a single sentence (and if we are, we should examine that sentence) we never use a substitute for the character's name just to vary the sound.

Character names become invisible to the reader and the use of a synonym or nickname draws attention to it. Again, just as "said" is invisible when tagging dialogue, names should be distinct but invisible as well. The reader shouldn't need to pause to figure out who we're talking about. Beyond using "he" or "she," we use nothing other than the character's name.

---

[81] Renée Miller, In the Bones.

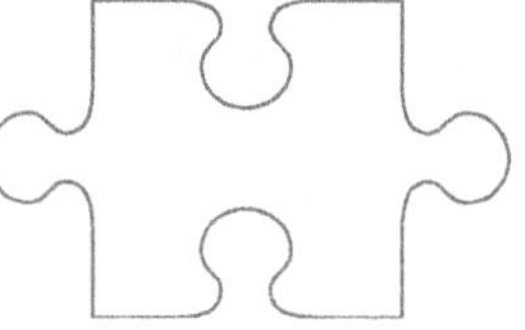

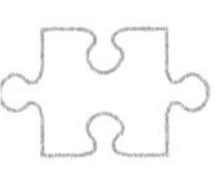

3.2 REVISION

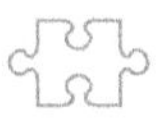

3.2.1 SELF EDITING

What is an editor? Editors are professionals of the highest order, a writer's best friend. The work they do isn't just about correcting spelling errors and chasing down rogue commas. An editor can revise our manuscript, checking for scores of unrelated errors on a single pass. Best of all, a good editor *will find* those errors.

As the editor reads, he addresses grammar, style, syntax, voice, POV, continuity, repetitions, pace, usage, and many other issues. We lesser mortals must plod, checking one item or a set of related items at each pass.

Novice writers sometimes ask: Then why not just send the draft to the editor? Because we should never waste their time and efforts. Writers must polish their manuscripts to the best of their ability before submitting. The same is true before sending the manuscript to first-line readers. Having to stop at every other line to repair typos, grammar and syntax errors, missing words, etc., stresses readers to such an extent they can't to concentrate on plot, continuity, story flow, pace, and characterization, which is what we want from our indefatigable beta readers. As our colleague Wendy Swore once aptly remarked "...it would be like showing your filthy kitchen to your friends, while asking them to pretend it's not covered in vomit. Clean up your mess first. Then show it."

To prepare a manuscript for readers, it's critical to do a good line edit. The readers will suggest all kinds of changes, and yes, we'll have to edit again, but the second pass will require less work because we've already taken care of the many bits with our line edits.

Once we receive the manuscript back from our readers, littered with all kinds of graffiti if we're lucky, we must weigh each suggestion and address it accordingly. Then it's the time to tackle the final edit to end up with a polished manuscript that is suitable for an editor's eye.

Thus, the procedure is:

●   **Write the first draft**

This is writing at full tilt. We don't pay attention to anything beyond getting the story on paper. Of course, obvious errors we'll correct along the way, but we don't backtrack or pause. We simply write.

●   **Let it rest**

This is the hardest part, leaving our baby alone for at least a week. We work on a new project, write a synopsis and a query, paint our toenails or twiddle our mustache while pondering another outline. We do not even glance at the draft during this time.

Read and annotate

After a week we pull our beloved out and read, making notes on changes, problems, etc. No changes just yet. Just read and make note of issues, errors, plot inconsistencies, areas we want to add to or remove and why—and when we're done, the real work begins.

Rewrite

We now address each note we made on the read-through and make any changes necessary to improve plot, continuity, etc.

Let it rest

By this point our toenails and mustaches are a mess while a new project simmers in our minds. We set aside the manuscript once more and work on something else. Again, we don't even glance at the manuscript for at least a week.

Read and tweak

The week has passed and we pick it up again. This time we read each page and tweak issues such as spelling, grammar, tightening POV, etc.

First edit

Then the real fun begins. Line edits. We go through the manuscript from the end to the beginning. We'll explain the reason behind the reverse order in the following sections.

Beta readers

We now bundle our darling and send it off to readers for feedback. Beta readers are crucial to the editing process. Writers need this feedback to properly edit things we either can't see or refuse to see. We'll discuss beta readers in more detail later.

Address reader's suggestions

When we receive the readers' feedback, we address every comment. Some, we might think are silly, but still, make a note. If more than one reader makes the same comment, or one along a similar vein, we consider the comment—no matter how silly it seems—more seriously.

Final edit

Once we've addressed the readers' suggestions, we make a final pass. Clean up the prose, correct formatting, punctuation, and anything that isn't polished and perfect.

Fireworks and bubbly

We're done. Break out the bubbly, light some fireworks, and celebrate. Time to start looking for a home for our baby.

In the following sections we'll address each step in more detail.

3.2.1.1 LINE EDIT

Line edits are a massive undertaking and possibly the most intimidating step when rewriting our draft. We've heard many writers claim it's not necessary, that's for the editor to worry about. Those writers are wrong. The line edit finds many errors we wouldn't ordinarily see. Publishers want a ready-to-read manuscript, and without a line edit we don't even come close to that.

To begin, we start at the end; at the very last sentence. Why? We know what we've written, so if we begin with the first sentence, our brains fall into the rhythm of what we've read over and over and ignore possible errors. *It* knows what comes next, and *it* knows what *should* be there. Starting with the last sentence enables us to see the words clearly.

One sentence at a time we examine it, search for grammar, syntax, beginnings, ends, dangling modifiers, comma splices, fused sentences, sentence length and construction variety, vocabulary variety. Address each sentence in isolation.

Once we've done this, we begin a list. Even the best editors cannot edit without a list and often their list spans several pages. Typically, a page is given per letter of the alphabet. Then we note words beginning on page one. Which words? Repeated words, unusual words, misused words, etc. Then beside the words, we note the pages on which they appear.

On a separate page, we list character names, and next to those names, we list eye color, hair color, age, build, and any distinctive features. Beside all of that, we list the page where the detail is mentioned.

We're not done yet. Next we list places, dates, addresses, makes of car, unusual words, foreign words, and anything that may be later mistaken.

When finished, we'll have pages and pages of issues. If we don't, then we've done it wrong and must begin again. Using these lists, we address and correct the errors found. For example, we might find we've cited someone as fourteen years old on page 12, and on page 232 he's suddenly eleven years old. Strange things happen from the moment we begin to write. We change our minds about elements in the story, we pause for a period of time and come back, and although we try to be thorough, we miss minor issues like someone's age, or how often we've used a particular word.

This seems rather involved and possibly unnecessary, but it's useful. Carlos happens to be an attentive self-editor. When his novel *Perfect Circle* was edited, he received with his original manuscript no fewer than thirty pages of issues to address. For example, he used one unusual word on seven pages. No matter how attentive we are, there will be things we miss. The line-edit and the list cuts down those missed errors significantly.

We recommend using a spreadsheet to make the list, but if mastering MS Excel or other similar programs is beyond the writer's patience or abilities, pen and paper work just as well.

Some common problems to look for first:

Contractions vs. possessives and sound-alikes, such as:

It's/Its	They're /Their/There
Who's/Whose	You're/Your
There's/Theirs	Let's/Lets

Hint: Possessive pronouns never use apostrophes, so if you've used one, make sure you're intending to use a contraction and not show possession. Another common mistake is to use an apostrophe for plural forms. Search for these as well.

● Overworked Sentences

Look at each sentence to determine whether it contains enough or too much. Don't expect too much from a single sentence. Shorter sentences are ideal because they don't ask a lot from the reader; they're clear and concise (if written properly). If we find words like <u>that</u>, <u>however</u>, <u>because</u>, <u>or,</u>, and <u>as</u>, and <u>while</u>, it's likely we have a sentence that should be shortened or rewritten to make more than one sentence.

> <u>Overworked:</u> If Matt couldn't find the key, all would be lost because the key unlocked the future, and without the future, what did mankind have to look forward to?

> <u>Better:</u> If Matt couldn't find the key, all would be lost. The key unlocked the future. Without the future, what did mankind have to look forward to?

Three sentences. Three ideas. The sentence isn't hard to digest when it is broken down into simpler ideas. However, sometimes we don't let one sentence do enough and spread one idea through several, risking too much repetition in sentence structure.

> <u>Underworked:</u> She ran. She pumped her legs until they burned. She had to get to the castle.

> <u>Better:</u> Pumping her legs until they burned, she ran toward the castle.

● Dangling Modifiers

"Dashing to the door, the phone rang in the background."

The phone dashed to the door? As we discuss in section 4.2, the first part of the sentence is the dependent clause, and it must have the same subject as the independent clause in the second part. This sentence should be rewritten to avoid the dangling modifier.

> Better: "As he dashed to the door, the phone rang."

● Punctuation

Missing periods, misplaced commas, open quotes, and all kinds of strange punctuation can squeak past our eyes on the first revision. When we line edit, we examine each sentence and make sure we've crossed every T and dotted each I. In other words, we fix any punctuation mistakes we find.

● Overusing weak words

Most writers tend to favor certain words, many of them weak. Often, writers use "maybe," "so," "just," "that," "move," "walk," "well," and "like." We don't intend to, but they creep in anyway. (Anyway is another weak word we can search for). When line editing, make note of weak words from the beginning, and each time you see those words, note the page number. When we've finished, we'll see how often we use certain words so we can correct them.

 **3.2.1.2 REPETITIONS**

Repetitions are not bad when done for effect. If the writer has repeated words on purpose and with good reason, then a repeated word is not an error.

> "... he kissed me under the Moorish wall and I thought well as well him as another and then I asked him with my eyes to ask again <u>yes</u> and then he asked me would I <u>yes</u> to say <u>yes</u> my mountain flower and first I put my arms around him <u>yes</u> and drew him down to me so he could feel my breasts all perfume <u>yes</u> and his heart was going like mad and <u>yes</u> I said <u>yes</u> I will <u>Yes</u>." [82]

The repetition of "yes" in this passage creates a breathtaking effect. Each time we read "yes" we aren't distracted, but drawn into the emotion of the moment and Molly's speech., and no, we've not made a mistake; the original is orphaned of punctuation. Some more examples of necessary repetition are:

> He touched his finger to his nose. A nose that had experienced many a fist.

> Jacob traced her lips with his tongue, and her lips warmed.

> She walked on the grass. Grass that would never be the same because her bare feet had touched it.

We mention in section 3.1.10.2 that with names, sometimes repetition is necessary. In these cases, we examine the repetition, determine that it must be repeated and leave it alone. It's silly to refer to the same person as Mr. Jones, Professor Jones, the professor, the speaker, and James Jones. In these cases we'd use either he or the name we've given him. Use one name and stick to it.

The problem we're looking for with repetition is when it is unintentional. We search the manuscript for too many articles, or crutch words, or the same adjective at close quarters. There is a wonderful program called Repetition Detector at:

http://www.freewarefiles.com/Repetition-Detector_program_34904.html

This program will cut down a writer's editing time. We still must search the document to ensure we've covered them all. Names used like we've just discussed won't show on the detector, but we recommend writers use this program when editing.

3.2.1.3 CONTINUITY

We've tossed this term around several times now, so let's explore it a bit more. Continuity in writing refers to how we order events and facts to make them consistent. Any issues in continuity can ruin a good novel. For example, perhaps a young woman's hair is short in the first description given, but later the writer shows her flipping it over her shoulder. What? How? These are things the reader will remember, whether they're major details, or tiny slips.

---

[82] James Joyce, Ulysses.

Continuity flaws are not for the new writer alone to worry about. Every writer makes mistakes. Consider that as we write our story—becoming more and more involved in the plot—characters, and such, the chances we'll slip here and there increase with each page, with each new character or event. Problems arise in positions, dialogue, and actions. We don't see them because we're engrossed in the world we're creating.

This is where our list, the one we make while line editing, is vital. We list small details about characters as well as the large ones. We'll see the slips at once, and because we list page numbers beside these items, we can quickly correct them. We also list events, whether characters are involved or not, to track them and determine if we've made any errors in the timeline.

For example, on page 34, they're approaching Christmas. A character says she can't wait to see her son's face next week when he opens his present. Strangely, the event does not occur on stage, as though Christmas is forgotten. This is a continuity error. Another more likely example occurs when we begin a scene with a character tossing his alarm clock across the room. He hates early mornings. He gets up, dresses, chats with the paperboy, and eats breakfast. His neighbor across the road waves, the setting sun casting a golden halo around his head.

How can the sun be setting already? When line editing, we write each event, no matter how insignificant, into our list.

Singulars and plurals

Watch out for subject-verb disagreement in singular and plural forms as well. Sometimes writers either forget or confuse them, maybe by adding in an extra subject and forgetting the verb is singular, but readers notice. Even if readers don't know what they notice, they feel the disjointed effect.

> No: My aunt and my grandmother is crazy.
> Yes: My aunt and my grandmother are crazy.
> Or: My aunt or my grandmother is crazy.

> No: Joe's feet is planted on the ground.
> Yes: Joe's feet are planted on the ground.

> No: She sleep in the car.
> Yes: She sleeps in the car.

Spelling

Fiction writers often make up names, towns, streets, and countries when creating our make-believe worlds. It's easy to pick up an alternate spelling partway through the manuscript and then to switch back to the original spelling.

> Carroll/Carol
>
> Catherine/Katherine
>
> Jerry/Gerry/Geri
>
> Rachel/Rachael
>
> Mary/Marie/Marry

When editing, we must use our lists with names we've used and how we've described the characters. We spot the inconsistencies in spelling by checking subsequent references to these characters against our previous notes.

Autonomous Body Parts

These errors are common. However, a part of the body cannot act alone, unless it's a horror story and a possessed limb terrorizes a small town somewhere. The characters must lift their hands, dart their gazes, and stand on their tiptoe. Body parts should not move without the character making them do so. The images given to the reader with autonomous parts acting up all over the place can be horrific, or funny. In most cases, it's not good for the writer. For example:

Horrific: Her eyes dropped.
Correct: She lowered her gaze.

Horrific: His feet stomped away.
Correct: He stomped away.

Horrific: Her lips smacked.
Correct: She smacked her lips.

Horrific: His fingers tangled in her hair.
Correct: He tangled his fingers in her hair.

Cause before Effect

Sometimes we unintentionally put an effect before the cause, or a reaction before an action. This is easy to spot if we search for words like "when," "as," "before," "during," "while," "until," "after," and "since." These words often signal that we've made a syntactical error and put the sequence of events in the wrong order. When we find these, flip the phrases so that the events happen as they should and the continuity is improved.

Incorrect: Cheryl froze when the doorbell rang.

Correct: The doorbell rang. Cheryl froze.

Incorrect: The dog barked as the mailman walked up the step.

Correct: The mailman approached the step and the dog barked.

Incorrect: Bob answered the ringing phone.

Correct: The phone rang. Bob answered.

These are small slips, but they're a big deal when the reader notices them, *and she will.*

3.2.1.4 DATA

The make of a car, historical events, distances, times, or movies and television shows we've included in our story might pose problems later on. Editing for data errors can only be done with our lists. Why? It's impossible to track all of these, and we really don't want to pause in editing, look up what we've written, and then go back to editing, do we?

In her novel, *I Do… and other Lies we Tell,* Renée described a vehicle, a beaten up old rust bucket of a truck that a despicable character named Warren drove. The problem? The color of the truck's interior was impossible. The manufacturer didn't use anything remotely close to the color she'd given in the initial description. How did she realize this? She made her list. Under "descriptions" she'd written "Warren's Truck" and its description. Later, when checking back through the list, she researched Dodge trucks made in1966, and found to her dismay, that Dodge didn't make this color interior until much later. Because she'd written in her list the other pages she'd mentioned the truck's interior, she was able to correct every entry.

Data cannot be edited without using a list of some sort. We cannot catch or track all of the data contained in a manuscript without a reference.

Make note of travel, timelines, distances, dates, figures, factual information, and names. Editors will check these things, and whether we've misrepresented facts by error or simply didn't bother to check, our editor won't be impressed. We must edit basic information ourselves.

For example, our character must drive from Alberta to Ontario. Let's say we have him drive the distance in a day. It is physically impossible for anyone to drive that distance in a single day. The distance from Edmonton (in Alberta) to Toronto (in Ontario) is over 2,800 kilometers. If we factor in the speed limit of most Canadian highways, which is between 80 and 100 kilometers per hour, and we're looking at a minimum driving time of twenty-eight hours, this means driving round the clock. No rest, no breaks for gas, bathrooms, or food. Odds are no one would or could do this.

When we include items like this, we must make notes and check our data to ensure it is accurate.

Another example:

A child is watching the television in 1982. He's eating his Cheerios while engrossed in the radical antics of the Teenage Mutant Ninja Turtles, as he does every morning. We vaguely remember the eighties and the Ninja Turtles were really popular. Right? Nope. He can't be watching them in 1982, because the cartoon didn't appear on television until the late eighties. We remembered the correct decade, but the minor detail of the specific has made our data incorrect.

In settings that are current, we must be sure we're just as accurate. Of course, we know what's on television now, and which manufacturer makes what. After all, we see these things daily. Mistakes are still possible. Perhaps our character has stolen an electric blue Hummer H3 right off the car lot. It's a brand spanking new 2010 model. Well, that would be great, and we hope he doesn't get caught, but the Hummer H3 2010 line isn't factory-produced in electric blue. Nope. One might be able to order such an animal or have one repainted that color, but off the lot we'll get shades of black, red, white, green, silver, and an "all-terrain blue" which resembles a very dark shade of blue, but not electric blue. These small details seem meaningless and might not be noticed by some readers, but we guarantee someone will notice. Will it ruin the story? Maybe not, but too many data errors will undermine our writing and make readers believe we're either lazy or not very bright.

When editing for setting, we list dates along with setting descriptions and locations. November in a southern state like Florida would be rather pleasant, while in New York it would be on the chilly side. We'd describe these settings in several ways, and the characters living in these locations would wear different clothing and participate in disparate activities.

We also check our facts to make sure we haven't fallen victim to clichés or stereotypes. For example, Canada is not snowbound everywhere, and it's not cold year round. Each province's climate is different at different times of the year, just as it is in America. If we're writing a story set in British Columbia, the climate is much different than what we'd find in Quebec. Similarly, while it rains often in parts of England, it doesn't mean that every day should include a thunderstorm. We make note of these little bits and research to make sure we've accurately described the setting.

 **3.2.1.5 INDIVIDUAL WORDS**

Finding words that indicate passive constructions, terminations, hyphens, weak verbs, and such is a tedious job but a necessary one. To list every one of them is also tedious, so we won't ask writers to do that. Instead we use the "Find" feature under the "Edit" menu. We punch in each of the words we have listed along the way and then click "Find all," and the program will highlight each time we've used the word. Let's say we begin with one of the usual suspects and type in "was". We scroll through and examine each use of the word and rewrite to eliminate it whenever possible. Then we type in the next word, and do the same. For adverbs, it's even easier. We just type in "ly," and the handy little function highlights every word that includes "ly" for us. We examine each one again and correct when we can.

  **Look for the word "that." We can often delete ninety-five percent without losing meaning**

Don't: He sank into the chair that faced the window.
Do: He sank into the chair facing the window.

Don't: Bob told me that you hated me.
Do: Bob told me you hated me.

Don't: Catherine pulled out the book that he'd given her.
Do: Catherine pulled out the book he'd given her.

  **Search for to her, to him, for her, for him, at her, at him, etc. These are often implied and can be deleted. Prepositional phrases placed at the end of a sentence weaken it**

Don't: Following the trail, she realized he'd never come back to her.
Do: Following the trail, she realized he'd never come back.

Don't: Mike stared at him.
Do: Mike stared.

  **Evaluate each "ly" adverb we find and try to replace it with a stronger verb**

Weak: She leaned to his ear and spoke softly.
Strong: She leaned close and whispered.

Weak: The maid raked the brush through her impossibly tangled hair.
Strong: The maid raked the brush through her tangled hair.

 **"Seemed to," "tried to," "began to," and "started to" weaken our prose. When we see these, we delete and use the simple past tense of the verb to make the sentence active** 

Weak: Julie's face seemed to crinkle.
Active: Julie's face crinkled.

Weak: He tried to begin the story again.
Active: He began the story again.

Weak: Mark started to run.
Active: Mark ran.

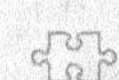 **Search for all uses of the word "eye" and if it refers to an action an eye makes. We replace "eye" with the word "gaze"** 

Incorrect: Her eyes dropped to the floor.
Correct: Her gaze dropped to the floor.

When we're using "eyes" to describe their color or state, then we can leave it.

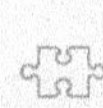 **Avoid using the word "it" too often as a subject. In most cases, we can strengthen the sentence by replacing vague pronouns with strong nouns** 

Example: It sapped all of her energy just to walk up the stairs.
Better: The climb up the stairs sapped her energy.

Example: It was nice to see him.
Better: She enjoyed seeing him.

Weak verbs are rampant in many rough drafts. Search for the following and replace with a more visual verb to make the action stronger 

Move, push, pull, press, bring, brought, reach, went, came

Sometimes, as in the case of "reach," we don't need the word at all. Search and replace or delete common words 

Check beginning interjections such as "oh" and "well" and make sure the comma is present 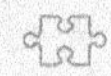

Well, I wanted to go, but he didn't ask.
Oh, you're in trouble.

 **Watch out for telling verbs** 

Watch for weak verbs like "saw," "watched," "heard," "thought," "felt," "knew," "moved," and "reached." These are often unnecessary and tend to pull the reader away from the present story. Telling phrases that include these words can be rewritten so that they're no longer redundant.

3.2.2 TIMELINE

A timeline is the sequence of chronological events, past, present, and future, which will affect our story. We create a timeline when revising our manuscript, to ensure that our times, dates, ages, and events occur as they should and there are no inconsistencies in the plot.

For example, let's say we have this story:

> John, age thirty-four, has a problem. His wife, eight years younger than him, seems to be losing interest in their marriage. John's first wife, who he married when he dropped out of high school at sixteen, (she was his math teacher) suddenly surfaces and wants him back. John always harbored feelings for his ex, who is twelve years older than he is, and part of him knows he married a much younger woman (second wife was just eighteen when he was twenty-six) to salve his fractured ego.
>
> Now his current wife sees this change in John's relationship with his ex-wife and realizes she does love John. The birth of their son and his promotion have caused them to drift further apart, and a week before their tenth anniversary, she makes a decision. She won't allow that slut to steal her husband. She plots to win him back. First task; kill the ex-wife.

We plan to tell this story beginning with present time, and shifting back to John's first marriage. If this were a story where events happen in chronological order, the timeline would be simpler and we'd have less chance of making mistakes. Still, a timeline is useful because mistakes will creep in.

In this timeline we've concocted for John's story, we have several things to take into account. When did John and his first wife marry? If he was sixteen, and she was twelve years older, then she was twenty-eight when they married. Let's forget about the legality of this for the moment. If the story took place in 2011, then John would have been sixteen in 1993, and eighteen years have passed since he found he was hot for the teacher.

We have to determine what happens from the earliest time to the present. So we set the first year as 1993, the year John and his first wife met, and mark each year until the present time, or the year in which John's present time takes place. Then we enter into that timeline when events happen.

Hard? Not at all. We read through the story and on the first page, we have John's marriage to his first wife. Then perhaps they have a child in 1994, we add that event. They break it off in 2002. In 2011 we note that John and his new wife will celebrate their tenth wedding anniversary.

1993 – John and first wife marry.

1994 – Junior is born.

1995 – First wife's first affair.

1998 – John loses his job and goes into a depression.

2000 – Trial separation.

2001 – Renew their vows.

2002 – First wife disappears with child.

2003 – John meets second wife and they marry in Vegas two weeks later.

2003 to 2009 – Wedded bliss.

2010 – John's second child is born.

2011 – John gets a promotion, but works more hours.

Ex-wife shows up asking for a second chance.

Celebrate tenth anniversary with second wife.

Then we notice the first problem. If he broke his marriage off with wife number one in 2002, it's impossible for him to be married ten years to the second wife in 2011, unless of course, he's one of those multiple-wife kind of guy, which he isn't. We have to fix this. But we've made her eighteen at the time they married for logical reasons. John wouldn't have married a kid, he's a good guy. But for them to be married ten years, he'd have to marry her in 2001 when she was just sixteen. How do we fix this? We could adjust her age and John's, but that would mean also adjusting when and how he met his first wife. It would be simpler to change the anniversary they're celebrating to eighth instead of tenth. Whatever we decide, the timeline helps us to see major flaws in the chronology of our story's events.

Perhaps we've listed a couple of other events in the timeline which don't mesh. What about this first child, who would be a teenager now? Where is he or she? Shouldn't we include something about this kid? Did he die, perhaps? This might drive the ex to seek John out.

We won't often spot these mistakes by just reading. The concept of a timeline is to keep our times accurate, lest we discover that things couldn't have happened as written.

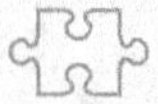

3.2.3 GESTALT VIEW

This sophisticated evaluation tool is appropriate for stories with complex plots. It helps the writer visualize the relationship between individual scenes and see the manuscript as a whole.

> Gestalt. *Noun.* A configuration or pattern of elements so unified as a whole that they cannot be described only as a sum of its parts.

A story with a complex plot is gestalt, for it contains many interwoven elements that combine to make a whole that is more than the sum of its parts.

Structuring a novel in parts, chapters, scenes, and scene details, affords a writer the possibility to "walk" through the story to explore the interaction between its elements, its flow, and its pace. This is a unique method to determine during rewrite if the story works not only as a whole but also on the level of its constituent parts. By focusing on the details of a scene and tracking them back to their place within the story part, the writer can compare and assess their impact on the "whole."

This technique is useful for those writers who, knowing they have a good manuscript, have suffered substantial rejections. Not any type of rejection, though, but those mentioning that the writing is good but the novel, as a whole, doesn't hold. We stress this point because most manuscripts are rejected early because of poor writing. A rejection naming poor technical execution implies that the editor has read the manuscript, or at least part of it, and not just a couple of pages.

Without the professional counsel of a good editor, it's impossible to address plot, pace, tension and other technical aspects that a line edit cannot repair. The gestalt tool can help, though it's difficult and time consuming. It means breaking down the manuscript into parts, the parts into chapters, the chapters into scenes and the scenes into sections. Naturally, this means separate documents.

The next step consists of a MS Excel spreadsheet or a few large sheets of paper, though doing a gestalt by hand can be soul destroying.

Part. The first division concerns the parts of a novel. Often there are three: beginning, middle, and ending. If the novel can be divided into more clearly defined parts, it would mean more divisions. Once those divisions are made, the next step is to resume as succinctly as possible the gist of what that part is supposed to achieve: beginning, middle, and ending.

Chapter. The second division concerns the chapters. Each chapter is allocated on its corresponding part. We might end up with part one comprising chapters one to ten, second part with chapters eleven to thirty-two and so on. Next comes a short resume of the plot within the chapter and its task relative to plot, once more with: beginning, middle, and ending.

Scene. This is the third division, dividing the text into scenes and allocating each to a given chapter., and yes, each scene needs a mini-resume and the mandatory beginning, middle, and ending.

Scene parts. So far we have insisted doggedly on beginnings, middles, and endings because these should mark natural breaks in the story: the part should have a chapter or chapters covering its beginning, other chapter or chapters to its middle, and the rest of the chapters to its ending. The same happens with chapters. Sometimes, a chapter consists of a single scene containing the three sections. If there are two scenes, one will correspond to the beginning and the other to the ending. If there are more scenes, some will correspond to the middle.

And we come to the scenes. Since these should have three sections, the writer's task is to split the scene into its parts. In other words, we need a line to outline the purpose of each scene section.

When done, we will have hacked the manuscript and reduced to its constituent parts. By compiling our resumes in the right order, we will have a diagram looking something like the diagram on page 206.

In the diagram, we have apportioned three chapters to a section, thee scenes in each chapter, and three sections to each scene. Of course,, no book fits these parameters. We've used three units each for simplicity, but the concept holds regardless of the number of items in each division. Some parts might have any number of chapters, divided into any number of scenes.

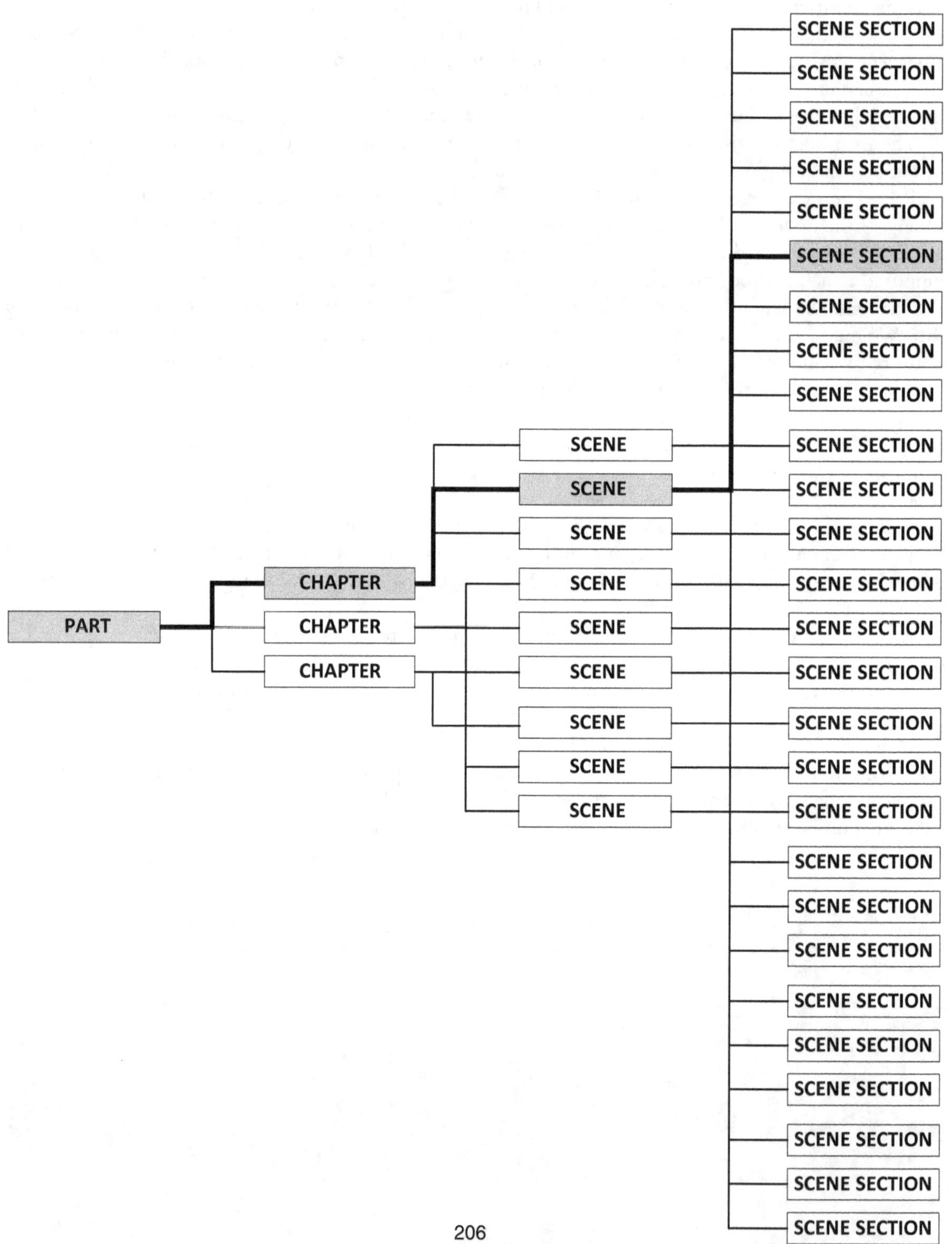

PART
CHAPTER
CHAPTER
CHAPTER
SCENE
SCENE
SCENE
SCENE
SCENE
SCENE
SCENE
SCENE
SCENE
SCENE SECTION
SCENE SECTION
SCENE SECTION
SCENE SECTION
SCENE SECTION
SCENE SECTION
SCENE SECTION
SCENE SECTION
SCENE SECTION
SCENE SECTION
SCENE SECTION
SCENE SECTION
SCENE SECTION
SCENE SECTION
SCENE SECTION
SCENE SECTION
SCENE SECTION
SCENE SECTION
SCENE SECTION
SCENE SECTION
SCENE SECTION
SCENE SECTION
SCENE SECTION
SCENE SECTION
SCENE SECTION
SCENE SECTION
SCENE SECTION

The gestalt diagram is most useful when combined with a tension graph, explained from pages 85 to 90. Once the writer determines that some sections of the story don't keep to adequate levels of tension, or where the levels don't change, he or she can address the story constituents intervening in that section.

As an example, we have highlighted in gray one particular scene section and linked it through the diagram with a bold line. This way, it's clear to follow the origins of such scene section through scene, and chapter to the part of the book it belongs. Since the story "part" is concerned with beginning, middle, or end of the book, the writer must address the contents of each constituent to determine in which way, if any, the element under study contributes to the overall story line.

If the usefulness of any particular story element is doubtful, the writer can incorporate whichever content is vital to the overall storyline, slot it into another section, and delete the rest.

We don't need to repeat that this is one major undertaking that can absorb an inordinate number of hours, requiring concentration and much soul-searching. But in the absence of a good editor, or the money to pay for the services of one, the gestalt approach is the only procedure we know of to address major story-flow problems.

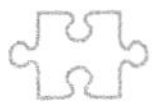 **3.2.4 TENSION**

So we've messed about with our manuscript and removed the errors and tightened the prose. It reads well. Great. What about the tension? The tension in any given story should rise through each scene and each chapter. Our goal is to build tension until the story reaches the climax and then slowly fall back down until we reach the end.

How does one edit for tension? We have a simple method, but the catch is that as writers we must be honest with ourselves, or else it will never work.

First, take the manuscript and begin on page one. Read the first scene. What happens? How does it end? Is the tension increased from the scene opening until it closes or does it fall flat? On a scale of one to ten, rate the scene. "One" means it lacks tension, and "ten" means it's awesome. If we have a scene where nothing happens to move the story forward, then that scene should score low. Let's say the first scene is a three because, although something happens, it's rather slow. So on a piece of paper we write 1-1-3: Chapter one, scene one, tension rating (3).

Go to the second scene and repeat the process. Do the same with the third. Let's say we gave the second a rating of four, because it was a bit more intense than the first, and the third scene we gave a five. We have now a set of ratings of 3, 4, and 5. Not bad. The tension is rising. This is good. We move onto chapter two and repeat the process. Let's pretend both chapters contained three scenes. In chapter two the tension has dropped and scored 1, 3, and 1.

We continue reading and then rating through every chapter. When we finish reading and rating every scene, we make a graph of chapters and scenes using the scores we gave each.

Now, if we've been honest, we'll see areas where the tension falls dramatically or is flat. These are the areas where we have to go in and rewrite to increase the tension. If we have three or four in a row that do nothing, then we've got a flat line, and a problem. To fix this we have to determine first if the scenes are necessary. If they aren't, we rewrite to remove them. If they are, we need to insert conflict or an event that will improve the tension and push the story forward, giving our flat line a little spike upward.

It's the plot and the characters that matter, isn't it? Tension *is* part of plot. If we want to be published, we'll make sure that everything is perfect, including the tension.

If we aren't brutally honest while editing for tension, we're only hurting ourselves. So be brutal. Only when we give it an honest rating can we rewrite as needed.

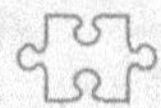 **3.2.5 BETA READERS**

What are they, and why do we need "beta readers?"

A beta reader is someone who reads our book when it's almost polished. After we've edited it to the point that we can no longer improve it, we find a group of people willing to give it a read.

Beta readers are not editors, but they can provide a critique or feedback on the things we cannot see ourselves, no matter how hard we may try, such as plot, tension, characterization, pace, too much description, too little, too much sex, not enough sex, POV shifts, etc. Beta readers are not for picking out things like grammar, spelling mistakes, etc., but if they do, that's a bonus. We find that some beta readers are great at spotting certain inconsistencies, while others are more visceral and spot character flaws. This is why we need more than one reader.

"Beta reader" is much like the term "beta tester." In the software industry, a beta tester takes a piece of software almost ready for the market and tests it out. Typically, a beta tester is unfamiliar with the software's design, so the tester won't avoid using the software in such a way that he avoids bugs. Because the beta tester approaches testing the software without assumptions or previous knowledge, he finds things the creators miss.

This is how beta readers work for our writing. We are the alpha tester, or the creator. We ready the product and tweak it until we feel it is fit to send off. The beta reader takes it, without knowing what we intended to say, and reads what is there. He sees what we might have missed.

So what makes a good beta reader? That depends on what we, as the writer, want. As we've said, different readers notice different things. One, a teacher for example, might notice grammar issues and technical flaws. A librarian might notice characterization issues. It's tough to find the right beta readers because it isn't simply a matter of saying, "Hey, do you like romance novels? Great, give this a read for me."

When we do find our readers, we must decide how best to utilize their efforts. In the following sections we'll discuss review groups, etiquette, and some words of caution for writers when working with beta readers.

 **3.2.5.1 SPELLING**

Review or critique groups provide feedback in exchange for our feedback on their manuscripts, to help us prepare our novel to the best level it can be. These groups may function on a chapter-by-chapter basis, exchanging just portions of work, or they may act as beta readers, exchanging entire manuscripts. There are several ways we can find review groups. The first task is to find one that suits our needs.

New writers should search for groups with at least a few published writers. We need someone with enough knowledge to teach us. A group of new writers won't be helpful, because everyone is still learning the ropes. If we're unsure how to proceed, or how to fix this or that, then their efforts may fail to help improve our manuscript.

Writers have several options when searching for review groups.

 **3.2.5.2 FACE-TO-FACE GROUPS**

Writers often form groups that meet in person. Small groups meet at restaurants, coffee houses, or local libraries. Some meet at members' home or at a local park. These groups offer support and critique face-to-face, which means the writer can ask questions and get feedback at once. Many writers' organizations have listings of this type of group on their websites. We have to find the one closest to us. Of course, many of us feel better sharing our work in person with people we know. Face-to-face groups can also be found at local bookstores, which announce meetings on local websites regularly. Local arts councils also list groups available for writers. Writing classes provide this type of beta reader, and often these groups are guided by instructors or published authors.

 **3.2.5.3 ONLINE GROUPS**

The easiest to find are online groups. Many writing organizations—like OFW— list resources such as online critique groups on their sites. From these groups, it is possible for a writer to find trustworthy and competent beta readers. The key to finding the right group online is research. The Science Fiction, Fantasy, and Horror Online Writing Workshop (OWW), for example, provides writers in these genres a great place to learn, critique, and polish their work.

However, a children's fiction or romance writer looking for beta readers is not going to find this site helpful. Google is a handy tool and will list associations, clubs, etc., that we can explore to find groups to suit what we write. It's up to us to determine whether the members are helpful, knowledgeable, and serious about writing. We've seen a few groups online that are a gathering place rather than a review group. Search the group's forums, ask other writers for suggestions, and search writer's pages to find sites that will provide the level of beta readers sought.

 **3.2.5.4 ETIQUETTE**

Beta reading comes with some unspoken rules, both for the reader and the writer. We've experienced readers who offer little to no help because they either do nothing but gush about our brilliance, or their critiques are harsh and unfounded. The first is the most harmful. While we all enjoy a good pat on the back, we don't want it from our beta readers. The second, while not always harmful, makes the experience difficult, and often the critique is useless because we can't put aside the anger or hurt feelings at the reader's insensitive manner. On the other side, we've seen writers who can't handle critiques and become defensive or hostile with their readers. Their work is genius and they dare anyone to say otherwise. Good luck keeping beta readers that way.

Beta Reader Etiquette

Don't be vague. When pointing out problems, don't use vague generalities, such as: "This is awkward." Be specific, what is it that is awkward? Is it the sentence, the idea, the entire paragraph?

Make suggestions. Show the writer how you would solve the problem. Of course, these suggestions may be ignored, and that's fine. When you make suggestions, remember to watch your tone. Be firm and decisive, but respectful. Avoid personal or potentially offensive comments, even if joking.

Some writers will advise beta readers to point out good points for every bad point. We're going to stray away from the herd here and say that, yes, we should point out good points, but the entire purpose of the beta reader is to fix what's wrong. Positive feedback doesn't do that. It is polite and makes it easier for the writer to digest all of these criticisms, so now and then, add a point about what was done well, but these need not balance the negative comments.

Be honest. As readers, it's crucial that we are honest. We can't sugarcoat or leave out problems because we worry it might upset the writer. If said writer can't handle the comments, then that writer isn't ready to publish. Also be honest about time. Typically, when we hand off our manuscripts, we have an idea of how long we want the reader to take. If the writer asks for it back in a couple of weeks and the reader can't do this, we need to know. Nothing is more frustrating than waiting for that reader to finish.

<table><tr><td>●</td><td>Writer Etiquette</td></tr></table>

No matter what the feedback might be, we always thank our beta readers for their time. Even if there isn't a single suggestion we can use, the reader took time out of their lives to read our manuscript, and we should show appreciation for that effort.

Examine each suggestion with the same attention. The ones that we instinctively reject should get extra attention. Not everything the beta reader suggests will be helpful, but we have to remember that they see things we cannot because we're too close to the work. If more than one reader comments on a certain point, it's likely we need to examine the issue and make changes.

Resist the urge to explain. If we choose not to use a suggestion, we don't have to rifle off an email stating which one we're ignoring and why. Once we have thanked the reader that is the end of it. We make the decisions privately, and we don't debate areas we don't agree with.

Watch what we say and where we say it. The Publishing Industry is a small world, in particular among genre writers. If we've selected a beta reader from a critique group for example, who ends up being less than helpful, we don't share this with other members or on our blogs, Twitter, or Facebook updates. Why? Odds are it will go back to the reader, or someone who knows the reader. Sure, we might not care to have that person read for us again; but what about the twenty other potential readers who witness our unprofessional behavior? If we're not happy with a critique, we keep it to ourselves.

<table><tr><td>●</td><td>Caveats</td></tr></table>

When sending a manuscript to beta readers, there are a few words of caution we'd like to offer for writers.

<table><tr><td>🧩</td><td>Be clear on what you want but don't dictate</td><td>🧩</td></tr></table>

In other words, don't ask for anything specific such as grammar edits or characterization comments. We want a reader's point of view of the manuscript overall. When the reader asks what we are looking for, we ask for his thoughts and suggestions for improvement. We don't list a bunch of instructions. Why? The reader will focus on the details of our list and miss other issues they may have noticed without the distraction. The reader might also see the error, but leave it because it involves something we didn't ask for.

Don't argue or discuss

Never assume that our readers should understand any part of our manuscript. If the idea or scene is misconstrued by the reader, it's up to us to examine it and determine if the issue is muddy. The only time discussion is necessary is when a reader makes a comment that we don't understand. For example, he says "This is awkward. Why do they have these?" but hasn't highlighted anything so that we know what he means. We can discuss to clarify these points. Sometimes readers use unfamiliar terms or symbols. These are also okay to discuss and clarify.

Record each item and compare

Do not edit the manuscript each time it comes back from a reader. We compile the feedback and wait until all readers have offered suggestion and then we examine and make changes. The reason for this is simple. If each reader makes a different suggestion for a single scene, then we're looking at multiple changes which can lead to ruining what we had in the first place. Also, we might be tempted to ignore a comment that is made by subsequent readers as well. We see this at once when it's all there in front of us. More than one reader noticing something often means there is something there that we should consider changing.

Choose the right beta readers

If the beta reader we've chosen doesn't suit our style, genre, or knowledge of writing, it just won't work. Family, friends, and other writers aren't often ideal readers. Why? Family and friends don't want to hurt our feelings and often their comments are skewed because they want to be as gentle as they can. Of course there are exceptions to this; some writers have family members who are brutal readers. These people are lucky. Most of us don't have that resource.

The problem we find with other writers as beta readers lies in a few areas. First, does the writer have the same amount of knowledge and skill as we do? Less? Nope. More? Great. If the writer doesn't know about plot or characterization, or if she is still working out the kinks in her own voice she won't be able to spot what we need her to spot. We also need writers that write the same genre, as these writers will know what readers like and dislike.

Great beta readers include teachers, librarians, avid readers, and experts in the fields we've depicted. If we've written a courtroom drama or a legal thriller, a lawyer or someone in law enforcement can provide excellent feedback on our information. This type of reader can suggest improvements as well. A nurse or physician might provide valuable characterization tips for our protagonist who is in his first year of medical school. These are the readers who provide the feedback we need.

Teachers are a great choice because often grammar and language usage won't slip by their astute eyes. English teachers are often well read and accustomed to a variety of genres and writing ability. Tips, suggestions, and some feedback on where we are weakest are commonly what we'll get from this beta reader.

Avid readers know what they like and what they don't. These beta readers may not know why they don't like it, but they're sure about the problem areas and this is what we want.

And again, we always remember to thank our readers. Let each reader know he was helpful (even if he wasn't) and thank him for taking the time to read.

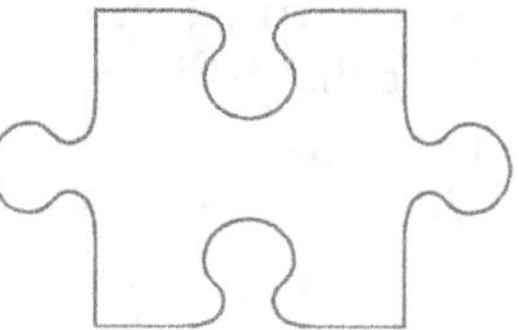

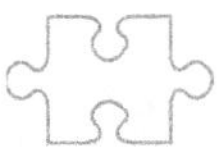 # 3.3 ANALYSIS

Writers construct novels in several ways. Some use a prologue, while other swear it's a waste of time. Stephen King often includes a foreword in his novels, in which he speaks directly to the reader. Sometimes an author includes an endorsement from another established author, which also speaks directly to the reader. Throughout the body of the novel we have chapters and scenes, which may or may not be broken into books or parts.

We've discussed these tools in terms of what they are and how they're used in sections 1.5 and 1.6. When we look to editing and revising, we need to analyze each of the tools we've used to format our book and ask a number of questions.

Do we need a prologue? Does the foreword do its job or is it really a prologue? Are the chapters and scenes complete and relevant to the plot and its forward progression? Do we need to divide chapters into separate parts?

These are just a few of our concerns. Nothing annoys a reader more than a chapter dressed up as a prologue or scenes that end on a whimper instead of a bang. This is why it's important to mull over each in detail.

 ### 3.3.1 PROLOGUE

The prologue should work as a way to tell our story from two different points, or to include information which is crucial to the plot that we cannot include in the body of the story.

When revising a prologue, we have to ask a few key questions:

 **Do we need a prologue?** 

Unnecessary prologues are a pet peeve of many readers. We don't want to do something to annoy the reader from the first page, if we can avoid it. The reason for a prologue is that it must be vital to the reader's understanding of the plot. A quick way to determine if the prologue we've written is necessary is to remove it and read the story. Are we missing anything important? Does the absence of the prologue remove information necessary to the rest of the plot? Then we change the prologue to Chapter One and read again, looking for the same details. If it changes nothing, the prologue is not needed. If it does no more than create atmosphere before the reader begins the real story, then delete it or slap a chapter on it and call it a day.

 ## Can the contents of the prologue be doled out within the plot?

Many times, we think we need the prologue to provide backstory necessary to the plot. However, we can include this in small bits over several chapters. Look at the information contained in the prologue. If it can be dispersed or woven (not dumped) into another spot, then do so and eliminate it.

 ## Is it written from the POV of a major player?

Although we stated that this is not a hard and fast rule, it is wise to set the prologue in the POV of a major character because the voice of the prologue should fit in with the genre and storyline of the main text. It can be written in the voice of a non-physical entity as well. If the POV character of the prologue doesn't appear later, then we must make sure his presence is justified on the timeline.

 ## Does it fulfill its function?

The prologue is the introduction to the story. It should establish setting and provide essential information that is impossible to convey in any other way. If we've done this, we go back to the first question and determine if this is information that the reader must have before chapter one. The prologue should not be used to mask a weak opening chapter or to set a better picture than we've built in the opening pages. It shouldn't be an opening into the story itself. It should not be directly connected to the story at all. The prologue should be distinct and the reader should notice the change when moving from prologue to chapter one. If it does any of the "should nots," odds are it is a chapter. The place to set the atmosphere is in our story, not in the prologue. If we've included information in our prologue that is factual, filling the reader in on certain events or details, then our prologue may be a foreword.

3.3.2 FOREWORD

The foreword is a piece of writing set at the beginning of a book or other piece of literature and before the main text. We've discussed just what is contained in a foreword in section 1.5.2. In this section we'll look at how we approach revising our foreword.

Like we did when we revised the prologue we have to ask ourselves a few questions.

 ## Is it a foreword?

Forewords in fiction writing contain factual information necessary to the story or they act as an endorsement from another author for the book. If we've written part of the story, a previous event, a character's commentary, or something that is part of the story, it is not a foreword. It is a chapter or a prologue.

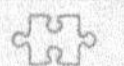 ## Does it serve its function?

Does the foreword prepare the reader for what she is about to read. Is the information contained in it absolutely necessary to the reader's understanding of the story? Or, does it introduce the reader to the author and how he came to write the book? If it does none of these, we must either rewrite it so that it does, or remove it.

Is it complete?

Does it have a beginning, middle, and ending? If not, we must rewrite to make sure it does. For example, if the foreword is an endorsement, then it should include why its author has written the foreword. Why is the book unique? What about it makes it worth reading?

3.3.3 PREFACE

A preface is a short introduction before the body of the novel, and the author writes it herself. The term, as we discuss in Section 1.5.3 means any preliminary statement that covers how the book came about, or how the idea for the book was developed.

A preface is similar to a foreword, but the two aren't interchangeable. Prefaces feature backgrounds, historical content, scope, and the intentions of the author in writing it. When revising, we must analyze a few key details to ensure what we have is actually a preface and to ensure it is necessary.

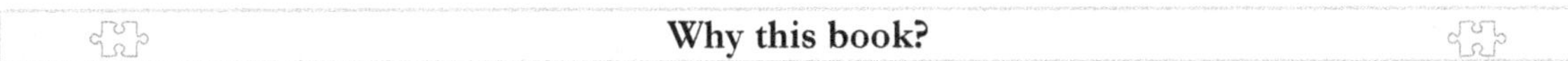

Why this book?

The preface should answer for the reader just why she should read this book as opposed to the many others like it. What is it that makes this one unique and worth her time?

Why now?

Often this question can be answered in how the book came to be written or what made the writer decide it should be written.

Who is this person? Why this author?

The author must be identified in terms of what makes him ideal for writing this book. In a preface, we should include education or experience that makes this author suited to the job of writing this book.

If the preface doesn't answer these questions, or it is intended to set the story's tone or atmosphere, then we have either a prologue or a chapter, and not a preface.

3.3.4 SCENE

We discussed scenes and chapters in sections 1.5.4 and 1.5.5. When revising, we must look at several elements to ensure our scenes are tight and that we've included all of the necessary elements.

Does the opening hook the reader?

We examine the first lines of each scene, as we'd examine the first page. Does the line drag the reader in? Does it make her want to continue? Is it active? If the opening lines don't hook the reader all over again, she might set it down. We must analyze these openings on their own, without considering the lines that follow. On their own, they should raise questions and interest. If they do not, we consider starting at a more active place in the scene, or rewriting the lines to provide a hook. For example:

Julie stretched and opened her eyes. The sunlight pressed into her brain. *Relentless son of a bitch.* Just like her husband.

This is good. The third and fourth sentences will intrigue the reader, but the first two kind of weigh it down. Let's polish it:

Relentless son of a bitch. Just like her husband. Julie stretched and cursed the sunlight that pressed into her brain.

Good: Martin slowed the car, eyeing the crowd outside his house. "Looks like they found the body."

Killer: "Looks like they found the body." Martin slowed the car, eyeing the crowd outside his house.

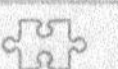
What about the closing lines? Killer as well?

The closing lines must persuade the reader to continue to the next scene. We examine these as we would the opening lines. Look at them in isolation to of the previous text. Do they make us want to read more?

Good: "I'm leaving you." She slammed the door.

Bob sank into the chair. He stared for a moment at the empty room, and he smiled. "Good riddance."

Killer: "I'm leaving you."

We would then take the last lines into the next scene, creating a killer ending and another great opening.

Sentence openings. Are they varied?

Now that we know the openings and closings will pull the reader along, we examine the structure of each scene opening. Are they varied, or do they repeat? We've discussed varying our scene openings in section 3.1.5. If we've repeated openings, creating an echo, we need to rewrite so that each scene opens differently than the scene before and after.

Does the scene further the plot?

Each scene must have a purpose; it must contain conflicts or resolutions that show the reader something about the plot or the characters. If it does not do this, it has no reason to be in our novel. What does the scene do? What happens? If the scene does nothing to further the plot, we rewrite or cut. If we rewrite, we include something to further the plot or to deepen characterization.

Is the POV tight?

Check internal dialogue and search for slips in POV, which we discussed in section 2.2.1. Also examine whether we've used the right POV for the scene. If it could be shown better in another POV, then we should rewrite it in that POV.

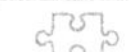 **Is there a resolution?** 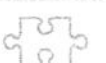

The conflict that we introduce in the beginning of the scene should be resolved at its ending. Throughout the scene, we build a new conflict, which doesn't have to be resolved, but the reader must find an answer of some kind by the last lines.

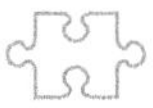 ### 3.3.5 CHAPTER

Chapters must contain a scene or a group of scenes. They should be built around events that belong together and either push the plot forward or build the tension. When analyzing chapters, we must ask:

 **Does the chapter build tension?** 

In section 1.5.4 we discuss how to evaluate the tension in a given scene or chapter. If we find a chapter that has fallen flat or that contains no tension at all, we must determine if the chapter is needed. If it is, then rewrite to increase the tension.

For example, Renée's novel In the Bones had no tension in the second and third chapters. Each served to introduce the characters and little more. By adding conflict in the form of the protagonist finding clues to a mystery left by his grandparents and the villain's plot to get rid of the protagonist— whom he believes is out to ruin the sweet deal he has in his town—the tension was increased. Why did these minor details fix the problem? They created questions, which helped to build tension. If we have no question to answer, then what is the purpose of the chapter?

 **Is the chapter complete?** 

Chapters must have a beginning, middle, and ending. We must resolve one conflict and build to another before the ending. If the chapter doesn't do anything, then it's incomplete or unnecessary.

 **Is the opening a killer?** 

Like a scene, the opening of a chapter must work to hook the reader all over again. To do this we open more often with action or dialogue rather than exposition because exposition almost always slows the pace. We don't want to do that. For each chapter, we read the opening paragraph. Does it form a question in the reader's mind or grab her attention? Is it different from the chapter before it? As we mention in section 3.1.5, chapter openings should be varied so that we avoid repetition. The reader does notice if we open chapters the same way each time. For example:

Chapter 1: John pulled into the driveway and picked up his gun.

Chapter 2: Maria screamed, and he covered his ears.

Chapter 3: John tossed the rope over the beam and pulled.

These all begin in similar ways; John pulled, Maria screamed, John tossed. These create an echo. While the reader might not realize why she hears it or what is causing it, she'll notice. If we see chapter openers that repeat like this, we rewrite to show variety.

Chapter 1: John pulled into the driveway and picked up his gun.

Chapter 2: Covering his ears didn't silence Maria's scream.

Chapter 3: "Up you go," John tossed the rope over the beam and pulled.

Each of these begins differently, eliminating the echo, but still showing what the writer needs to show.

Is the POV clear in the first line?

Readers step away, as we've mentioned many times before, and they may not return for days or even weeks. Often we stop at the beginning of a new chapter or scene, so it's important that the POV character is clear in those first lines. The reader doesn't like flipping back and rereading the previous pages to recall what is going on. Besides, after a week or two away from the book, she may not bother flipping back, having lost her interest. So we check that POV is well established in the first paragraph. If it is not, consider beginning the chapter where the POV is clear, or rewriting to show.

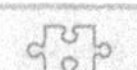

What about the ending?

Does the chapter ending entice the reader to turn that page just one more time?

Chapters should end with a question that will be answered in the following chapters. In other words, although they contain a beginning, middle, and ending, they do not actually end. For example, if a woman were spending the afternoon locked in the gardener's embrace, the chapter wouldn't end after her husband walks in and shoots the man. It should end just before that. The next chapter opens with the gun trained on the gardener's head.

We read each ending and check that it either includes a cliffhanger, a revelation, interrupted conversation, or some kind of unresolved development. If we've ended the chapter completely, then we move the ending to a point before the resolution and move the resolution to the next chapter.

3.3.6 PART / BOOK

A part or a book is crafted from several chapters to indicate a shift in time, place or point of view. Unlike chapter endings, parts must end without unfinished business such as a cliffhanger. For example, a novel following a family through generations might divide each into parts. Each generation faces its own struggles and resolves those conflicts by the end of their part, and then the next generation takes over.

When analyzing how we've divided our book parts, we must first we check the openings. Do they hook the reader? Just as a novel's first page must yank the reader into the story, so should the first lines of each of its parts.

Is it clear that we've entered a new time, place, or viewpoint? This different setting should be clear to the reader so she isn't struggling to ground herself in the current part of the story.

We then look at the ending. Is the major conflict for this group of chapters resolved? Does it entice the reader to read more?

Writers should also question why the book is divided into parts. Should it have parts? What purpose does the division serve? If there is no clear reason, such as time periods or different POV characters, then we should consider removing the divisions.

 ### 3.3.7 EPILOGUE

An epilogue is the section following the final chapter that tells the reader what happened after the main story is over. Often epilogues are used to wrap up questions about the story that haven't been answered in the main story arc. This can be a powerful tool, but often it isn't needed. Part of analyzing our epilogue is making that determination.

 ### Can this information be included in the story? 

If we've used the epilogue to tie up plot strings that we were too lazy to complete in the main story, the reader will realize this. Examine the epilogue. If we can finish the book using another chapter instead, then that is what we should do. The epilogue is an afterword, meant to show the characters beyond the story's timeline.

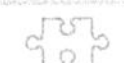 ### Is it full of explanations or revelations that set up a second book? 

These tricks will not pull readers into the next novel. Most times, an epilogue that does this has the opposite effect. If the epilogue introduces another sort of cliffhanger, or a preview of another story that is intended to hook the reader in all over again, we should delete it. The reader will be more open to the next book if she's not shoved toward it with the current one.

Is the ending clear without the epilogue? 

If the ending is clear without it, we have to decide whether or not the epilogue can be eliminated. Many writers enjoy using an epilogue to give the reader a glimpse of "after happily ever after" but if it's not necessary, we should consider the possibility that it may serve to irritate the reader, rather than amuse her.

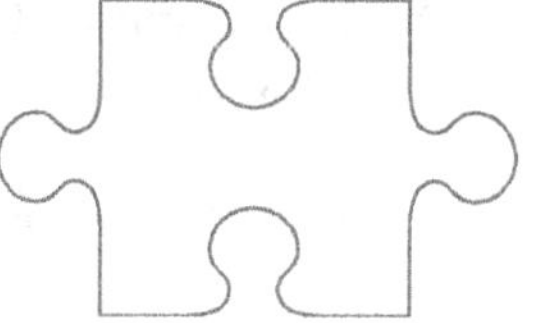

4 THE RULES OF WRITING

Of all the technicalities of writing well, grammar has the worst image. Mention grammar, and pictures of mind-numbing lectures dished out by monotone voices swim to the forefront of our memories, with endless lists of prepositions, irregular verbs, and other unsavory bits.

Bridge, Poker, Whist, and other fun card games have rules. Some are set, and failing to observe them will result in the player being unceremoniously kicked out of a competition. Other rules are flexible. If the player knows them well, he may spot the opportunity to bend one to suit a particular hand, and in doing so, defend an otherwise hopeless contract. Still other rules are unwritten. The player ignores them at his peril and suffers the inevitable fallout.

The common thread in these examples is knowledge of the rules. A player who sits down to play ignoring the game, house, or a particular table's rules is a fool. With luck, he will lose his money, and depending on the players and venue, keep the integrity of his skin and bones.

Thus, a writer, any writer ignoring the rules of this "game," is similarly misguided. The gorgons out there (agents, editors, readers, and other writers) will eat him alive.

Grammar consists of a set of rules governing the way we string words together to convey concepts. Some are clear-cut, while others—nebulous and fewer still—are left to the interpretation of the writer according to the subjective tenets of something called "style."

In the following sections, we aim to highlight these rules. We have neither the space nor the inclination to write a comprehensive grammar treatise and have limited the explanations to the basic concepts. We will attempt to lay down this necessary theory not in the style of a school primer but as tools for fiction writers.

"But... grammar is grammar, no?"

Not quite. In day-to-day communication with other members of our species we use words loosely. We rely on noises, gestures, volume, jargon, tone, and texting shorthand (RU1?, LMAO, ROFL, LOL), dispensing with niceties to convey information. That's communication in basic form. Writers strive to convey complex pictures and deep sensations with the sole help of text. This is a different ballgame.

We have structured the grammar sections into three parts:

Parts of speech

Clause/Sentence

Punctuation

Writers must understand not only the rules but their power to transform the rows of letters on a page into magical images. To do so, it's not sufficient to understand the laws of composition but rather their effect on prose. To this end, we have structured the grammar sections with emphasis on how each part of speech affects fiction writing.

Rules have origins. Some are sensible, others picturesque, and a few downright questionable, but no writer can decide which is which unless he's familiar with them.

First, let's return to school.

Language is constructed with words, the building blocks from which sentences are made. Words, which experts term "lexical items," fall into different categories as defined by their use or syntactic behavior. We name these groups: parts of speech, word class, lexical class, or lexical category. For our reference, we'll stick with "parts of speech."

The number of parts of speech depends on source and uses. Linguists and grammarians need scores of these categories to analyze language, while most dictionaries name only eight. Here we have chosen the short list with one exception: Determiners. Though most sources include these with the adjectives, we have given them their own group. Therefore, we will investigate nine parts of speech:

Verb

Noun

Pronoun

Adjective

Determiner

Adverb

Conjunction

Preposition

Interjection

We'll examine each part of speech under these regular headings:

What's a verb?

How do verbs work?

For writers, what's in a verb?

Feel free to go straight to the heading most appropriate for your needs, but remember that familiarity with all of them—concepts and uses—will strengthen your prose. As our incombustible Wendy Swore remarks:

"Grammar is good for you—like vegetables: they keep the strength up and help things come out smooth."[83]

---

[83] She's a farmer and knows her subject matter.

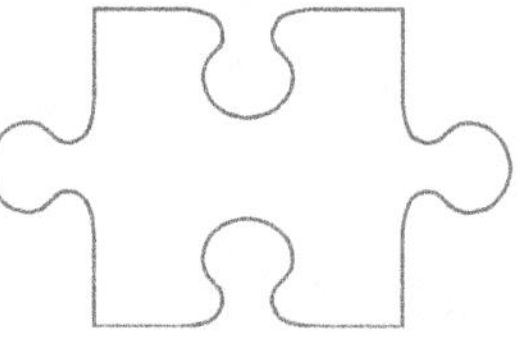

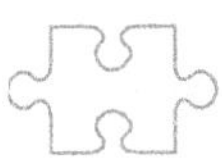

4.1 PARTS OF SPEECH

There's no reason behind listing parts of speech in any particular order. In prose, every part of speech has an important role. After considering that verbs are the soul of good writing, our choice was inevitable.

4.1.1 THE VERB

4.1.1.1 WHAT'S A VERB?

A verb is the part of speech indicating thoughts and actions.

Eat, sleep, jog and write are verbs.

4.1.1.2 HOW DO VERBS WORK?

Complete sentences don't exist without verbs (sentence fragments do, and that's why we call them "fragments"). Just as we use nouns to name things, we need verbs to express what those things do. Even the shortest of sentences use verbs: I am; Jesus wept; She froze; Beer flowed.

In syntax, the verb teams with the subject—and shares its form—to tell us *who*, *when*, and (sometimes) *how*.

A word about the infinitive. The infinitive is the *name* of the verb, not a verb form or tense. To eat, to sleep, to jog, and to write are infinitives. Infinitives don't add information. They don't tell us *who* or *how* or *when*. You will recognize them when the preposition "to" precedes the name of the verb.

Person and Number

To work with a verb, we use a number form matching that of the subject to determine who the verb is attached to. We classify a subject by its person—first, second, or third—and by its number—singular or plural.

	Singular		**Plural**
First	I <u>write</u> silly lines.	First	We <u>write</u> silly lines
Second	You <u>write</u> silly lines	Second	You <u>write</u> silly lines
Third	He/she/it <u>writes</u> silly lines	Third	They <u>write</u> silly lines

The first person names the person speaking, whether it's a single person (singular *I*) or a group including that person (plural *we*).

The second person names the person spoken to, whether it's a single person (singular *you*) or a group including that person (plural *you*).

The third person indicates the person spoken about, whether it's a single person (singular *he, she, it*) or a group including that person (plural *they*).

Tense

To determine the "when" of a verb, we use tense. Verbs describe actions or states of being which must take place in time, and the only three stages of time are past, present, and future.

<u>She wrote</u> signifies that the action of writing took place in the past. <u>She writes</u> grounds the action in the present. <u>She will write</u> points to an action that will take place in the future.

With tense, verbs can also give us information about *how*, or the quality of an action.

Is the action in progress? The progressive or continuous forms, such as <u>she is writing</u> show that the action takes place over a period of time.

Is the action completed? Past forms such as she <u>wrote</u> or past perfect forms like she <u>has written</u> show that the action is complete.

Other Verb Eelements

There are other aspects of verbs, such as active and passive voice, class, mood, modal auxiliaries, and verbals. While prose can be improved through knowing these aspects and how to manipulate them, these more advanced details need explanations fit for a grammar book. In the resources pages (450 to 451) we've listed a number of grammar manuals for those in search of deeper knowledge.

4.1.1.3 ARE THERE DIFFERENT TYPES OF VERBS?

Yes, about forty, from andative, momentane, and semelfactive to zero copula.[84] But, as stated earlier, this book is not a treatise on English grammar. For our purposes we'll limit the verb types to major divisions: intransitive, transitive active, transitive passive, linking, and helping.

Intransitive verbs

These are verbs of action that never have direct or indirect objects to receive those actions.

> Sonia always prays before eating.

The verb is "prays," which is active, but the sentence construction supports no object to receive the action. "Before eating" is a prepositional phrase modifying "prays." It tells us when.

Transitive active verbs

These express direct actions (hit, pinch, carry, load) or possession (give, take, get, have).

Transitive active verbs have a direct and/or, sometimes, an indirect object. By "object" we mean the noun that receives the action of the verb. To determine the direct object, we ask whom or what receives the action of the verb:

---

[84] Michael Keyton, one of the writers who waded through the rough manuscript, was troubled with this term. He always thought it was a synonym of abstinence.

Sonia kicks the rock.

Sonia kicks what? The rock. Hence, the rock is the direct object of "kicks."

To identify any indirect object, we ask "to whom," "for whom," "to what," or "for what."

Sonia gave Joe her cookie.

Here, the verb is "gave." What did Sonia give? Her cookie, which is the direct object of the action. To whom did Sonia give it? To Joe. Joe is the indirect object.

Sometimes this example is seen in a sentence as:

Sonia gave her cookie to Joe.

Transitive passive verbs

These verbs also show action, but the action of the sentence is directed at the subject rather than the object of the sentence within the construction. These constructions are best avoided in fiction because they create a slower pace and a "telling" construction.

Sonia was hit by the cookie.

In this sentence, for example, "Sonia" is in the subject position. "Cookie" is in the object position. A natural active construction would say either "Sonia hit the cookie" or "The cookie hit Sonia." Neither example is an exact translation of the example. If Sonia stands there and a cookie hits her, Sonia certainly does not hit the cookie. However, the cookie cannot (unless this is plausible within a fantasy) hit anyone without being propelled through the air. A better construction would be: "Steve hit Sonia with a cookie." If we don't know who threw the cookie, the transitive passive example is the best construction to convey this meaning.

Linking verbs

Linking verbs describe states of being. These verbs are conjugations of the infinitive "to be." They connect the subject of a sentence to a word—a noun or an adjective—or phrase that describes it:

Joe is the champion.

Joe is the subject and "is," the linking verb. "Champion" is a predicate noun, meaning a noun positioned after the verb, which is another word for Joe.

Joe is handsome.

Again, "Joe" is the subject with "is" linking it to the predicate adjective "handsome."

Helping verbs

These verbs also termed auxiliary verbs, team with other verbs to add information. Together, they become a verb phrase.

The cow has jumped over the moon!

In this intransitive sentence, the helping verb "has" lends a hand to the main verb "jumped." Together, they tell us the jump occurred in the past. "Has jumped" tells us when. We know the cow performed an action, but there was no object to receive it. "Over the moon" told us where the cow went.

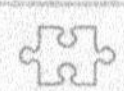 **4.1.1.4 FOR WRITERS, WHAT'S IN A VERB?**

Verbs do more than show action: they indicate when the action happened, how many things were acting, and can add description. This last bit is what matters most to us writers: describing actions.

The choice of a verb can describe the action. A good choice makes it real. To depict consuming food we use the infinitive "to eat." "Mary <u>eats</u> pancakes" names the action; it tells us *what* happens (eats) and names *who* does the action (Mary). But the verb doesn't tell us *how* Mary eats. Yet, other verbs can add information about Mary's action. She may:

Pick at, sample, taste, nibble, devour, gobble, wolf, scoff, gorge, demolish, scarf, etc.

All verbs tell us *what*, but not all verbs tell us *how*.

Mary batted her eyelashes demurely and ate her pancakes.

This sentence paints an unclear image of a shy or coy female but doesn't tell us much else. Why does she bat her eyelashes before eating? Beats us. She may have troublesome contacts or blurry eyesight. She may be making a move on the yummy waiter. Your guess is as good as ours since the sentence doesn't help.

Mary batted her eyelashes demurely and nibbled at her pancakes.

This sentence paints the image of a shy female, perhaps with a sheltered upbringing. "Nibbling" buttresses the batting eyelashes and delivers prim images to mind.

Mary batted her eyelashes demurely and scarfed her pancakes.

Finally, this sentence paints a disturbing image. Perhaps she's famished or ravenous ("hungry" wouldn't give us a measure of her appetite). Batting her eyelashes before wolfing down her pancakes adds strangeness to an otherwise tame scene. Why? Because batting one's eyelashes (demurely, don't forget) before pouncing on the pancakes is unnatural and unexpected. We wouldn't be surprised if the yummy waiter cringed at the sight.

"Nibble" and "scarf" are *how* verbs, while eat is a *what* verb. Writers must strive to use *how* verbs whenever possible. This harkens back to our pitting weak against strong verbs. Adding "how" and "why" to the explanation fleshes out these vague concepts.

When settling down to rewrite, or line edit, or otherwise polish prose, stop at verbs and query them. Ask are you a *what* or a *how*? If a *what*, consider replacing. Naturally, not all *what* verbs have a list of *how* relatives to choose from. Replacing those that do can change your prose.

Check the following passage:

Count Lecter and Lady Murasaki enter Hannibal's room. He has bitten the pillow with his teeth and feathers are flying. Hannibal moans and screams, moving, fighting, clenching his teeth. Count Lecter puts his weight on him and holds the boy's arms in the blanket.

There's nothing wrong with the passage, but Thomas Harris is a master, and a lover of how verbs. His choices are a joy to read and elevate his prose to dizzying heights. This is how he wrote it:

Count Lecter and Lady Murasaki burst into Hannibal's room. He has ripped the pillow with his teeth and feathers are flying. Hannibal growls and screams, thrashing, fighting gritting his teeth. Count Lecter puts his weight on him and confines the boy's arms in the blanket.[85]

For "holds" (the boy's arms in the blanket), he could have used "secures," "grips," "grasps," "clutches," "clasps," "grabs," "seizes," "clenches," etc. He didn't. He chose "confines," a beautiful *how* verb that reflects the anxious mood. His choice marks a subtle difference between everyday prose and literature.

4.1.2 THE NOUN

4.1.2.1 WHAT'S A NOUN?

A noun is a word that represents a person, place, thing, or idea. Nouns can be proper (Fred) or common (book).

Yvonne, woman, radish, Ireland, dog, love, water, and hydrogen are nouns.

4.1.2.2 HOW DO NOUNS WORK?

Once we have determined which noun is most appropriate to represent our concept, and depending on the sources, there are between five and eight ways in which nouns are used. These use are: subject, direct object, indirect object, object of preposition, predicate nominative, appositive, direct address, and objective complement. Since we already warned that this is not a treatise on grammar, we'll review the first four.

Noun as a subject

Writers write.

Yvonne is a famous writer.

Writers and Yvonne are the subjects of these sentences.

Noun as direct object

The woman shampooed the skunk.

The jury murdered Rita.

We can identify a direct object by asking *what* or *whom*.

First sentence. The woman shampooed what? Answer: skunk. "Skunk" is the direct object of the verb "shampooed."

Second sentence. The jury murdered whom? Answer: Rita. "Rita" is the direct object of the verb "murdered."

---

[85] Thomas Harris, Hannibal Rising, p 85, Bantam Dell 2007

● Noun as indirect object

I mailed Vlad the bribe.

He gave the <u>werewolf</u> a collar.

We can identify an indirect object by asking *to what, for what,* or *to whom/for whom.*
First sentence. I mailed the bribe to whom? I mailed it to Vlad. "Vlad" is the indirect object.
Second sentence. He gave a collar to whom? He gave the collar to the werewolf. "Werewolf" is the indirect object.

● Noun as object of a preposition

He pushed the stolen car to the garage.

Yvonne ate mouse with <u>ketchup.</u>

First sentence: The preposition is "to," and the object of that preposition is the noun "garage."
Second sentence: The preposition is "with," and the object of that preposition is the noun "ketchup."

4.1.2.3 ARE THERE DIFFERENT TYPES OF NOUNS?

Nouns fall into four classes with seven types: common and proper, countable and uncountable, concrete and abstract, and collective.

● Common and proper nouns

Common nouns denote types, like animal, person, and country as opposed to proper nouns that denote unique entities like Fido, Yvonne, and Ireland. Common nouns are generic and proper nouns specific.

● Countable and uncountable nouns

Countable nouns can take plurals and/or combine with quantifiers (most, several, a little, etc.) and numerals (seven, eleven, etc.) A countable noun can take an indefinite article (a or an). Examples for countable nouns are dog, woman, and radish.
Uncountable nouns are the names of elements or abstract ideas, which we do not see as separate objects. Most uncountable nouns are singular and have no plural forms. We do not use numbers with uncountable nouns. Rice, laughter, and hydrogen are uncountable nouns. For example, we say water, but not "a water" or "two waters." (Yes, we know people ask for "two waters" at the bar, but that's colloquial, which means acceptable in dialogue but not in narrative). Similarly, we say, "hydrogen," but not "a hydrogen" or "two hydrogens."

● Concrete and abstract nouns

Concrete nouns belong to elements that can be experienced with the physical senses; for example, dog, radish, and Yvonne. By contrast, abstract nouns refer to concepts or ideas; for example, happiness, justice, and love.

Collective nouns

Collective nouns are those that refer to a group consisting of more than one entity; for example, crowd, school, or committee.

4.1.2.4 FOR WRITERS, WHAT'S IN A NOUN?

To write details, the writer needs specific nouns that create an image. To give an example, the generic noun "dog" gives us an idea of an animal with four legs and a tail, which is often wagging when happy. But the specific noun "Dachshund" draws a particular image into the reader's mind. If Yvonne hears noises downstairs and she's alone in the house but for her fearless Dachshund, the reader will smile and form a picture of the sausage-shaped animal running on his short legs to yelp at the intruder. The reader's mental image would be different had the writer named Yvonne's dog a Rottweiler. Good writing needs specific nouns and few, if any, generic ones.

The noun "bird" conjures images of something with wings and feathers. The noun "cardinal" paints a picture of a bright red bird with its distinctive crest of feathers giving a triangular profile.

Strong nouns give readers more information. Writers should seek specific nouns to season their prose. Naturally, a specific noun should be familiar to the reader, otherwise it will require description. If the canoe you're using in a scene is a "pipante," you shouldn't assume the readers are conversant with the craft of Honduran natives.

Often, writers rely on adjectives to buttress nouns. This is lazy writing. Earlier on, we read about a teenager with a bad case of acne. The writer described "a large spot on her nose." "Large" in this context is an adjective conjured to strengthen a weak noun. Replacing "spot" with pustule, carbuncle, boil, cyst, or abscess would have made most readers cringe.

Abstract nouns present a different set of problems. Concepts like "beauty" or "justice" don't provide the reader with much information and usually harbor the writer's idea of what those words mean. This can be dangerous in careless hands. A thunderstorm may have beauty, but not for those whose home has been demolished by lightning. Our understanding of beauty or justice may have nothing to do with the reader's; he can't see, touch, or hear beauty or justice but may relate to concrete examples of such.

Purists maintain that true synonyms are rare, and we concur. Object, device, contraption, and artifact are not synonymous, each noun carrying a particular nuance.

The *man* checked his parachute and jumped.

Doesn't carry the punch of:

The pilot checked his parachute and jumped.

In particular if the scene takes place in a passenger aircraft, By the same token, there's a difference between the "aircraft" being a Cessna or a Boeing 747. (We can take the analogy further if we consider that a 747 requires two pilots and a Cessna only one).

In a nutshell:

A. Choose your nouns with care.

B. Strive for common nouns conveying extra information.

C. Beware of abstract nouns and illustrate their specific meaning or degree.

D. Substitute whenever possible adjective + noun constructions with a single, stronger, noun.

 **4.1.3 THE PRONOUN**

 **4.1.3.1 WHAT'S A PRONOUN?**

A pronoun is a word that substitutes for a particular noun or another pronoun. The specific noun that a pronoun substitutes for is called an "antecedent."

She, him, her, it, and our are pronouns.

 **4.1.3.2 HOW DO PRONOUNS WORK?**

If we didn't have pronouns, languages would read stilted and awkward, full of repetitions. Take the following passage:

> Arius cut straight through the vineyards, holding back the branches for Thea not out of courtesy, but because Thea would slow Arius down if Thea had to fight Thea's own way through.

Besides the horrid noun repetition, the passage above should be in first person, a lost cause without the concourse of pronouns. Kate Quinn will blow a fuse at the liberties we've taken with her prose. This is how she wrote it:

> Arius cut straight through the vineyards, holding back the branches for me not out of courtesy, but because I would slow him down if I had to fight my own way through.[86]

Although pronouns are small words, they are irreplaceable.

 **4.1.3.3 ARE THERE DIFFERENT TYPES OF PRONOUNS?**

Pronouns can have several cases and different roles:

● Subject pronouns

I, you, he, she, it, we, and they are the subjects in a sentence and team with linking verbs. Examples:

> He and I are going to massacre the town.
>
> Yes, this is he, formerly known as she.
>
> Robin and he brought a stripper's pole.
>
> He is wider than she.
>
> We girls will be back in time for the sacrifice.

---

86 Kate Quinn; Mistress of Rome, p 361, The Berkley Publishing Group, 2010

<u>We</u> are smellier than <u>they</u>.

The sentences above are grammatically correct. They might read strange because we often hear people use object pronouns where subject pronouns are required.

What is a writer to do? Shouldn't dialogue sound like real people? Above all, the writer needs to know correct usage. If he then chooses to use incorrect grammar to match the speech of a character, he can do so. This said, some writers publish children's books full of grammatical errors because "this is how kids talk." Children are learning to talk. Filling their stories with errors does not serve their learning.

Object pronouns

<u>Me</u>, <u>you</u>, <u>him</u>, <u>her</u>, <u>it</u>, <u>us</u>, and <u>them</u> are objects of verbs or prepositions.

Jason's dog peed on <u>me</u>.

"Me" is the direct object of the verb "peed."

Hal gave <u>us</u> tickets to the game.

"Us" is the indirect object of "gave."

Hal gave the corpses to Frank and <u>me</u>.

"Me" is an object of the preposition "to" as well as an indirect object.

Possessive pronouns

<u>Mine</u>, <u>yours</u>, <u>his</u>, <u>hers</u>, <u>its</u>, <u>ours</u>, and <u>theirs</u> show ownership.

Is this <u>your</u> finger? Yes, it's <u>mine</u>.

Is this <u>hers</u> or <u>yours</u>? <u>Hers</u>.

No apostrophes are used with possessive pronouns (like its) but are used with contractions (like it's for "it is").

The prize is <u>ours</u>.

The dragon wagged <u>its</u> tail.

Rudy and Jan said the wagon is <u>theirs</u>.

Possessive pronouns are used before gerunds (verbal forms ending in "ing" that function as nouns).

Terry's aunt applauded <u>his</u> sailing in the race.

Reflexive pronouns

<u>Myself</u>, <u>yourself</u>, <u>himself</u>, <u>herself</u>, <u>itself</u>, <u>ourselves</u>, <u>yourselves</u>, and <u>themselves</u> show that someone or something is acting for itself or on itself. Reflexive pronouns are often used as intensifiers.

I can do it <u>myself.</u>

They, <u>themselves</u>, are responsible for this mess.

The cat groomed <u>itself</u> with tongue and paw.[87]

Demonstrative pronouns

<u>This</u>, <u>that</u>, <u>these</u>, and <u>those</u> refer to objects and sometimes to people.

<u>These</u> pants are dirty.

Do you prefer <u>these</u> colors or <u>those</u>?

<u>This</u> is she. (telephone response to e.g. "May I speak to the person in charge?")

<u>This</u> is my family.

Relative pronouns

<u>That</u>, <u>which</u>, <u>who</u>, <u>whom</u>, and <u>whose</u> show the relationship of a dependent clause to a noun in the sentence.

Relative pronouns link two phrases or clauses. The relative pronouns are similar to the interrogative pronouns but they are not used to ask a question.

This is the bull <u>that</u> gored the matador.

A "loser," <u>which</u> consists of decaf, milk substitute, and saccharine, is a parody of coffee.

Interrogative pronouns

<u>Who</u>, <u>whom</u>, <u>whose</u>, <u>which</u>, <u>what</u>, <u>whoever</u>, <u>whomever</u> and <u>whichever</u> are used to ask questions.

<u>Whose</u> sandals are these?

<u>Which</u> flavor do you prefer?

Indefinite pronouns

These make indefinite reference to nouns and are grouped as a function of their requirements.

Some indefinite pronouns require a singular verb: <u>anyone/anybody</u>; <u>everyone/everybody</u>; <u>someone/somebody</u>; <u>everything/nothing</u>; <u>either</u>; <u>one</u>.

Other indefinite pronouns require a plural verb : <u>both</u>, <u>few</u>, <u>many</u>.

Finally, some indefinite pronouns can be either singular or plural, depending on the meaning of the sentence: <u>some</u>, <u>none</u>, <u>more</u>, <u>most</u>, <u>any</u>, <u>all</u>.

<u>Everybody</u> is here.

<u>Many</u> are called, but <u>few</u> are chosen.

<u>Most</u> of my work is finished.

---

[87] In creative writing, reflexive pronouns are often omitted unless essential for clarity.

4.1.3.4 FOR WRITERS, WHAT'S IN A PRONOUN?

We've listed below a number of problems plaguing writers of all levels of competence. These are issues to watch when rewriting or line editing.

Keep antecedents close to the pronouns

A pronoun refers back to a nearby noun. If this convention isn't observed, pity the poor reader who has to wonder "who is who" or "what is what."

> The argument started when John and Mark refused to pay for the burnt pancakes. The rain fell unabated, the humidity unbearable. On the windowpane, one drop joined another and raced all the way down to the windowsill. Mary thought they were cute.

Great stuff. Who is cute? The drops, the burnt pancakes, or John and Mark?

Depending on what's in Mary's mind, replacing "they" with "the boys," "the pancakes," or "the drops" would solve the issue. Writers should avoid repetition whenever possible, but never at the expense of clarity.

The above example is extreme—the antecedents being all over the place and some far removed—but the same problem can ruin short sentences:

> If the cat doesn't like raw fish, cook it.

Poor cat. Rewriting the sentence will spare the feline:

> Cook the fish if the cat doesn't like it raw.

Avoid using a single pronoun with paired antecedents

When there are two or more nouns involved, careless sentence construction can confuse the reader. For example.

> Mary told Gladys she couldn't go to the party.

> The mosquito bit his nose, and he was angry.[88]

In the first sentence, we don't know who can't go to the party. In the second, we gather the mosquito was angry (as the nose soon would be), but we don't think that's what the writer intended to convey.

> Mary couldn't go to the party, she told Gladys.

Or

> I can't go to the party, Mary told Gladys.

Would solve the first problem.

> He got angry when the mosquito bit his nose.

---

[88] Only female mosquitoes suck blood, but we cheated and used the masculine form.

Would take care of the second.

⬤ That

In most instances, a writer can improve his prose by omitting the relative pronoun "that," without loss of meaning.

The dress that she bought was too large.

The dress she bought was too large.

⬤ It/Its

A universal rule of good writing is to avoid repetition. Pronouns can be handy to avoid using a word twice, but sometimes the remedy can be worse than the disease and introduce an element of vagueness. In particular, writers should be wary of "it" and "its."

The "it" pronoun, by its very nature, is vague at best and even abstract at times. Careless or frequent use can weaken the strongest writing. Of course, sometimes its use is unavoidable:

Mary folded her napkin and set it aside.

The reader is likely to understand that "it" refers to "napkin." Without the pronoun, the sentence would read:

Mary folded her napkin and set the napkin aside.

Definitely clunky.

In the next example, the inherent vagueness of the pronoun should be self-evident.

Mary charged into the room holding her key and cringed at its size.

When the reader comes across a pronoun, his gaze instinctively seeks its antecedent: the nearest noun. In the example above, the reader would initially assume "its size" refers to the key. If Mary lives in a castle, the reader may think the key is a foot long. On the other hand, the room she's entered may be vast. In any case, the reader will pause and puzzle out the sentence. If he stops, the story will lose its forward momentum.

We could change the sentence's structure:

Holding her key, Mary charged into the room and cringed at its size.

The above construction is clearer, but leaves the abstract pronoun in place. "Its" does not conjure the vivid image of "room." To remove the pronoun we must rewrite:

Mary charged through the door holding her key and cringed at the room's size.

Holding her key, Mary charged through the door and cringed at the room's size.

Finally there's an issue of style and sentence strength. As a rule, avoid ending sentences with a vague pronoun. The most important part of a sentence is its ending. "It" doesn't convey an image, but a reference to one.

Mary flung a pan at the thieving raccoon, then hurled her rolling pin at it.

Flinging a pan conveys a vivid image. So does hurling a rolling pin. But the "it" ending flattens a sentence with such strong imagery.

We could repeat "raccoon," but rewriting the sentence to remove "it" is a better proposition.

Mary flung a pan then hurled her rolling pin at the thieving raccoon.

"It" and "its" have their place in good writing. When found in sentences, pause and consider if rewriting will deliver clearer and more powerful images.

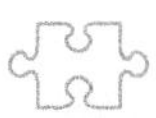 **4.1.4 THE ADJECTIVE**

 **4.1.4.1 WHAT'S AN ADJECTIVE?**

Adjectives are descriptive words that qualify, show, or point out distinguishing marks or features of the noun. Grammarians also consider articles or Determiners (the, a, an) to be adjectives. In this section, we have listed them as a separate part of speech. (See pages 240 t0 243.)

Playful, old, dark, greasy, seven, and bile-colored are adjectives.

 **4.1.4.2 HOW DO ADJECTIVES WORK?**

An adjective modifies a noun or a pronoun by describing, identifying, or quantifying them.

His large and brave piranha swam away.

Where we learn features or virtues about his piranha.

Her brown and frizzy hair hid her ears.

Though her color is consistent, here we learn her hair is in a mess.

The playful cat climbed the tree.

Now we know Puss is inclined to do tricks.

Daisy painted her kitchen walls with bile-colored paint.

Besides Daisy's arguable tastes in color, we discover that "kitchen," a solid noun, can metamorphose into an adjective to qualify "walls."

The pizza parlor is dated, dark, and greasy.

Another example of how a substantive (pizza) can be an adjective to describe the parlor.

An old music box sat on the pine bough.

And another (pine), to drive the nail home.

 **4.1.4.3 ARE THERE DIFFERENT TYPES OF ADJECTIVES?**

There are six classes of adjectives in the English language:

Numeric: five, eleven, four hundred

Quantitative: more, all, some, half, enough

Qualitative: <u>red</u>, <u>soft</u>, <u>sweet</u>, <u>thick</u>

Possessive: <u>my</u>, <u>his</u>, <u>their</u>, <u>your</u>

Interrogative: <u>which</u>, <u>whose</u>, <u>what</u>

Demonstrative: <u>this</u>, <u>that</u>, <u>those, these</u>

Each category of adjectives will describe nouns in a different way.

Descriptive adjectives

Numeric, quantitative, and qualitative adjectives modify nouns, adding features, nature, feel, personality, age, or number. Asking of the noun what kind identifies a descriptive adjective.

Paula has a <u>large</u> tree house.

What kind of tree house? A <u>large</u> one.

The pet alligator is <u>spotted</u>.

What kind of alligator? A spotted one.

Common adjectives

These describe nouns or pronouns.

<u>Intelligent</u> man

<u>Red</u> rose

<u>Awesome</u> view

Proper adjectives

These are adjectives formed from proper nouns.

<u>Mexican</u> food

<u>European</u> fashion

Compound adjectives

These are made up of more than one word.

<u>Far-off</u> state

<u>Sage-green</u> dress

Possessive, demonstrative, and indefinite adjectives

These adjectives are similar to possessive, demonstrative, and indefinite pronouns, except that they modify a noun phrase, pronoun, or noun. Asking of the noun whose identifies a possessive adjective

Bart loved <u>his</u> lizard.

Whose lizard? <u>His</u>.

Chloe often gave comfort to <u>her</u> brother.

Whose brother? <u>Her</u>.
Interrogative Pronouns like <u>which</u>, <u>what</u>, <u>who</u>, or <u>whose</u> can act as Determiners.

<u>What</u> referee did Josh offend?

It doesn't matter <u>which</u> pizza you order.

<u>Which</u> runner arrived last?

He doesn't know <u>whose</u> wine he drank.

Asking of the noun <u>which</u> identifies a demonstrative adjective

Eryn drew <u>this</u> cat.

Which cat? <u>This</u> cat.

A woman bought <u>these</u> books.

Which books? <u>These</u> books.

 **4.1.4.4 FOR WRITERS, WHAT'S IN AN ADJECTIVE?**

We need adjectives to spruce up our sentences, but like everything in writing, the trick is to insert the right word in the right place.

Think of a cake. We have a piece of sponge cake of a given shape and size. This is the plot. Next, we cover the sponge with icing. This is the story. Rather than slapping colored stuff all over the cake and emptying a boxful of sequins and rhinestones over it, a sensible confectioner will stand back, ponder the overall design he dreams for his creation and set to work. He will pipe a little dab here, lacy bits over there, curlicues on the edges and feathery patterns on the sides. Gradually, the lump of baked dough and sugar will metamorphose into an object of rare beauty. Of course, besides sensitivity, aesthetic, and color sense, there's craft involved. The cake must taste good and have the right spongy texture, richness, and aroma. There are so-so cakes and scrumptious masterpieces.

At school, teachers advise students to use many adjectives to dress sentences and add interest to their writing. This is sound advice for learners, but fiction writing is an art form.

Take an average grade school student's story:

John, a <u>dark-eyed</u> boy with <u>unkempt</u> <u>dark</u> hair, about <u>five foot three</u> and <u>plump</u>, walked slowly down the street. He was coming to pick up his girlfriend to take her to the <u>ice-cream</u> parlor for her <u>favorite</u> <u>vanilla</u> sundae. Mary, his <u>red-haired</u>, <u>shapely</u>, and <u>gorgeous</u> girlfriend, sat calmly toying with her hair on the <u>wooden</u> steps leading to the <u>wraparound</u> porch fronting her <u>stuccoed</u> house.

There's nothing wrong with the tale. The student has a good grasp of vocabulary: unkempt, shapely, wraparound, stuccoed... nice. It's a descriptive passage, *telling*, and empty of meaning beyond that of the words themselves. Both John and Mary are over-described and one wonders if glossing about their plans, or the house's construction, adds anything to the scene. Fourteen adjectives are unnecessary.

A fiction writer would zero in on the relevant issues: John is shabby and overweight. Mary is beautiful. John is on his way to pick her up. She's waiting for him.

John strolled down the street, the breeze toying with his <u>tousled dark</u> hair. A smile tugged at his lips when he spotted Mary on the front steps of her porch. She flicked her <u>flaming</u> mane, and John sucked in his belly, once more awed that such a <u>beautiful</u> creature was his girlfriend.

Four adjectives and no adverbs tighten the prose. But the important issues in the scene are shown rather than told. John is chubby and self conscious. His hair is in a mess. He's in love with a gorgeous redhead. We have hinted at her beauty and his ungainly appearance, but the rest is only implied.

The soul of prose is in the verb, followed closely in importance by the noun. Choosing these with care will enrich any writing. Next in the list are adjectives followed by the remaining parts of speech.

"The dog ran down the street" is an excellent sentence; it tells us about *who* does *what* and *where*, but it doesn't mention or hint at anything beyond "dog" and "ran." A student may succumb to temptation and add handfuls of icing to decorate an otherwise dry sentence. Add a couple of adjectives plus a couple of adverbs and the sentence reads: "The scruffy and multi-colored dog ran very quickly down the road." Not bad. Now we know much more about the dog and how it ran. But the question is: Do we need the adjectives and adverbs?

"Scruffy and multi-colored dog," begs for a wonderful and descriptive noun: "mongrel." "Ran very quickly," begs for a precise verb signifying exactly the action: bolt, dash, fly, etc. "The mongrel bolted down the road," describes the dog and how it ran.

Using few adjectives and fewer adverbs compels the writer to seek strong verbs and nouns, which brings us to the gregarious nature of adjectives and the bent many writers have to let them get away with it. "The tall, buxom, and beautiful woman," carries a fraction of the weight of "The statuesque woman."

Piling up adjectives is a serious flaw in fiction writing, to be avoided at all costs by choosing the correct descriptor.

When settling down to straighten a first draft, scour the text for nouns qualified by two or more adjectives. In every instance, select the strongest, the one that conveys the image you want to portray and discard the rest. Whenever possible, conjure stronger verbs and nouns to remove adjectives, and the prose will grow.

There's a joke about adjectives going round editorial circles and expressed in equations:

$1 = 1$

$1 + 1 = \frac{1}{2}$

$1 + 1 + 1 = 0$

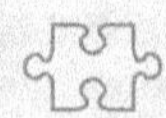

4.1.5 THE DETERMINER

Some grammarians do not consider Determiners to be adjectives and give them a class of their own. In this manual, we've followed that trend.

4.1.5.1 WHAT'S A DETERMINER?

Determiners "mark" nouns. That is to say, determiners are words placed in front of a noun to clarify which or how many, for example. Determiners belong at the beginning of noun phrases.

<u>A</u>, <u>my</u>, <u>the</u>, <u>this</u>, <u>those</u>, <u>each</u>, <u>either</u>, <u>some</u>, <u>few</u>, <u>all</u> and <u>both</u> are determiners.

 **4.1.5.2 HOW DO DETERMINERS WORK?**

Determiners can:

Define something or someone (specific or unspecific).

Define the number of people, things, or other nouns.

Attribute possession.

Define how things or people are distributed.

Specify the difference between nouns.

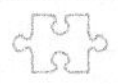 **4.1.5.3 ARE THERE DIFFERENT TYPES OF DETERMINERS?**

There are about fifty different Determiners in the English language. Their type depends on that of the noun and can be listed under the following classes:

Articles: a, an, the

Demonstratives: this, that, these, those, which, etc.

Possessives: my, your, our, their, his, hers, whose, etc.

Quantifiers: few, a few, many, much, each, every, some, any, etc.

Numbers: one, two, three, twenty, forty, etc.

Ordinals: first, second, 1st 2nd, 3rd, last, next, etc.[89]

 **4.1.5.4 FOR WRITERS, WHAT'S IN A DETERMINER?**

In our experience, when editing, beta-reading and reviewing fiction prose, we've discovered that many writers struggle with article choice, when the rules (for once) are clear-cut and easy to follow.
There are three articles: the, a, and an.
<u>The</u> is a definite article, which means that it's used to specify.

 **To refer to something that has already been mentioned** 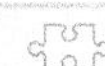

A fly and a fish fell in love.

The fly loved the fish's silvery scales, and the fish loved the fly's taste.

In the first sentence, "a fly" and "a fish" are introduced to the reader; hence, the indefinite article "a" is correct. In the second sentence, since we're already acquainted, we change the article to definite.

---

[89] Martha Kolln, Understanding English Grammar, 4th Edition. MacMillan Publishing Company: New York. 1994.

If it hadn't been for the name, Cain would have missed the face.
"Cesar Brown."
One finger poised over the channel button on the remote, Cain waited.
Applause, whistles; a few catcalls and a small man with a mop of silver hair struggled across a garish stage, leaning on a much younger woman.
Off camera, a voice with mushy vowels droned a stream of platitudes while Cain thought that Mr. Brown senior must have been an optimist.
Then, Cesar straightened and turned toward the camera.[90]

These are a first chapter's opening lines. Even if the character is familiar with his environment, the reader has not been introduced to the TV images. Hence "a small man," "a garish stage," and "a much younger woman." If these lines were in a later passage, after the show has been described, the writer would use "the small man," "the garish stage," or "the much younger woman."

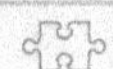

When the matter is known, even if it wasn't mentioned before

"Where's the hardware section?"

"It's on the fourth floor."

But it would be different if one or both of the characters didn't know.

"Is there a hardware section in this store?"

"Yes. The hardware section is on the fourth floor."

A and an are indefinite articles and used the same way grammatically, before a singular noun, or before the adjective that describes the noun but never with plural or uncountable nouns.

Most texts we've consulted state that the choice between a and an depends on whether or not the noun begins with a vowel. This is incorrect and confusing to many writers. There are no spelling rules to determine the correct a/an usage, except for pronunciation. Words opening with a vowel *sound* merit the an, those opening with a consonant *sound* get the a.

The full rule reads:

A, before a consonant sound, including the palatalized "y."

An before a vowel sound or unvoiced consonants.

Problem is not every word opening with a consonant has a consonant sound nor all words starting with a vowel have vowel sounds. Take "uniform." Though "u" is a vowel, it doesn't sound like one; hence "a uniform." (Pronounced "yuniform.")

Pronunciation can be dicey with words starting with "h," but fear not. Only four words starting with "h" in the English language merit an "an:" heir, honest, honor, and hour. Why? Because the "h" is silent; we hear a vowel sound. Although it was once taught that one should say "an hotel," modern usage is "a hotel" because the initial letter "h" is now sounded, ignoring the French origin of the word.

We write a European, a university, a unit, and a unicorn, even though the words start with a vowel.

Another structure to watch is when letters are said rather than pronounced. Example:

---

[90] Carlos J Cortes, Rent-a-Friend.

An FBI agent and a CIA agent walked into the bar where an S.O.S. symbol blinked in its window.[91]

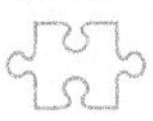

4.1.6 THE ADVERB

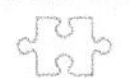

4.1.6.1 WHAT'S AN ADVERB?

An adverb is the part of speech that modifies a verb, adjective, or another adverb. <u>Quickly</u>, <u>well</u>, <u>there</u>, <u>still</u>, <u>very</u> and <u>almost</u> are all adverbs.

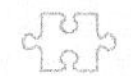

4.1.6.2 HOW DO ADVERBS WORK?

By modifying or adding information about a verb, adjective, or adverb.

Uses as verb modifier

John walked <u>quickly</u> toward the window.

Mary sat <u>silently</u> waiting for her tea and cake.

Uses as an adjective modifier

The new gardener was <u>impressively</u> dishy.

The sandals were <u>outrageously</u> expensive.

Uses as other adverb modifier

Mary typed <u>extremely</u> quickly.

The boat sailed <u>incredibly</u> swiftly.

4.1.6.3 ARE THERE DIFFERENT TYPES OF ADVERBS?

Yes, to indicate manner, place, time, frequency, or degree among others, and often answering questions such as how, when, where, or how much?

 Adverbs of manner

These answer the question, how?

John plays the piano <u>beautifully</u>.

Mary bakes <u>well</u>.

---

[91] Rita Webb

John must drive his motorbike <u>carefully</u>.

Sleep <u>soundly.</u>

Adverbs of place

These answer the question, *where?*

We saw Mary <u>there</u>.

We were waiting <u>here</u>.

We looked <u>everywhere</u>.

Have you seen my glasses <u>anywhere</u>?

I'm sure I left them <u>somewhere.</u>

Adverbs of time

These answer the question, *when?*

<u>Afterward</u> we decided to go by train.

I've played that game <u>before</u>.

We haven't started baking <u>yet</u>.

She is <u>still</u> a teenager.

Adverbs of frequency

These answer the question, *how many times?*

She's <u>always</u> honest.

They <u>sometimes</u> spend Sunday singing with the choir.

I have <u>often</u> wondered about the gender of the angels.

John <u>never</u> has any trouble with his neighbors.

Adverbs of degree

These answer the question *to what extent?*

The bottle is <u>almost</u> full.

I <u>quite</u> understand your concern.

We had <u>almost</u> reached the crossing when the train thundered by.

I am <u>just</u> beginning macramé lessons.

 ## Conjunctive adverbs

To join clauses we use conjunctive adverbs, such as: also, consequently, finally, furthermore, hence, however, incidentally, indeed, instead, likewise, meanwhile, nevertheless, next, nonetheless, otherwise, still, then, therefore, and thus.[92]

4.1.6.4 FOR WRITERS, WHAT'S IN AN ADVERB?

Adverbs are the tool of the lazy writer. Mark Twain

Amen. But since lazy writers don't read writing manuals, the quote is likely not applicable.

Adverbs modify other words, so they provide more information and add dimension to sentences. Therefore, there is nothing uncouth or bad about adverbs. Since we're against fanaticism of all kinds, including the current bigotry toward adverbs, let's try to shed a little light on the issue.

Like every other part of speech, adverbs have their place in fiction writing. With adverbs, it isn't a question of love or hate, moderation or extravagance, but usage.

The *misuse* of adverbs empurples prose and makes it look amateurish. But there's worse to come. Reckless use of adverbs can wreck a reader's experience by demystifying the story. The pleasure of reading derives from filling in *what the author doesn't tell*. If the writer decorates actions or statements with adverbs, there's no room for the reader's imagination. There is no ambiguity—a necessary aspect of literature. Most of the time people do things. They don't do things surreptitiously, succinctly, bashfully, imaginatively, or coyly. They just do them.

Adverbs provide a quick and effortless way to characterize, and inexperienced writers often neglect ways to describe a character in better, more meaningful ways.

Master editor Sol Stein names two rules for using adverbs:

> Keep an adverb that supplies necessary information. Example:
>
> "He tried running faster and fell."
>
> If he's already running, you must keep "faster." If you remove the adverb, the sentence means that he fell as soon as he started running.
> Keep an adverb that helps the reader visualize the precise image you want to project. Example:
>
> "She drove crazily, frightening the oncoming traffic."

And he goes on to add:

> "Don't let these exceptions make you lose sight of the fact that most adverbs can be eliminated."[93]

The real problem with sloppy adverb usage is that they often add unnecessary dimension—the adverb is redundant or a weak alternative.

---

[92] A conjunctive adverb is not strong enough to join two independent clauses without the aid of a semicolon.

[93] Stein on Writing, St Martin's Press, 1995, p 202.

Redundant adverbs can weaken strong verbs with sloppy tautologies.[94]

> The TV set blared loudly. Totally flabbergasted, John clenched his teeth tightly. In a few effortlessly easy strides he crossed the slightly Spartan room, violently yanked the cord from the wall socket and grinned widely.

Come on… How can you be a bit flabbergasted or even partially so? Clenched tightly? How on Earth can you clench your teeth if not tightly? Effortlessly easy? Slightly Spartan? It is, or it isn't. Violently yanked? And a darling of careless writers: "grinned widely." Can you "grin narrowly"? Each of these strong verbs and adjectives already implies the message of the adverb.

> "Hurry up," John said quietly. Then, they walked carefully past the Police Station.

In the first sentence, "said quietly" is weaker than "whispered" or "murmured." In the second, "walked carefully," is weaker than "sneaked" or "crept."

> "Hurry up," he whispered softly.

"Softly" adds nothing to the sentence, as a whisper is soft by definition.

So, which adverbs should we be wary of? Answer: The ones we use as fillers.

When used as modifiers of verbs, adverbs are ambiguous; they don't answer "to what degree" or "to what extent," despite what grammarians might say.

From a better-left-unnamed romance novel—by one of the sacred cows in the business—we've chosen this rare gem: *She crossed the room, moving determinedly.* Leaving aside that the writer has wrung a verb into a participle and then contorted it to adverbial form, what does "moving determinedly" mean? Did the woman sail, sweep, or march? Did she stomp, strut, or sashay?

We won't suggest that the use of adverbs in speech or writing is against the rules of the English language. We are saying that, with rare exceptions, *careless* use of "ly"-ending adverbs, *particularly*, makes bad writing.

This most common writing fault is also one that, when pointed out, writers—including experienced ones—will defend to the death. Why would decent writers support bad writing? There are many reasons, like ingrained habits, sheer pigheadedness, and an unpalatable detail: library shelves are chockablock with published works brimming with "ly"-ending adverbs.

A point to ponder is that these works are published *despite* sloppy adverbs, not *because* of them. One "ly" adverb every couple of pages (or, better still, every couple of chapters) may be acceptable. We've read pages and even paragraphs with scores of these horrors.

Adverbs are often found littering fiction writing. Some writers realize that their verbs are weak and tack on adverbs in hopes of adding intensity or precision. This mechanism often falls flat. Most adverbs are flab, or as a dear friend once said: "Adverbs are flatulence pushing on prose tissue."

> Frowning angrily, John moved swiftly toward Mary, saying very harshly, "You slut."

How's that for cheesiness?

> Scowling, he stalked toward Mary. "You slut!"

---

94 A tautology is an unnecessary repetition of meaning or, as Fowler described it "saying the same thing twice." Check Tautology, on page 568.

Why search for a perfect verb like "stumped" when "seriously confused" will do? Or "sprint" when "run swiftly" sounds good? Why bother to come up with "castigate" if we've written "berated harshly?"

Please, don't have your characters "teasing mercilessly" or "crushing terribly" or "roaming aimlessly" or "touching tenderly" or "wanting badly" or "thinking deeply." Instead, have them taunting, mangling, wandering, caressing, craving, or pondering.

Yet, the mortal sin of adverb use is in dialogue attributes, perhaps in a misguided attempt to break up the monotony of using only "he said" or "she said."

"Oh, no," said Hermione, stopping abruptly.

"Who?" said Harry as they backtracked quickly.

"Careful not to walk through anyone," said Ron nervously.[95]

That writers who sell a zillion books are so careless and disrespectful to their readers—not to mention staff editors who prostitute themselves into accepting such lines—is a disgrace. "Ly"-adverbs in tags and attributes are the writer's attempt to explain dialogue and palm emotions that belong in the dialogue itself. Good dialogue doesn't need props.[96]

What can we do about it? Upon completion of a first draft, use the "Edit/Find" feature of your word processor. Type in "ly," hit "find," and study any sentence that contains the "ly" adverb. (Beware: not every "ly"-ending word is an adverb.) If the adverb is the best choice or the only option, leave it. If the adverb is redundant, weak, or susceptible to being replaced by a stronger construction, rewrite.

In an interview, Nobel Prize winner Gabriel Garcia Marquez, said:

"...before Chronicle of a Death Foretold, there are many adverbs in my writing. In Chronicle, I think there is one. After that, there are none."

But this declaration can be misinterpreted (and often is). Mr. Garcia Marquez was referring to adverbs ending in "mente," the equivalent of "ly" in English, not *every* adverb. There are thousands of adverbs, both in the Spanish and English languages, without which meaningful prose would be impossible

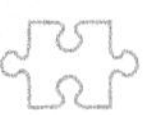

4.1.7 THE CONJUNCTION

4.1.7.1 WHAT'S A CONJUNCTION?

"Conjoin" means to link, to unite, or to join. Therefore, a conjunction is the part of speech that joins, links, or unites other words or groups of words in a sentence.

<u>And</u>, <u>but</u>, <u>or</u>, <u>either</u>, <u>when</u> and <u>as</u> are conjunctions.

---

[95] J. K. Rowling, Harry Potter and the Chamber of Secrets.

[96] In dialogue (not tags or attributes) adverbs are often justifiable because people often riddle their speech with "naturally, definitely, really," etc.

 **4.1.7.2 HOW DO CONJUNCTIONS WORK?**

Conjunctions work by joining words, phrases, and clauses, as in the following examples:

Gladys <u>and</u> Maria are students.

The conjunction "and" connects two nouns.

She will read <u>or</u> write.

The conjunction "or" links two verbs

It is late, <u>but</u> the shop will still be open.

The conjunction "but" joins two independent clauses.

 **4.1.7.3 ARE THERE DIFFERENT TYPES OF CONJUNCTIONS?**

There are three types of conjunctions: coordinating, subordinating, and correlative.

Coordintaing conjunctions

These conjunctions connect two elements comparable in importance and structure. These elements may be single words or groups of words, as long as they are grammatically equal or similar, like two nouns, two phrases, or two independent clauses.

The seven coordinating conjunctions in English are:, and <u>but, or, nor, for, so, yet</u>. Of these,, and <u>but, or,</u> and <u>so,</u> are used the most.

Spring <u>and</u> fall are usually mild in this state.

The coordinating conjunction "and" links two nouns.

This meat cookery book is particularly bizarre, <u>for</u> a vegan wrote it.[97]

The coordinating conjunction "for" links two independent clauses.

Sonia spent last summer hacking through jungle <u>and</u> nursing insect bites.

The coordinating conjunction "and" links the participial phrases "hacking through jungle" and "nursing insect bites."

Subordinating conjunctions

A subordinating conjunction connects two unequal parts of a sentence, linking a dependent clause to a main clause.

I ate the porridge (main clause), <u>although</u> it was stone-cold (dependent clause).

---

[97] "Take the bloody hunk of flesh that you ruthlessly ripped from a living being and bake it until your murderous guilt burns away…" Wendy Swore.

The most common subordinating conjunctions are <u>after</u>, <u>although</u>, <u>as</u>, <u>because</u>, <u>before</u>, <u>how</u>, <u>if</u>, <u>once</u>, <u>since</u>, <u>than</u>, <u>that</u>, <u>though</u>, <u>till</u>, <u>until</u>, <u>when</u>, <u>where</u>, <u>whether</u>, and <u>while</u>.

Unlike coordinating conjunctions, which always come between the words or clauses they conjoin, subordinating conjunctions usually come at the beginning of the subordinate clause.

John felt drowsy <u>after</u> he finished his supper.

"After" introduces the subordinate clause "he finished his supper."

<u>If</u> Ben is a good boy, he can watch cartoons after supper.

"If" introduces the subordinate clause "Ben is a good boy."

Peter had to begin counting marbles over again <u>when</u> he lost count.

The subordinating conjunction "when" introduces the dependent clause "he lost count."

Frequent travelers argue that aisle seats are better <u>because</u> passengers can stretch their legs.

In this sentence, "because" introduces the dependent clause "passengers can stretch their legs."

Correlative conjunctions

Correlative conjunctions always appear in pairs and consist of a coordinating conjunction and an adjective or adverb. Their role is to join grammatically equal sentence elements. The most common are <u>both</u>/<u>and</u>, <u>either</u>/<u>or</u>, <u>neither</u>/<u>nor</u>, <u>not only</u>/<u>but also</u>, and <u>as</u>/<u>as</u>.

<u>Both</u> my cousin Jack <u>and</u> my uncle Bubba are over six feet tall.

In this sentence, the correlative conjunction "both...and" is used to link the two noun phrases.

Take <u>either</u> a savory sandwich <u>or</u> a slice of apple cake.

Here the correlative conjunction "either...or" links two noun phrases: "a savory sandwich" and "a slice of apple cake."

4.1.7.4 FOR WRITERS, WHAT'S IN A CONJUNCTION?

Beginning a sentence with a coordinating conjunction breaks no modern grammatical rule.

Of course, some high school English teachers and even Strunk and White in their *The Elements of Style* would disagree. They would argue that a coordinating conjunction implies a previous clause to which the sentence should be connected. They would further contend that the practice would result in a sentence fragment.

We are on shaky ground here. The arbitrary rules dictating that (a) sentence fragments, (b) opening a sentence with a coordinating conjunction, or (c) failing to insert a comma between two conjoined sentences are wrong practices belong to another era. Writers have ignored these restrictions since Guttenberg.

But issues are seldom simple. The truth is that a sentence starting with a conjunction draws attention to itself. Writers should be aware of this detail and measure such syntax fireworks with care. After perusing the sentence starting with a coordinating conjunction, the writer should question if the passage functions without it and determine if the sentence in question should be connected to the previous one. If the answers are negative, stet.[98]

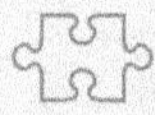 **4.1.8 THE PREPOSITION**

 **4.1.8.1 WHAT'S A PREPOSITION?**

A part of speech that links nouns, pronouns, and phrases to other words in a sentence. The word or phrase that the preposition introduces is the object of the preposition. Here is a short list of the most common, single-word prepositions:

About, above, across, after, against, along, among, around, at, before, behind, below, beneath, beside, between, beyond, but, by, despite, down, during, except, for, from, in, inside, into, like, near, of, off, on, onto, out, outside, over, past, since, through, throughout, till, to, toward, under, underneath, until, up, upon, with, within, and without.

4.1.8.2 HOW DO PREPOSITIONS WORK?

A preposition indicates the temporal, spatial, or logical relationship of its object to the rest of the sentence.

The heart is on the chest.

The heart is in the chest.

The heart is beneath the chest.

The heart is leaning against the chest.

The heart is beside the chest.

She held the heart over the chest.

She rested the heart on her lap during breakfast.

In each of these sentences, diverse prepositions locate the noun "heart" in space or in time.

One of the wonders of prepositions is their ability to fashion prepositional phrases, or groups of words we can use as one. A word such as "in" or "after" is meaningless and hard to define with reference to itself. For instance, if we attempt to define prepositions like "in" or "between" or "on," we invariably use other words to show how something is situated in relationship to these. In the glass means contained, just as between can be hemmed or gripped. Most of the time, prepositions combine with other words in structures called prepositional phrases, which are formed by joining the preposition, its object, and any associated adjectives or adverbs. Then, the prepositional phrase becomes a modifier. It acts as an adverb or adjective to modify nouns; locate elements in time and space; or detail where, when, or under what conditions something happened.

The underscored words in the following sentences are prepositions:

---

[98] "stet" is a Latin word used by proofreaders and editors. It means "let it stand."

Mary aimed the dagger <u>at</u> the target.

In this sentence, the preposition "at" introduces the noun phrase "the target." The prepositional phrase "at the target" functions as an adverb describing where Mary aimed the dagger.

The rabbit hopped <u>across</u> the lava.

The preposition "across" introduces the noun phrase "the lava" and the prepositional phrase "across the lava" acts as an adverb, describing where the rabbit hopped.

4.1.8.3 ARE THERE DIFFERENT TYPES OF PREPOSITIONS?

Prepositions belong to different groups, although textbooks don't adhere to particular divisions. The most common groupings are:

Place: <u>at</u>, <u>on</u>, and <u>in</u>.

Location: <u>above</u>, <u>beneath</u>, and <u>around</u>.

Movement: <u>to</u>, <u>from</u>, and <u>toward</u>.

Time: <u>before</u> and <u>since</u>.

Then there are prepositions paired with nouns, adjectives, and verbs. Prepositions have the unique trait of latching to other words. Usage fuses them so they become one word for communication.

With nouns

confusion <u>about</u>

desire <u>for</u>

success <u>in</u>

understanding <u>of</u>

With adjectives

familiar <u>with</u>

interested <u>in</u>

married <u>to</u>

worried <u>about</u>

With verbs

grow <u>up</u>

pay <u>for</u>

think <u>about</u>

trust <u>in</u>

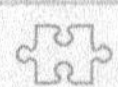 **4.1.8.4 FOR WRITERS, WHAT'S IN A PREPOSITION?**

You might have heard that ending a sentence with a preposition is iffy grammar.

Based on a dicey historical precedent, the rule took hold until grammarians pointed out the nonsense.

Bill Bryson wrote:

> The "rule" was enshrined by one Robert Lowth, an eighteenth-century Bishop of London and a gentleman grammarian. In his wildly idiosyncratic but curiously influential *Short Introduction to English Grammar*, Lowth urged his readers not to end sentences with prepositions if they could decently avoid it. Too many people took him much too literally and for a century and a half the notion held sway. Today, happily, it is universally condemned as a pointless affectation. Indeed, there are many sentences where the preposition could scarcely come anywhere but at the end: "This bed hasn't been slept in;" "What is the world coming to;" "I don't know what you are talking about."[99]

Ending a sentence with a preposition is not a grammatical error but... (In English grammar, there's always a "but"). One of the *real* rules of fiction writing is to make every word count, something we repeat to exhaustion in this manual. The corollary is that every word we write must be justified. Nothing advances more the quality of a writer's output than ruthless inquisition: "What are you doing here?" If the text answers, "I don't know," or "looking pretty," the word, clause, sentence, paragraph or chapter should go. Extra prepositions—when the meaning is clear without them—is a case in point.

Where did Mary go <u>to</u>?

John will go later <u>on</u>.

Where did Mary get this <u>at</u>?

In the three previous examples, we don't need the prepositions. Another common problem is to pile up prepositions one after the other:

The glass fell off <u>of</u> the table.

Mary looked out <u>of</u> the window.

John tore the photo <u>up</u> into small pieces.

In these examples, the underscored preposition is redundant.

"Gotcha! You used 'pile up' in the earlier explanation."

Indeed, we did. "Pile up" is a phrasal verb, a two-word verb or a verb-preposition phrase, not unlike pile on, pile down, pile in, or pile out.[100]

For native English speakers, choosing the right preposition seldom presents a problem. For those for whom English is a second language, the subtle distinctions can be difficult. Even the mighty

---

[99] Bill Bryson, Troublesome Words, 2002 Penguin Books, p 161.

[100] George A. Meyer, The Two-Word Verbs: a Dictionary of the Verb-Preposition Phrases in American English, 1975, de Gruyter Mouton.

Conrad struggled with his English prepositions. Carlos? He's a lost cause when it comes to prepositions.

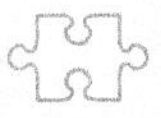 **4.1.9 THE INTERJECTION**

 **4.1.9.1 WHAT'S AN INTERJECTION?**

Interjections are words used to convey sentiments or emotions.

We've listed below a few of the most common interjections, though many of them are archaic and should be chosen with care, matching them to the character and setting of the fiction work.

Ah, alas, darn, dear, eh, er, good, goodness, gosh, great, ha, hah, hello, help, here, hey, hi, hmm, ho, huh, humph, hurrah, hush, indeed, lo, now, o, oh, oops, ouch, so, stop, there, tush, tut, ugh, uh, uh-huh, um, well, what, whoa, whoopee, whoops, why, wow, yay, yes, yo, yuck.

 **4.1.9.2 HOW DO INTERJECTIONS WORK?**

By conveying an emotional item such as surprise, pleasure, sorrow, recognition, resignation, delight, pity, grief, shock, pain, reluctance, doubt, etc.

In most instances, interjections are set at the beginning of a sentence or clause, to express various emotions. Interjections are seldom grammatically related to any other part of the sentence.

Examples:

"Phew, that was close."

"Hey! Leave her alone!"

"Jumping jehosaphat! What a pleasant surprise."

"Great! Let's do it again."

 **4.1.9.3 ARE THERE DIFFERENT TYPES OF INTERJECTIONS?**

Besides exclamations and filled pauses, discussed in the next section, some introductory expressions such as yes, no, indeed, and well also work as interjections.

Examples:

"No! You can't have my marbles."

"Indeed, a fine figure of a man."

"Yes, this is for real."

Some interjections are onomatopoeias (sounds) without any other meaning.
Examples:

"Shh… you'll wake her up."

"Argg! I forgot to stir the sugar."

"Mmmm, this tastes delicious."

4.1.9.4 FOR WRITERS, WHAT'S IN AN INTERJECTION?

Interjections are dialogue devices to transmit the emotion of the speaker or narrator. For fiction writers, creating realistic dialogue is one of the most difficult aspects of the craft. Interjections, if used with care, can convey natural-sounding lines.

Let's try a silly game. In a room, we have a group of males waiting for the bride: the groom, a teenager, a grandfather, a young brother, and the father. We have lines of dialogue but we forgot to append their attributes. Can you tell who said what?

"You look nice."

"Hey, you look nice."

"Wow! You look nice!"

"Mmm… you look nice."

"Er, you look, hum, nice."

"You look nice." Is dry, sober and serious; it could be the grandfather.

"Hey, you look nice." This is a little more zesty, but restrained, no exclamation marks; it could be the father.

"Wow! You look nice!" Enthusiastic. Perhaps the young brother?

"Mmm… you look nice." The filled pause points at the groom. Yet, one of the writers of this manual pointed out that if anyone but the groom had said "Mmm…" it would make for an interesting story. Go figure.

"Er, you look, hum, nice." Finally, this sentence ripe with filled pauses could belong to the teenager.

With nouns

These interjections add realism to prose because we often use them in our conversations. But like every device in fiction writing, using interjections for effect or characterization wants careful dosing. This implies limiting their use to specific situations or the mannerisms of individual characters. Excessive use of interjections in writing is a flaw that signals stylistic immaturity.

Either a comma or an exclamation mark can punctuate an interjection. This opens possibilities to "grade" the emphasis of a sentence. For a mild effect, use a comma, and an exclamation mark for a stronger show of surprise, emotion, or deep feeling. Another exclamation mark on the following sentence will increase the effect.

"Hey, that horse is huge."

"Hey! That horse is huge."

"Hey! That horse is huge!"

In the previous examples, the first is declarative, lifeless. It doesn't convey anything beyond the information contained in the words "horse" and "huge."

The second example adds a tone of excitement and in the third the agitation multiplies.

Filled pauses

Another form of interjection, also useful for adding realism to dialogue, is the filled pause. Filled pauses are seldom "real" words, but onomatopoeias we introduce in our speech patterns when unsure, nervous, searching for the right word, or pausing. Examples of filled pauses are: um, mmm, hmm, er, uh, etc.

In fiction writing, the filled pause can convey character traits and emotions, awkwardness, impatience, doubt, nervousness, and lies.

> "Er, um, Dad, I, er, was wondering if, uh, you would, um, lend me your, er, car…"
> "No way.
> "Um, Dad… please?"
> "Forget it. Are you crazy? What do you want the car for?"
> "Uh, well, you see…."
> "No, I don't."
> "Um, I have a, uh, date."
> "A date? Zoinks! Why didn't you say so? Come here, son. Sit down and tell me about it. You'll need money. Here. A date you said? Someone we know?"

Context and the acceptable language conventions by the characters in the given scenes or settings are important before applying any literary devices.

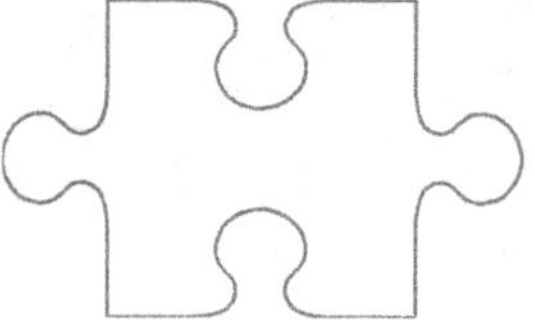

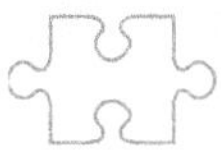 # 4.2 CLAUSE

While this book only scratches the surface of the subject of grammar, our goal is to list elements and concepts that every user of the language should recognize and know how to manipulate. We also strive to convey a rough idea about the roles of the different parts of speech and elements of syntax.

Sentences develop through phrases and clauses. Before we attempt a few examples, we must explain classification for each constituent of a sentence.

Different authors and texts confuse their readers by giving the same element contrary names. For instance, if we were asked to describe a book, we might say:

A. A stack of bound paper pages.

B. A vehicle to share facts, concepts or dreams.

If we wanted to describe a tool, we could use similar approaches. What's an Allen key (also called an Allen wrench or Hex key)?

A. A length of hexagonal-section steel bent in different shapes.

B. An implement to loosen and tighten screws with an Allen head or slot.

In answer A, we describe what it is.
In answer B, we describe its functions.
In the sentence, "<u>The old woman</u> carried a pail of water to the chicken coop":

A. "The old woman" is a noun phrase, (and a noun phrase is what it is).

B. "The old woman" is a subject, (that's its function within the sentence).

Both are correct, depending on perspective.

While grammarians may blow a fuse at the lightness with which we sail over intricate or complex definitions, we aim to explain functions, not technicalities. Unless we plan to write about the language—instead of using it—knowing how to parse non-identifying relative clauses won't help as much as knowing how clauses work within sentences.

In the English language there are two kinds of clauses: independent and dependent. Independent clauses contain a subject and verb that represent a complete idea. Dependent clauses, though they also contain a subject and verb, cannot stand alone. They need to be joined with an independent clause to make sense. Dependent clauses are of three types: noun, adjective, and adverb.

In other words, a clause can be a sentence that conveys a complete idea or a part of a sentence that does not. Either way, it contains its own subject and verb.

"Jesus wept," is a clause. It has a subject and a verb and conveys the full idea.

"When Jesus wept," is a clause. Though it has a subject and a verb, it doesn't convey an idea in full. This clause is dependent because it needs an independent clause to finish it.

Over the next few pages, we'll examine the main classes and types of clauses.

Why waste time with silly grammar concepts, rules, and regulations? I only want to write a novel.

Rewriting and editing, major components of successful fiction writing, demand that we understand the roles of different bits and pieces of prose. We need to acquire tools for streamlining our work, because tight, lean, and energetic prose keeps manuscripts out of the slush pile.

To work with sentences and identify their different types, we need to know how clauses work. Detecting fiendish errors like run-ons, comma splices, and the like that editors don't want to see will become child's play.

4.2.1 INDEPENDENT CLAUSES

An independent clause—also called a <u>primary</u>, <u>main</u>, or <u>principal</u> clause—is a group of words that contains a subject and verb, expresses a complete thought, and can stand alone as a sentence.

Mary shuffled back to the hut.

This is a sentence containing a single clause. Therefore, an independent clause can be a sentence. Why "independent?" Because it expresses a complete thought or idea and stands alone. We could use the above sentence to open or close a paragraph, scene, or chapter.

Mary shuffled back to the hut after watering the chickens.

In this example, "Mary shuffled back to the hut" retains its role as the primary clause, because it contains the subject and predicate (verb) of the full sentence.

The primary clause "Mary shuffled back to the hut," contains a complete idea. The rest is additional information. Do we need "after watering the chickens?" That's a decision the writer must make when editing. Have we mentioned where Mary was in the last few lines? If affirmative, the information may be redundant.

Remember that we underlined <u>primary</u>, <u>main</u>, and <u>principal</u> earlier on? We did so because learning to separate concepts or ideas from additional information is an essential part of the writer's craft. Full ideas are seldom superfluous, but the information we append to them often is. On rewrite, a tool to tighten the prose consists of identifying independent clauses and then questioning with open hostility whatever we've added to them: is the added detail necessary? Have we already mentioned, hinted, suggested, or otherwise implied the same aspect? If so, we delete.

4.2.2 DEPENDENT CLAUSES

Some clauses are groups of words that, although sporting a subject and verb, do not express a complete thought. These are dependent or subordinate clauses. They add information to the sentence by acting as an adjective, adverb, or noun (hence the terms adjective clauses, adverb clauses, and noun clauses). Often, a conjunction introduces a dependent clause.

When Mary shuffled back to the hut…

The burly Cossack was running a bath? The Big Bad Wolf sprang out of the closet?

The conjunction "when," also called a <u>dependent marker word</u>, has turned our independent clause into a dependent one. Why dependent? Because the idea or thought is not complete; it "depends" on something else. Therefore, a dependent clause cannot be a complete sentence.

A dependent marker word, added to the beginning of an independent clause turns it into a dependent one. Some common dependent markers are: <u>after</u>, <u>although</u>, <u>as</u>, <u>as if</u>, <u>because</u>, <u>before</u>, <u>even if</u>, <u>even though</u>, <u>if</u>, <u>in order to</u>, <u>since</u>, <u>though</u>, <u>unless</u>, <u>until</u>, <u>whatever</u>, <u>when</u>, <u>whenever</u>, <u>whether</u>, and <u>while</u>.

"The boy wolfed down his sandwich," is a robust independent clause; it doesn't need anything else to convey the image of a ravenous boy doing what boys do best with sandwiches. But add a dependent marker, any of them, and the clause's independence vanishes:

<u>As</u> the boy wolfed down his sandwich,

<u>Even though</u> the boy wolfed down his sandwich,

<u>When</u> the boy wolfed down his sandwich,

These dependent clauses now beg for more, else their meaning is missing. The boy is still attacking the sandwich, but something else happened, is happening, or is about to happen.

As the boy wolfed down his sandwich, Fido wagged his tail.

Even though the boy wolfed down his sandwich, he missed his favorite cartoon.

When the boy wolfed down his sandwich, Grandma brought another one.

Now the sentences are complete and their meaning clear. Are they stronger? Weaker? These are questions a good editor asks him/herself.

Knowing the difference between independent and dependent clause can help avoid common errors, rife in early drafts, like comma splices, fused sentences and fragments.

 **4.2.3 ESSENTIAL AND NONESSENTIAL CLAUSES**

The construction of a sentence determines if a clause is essential or nonessential. Unlike other mind-boggling aspects of English grammar, the distinction between these is gentle on the mind and easy to remember. We need essential clauses to clarify a sentence. A nonessential clause adds detail the writer might want to include for a number of reasons, but it's not necessary to improve meaning. In other words: A nonessential clause can often be deleted without changing its sense.

On rewrite, the difference can be capital. Nonessential clauses contribute details, nuances, and color to flesh the narrative style. However, they may also clutter otherwise powerful sentences and render them listless.

Call me, so we are on first-name terms, Ishmael.

We cringed with aesthetic horror as we wrote "so we are on first-name terms." The clause is cliché, unnecessary and telling. Mr. Melville's bones would rattle. Many writers would defend such an aberration on the grounds that the sentence "needs" the information. In doing so, they would underestimate the average reader's imagination and the beauty of showing.

"Call me Ishmael,"[101] besides being one of the most rotund first lines in English literature, already implies what we've added. Rather than additional information, the additional clause is redundant.

Before we delve further, it's important to point out that U.S. grammarians often refer to essential and nonessential clauses as restrictive and nonrestrictive and the British as defining and non-defining. These are different words to name the same classifications.

So then, essential or non-essential. What's the difference?

When a sentence is vague, an unclear noun—which may or may not be the subject of the sentence—is often the culprit.

The <u>boy</u> ran to join his friends by the pond.

Unless we have disclosed the boy's identity on previous lines, a reader might frown: which boy? There are many boys in the neighborhood.

The <u>man</u> has landed a leading role in the Pirate's play.

If we have introduced several men in our tale, trying to determine which man is on his way to stardom may prove difficult.

To help the reader work out which boy or man we're writing about, we need a helping clause. And that's the role of essential clauses.

An essential clause is a group of words that adds precision to an ambiguous noun. Check these reworked examples:

The boy <u>who wolfed down his sandwich ran</u> to join his friends by the pond.

Okay, now we know. It's the boy with the big appetite.

The man <u>who owns a chatty parrot</u> has landed a leading role on the Pirate's play.

That man? Now we wonder who's landed the job; the man or the parrot.

These clauses have helped clarify the nouns "boy" and "man" by adding information.

Next we can turn the essential clauses above into nonessential clauses by tweaking the sentences a little:

Timmy, <u>who wolfed down his sandwich</u>, ran to join his friends by the pond.

Mr. Burns, <u>who owns a chatty parrot</u>, has landed a leading role on the Pirate's play.

In place of indefinite nouns like "boy" or "man" we have specific proper nouns: Timmy and Mr. Burns.

Changing the nature of the nouns has had a deeper effect on those sentences. The clauses are now nonessential. Although the detail in these clauses might be colorful or interesting, it's not necessary, for we know which boy and which man because they are named. To signal the nonessential nature of these clauses, we have surrounded them with commas to separate them from the rest of the sentence.

A word of warning. Nonessential clauses interrupt the flow of a sentence and can affect the pace because the reader will pause at the information. If the information is not essential for clarity, it should be deleted.

---

[101] First line. Moby-Dick, Herman Melville, 1851.

To sustain pace and narrative flow, it pays to remove nonessential clauses. The removed clause can be crafted into a short sentence to follow the original or, if it contains important details, we can rewrite the complete sentence.

The man, who runs the cafeteria, is the only Tutsi in Queens.

The man is the only Tutsi in Queens. He runs the cafeteria.

In many instances, and to control pace, a pair of terser sentences might be more effective than one containing commas.

And another word of caution. Punctuation is not without risks, and writers should exercise great caution, lest they alter the meaning of their sentences with a comma.

The hobo, who leans on a lamppost, will make a killing from churchgoers.

This example, with commas, contains a nonessential clause. It refers to a specific hobo. It tells us his whereabouts, then about his profits.

The hobo who leans on a lamppost will make a killing from churchgoers.

The second example uses an essential clause. Without the commas, the sentence states that any hobo who leans on a lamppost will benefit from the churchgoers' largesse.

4.2.3.1 HOW TO PUNCTUATE ESSENTIAL/NONESSENTIAL CLAUSES

To surround a clause with commas or not will depend on the clause's nature. This detail can be an unexpected gift for a weary writer when laboring on rewrite. If a sentence contains a well-defined common noun, the nonessential clause is often a mere accessory. And "accessories" can be pruned to tighten the prose.

On rewrite, a shrewd writer will peruse clauses surrounded by commas with murderous intent. Check the following example:

As we entered the bar, we spotted a group of tall women slurping Margaritas. They didn't eye us as we expected. The women, built like linebackers, carried on drinking.

The clause "built like linebackers" is nonessential since we know which women. Thus the clause requires commas.

If an essential clause provides necessary information about the vague noun it describes, we shouldn't use punctuation around it.

The coffeemaker <u>that Paul purchased from E-Bay</u> makes a farting sound whenever he switches it on.

The moles are nesting in the room <u>where Kurt hides his still</u>.

The attendant <u>who manned the pumps</u> didn't know that Renée's Ferrari doesn't run on diesel.

But if the underlined clauses are decorative and unnecessary—or nonessential—we must punctuate them.

The Studebaker coffeemaker, <u>which Paul purchased from E-Bay</u>, makes a farting sound whenever he switches it on.

The moles are nesting in the basement room, where Kurt hides his still.

Carlos, <u>who manned the pumps</u>, didn't know that Renée's Ferrari doesn't run on diesel.

In these examples, the clause surrounded by commas adds information to an already defined noun. It's up to the writer to determine if the detail is redundant:

The Studebaker coffeemaker makes a farting sound whenever Paul switches it on.

The moles are nesting in the basement.

Carlos didn't know that Renée's Ferrari doesn't run on diesel.

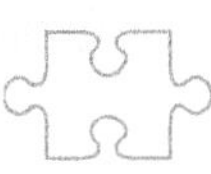 # 4.3 SENTENCE

What is a sentence? A sentence is a construction of clauses. A sentence starts with a capital letter and ends with a period, question, or exclamation mark. Examples:

I am.

Jackdaws love my big sphinx of quartz.

The only people for me are the mad ones, the ones who are mad to live, mad to talk, mad to be saved, desirous of everything at the same time, the ones who never yawn or say a commonplace thing, but burn, burn, burn, like fabulous yellow roman candles exploding like spiders across the stars and in the middle you see the blue centerlight pop and everybody goes "Awww!"[102]

The first example is the shortest sentence in the English language; the second is a thirty-one letter pangram—a composition using all the letters of the alphabet. The third is… a holistic jewel from one of the finest novels of the 20th century, written in three weeks on a 120-foot long roll of paper by a writer we love. All three have one thing in common: they are sentences.

Sentences are the largest element of the English language ruled by grammar. Any text or conversation containing more than one sentence falls outside the competence of grammar and enters into the realm of discourse.

We create language from words, but the unit of grammar is the clause. It follows that the building blocks of sentences are clauses. This is the reason we insisted a writer must be familiar with the concept of clause before we begin our work with sentences.

The English language has two sentence classifications:

According to their clause structure.

According to form.

Structurally there are four sentence types:

Simple

Compound

Complex

Compound–Complex

In relation to form, sentences fall into another four groups or kinds:

Declarative

---

[102] Jack Kerouac; On the Road.

Interrogative

Exclamatory

Imperative

In the following sections, we will examine both sentence classifications.

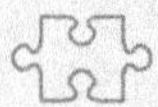 **4.3.1 SIMPLE SENTENCES**

The simple sentence is the most natural sentence structure. It contains a single clause, usually consisting of only a subject and predicate.

Jenny ate a dog.

Peter stole another billfold.

Mother scratched.

This is the first type of sentence children learn, and the most common in everyday speech. For writers, simple sentences are priceless to capture the reader's attention and drive the plot forward. Of course, like all good things, simple sentences must be meted with care; overusing them can result in choppy and immature writing.

All simple sentences consist of a subject and predicate.

Subject—Predicate

The lover—climbed the fence

The dandelion seeds—have blown all over the place.

That Timmy loves hanging out with lovely Brenda—doesn't surprise his dad.

Purple—is Courtney's favorite color.

Finally, a simple sentence may consist of one or many words:

Grow!

Flowers grow.

Flowers grow wildly.

Flowers grow wildly on the edge of the forest.

The flowers that are cosseted under the shade of tall trees grow wildly on the edge of the forest.

We've constructed the above example to dispel a myth dear to many writers; namely, that one can tell a simple sentence from a compound or complex one by its length. Not so. A simple sentence can contain any number of words. But writers should be wary of long simple sentences, as they tend to be difficult to read and comprehend.

4.3.2 COMPOUND SENTENCES

A compound sentence contains two or more clauses or simple sentences. These may be connected by coordinating conjunctions or punctuation. (A traditional mnemonic device to remember coordinating conjunctions is FANBOYS: For,, and Nor, But, Or, Yet, So.)

> I wanted to practice a jig.

The previous clause is a simple sentence, and so is:

> Donna wasn't in the mood.

Add a conjunction and we have a compound sentence:

> I wanted to practice a jig, but Donna wasn't in the mood.

The simple sentences might have dissimilar lengths, as in "Timmy brought two peanut sandwiches to the riverside," and "Brenda brought two cans of soda." Adding a conjunction and getting rid of the repeated verb transforms them into a passable compound sentence:

> Timmy brought two peanut sandwiches to the riverside, and Brenda two cans of soda.

One more example:

> Sonia is cute. I hate her.

> Sonia is cute, but I hate her.

In creative writing, the compound sentence is an excellent device to show balance between two concepts or strike a contrast between two similarly structured ideas. Example:

> The negotiators did not agree.

> The generals drew their swords.

Each of the above sentences contains well-defined ideas. Joining them, the compound sentence gathers strength.

> The negotiators did not agree, so the generals drew their swords.

Children use compound sentences early to connect ideas and deliver them chatterbox-fashion when excited:

> "I was at the back and Timmy had a coconut and he hit it with a stone and it didn't break and I took a turn and it breaked...broke... and it was full of water and..."

Though a silly example, it highlights the danger of joining too many simple sentences. Aware of the need to balance paragraphs with short and longer sentences, many inexperienced writers use conjunctions with abandon and string their sentence pearls into childish necklaces.

To get rid of choppy constructions, the writer can join multiple simple sentences to add variety. Three simple statements like:

> Sue bought the small-sized dress.

The dress fit like a glove.

She's elated.

We can rewrite as:

Sue bought the small-sized dress; it fits like a glove, so she's elated.

As we pointed out earlier, punctuation is another way to join simple sentences into compound ones. In some instances, a semicolon might be appropriate to replace a coordinating conjunction.

Michael has a drinking problem; his wine cellar is empty.

I am twelve years-old; she is only eleven.

There's magic in prose, a wonder that expresses itself in the nuances. These are the humble details that separate good writing from keyboard diarrhea. The difference between the simple sentences "Sonia is cute" "I hate her" and the compound "Sonia is cute, but I hate her" goes beyond a comma and a conjunction.

Yin and Yang in their construction, the first sentence is affirmative and the second negative. The first is positive, the second pejorative. Yet, there's no connection between the two statements; they could belong to different players, even different books, or chapters. Add a humble coordinating conjunction and a comma to transform these two sentences into the clauses of a compound one and magic happens:

Sonia is cute, but I hate her.

Same ideas, same ingredients, save for one extra word. The writer has tamed hate; he didn't need the first clause to express abhorrence. Rather than loathe, the new compound sentence blushes with the feeling of an endearment.

Writers who carelessly fling their words onto paper like chicken feed miss out on the endless possibilities of prose.

Now a warning about the effect of the dreaded comma splice and the run-on sentence. Although we'll highlight these horrors in several pasages this is an excellent place to warn about their mechanics.

As we've seen above, we need at least one independent clause to have a complete sentence.

Shermaine has polished her manuscript.

But there's nothing to stop our adding another independent clause to the first, such as:

She's over the moon.

Whether we end with a comma splice, a run-on, or a well-written sentence depends on the way we join these two independent clauses.

If we add them with nothing in between, we create a run-on.

Shermaine has polished her manuscript she's over the moon.

We can join them with a comma for a comma splice.

Shermaine has polished her manuscript, she's over the moon.

But if we summon a comma *and* a handy coordinating conjunction, we have a correct compound sentence.

Shermaine has polished her manuscript, and she's over the moon.

Of course, there are other ways. Rather than a compound sentence, we might strive for a complex one. If so, we can begin it with a subordinating conjunction:

Since Shermaine has polished her manuscript, she's over the moon.

This leads us to the next section.

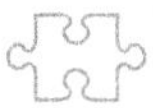 ### 4.3.3 COMPLEX SENTENCES

As we encounter the third kind of sentence, we can put our knowledge of dependent and independent clauses to the test.

Complex sentences contain one independent clause and one or more dependent clauses. By using the sentence constructions so far reviewed, we hope to show a logical progression from simple to complex.

Simple

> Sonia is cute. I hate her.

Compound

> Sonia is cute, but I hate her.

Complex

> Although Sonia is cute, I hate her.

In the third example, the use of a subordinating conjunction, also called a subordinator, transforms a simple sentence into a dependent clause. (The most common subordinating conjunctions are <u>after</u>, <u>although</u>, <u>as</u>, <u>because</u>, <u>before</u>, <u>how</u>, <u>if</u>, <u>once</u>, <u>since</u>, <u>than</u>, <u>that</u>, <u>though</u>, <u>till</u>, <u>until</u>, <u>when</u>, <u>where</u>, <u>whether</u>, <u>while</u>, etc.)

The order of dependent/independent clauses is not important in this sentence classification. Examples:

Dependent Clause—Independent Clause

Because of the weather,—we didn't go sailing.

Although we had to run,—we made it to the airport in time.

Independent Clause—Dependent Clause

I missed the shooting stars,—although I stayed up late.

I will go home,—after I buy the dynamite.

Dependent Clause—Independent Clause—Dependent Clause

Even though Lisa enjoyed the book,—she will not buy its sequel—because the reviews are awful.

After a swim,—we strolled along the promenade—before we dressed.

For writers, these three sentence kinds, their nature and iterations are important to convey the weight or importance of correlative ideas. Let's examine once more the examples above, this time in terms of "weight."

In the first example, though tone and meaning differ, both sentences have equal weight. Both express clear ideas. "Sonia is cute" is a complete statement. Of course, its meaning will hinge on Sonia's age. If she's a toddler, the sentence conveys the image of a cuddly little princess. If she were in her twenties, the image would remain positive but with ambiguous undertones. "Cute" is often a crutch adjective to describe someone who doesn't merit "gorgeous" or "beautiful." The second sentence is equally direct: "I hate her." It shares the properties of the first sentence. If Bobby (aged six) were to stomp out of his older sister's room, complaining she stole (make that borrowed) his computer game, the scene wouldn't have the same meaning if Bobby was forty, drunk, and in possession of a baseball bat.

In other words, both sentences in the first example are round, and the reader wouldn't know which of these ideas has more weight in the story. The writer must understand the construction well enough to know if the thoughts have equal value.

In the compound example, "Sonia is cute, but I hate her," there's added nuance. However, unless the surrounding text bolsters one or the other idea, the reader cannot determine which is more important, since both clauses could still stand as independent sentences.

In the third example, however, the sentence has changed. The first clause "Although Sonia is cute," is an incomplete thought, or in grammar parlance a dependant clause. We need something else to finish the idea; we need a dependent clause such as "I hate her."

A complex sentence is different from a simple sentence or a compound sentence because it shifts the focus over to the most important idea. In, "Although Sonia is cute, I hate her." The subordinating conjunction drains the first clause of its importance. Now we know that regardless of Sonia's cuteness, hate wins the day.

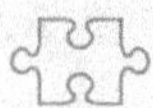 ### 4.3.4 COMPOUND-COMPLEX SENTENCES

The fourth and final sentence structure is the compound-complex sentence. Now that we have an idea of the other sentence types, the forbidding "Compound-Complex" title shouldn't cause much trepidation. Just as two or more simple sentences formed compound ones, compound-complex sentences are nothing more than combinations of one or more compound sentences and one or more complex sentences. A more precise definition would be: Sentences with at least one dependent clause and two or more independent clauses are compound-complex.

Example:

Sonia went to the beach because she wanted to get a tan, but she forgot the cream.

Here we have an independent clause:

Sonia went to the beach

Followed by a dependent one:

because she wanted to get a tan

Together, they form a complex sentence:

Sonia went to the beach because she wanted to get a tan

If we append the independent clause "She forgot the cream" with the conjunction "but," we have a compound-complex sentence.

We can link the clauses with coordinating or subordinating conjunctions.

Unless we hurry up, your dad will complain, **so** get your socks on.

<u>Dependent</u>   <u>Independent</u>   <u>Independent</u>

Familiarity with sentence structure is critical for creating sentence variety, which is the soul of rhythm in creative writing, a major component of voice and style. Too many consecutive sentences sharing a similar construction soon give the prose a monotonous flavor.

Opening a passage with a simple sentence, following with compound or complex sentences, or interspacing simple and complex sentences will result in forceful and agile prose.

A few children played with marbles. Over in a corner, two cats turned something with their paws. A man with a white, many-chinned face and an under lip that stood out like a ledge, sat outside a dark entrance reading a paper and darting vigilant glances at the boys and the cats. The streets teemed with life and hope. Somewhere, fingers tore from a slightly off-key piano an old Russian melody; a lament with the bitter calmness of dawn after a pogrom.[103]

4.3.5 SENTENCE CLASSES

We have now reviewed how we construct sentences and have analyzed them in terms of structure. Another sentence classification describes why we wrote the sentences in the first place.

We craft sentences to describe things, people, or situations; we make statements or requests and we issue orders and exclamations to convey strong emotions. Since we have countless uses for them, it seems there should be hundreds of sentence types.

Yet, every sentence we write can only have one of four purposes: to state, command, question, or exclaim.

According to their uses, sentences can be:

Declarative

Interrogative

Exclamatory

Imperative

While it's true that sentences have similarities—all convey information—they are more easily recognized by their differences.

To identify a sentence's role, we only have to question the sentence with, "what are you doing?"

If the sentence describes, illustrates, declares, or explains something, it's a declarative sentence and will end with a period.

---

[103] Carlos J Cortes, Mahdi.

The dog ate the newspaper.

If the sentence poses a question or requests information, it's an interrogative sentence and will end with a question mark.

Where did the paper go?

If the sentence states something, more or less forcefully, or proclaims shock, or a strong emotion, it's an exclamatory sentence and will end on an exclamation mark.

The newspaper is gone!

If the sentence gives an order or instructs someone to do something, it's an imperative sentence and as the declarative type, it will end with a period.

Catch that dog.

Of course, nothing in English syntax could be so straightforward. Take the following exchange:

Man: "Excuse me, madam; is there a long way to Tipperary?"

Woman: "Go to hell."

The first sentence is clearly interrogative (it ends in a question mark.)

But, what about the second one? In theory, it's an imperative sentence since it gives a directive. We issue directives for someone to act a given way, and we don't think "madam" intended for the man to carry her recommendation to the letter.

Mary comes home after a night out on the tiles. John is waiting. As she enters the house, he barrels down the stairs hefting a baseball bat. Mary trains a large revolver on her beloved's chest and flutters her eyelashes.

"Go on. Hit me."

Though "Hit me," is an imperative sentence, we doubt Mary expects John to follow instructions.

And the moral behind these examples is? Though their classification is clear, sometimes the sentence's purpose doesn't fully adjust to its discourse function.

We will review this classification's syntactic forms in the following sections.

 **4.3.6 DECLARATIVE SENTENCES**

The declarative sentence is by far the most important, and the most common in English literature. Check any book you're reading to discover that most of the sentences in the prose are declarative. We can write scenes, chapters, and even full narrative novels using only this form. This is so, because declarative sentences don't require answers or reactions from other players—or the readers. The role of a declarative sentence is to convey information, and most sentences follow this pattern.

Miro's art is over my head.

I've always loved ducks because they have a sexy walk.

Why you draw your gun when I show you my new bat is beyond me.

After a while, she often pondered, commuters become inured to off-key music, mangled limbs, and poorly written cardboard signs pitching man's miseries.[104]

The third sentence contains an indirect question, "Why should you draw your gun?" but only direct questions punctuated with a question mark justify an interrogative sentence.

As in the examples above, declarative sentences may be short and simple or lengthier and complex; structure doesn't affect their purpose. A declarative sentence does not command, question, or proclaim but make statements.[105]

I like buttered fettuccini.

I used to be snow white, but I drifted.[106]

Urbanites often refer to pigeons as "winged rats" because of their predatory behavior.

When we go to the movies, I love candied popcorn, but only if we share.

Marcia has a pert nose and lots of freckles.

We always punctuate declarative sentences with a simple period and use ordinary word order, placing the subject before the verb.

 ### 4.3.7 INTERROGATIVE SENTENCES

The next kind of sentence is the interrogative. These are also known as questions. Most interrogative sentences expect answers, information, confirmation, or the denial of a statement. Often, they begin with a question word (what, who, or how) or an auxiliary verb (be, do, can, or would).

What are you doing this evening?

Can I have more meatloaf?

Has your new dress shrunk?

We must be careful to distinguish between direct and indirect questions. Direct questions normally reverse the word order, placing the verb before the subject, and end with a question mark.

 ### 4.3.7.1 DIRECT/INTERROGATIVE SENTENCES

Is that a Rottweiler?

What did she do to her dress?

---

[104] Carlos J Cortes, Where's me man?

[105] There's an anecdote, perhaps an urban legend, about Maurice Saatchi, the advertising wizard. During the Christmas season, Maurice was on his way to a meeting when he spotted a beggar huddled behind his "I'm hungry" sign and an empty bowl. Marker in hand, Maurice approached the beggar for permission to edit the sign. The meeting over, Maurice returned to check the beggar's fortune, and determined with satisfaction that his bowl brimmed with coins. The sign now read 'I'm hungry, and it's Christmas." Yes, words matter.

[106] Mae West

Indirect questions normally do not use the inverted subject-verb order or end with a question mark.

 **4.3.7.2 INDIRECT/DECLARATIVE SENTENCES**

I wonder if other dogs think Rottweilers are the Gestapo.

I want to know what she did to the dress.

According to form, we can classify interrogative sentences into the following categories:

Yes-No

Alternative

Adverb-pronoun interrogatives

Tagged

Rhetorical

 **4.3.7.3 YES-NO INTERROGATIVE SENTENCES**

These sentences require answers limited to yes or no:

Are you lonesome tonight?

Is this seat taken?

Have you taken the garbage out?

 **4.3.7.4 ALTERNATIVE INTERROGATIVE SENTENCES**

These offer different responses, which are not yes or no.

Should I wear the leopard-print windbreaker or the gray coat?

Do you want apples, pears, or a tot of malt whiskey?

Is she Fifi, Mary, or Genevieve?

 **4.3.7.5 ADVERB/PRONOUN INTERROGATIVES**

These sentences are introduced by interrogative adverbs or pronouns, such as what, where, or who.

What's going on here?

Where is my new shirt?

Who wrote Naná?[107]

---

[107] Just in case you're wondering; Anaïs Nin.

 **4.3.7.6 TAG QUESTIONS**

These consist of auxiliary verbs followed by a pronoun and are tagged onto the end of declarative sentences.

> Sonia has grown since we last saw her, hasn't she?

> The kids are having fun, aren't they?

> My Bouillabaisse is magnificent, isn't it?

 **4.3.7.7 RHETORICAL QUESTIONS**

These are excellent devices for writers—as long as we use them in moderation. These questions have interrogative form (they are punctuated with a question mark), but they are statements since we don't expect direct answers.

> Why should I care?

> Why do Americans bellyache about their presidents? They voted them into power.

> Who does she thinks she is?

The most powerful way to handle these questions is by carefully inserting them in description or internal dialogue:

> That couldn't be their baby, it couldn't. The memory of the hideous creature wouldn't leave his head, joining that image one of Dana crouched on the floor sobbing. He knew they'd fought, and he'd kicked her, but surely that didn't cause their baby to look like that. It probably was bad genetics. Obviously, her gene pool was pretty shallow.[108]

"Surely that didn't cause their baby to look like that," is an excellent example of a rhetorical question.

4.3.8 EXCLAMATORY SENTENCES

Exclamatory sentences or exclamations are emphatic versions of declarative sentences, punctuated with exclamation marks.

> Fancy that!

> I've won the lottery!

> Yes! She'll marry me.

Often, exclamations consist of a single word or sentence fragments, or are tagged on at the end of imperative sentences. Beginning writers love to pepper their writing with exclamation marks when

---

[108] Renée Miller, I Do… and other Lies we Tell.

these should be a rarity in fiction. Exclamatory sentences are one of the warning signs of telling. Some writers rely on exclamation marks to express strong emotions, instead of showing to the reader what is exciting or not with powerful description.

When writing fiction, we must exercise great care with exclamatory sentences for a number of reasons:

Most exclamations are informal.

> Gorgeous!

> Lovely day!

Formal exclamations—according to grammarians—must begin with "what" or "how." In modern prose, these constructions read contrived.

> How gorgeous!

> What a lovely day!

Most exclamations are "telling," and unnecessary. The exception would be when used to reveal character in dialogue. Usually, we can better convey emotions through the careful use of context.

> "Gorgeous." He pawed the rug like a bull about to charge.

> Her face lit up like one of those alabaster statues with a lamp inside. "Look at this lovely day."

Sometimes, we can form exclamations with interrogative sentences.

> What have you done to the dress!

> Who is this!

Comedians have exploited this ambiguity through the ages, such as Abbott and Costello in their unforgettable "Who's on First?"[109] (Where a baseball player is named "Who"). In a similar vein to a South Park episode where a comedy pair engaged on a preposterous parody:

> "Excuse me, sir. Do you know Who farted?"

> "He sure did."

Finally, a caveat. Though we pointed out earlier that we punctuate exclamatory sentences with exclamation marks, slapping one at the end does not automatically change a declarative sentence. Exclamatory sentences must also convey strong emotions or feelings.

4.3.9 IMPERATIVE SENTENCES

The two types of sentences ending with periods are the declarative and the imperative. Though they are often confused, writers shouldn't have much problem if they question the sentence's role. If they convey information, the sentences are declarative. If they tell someone to perform an action, these are imperative.

---

[109] In 2005, the line "Who's on First?" was voted one of the top 100 memorable movie quotes by the American Film Institute.

Imperative sentences give commands or directives. In other instances, they make demands or requests.

Please, go away.

Stay away from the chocolates and nobody gets hurt.

Stand aside while we secure the place.

We can use imperative constructions as exclamations.

Go!

Stop!

Lower your heads!

But writers should refrain from using exclamation marks in a sentence containing "please."

Another trait of imperative sentences is that the subject is seldom expressed—the subject may not be visible. But it's understood that the subject is always "You." The person making the command or request asks 'you' to do something.

Go figure.

Mow the lawn.

Give freely to the needy.

Take out the trash can.

In these four sentences, the subject "you" is implied:

You go figure.

You mow the lawn.

You give freely to the needy.

You take out the trash can.

In this sentence classification, we can also add tags to the end of imperatives to reduce the vehemence of a command to show politeness.

Bring me a glass of water, will you?

Write soon, won't you?

Imperative constructions—like declarative sentences—may be short or long, simple or complex. An imperative form can have any structure and still be an imperative sentence.

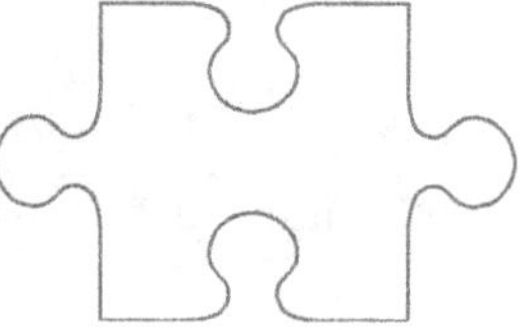

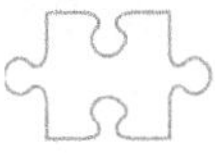 # 4.4 PUNCTUATION

The argument about punctuation has raged for years in writing circles. Defenders of rules and usage have dug their heels in, while their opponents accuse them of being grammar fascists or punctuation zealots.

We observed the battle at our old writer's group, a lively crowd with close to fifteen-hundred members, including both established writers and those struggling through their first manuscript. Many newcomers to the profession displayed varying degrees of contempt for the elementary rules of grammar and syntax. Not surprisingly, punctuation was one of their pet peeves.

In our opinion, the issue is straightforward: some writers can do whatever they want; others cannot.

To answer who belongs in each group we'll use an example:

Picasso (or to give his full name, Pablo Diego José Francisco de Paula Juan Nepomuceno María de los Remedios Cipriano de la Santísima Trinidad Ruiz y Picasso) was one of the foremost modern painters. Unlike most of his contemporaries, his works commanded millions of dollars while he could still spend them. A sample of his synthetic cubist style is *Musiciens aux masques*, which is *Musicians with Masks* or *The Three Musicians*. You can view it at:

> http://en.wikipedia.org/wiki/Three_Musicians

Much of his later work was considerably simpler-looking. Sometimes, only a few brush strokes graced a canvas.

We've heard many ironic or downright pejorative comments about his work:

"My seven-year old could do better."

"I wouldn't hang that on my barn."

"I could do that with one hand tied behind my back."

A few years back, at Barcelona's Picasso Museum, we spent a good fifteen minutes drinking-in his awe-inspiring oil on canvas *Primera Comunión*, or *First Communion*. You can have a look here:

> http://www.flickr.com/photos/8449304@N04/2628035831/

Picasso painted his "*Primera Comunión*" at age fourteen. Later, he changed the rules because *he could*.

There's an intrinsic fallacy in the cliché "rules are there to be broken." It doesn't mean all *the rules*, but only those a particular artisan has mastered. Sidestepping a norm without knowledge is the trait of fools, not writers. Musicians must study a composition and know it inside out before attempting to imprint their own style on it, and the same goes for ballet dancing and figure skating. Artists must learn the rules intimately, to discover why, where, and how to break them.

To determine in which group we belong there's a simple test. A writer has only to type a standard 250-word page eschewing punctuation. If said writer can then list on a separate page every missing punctuation mark, like Picasso he can write prose as he pleases. (His publishers and readers might take a dim view, but that's another matter).

In other words, to disregard punctuation rules *intentionally* is the right of every modern writer, but to eschew punctuation out of laziness or ignorance is a recipe for disaster.

> That punctuation is important all agree; but how few comprehend the extent of its importance! The writer who neglects punctuation, or mis-punctuates, is liable to be misunderstood—this, according to the popular idea, is the sum of the evils arising from heedlessness or ignorance.[110]

Punctuation is the soul of rhythm, style, and tone in literature. Its use and misuse can alter the meaning of sentences, and even full paragraphs as displayed in this classic:

> Dear John:
>
> I want a man who knows what love is all about. You are generous, kind, thoughtful. People who are not like you admit to being useless and inferior. You have ruined me for other men. I yearn for you. I have no feelings whatsoever when we're apart. I can be forever happy–will you let me be yours? Gloria

> Dear John:
>
> I want a man who knows what love is. All about you are generous, kind, thoughtful people, who are not like you. Admit to being useless and inferior. You have ruined me. For other men, I yearn. For you, I have no feelings whatsoever. When we're apart, I can be forever happy. Will you let me be? Yours, Gloria[111]

Take the humble apostrophe. Its use can turn a passage from friendly to bureaucratic: from easy to stiff.

> I don't know if they'll be in town.

> I do not know if they will be in town.

And what about commas? Like everything else in writing, there are norms for their use. "Eats shoots & leaves" [112] is a description fit for a panda, but "Eats, shoots, & leaves," is for gunslingers.

Every other day, we hear someone's remark about the best-selling author who writes with *too many* commas. A sentence or paragraph with *too many* commas belongs to someone who didn't know what to do with them. Sometimes, a sentence requiring more than two commas betrays our irrational urge to string too many ideas before a period. Punctuation signs are *not* optional—unless a writer knows what he's doing—and commas are no exception. Their role is to render the meaning of sentences clear, not *to take a breather*, as taught in some schools. Why? Because not everybody breathes with the same intensity or cadence.

---

[110] Edgar Allan Poe, Graham's Magazine, February 1848.

[111] We've searched for the author to credit this masterpiece, but our efforts have been in vain.

[112] Eats, Shoots & Leaves: The Zero Tolerance Approach to Punctuation. Lynne Truss. Gotham, 2004.

This section covers the rules governing punctuation and the norms every writer must know intimately before dreaming of being a literary Picasso. As Kant remarked: "Theory without practice is empty; practice without theory is blind."[113]

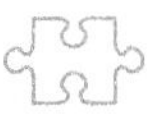 **4.4.1 THE APOSTROPHE**

Writers may omit commas and other punctuation marks to impart a particular rhythm to a sentence, paragraph, or passage. As long as they know what they're doing, such omissions may be justified under the nebulous cloak of style. Apostrophes are universally misused, and they should be treated with respect because they alter the meaning of words. A missing apostrophe can render a sentence confusing. Worse still, a misplaced apostrophe sticks out like a sore thumb.

Most punctuation signs have unique uses. Commas, periods, semicolons, colons, and em-dashes add pauses of varying lengths to prose. Other signs, such as question and exclamation marks, signal changes in intonation. Apostrophes, on the other hand, have three dissimilar applications:

We use apostrophes to form:

Possessives

Contractions

Plurals

 **4.4.1.1 POSSESSIVES**

Forming possessives (genitive case)

Unlike other aspects of English grammar, using apostrophes to form possessives obeys straightforward rules with few exceptions. There's no need to memorize long lists of cases that depart from the norm.

First, we need to determine if there is room for a possessive. To find out, we check sentences for "of" or "of the," preceding a noun. Examples:

The pelt <u>of the</u> cat looks shabby.

This is the dress <u>of</u> Maria.

The legs <u>of the</u> chair are crooked.

Once established we *can* use a possessive, the decision whether to use it or not belongs to the writer. Does the sentence have the right tone in its context? Does it sound better with a possessive?

The cat's pelt looks shabby.

This is Maria's dress.

The chair's legs are crooked.

---

[113] Take heart. The quote is not only applicable to lazy people, but to the editors and grammarians who regardless of their theoretical excellence are lousy fiction writers.

And now for the norms:

● Possesives of singular nouns

<u>One</u>. To form the possessive case of a singular noun we add an apostrophe and the letter s. Examples:

> The cat's pelt
>
> Maria's dress
>
> The chair's legs

<u>Two.</u> The previous rule also applies if the singular noun ends in *s*.

> Carlos's beguiling mustache
>
> The boss's lovely daughter
>
> Mars's canals don't exist.

Exceptions:
Two notable personal names are Moses and Jesus. These form their possessive form by adding only the apostrophe:

> Moses' tablets
>
> Jesus' miracles

Other exceptions concern some names with more than one syllable, and those unaccented endings in *s* or *z*, such as: Sophocles, Chavez, Achilles, Fergus, Cornelius, Beatriz, etc. Authorities disagree; some favor Chavez' and others Chavez's. As with other disputed rules, it's difficult to follow one without incurring someone's wrath. Whichever the writer's personal choice, what matters is to sustain consistency throughout the text.

● Possessives of indefinite pronouns

Indefinite pronouns don't refer to a specific person or thing. Examples are: one, anyone, other, no one, and anybody.

To form the possessive of an indefinite pronoun, we add an apostrophe and the letter *s*.

> Nobody's answer was correct.
>
> Is this anyone's beer?
>
> The dirt marks on the door weren't anybody's fault.

● Possesives of plural nouns

<u>One</u>. To form the possessive, if the plural noun ends in s, we add only an apostrophe.

> Light crept over the mountains' ragged lines.
>
> The bosses' offices are clad in pink marble.
>
> Fido is the puppies' father.

<u>Two.</u> To form the possessive, if the plural noun doesn't end in *s*, we add an apostrophe and an *s*.

The men's section is closed.

These are the children's clothes.

Geese's eggs are huge.

Possessives of compound words

To form the possessive case of a compound noun, add an apostrophe and an s to the last word.

My sister-in-law's car is falling to pieces.

You have taken somebody else's umbrella.

She sat on the merry-go-round's platform.

Possessives of two or more nouns

<u>One</u>. If two or more nouns have joint possession of something, we add an apostrophe and an s to the last noun.

Fido and Tina's kennel needs cleaning.

Laurel and Hardy's films are classics.

<u>Two.</u> If two or more nouns each have individual claim to something, we add an apostrophe and an *s* to each noun.

The director's and the shareholder's lawyers don't agree.

Paul's and Michael's cars are Mercedes.

The cop's and the gangster's law book is different.

Common errors when using apostrophes

Its-It's / Who's-Whose

By far, the most common error we come across in manuscripts involves the possessives of personal pronouns.

Pronoun	Possessive form
He	His
It	Its
She	Hers
They	Their
We	Your
Who	Whose
You	Your

Its is the possessive form of *it*.

The castle and its crenellated walls

Like a dog chasing its tail

The river reversed its course

It's is not a possessive, but a contraction of *it* + *is* or *it* + *has.*

It's clear to me. = It is clear to me.

Hurry up, it's getting dark. = Hurry up, it is getting dark.

It's been a killer of a day. = It has been a killer of a day.

Whose is the possessive form of *who*:

Whose clothes are these?

I know a woman whose husband is a street artist.

Mary, whose lips quivered, remained silent.

Who's is not a possessive, but a contraction of *who* + *is* or *who* + *has.*

Who's already finished the essay? = Who has already finished the essay?

Guess who's coming for dinner? = Guess who is coming for dinner?

Who's that gorgeous creature? = Who is that gorgeous creature?

Possesives of inanimate objects

One of the myths championed by pseudo-purists shuns the use of possessives with inanimate objects. The sages argue that objects cannot possess other things. According to these experts, "that car's radio," "the ship's rudder," or "a day's notice" are wrong. They aren't. There is nothing wrong with using 's with inanimate objects.

The term "possessive case" can be misleading. Instead, we should use the term genitive. And descriptive genitives are "the mountain's top" and "a day's pay."

> "In fact, the genitive case—in English as in Latin before it—has always had many more purposes than simply indicating possession, and descriptive (and other nonpossessive) genitives are and long have been Standard English." [114]

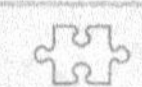 ## 4.4.1.2 CONTRACTIONS

Forming contractions

A contraction occurs when we combine two words and remove one or more letters. We then use an apostrophe to signal where the letters have been omitted. Some examples are:

do not (do**not**) = don't

I am (I**am**) = I'm

he will (he**will**) = he'll

---

[114] Kenneth G. Wilson, Columbia Guide to Standard American English; Descriptive Genitive, Columbia University Press, 1993.

who is (wh**oi**s) = who's

should not (shouldn**ot**) = shouldn't

did not (did**no**t) = didn't

could have (could**hav**e) could've

cannot (can**no**t) = can't

they have (they**ha**ve) = they've

I would (**I**wo**ul**d) = I'd

I had (**I**had) = I'd

it is (i**ti**s) = it's

it has (it**ha**s) = it's

we have (we**hav**e) = we've

they had (they**had**) = they'd

let us (let**us**) = let's

In the above examples, we substitute the bold letters with apostrophes.

We write certain words with an apostrophe to mark that they are a shortened form of the original word. Examples are:

'phone = **tele**phone

'flu = **influ**enza

This usage is dated and most house styles favor the shortened word without the apostrophe, as in "phone" and "flu."

We can also use the apostrophe to substitute for omitted numerals in dates. In these instances, we omit the first two figures:

Elizabeth was born in '54. (Where '54 stands for 1954)

The roaring '20s (Where '20s stands for 1920s)

Special cases

We use the apostrophe in certain words that are traditionally spelled with their silent letters omitted to better represent pronunciation.

o'clock = **of the** clock

fo'c's'le = for**e**ca**s**tle

sou'wester = south**w**ester

bo's'n = bo**at**swai**n**

ne'er-do-well = nev**er**-do-well

rock 'n' roll = rock **and** roll

o'er = over

cat o' nine tails = cat of nine tails

We can use the apostrophe in place of the letter *e* in the adjectival suffix *ed* when the root word ends in a pronounced vowel.

shampoo'd = shampooed

subpoena'd = subpoenaed

shanghai'd = shanghaied

These last practices might be outdated, which means inappropriate for some genres and recommended in others. Perhaps they will violate the house style of particular publications or publishing houses, but they are nevertheless correct.

 **4.4.1.3 PLURALS**

In our last use for apostrophes, we explore their role in the formation of plurals.

Plurals of lowercase letters

Although the rule is more typographical than grammatical, we use apostrophes to form the plural of lowercase letters.

Dot your i's and cross your t's.

She usssses too many s's.

Mind your p's and q's. [115]

Two t's in patter.

Plurals of uppercase letters

If the plural is clear, apostrophes after upper-case letters are not necessary but, in any other instance, the use of apostrophes is recommended:

Rather than: Peter got three Bs and many Cs.

Use: Peter got three B's and many C's.

Plurals of numbers

Though many editors still use them, some publishers no longer consider them necessary or even create the plural of years or decades with an apostrophe:

Rather than: I love music from the 1960's

---

[115] The phrase dates from the early days of the printing press, when letters were composed backward in boxes so they would appear the right way on the printed page. The expression meant "Don't make mistakes." Nowadays we use the term to recommend politeness.

Use: I love music from the 1960s

⬦ Plurals of abbreviations

We form the plurals of abbreviations without periods by adding an s, as in:

There are several PhDs working at our laboratories.

Martha and Susan have high IQs.

With periods, we would add an apostrophe before the s:

There are several Ph.D.'s working at our laboratories.

Martha and Susan have high I.Q.'s.

⬦ Plurals of words used as words (rathar than for their meaning)

For clarity, letters or words we use to represent themselves must be underlined or set in italics. But the apostrophe and the *s* are not.

His argument consists of *but*'s

After checking my list of *to-do*'s, I'm depressed.

One final note to those writers struggling with apostrophes. Proofreading, after finishing the manuscript, is easy with the "search" function in most word processors.

Those writers who tend to leave out apostrophes can search for words ending in *s* or *es*, to determine if they need apostrophes.

If the writer dusts his prose with too many apostrophes, he can search for words containing (') to check if they follow the rules.

4.4.2 THE COLON

The colon is a pause device, similar to the semicolon but stronger. Though there are different ways to use the colon, the most important concept is: Colons follow independent clauses (whatever precedes a colon must be able to stand on its own). The independent clause preceding a colon implies a promise, and what follows the colon makes good on that promise. We use the colon in the following cases:

Emphasis

Lists

Explanations

Quotations

Other uses

Since English has exceptions to every rule, we have addressed these under the heading "other uses."

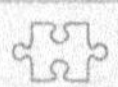 **4.4.2.1 EMPHASIS**

To add emphasis or a degree of formality, we use colons to introduce words, phrases, or clauses (used in apposition to a noun or noun phrase in the introductory statement). Some examples include:

To emphasize a word

A writer is a sentient entity who cannot exist without one thing: writing.

Happiness is to cuddle in a warm blanket next to my lover: chocolate.

My girlfriend has an irresistible magnetism: money.

To emphasize a phrase

I have a soaring goal: the Everest.

The intruders had a target: the strong room's gold.

My neighbor has a new live-in pet: the gardener.

To emphasize a clause

The family gathered to ponder one issue: who stole the cookies?

My recipe for a successful marriage is foolproof: she's always right.

Congress unveils plans to deter extremists from traveling into the U.S.: Airlines will only serve pork pies.

 **4.4.2.2 LISTS OR SERIES**

After introductory statements, we use colons to indicate that a list or an enumeration will follow in run-in lists (those built into the flow of the text). Some examples are:

For the picnic, we put together all the necessary trappings: sandwiches, cookies, soda, fruit, and Fido.

After the party, a number of unexpected problems cropped up: somebody stole my wallet, the car wouldn't start, and Melanie left with a waiter.

My goals for the next year are as follows: self-publish my novel, win the Nobel Prize, win the Pulitzer, and find a roommate.

Vertical or display lists

Though seldom used in fiction, vertical lists have specific requirements. Reference manuals offer different advice, and writers must check the house style of the text's recipient. In any case, the single most important detail is to use punctuation consistently.

As mentioned earlier in this chapter, the introductory statement must be an independent clause.

Numbers

A new writer needs three things:

1) a killer manuscript;

2) friends in the industry;

3) bushels of luck.

Note that we use parentheses around the numbers and semicolons to separate the items with a period after the last entry.

Capitalization

a. If the entries are unnumbered sentence fragments, no capitalization or punctuation is necessary.

A new writer needs three things:

a killer manuscript

friends in the industry

bushels of luck

b. If a vertical list contains complete sentences, we use standard punctuation.

A new writer needs three affirmative statements:

I have a killer manuscript.

I rub shoulders with the directors of one major publishing house.

I have the luck of the devil.

c. For lengthy or complex elements, we treat the series in the list as a sentence and punctuate the items with semicolons, except for a period after the last statement.

A new writer needs three items to secure publication:

He will have written a killer manuscript with guaranteed advance sales of zillions;

hangs out with the industry's heavyweights;

and has the luck of the devil.

Notice that we haven't used capitalization with the incomplete sentences. Also, some reference manuals have conflicting advice about using the conjunction (and) before the last item. [116]

To recap: If the introductory statement is a complete sentence, we use a colon, in particular if it contains the phrases "the following" or "as follows." We also use colons before numbered or prioritized lists.

---

[116] Typically, UK usage uses a conjunction and omits the separator, thus: We brought: ham, hard-boiled eggs and bread. U.S. usage would have: We brought ham, hard-boiled eggs, and bread.

 **4.4.2.3 EXPLANATIONS**

We use a colon before explanations when the introductory statement is a complete sentence or a standalone clause.

> We are ready here: finish your cigarette and we shoot.

> *Queimada* has a simple recipe: drop lemon peel into spirits, add sugar, set alight, and stir.

> The captain has jumped overboard: you can follow or sink with the ship.

 **4.4.2.4 QUOTATION**

We use colons to separate independent clauses from the quotation that the clause introduces.

> The literary agent framed his reply with care: "In my next incarnation I want be a potato farmer."

> She had only one thought before the slush pile: "No prisoners."

> The instructor issued a clear message: "This is a compassionate workshop; either you learn to write or I'll put you out of your misery."

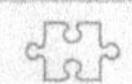 **4.4.2.5 OTHER USES**

We use the colon after the salutation in letters, between title and subtitle of a published work, in divisions of time, and biblical citations.

In these instances, it's not necessary that whatever comes before the colon is a complete sentence.

Salutation

For friendly and/or informal letters, a comma after the salutation is sufficient:

> Dear Tibbs,

In formal letters, the colon is more adequate:

> Dear President Kabolo:

To separate title and subtitle in published works we also use the colon:

> The Guantanamo Inmates: Going, Going, Gone.

In time, we separate hours and minutes with a colon.

> We have re-scheduled the meeting for tomorrow at 9:30.

In Biblical citations, we use a colon to separate chapter and verse.

> The parson read Deuteronomy 28:16

 **4.4.2.6 SALUTATION**

In the opening of this section we explained that the clause preceding the mark should be independent. If its purpose is to introduce whatever comes after the colon, it may feel incomplete but grammatically must have both a subject and a predicate.

We wouldn't use a colon in the following example:

> <u>Her recipe for "Brownie in a Mug" includes</u> flour, sugar, egg, cocoa, water, and a few minutes in the microwave.

The underlined clause is dependent.
We don't use a colon to separate a preposition from its objects.

> Incorrect: He was hired to: run the company, park the cars, and make the coffee.
> Correct: He was hired to run the company, park the cars, and make the coffee.

We don't use a colon to separate a verb from its objects.

> Incorrect: She likes to dance: salsa, quickstep, and polka.
> Correct: She likes to dance salsa, quickstep, and polka.

We don't use a colon after "such as."

> Incorrect: I like to eat simple food such as: caviar, lobster and sturgeon.
> Correct: I like to eat simple food, such as caviar, lobster and sturgeon.

Finally, once a colon has introduced an element, the sentence must end with the introduced element. To continue is a common error among inexperienced writers, perhaps eager to append information after a list.

> Incorrect: The bartender had a grand selection of whiskeys: Lagavulin, Bunnahabhain Laphroaig, and Bruichladdich, but I passed out before I could sample them all.

> Correct: The bartender had a grand selection of whiskeys: Lagavulin, Bunnahabhain, Laphroaig, and Bruichladdich. I passed out before I could sample them all.

 **4.4.2.7 PUNCTUATION**

There's disagreement among reference manuals about capitalization following a colon.
The *NYPL Writer's Guide* and the *Chicago Manual of Style* suggest beginning independent clauses after a colon with a lowercase letter with two exceptions:

1. When two or more sentences follow the colon

2. When a quotation follows the colon.

The *APA Publication Manual* and the *Gregg Reference Manual* advise to capitalize any independent clause following a colon.
Whatever the writer's choice, the important issue is to remain consistent throughout the manuscript.
In our opinion, any complete sentence after a colon should be capitalized.

There's an instance where regardless of the style chosen, sentences after a colon should be capitalized. If the introduction to a colon is brief, sometimes consisting of a single word, *and* the clause after the colon represents the gist of the idea, it should always be capitalized.

Remember: The Egyptians may appear backward, but they performed eye surgery when we still lived in caves.

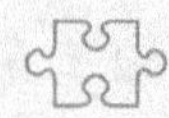

4.4.3 THE COMMA

Of all punctuation marks, the comma is the most misunderstood, and generally abused by many writers.

Seldom has a day gone by when we don't have to endure (yet again) another rendition of the most prevalent myths:

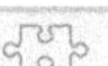 **Long sentences need commas.** 

False. One can readily write the grammatically correct and exceedingly long sentences that would definitely force a cyanotic reader into hurriedly gasping for his dear life or risk further depleting the already scarce and quickly-waning oxygen supplies from his stressed respiratory system to a point where collapse and loss of consciousness would ensue. The question is: why would a writer want to do that?

Add a comma wherever you pause. 

Risky. This is tantamount to saying, "Where the writer *thinks* readers should pause if reading the sentence aloud." Some people read quickly; others take their time. If an agent or editor pauses differently....

Insert commas where they sound good. 

Riskier. To insert commas where they sound good is a delicate subject, perhaps closer to the philosophy of aesthetics—or literary experimentation—than genre writing. As with pauses, "sound good" is subjective. Readers may have a different opinion (not to mention agents and acquisition editors). Sound is a tricky thing. Once upon a time, a musician who created a score (almost five minutes-long and for a full orchestra) demanded that musicians remained silent for the duration. In effect, the composition was a five-minute silence. We don't know much about music or art forms, but we are under the impression that music is sound, and silence the absence of it.

My editor doesn't like commas. 

Fire your editor.

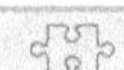 **Writer so and so uses very few commas.** 

Every writer is entitled to write anyway he wants, experiment, and create unique prose with a unique format. There's nothing wrong in having a unique voice with a unique style. The point to ponder is the effect that such literary stunts can have on the prospects of a new writer. There's an anecdote about

Stephen Hawking, the physicist genius. When he wrote a book on black holes, his editor warned him that every formula on the manuscript would mean 5,000 fewer sales. He wrote the book without one single formula. Our task when composing this Companion is to explain the standard rules of Common English, not to dictate style. Whether a writer follows the norms or not is a matter of preference, and a personal decision.

Rules are flexible.

Some rules are but others are not. While there is flexibility in some aspects of comma use—where a writer can use his own judgment—there are specific rules that dictate how to separate parts of a sentence into logical elements.

Commas help readers figure out which words go together and which parts of the sentence are most important. For a writer, using commas incorrectly may have one of these consequences:

It may confuse agents, editors, and readers.

It may give agents, editors, and readers a reason to think the writer ignores basic writing rules.

It may give agents, editors, and readers a reason to think the writer is careless.

None of these can benefit a writer's career or book sales.

4.4.3.1 ONE

We use a comma before a coordinating conjunction if it connects two independent clauses.

Coordinating conjunctions, as found in the mnemonic FANBOYS, are for, and, nor, but, or, yet, so. An independent clause is one with both a subject and predicate that is capable of standing on its own.

She wants to major in Etruscan, and my father thinks it's a dead end.

I hate your spiky hair, yet I can't live without you.

Mary ate all the muffins, for she didn't want to share.

You could stay home and sulk, or we can paint the town red.

If the sentences are well balanced, this is an instance when the writer may flaunt his personal style and omit commas. Some writers contend that the conjunction gives adequate pause. As long as the omission is consistent, we doubt many editors will blow a fuse. When in doubt, we recommend to use the comma. In this instance, it's always correct. In any case, familiarity with the linking mechanism might be a useful tool on rewrite.

In the previous examples, each clause is independent. We can list them in isolation and check that they make sense:

She wants to major in Etruscan.

My father thinks it's a dead end.

I hate your spiky hair.

I can't live without you.

Mary ate all the muffins.

She didn't want to share.

You could stay home and sulk.

We can paint the town red.

Sometimes "choppy sentences" (a staccato sensation) creeps into the prose when the writer strings too many short sentences together without cause.

If we want to convey a sensation of stress, danger, or urgency, short sentences are a handy device.

I can't stand your spiky hair. I can't live without you. You could stay home and sulk. We can paint the town red.

This is choppy and disjointed. Though the concepts are there, these sentences don't make much sense as written. With coordinating conjunctions and commas added, we can collapse four sentences into two.

I hate your spiky hair, yet I can't live without you. You could stay home and sulk, or we can paint the town red.

If the clause following the conjunction is incomplete (missing a subject or predicate), we don't use a comma.

She wants to major in Etruscan but thinks it's a dead end.

I hate your spiky hair and to live without you.

Mary ate all the muffins and forgot to share.

You could stay home and sulk or paint the town red.

There's a major difference between the two next examples:

She went to the boutique, and she bought a skirt.

She went to the boutique and bought a skirt.

In the second example "and bought a skirt" is not an independent clause. It cannot stand on its own as a complete sentence. Therefore, we use no comma.

If the second clause opens with an introductory element, its treatment is different. For example:

She went to the boutique and after that she bought an ice cream.

Here we have two independent clauses:

She went to the boutique.

She bought an ice cream.

We also have a coordinating conjunction (and).
"After that" is an introductory element.

In the following instances, the comma placement would be incorrect.

She went to the boutique, and after that she bought an ice cream.

She went to the boutique and after that, she bought an ice cream.

She went to the boutique, and after that, she bought an ice cream.

The correct comma use is to separate the conjunction and introductory element, leaving both independent clauses to speak for themselves.

She went to the boutique, and after that, she bought an ice cream.

A frequent error in comma usage is placing it *after* a coordinating conjunction.

She shouted at the mole, and since the animal ignored her, she shouted some more.

We find the reason for this common error in everyday speech, since we often pause after the conjunction. In writing, it's incorrect. Therefore, the correct punctuation in the previous example would be:

She shouted at the mole, and since the animal ignored her, she shouted some more.

 **4.4.3.2 TWO**

We use commas to set off introductory words, phrases, and clauses.
The comma warns the reader that the meat of the sentence—main subject and verb—come later.

Although the evidence suggests otherwise, I didn't eat the cookies.

After lunch, you can buy the coffee.

Though he was tired, Kurt mowed the front lawn.

Anyway, you're out of luck.

When striving for variety, writers can reverse the order of some sentences. This is a useful device if handled with care. Sometimes the punctuation will change or might be absent altogether, as in the second example below.

I didn't eat the cookies, although the evidence suggests otherwise.

You can buy the coffee after lunch.

Kurt mowed the front lawn, though he was tired.

You're out of luck, anyway.

A comma after an introductory element is never wrong, but this is another instance where writers might eschew its use if the introductory element is short. However, if the omission results in confusion or hesitancy in reading, the comma is mandatory.

When Mike sat to eat the parrot pecked on the table.

After thirty athlete's careers are often over.

The first example reads as if Mike is about to eat the parrot, before the sentence turns confusing. The second example *is* confusing.

> When Mike sat to eat, the parrot pecked on the table.

> After thirty, athlete's careers are often over.

 **4.4.3.3 THREE**

We use commas to separate item series of three or more words, phrases, or clauses.

> I will order soup, steak, and a banana.

> My week consists of Monday, Monday, Monday, Monday, Monday, and deliverance.

> We're ready after you load the car with the hamper, drinks, and Fido.

Throughout this Companion we've used the serial comma. (Some sources name it Oxford comma or Harvard comma. Please check page 563 for explanation). Briefly, it's a matter of using or not using a comma before the conjunction in a series:
Using the serial comma:

> She stored books, laptop, underwear, and chocolates in her backpack.

Not using the serial comma:

> She stored books, laptop, underwear and chocolates in her backpack.

If the absence of comma doesn't make the sentence ambiguous or confusing either way is correct. The only caveat is consistency. Once a writer chooses one style over the other, it should remain uniform throughout the manuscript.
Simple series seldom present ambiguity if the comma is left out.

> Connie lives with a tortoise, a snake, a pelargonium and a nice boy from Ohio.

However, lists containing phrases with internal conjunctions can be confusing, or cause readers to pause and frown.

> George decided to buy bell peppers instead of cucumbers and carrots, sirloin instead of brisket and bacon and wine instead of beer.

In the previous example, a comma before "and wine" would ease its reading.

4.4.3.4 FOUR

We use commas between coordinate adjectives.[117]
Coordinate adjectives are those that equally modify the same word. (In one of these examples the comma is used incorrectly).

---

[117] We can also use commas to separate coordinate adverbs, but since most adverbs are weak, to string them would add insult to injury. "She slurped swiftly, noisily, greedily her smoothie."

Four sleek, fast boats sailed past the lighthouse.

He was a tall, debonair pirate.

The frail, wizened old lady was a vampire.

The dark, blue negligee was her husband's favorite.

To determine if the adjectives are coordinate, we can try several approaches:
First, we add "and" before the adjectives. If the sentence still makes sense, the comma is correct.

Four sleek and fast boats sailed past the lighthouse.

He was a tall and debonair pirate.

The frail and wizened old lady was a vampire.

The dark and blue negligee was her husband's favorite.

The first three examples make perfect sense. In the fourth example, replacing the comma with "and" renders the sentence meaningless. What color is "dark and blue," anyway?
If the adjectives are coordinate, the sentence should still make sense if we reverse their order.

Four sleek, fast boats sailed past the lighthouse.
Four fast, sleek boats sailed past the lighthouse.

He was a tall, debonair pirate.
He was a debonair, tall pirate.

The frail, wizened old lady was a vampire.
The wizened, frail old lady was a vampire.

The dark, blue negligee was her husband's favorite.
The blue, dark negligee was her husband's favorite.

Once more, the first three examples work; the fourth doesn't.
There's still another test to determine if the adjectives in a series are coordinate. Each should make sense if used separately:

Four sleek, fast boats sailed past the lighthouse.
Four sleek boats sailed past the lighthouse.
Four fast boats sailed past the lighthouse.

He was a tall, debonair pirate.
He was a tall pirate.
He was a debonair pirate.

The frail, wizened old lady was a vampire.
The frail old lady was a vampire.
The wizened old lady was a vampire.

The dark, blue negligee was her husband's favorite.
The dark negligee was her husband's favorite.
The blue negligee was her husband's favorite.

In this last example, using the adjectives separately result in different messages. In the sentence, "The dark, blue negligee was her husband's favorite," "dark" modifies "blue" not "negligee." In this instance, "dark blue" is a cumulative adjective. Therefore, the sentence needs no punctuation: "The dark blue negligee was her husband's favorite."

We must never separate cumulative adjectives. A good way to identify cumulative adjectives is to determine if the one nearer the noun is closer in meaning.

In the example, "The dark blue negligee was her husband's favorite," "blue" describes how the garment looks; "dark" is vague.

One final word of warning: Do not insert a comma between the last adjective and the noun it describes.

The following examples are wrong.

> He was a tall, debonair, pirate.

> The frail, wizened, old lady was a vampire.

 ## 4.4.3.5 FIVE

We use commas to set off nonrestrictive elements.

In a sentence, we class as nonrestrictive those elements (word, phrase, or clause) that can be removed without altering its meaning. Conversely, restrictive elements are essential to retain the meaning of the sentence.

> The neighbor, who moved in last week, is still celebrating.
> The neighbor who moved in last week is still celebrating.

In the examples above, the commas around "who moved in last week" signal that the element is nonrestrictive. The sentence implies that we know the neighbor's identity (perhaps he's our only neighbor). The second sentence, without commas, signifies that there is more than one neighbor. We need to specify we mean the one "who moved in last week."

Let's try another:

> She loves her baggy pants, which are really old.
> She loves her baggy pants that are really old.

The first sentence declares that her baggy pants (meaning every pair of baggy pants she owns) are old. The second sentence is different. It states that out of her baggy pants, she likes the old ones.

Often, nonrestrictive clauses begin with a subordinating conjunction ("who," "whom," "whose," "which," or "that"). Grammarians advise to use "that" before restrictive elements and "which" with nonrestrictive clauses.

If the concept of restrictive/nonrestrictive is still nebulous, the example below might clarify the matter. Say you have one sister: Mary.

> My sister, Mary, has a new boyfriend.

In this instance, "Mary" is nonessential; you've appended her name to give additional information. If we remove it, "My sister has a new boyfriend" conveys the full message.

If you had several sisters:

My sister Mary has a new boyfriend.

"Mary" is essential to determine which sister is over the moon.
Nonrestrictive elements may be at the end of a sentence, as in the following example:

I've met Parson Williams, who is younger than I thought.

Here, "who is younger than I thought" is a comment. We can remove it and the sentence's meaning remains intact: "I've met Parson Williams."

 **4.4.3.6 SIX**

We use commas to set off nonessential elements.

As we reviewed earlier, nonrestrictive elements can be removed from sentences without altering their meaning. There are many more elements that, while not essential to the meaning of the sentence, add color and depth. We have grouped these under the generic "nonessential elements."

To separate nonessential from nonrestrictive elements there's an easy test: If the element refers to a specific idea or word in the sentence, it's nonrestrictive. If the element doesn't refer to a specific idea or word in the sentence, it's nonessential.

Let's use an example from the previous section:

The neighbor, who moved in last week, is still celebrating.

Here, "who moved in last week" refers to the neighbor; therefore, it's a nonrestrictive element.
If we add a mild interjection:

Well, the neighbor, who moved in last week, is still celebrating.

"Well" doesn't refer to anything in the sentence; it's an add-on. In this instance we would class "well" as a nonessential element. Nonessential elements include:

Parenthetical elements

Absolute constructions

Contrasted coordinate elements

Tag questions

Direct address

Mild interjections.

Six/A

We use commas to set off or around parenthetical elements.

These are also termed "interrupters." Why? Because they interrupt the sentence flow. In fiction we must use these constructions judiciously and always be aware of their effect.

Benjamin was the brightest boy in the class.

Benjamin was, in fact, the brightest boy in the class.

In the second example, "in fact" is a parenthetical element of a type that should never be used in fiction narrative, only in dialogue if the emphasis is necessary.

Other parenthetical elements, add information:

Officer Williams, a chubby and clumsy cop, patrols our neighborhood.

My OFW Companion, an impressive tome, is a writer's best friend.

Like nonrestrictive elements, parenthetical items can be removed without changing the essential meaning of a sentence. This is the reason parenthetical elements are sometimes called added information.

It can be difficult to determine what qualifies as added information, as opposed to essential information. We insist writers should master the use of commas, because only they know with certainty if the item is crucial to the sentence—and the story—or not.

In the previous examples, "a chubby and clumsy cop" and "an impressive tome" are surrounded by commas as added information. A good reader will interpret these as parenthetical. We are telling him or her that the words within the commas are not necessary to understand the rest of the sentence.

But imagine the cop's physical description was essential to the story.

The robber sprints ahead to the echo of Officer Williams's huffing and puffing like ruptured bellows.

The book's size might be pivotal.

Mary rubbed her hands to restore circulation. No fuel left, and the temperature continued to drop. Then her gaze fell on the OFW Companion.

If Officer Williams and the OFW Companion's respective sizes are not described elsewhere, these snippets don't qualify as added information, but necessary. In such an instance, the writer should rewrite the sentences to remove the parenthetical commas.

This seemingly trivial distinction can have dire consequences for a writer. We insist because the issue of surrounding parenthetical expressions with commas is important in fiction writing. Editors never remove anything from a manuscript without a writer's consent. But writers, like most humans, often have lousy memories. If in the rush of a tight deadline, an editor suggests removing a few parenthetical expressions to tighten up a scene, chances are the writer (if he trusts his editor) will agree to do away with the "added information." Only the information wasn't "added" but critical to understand why Officer Williams huffed and puffed.

The bulky reading glasses, with thick tortoiseshell frames, made John look older.

Xu, a girl from Guangdong, has lovely almond eyes.

The first example is straightforward. The writer has only to determine if the tortoiseshell composition of the eyewear frames is necessary.

The second example is dicey. The writer should consider if readers will know that Xu is a girl's name. If the writer inadvertently removes the "added information," the reader will see that:

Xu has lovely almond eyes.

Without added description, readers could assume Xu is a boy. Worse still, some readers will be baffled.

A simple rewrite would get rid of the commas to make the information essential.

Xu is a girl from Guangdong who has lovely almond eyes.

Six/B

We use commas to delimit absolute constructions.

Absolute phrases are modifiers with a difference. Unlike other modifiers, absolute constructions modify entire sentences. They often contain a noun and a modifier of this noun, and not another noun in the sentence. They attach to a sentence with no conjunction and though they can be removed without altering its grammatical coherence their omission will take away much of the sentence's meaning.

To tell the truth, I would have never thought the neighbor was a vampire.

Stars sparkling in her eyes, she closed the door and ran toward the sea and freedom.

Teeth gnashing, Kurt hefted the saber and met his foe head on.

In the examples above, the underscored sections are absolute constructions. They attach to a sentence with no conjunction, and though they can be removed without altering its grammatical coherence, their omission will take away much of the sentence's meaning. In every case, absolute phrases provide details that place the whole sentence or idea in context.

For writers, absolute phrases are excellent linking devices, useful on rewrite to control the pace, add color, characterization, and sentence variety.

Her eyes were brimming with tears. Sonya hefted her bag and headed toward the docks.

They cuddled to watch dawn creeping over the horizon. Their bodies were aglow. Their minds were at ease.

Absolute constructions never contain finite verbs. This detail helps to transform those sentences that add detail into absolute phrases and attach to the sentence containing the gist of the plot or narrative.

Eyes brimming with tears, Sonya hefted her bag and headed toward the docks.

They cuddled to watch dawn creeping over the horizon, bodies aglow, minds at ease.

In this last example, the writer can juggle the absolute constructions around the main idea to convey the effect he wants.

Minds at ease, Sonya and Edward cuddled to watch dawn creeping over the horizon, their bodies aglow.

We class absolute phrases as parenthetical, separated from the rest of the sentence either with a comma (or a pair of commas), or a dash (or a pair of dashes).

At the mall, stomach fluttering in anticipation, Sonya headed for the ice cream parlor.

The monkey frowned—the banana a memory—and demanded another treat.

Six/C

We use commas to separate contrasted coordinate elements, also termed "phrases of contrast."

Marrying Peter should be a desire, not an obligation.

Your sloppy writing is due to carelessness, not lack of talent.

In these examples, we substitute a conjunction with a comma.

You should view mowing the grass as an opportunity to do something useful, not a burden.

The next-door neighbor needs less chocolate, more exercise.

Writers can use commas with contrasted coordinating elements to add sentence variety.

Mary won the beauty pageant. Sonya lost.

Sonya lost the beauty pageant. Mary was the winner.

On rewrite, these sentences can be joined if desired.

Mary, not Sonya, won the beauty pageant.

Six/D

We use commas to set off tag questions.

Tag questions, as their name indicates, are short items added to the end of positive or negative statements.

You didn't eat the cake, did you?

The pool boy is gorgeous, isn't he?

In fiction dialogue, we use tag questions for effect to color sarcastic remarks, or to make a strong point. Technically, tag questions can be used to verify information that the character thinks is true or to check information of doubtful accuracy.

I'm sure my new game was in the console slot, wasn't it?

That harpy can't be the parson's daughter, can she?

As in the examples above, negative tags follow positive statements, and positive tags follow negative statements.

Another point to note is that the verb from the main sentence must match that of the tag.

If we use an auxiliary verb in the statement, the verb in the tag must share its tense.

You are—aren't you?

She is—isn't she?

You are not—are you?

She is not—is she?

If we use modals, ("can," "will," "would," "could," "should," "must," etc.) in the statement, then we must use the same modal in the tag.

You can knit socks, can't you?

He shouldn't borrow my belt without asking, should he?

If we don't have an auxiliary verb in the main sentence, then we use the auxiliary **do** in the tag.

He drinks beer, doesn't he? (He **does** drink.)

She had many presents, didn't she? (She **did** have.)

Something happened, did it? (Something **did** happen.)

Six/E

We use commas for direct address.

Commas are confusing punctuation marks because there are so many rules dictating when and how they should be used. Some of these rules allow writers a degree of freedom, others don't.

Each day we receive hundreds of e-mails where the salutation is invariably wrong.

Hi Carlos,

Hello Donna,

These are friendly ways to begin a message, but they violate one comma rule. The correct punctuation is:

Hi, Carlos,

Hello, Donna,

We must always use a comma when directly addressing someone, regardless of whether the direct address opens or closes a sentence.

Dearest, can I borrow some money?

Tess, you must read this book.

Your generosity is boundless, madam.

Come here, buster.

If the direct address falls in the middle of the sentence, then we must surround it by commas.

Thank you, my friends, but you shouldn't have bought me a Ferrari.

Enough excuses, Peter, so where's the cake?

Often, sentences opening or ending with a name do not require a comma if a qualifier precedes the noun or if the other person is being told something but not addressed.

Beloved Carlos,

Dear Donna,

These salutations need no comma because "beloved" and "dear" are qualifiers.

Did you eat the roast, Fido?

Has someone seen Fido?

Dad, can I borrow your car?

Dad could lend me his car, but he won't.

Six/F

We use commas to set off mild interjections.

Oh, I like your necklace.

Wow, have you painted your dress on?

Well, it goes this way.

We also use commas to set off *yes* and *no*.

Yes, the large hut belongs to the shaman.

No, I don't want to kiss a toad.

4.4.3.7 SEVEN

We use commas to set off transitional expressions.

Transitions are important in fiction writing to provide logical organization and connectivity between thoughts and ideas.

Transitions indicate relations within a sentence or paragraph. We have listed below the most common transitions grouped according to use. Though a few are useful, many of these expressions are too formal, dated, or belonging to legal and commercial jargon. Writers should exercise great care with their use.

Addition

Addition words and phrases like "also," "again," "as well as," "besides," "furthermore," "in addition," "likewise," "moreover," and "similarly" need a comma.

I don't like peaches. Besides, I'm not hungry.

Again, where's the cake?

Consequence

Consequence words and phrases like "accordingly," "as a result," "consequently," "hence," "otherwise," "subsequently," "therefore," and "thus" need a comma.

As a result, he eloped with the schoolteacher.

Otherwise, the new roof looks great.

Contrast or Comparison

Contrast and comparison words and phrases like "conversely," "instead," "likewise," "on the other hand," "on the contrary," "rather," "however," and "still" need a comma.

I hate peaches. Instead, I'll try the melon.

On the other hand, we don't have to invite your mother over.

Direction

Words and phrases of direction, such as "here," "over there," "beyond," "opposite," "under," "above," "to the left," "to the right," and "in the distance," need commas.

In the distance, the armies massed.

Beyond, where sea and horizon mated, a tiny speck grew.

Generalizing

Words and phrases that generalize, such as "as a rule," "as usual," "for the most part," "generally," "generally speaking," "ordinarily," "usually," need commas.

Ordinarily, I don't touch the stuff.

As a rule, she doesn't get out of bed before noon.

Emphasis

Words and phrases that give emphasis, such as "above all," "chiefly," "with attention to," "especially," "particularly," and "singularly," need commas.

Above all, don't forget the potatoes.

Particularly, I hate lace-ups.

Exemplifying

Words and phrases that exemplify, such as "chiefly," "for instance," "in particular," "namely," "particularly," "including," "specifically," and "such as," require commas.

Specifically, what do you plan to do in my car?

For instance, have you ever watched Sirius before dawn?

Illustration

Words and phrases that illustrate, such as "for example," "for instance," "for one thing," "as an illustration," and "in this case," need commas.

In this case, I will forgo leniency.

For example, socks go there, underwear here.

Restatement

Words and phrases that restate, such as "in essence," "in other words," "namely," "that is," "that is to say," "in short," "in brief," and "to put it differently," need commas.

In other words, you have one hell of a problem.

To put it differently, my gun is loaded.

Sequence

Words and phrases that convey sequence, such as "at first," "to begin with," "later on," "meanwhile," "soon," "later," "earlier," "afterward," and "with this in mind," require commas.

Later on, we lathered each other.

With this in mind, Wendy attacked the cake.

Similarity

"Comparatively," "coupled with," "correspondingly," "identically," "likewise," "similar," "moreover."

Moreover, I've not finished my tea.

Likewise, she refused to shovel the snow.

Summarizing

"After all," "in any case," "on the whole," "in short," "in the long run," "on balance," "finally."

After all, we are alone.

In the long run, you always lose at roulette.

4.4.3.8 EIGHT

We use commas to set off quotations.

Non-fiction and technical writers use quotations in the bodies of their texts. Fiction writers use them often in dialogue, inner dialogue, and exposition.

We use commas to separate quoted excerpts from the rest of the sentence that explains or introduces the quotation:

Jonas's warning was succinct, "if my dinner is not ready when I come home tomorrow, I'll take you out to a restaurant." No wonder I love him.

The police officer didn't waste any time, "the law is clear. You can't have a live hippopotamus in your pool."

If the attribution (or dialogue tag) of a quoted element comes in the middle of the quotation, it should be surrounded by commas.

My parents were arguing. "Let me be clear," Dad said, "that I didn't touch your chocolates."

My girlfriend has lived a sheltered life. "I don't know where to plug this." Hose in hand, she eyed the vacuum cleaner. "It won't fit."

But we don't use commas if "that" introduces the quoted element or if small quotes are embedded in larger structures.

Sheila writes that "the result was as expected."

What do you mean by "Cake?" I want to know who raided the fridge.

 **4.4.3.9 NINE**

We use commas in dates, addresses, place names, numbers, and titles.

Since we use these in everyday routine and not only in fiction writing, we should be conversant with the correct comma use. Just in case, in the examples below we've noted the exact places where commas should go in dates, addresses, place names, numbers, and titles.

I wrote my first book in June 1940, and published it April 1, 2010.

Kattia was born on a windy night, September 1990.

She lives at 84 Troestralaan, Utrecht, 03445, Holland.

San Francisco, California.

Madrid, New Castile, is Spain's largest city.

If the city name includes a period, the comma goes after the period.

Washington, D.C., Gore Vidal.

We use a comma for numbers over 999 to separate thousands, but never within a date, street numbers, telephone numbers, Social Security numbers or ZIP codes.

The bridge weighs 1,600 tons.

Rita's phone number is 123-456-7890

After entering a contest, Mike won 6,325,600 boxes of matches.

Please note: In English, commas separate thousands and periods separate decimals. Many other languages use the opposite system:

English: 6,754,316.75
Other languages: 6.754.316,75

English: 0.5 pounds
Other languages: 0,5 pounds

We use commas to set off a title that follows a name.

Bernard Hotts, Professor of Divinity
Arthur Rimbaud, Editor in Chief

But if the title includes a period, that period comes before the comma.

Paul Vernier, Jr., follows in the family tradition.
Senta Whiggs, Ph.D., couldn't figure out how to load the dishwasher.

4.4.4 THE DASH

We use dashes to emphasize parts of a sentence, indicate breaks in tone or thought and for clarity when setting off sections with internal punctuation. No spaces come before or after the dash.

There are two kinds of dashes. The em dash (—) has the width of the letter M—though in some word processors is wider, perhaps in a bid to highlight their relative sizes—and the en dash has the width of the letter N (–). Some sources list dashes and include the hyphen.

Hyphen = -

En dash = –

Em dash = —

In this Companion, we have reviewed the uses of the hyphen in a different section (pages 310 to 313).

 **4.4.4.1 THE EM DASH**

"The em-dash is perhaps the most underused mark in American writing. Whatever the type of writing, dashes can often clarify a sentence that is clogged up with commas—or even one that's otherwise lusterless."[118]

We use the em dash to set off parenthetical or nonessential material for emphasis, or for clarity if it contains internal punctuation.

> Three of our colleagues—Tom, Dick, and Harry—are co-writing a romp.

> Though Lisa knows Peter well—they have been married for over twenty years—she doesn't know how to tell him about her boyfriend.

> Supper—a bowl of cucumber and lettuce, with a flourish of watercress—was uneventful, though most appropriate for ruminants.

Sometimes we use the dash between a series of elements and the statement that summarizes the series.

> Concept, craft, doggedness, luck—a writer doesn't need anything else to produce a bestseller.

> Gold, ochre, goldenrod, red—dusk set the dunes on fire.

> Weeds, straw, dust, desolation—where have all the flowers gone?

In dialogue, we use the dash to highlight breaks in speech continuity and shifts in tone:

> "Do you know what day it is." It wasn't a question.
> "Wha—" Mike's glance darted to the calendar and the bright circle around their anniversary date.
> "You won't forget again, will—" She squeezed the trigger.

> "I've met a girl at a party, mmm…"
> "Hot?"
> "You bet. She couldn't keep her hands off—"

---

118 Bryan Garner, *Garner's American Usage*, Oxford University Press, 2003.

"What's wrong?"

"My wallet!"

4.4.4.2 THE N DASH

The uses of the n dash, for spacing dates in chronological ranges, between numbers and letters in indexing schemes, and to join certain compounds, fall almost exclusively in the realm of technical and academic writing. As such, the n dash has rare applications in fiction writing and is out of this Companion's scope.

The *Gregg Reference Manual* and the *Chicago Manual of Style* have excellent sections detailing the specific uses of the n dash.

How to type dashes

At writer's haunts we have listened to writers complaining about the lack of dashes in their word processors—or the difficulties to coax them onto the screen. Here is how we place dashes on our manuscripts:

To produce dashes in MS Word, we use the minus symbol on the numeric pad of our keyboards:

en dash = Ctrl + minus symbol

em dash = Alt + Ctrl + minus symbol

To produce them in any other program or even a web browser:

en dash = Keep Alt pressed and enter 0150 in the numeric keypad.

em dash = Keep Alt pressed and enter 0151 in the numeric keypad.

One last detail. In some versions of MS Word, setting smart quotes (" ") instead of straight quotes (" ") after an m dash is tricky.

The closing quotes after the m dash always point in the wrong direction:

"What on earth—"

The only way we know around this glitch is to type one more letter after the m dash, plus the closing quote:

"What on earth—a"

And then delete the extra letter:

"What on earth—"

Unoriginal? Pedestrian? Hey, we're not very bright, else we would have chosen a different profession.

4.4.5 THE ELLIPSIS

The ellipsis mark, also called "suspension point" or "dot dot dot," looks like three dots or periods (...).

The ellipsis mark has two main uses, only one of which is relevant to fiction writers.

In non-fiction and academic writing, ellipses are set in place of missing words when quoting from original texts. In these contexts, their use is precise and follows tight rules. Also, the formatting and spaces between, before, and after obey particular house style. None of these are of use to fiction writers.

In fiction, we use an ellipsis mark to indicate a pause in speech or unfinished sentences.

> She turned to Henry, eyes welling with tears. "Sweetheart... I must tell you something... important... about...."
>
> "Please..." He hugged Lisa, her running mascara trailing huge skid marks across his white shirt.
>
> "I've totaled your car."

> "I wonder..." Jonas gestured to keep the conversation going and drew his gun.
>
> "The kitten is... kinda cute, and fluffy and stuff."

4.4.5.1 ELLIPSES MECHANICS

We mentioned above that an ellipsis mark looks like three dots. Coded ellipses—as used in this book—are single punctuation marks. In other words, they cannot be split because they are not constructed from three periods.

> Coded ellipsis (…)

> Ellipsis made from three periods (. . .)

This is important when formatting a manuscript. Why? Otherwise, they might be broken at the end of a line—we may end with two dots in one line and one in the next.

The ellipsis should be regarded as one unit, without a space before and a single space after.

> "Er... ellipsis... ellipses?"

The plural of ellipsis is ellipses. The dots that make up the ellipsis are called ellipsis points or ellipsis marks.

> "Yes, but how do we type these... coded ellipses?"

Nothing could be simpler. We hold Alt and Control with the fingers of one hand and depress the period (.) key. The result is… One beautiful ellipsis.

One last thought on the matter of ellipses. When writing dialogue, if the line ends with an ellipsis, the punctuation is different with tags and attributions.

Tags do not require a period after the ellipsis:

> "I think it was over there…" he said.

Attributions do:

"I think it was over there…." He leaned over the counter.[119]

 **4.4.6 THE EXCLAMATION MARK**

We use the exclamation mark after an emphatic declaration, interjection, or command.

At this point, we must warn that in academic and newspaper writing the exclamation mark is virtually nonexistent. In fiction writing it's grossly overused. A friendly editor—from a major publishing house—once commented over the rim of his glass that good writers only had ten exclamation marks to use over the course of their entire lifetime. We concur.

In most circumstances, the exclamation point is redundant.

Using exclamation marks is akin to writing in uppercase; it feels as if the character shouts.

"Come in!"

"Look at the state of your room!"

"In a minute? I mean, now!"

Problem is that shouters soon become irritating to readers. We hate people shouting all the time and we soon dismiss them.

Since in fiction writing the exclamation mark (or exclamation point) belongs in dialogue, writers have ample resources such as tags and structure to convey tones of voice.

Mary's eyes darkened. "Get in there!" she shouted.

In the example, either the tag "she shouted" or the exclamation point is redundant. Most beginning writers indulge this error, perhaps in a bid to infuse character into their writing.

We can write the paragraph without the exclamation mark:

Mary's eyes darkened. "Get in there," she shouted.

Or without the tag:

Mary's eyes darkened. "Get in there!"

But never with both.

An exclamation mark is "telling." There's no getting around it. By using it, we "tell" the reader rather than show.

Mary's eyes darkened. "Get in there."

The crowd hushed.

Perhaps this is not clear enough?

Mary's eyes darkened. "Get in there."

The crowd flinched.

Still not clear?

---

[119] Sir Paul Mitton

Mary's eyes darkened. "Get in there."

The windows rattled.

Do our readers need a better cue?

Mary's eyes darkened. "Get in there." Her bellow drowned the roar of a low-flying 747.

Banter aside, we counsel to use exclamation points sparingly and to avoid diluting their impact with overuse.

We can use exclamation marks to close questions if we mean to convey strong emotion, as in:

"What are you doing with that high explosive!"

Another use of exclamation marks is to accompany mimetically produced sounds.

"When I modeled my new negligee, Paul scraped the rug with his boot and bellowed, 'mooo!'"
"And then?"
"He charged."

"I told Mike I loved dogs."
"What did he say?"
"Woof!"

There are two final issues about punctuation and formatting involving exclamation marks.
If a sentence ends in an exclamation mark, we do not add a period.

Incorrect: "Look at this!."
Correct: "Look at this!"

If an exclamation mark is at the end of an italicized sentence, fragment or title, the exclamation mark must also be in italics.

Incorrect: *Omigod, he's coming over*!
Correct: *Omigod, he's coming over!*

 **4.4.7 THE HYPHEN**

A hyphen is a short horizontal line between words or syllables, not to be confused with an en dash (–) or an em dash (—), both of which are longer.

We use hyphens to join ordinarily separate words into single words. Another use of hyphens, namely to break single words between syllables, falls outside the scope of this book, since standard fiction manuscript formatting demands unjustified (ragged) right-hand margins.

Some punctuation rules are clear, but a definitive collection of hyphenation rules does not exist.

Those writers with hyphen anxiety should relax, bunch their toes, and keep a *current* dictionary handy. We stress *current*, because the rules of style that apply to hyphens are in continuous flux;

different manuals of style prescribe different usage guidelines and with every new edition dictionaries eliminate thousands of hyphenated entries.

Tom Little, in *The Great Hyphenation Hoax*, sums it up nicely.

> "Hyphens cause writers more trouble than any other form of punctuation, except perhaps commas. This may be because the hyphen has no analogue in speech; it is punctuation created purely by the needs of print."

Rather than rules, what follows are guidelines to avoid confusing constructions and promote ease of reading.

 **4.4.7.1 ONE**

We use hyphens to join words—to transform them into compound words—when their meaning would be different if apprised separately. Some self-explanatory examples are:

merry-go-round

pick-me-up

word-of-mouth

hush-hush

mother-in-law

 **4.4.7.2 TWO**

We use hyphens to make compound modifiers before nouns.

A good example comes to mind:

I'm calling you long distance before running a long distance in a long distance race.

Without hyphens, the contrived sentence from the example reads strange.

I'm calling you long-distance before running a long distance in a long-distance race.

Now it makes sense (to us it does) but the important issue is to determine why.

The first occurrence of long distance is tricky because "calling long-distance" is an idiom. What we mean is "I will place a long-distance call" and a "long-distance call" is different from "a long call" or "a distance call." The same is true of "a long-distance race." The middle "instance" doesn't qualify for possible hyphenation. Why? Because in "running a long distance" there's no noun in front to qualify.

The trick is to use a hyphen when one adjectives modifies another and *not* the noun that follows immediately after.

Bobby is a nice plump cat.

Here, both "nice" and "plump" modify the noun "cat." We can check by composing two sentences:

Bobby is a nice cat.

Bobby is a plump cat.

The same is true in the next example:

> Peter needs a hot water bottle.

Where Peter needs a water bottle that is hot.
If we want to signify a bottle for holding hot water, we need a hyphen:

> Peter needs a hot-water bottle.

Now, "hot" qualifies "water" and together, "hot-water" qualifies "bottle."
Here's another example:

> To get out of here, we need a carbon-tipped hacksaw.

In isolation, neither "carbon" nor "tipped" qualify the hacksaw.

> The hacksaw Renée smuggled in is carbon tipped.

Now "carbon" and "tipped" have no noun in front to qualify, therefore no hyphen is needed.
We'll repeat with a different order of words: If the qualifiers come before the noun and qualify each other, we use a hyphen.

> We are in a long-term relationship.

Where "long-term" comes before the substantive "relationship."
If they come after the noun, we don't.

> Our relationship is long term.

Now the substantive comes before the qualifiers.
When two or more modifiers modify another modifier before a noun, we use a hyphen for the meaning to make sense.
One exception to this guideline is never to hyphenate ly-ending adverb-adjective combinations.

> Mine is a nicely-appointed house.

> The room has a fully-stocked bar.

Both the previous examples are wrong. The correct punctuation is:

> Mine is a nicely appointed house.

> The room has a fully stocked bar.

 **4.4.7.3 THREE**

We use hyphens with prefixes like "non," "un," "ex," "self," "all," "pre," "post," "pro," "anti," etc., in particular if they come before a capitalized word or a number:

> Non-stick

> All-inclusive

> Pre-Mesozoic era

> Ex-wife

Anti-American feeling

Self-control

Post-1800 Australian culture

We also use hyphens if the prefix is a capitalized letter:

X-ray

A-list

T-shirt

 **4.4.7.4 FOUR**

We use hyphens to write out numbers from twenty-one to ninety-nine and fractions. For example:

Twenty-nine

Sixty-four

Three-eighths

Two-thirds

This is important for fiction writers, since most editors require spelling numbers from one to ninety-nine. (check "Number" on pages 223, 324, 523, 549 and 550.)

The twenty-one to ninety-nine rule also applies when we have hundreds or thousands before, such as:

Two hundred and seventy-four

Six thousand two hundred and seventy-four

 **4.4.7.5 FIVE**

We use hyphens for hyphenation, or to show that we have broken a word at the end of a line.

This is a headache when formatting a justified document, which doesn't apply to fiction manuscripts. The rules for hyphenating at line endings are so complex, varied, and changeable from one house style to another, that we can only hope typesetters and editors can keep track of them.

The *APA Publication Manual* recommends not breaking words at line-endings while *The Chicago Manual of Style* has many pages listing endless rules.

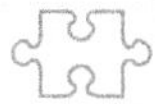 **4.4.8 THE PARENTHESES**

In fiction writing we seldom use parentheses ( ), but to be as thorough as possible we are including them in the Companion as a reference. We use these punctuation marks to separate incidental and other nonessential material used to expand, clarify, illustrate, define, or supplement the contents of the main part of the sentence.

Since parentheses indicate that the material inside them is not as important as the rest of the sentence, and does not affect its meaning, it follows that elements outside the parentheses should always make sense grammatically.

> Before torpor, some bears use a tompion (plug of mud crafted from dust and saliva) to seal their anuses and prevent the ingress of ants and other insects.[120]

Another use of parentheses is to contain labels for lists.

When submitting a manuscript we need: (1) a short synopsis of the work, (2) files with sample chapters or the first fifty pages, (3) the full manuscript, and (4) a cover letter.

We also use them for references or to append directions.

Check for the recommended files before submission (pages 413 to 427).

As we mentioned earlier, parentheses have little use in fiction writing, outside of references and other front or back matter. The principal reason is that these punctuation marks tend to de-emphasize text.

A few notes on punctuation with parentheses.

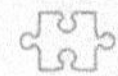 **4.4.8.1 ONE**

If the parenthetical expression or phrase falls in the middle of a sentence, we don't capitalize its first letter or add punctuation, unless the expression opens with a proper noun.

> Incorrect: On our trip to Wales (Last summer.), we sampled Paul's moonshine.
> Correct: On our trip to Wales (last summer), we sampled Paul's moonshine.

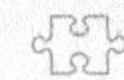 **4.4.8.2 TWO**

Parenthetical questions or exclamations are always capitalized. The punctuation goes inside the quotes.

> Incorrect: On our trip to Wales (have you ever been there)? we sampled Paul's moonshine.
> Correct: On our trip to Wales (Have you ever been there?) we sampled Paul's moonshine.

 **4.4.8.3 THREE**

A full sentence is always capitalized and punctuated inside the parentheses.

> Incorrect: On our trip to Wales, (he really is a darling man) we sampled Paul's moonshine.
> Correct: On our trip to Wales, (He really is a darling man.) we sampled Paul's moonshine.

---

[120] Please, refrain from looking up this meaning of "tompion." It doesn't exist. One of the Companion's writers has a weird sense of humor. To our knowledge, no bear adopts such wise precautions. Our Michael Keyton is mulling over a tompion's boundless benefits on extended picnics.

 **4.4.8.4 FOUR**

If the punctuation belongs to the sentence and not to the parenthetical contents, the punctuation goes outside the quotes.

> Incorrect: On our trip to Wales, we sampled Paul's moonshine (he didn't.)
> Correct: On our trip to Wales, we sampled Paul's moonshine (he didn't).

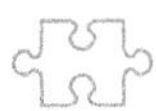 **4.4.9 THE PERIOD**

Fortunately, this is one of the easiest punctuation marks to master. We use periods to mark the end of a sentence, a command (but not an exclamation), or an indirect question, (but not a direct question).

 **4.4.9.1 STATEMENT**

I love sun-dried tomatoes.

Billy Blake is cool.

Spring is around the corner.

 **4.4.9.2 COMMAND**

Send your manuscript in by Monday morning.

Check the typo on the title of your book.

Put only one space after a period.

 **4.4.9.3 INDIRECT QUESTION**

I wonder if the editor will ever recover.

The agent asked if I've considered learning English.

When she will learn is a mystery to me.

We also use periods with some abbreviations.

> Mr. Taylor landed at Washington, D.C., shortly after 10 p.m.

As in the example above, when the period ending the abbreviation comes at the end of a sentence, it also serves as full stop. But if the abbreviation ends a question or exclamation, the appropriate mark must follow the period.

> Did you say, shortly after 10 p.m.?

It's worth mentioning that abbreviations with three or more letters seldom need periods:

EEC, IESNA, NATO, USAF, DNA, etc.

4.4.10 THE QUESTION MARKS

We use question marks after direct questions.

When will they ever learn?

Haven't we been married before?

Where have you hidden my pipe?

In the section dealing with interrogative sentences, (pages 271 to 273) we explored tag questions. We use these devices to turn statements into questions:

She's selfish, but aren't we all?

There were too many sailors in town, weren't there?

She has finished the rewrite in time, hasn't she?

Indirect questions don't take a question mark.

I wonder if Mary will accompany me to the theater.

I asked Jenny if she had finished the chapter on moles.

The instructor asked John to hold his saber correctly.

Since question marks close statements, the following sentence must be capitalized:

Are you ready? We've been waiting a long time.

Consecutive interrogative sentences are also capitalized:

You call that a pajama? Have you no shame?

When writing dialogue, we must differentiate between tags and attributions:

"Where's Fido?" He checked his watch.

"Where's Fido?" he grumbled.

A speech tag (see page 168) after a question mark, as in the last example, takes lowercase.
The same is true of concatenated short questions, regardless of the complaints and squiggly underlines of word processors.

"Who is responsible for this mess? the tailor? the baker? the candlestick maker? Fido?"

Some impulsive writers, eager to impress the reader with bursts of emotion, resolve to pile up question marks, which is *always* wrong.

"That's a nice coat. How much????"

Other times, they use them in combination with other marks:

"He did what!?"

This last example, sometimes termed an "interrobang," might live in hurried SMS texts or informal notes to pals, but no serious writer will ever use it in prose.

 **4.4.11 THE QUOTATION MARKS**

In fiction writing, we use quotation marks to surround dialogue and direct quotations.

Since this is a manual for fiction writers, we will not enter into the many rules, norms, and indications governing the use of quotation marks in journalism, non-fiction, or academic prose.

In the U.S., final punctuation goes inside quotation marks. This includes periods, commas, exclamation points, question marks, and em dashes. And what about colons and semicolons? In dialogue, there's no use for colons or semicolons as final punctuation. At least, none that we can think of.

In other parts of the world, the United Kingdom in particular, final dialogue punctuation falls outside the quotation marks. Writers considering submitting manuscripts to non-American publishers can check sundry details on formatting in pages 405 to 427.

We enclose complete sentences and paragraphs in quotes.

"He is happy now."

"As a voice memo. He never earned his trip, recouped the investment."

"A shame."

"The process left him a mad man, his psyche so shredded he was unable to voice more than five words, and that was a question." [121]

If the sentence or paragraph ends in an exclamation point, ellipsis, or question mark, we enclose these inside the quotation marks.

"Where have you hidden my treasure?"

"No more chocolates!"

"I will be a good girl..." [122]

If we quote a short passage from another book or work, this also goes in quotation marks.

Patrick eyed the savage hordes massing around him. A suitable greeting crossed his mind, "I am the Alpha and the Omega, the First and the Last, the Beginning and the End," until he spotted a black-frocked man at the rear.

Many writers use quotes around foreign words, jargon, or slang, to give a special effect or indicate irony or sarcasm. This is incorrect.

He hefted the "thing" and made a face.

---

[121] Michael Keyton, *Elizabeth's Head*, *Ménage à Twenty*. 2009

[122] For discussion on punctuation in dialogue, check pages 170 to 172.

Sonya rummaged inside her bag and drew her "tool."

In fiction writing, the primary function of quotation marks is to set off spoken language. To emphasize or show that we're using a particular word in a special or peculiar way, we use italics. Using quotes for emphasis is *always* wrong.

Her keyboard is in the table, *fused* with the glass top.

 **4.4.11.1 SINGLE QUOTATION MARKS**

In fiction writing, our only use for single quotation marks is for quotes within quotes in front or back matter, or quoted dialogue inside dialogue.

"And then he said, 'I'd rather blow my brains out than live without you'."
"And what did you say to that?"
"The first thing that came to my mind: 'my husband will let you borrow his regulation Smith & Wesson'."

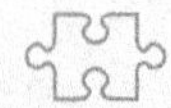 **4.4.12 THE SEMICOLON**

Semicolons indicate longer pauses than commas. The good news is that there are only three rules to learn.

 **4.4.12.1 ONE**

We can use semicolons between two independent clauses if:
The clauses are closely related in meaning.
The clauses are not joined by a coordinating conjunction.
As we explain on page 258, an independent clause is the group of words with subject and verb that expresses a complete thought.

Paul drew his gun.

Henry paled.

As in the examples above, sometimes independent clauses stand alone as a complete sentence.
If we want to join these into a compound sentence, we can use a comma with a coordinating conjunction or a semicolon. As long as he does it the right way, the writer has the last say.

Paul drew his gun, Henry paled.

To use the comma between two independent clauses is incorrect, the result being a comma splice.

Paul drew his gun, and Henry paled.

Here we use a comma, but to be correct, we've had to add a coordinate conjunction (and). In this instance, the comma is optional, we could also write:

Paul drew his gun and Henry paled.

But if we want to add a pause and dispense with the conjunction, the answer is a semicolon:

Paul drew his gun; Henry paled.

Whether to link two independent clauses with a conjunction, connect them with a semicolon, or separate them into two sentences is up to the writer, but we must stress that semicolons as joining devices are only indicated when the two clauses are closely related in meaning.

 **4.4.12.2 TWO**

We use a semicolon to separate main clauses joined by conjunctive adverbs. These include "also," "hence," "however," "instead," "meanwhile," "moreover," "nevertheless," "similarly," "then," "therefore," "thus," and "others."

Vladimir Nabokov's Lolita is a literary masterpiece; however, it has created much controversy because of its subject.

We can move the conjunctive adverb around and retain the syntactic integrity of the sentence.

Vladimir Nabokov's Lolita is a literary masterpiece; it has created much controversy, however, because of its subject.

Vladimir Nabokov's Lolita is a literary masterpiece; it has created much controversy because of its subject, however.

Rhythm, sound and the effect the writer strives to convey will determine the position of the conjunctive adverb.

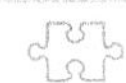 **4.4.12.3 THREE**

In the comma section (pages 290 to 305) we explored how to use commas to separate items in a series. If the items contain internal punctuation, we use semicolons.

To create the OFW Writer's Companion needed Renée, Carlos, Donna, and the best readers in the world.

But if the items contain internal punctuation, confusion might result:

To create the OFW Writer's Companion needed Renée, the whirlwind, Carlos, the slave driver, Donna, the ogre, and the best readers in the world.

Semicolons can add clarity to the list:

To create the OFW Writer's Companion needed Renée, the whirlwind; Carlos, the slave driver; Donna, the ogre; and the best readers in the world.

Even if just one item in the series contains a comma, we must use semicolons to separate all items:

To create the OFW Writer's Companion needed Renée; Carlos, the slave driver; Donna, and the best readers in the world.

4.4.13 THE SLASH

We've reached the last punctuation mark: the slash. Unlike other foes we have to wrestle with on a daily basis, the slash has practically no use in fiction writing. We use the "practically" caveat because fiction works sometimes include quoted poetry or non-fiction elements in the front or back matters, such as indices, forewords, etc.

The slash (/) is also known as the stroke, oblique, solidus, virgule, or forward slash. It is often used in a Uniform Resource Locator (URL) for World Wide Web addresses and also for top folders on Unix, Linux, and Apple machines. It should not to be confused with the backward slash (\) used for pathways in Windows PCs.[123]

We use the slash in informal writing to indicate "or," such as in and/or, apples/pears, or Mr/Mrs. The slash can also be used to indicate fractions, as in 1/2 or 3/4. None of these constructions—we repeat so there's no doubt—have a place in fiction writing.

In particular, the he/she, his/her; him/her constructions are horrid.

The only legitimate use of the slash in fiction that we know of is when quoting poetry, to indicate there's a line break.

> Black wing, brown wing, hover over;
> Twenty years and the spring is over;

We would quote these two lines from T. S. Eliot's *Landscapes*, thus:

> "Black wing, brown wing, hover over; / Twenty years and the spring is over;"

---

[123] Paul Mitton

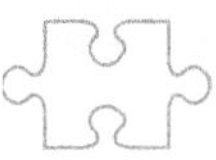 # 4.5 DOUBTS

English is a vast language, with more than one million words, according to some sources, and one billion people speak it with different levels of proficiency. Many thousands of words are added to the English vocabulary each year.

To the chagrin of those who hate its reach, English has become the Esperanto of the modern era, a *lingua franca* for the world. Frequent travelers know that English is by far the best baggage to own when visiting far removed countries. Tramping through the Kalahari, Gobi, or Sahara deserts, roughing it through the Amazon, Mosquitia, or the Ituri forests or traveling through Mongolia, China, or darkest Africa, one of the writers penning these lines always managed to discover English speakers.

Of course, the vastness of English is misleading. Most words have specialized uses and are seldom, if ever, used or read by ordinary citizens. This includes most of us. The average speaker uses between one and three-thousand words for everyday use and knows ten to twenty-thousand additional words passively—those that the subject understands but seldom uses.

Again, this is misleading. There are no serious or conclusive inquiries on word usage. Several linguists suspect that the figures are exaggerated and that most English speakers use fewer words, perhaps one thousand or thereabouts.

To those thinking that we are unduly pessimistic we would like to clarify that "one word" means a basic word, such as the infinitive "to be." "Being," "was," "were," "am," "are," etc. would be included with the basic verb and altogether count as a single word. Therefore, one thousand words imply several thousand word-forms.

In 2008, the Royal Spanish Academy published a study revealing that the average Spaniard uses no more than one-thousand common words, and that only the most educated individuals reach five-thousand. They went on to state that some young people use only 240 words daily—which, in the opinion of this writer, is wildly optimistic after listening to incomprehensible exchanges of grunts peppered with "thing" and "stuff" (synonyms for any noun). When "thing" and "stuff" don't convey the desired meaning, they enrich the conversation with "like" and "you know," failing which they would resort to gestures and mimicry.

It would be shortsighted to presume that Spaniards are less literate than other world citizens. This includes our brothers and sisters from the Unites States of America.

The paucity of our vocabulary should be apparent to anyone who takes a little time to peruse popular fiction. We are caught in a vicious cycle with writers striving for simpler, less complex word choices—to reach a broader audience—and readers demanding prose to be consumed with fewer intellectual burdens.

In an ideal world, we would counsel writers to enrich their vocabulary, but in view of the unstoppable decline of literacy, we won't. Our duty as writers is to create prose for the market and to do so in a way that our work reaches the widest readership. The added difficulty implies choosing our concepts with care and refraining from penning any word we wouldn't hear at the store. It demands much self-discipline and cunning to rewrite "the Count's stentorian discourse" as "he shouted," especially when it doesn't mean the same.

We have spent many hours compiling the list of words on the following pages, adding a few and deleting many. Our goal is not to expand the writer's vocabulary but to help him make the correct choice—since we use fewer words, at least we can try to use them correctly.

After poring over countless manuscripts, we've listed the words that, in our opinion and experience, are among those frequently confused in fiction writing.

Ernest Hemmingway should be an example to any modern writer; he wrote literature of the highest order with a basic vocabulary and boundless talent. It saddens us to ponder that even if Mr. Hemmingway could publish anything nowadays—which we doubt—his editors would insist that *For Whom the Bell Tolls* is an unnecessarily complicated title. They would rechristen it as *The Clanging Bell*, or a similar inanity.

4.5.1 FREQUENTLY CONFUSED WORDS

- A -

180 DEGREES /360 DEGREES—If we're looking north and turn 360 degrees to the right, we pass through east, south, west and finish were we started, looking north. If we want to describe a position opposite to the one we are at, we use 180 degrees. This way we would pass through east as we turn and end up looking south.

A /AN—Most spell checkers will gift harassed writers with a squiggly line under **a** if what follows is a word starting with a vowel. The squiggly line hovers under **an** if it is followed by a word starting with a consonant. The *rule* for the use of **a** and **an** is not based on spelling but pronunciation. Words <u>that</u> <u>sound</u> as though they begin with a vowel get **an**: an hour, an SAS officer, an honest man, an honor, an heir. Words <u>that sound</u> as though they begin with a consonant get **a**: a user, a university, a unicycle, a one-way ticket, a unicorn, a union.

ACCEPT / EXCEPT—"Accept" is a verb that means "to receive something given or offered" or "to be received." *We accept the gift given by the girls when they accepted us into their group.* Accept also can be used to mean "considered proper or right or to believe in or considered to have a certain meaning." *The accepted reply would be yes.* "Except" is a preposition that means other than or with the exclusion of. *She invited everyone except her boss.*

ACCURATE / PRECISE—"Accurate" doesn't imply precision. *Renée is taller than Carlos,* might be an accurate statement; she's 6' and he's 5'3." A "precise" statement would be *Renée is 9" taller than Carlos.*

ACCUSTOMED TO / FAMILIAR WITH—"Accustomed" is an adjective meaning usual or customary, while "familiar" means well-known or having great knowledge about something: *Sonya was accustomed to Paul's weak verbs. I am familiar with disgruntled literary agents.*

ADVICE / ADVISE—"Advice" is a noun, and "advise," a verb. *We love to advise new writers, by sharing with them our best advice.*

AFFECT / EFFECT—"Affect" is a verb meaning "to influence." "Effect" is also a verb, but means "to bring about or cause." It is also a noun meaning "a result." *The affected members of the board met several times in secret, hoping to come up with a solution that would effect great changes in the management structure.*

AFFLUENCE / EFFLUENCE—"Affluence" is wealth and prosperity; "effluence" is sewage. *Sewage, the effluence of affluence.*[124]

AGGRAVATE / IRRITATE—To "aggravate" is to make something worse. *Scratching that rash will only aggravate it.* Irritate means to arouse anger or annoyance. *Whining about the rash will irritate those around you.*

AGONIZE / ANTAGONIZE—"Agonize" means "to be in extreme emotional or in physical pain," while "antagonize" means "to bring about dislike or irritation." *He resisted the urge to agonize over the reasons why his brother chose to antagonize him.*

AID / AIDE—An "aide" is a person, an assistant. An "aid" is a device, like a hearing aid.

AISLE / ISLE—An "aisle" is the space between a row of chairs, seats, or shelving. The space between church pews or between grocery store shelves is an aisle. *She roamed the aisles pretending to examine this item and that, while watching the clerk's movements at the register.* An "isle" is a small island.

ALL READY / ALREADY—"All ready" means "prepared or set." "Already" means "by now" or previously." *Martha was all ready to stuff the turkey, but John had already done it.*

ALLUDE / ELUDE—If we "allude" to something, we are making an indirect verbal reference to it. To "elude" something means to escape or avoid it.

ALLUSION / ELUSION / ILLUSION—"Allusion" suggests a concept or thing without naming it. "Elusion" is to skirt or escape. "Illusion" is a fantasy, deception, or daydream.

ALOUD / ALLOWED—"Aloud" means "out loud," while "allowed" means "permitted." *The boy is not allowed to say curse words aloud when in his mother's presence.*

ALRIGHT / ALL RIGHT—In fiction writing we use "all right." "Alright" is considered non-standard or "old" English and shouldn't be used.

ALTAR / ALTER—An "altar" is a platform typically like the one at the back of a church. *They knelt in prayer before the altar.* "Alter" is a verb, meaning to change something. *She had to alter the dress, adding three sizes to squeeze her ample frame into it.*

---

[124] Carlos J Cortes, The Prisoner.

ALTERNATE / ALTERNATIVE—"Alternate" is an adjective or a verb. "Alternative" is a noun. Incorrect: *They met to discuss their plan on alternative Saturdays.* Correct: *They met to discuss their plan on alternate Saturdays.* Incorrect: *We need to find an alternate to this idea.* Correct: *We need to find an alternative to this idea.*

ALTHOUGH / THOUGH—"Although" and "though" are little buggers. Sometimes they come back corrected, other times the same usage slides by. Why? Is the editor suffering brain farts and not seeing the second and third usage? How can we know which is right? Not to worry, these words are interchangeable most of the time. The proper usage puts "although" at the beginning of its clause. *Although she finished the job in record time, her work proved quite shoddy.* "Though" can be placed elsewhere and is more commonly used to link words or phrases in a sentence. *She's fast, though not very thorough.*

ALTOGETHER / ALL TOGETHER—"Altogether" is an adverb meaning completely. *She stopped caring altogether.* "All together" is an adjective (all) and an adverb (together) meaning "in a group." *All together now class; let's begin.*

AMBIGUOUS / AMBIVALENT / INDIFFERENT—Let's imagine we go out for dinner. "Ambiguous" means we are uncertain if we want a full dinner, a snack, a drink, or a bag of popcorn **or** that we are not certain what something on the menu is. "Ambivalent" means being "torn between two opposing alternatives," such as crayfish on the beach or rabbit stew in the countryside. "Indifferent" means we don't care about where we eat.

AMID / AMIDST AND AMONG / AMONGST—"Amid" and "among" are American usage. "Amidst" and "amongst" are the British usage of the same words.

AMONG / BETWEEN—We use "among" to compare more than two elements. We use "between" to compare two elements. *It was hard to choose between Mary and Edna among the seething crowd of fans.*

AMORAL / UNMORAL / IMMORAL—While "immoral" means "opposed to current or accepted standards of morality," the words "amoral" and "unmoral" imply there is no concern for morality at all. *A judge found the painting immoral. The amoral artist couldn't understand why.*

AMOUNT / NUMBER—If something cannot be counted, we use "amount." If it can be counted, we use "number." Is this a problem for writers? Yes, very much so. *He consumed a large amount of food and then he exploded.* Food is a general term, we can't count it. *He ate four food.* Not good. Now, a specific item can be counted. *He ate four pies.*

ANCESTOR / DESCENDANT—Our forebears, father and mother, grandparents, great-grandparents, etc., are our "ancestors." We are their "descendants."

AND / BUT / SO—We use coordinating conjunctions to link the elements or ideas in a sentence. *I like beer, and she likes wine.* We don't use conjunctions to begin a sentence. *But I have better taste* is wrong. Occasionally, when we want to add emphasis, or when used in dialogue, it's okay to use "and," "but," or "so" to begin a sentence, but only occasionally. Often we can delete the conjunction at the beginning of the sentence, and it still retains its meaning and impact. We can also combine the sentences to make it flow much better. *I like beer and she likes wine, but I have better taste.* One more note;

rarely does a comma follow a conjunction. If we use a comma, it should come before the conjunction. Incorrect: *I like beer and she likes wine but, I have better taste.* Correct: *I like beer and she likes wine, but I have better taste.*

AND ALSO / AND / ALSO—"And also" is a redundancy. Either conjunction, "and" or "also" is enough.

ANTARCTIC / ANTARTIC / ARCTIC / ARTIC—To avoid misspelling, we remember that **Arc**tic and Ant**arc**tic Circles are "arcs."

ANTISOCIAL / ASOCIAL—Someone who avoids social interaction can be described as "asocial," not to be confused with "antisocial," which suggests hostility to the laws and customs of society.

ANXIOUS / EAGER—These adjectives are not interchangeable. "Anxious" is negative while "eager" is positive. "Anxiety" implies foreboding and unease. "Eagerness" is about wanting something very much. *They were anxious about finishing the ceremony and eager to get on the flight to Mexico.*

ANYMORE / ANY MORE—We know many writers who don't understand the difference between the variations of "anymore." They believe that it's simply a matter of preference. It's not. Each word refers to something different. "Anymore" is an adjective which refers to time. *They just don't make men like that anymore.* "Any more" is an adjective (any) and a noun (more) which refers to an amount. *Would you like any more chocolate?*

ANYPLACE / ANY PLACE—Let's include "someplace," "some place," and "no place" in this as well. These words are used to replace "somewhere," "anywhere," "everywhere," and "nowhere." While "anyplace," "someplace," and "no place" are not entirely wrong, when writing fiction we should avoid using them. Why? It's not proper usage. The two-word expressions are acceptable, but only when "where" cannot be inserted. So, when in doubt, we insert "where" instead of "place" and see if it works. *She takes a souvenir from every place she's ever visited.* Substituting "everywhere" doesn't create proper narrative so "every place" is okay. However *He throws his clothes any place* does not work. *He throws his clothes everywhere.* Better.

APART / A PART—"Apart" means separately, spaced out or distant. "A part" is a section or a component of the whole. *You are such a part of my life that I wilt when we're apart.*

APIECE / A PIECE—If we need a synonym of "each" the word we need is "apiece." *These watermelons weigh ten pounds apiece.* But if we refer to a part, slice or portion we use "a piece." *They sell melon halves of five pounds a piece.*

APPRAISE / APPRISE—"Appraise" means to evaluate something, such as the value of a house. *The jeweler examined the ring before appraising its value as worthless.* "Apprise" is to inform. *She apprised her parents of her plans for the evening.*

APPROXIMATELY / ABOUT—While they mean the same thing, writers should use the simpler term whenever possible, because the longer word screams for attention. The reader notices it. (Plus, it's an adverb we don't need to use.) Choosing the simpler term means that we can use it again and there is less chance of the reader noticing the repetition.

APT / LIKELY / LIABLE—These three words are often used interchangeably, but the words have distinct meanings and should be used accordingly. "Apt" is an adjective meaning "appropriate, inclined, or capable." *She proved an apt student, learning her way around any lock she came across. It would be an apt judgment to believe she was born to burgle.* "Likely" means "probable or plausible, something within the realm of possibility." It might also mean something is apparently suitable. *Maria is likely to punch him in the mouth if he calls her Julie one more time.* "Liable" is another adjective but means "legally responsible or at risk of suffering unpleasantness." Most often, this word is used to describe a negative outcome. *If she gets caught, she's liable to serve serious jail time.*

ARAB / ARABIAN / ARABIC—Arabs are the people from the Arabian Peninsula. They speak Arabic.

AROUND / ROUND—These are not always interchangeable. For example we "round" up to the nearest dollar, just as we might round up our kids. Two different meanings for the same word. However, we would walk "around" the corner, not "round" it. We'd turn "around," not turn "round."

AS / BECAUSE—"As" is commonly used to replace "because." *I went to the store as I was out of coffee.* This is the wrong usage. "As" should never replace "because." "As" also tends to be one of the most repeated words in a manuscript because it has so many meanings. Writers shouldn't be afraid to look for another word. "While," "because," "when," "though," "like" and the several other alternatives to "as" are much better than using "as" every time it comes up. Yes, simpler words escape notice, but not when used twenty times per chapter.

AS TO / SO AS TO—Writers should avoid these phrases. They aren't essentially wrong, but we should use the less wordy option whenever possible. These are overused, perhaps because we feel they make the writing look more proper or intelligent. They don't. They weigh it down. *She carried the laundry to the lake, stepping over the rocks so as to avoid tripping.* Too wordy. *She carried the laundry to the lake, stepping over the rocks to avoid tripping.* Much better.

ASCENT / ASSENT—To "assent" is to agree. "Ascent" is a climb. *They knew the ascent up the mountain would be perilous, but they assented to go anyway.*

ASCRIBE / SUBSCRIBE—We "ascribe" a belief by crediting or assigning origin or authorship. *The three laws of robotics are ascribed to Isaac Asimov.* "Subscribe" means "to concur" or "be in agreement." *I subscribe to your suggestion of another tot.*

ASSURE / ENSURE / INSURE—These three words all mean "to remove doubt," though their usage is different in some cases. "Assure" means "to remove doubt" and is the only one used to refer to setting a person's mind at rest. *The salesperson assured me the parts would be in on Monday.* "Insure" is also used when speaking about the process of covering one's property against damage. If we buy car insurance, we insure our car. "Ensure" is used when we want to indicate something is secured or guaranteed, or to make certain, secure, or safe from harm. *We lock the door to ensure no one can get in. The court might also send us a subpoena to ensure our presence at the trial.*

ASTROLOGY / ASTRONOMY—"Astrology" is an ancient pseudoscience concerned with divining the future by means of the relative positions of the planets. "Astronomy" is the scientific study of stars and celestial bodies.

ATHEIST / AGNOSTIC—"Atheists" believe that there are no gods. "Agnostics" believe that it's impossible to prove, and therefore cannot be certain if a god or gods exist.

ATTAIN / OBTAIN—To reach, achieve, or accomplish with a degree of effort is to "attain." To "obtain" means to get, without implied difficulty. *We attained a depth of sixty meters on the first drilling shift. She obtained a case of beer in exchange for a box of shells.*

AURAL / ORAL—Things concerning hearing or the ears are "aural." Those relating to speech or mouth are "oral."

AWHILE / A WHILE—"Awhile," one word, means "for a time." It is never preceded by a preposition. *For awhile* is wrong. *For a while* is correct.

AXEL / AXLE—An "axle" is a rod passing through the center of a wheel or cog. "Axels"—single, double, and triple—are figure-skating jumps with a forward takeoff.

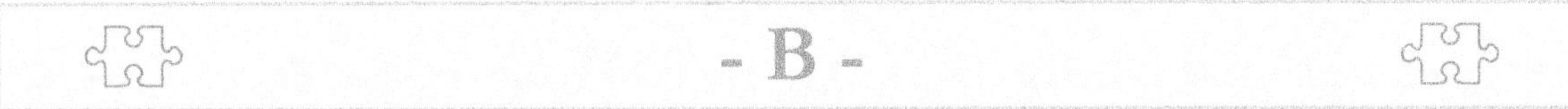

- B -

BACK UP / BACKUP—"Back up" is the verb and "backup," the noun. We should back up our work everyday, to have a backup in case our computer crashes.

BACKYARD / BACK YARD—The latter is a two-word phrase denoting the area where Fido chases the cat. Petra is sunning in the back yard. "Backyard" is an adjective. We have a backyard garden shed.

BAD / BADLY—No matter how much we want it to be so, people cannot feel "badly." Rather, they feel "bad." "Badly" is an adverb, describing how something is done. To say she felt "badly" means she did a crappy job of feeling. We won't get into how writers could find a much better way of saying that, showing us what "bad" feels like instead, because she felt bad isn't wrong. When compared to she felt badly, it's fabulous. Now, if she felt bad because she handled her mother's interference badly, then we're correct.

BAIL OUT / BAILOUT—"Bail out" is the verb and "bailout," the noun. *We have to bail out Timmy; he didn't steal the pumpkin. How much is the bailout?*

BARTER / HAGGLE—To "barter" is to trade goods or services without using money. *John bartered his baseball cards for a bicycle.* "Haggling" is the national sport in many countries where the buyer tries to lower the vendor's price.

BATE / BAIT—"Bate" is to take away or subtract. *Waiting with bated breath.* "Bait" can be used as a noun or a verb. To bait someone is to entice them or tempt them to something. "Bait" as a noun is an enticement or temptation. *Worms are bait for fish just as a young girl is considered jail bait for a lascivious old man.*

BATH / BATHE—A "bath" is a noun. We run a bath, or sit in a bath, or do whatever else we like to do in a vessel full of water with which we might clean ourselves. "Bathe" is a verb, an action. *We bathe an infant or a dog, but never both in the same bath.*

BEAT UP / BEAT-UP—"Beat up" is the verb and "beat-up," the adjective. *After the bandits beat up the guards, they drove away in a beat-up truck.*

BEGAN / STARTED—Let's remember that "began" and "started" usually lead to an infinitive (to) or a gerund (ing), which can create a passive construction. Often we use "began to," "started to," and such when an action verb would be much better. *She started drinking the wine.* No, she drank the wine. *Joe began to jog up the street.* No, Joe jogged up the street. We use "began" and "started" only when the action truly begins. *He began his complaint, but the clerk walked away. Joe began to run but tripped over his shoelace.*

BEMUSE / AMUSE—We "bemuse" someone when we cause emotional confusion. To "amuse" is to occupy in a pleasant or entertaining fashion. *Sarah liked to amuse herself by breeding alligators in her backyard—a habit which bemused her doting father.*

BESIDE / BESIDES—"Beside" means "next to." *I stood beside the smelly man on the subway.* "Besides" means "in addition to." *Besides me, there were four people who passed out from the smell of his breath.*

BLAST OFF / BLASTOFF—"Blast off " is the verb and "blastoff," the noun. *We are ready to blast off. Blastoff cancelled.*

BLATANT / FLAGRANT—A woman blatantly ignoring her husband is obvious action, offensively so, obtrusive even. If our music is annoyingly loud then it is also blatant. "Flagrant" is often used in place of "blatant," and although it also means obvious, it's a bit different. To be "flagrant," we must be shockingly obvious. *The bride's large belly and blatant affair with the best man showed flagrant disregard for the bonds of holy matrimony.* The difference between the two is that "blatant" is a failure to conceal an act, while "flagrant" describes offense in the act itself.

BLIND / VISUALLY IMPAIRED—Many writers are wary of causing offense and resort to the unlikeliest euphemisms to please everybody. Someone who is "visually impaired" has problems with his vision. Someone without eyesight is "blind." We'll include "deaf" and "hearing impaired" here as well. "Deaf" means that one cannot hear. "Hearing impaired" means that one has severe trouble hearing.

BLOG / POST—"Blog" is a shortening of the term Web log. The activity of updating blogs is called "blogging." The term blog means a journal or diary where people lodge periodic entries called "posts." We don't "write new blogs" or "post new blogs." Rather, we put—or publish—new posts in our blogs.

BLOND / BLONDE—The usage of these two forms of "blond" is widely debated. When using as a noun, the proper usage is "blond" in the masculine form. *The blond turned his head, distracted by the horn of a cab speeding past, and tripped over the body.* "Blonde" (with an e) is the feminine form. *The blonde stepped over the body as though she hadn't noticed it lying in the middle of the sidewalk.* When using "blond" as an adjective, we always use the masculine form. *Her blond hair hung about her face in a tangled mess of knots and dirt.*

BLOW OUT / BLOWOUT—"Blow out" is the verb and "blowout," the noun. *Blow out the candles and make a wish. The meeting with the Japanese delegation was a blowout.*

BLOW UP / BLOWUP—"Blow up" is the verb and "blowup," the noun. *Unless we blow up that pillbox, they have us pinned. Complaints about her squirrel stew led to a blowup.*

BOIL OVER / BOILOVER—"Boil over" is the verb and "boilover," the noun. *Don't let the mush boil over, else we'll end up with a boilover when Mom gets back.*

BOLDFACE / BOLD-FACE—"Boldface" refers to a type font. *Titles and name must be typed in boldface and centered on the page.* "Bold-face" means "brazen or cocky." *That's a bold-faced lie.*

BORED OF / BORED WITH—When we get tired of something, we are "bored with" it. "Bored of" it is non-standard English.

BOTH / EACH—These two terms can be confusing if used carelessly. I gave both of the Mexican officers $100 can be construed as having given them $100 to share. If this is the case, "both of" is redundant. Otherwise, I gave each of the Mexican officers $100 is clearer, and probably more accurate.

BRAKE / BREAK—"Brake" is an action verb meaning to slow down, and it also refers to the pedal in the car which slows it. "Break" means "to fracture, damage, or ruin something." *We should brake to slow down a vehicle or risk breaking our necks when we collide with that tree.*

BREACH / BROACH—If someone violates a contract or makes a hole or an opening into an object, he's "breached" it. If we bring up a subject for conversation, we've "broached" it.

BREAK / BROKE—We have spotted this hilarious gaffe in several bestsellers. *Igor leaped from the third floor and broke his leg.* Why would Igor break his own bone? We need a direct action to break something. "Sandra broke her glass" is acceptable but "Sandra broke her arm" isn't, unless she actually snapped the bone with her own hand. *Igor leaped from the third floor, and the fall broke his leg.*

BREAK AWAY / BREAKAWAY—"Break away" is the verb and "breakaway," the noun. *John and Mary want to break away from the daily grind of life. The thugs made their breakaway on skateboards.*

BREAK DOWN / BREAKDOWN—"Break down" is the verb and "breakdown," the noun. *We must break down their defenses. When a drunken guest tore down the curtains, Alice suffered a breakdown.*

BREAK OUT / BREAKOUT—"Break out" is the verb and "breakout," the noun. *The Joneses break out from prison each time they are captured, and the guards do nothing to prevent the breakout.*

BREAK UP / BREAKUP—"Break up" is the verb and "breakup," the noun. *So the neighbors are ready to break up because of their dog? I've never heard a more outlandish reason for a breakup.*

BREATH / BREATHE—"Breathe" is a verb, and "breath" a noun. *I took a breath and knelt. She breathed peace deep into her spirit, smiled, and said, "yes."*

BRING / TAKE—We use "bring" to move objects toward us and "take" when the object moves away from us. *Please bring the bricks and take the rubble to the dump.*

BRITISH / ENGLISH—These terms are not interchangeable. The United Kingdom or Great Britain is made up of England, Scotland, Wales, and Northern Ireland. If we refer to a native of the British Isles, the term is Briton, and their nationality is British. Those from England are English, Scottish folks are Scots, and people from Wales are Welsh.

BRUNET / BRUNETTE—"Brunet" describes a man with dark hair; "brunette," a woman.

BRUSH OFF / BRUSHOFF—"Brush off" is the verb and "brushoff," the noun. *Brush off the crumbs from your clothes. Otherwise, your date may give you the brushoff.*

BUILD UP / BUILDUP—"Build up" is the verb and "buildup," the noun. *We must build up our savings. There's a buildup of dead leaves in the gutter.*

BULLION / BOUILLON—When we're speaking of the gold bricks that we lifted from Fort Knox last weekend, we are speaking of "bullion." If we're making a stew, we use "bouillon," or boiled down beef/chicken/vegetable stock, for flavor.

BURN OFF / BURNOFF—"Burn off" is the verb and "burnoff," the noun. If you burn off calories, you won't get fat. *The rocket caused a severe burnoff on the grass.*

BUTTOCKS / BUTTOX—"Buttox" is not a word. Let's get it out of our brain right now. The proper spelling is "buttocks," the plural of "buttock."

BUY IN / BUY-IN—"Buy in" is the verb and "buy-in," the noun. *We need investors to buy in. A buy-in from investors is what we need.*

CACAO / COCOA—The small evergreen tree is a "cacao" tree, or simply a "cacao." Its fruit, beans, and the resulting powder is "cocoa."

CALL BACK / CALLBACK—"Call back" is the verb and "callback," the noun. *Call back your goons. There's no reply; I'll try a callback later.*

CALLOUS / CALLUS—"Callus" refers to the hardening of skin or bone after an injury. "Callous" means insensitive or unsympathetic. This might be physically, such as the nasty callused skin on someone's feet, or it might mean emotionally. For example, we might be angry at the callous manner in which he mentioned the nasty calluses on our feet.

CANCELED / CANCELLED / LABELED / LABELLED—The second spelling of each word looks right, but it isn't. The American spelling with one "L" is correct. The rule is that with words like these, when the emphasis is on the first syllable (as it is in cancel and label), we do not double the consonant on the end when adding suffixes such as "ed."

CANVAS / CANVASS—"Canvas" is a noun. The thing an artist paints on is called a "canvas." "Canvass" is a verb meaning "to inspect, study, or examine." *To find his lost dog, Billy would canvass his neighborhood. If he doesn't turn up, Billy might canvass the entire city.*

CAPITAL / CAPITOL / CAPITOL—"Capital" refers to a city or town. *Toronto is the capital of Ontario.* It also refers to uppercase letters. *The first letter in every sentence should be a capital.* "Capitol," spelled with an uppercase "C" refers to the building in Washington D.C., where the United States Congress meets. Spelled with a lower case "c," "capitol" refers to the building in which a state or city legislative assembly meets. *Of course, when starting a new business venture, it's a capital idea to attract plenty of venture capital to the capitol.*

CARRY ON / CARRY-ON—"Carry on" is the verb and "carry-on," the noun. *If you carry on another bag you must pay. Place your carry-on on the belt.*

CAVE IN / CAVE-IN—"Cave in" is the verb and "cave-in," the noun. *When he unwrapped the diamond tiara, I caved in. We don't expect survivors at the Mason Tunnel's cave-in.*

CEMENT / CONCRETE—"Cement" is one of the ingredients of "concrete," the others being water, gravel, sand and—sometimes—additives to speed or delay hardening. More cement in the mix usually results in stronger concrete. "Cement" is also a verb and a synonym of "adhesive." *That concrete is too light; add more cement.*

CENTERED ON / CENTERED AROUND—We don't "center around" anything. We "revolve around." We "center on" something.

CHANGE OVER / CHANGEOVER—"Change over" is the verb and "changeover," the noun. *We must change over to the new cable system. We'll have three-thousand new channels after the changeover.*

CHECK IN / CHECK-IN—"Check in" is the verb and "check-in," the noun. *We must check in before raiding the duty-free. The check-in gauntlet now entails fondling.*

CHOOSE / CHOSE—"Choose" is present tense, meaning "to select" something. "Chose" is past tense, meaning "to have selected" something. *Will she choose the same door the contestant before her chose?*

CITE / SIGHT / SITE—"Cite" means "to quote or document a statement or events." We cite quotes or rules. "Site" is a position or a location. *We'd show up late to the job site after our adventure in Mexico with the mule and the pretty little maid.* or *We'd love to find a web site that offered maps of Mexico and the places to avoid.* "Sight" might seem obvious but is occasionally mixed up with the others. "Sight" means vision. We'd use this when speaking of seeing things visually. *A mule in a wedding dress is a peculiar sight, but not to a cowboy.*

CLAMP DOWN / CLAMPDOWN—"Clamp down" is the verb and "clampdown," the noun. *The authorities will clamp down on sales of unlabeled bananas. There was a paucity of hookers after the clampdown.*

CLASSIC / CLASSICAL—"Classical" relates to ancient Greek and Latin culture, literature, or art. Exceptions are classical music, or things from Rome or analogous ancient periods like classical Sanskrit poetry, ballet, or other traditional art forms. "Classic," refers to "outstanding examples," such as a classic soufflé, a classic car, or a classic pair of legs.

CLICHÉ / CLICHÉD—To say that a book, story, or play is "cliché" is undoubtedly wrong. "Cliché" is a noun and "clichéd" the adjective. A story can be "clichéd" and be full of "clichés."

CLICK THROUGH / CLICKTHROUGH—"Click through" is the verb and "clickthrough," the noun. *Click through to access the members-only section. Clickthrough rates have gone down.*

CLIMACTIC / CLIMATIC—An event ending in a climax accepts the adjective "climactic." "Anticlimactic" is another adjective implying a disappointing end to an exciting event or series of events. "Climatic" has to do with climate or weather conditions.

COARSE / COURSE—"Coarse" is an adjective meaning rough, like when describing sandpaper. "Course" is a noun referring to a college class, movement, direction, or path. *The storm raged on, its powerful winds turning the ship from its course.*

COLOMBIA / COLUMBIA—Washington, the U.S. capital, is the District of Columbia, but the country in South America is Colombia.

COME DOWN / COMEDOWN—"Come down" is the verb and "comedown," the noun. *Come down and spend a weekend with us. The rented apartment was a comedown after growing up in a mansion.*

COME ON / COME-ON—"Come on" is an expression or imperative. Come-on is a noun. *Come on, this is too heavy. "Free strawberries" was only a come-on; they had none left.*

COMPRISE / COMPOSE—The whole "comprises" the parts and the parts "compose" the whole. *Sixty minutes compose* (make up) *an hour.* "Comprised" means "composed of," so "comprised of" would be incorrect in this sentence. *A dozen comprises twelve items.* "Comprise" is used correctly in this one.

CONFIDANT / CONFIDANTE—"Confidant" refers to a man. "Confidante" refers to a woman. If we're sharing our deepest secrets to the bartender with the six pack abs and a lovely tattoo on his neck, he's our confidant. The woman in the bathroom an hour before was our confidante, when we shared with her the state of our pathetic love life.

CONNOTE / DENOTE—The "denotation" of a particular word is its literal meaning; the "connotations" are the broader senses or implications of the same word. "Silly" and "stupid" both denote asinine dullness, but their connotations differ; the first can even be used as an endearment while the second is definitely pejorative.

CONSCIENCE / CONSCIOUS—"Conscience" is that annoying little voice that we tend to ignore at the crucial moment before indulgence. It is our sense of right and wrong. "Conscious" means that we're awake. *"I cannot in good conscience perform this wedding ceremony," said the minister to the mule. "Your groom is not even conscious."*

CONTAGIOUS / INFECTIOUS—"Contagious" diseases spread from one organism to another by direct or indirect contact. An "infection" is the presence of a virus or other pathogen in an organism, which may or may not be contagious. *My vines are infected with Phylloxera. You can touch it; luckily it's not contagious.*

CONTINUOUS / CONTINUAL—"Continuous" means without break or interruption. *The music was continuous through the night.* "Continual" means again and again. *The door bell rang continually, but she ignored it.*

COULD / COULDN'T CARE LESS—We're addressing two issues here. First, "could" is the past tense of can. We try to avoid using "could" because it can lead to a needlessly wordy or passive construction. *He could see the car crossing the median.* That reads better as, *He saw the car cross the median.* Better: *The car crossed the median.* Second, it is incorrect to use sentences like *"She could care less about his opinion."* Although we hear it often in speech, it is the bastard form of the proper phrase: *She could not care less.* "Could care less" implies that she does in fact care just a little, which is not what is usually intended with this saying. Writers must remember to include "not" if we must use this phrase.

COUNCIL / COUNSEL—A "council" is a group that gathers to consult or advise (noun), but to "counsel" means to give advice (verb). They are similar, but their usage is different. *The council of elders met to decide the fate of the man in chains. His lawyer counseled him to keep his mouth shut about his relationship with the duck.*

CREVICE / CREVASSE—Though both these words refer to cracks, their difference is the size. "Crevices" are small, while "crevasses" are large: *I floss my teeth by running the silk thread through the crevices. We had to walk two miles around a new crevasse at the base of the Denali.*

CRITICIZE / CRITIQUE—To "criticize" is to censure or emit a disparaging verdict, while to "critique" means to analyze or evaluate something in detail. *Rita critiqued my latest manuscript and found it excellent, but she criticized two POV blunders.*

CROSS / CRUCIFIX—These two words refer to items of a similar shape but different construction. A "cross" is a shape made from one upright element and a transverse piece, usually set at right angles. A "crucifix" is a cross with a human figure nailed to it.

CROTCHET / CROCHET—Though vastly different in meaning, some writers still confuse these words. "Crotchets," besides elements of musical notation, are whimsical, perverse, or unfounded beliefs or notions. *Peter holds dear to his crotchet about the Earth's flatness.* "Crochet," is what we do with a crochet hook and yarn to pass the time while we wait for Mary to empty the shops.

CUT BACK / CUTBACK—"Cut back" is the verb and "cutback," the noun. *I will cut back on hamburgers, but I'll keep my Godiva chocolates. The Council plans a cutback on complimentary drinks.*

- D -

DAMN / DAM—"Damn" is a curse word, sometimes replaced by the euphemism "darn." A "dam" is a structure that holds back water. *The damn hurricane broke the dam, and the water gushed over the town.*

DAMPENED / DAMPED—Our hair is still "dampened" after we towel it. We "damp" something through a device to limit or control its movement. Motors are usually set on dampers—blocks of neoprene or other elastomer—to impede the transmission of vibration.

DARK / DARKENED—"Dark" is an adjective that means lacking light or brightness. "Black" is a dark color. *It is dark at midnight.* "Darkened" is a verb meaning "to make dark or darker." We would "darken" a doorstep, or we might add color to "darken" paint. "Darkened" is not and never should be an adjective.

DESERT / DESSERT—These two words are confused quite frequently. "Desert" refers to an arid piece of land or to abandon something or someone. "Dessert" is the sweet treat that follows a meal if we've eaten all of our vegetables. An easy mnemonic is that we would like double helpings of "dessert" (the double "s").

DESPITE / IN SPITE OF—There isn't a literal difference in meaning between these two. There is however a difference in intent when using them that should determine our choice. "Despite" implies an attempt to avoid. *He walked to work, despite my warning that it would snow.* "In spite" is used when everything possible was done to avoid failure, but it still prevailed, which is why it's usually phrased with "best efforts." *In spite of the players' best efforts, the team lost the championship.*

DIFFERENT FROM / DIFFERENT THAN / DIFFERENT TO—"Different from" is what we should use. *This book is different from any other.* While "different than" and "different to" (British) are not wrong, they are not accepted as proper usage in all sources.

DISASSEMBLE / DISSEMBLE—To "assemble" something, we put it together, and we "disassemble" it by taking it apart. *I'm afraid, honey, Timmy has disassembled your hi-fi system.* We "dissemble" by concealing our true intentions, motives or feelings. *She can't dissemble her motives; her eyes would give her away.*

DISCREET / DISCRETE—Often these two words are simply misspelled. "Discreet" refers to showing restraint or prudence in speech or behavior. *His part in the fraud was discovered because he wasn't discreet in his spending.* "Discrete" is not often used correctly, but means "distinct or separate." *The machine consisted of several discrete parts.*

DISINTERESTED / UNINTERESTED—"Disinterested" means "impartial or unprejudiced." *We need disinterested experts to examine our security measures.* "Uninterested" means "distracted or unconcerned." *I asked her to marry me but she was uninterested.*

DISPOSE / DISPOSE OF—The difference is in the use of the preposition. To "dispose of" means getting rid of something. *He disposed of his inheritance at the local cat house.* To "dispose" (without "of") means "to arrange in a given order or to bring someone into a particular frame of mind." *She disposed glasses, cutlery, and plates on the table. After Mary vented out steam, yelling at the top of her lungs, she was disposed to strike a truce.*

DIVED / DOVE—"Dove" is accepted by many sources as a correct past tense of "dive." But "dived" is preferred, and causes fewer misinterpretations.

DOUGHNUT / DONUT—Though "donut" is increasingly popular, the correct spelling is "doughnut."

DOWNGRADE / DENIGRATE / DEGRADE—To "downgrade" is to reduce to a lower grade or level of importance. *Our book has been downgraded to number two on the bestseller's list.* In itself "downgrade" doesn't imply a reduction in value. To "denigrate" means to belittle with unfair criticism, insult, defamation, or slander. "Degrade," like "downgrade," also denotes a reduction in rank or importance, only in this instance it implies a reduction in value. Another meaning of "degrade" is to corrupt or treat someone with contempt or disrespect.

DRAG / DRUG—"Drag" is a verb, meaning to pull. "Drug" can be used as a noun or a verb. "Drug" as a noun, means medication or narcotics. *The doctor would prescribe drugs, or we might buy them from that shifty looking fellow who hangs out by the post office.* "Drug" as a verb means to administer or give medicine or narcotics. *The only way she could escape was to drug him into unconsciousness.* "Drug" is not the past tense of "drag." We would use "dragged."

DRAW BACK / DRAWBACK—"Draw back" is the verb and "drawback," the noun. *If you draw back and release the cookies, nobody gets hurt. Grass has a big drawback; it grows.*

DRINK / DRANK / DRUNK OR SINK / SANK / SUNK—We've seen these words debated many times. The main issue is that no one can seem to agree whether or not "drunk" or "sunk" is proper. "Drunk" or "sunk" as a past participle is correct usage. *He drank too much beer. He drinks too much beer. He has drunk too much beer.* All are correct. *She will sink the ship. She sank the ship. She has sunk the ship.* Again, all are correct, even if the latter isn't often used.

DRIVE BY / DRIVE-BY—"Drive by" is the verb and "drive-by," the adjective. *Drive by the bank. The guards are on their lunch break. We passed through a drive-by watering hole.*

DROP OUT / DROPOUT—"Drop out" is the verb and "dropout," the noun. *I will drop out from macramé classes. That boy is a dropout.*

- E -

EARTH / EARTH—If we're referring to the planet Earth, then we capitalize this word. If we're not, we don't capitalize. *The aliens landed on Earth on Sunday.* This is correct. *She stepped off the ship, eager to sink her bare feet in the soft Earth on shore.* This is not correct.

ELAPSE / LAPSE—"Elapse" refers to the passage of time. *Six hours elapsed before Dad forgave Timmy for painting the cat bright orange.* To "lapse" can mean a change of state or a termination of an arrangement or right. *After hugging the lamppost for a few minutes, Mike finished the bottle and lapsed into oblivion. I'm sorry, sir, but your license to kill has lapsed; you're under arrest.*

ELICIT / ILLICIT—These two are often mistaken but have different meanings. To "elicit" is to draw or bring out something. "Illicit" means "illegal." *The officer stood, arms crossed, hoping his silence would elicit a confession from the man cuffed to the chair. They knew all about the illicit drugs he'd smuggled into the country using that poor mule.*

EMINENT / IMMANENT / IMMINENT—"Eminent" means "famous or respected," while "immanent" is "inherent or intrinsic." "Imminent," means "about to happen or ready to start." Writers often mix the three of these up, although sometimes it's more a matter of misspelling than not understanding the difference. We'll provide an example of their usage anyway. *The eminent priest, next in line for pope according to rumor, read the strange letter. Its meaning was immanent, not easily recognized, but one thing became clear to him as he read the words again: The end was imminent.*

EMULATE / IMITATE—To "emulate" is a specialized word meaning "to match or surpass a deed or achievement by positively imitating someone." *She wanted to emulate her sister and run the transcontinental marathon.* To "imitate" something or someone is "to follow suit or copy a fashion or behavior." *Other models try to imitate her walk, but they don't have the hips to go with it.*

ENDEMIC / EPIDEMIC—"Endemic" is an adjective qualifying a disease or condition regularly found among particular species or restricted to certain areas. "Epidemic" refers to the widespread occurrence of an infectious disease or situation. *In Nigeria, organized crime is endemic. The country also suffers a flu epidemic.*

ENGINE / MOTOR—An "engine" is a device to internally exchange chemical energy into mechanical energy. A "motor" converts electrical or other externally supplied power into mechanical energy.

ESPRESSO / EXPRESSO—We may want it in a hurry or expressly made for us, but the correct spelling is "espresso," meaning "squeezed through." Espresso machines squeeze water through the coffee grounds.

ETHICS / MORALS—While "ethics" are beliefs, "morals" concern behavior. *Father Jonas preaches lofty ethics, but his morals are suspect; yesterday he parked his Hummer before the soup kitchen.*

EVERY DAY / EVERYDAY—"Every day" means "each day." *We'd milk the cows every day so the poor girls don't explode.* When referring to something commonplace or routine, then we'd use "everyday." *When Superman returns home from his day job, he changes from his everyday clothes into a blue leotard and shiny red cape.*

EVOKE / INVOKE—Bringing into the conscious mind or reminiscing is to "evoke." *He evoked with nostalgia the days when one could fly inside the Grand Canyon.* "Invoke" can mean to cite or appeal to someone in authority as in: *"She invoked Martha's help to defeat the intruders."* More often, invoke is used to mean summoning gods or spirits. *Charles set the Ouija and invoked Rasputin's spirit.*

EXAGGERATED / OVER-EXAGGERATED—"Exaggerated" means that something is depicted as larger, greater, better, or worse than it really is. "Over-exaggerated" is non-standard English.

EXASPERATE / EXACERBATE—Think of "irritate" vs. "aggravate" and similar distinctions apply here, but with a slight difference. When people are irritated to the point of fury, we say they are "exasperated." *Yet another disaster exasperated the weary inhabitants.* To "exacerbate" means to worsen an already bad situation or feeling, and can't be used with people. *The oil spill exacerbated the havoc caused by the hurricane.*

EXULT / EXALT—We "exalt" something or someone by having a high opinion or dignifying. *Mary exalted Susan's prowess at tossing pancakes.* To "exult" is to show or feel elation, generally after a successful deed. *He exulted at Caesar's victory.*

- F -

FALL BACK / FALLBACK—"Fall back" is the verb and "fallback," the noun. *After the raid we can fall back toward the barn. If we need a fallback there's always your mother.*

FEEL / BELIEVE / THINK—Writers should save "feel" for when we really mean to feel something. We don't use "feel" when we mean "think" or "believe." *He felt the date went well.* Better: *He thought the date went well.*

FEINT / FAINT—A "feint" is a deceptive move, especially in fencing or boxing, designed to divert the opponent's attention. *He parried, feinted left, and kicked his opponent's chin.* "Faint" means something is barely perceptible by the senses, or to lose consciousness. *Dawn painted a faint blush on the rolling hills.*

FEWER / LESS—Use "fewer" when referring to countable elements and "less" with uncountable ones. *We could do with less drought and fewer hurricanes.*

FIANCÉ / FIANCÉE—A "fiancé" is an engaged man, like Bob, and the woman Bob is betrothed to is his "fiancée." The man Bob proposed to the month before is also his fiancé. *No, his fiancé and his fiancée haven't met, but they will.*

FILM / VIDEO—Trying to make sense of this to the younger generation is a lost battle, but we are gluttons for punishment. A "video" is a system of recording or a physical item imprinted with a recording. A "film" is a story or event recorded by a camera. We can enjoy films or movies on video, but we can't watch a video. Casablanca will always be a film, never a video.

FLAMMABLE / INFLAMMABLE—Both words are synonymous and mean that whatever these adjectives qualify catches fire easily. Problem is that some people interpret the prefix "in" as a negation. When in doubt about the reader's vocabulary prowess, use "flammable."

FLAUNT / FLOUT—We "flaunt" when we show off (or follow the sage's counsel: If you've got it, flaunt it). To "flout" means "to openly disregard a rule, norm, or convention." *The sign clearly stated no topless sunbathing. Elsa flouted it.*

FLOUNDER / FOUNDER—"Flounder" means "to struggle or stagger in water or mud." "Founder" means "to fill with water and sink" or—figuratively—to break down or fail. *When the pirogue foundered, the men swam ashore while the chickens floundered.*

FLY BY / FLYBY—"Fly by" is the verb and "flyby," the noun. *Lost in the promise of her décolletage, the afternoon flew by for him. We have enough fuel for another flyby over the herd.*

FONT / TYPEFACE—A "typeface" refers to the design of the letters, such as Arial, Courier New, and Times New Roman. These, in turn, are made up of "fonts," like Arial Narrow, Arial Bold, Arial Black, Arial Unicode, etc.

FOR SALE / ON SALE—Items in a shop window or the house down the road are "for sale." If they lower the price, then the house or the items in the shop go "on sale."

FORMER / LATE—"Late" husbands, wives, or lovers are dead ones. If they've survived the experience, the term we use is "former."

FORTUITOUS / FORTUNATE—"Fortuitous" events happen by chance rather than design and need not be "fortunate" or positive. *It was fortuitous that the tornado razed our house rather than Patrick's. I didn't borrow your new car, a fortunate decision. I've totaled mine.*

FREAK OUT / FREAKOUT—"Freak out" is the verb and "freakout," the noun. *Please, don't freak out; this won't hurt. The party was a freakout.*

FUN—"Fun" is not an adjective. It is a noun. In spoken English it is often used as an adjective, but in writing it must be used correctly. The only exception is when it's used in dialogue. "I had a fun time at the dance." Whereas, "He had a fun time at the dance" is wrong, because we're using fun as an adjective in narrative. "He had fun at the dance." This is the correct way to use "fun." What did he have? He had fun. A noun.

FURTHER / FARTHER—"Further" and "farther" have their own distinct meanings. "Further" refers to abstract situations, and "farther" refers to measurable distances. *If he walked much farther, his injury would worsen, causing him further debilitation.*

GAGE / GAUGE—A "gage" is a precious object—even one's life—deposited as a gesture of good faith. In the Middle Ages, the glove thrown down to challenge someone to a duel was a gage. A "gauge" is a measuring tool, such as a blade or rod of certain length and thickness.

GET AWAY / GETAWAY—"Get away" is the verb and "getaway," the noun. *I need to get away from it all. We could try a mountain getaway.*

GIVE AWAY / GIVEAWAY—"Give away" is the verb and "giveaway," the adjective. *Though I tried to give away copies of my new novel, there were no takers. Customers preferred sweets as giveaway gifts.*

GO AHEAD / GO-AHEAD—"Go ahead" is the verb and "go-ahead," the noun. *If we go ahead with the revamp, we'll need paint. Dad just gave me the go-ahead.*

GOODBYE / GOOD-BYE / GOOD-BY—Any one of these is fine, although the preferable spelling is "goodbye." The one thing we advise is that writers use the same spelling throughout the manuscript. We don't shift between them.

GRAY / GREY—Neither of these is wrong. "Gray" tends to be preferred, but no one will rap our knuckles for using "grey" (which is the common British usage). We must be consistent, however, and use one form only in our manuscript.

HAND OUT / HANDOUT—"Hand out" is the verb and "handout," the noun. *Please, hand out leaflets to the faithful leaving the hall. I'm sick of handouts.*

HANG OUT / HANGOUT—"Hang out" is the verb and "hangout," the noun. *I will go downtown to hang out with my buddies. The Doldrums is a popular hangout for bikers.*

HANGAR / HANGER—We've seen a "hanger" dangling in our closet. It's that wire or plastic thing that we're supposed to hang our clothes on. A "hangar" is an enclosure used to park airplanes. We would never find a "hangar" in our closet.

HANGED / HUNG—"Hanged" is only used as the past tense of hang when we mean the past tense of "put to death by hanging." *They hanged him at noon.* In all other cases, when we're writing the past tense of "hang," we would use "hung." *He hung his coat on the chair.*

HE OR SHE—Political correctness is driving us insane. Using "he or she" when trying to depict an individual without sounding sexist results in wordy and clunky prose. If we want to be politically correct, we go for the plural form instead, which is less wordy. If writers want to avoid accusations of sexism, **they** often use "he or she" in place of he. Ick. Let's try this instead: *Writers who want to avoid accusations of sexism often use he or she in place of he.*

HEAR / HERE—"Hearing" is an auditory sense, the act of processing sound through the ear. "Here" means "in this location." *I can't hear anything here because everyone is yelling.*

HISTORIC / HISTORICAL—"Historic" refers to important actions or events in history. "Historical" refers to any past events. *The European Community is a historic blunder. Historical evidence should have been enough to prevent it.*

HOLD BACK / HOLDBACK—"Hold back" is the verb and "holdback," the noun. *He couldn't hold back any longer and reached for another sweet. Until we deliver in full we cannot recover the holdback.*

HOME / HOUSE—A "home" is where one lives permanently as member of a family unit. A "house" is a building. "Home" has the household emotional connotations that "house" lacks. *This is my house, but now that Mary has eloped with the preacher, it will never be a home.*

HOOK UP / HOOKUP—"Hook up" is the verb and "hookup," the noun. *I'll hook up with James and head for the mill. Is he permanent or just a hookup?*

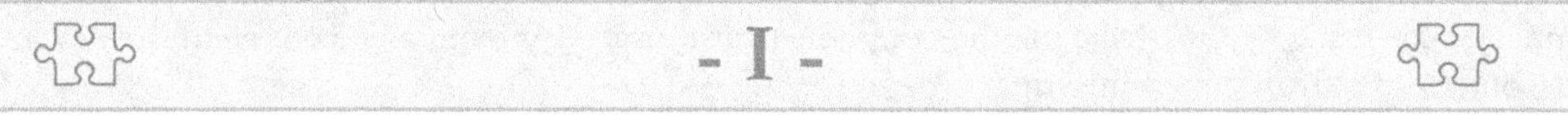

- I -

IF / WHETHER—"If" is used when implying a true or real condition. *We'll give you five bucks if you can eat his cooking.* "We will give the five bucks if he survives the meal," which makes it a real condition. "Whether" is used when providing alternatives. *Whether or not you give me the money, I won't eat that man's food.*

ILLEGIBLE / UNREADABLE—"Illegible" means not clear enough to be read. *Erosion has rendered the carvings illegible.* "Unreadable" means too dull or badly written. *What's that? Another unreadable manuscript?*

IMAGINED / ASSUMED—We never use "imagined" in place of "assumed" or "believed." They are not interchangeable. Because we often make the exchange in speech, it is acceptable to do this in dialogue.

Carrie imagined they'd prefer to spend the night at a motel. This is wrong. It should read: *Carrie assumed they'd prefer to spend the night at a motel.* But if Carrie is saying the line, we can keep imagined. *"I imagine you'd prefer to stay at a motel,"* Carrie said.

IMPACT / IMPACTED—"Impact" is a noun meaning either "a collision" or "the effect of one thing on another." *His impact on the lives of others was minimal.* "Impacted" is an adjective meaning "wedged in" or "blocked." Bowels can become impacted, as can a tooth, but we can't impact someone's life unless we manage to jam it into a passage. "Impact" is often used as a verb like this. If we find ourselves writing "have an impact on," we're using the word incorrectly.

IMPLY / INFER—These are often used as though they have the same meaning. They do not. "Imply" refers to what the speaker does. *He implied that she might be a loose woman.* "Infer" refers to what the listener hears. *She inferred from his words that he thought she was attractive.*

IN / INTO—"In" is used to indicate something is within the limits of something or a location. We would be hit *in* the face or eat *in* the dining room. "Into" means "to go inside of something." It also can be used to mean going into the occupation of or to the condition or form of something. We would walk *into* a room, go *into* nursing, or change *into* a dog.

INTER / INTERNMENT—To "inter" someone is to bury him, once he's dead of course. To suffer "internment" is to be locked up.

IRREGARDLESS / REGARDLESS—Once and for all: "Irregardless" doesn't exist as a word. The word is "regardless."

ITS / IT'S—Editors all over the world cringe when they read this basic mistake and writers gnash their teeth trying to remember which is which. "Its" means "of or belonging to," showing possession. "It's" is a contraction for "it is." *It's terrible to see a dog that has lost its bone.*

JACK / PLUG—To the chagrin of many SF writers, a "jack" is the female part where one shoves the plug or male thing. Usually, jacks are located on the appliance and "plugs" are at the end of cords. *She rammed the jack of her earphone into the socket* is wrong. The correct usage would be *she rammed the plug into the jack.*

JEALOUSY / ENVY—We are "envious" of what others have. "Jealousy" involves wanting to hold onto what we have, even though possession might be imagined. We are envious of Jack's charisma with women, and jealous when "our" Mary salivates at the sight of him.

JOURNEY / SOJOURN—This pair is often confused. To "journey" implies movement, while to "sojourn" implies a rest or stay. *We journey through the steppes and enjoy a sojourn at a nice village.*

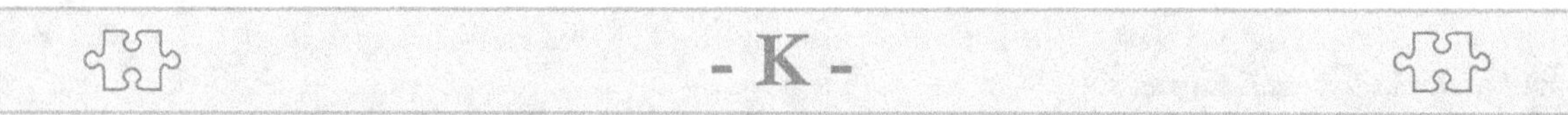

KNOCK DOWN / KNOCK-DOWN—"Knock down" is the verb and "knock-down," the adjective. *I will knock down the greenhouse. They are getting rid of tires at knock-down prices.*

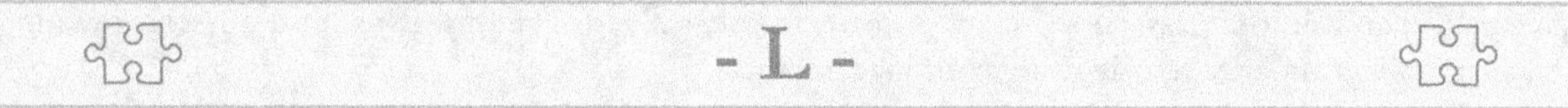

LANGUISH / LUXURIATE—To "languish" is to grow weak and feeble: *He languished under the apple tree as sickness took its toll.* Other uses include pining after a loved: *For twelve years she languished after Don Fernando.* Also, enduring internment: *He languished in a Turkish cell until he consented to pay his debts.* In all cases, it denotes an undesirable situation. To "luxuriate" is to enjoy something, like a bubble bath or a box of chocolates. *She luxuriated on the grass, its coolness, balm to her fevered skin.*

LAY OUT / LAYOUT—"Lay out" is the verb and "layout," the noun. *Lay out the mulch over the strawberry beds. The cover layout shows appalling bad taste.*

LEAD / LED—"Lead" and "led" sound the same. (Unless we're speaking of lead, pronounced "leed," which is a verb.) "Lead," when it sounds like led, is a type of metal. "Led" is the past tense of the verb "lead" (pronounced "leed"). *He led the man downstairs, where his wife waited with a lead pipe. He will lead us into battle.*

LEFTWARD / RIGHTWARD—These two words aren't technically wrong in that they are words, but before using them, a writer should try saying a sentence aloud when it includes "rightward" or "leftward." Do they easily roll off the tongue? No, they don't. "Leftward" and "rightward" are noticeable, making the reader stumble or remember them later so that if we use them again in the manuscript, the echo will be evident. It's always best to use the simplest word. So let's all use "right" or "left" instead.

LET DOWN / LETDOWN—"Let down" is the verb and "letdown," the noun. *Here, let down your hair and bunch your toes. I had high hopes for Brenda's manuscript, but it's a letdown.*

LETS / LET'S—"Let's" is the contraction of "let us." "Lets" means allows.

LIE / LAY—Oh the agony these two tiny words cause writers. Which one and when and why and how are they used? "Lie" means for a person or animal to lie down. A good way to remember is that people lie, so Jane would lie on the bed. It is a state of being. "Lay" is the action or the past tense of lie. *She lay there all day waiting for him to come.* "Lay" is used in present tense when we're referring to setting an object down. *She lay the blanket down so that she could lie on it.*

LIE DOWN / LIE-DOWN—"Lie down" is the verb and "lie-down," the noun. *Why don't you lie down and relax? I need a good lie-down.*

LIFT OFF / LIFTOFF—"Lift off" is the verb and "liftoff," the noun. *We request permission to lift off. Liftoff denied.*

LIGHTENING / LIGHTNING—When we bleach our hair, we're "lightening" it. When electrical activity in the air gives us even lighter highlights, we've probably been struck by "lightning." "Lightening" is a verb; "lightning" is a noun.

LIGHT-YEAR—We use the term "light-year" to measure distance, not time. "Light-year" is the distance light travels in one year.

LIKELINESS / LIKENESS—"Likeliness" is the probability of something happening. A painting, drawing or portrait can show a good "likeness."

LITERALLY / VIRTUALLY—"Literally" means "word for word", or actual fact. Writers often use this word when what we mean is "practically" or "figuratively." What we should be using is "virtually" in most cases. Use of the word "literally" can often have an amusing effect, even when humor isn't intended. *I literally died when he looked at me.* Really? She died? Well, how is she still telling the story? We avoid using "literally" unless we literally mean what we're saying.

LIVE IN / LIVE-IN—"Live in" is the verb and "live-in," the adjective. *I wanted a woman to live in, but I got two live-in parrots instead.*

LOATH / LOATHE—"Loath" is an adjective that means reluctant or unwilling. *She was loath to take risks and didn't bungee jump.* Loathe is a verb meaning intense dislike, hate, or disgust. *I loathed her at first sight.*

LOCK UP / LOCKUP—"Lock up" is the verb and "lockup," the noun. *Don't forget to lock up the barn. She spent the night in lockup, until she sobered enough to be brought before the judge.*

LOOK / LOOKING—Often "look," "looking," and even "looked" can be replaced with a more active verb. The temptation to add "-looking" to an adjective is irresistible, we know. However, that is the lazy writer's way of writing. Good writers find the word we're searching for and avoid "look" in all its forms. *She looked cheap.* Really? And how exactly does cheap look? We must show the reader what is meant by cheap, rather than relying on the easy way out. *Her red dress strangled her body in all the wrong places. Her panties peeked from beneath the frayed hem, and her breasts clamored to escape the strained neckline.*

LOOK IN / LOOK-IN—"Look in" is the verb and "look-in," the noun. *Look in the "new" section at the library. I'll give the new janitor a quick look-in.*

LOOK OUT / LOOKOUT—"Look out" is the verb and "lookout," the noun. *Look out for spluttering oil when you fry squid. Our lookout hasn't reported movement in the enemy lines.*

LOSE / LOOSE—If writers everywhere would stop confusing "lose" and "loose," we know a few editors who would appreciate it. Pet peeves of many, these words are confused far too often. "Lose" is a verb meaning to misplace or to not win something. *Every time I set my keys down, I lose them.* "Loose" is an adjective meaning not tight. *His pants were so loose they slipped over his hips.* It is also used as a verb, although not used as often, meaning to release or let go. *"Let her loose!" the cop yelled to the gunman. "You hurt her, and we all lose."*

LUSTY / LUSTFUL—"Lusty" means healthy and strong, full of vigor. *The lusty sons of Farmer Smith painted the town red.* Lustful, defines strong sexual desire. *Mrs. Cunningham eyed Farmer Smith's sons with a lustful gaze.*

- M -

MAKE UP / MAKEUP—"Make up" is the verb and "makeup," the noun. *Make up your mind, whiskey or rye? She must slap on her makeup with a trowel.*

MANTEL / MANTLE—Both spellings can refer to the shelf over the fireplace that holds pictures, trophies and dust, but if we're referring to the cloak, we use "mantle." If the shelf is spelled as "mantel" consistently and the cloak is spelled as "mantle," then we avoid unnecessary confusion.

MARK DOWN / MARKDOWN—"Mark down" is the verb and "markdown," the noun. *When they mark down your book, I might buy one. I've heard there's a big markdown on "I Love Billy Blake" T-shirts.*

MARSHALL / MARTIAL—If we're referring to the law enforcement or military figure responsible for seeing justice done, we use "Marshall." Now, if we're speaking of the process in which the military tries one of its own members, we want "martial," as in "court martial." Martial is also used when referring to karate, jujitsu, and other "martial" arts.

MASH / MASHED—Only after we "mash" peas or potatoes can we enjoy "mashed" peas or "mashed" potatoes.

MAY / CAN / MIGHT—"May" asks for permission. "Can" is used in reference to ability. "Might" indicates a situation that is contrary to fact or a probability that is weaker than "may." *Can I go to the store?* Of course, we have the ability to go to the store. What we're asking for is permission to go to the store, so we replace "can" with "may" in this sentence, and we've got it right. *Might I borrow your pen?* Again, replace "might" with "may" because we are asking permission. *I might say yes, if you include dinner.* This means we are less likely to say yes than if we say I may say yes, if you include dinner; however, it is correct usage.

METEOR / METEORITE / METEOROID—This one might be useful to SF writers. The space rocks are "meteoroids," not "meteorites." If one of these rocks travels close enough to be displaced by Earth's gravity and plummets down through our atmosphere, the streak of light it leaves behind is termed a "meteor." *The meteoroid hurtled toward the surface, its fiery tail clearly visible.* Only when the rock hits the ground, whatever is left of it is called a meteorite.

MINUTE / MOMENT—Let's count to sixty. That's a long time, eh? A "minute" is actually a long time and often we use it without thinking. In fiction writing, we should strive to use the most appropriate word. If they kissed for several minutes before he boarded the plane, they kissed for a long time. If she knelt in the closet for a minute, we should consider how long she must be down there and just what the heck is she doing? In many cases, "moment" is the word we want to use. A moment is brief, but a minute is sixty long seconds.

MIX UP / MIX-UP—"Mix up" is the verb and "mix-up," the noun. *Mix up the ingredients, else the cream will curdle. There must have been a mix-up at the grocery; I never purchased these chocolates.*

MOP UP / MOP-UP—"Mop up" is the verb and "mop-up," the noun. *Mop up the mess and take the dog outside. In the mop-up operation they found seven bud plantations.*

MORAL / MORALE—A "moral" is a lesson or principle. *The moral of the story is that one should never spit against the wind.* "Morale" refers to an emotional state. *The captain improved morale by allowing his crew more time on shore.*

NAKED / NUDE—"Naked" is merely to be without clothes, while "nude" has positive or artistic undertones. *Buck naked, he ogled her nude splendor.*

NEITHER-NOR / EITHER-OR—"Neither" and "nor" belong together in a construction. "Either" and "or" belong together. We use them in sets and we do not mix them. "Neither" is used in the negative. *Neither Jane nor her friends are going to the party.* "Either" is used to indicate an alternative. *Either Joe or his brother will pick Jane up after the party.*

NEVER THE LESS, NOT WITHSTANDING / NEVERTHELESS, NOTWITHSTANDING—Always spell them as single words: "nevertheless" and "notwithstanding."

NOW / AGO / YESTERDAY / TOMORROW / TODAY / ETC.—When writers use such words, we're reminding the reader that he is reading, an undesirable effect in fiction writing. The only time we should use them is in dialogue. When writing past tense words that are almost present tense, like some of these are, we pull the reader into the present as well, and out of the world we're trying to create. Avoid words that don't belong in the narrative. For example, instead of "yesterday," we use "the day before." Instead of "today," we write "that day." It may go unnoticed, or it may not. These tiny details add up to give the reader an impression, and paying attention to these details means the difference between a good writer and an excellent writer.

OBSOLESCENT / OBSOLETE—We have noticed this term incorrectly used in several publications. "Obsolete" means something is no longer available or out of date. "Obsolescent" is something on its way to becoming obsolete. "Obsolete" things underwent a process of obsolescence.

OCTOPI / OCTOPUSES—We're sorry to disappoint "octopi" lovers. The plural of octopus is "octopuses." Although, we must admit, "octopi" is great fun to say.

OF / HAVE—When we speak, we frequently use words that are grammatically incorrect. *I could of used a cup of coffee.* This is how we say it, but it is not how we should write it. This sentence written would be: *I could've used a cup of coffee.* "Could've" is the contraction of "could have," which is correct.

OL' / OLE—"Ol'" means old. It's often used when depicting a Southern dialect. "Ole" (pronounced "olay") is Spanish and is similar to saying "Hooray!" Trust us, we know. We should not use "ole" (that English word you remember was "olde") when writing dialect, unless the speaker is Spanish and very happy about something.

OVER / MORE THAN—Writers must never use "over" to mean "more than." "Over" should only be used in its literal meaning. *The ball went over the fence, which was more than eight feet high.*

OVERSEE / OVERLOOK—To "oversee" is to supervise. To "overlook" is to fail to see something. *Henry planned to oversee filling the pool, but he overlooked the leaking facet.*

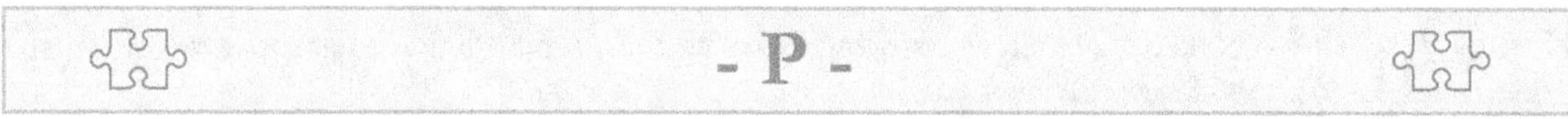

PASSED / PAST—"Passed" is a verb, the past tense of "pass," meaning "to have moved on or ahead." *They passed in the hallway but rarely spoke a word.* "Past" means a former time or place, no longer current, or over. *In his past, he'd made many mistakes.*

PAY OFF / PAYOFF—"Pay off" is the verb and "payoff," the noun. *If you don't pay off the debt, we'll send over our cousin. The payoff from our gamble was smaller than we expected.*

PEAK / PEEK / PIQUE—"Peak" may be used as a noun, an adjective, or a verb. It refers to a tapered point like the summit of a mountain, the mountain itself, or the highest point or amount. As a noun: *The store's sales hit their peak the day before Christmas.* As a verb: *Sales peak just before the holidays.* As an adjective: *The supervisor observed that employees work at peak efficiency before lunch.* "Peek" is a noun meaning "a furtive or quick look." *We may peek at our presents before Christmas, but we don't dare unwrap them completely.* "Pique" is a sudden outburst of anger, to cause feelings of resentment, or to stimulate. *In a fit of pique, after your stupid remark piqued me, I thought—perhaps you're right after all. My interest piqued, I began to research.*

PERFORMED / PREFORMED—"Perform" is the act of doing something. *The actress performed the role of evil seductress with stunning believability.* "Preformed" means "to form something beforehand." We'd preform sugar cookies before baking them, for example.

PERSECUTE / PROSECUTE—We "persecute" someone when we harass or treat him with hostility. Only lawyers can "prosecute." Though we're sure some husbands or wives prosecute their spouses for their crimes on a daily basis.

PERUSE / GLIMPSE—"Peruse" is to look something over in great detail. "Glimpse" is a glance. The two are not interchangeable. Writers must be sure to use the one we mean.

PHASE / FAZE—"Phase" is a stage of development, a temporary attitude, a behavior, or a part or aspect of something. *They moved into phase three of their plan for total world domination.* "Faze" means to disrupt one's composure. *That she would have to kill her darlings didn't faze her.*

PHENOMENA / PHENOMENON—"Phenomenon" is the singular form and "phenomena," the plural. *We observed the falling stars, a most amazing phenomenon. These phenomena are seldom visible in our hemisphere.*

PICK UP / PICKUP—"Pick up" is the verb and "pickup," the noun. *I must pick up the baby's toys. John has bought a new pickup.*

PIG OUT / PIGOUT—"Pig out" is the verb and "pigout," the noun. *Must you always pig out at the buffet? You don't look too chirpy after yesterday's pigout.*

PIN UP / PIN-UP—"Pin up" is the verb and "pin-up," the noun. *I must pin up the cover to dry. She's gorgeous, like a pin-up.*

PLACE / DO / BE—Words like "place," "do," and "be" are weak. There are so many stronger options, and we should always use the better word when one is available. *She placed the glass on the table.* "Placed" could be replaced with "slammed" or "set." *Undo your pants.* Well, that's interesting as it is, but it could be better if we used "unzip," "unbuckle," "open," or even "remove."

PLAY BACK / PLAYBACK—"Play back" is the verb and "playback," the noun. *Play back our favorite tune. I hate when these people use playback.*

PLUG IN / PLUGIN—"Plug in" is the verb and "plugin," the noun. *I forgot to plug in the lawnmower. The program won't work without the latest plugin.*

PODIUM / LECTERN—A "podium" is a raised platform. A "lectern" is a piece of furniture where we rest our papers while giving a lecture or speech.

POP OUT / POP-OUT—"Pop out" is the verb and "pop-out," the noun. *Her deep breath caused the buttons on her bodice to pop out all over the place. I love these children's books full of pop-outs.*

PORE / POUR—We "pour" a drink, while we exfoliate our "pores." Well, not at the same time. "Pour" means to send forth in a stream or a flow. *He poured the sugar into the coffee.* "Pore" can be either the tiny holes in our skin or refer to reading, studying, staring, or pondering intently or deeply. *She pored over her notes line by line in an effort to commit them to memory.*

PRECEDE / PROCEED—"Precede" means to come before and "proceed" is to go forward. *The outline would precede the writing of the story. We can only proceed to write after we've established what the story is about.*

PRINCIPAL / PRINCIPLE—"Principal" is a noun meaning "a person who has authority" or an adjective meaning "most important." *The school's principal was the principal figure in the establishment.* "Principle" refers to a truth, such as the principle of gravity.

PROPHECY / PROPHESY—"Prophecy" is a noun, while to "prophesy" (pronounced "prophi sigh") is a verb. *He prophesied rain, but prophecy is not the shaman's strong point.*

PULL DOWN / PULL-DOWN—"Pull down" is the verb and "pull-down," the adjective. *Pull down the "closed" sign and come here. The pull-down menu is too long.*

PULL OFF / PULL-OFF—"Pull off" is the verb and "pull-off," the noun. *Well, if she can pull off the heist she's in. Please, stop at the next pull-off.*

PULL OVER / PULLOVER—"Pull over" is the verb and "pullover," the noun. *Pull over, hands on the steering wheel, relax. Grandma knits great pullovers.*

PUT ON / PUT-ON—"Put on" is the verb and "put-on," the noun. *Why don't you put on the purple slacks? She said no, but it was just a put-on.*

- Q -

QUITE / QUIET—We know that this is usually a typo, but just in case there are writers who still confuse these two we'll clarify. "Quite" means to a degree. *I was quite dismayed at his behavior.* "Quiet" is used to mean without noise. *The quiet room made it impossible for her to hide the gas that erupted from her body. She hid her face, quite embarrassed.*

- R -

RAISE / REAR—We "rear" children and "raise" animals, though the distinction is becoming increasingly rare.

REBUT / REFUTE—"Rebut" is to claim that evidence or an accusation is false. "Refute" is to prove it. *After much rebutting the claims, Marcus refuted the accusation.*

RECUPERATE / RECOUP—We "recuperate" from an illness, accident, or exertion. To "recoup" is to recover something we've previously lost.

RELUCTANT / RETICENT—Though both adjectives have become synonymous, there's a difference. They both imply unwillingness and hesitancy, but "reticent" should only be used when a character is reluctant to speak.

REVENGE / AVENGE—We "avenge" a wrong by taking "revenge." *I will avenge the capture of my bishop with an appropriate revenge. Mate in three.*

RIFLE / RIFFLE—To "rifle" is to steal while to "riffle" means to turn something over casually, especially the pages of a book. *He opened the drawer, riffled through her papers and rifled her latest testament.*

RIP OFF / RIP-OFF—"Rip off" is the verb and "rip-off," the noun. *We must rip off the paper before painting. This cap was a rip-off; it's already falling apart.*

ROLE / ROLL—Role: a part or a function, a character, or a position. *His role in the debacle remains unclear.* Now, "roll" is that tasty roundish hunk of bread we enjoy at dinner, or it might be the forward motion that our body would follow while tumbling down a hill. *Had he just eaten the roll, it wouldn't have rolled onto the floor.*

RUB DOWN / RUBDOWN—"Rub down" is the verb and "rubdown," the noun. *You should rub down a little ointment to ease the stiffness. Mmmm, let me see... definitely; you need a rubdown.*

RUN OFF / RUNOFF—"Run off" is the verb and "runoff," the noun. *Run off to the store and get a loaf. The runoff from the sewers stinks.*

- S -

SACCHARIN / SACCHARINE—Depending on its usage, this word is spelled two ways. Writers shouldn't feel too bad about confusing these two. One of us was in the dark on this one too. Without the "e" on the end, "saccharin" is a white powder. With the "e," "saccharine" means relating to or characteristic of sugar. More simply, it means sweet.

SAID / STATED—*Mary stood, arms akimbo. "You are horrible, but I love you," she stated.* Nope. Only the written word is stated; the spoken word is "said." *In her letter, she stated that enough was enough.*

SARCASTIC / IRONIC—Something "sarcastic" has a pejorative connotation; it's meant to cause harm or wound. "Irony" has no such connotation of malice.

SAT THERE / STOOD THERE—These lack action and weigh down prose. We want the narrative to be tight, and the fewer unnecessary words we use the better the narrative will read. *I sat there staring at him.* This would be much better written as, *I stared.* Note, we deleted "at him" too. Bonus tip: If it is clear who the subject is, we don't need "at him," "at her," "to him," "to her," etc. on the end. It's just clutter.

SCREW UP / SCREWUP—"Screw up" is the verb and "screwup" the noun. *This is a gun and that is a very angry rhinoceros, so try not to screw up. After the screwup at the bank heist, he's taken up ballet lessons.*

SET BACK / SETBACK—"Set back" is the verb and "setback," the noun. *Countless rewrites set back the manuscript's publication date. To discover that the plot made no sense was a terrible setback for Sonya.*

SET UP / SETUP—"Set up" is the verb and "setup," the noun. *We can set up the beer stall over there. There was no free beer to be had; it was a setup.*

SHEAR / SHEER—"Shear" refers to a pair of scissors or to remove hair (or fur). We would use shears, for example, to shear a sheep of its wool. In physics, shear refers to a force or a system of forces that produces a shearing strain. "Sheer" has several meanings and not one is the same as "shear." If we're describing something thin or transparent, like a gauzy material, we'd call it sheer. It might also mean steep or unqualified. *His sheer ignorance astounded the girl.* "Sheer" can also be used when referring to a swerving course or causing someone or something to swerve from a course.

SHINNY / SHINY—Sadly these two are often confused. "Shinny" (yes, it's a word) is a game, field hockey, played with curved sticks and a ball. "Shinny" is also what the curved stick is called in this game. "Shiny" is an adjective we'd use to describe something bright or lustrous. *His bald head was so shiny under the bright lights that it blinded me.*

SHOCK / ELECTROCUTION—We get a "shock" if we touch a live electrical wire and can die by "electrocution" if we can't remove our fingers. "Electrocution" implies death.

SHOW OFF / SHOW-OFF—"Show off" is the verb and "show-off," the noun. *She likes to show off her cosmetic surgery. Pay no notice; he's a show-off.*

SIGN IN / SIGN-IN—"Sign in" is the verb and "sign-in," the noun. *After you complete the sign-in sheet, you can proceed to the front gate and sign in.*

SIT DOWN / SIT-DOWN—"Sit down" is the verb and "sit-down," the noun. *You could sit down a little closer. I'm tired. I hope the lecture is a sit-down affair.*

SLEEP OVER / SLEEPOVER—"Sleep over" is the verb and "sleepover," the noun. *Bad boy. You can sleep over in the corner. Tatiana asked if I would like a sleepover.*

SNEAK / SNEAKED / SNUCK—We say "snuck" when we speak, but it's not correct usage. When writing fiction, we should strive to use the correct term whenever possible, unless writing dialogue. "Sneaked" is the past tense form of "sneak." "Snuck" is not.

SPIN OFF / SPIN-OFF—"Spin off" is the verb and "spin-off" the noun. *Leave the end open and you can spin off a sequel. She's only written one novel, the other fifty were spin-offs.*

STAND OUT / STANDOUT—"Stand out" is the verb and "standout," the noun. *Although short and chubby, Ophelia will stand out among the pygmies. Look at him, he's a standout.*

START UP / STARTUP—"Start up" is the verb and "startup," the noun. *I'll load the gun while you start up the engine. OFW is a great startup.*

STATIONARY / STATIONERY—"Stationary" means "still, unmoving." A wall is a stationary object (most of the time). "Stationery" refers to that pretty paper we write letters or grocery lists on.

STICK UP / STICKUP—"Stick up" is the verb and "stickup," the noun. *Mind the corners when you stick up the cards in the album. There was a stickup downtown.*

STRAIT / STRAIGHT—A "strait" is a narrow canal or passage between two bodies of water, such as the Gibraltar Strait between the Mediterranean Sea and the Atlantic Ocean. "Straight," describes something without curves. It follows that the phrase "dire straights" is wrong. Try "dire straits."

SUPPOSE / SUPPOSED—"Supposed" (combined with "to") means obligated to. Incorrectly, writers often use "suppose to." *You're supposed to pick the kids up from school every day.* "Suppose" refers to conjecture or to guess. *I suppose that's not too much to ask.*

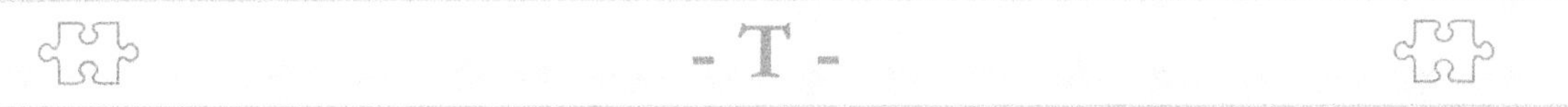

TACT / TACK—"Tact" refers to sensitivity to the right way in dealing with or talking to others. *Of course you don't look fat, honey. He decided tact would be wise in this situation. Like he'd tell her the dress reminded him of a sausage casing on her body.* "Tack" is often used as a nautical term meaning trail or course. It also refers to those sharp little things that teenagers use to post pictures on their walls, the ones we step on, scream in agony, and try not to cry as we rip them out of our foot. Yes, those tacks.

TAKE OUT / TAKEOUT—"Take out" is the verb and "takeout," the noun. *You can take out the dog; he looks restless. I don't feel like cooking. Why don't we get Mexican takeout?*

TAKE OVER / TAKEOVER—"Take over" is the verb and "takeover," the noun. *Please, take over the machine gun while I have a smoke. We better brace ourselves; Amazon has singled us out for takeover.*

THAN / THEN—"Than" is used to compare. *I'd rather lay in a bed filled with snakes than spend one minute with his mother.* "Then" means "next" or "at that time." *She went to the kitchen then slipped out the back door.*

THEIR / THERE / THEY'RE—The confusion between these three words is very common. Let's look at meaning to clear things up. "Their" is the possessive form of "they." *Their car resembled a boat.* "There" refers to location. *Don't put your shoes there.* "They're" is the contraction of "they are." *They're going to vacation in Peru.*

THROUGH / THREW / THOROUGH / THOUGH / THRU—So many words with distinct meanings, and yet, difficult for many writers to differentiate among. "Through" refers to going into or out of, finished, or by means of. *He entered through the door. I'm through with your nonsense. It is only through practice that one achieves skill.* "Thru" is slang for "through" and shouldn't be used. "Threw" is the past tense of "throw." The "w" should be our clue when deciding. Both "threw" and "throw" have the "w," while none of the others do. "Thorough" is often a matter of misspelling "through." "Thorough" means careful or complete. *I hoped that you'd thoroughly clean your bathroom so that you wouldn't leave germs behind.*

"Though" is usually a simple case of poor spelling as well. "Though" replaces "however." *She's a pretty girl, though her constant scowl makes that hard to see.*

TIC / TICK—Clocks "tick" and we may have to endure being bitten by "ticks" if we travel a savanna or any other place with high grasses. But if someone has a spasmodic twitch, the noun to describe it is "tic."

TO / TOO / TWO—"To" means toward. *We would walk to the living room and give a gift to our friend.* "Too" means excessively or also. *We may eat too much cake. We consume a lot of pie too.* "Two" is the number that comes after one.

TOLLED / TOLD—No, it's not "all tolled" but "all told." *All told, there were sixteen people in a theater with a thousand seats which tolled the play's death knell.*

TOUCH DOWN / TOUCHDOWN—"Touch down" is the verb and "touchdown," the noun. *We will touch down in four, three, two... After touchdown the captain resumed breathing.*

TOUSLE / TUSSLE—While a "tussle" is a struggle, fight, or scuffle, to "tousle" is to mess somebody's hair, usually as an endearment.

TRANSLUCENT / TRANSPARENT—Though "translucent" means that light can go through, the term is used frequently to describe frosted or patterned materials that don't display what's on the other side, like a paper or parchment screen. "Transparent" means clear. Ice can be either transparent or translucent. Pure water is transparent, while a silk negligee is translucent.

TURN ON / TURN-ON—"Turn on" is the verb and "turn-on," the noun. *As soon as they cross the line, turn on the lights. His charisma and roguish smile was a turn-on for the ladies.*

TURN OVER / TURNOVER—"Turn over" is the verb and "turnover," the noun. *You're snoring again. Could you, please, turn over? I ate six turnovers.*

UNHUMAN / INHUMAN / INHUMANE—"Unhuman" refers to a being not resembling or having human characteristics. "Inhuman" is cruel and barbaric. "Inhumane" means lacking pity or compassion.

UP / DOWN—Usually we don't need the words "up" or "down" in narrative. *She stood up* should read *she stood.* How else does one stand? *He knelt down* is also incorrect because knelt implies the downward action. "Down" is not needed.

VICE / VISE—A vice is a bad habit, custom, or mannerism. A vise is a tool with movable jaws to grip something while we mess about with it.

VICIOUS / VISCOUS—"Viscous" is an adjective used to describe something thick, like molasses. "Vicious" means spiteful or malicious, like an ex girlfriend.

WAIT FOR / ON—"Wait on" and "wait for" do not mean the same thing. We often use the two interchangeably in speech, but in writing we shouldn't do this. "Wait on" means to serve and "wait for" means awaiting something or someone. Avoid using one for the other.

WAIVE / WAVE—"Waive" is to set aside or let go of. A criminal may waive his right to a lawyer. "Wave" means to move back and forth, as we would when waving a flag.

WAKE UP / WAKE-UP—"Wake up" is the verb and "wake-up," the adjective. *If we want to wake up in time, we better ask for a wake-up call at reception.*

WEATHER / WHETHER—"Weather" refers to the atmospheric conditions around us. More simply, if it's raining, the weather is wet or damp. If it's winter, the weather may be cold or frigid. Often writers use this word when we really want whether. "Whether" is a conjunction that refers to alternate possibilities. *We wondered whether you'd like a chocolate or a vanilla cake for your birthday.*

WHO / WHOM—"Who" is used as a subject. *Who is your father? The winner is the player who collects all of the items on his list.* "Whom" is used as an object. *Whom did you select to go with you?*

WHO'S / WHOSE—New writers often struggle with this. Not because they don't realize that these are different words, but which to use and when. "Who's" is the contraction of "who is," and should only be used then. *Who's going to pay for this?* "Whose" shows possession (possessive form of who). *Whose car is this? Her father, whose booming voice could frighten even the toughest man, turned to wipe a tear. "Who's going to look after you?" he asked.*

WOOD / WOULD—We get "wood" from a tree. We burn it in our fireplace. Sometimes we sit on a wooden chair. "Would" is the past tense of will. *We would have liked to go on vacation but we had to get the wood cut for winter.*

WORK OUT / WORKOUT—"Work out" is the verb and "workout," the noun. *I must work out on the treadmill. I can't skip my daily workout.*

WRITE UP / WRITE-UP—"Write up" is the verb and "write-up," the noun. *He plans to write up a scathing report. There's a great write-up about your new book in the local paper.*

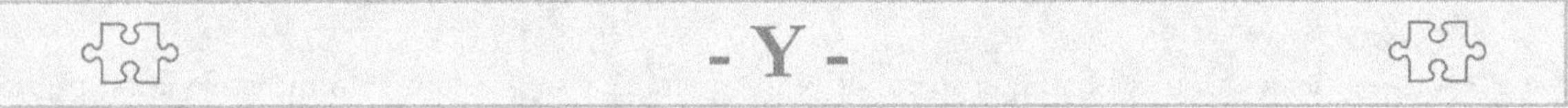

YOUR / YOU'RE—Writers, pay attention, this confusion must end right now. "Your" is the possessive of you: your car, your house, or your mistake. "You're" is the contraction of "you are."

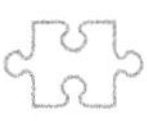 **4.5.2 USAGE DOUBTS**

Unlike the previous chapter, which focused on pairs of words commonly confused, this section looks at words most often used incorrectly. "Usage" means application of a given tool, or in this instance, a word.

Usage is in flux in all living languages. Daily we come across words deployed in unusual ways. Often, the idea catches on and the new usage becomes accepted. Until such a moment arrives, word usage is defined by rules laid down and endorsed in dictionaries and style guides. A wise writer will bear this in mind.

Unless we target our work to a limited or focused segment of the market, such as literary fiction, gay/lesbian, or religious/inspirational among others, our goal should be to reach the broadest number of readers. Many might see the word usage recorded in dictionaries and style guides as outdated, dictatorial, and sometimes patronizing, but these reflect "common usage." This is a reflection that the majority of the population has been brought up attaching specific meanings to words.

English has a vast diffusion. We've mentioned elsewhere that the number of English speakers nears one billion. We've heard writers complain about usage rules, adducing that in their street, village, town, city, state, or country people say "don't aggravate your mother" to mean "don't disturb or upset her." We've had writers heatedly arguing that "irregardless" is a common word where they come from, that "niggard" is a racial slur and that their novel touches the "Catholic religion."[125]

Even if these usages are commonplace in a region, we beg writers to stand back and look at the broader picture. Why defend local usage? If the number of prospective readers accustomed to the standard meaning is larger, shouldn't that be reason enough to adopt the current broader usage?

The hurdles that writers face grow and multiply with each passing day. Not only the competition increases, but more than ever, agents and editors look for the slightest excuse to reject a query, proposal, or manuscript. Gone are the days when publishing houses had an army of style and copy editors. Ever large publishing houses expect manuscripts to be print-ready before they will consider glancing at it.

Self publishing is an option, but this road has attracted some criticism because of the work of lazy or careless writers who haven't even bothered to use a spell-checker, much less a usage guide. We don't doubt that there must be self-published books with high editorial standards, but to date we haven't been able to find one. The difference has little to do with plot or characterization, but with grammar, syntax, usage, careful writing, and painstaking editing. We believe that if self-published books were indistinguishable in quality from those published by a major house, the industry would have to think twice and act, or close down the shop.

To work for months or years on a good story that could enrich the lives of millions and have it discarded because of a few usage errors is a tragedy. To lose an irreplaceable writer, disheartened after countless rejections, is a calamity.

The rules are there as the norms. We may hate them and despair at the burden of mastering vocabulary and usage, but the great public, our readers, expect to read competent prose.

---

[125] Irregardless is not a word, niggard means stingy or tightfisted, and Catholicism is not a religion, but a faith. The religion is Christianity.

Of course, we don't have to slavishly follow *every* established rule *every* time. After all, some of us live in free societies, but we ignore the norms at our peril. Our goal, when listing usage doubts on the following pages, has nothing to do with writing "proper English" or even "Queen's English." We merely hope to help writers improve their chances in a ruthless market.

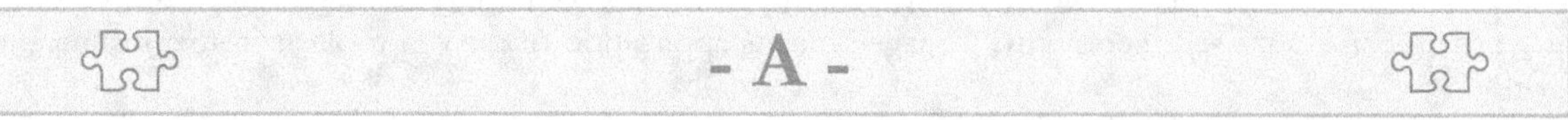

A LOT—Space or no space? Here's a simple way to never ever get this wrong: Don't use it unless referring to a noun. "A lot" is a parcel of land. Consider "a lot's" meaning when using it. Often we use it to mean a great deal, several, often, many, so why not use those words instead? Reserve "a lot" when referring to an amount for dialogue (because we tend to use *a lot*, a lot in dialogue) and for plots of land, and save everyone a lot of headaches.

A.D./B.C./ C.E./ BCE—The distinction verges on stupidity, as common sense often does when touched by religious beliefs. *anno domini* (A.D.)—Year of the Lord—and Before Christ (B.C.) have been deemed offensive to non-adherents to the Christian faith. The proposed alternatives Common Era (C.E.) and Before the Common Era (BCE [126]) refer to the same religiously-based calendar. Go figure. Newspapers favor the first set of abbreviations and scientific publications the second. In fiction, we can use either, and choose whom to anger.

A.M./P.M.—Let's say first that avoiding the use of either of these abbreviations (which stand for ante and post meridian) in fiction writing is preferable. For example: *He went to bed at 12:00 p.m.* isn't so great. *He went to bed at noon.* Preferred. Of course, if they must be used, never use them with morning, afternoon, or night. *He went to bed at 1:00 p.m. in the afternoon* is wrong. Never write them in large caps like this: A.M. or P.M. They must always include the periods. Avoid using these abbreviations in dialogue. *"He went to bed at noon."* Or if we're citing a different time like 12:30p.m., we'd write *"He went to bed at twelve thirty."* What if he went to bed at 7:04 p.m.? In dialogue we'd write *"He went to bed at four past seven."* Even better would be: *"He went to bed just past seven this evening, right after dinner."*

ABOUT—If using with measures or numbers this word is better to avoid because it's vague. If using a concrete number use "approximately," otherwise a range might be more precise. *There were about 250 vampires at the gathering.* Better: *There were approximately 250 vampires at the* gathering. Or *There were 200 to 300 vampires at the gathering.* Of course, why a writer would need such precision is debatable.

ACRONYMS—Some of us mistake acronyms for initials. Acronyms are made up of initials. Their usage is slightly different. "Scuba," for example, contains the initials that are in "self-contained underwater breathing apparatus." AIDS is the acronym for "acquired immune deficiency syndrome." Anything common in these groups of initials? Consider this: Carlos J. Cortes (CJC) could not be considered an acronym. Renée Miller-Johnston (RMJ) also would be unsuitable. On Fiction Writing? (OFW) Nope. Why is this? They can't be read as a word. If the initials cannot be read as a single word when put together, they can abbreviate, but they are not acronyms.

---

126 Acronyms with three or more letters dispense with periods. Check Period, page 315

ADDRESSES—How many times have we read something like, *Deliver to 404 Mistaken Blvd.?* Boulevard, avenue, street, lane, route, highway, etc. must be written in full in fiction. Do not use an abbreviation. North, East, South, and West must also be spelled unless used with street addresses in some city names.

ADJECTIVES—*The big, buxom, sexy, blonde, beauty winked her glorious, sparkly, sapphire-blue eye at me.* Don't do this. Avoid stringing a bunch of adjectives together. One is enough per sentence—two at the most. Descriptions should come a little at a time. Too much diminishes their effect.

ADMIT TO—This is usually a style error. In most instances, removing the "to" is enough. *Tochi will not admit to having raided the fridge. He admitted to sprinkling garlic on the pizza.* Or, better: *Tochi will not admit having raided the fridge. He admitted sprinkling garlic on the pizza.*

ADVERBS—Most adverbs aren't needed. We can delete these and never miss them. If an adverb is used, think of it as a sign that the writer needs to find more powerful verbs. Instead of: *She walked quickly.* Try: *She jogged.* Instead of: *He slowly made his way across the room.* Try: *He sauntered.*

ALL CAPS—Nothing is written in all caps in fiction writing except acronyms (AIDS, MADD) or chapter titles.

ALL OF—Incorrect. Remove the "of," and whenever possible, do away with the "all" too. *The children ate all of the cupcakes.* Or, better: *The children ate all the cupcakes.* Best. *The children ate the cupcakes.*

ALMOST—Vague. "Almost" is indistinct; it robs sentences of precision. In addition, some "almost" constructions are worthy of politicians, not writers. *We almost made it.* This means, we didn't. *We almost won.* Translation: we lost. *When his torrid breath seared her neck, she almost fainted.* We must always place "almost" immediately before the word or phrase it modifies: *Paul almost bought one gallon of moonshine,* doesn't mean the same *as Paul bought almost one gallon of moonshine.* In the first example, he didn't buy anything. In the second, well... "almost" a gallon.

AMBIGUITY—The English language has many words that mean several things. We deal with several in this and the vocabulary-doubts sections, but listing them all would mean another book. "Tear," for example, can mean that annoying moisture that leaks from the eye. It might also mean "a rip in your clothing or a piece of paper." Be clear or use a different word or phrase. *Her sobs made him turn in time to see her rip the paper in two pieces, then four. He turned to the door. The tear broke his heart.* What tear? Her tear? The paper tear? *Her sobs made him turn in time to see her rip the paper in two pieces, then four. He turned to the door. The shredding of his only copy of the manuscript broke his heart.* Better.

AMOUNT OF—Can often be deleted. *The amount of sugar in the coffee was overwhelming.* We could rewrite as: *The sugar in the coffee was overwhelming.* But *the coffee was too sweet,* would do the job, or *the coffee was like syrup,* if we feel creative.

AMPERSAND—&-When writing fiction, don't use symbols to replace words.

AND ALSO—The two words mean the same thing, making this phrase redundant. Just use either "and" or "also," not both.

ATM—The initials stand for Automated Teller Machine. To write *ATM machine* is a redundancy, and equivalent to Automated Teller Machine machine.

ATTRIBUTIONS—Attributions such as said, asked, muttered, mumbled, replied, etc. should be avoided if possible in dialogue. Use only as many attributions as are necessary to keep the speaker clear. Don't be afraid to use the standard "said" or "asked," because these are less intrusive than their fancier cousins. Show who is speaking through action instead. Replace *John asked* with *John crossed his arms over his chest*. Writers often try to use attribution with action. *John said, as he crossed his arms over his chest*, is wrong. Use only the action. Never both.

AUTHOR INTRUSION—Often writers slip in a minor author intrusion. *She was beautiful.* Beautiful is a personal opinion and not a true description. Describe her instead to avoid intrusion. *Her pale blue eyes dominated a heart-shaped face.* A major intrusion occurs when the writer stops the action to explain something. *She wept. She felt awful because…* This can be shown through dialogue with no intrusion. *She wept. Oh, why hadn't she answered his call? She was so selfish.*

AUTHORED—"Author" is a noun, not a verb. Writers, who are the authors of the deed, write books. Masons carve lintels. *Who is the author of that lintel? John is a master mason.* We doubt the mason would have name cards with John Smith—Author.

AWFUL—This overused adjective is prone to misuse. Awful means something unpleasant or negative, even dangerous, not merely appalling. *The advancing hoplites were an awful sight.*

AWKWARD SENTENCES—occasionally we see elements spread too far apart in a sentence. This makes it awkward. *She pulled the card, tattered, and chipped at the corner from the time she washed it in her pants by mistake, from her pocket and placed it in the machine.* Find a clearer way of saying this to make it less awkward. *She pulled a tattered card from her pocket and placed it into the machine.* Sometimes a sentence can be broken into two or more, to make the ideas clear, but often, the writer doesn't need so much in the sentence anyway.

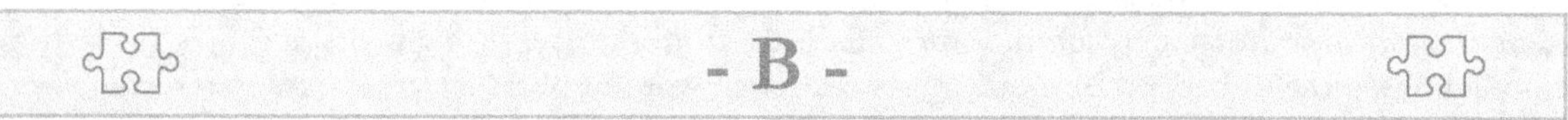

BETWEEN—To establish a relationship "between" dates or numbers: *Between 2002 to 2011 he was bedridden*, or *there were between 70 to 80 marchers at the demonstration*. The use of **to** is incorrect. The sentences should read: *Between 2002 and 2011 he was bedridden*, and *There were between 70 and 80 marchers at the demonstration*.

BISCOTTI—This is a plural form. The singular form is "biscotto."

BLATANT—Blatant means bad or objectionable behavior done openly and unashamedly. As such, it has pejorative connotations. To use it in a positive sense, as in *his book was blatantly excellent*, is wrong.

BRACKETS—Rarely do we have an occasion when brackets need to be used in fiction writing. Let's clarify that we are not talking about parentheses ( ), but brackets [ ].

BRAND NAMES/TRADEMARKS—Brand names and trademarks, even when used in fiction writing, must be capitalized and then followed by their generic name. (Although not always necessary, it is preferred). Trademark owners would rather we didn't pluralize their products either. No "Kleenexes" or "Cokes," please. The best way to avoid issues with brand names and trademarks is to use the generic name instead. Instead of "Kleenex," she used a "tissue." Rather than drink a "Coke," he drank a "soda," "cola," "pop." However, sometimes the brand name reveals something about the character or scene. If so, remember to capitalize and do not pluralize.

BRUSSELS SPROUT—No, we didn't make a mistake by adding an "s" to the end of Brussels. The tiny cabbage-like vegetable that is the bane of our childhood dinner experience is spelled like the city of Brussels. Many spell it without the "s," so many that we have forgotten the proper way to write it. Use the "s."

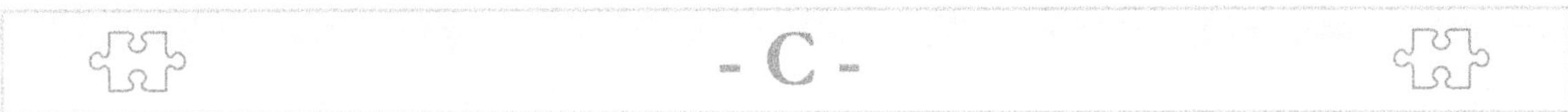

- C -

CAPITALIZATION—Capitalization can confuse even the most attentive writers. Nicknames and titles tend to be the most troublesome. Simply put, if the name or title is replacing a proper noun or is used as part of a name, we capitalize it. For example: "Aunt Betty"—not "aunt Betty." *Sorry, Honey, Dad said you can't go to that party.* We don't capitalize if the noun or title isn't replacing a name. *My dad said I can't go. I have to stay at my aunt's house.* A good way to decide whether or not to capitalize is to stick "the," "a," or "an" in front of the word. If it doesn't take away from the meaning of the sentence, then it should not be capitalized. Often we try to capitalize words that don't need capitals because they're what we consider proper names. The names of plants (oak, elm, maple tree), titles that aren't part of a proper name (my doctor, his aunt), and the titles of classes (biology or science—language classes are the only ones capitalized) shouldn't be capitalized. Proper names (Joe, Carol, Maria), Cities, Street names, Trademarks, and directions when they're used to name areas of a country (He lives up North) are capitalized. General directions (The arrow pointed west) are not capitalized.

CAUCASIAN—Black and white have become dirty words, or at least objectionable. But using Caucasian to name white-skinned people is wrong. The term refers to people from the Caucasus Mountains in Georgia (Europe) and should be used only in reference to these natives.

CHAISE LONGUE—The correct term is *chaise longue,* meaning long chair (which it is). "Chaise lounge" is a silly construction much laughed at by French folks. Yes, we lounge in the chaise, but that's no reason to change its name.

CHEMICALS—Please, refrain from describing "organic" produce as raised "without chemicals." To do so flaunts scientific illiteracy. Everything in the universe—except a few forms of energy and odd subatomic particles—has chemicals. Water and air are chemical compounds, and we can hardly raise a head of lettuce without them. Even the term "without added chemicals" is nonsense.

CIVIL WAR—When we're referring to any civil war, it isn't capitalized but when referring to a specific civil war, capitalize. *The American Civil War* is correct. *The country's history is marked by Civil Wars* is wrong.

COMPASS POINTS—North, east, south, and west are only capitalized when they are used to name places. Adjectival forms such as northern or westward follow the same rule. We traveled north, to South Dakota.

CRAFT—Whenever we refer to vehicles, "craft" covers both singular and plural uses: one aircraft or three aircraft.

CRITICISM—By definition, criticism is a neutral term meaning analysis or evaluation, and doesn't imply anything pejorative. Criticism can be devastating, though not necessarily so. Glowing praise is also criticism.

CURRENTLY—We've established that adverbs aren't often needed, but we felt it necessary to point out this adverb specifically because it **never** adds to the sentence. *I'm currently working at the bar. He currently resides at his mother's house.* Take out "currently." It is unnecessary and only adds to the wordiness of the narrative.

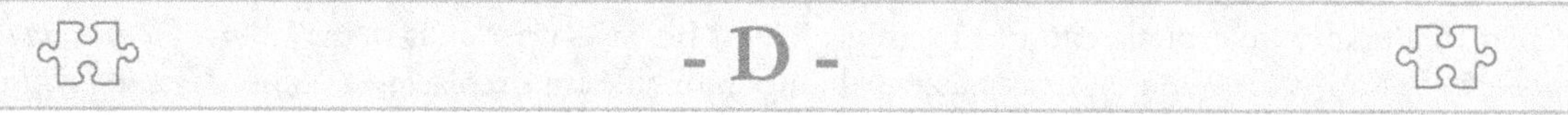

DECIMATE—Like many other words, this one has suffered great changes, to the point of being meaningless. "To decimate" was a Roman punishment for rebellious soldiers. The culprits were rounded up and one in ten was killed as an example to others. "Decimate" means "to kill one out of every ten." We can stretch the meaning to signify killing or destroying a great proportion, but never as a synonym of "annihilate," "wipe out," "extinguish," "eradicate," "exterminate," etc.

DIAGNOSE—"To diagnose" is to identify the nature of a disease or condition by studying its symptoms. *The doctors failed to diagnose the patient,* is wrong. *The doctors failed to diagnose her advanced pregnancy* may imply malpractice, but the sentence is grammatically correct.

DILEMMA—"Dilemma" does not mean a single problem but two problems when the solution to either problem is not desirable. More simply, we have two options and each poses a problem because they are both contrary to the objective. A "dilemma" means "stuck between a rock and a hard place."

DRASTIC—Drastic should never be used in positive or neutral statements. Declarations such as "drastic improvement," "drastic recovery," or "drastic enhancement," are wrong; try "dramatic" or "momentous" instead. The literal meaning of "drastic" is "severe," and has pejorative connotations, as in *John suffered a drastic relapse*, or *the currency suffered a drastic devaluation*.

DUE TO—*Due to the fact that we are sick of seeing this, we've decided to include it.* That is wrong. When tempted to write *due to the fact that*, we are sentenced to knock our heads on the wall and then replace it with *because*. Don't use "due to" to replace "because." Why? Because "due to" implies obligation and that's how it should be used when we're writing. We can't see *because* of the lady's big ugly hat. We pay the rent *due to* the landlord.

EACH—When "each" is the subject, it always takes a singular verb. *Each of us has to memorize the access code.*

ENORMITY—This word doesn't mean big or huge in a positive sense but describing something with the pejorative connotations of monstrous or horrible. *Sabine was appalled at the enormity of his beer gut.*

ESTIMATES—If we're going to imply an estimated number, then it, by nature, cannot be exact. *He visited about 232 people.* Read that sentence a few times. Now think about it for a moment. Using "about" to imply a rounded or estimated number makes no sense if we're using a number that is exact like 232. Either use "about two-hundred people" or "232 people."

ETC. / ET CETERA/IE/G—Et cetera, usually written etc. is Latin for "and so on." Latin phrases like this should be avoided. Never use "and" with this particular phrase either. *She recited the numbers one, two, three, and etc.* is incorrect. If we must, then *one, two, three, etc.* is the correct way to write it. Avoid using Latin abbreviations when writing fiction. Just spell it out in plain English; for example: *and so on.* In addition, if we use any Latin word or locution, don't capitalize it. Latin has no uppercase letters.

EVERY—With "everybody," "everyone," "everything," or "everyday," to give a few examples, "every" is treated as singular. *Every tree is covered in moss* or *everybody is fine.*

EYES—Avoid using "eyes" when we can use "gaze," "look," or "sight" instead. When using "eyes," the literal meaning becomes ridiculous. *Her eyes dropped to the floor.* Oh my! I hope someone picked them up for her. Unless we intend the character's eyes to literally fall from her head, *her gaze dropped to the floor* is the sentence we are looking for.

FLUKE—*The accident was a fluke* is incorrect. "Fluke" means a stroke of luck and must be always used to express fortunate, not unfortunate events.

FOREIGN LANGUAGES—Words written in another language should be in italics. For example: *Parlez-vous Francais?* the woman asked. "Uh, yes?" I had no idea what she asked, but it sounded awesome.

FRANKENSTEIN—Baron Frankenstein created a monster, but Mary Shelley never named the thing.

FROM WHENCE—"From whence" is redundant because "whence" means "from where." We know, "from whence" sounds better, but we've merely become accustomed to the error.

GOD—If we use it as the name of a particular Judaic, Islamic, or Christian god, we must capitalize the word like any other name. *My church is the house of God.* Whenever we use it as a generic term, it needs no capitalization. *...and the mountain god rumbled his displeasure.*

GOT—"Got" tends to be overused because it has so many potential uses. It also sounds… rough. While we aren't advocating removing it from our vocabularies, we should try to use the stronger word when there's an option. Rather than writing *he got up*, we write, *he stood. I got it.* Familiar. *I have it.* Better.

HAD—When using "had" to describe an action that is past or finished, we don't need to repeat it in every single sentence. Use it once or twice and then shift into past tense. *He had called her several times. She had promised she would be home.* Clunky. *He had called her several times. She promised she would be home.* Better.

HOPEFULLY—"Hopefully" means "in a hopeful manner." It is often used as an adverb. *Hopefully, I'll get an A on the next report.* This usage is wrong. Either shift the words around or, even better, rephrase the sentence to eliminate it. *I hope I get an A on the next report.*

HOWEVER—"However" is used incorrectly quite often because it can have many meanings. When used as a conjunction (linking two or more items) then it must be preceded by a semicolon and followed by a comma. It should not start a new sentence if the thoughts can be joined. So, let's look at some examples. In whatever way: *However, he did say he'd like to see her.* To a degree or extent: *...did say he'd like to see her, however grudgingly, and he agreed to come on Sunday.* In what way (how): *However did you do that?* Yet, in spite of or on the other hand: *The place is filthy; however, the waiters are hot.*

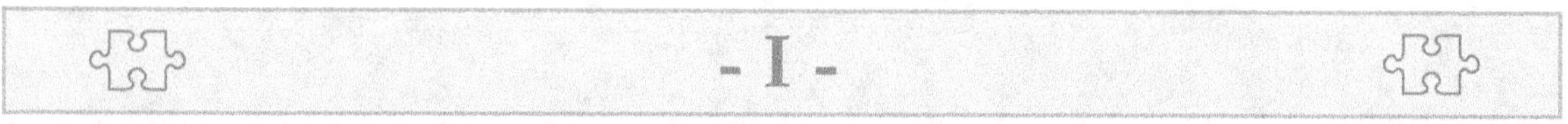

IN ORDER TO—This is just wordiness and isn't needed when writing fiction unless used in dialogue by a very stuffy, proper character. Often, when using "in order to," we can delete "in order" and the sentence keeps its meaning.

INCREDIBLE—"Incredible" means "unbelievable" or "impossible to be believed." To say *I fielded an incredible offer* means that I didn't believe a word of it. *An incredible plot, incredible characters, or an incredible ending* affirm that none was credible.

INDEED—Using the word "indeed" (except in dialogue) tends to lean on the bad side of author intrusion. In most cases, it can be deleted and not missed. In all cases of fiction writing, except dialogue, it can be avoided.

INFINITE—"Infinity" is relegated to matters mathematical or having to do with spirits. There are no "infinite" stars or "infinite" atoms in the universe, or "infinite" ways to combine the letters of the alphabet. We can use "infinite" in a figurative sense, as in *my love for thee is as infinite as the ocean*, or similar exaggerations, but never as factual.

IRREGARDLESS—This is not a word. If used at all, it is best suited for dialogue, depicting the limited education of a character.

- J -

JUST—Avoid it. "Just" has numerous meanings: "precisely," "exactly," "barely," "merely," "simply," "certainly," "possibly." The solution is to avoid both "just" and the adverbs. Adverbs are often not needed. Use "just" only when referring to justice.

- K -

KOALA—Let's be proper about this. However cuddly and adorable they may be, koalas are marsupials, not bears. Rather than koala bear, koala describes the animal.

- L -

LITERALLY—When we want to stress that a sentence has a literal, rather than a figurative meaning, we use literally. To use it as a replacement for lame intensifiers such as "in fact," "positively," "absolutely," or "really" is wrong. *Her eyes literally popped out of her head,* is nonsense.

LOCATED—Don't use located as an adjective. *The bar was located on Elm Street,* it's redundant. *The bar was on Elm Street.* Located is a verb meaning to find. Use it as such. *Amy located the gun in his pocket.*

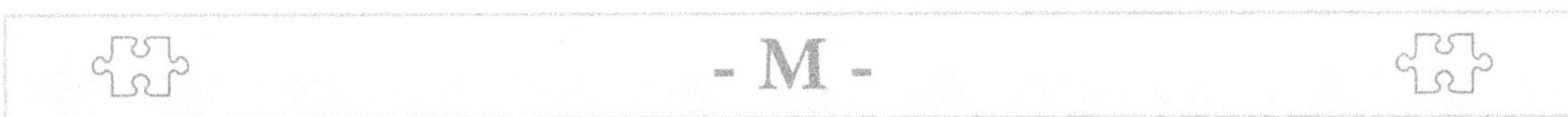

- M -

MAKE—Consider that "make" can be used to mean "produce," "cause," "lead to," "create," "bring about," "form," "compose," "force," "compel," "coerce," "oblige," "generate," "assemble," "manufacture," "cover," "go," "head," "bear," "get," "draw," "earn," "win," "name," "designate," "enact…" With so many words at our fingertips with similar meanings, choose the stronger word.

MOOT—We've seen this word used incorrectly too many times. Moot does not mean pointless. It means arguable or hypothetical. It's so widely misused in regular speech and in fiction writing that many probably don't realize they're using it incorrectly.

NIGGARD—The word has nothing to do with skin color or race. "Niggard" means stingy or tightfisted.

NOD IN AGREEMENT—Let's really examine this phrase, shall we? We wouldn't want anyone to think we were nodding to disagree, because that happens all the time. Wait a second, that's not right. No one nods to disagree. We should use nod and nothing more.

NONPLUSSED—Several writers have used this term to mean "at ease," "calm," or "controlled." Nope. It means to be confused or puzzled to such an extent that the "nonplussed" individual doesn't know what to do next. *When Richard suggested tackling the pizza with chopsticks, Gwen was nonplussed.*

NOTORIOUS—To use this term in a positive sense is wrong. "Notorious means" that someone or something is well known or famous on account of something bad. *Her notorious squirrel stew* indicates that the concoction was vile.

NUMBERS—This is confusing for some, especially when they either write, or are used to reading nonfiction. AP (Associated Press) style requires that the writer spell out numbers under ten and use numerals for numbers ten and higher. It also requires that numbers used in measurements, dates, and times be written as numerals. This is for nonfiction writing only. When writing fiction, spell numbers out, unless we're writing a date such as 1995. Numbers up to ninety-nine must be spelled as well as numbers accompanied by hundred, thousand, million, etc. *She walked 100 miles to reach the shore.* This is incorrect. It should read *one hundred miles.*

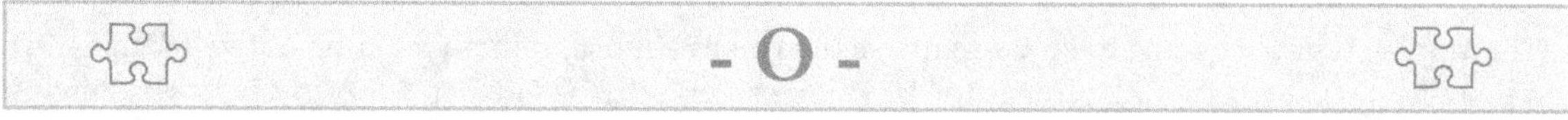

OF COURSE—Commercialese. This expression is unnecessary in fiction writing, with the exception of rare instances in dialogue.

ONLY—Use "only" immediately before the word it is modifying. Moving it around will change the meaning of the sentence. *Only Carrie had five dollars. Carrie only had five dollars. Carrie had only five dollars.* Do not use "only" when we mean to use "except." *I wanted to go, only I couldn't find my passport.* This is wrong. *I wanted to go, except I couldn't find my passport.* This is right.

OPPORTUNIST—"Opportunist" has negative connotations when applied to humans. It labels a person who exploits circumstances to obtain an unfair advantage. It shouldn't be used as a synonym of "resourceful" or "enterprising."

ORGANIC—See Chemicals.

PAIR—When using it to represent a number, pair is singular. *This is a pair of lovebirds. There is a pair of Ming vases flanking the entrance.*

PANINI—This is a plural form. The singular form is panino.

PERCENT—One word and spell it out. In fiction writing, we don't use symbols. We spell it out. Use "percent" when speaking of a fraction of a value is a single word and not written as "%."

PER—Replace with "a" or rewrite. "Per week," "per year," "per gallon," "per specification," are unsuitable constructions in fiction.

PIQUE—We can use this term as a noun or a verb. As a noun, it means "a feeling of wounded pride." As a verb, "pique" means "to provoke or arouse." When something interests us, it might pique our curiosity.

PRESENTLY—"Presently" means "in a short time." If we are inspired to write "presently," when we mean "currently" or "now," we should delete it. As we said before, "currently" is rarely needed anyway. Reserve "presently" for when we mean in a short amount of time. *We presently have two dozen girls in the class.* This is wrong. *I'll be with you presently.* This is correct.

PRETTY—Don't use "pretty" to mean "very," unless appropriate in dialogue. The word means "attractive," so use it only when referring to that.

PRONE—"Prone" means "to be lying face down." Also "likely or liable to do something."

QUALITY—Quality is not an adjective, but a noun. Items have quality or they do not. In *She drank high-quality wine*, high is redundant. Either the wine has quality or it hasn't.

- R -

REALIZED—If we find ourselves writing "realized" in our narrative, we must realize we're probably about to shift into telling. Instead of using "realized," take the opportunity to show the scene, rather than tell it. *He realized he forgot to eat dinner.* Horrible sentence. Try this: *His stomach gurgled in protest and he stumbled. "Damn, I forgot about dinner."*

REALLY—Although "really" sometimes serves a purpose in narrative, it's rare. Most times we can delete it or use a stronger word in its place. *He pushed her aside, rolled up his sleeves, and prepared to show her how cooking was really done.* Delete "really." The sentence does not change. Use "really" to mean "actual truth or fact," (*The Boogie Man doesn't really exist.*), truly (*I really did like him.*), or indeed (*Really, she must stop drinking so much coffee*).

REAL—Yet again, crafty writers are trying to sneak a word in when they want to use "very." *He wanted her real bad.* Come now, does this sound right? When we feel the urge to use "real" in place of "very," we hit the backspace key and begin again. Either delete the word or come up with something stronger. *He wanted her desperately.* Yes, it's an adverb, but it is preferable to the first sentence.

RELIGION—A "religion" is a set of beliefs, such as Christianity. Catholicism, Protestantism, and many others are faiths or churches. Catholics, Protestants, Baptists, etc, are variations on the Christian religion.

RENDEZVOUS—This is a noun, though some people use it as a verb. One can't "rendezvous" with Mary but can arrange a "rendezvous" with her.

RESTIVE—To be "restive" means "unable to keep still because of impatience, stubbornness, or restlessness." To use it as synonym for "calm" or "relaxed" is wrong.

- S -

SAID AS…—Dialogue is tough, we agree. Tags are probably the most difficult art to master. When do we use them? How do we use them? What types of tags? Let's help solve at least one part of the dialogue puzzle. If we find ourselves writing "said as he," "as she," "as they," or "as we," we stop and delete it. *"I bet you're sorry," she said as she kicked his shin.* "She said as she" is just filler, not needed at all. *"I bet you're sorry!" She kicked his shin.* It says the same thing without all the clunk. Plus, we don't remind the reader that he is reading.

SO—Avoid the temptation to use "so" in place of "very." Proper use requires that "so" be followed by "that" and never used to mean "very" or "really." *She was so smart.* This is incorrect. If we want to imply that she was exceptionally smart, we can try a stronger word like "brilliant." *I was so angry that I punched the keyboard.* This is the proper usage, although the sentence is rather crappy.

SCATTERED—"Scattered" means "thrown, tossed, or flung in various random directions." It follows that constructions such as *the force of the explosion scattered the bank notes in all directions*, contain a redundant "in all directions."

STATES/PROVINCES—States and provinces must always be spelled in full in fiction writing. Ontario should not be written as ON, and Wyoming should not be WY. This is true even if the state or province follows a city. Tweed, ON is incorrect. Tweed, Ontario is the proper way to write it. Of course, as with most rules, there is an exception. District of Columbia is acceptable for abbreviation. Washington, D.C. is preferred in this case.

STRAITJACKET—No, it's not "straight" but "strait," denoting tightness or narrow confines. The same concept applies to "strait-laced."

SUDDENLY—Like most adverbs, "suddenly" adds nothing to a sentence. Writers often use it to add intensity to a scene. *Suddenly the lights went out.* This is lazy. A well-written scene doesn't need the use of "suddenly" to add intensity.

SUPINE—To be lying face up.

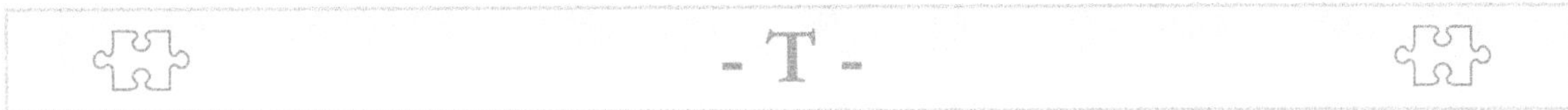

- T -

THAT—"That" pops up in prose so frequently that we barely notice it while editing. "That" is overused and can be deleted without changing the meaning of the sentence. *I hoped that he would call.* Go ahead, take it out. *I hoped he would call.* Much tighter, and we don't miss "that" at all.

THE—Avoid using "the" when "a" works instead, which is before the noun that follows it becomes familiar. "The" tends to become repetitive, much like "that." Use it when referring to a specific item. *She ran to the house and opened the door.* "The" in this sentence implies a specific house, probably hers (the owner's). Consider how "a" changes the sentence. *She ran to a house and opened the door.* This implies she's running to any house, not her own or any she might be familiar with, or one the narrator has not yet introduced to the reader.

TIME PERIOD—"Time period" and "a period of time" are redundant constructions. In this context, "a period" implies a length of time. Either "time" or "period" will do nicely.

TRY AND—The correct form is "try to." Often we read manuscripts with "try and" instead. We know that people speak this way, but as we mentioned before, when writing narrative, we strive to use the correct terms in the proper way. You don't "try *and* get an A" on your test. You "try *to* get an A" on your test.

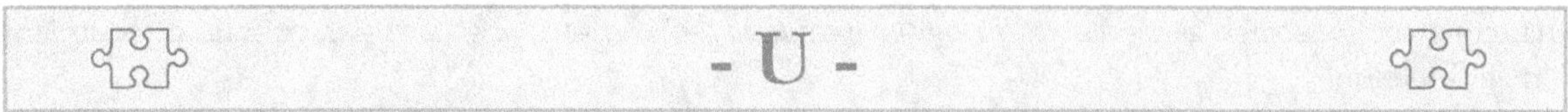

UNIQUE—"Unique" means "unparalleled, without equal or one of a kind." Now, look at this sentence: *She found his approach very unique.* Very unique? Unique stands alone, and should not be paired with words like "most," "very," "almost," or "somewhat." It either is the only one like it, or it isn't.

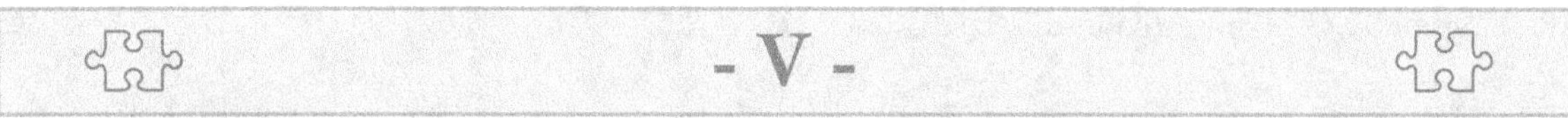

VERY—Mark Twain once said, "Substitute damn every time you're inclined to write very; your editor will delete it and the writing will be just as it should be." "Very" does not add emphasis to a sentence. It adds an extra word. If we feel the need to add emphasis, we find a strong word and avoid "very." Instead of writing "very attractive," use words like "stunning" or "gorgeous." Rather than "very hot," use "sweltering" or "scorching." We could also do as Mr. Twain suggests and insert "damn." It would make editing *damn* interesting.

WHEREABOUTS—"Whereabouts" is singular, and takes singular forms of the verbs. *The whereabouts of the fugitives is unknown.*

WITHOUT WARNING—Do things ever really happen without warning? Even tornadoes usually have a bit. It's like "suddenly" in fiction writing—a lazy attempt to add intensity to a scene. It adds nothing and often leaves the writer looking foolish. Consider this: *Without warning a hand clamped over her mouth and something cold and hard pressed into her back.* First, when does an attacker warn the victim? *Excuse me, Miss, I'm going to attack you now with my cold, hard weapon.* To use "without warning" in such a context trivializes the action.

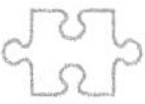 **4.5.3 SENTENCE DOUBTS**

Several of the sentence "errors" we'll examine on the following pages are not *really* errors in fiction, as long as the writer uses them to achieve a particular effect. There's nothing wrong with sentence fragments, split infinitives, passive voice, and many other issues—if used well. The rules are:

A. The writer knows to what extent he's bending or flexing the rules to suit his purposes.

B. The writer has a keen sense of voice and avoids overusing any tool or device.

The first rule is capital and we have stressed it before: We cannot bend a rule if we do not know and understand it. Ignorance makes us bad writers, not creative writers.

The second rule hides a universal truth: excellence resides in measure. Too much of anything will eventually set us on the road to hospital, prison, ostracism, or unhappiness. In writing, too much of one thing or not enough of another will send our manuscripts to the slush pile.

Getting rid of gross sentence errors is much easier if the writer takes a refresher course on clause and sentence types (pages 257 to 277). In the corresponding sections, we have included tips and copious comments on punctuation.

 **4.5.3.1 SENTENCE FRAGMENTS**

A sentence fragment is a group of words masquerading as a grammatically complete and independent thought, yet lacking a subject or predicate, erroneously including a subordinating conjunction, or containing incorrect punctuation. In fiction writing, particularly in dialogue, we use many fragments. Realistic dialogue often contains unfinished thoughts.

> The door opened. <u>Closed.</u>
>
> "Here you are." Jeff made a beeline toward the drinks sideboard. He held a crystal decanter. <u>Ambrosia.</u> "We have to talk."
>
> "<u>Yes?</u>" Her voice carried a raspy slur.
>
> "<u>Already…</u>"
>
> Sonya parted her flimsy housecoat to flaunt her contempt for underwear. "<u>Wasted.</u>"
>
> He downed his drink. "<u>Slut.</u>"

Seven lines and six (underscored) fragments, typical of some passages involving dialogue.

The preceding sentence is also a fragment. Unlike the dialogue exchange—which we can try to justify with dubious claims of arcane artistry—we offer no excuse for this one.

Seven lines and six (underscored) fragments **are** typical of passages involving dialogue.

In the dialogue, we wrote the fragments, knew they were fragments, and chose to keep them.

> Susan, the beekeeper. She keeps, scattered over the hills surrounding her property, scores of wooden boxes with slanted covers. Her hives, native to Montana.

The previous paragraph has two fragments hemming the central sentence.

Susan, the beekeeper.

And

Her hives, native to Montana.

In this instance the fragments do nothing for the prose and cannot be justified. The paragraph is badly written.

We could rewrite as:

Susan, the beekeeper, keeps—scattered over the hills surrounding her property—scores of wooden boxes with slanted covers; her hives are native to Montana.

Alternatively, if we need shorter sentences, we could try:

Susan is a beekeeper. Scores of wooden boxes with slanted covers are scattered over the hills surrounding her property. These are her hives, which are native to Montana.

Let's explore a different example. Often, when we reply to questions, we use fragments.

"Why did you run this morning?"

"Wanted to stand in line early."

The reply has no subject. Who wanted to stand in line? "I wanted to stand in line early." Sometimes we omit the subject when we speak because we assume the listener knows who the implied subject is. In fiction, however, this is often not the case.

Some situations can be tricky.

Carlos, being my favorite writer.

Here we have a subject (Carlos) and a verb (being). Right? Not at all. "Being" is a participial form that is not working as a verb. We can either write: "Carlos is my favorite writer," or "Carlos, being my favorite writer, is also my favorite person."

When we start a sentence with a subordinating conjunction, the presence of subject and predicate doesn't remedy the problem. A subordinating conjunction restricts a clause; it makes it incomplete.

Although we tried to find a better example.

Go on… what comes next? "Although" sets up a contrast, meaning that we must offer a complementary explanation. Unless we attach it to an independent clause, we have a fragment.

Although we tried to find a better example, we drew a blank.

 **4.5.3.2 MISPLACED AND DANGLING MODIFIERS**

Placing modifiers or descriptive phrases far from the words they describe leads to confusing sentences. The rule is to place modifiers as close as possible to the word they describe or modify. Modifiers are adjectives, adverbs, and their phrases and clauses acting as adjectives or adverbs.

The writer states that overpopulation is caused by people shunning contraceptive measures in the first chapter.

The contraceptive measures are not in the first chapter; the statement is. Since the modifying clause "in the first chapter" should be close or next to the element it describes, we can rewrite the sentence:

> In the first chapter, the writer states that overpopulation is caused by people shunning contraceptive measures.

When it is unclear what the modifier describes, the result is misleading and ambiguous.

> A manuscript sat on the pile of papers that Paul had written.

In the previous sentence, it's unclear what has Paul written. Is it the manuscript or the pile of papers?

> A manuscript that Paul had written sat on the pile of papers.

In the next sentence, "running through the fields" appears to modify "grass," though we doubt grass runs anywhere.

> Running through the fields the grass caressed my legs.

A little tweak and the sentence will gather more sense.

> As I ran through the fields, the grass caressed my legs.

Sometimes the dangling phrase is so far removed from the word it modifies that the reader must stop and retrace his steps to work out the writer's intention, as in:

> Mike inhaled spluttering on the barbecue the aroma of garlic and herbs.

This sounds painful. We cringe at the thought of dear Mike roasting away, regardless of what he's basted himself with.

> Mike inhaled the aroma of garlic and herbs, which he'd basted on the leg of lamb spluttering on the barbecue.

At times, the sentence structure doesn't clarify which of two possible words the modifier varies:

> Rita is frightened of stuffed alligators and spiders.

Is Rita frightened of stuffed spiders or all sorts of spiders?

> Rita is frightened of spiders and stuffed alligators.

Naturally, the revised sentence takes care of the spiders, but we're left with a worrisome doubt: Is Rita not scared of live alligators? In such an instance, a better solution would be to rewrite the sentence until it conveys the writer's intentions:

> Rita is frightened of spiders. She dreads alligators, even stuffed ones.

In fiction, dangling modifiers involving the lack of a subject are common, and often impossible for the writer to detect. This is even more likely if we use passive forms. When we write, we have the scene and the protagonists in our mind; we know what's happened and who is doing what. Unfortunately, the reader may not be so lucky.

> Having bought the chicken, it now needed skinning.

The problem here is that we don't know who has bought the bird or whose task is to undress it. Faced with such a silly sentence, a reasonable approach is to stop beating around the bush and name the party responsible.

> Having bought the chicken, Deb needed to skin it.

When using as modifiers adverbs like "almost," "even," "hardly," "just," "only," and "nearly," chances are we'll forget about placing them in the correct slot.

> Overcome with desire, Richard almost dragged Wendy to the rug as soon as he entered the house.

The translation is that Richard didn't drag Wendy to the rug. Tough luck.
Repositioning the pesky adverb improves Wendy's fortunes.

> Almost as soon as he entered the house, overcome with desire, Richard dragged Wendy to the rug.

 **4.5.3.3 FAULTY PARALLELISM**

Whenever we express two or more matching concepts or items in a series, it's important to use grammatically equal elements. Parallelism is a pretty word signifying that each part of a sentence must mach the other parts when listing actions or establishing relationships between ideas.

> The writer's tasks involve weaving a fantastic plot, a manuscript, and a synopsis.

On the first clause we have the robust verb "weaving" and the adjective "fantastic." If we mean that the verb and qualifier affects the three items in the series, rewriting and altering the punctuation will improve the sentence's meaning:

> The writer's tasks involve weaving: fantastic plots, manuscripts, and synopses.

If verb and qualifier only concern the first clause, we must ensure the remaining items on the list contain similar elements:

> The writer's tasks involve weaving a fantastic plot, writing a superb manuscript, and composing a killer synopsis.

When building a list, these do not work:

> Barbara likes to dance, traveling, and to laze about.

> Barbara likes dancing, to travel, and to laze about.

> Barbara likes to dance, to travel, and lazing about.

The three previous sentences suffer from lack of parallelism; the verb tenses are unequal. To straighten them, we've only to choose a tense for all items on the series and stick to it:

> Barbara likes to dance, to travel, and to laze about.

> Barbara likes dancing, traveling, and lazing about.

 **4.5.3.4 PRONOUN AGREEMENT**

A pronoun must agree with its antecedent or referent—the noun the pronoun refers to.

> Everyone should pay for their own beer.

> One might realize that his book may be impossible to sell.

> A person should ensure that he or she keep to the clearly marked path.

"Everyone," "one," and "a person" are singular nouns. In the first two examples, replacing the pronoun is enough:

> Everyone should pay for his own beer.

> One doesn't realize that her book may be impossible to sell.

Of course, we can use the "his or her" formula, but it's unwieldy.

> People should ensure that they keep to the clearly marked path.

In the third example "keep" is a plural form, as is the pronoun "they." In this instance, using "he or she" is not appropriate.

 **4.5.3.5 PRONOUN CASE**

We must determine whether the pronoun functions as a subject (the actor), object (the acted upon), or possessive (owner of another noun) in the sentence. The form we select must match its case (what it does in the sentence).

> James's plans soon sparked a conflict between he and Susan.

> Since the officers recommend strict adherence to the letter of the rules, them object to partisan interpretation.

Both examples are wrong. To rewrite, we should choose the correct pronoun cases:

> James's plans soon sparked a conflict between him and Susan.

> Since the officers recommend strict adherence to the letter of the rules, they object to partisan interpretation.

 **4.5.3.6 RUN-ON OR FUSED SENTENCES AND COMMA SPLICES**

Although these horrors elicit much dread from writers, they are easy to avoid by revisiting the section on clauses and memorizing the difference between dependent and independent clauses. (see pages 257 to 263)

Run-on sentences and comma splices share the same origin and mechanics. Let's start with a nice independent clause:

> Mark loves jam tarts.

Why independent? Because the clause—or full sentence in this instance—doesn't need anything else to make sense; it contains a full idea. "Mark loves jam tarts."

<u>We know the **who.**</u> Who is into jam tarts? Mark.

<u>We know the **how.**</u> How does Mark feel about jam tarts? He loves them.

<u>We know the **what.**</u> What does Mark love? Jam tarts.

And now let's produce another:

He likes to dip his finger in the filling.

This is also an independent clause with a "who" (he), a "how" (likes to dip), and a "what" (his finger in the filling.) Yum.

Independently, these sentences work well. If we set them one after the other the result is:

Mark loves jam tarts. He likes to dip his finger in the filling.

We have a superb line with two good sentences, which are correctly punctuated and capitalized. Our problems start when we try to join them. First we dispense with punctuation and pair them up:

Mark loves jam tarts he likes to dip his finger in the filling.

The result is a run-on or fused sentence and both appellatives are graphically representative: The sentence runs on past where it should stop with a period, and we've fused all the words into a single block.

Unless we have detoured through the section on clauses and discovered how to join independent elements, we might be tempted to use the easy way out and insert a comma. After all, it reads as if our new fused sentence is screaming for one. Here:

Mark loves jam tarts, he likes to dip his finger in the filling.

And we end up with a comma splice, or two sentences spliced with the wrong glue.

Both errors, the run on and the comma splice, demand similar remedies because they are two views of the same problem. The first option is to leave the sentences as they were when we started, which was independent and separated by punctuation:

Mark loves jam tarts. He likes to dip his finger in the filling.

But there are other punctuation marks we could use:

Mark loves jam tarts? He likes to dip his finger in the filling.

Mark loves jam tarts! He likes to dip his finger in the filling.

Mark loves jam tarts: He likes to dip his finger in the filling.

Mark loves jam tarts; he likes to dip his finger in the filling.

Mark loves jam tarts—he likes to dip his finger in the filling.

The first two are iffy. The question mark and exclamation point alter the voice by adding expression, which may or may not be appropriate to the passage. The third, or using a colon, is overkill and would depend on context whether is appropriate or not. The last two options work well.

There's nothing wrong with the punctuation approach. But if the writer is in the middle of a passage already riddled with short sentences only the last two are eligible to make a longer one.

Yet, this is deceptive because semicolons and em dashes create longer pauses, and their use might interfere with the rhythm the writer seeks.

Our second option is to use a comma and a coordinating conjunction. Coordinating conjunctions are "and," "or," "for," "nor," "so," and "yet."

> Mark loves jam tarts, and he likes to dip his finger in the filling.

> Mark loves jam tarts, for he likes to dip his finger in the filling.

Another, more involved way, to correct a run-on sentence or comma splice is to make one of the clauses dependent on the other. To do so we use a subordinator:

> Mark loves jam tarts, because he likes to dip his finger in the filling.

> Mark loves jam tarts, since he likes to dip his finger in the filling.

This device must be used with care, because the meaning of the new compound sentence varies slightly, depending on the way we choose to join them.

Warning: In our experience editing and revising scores of manuscripts, the cause of frequent problems when attempting to join sentences is the mistaking of a conjunctive adverb for a conjunction. These cannot be used to join two independent clauses. Some conjunctive adverbs are "also," "hence," "however," "in fact," "likewise," "so," "thereby" and "yet," among many others. (For an expanded section on conjunctive adverbs see pages 243 to 245).

Conjunctive adverbs may be inserted as modifiers within an independent clause. But to use them between two independent clauses we must separate them with a full stop.

> Mark loves jam tarts, in fact he likes to dip his finger in the filling.

> Mark loves jam tarts, also he likes to dip his finger in the filling.

> Mark loves jam tarts, so he likes to dip his finger in the filling.

These constructions are incorrect. Instead we can rewrite as:

> Mark loves jam tarts. In fact, he likes to dip his finger in the filling.

> Mark loves jam tarts. Also, he likes to dip his finger in the filling.

> Mark loves jam tarts. So, he likes to dip his finger in the filling.

Obviously, using a conjunctive adverb doesn't join the sentences; these remain separate entities.

 **4.5.3.7 FORMS OMITTED COMMAS**

It's essential to check sentences with introductory words, phrases, or clauses. Here we might go against the grain of these writers who defend omitting commas after introductory elements. While it's true that often short introductions don't need a comma, readers benefit from short pauses separating introductory ingredients from the rest of the sentence. We prefer to err on the side of over-correctness, rather than confuse the reader. The truth is a writer is never wrong using commas after introductory words.

> If there were enough time, he would have another pizza slice.

> However, that was not to be.

When it comes to whiskey, Scots, Irish, and Canadians have different tastes.

 **4.5.3.8 SUBJECT-VERB AGREEMENT**

In every sentence, the subject specifies who or what the sentence is about.

Amy neared the window.

To the question, "who neared?" the answer is "Amy." Therefore, "Amy" is the subject.

After a whistling sound, the aircraft exploded in midair.

To the question, "what exploded?" the answer is "the aircraft." Therefore, "the aircraft" is the subject.

This is an oversimplification, because subjects can be simple or complete. In the previous examples, "Amy" and "the aircraft" are simple subjects. A complete subject consists of the simple subject and the word or words that modify it. Examples:

Gorgeous Amy neared the window.

After a whistling sound, the enemy aircraft exploded in midair.

Where "Gorgeous Amy" and "the enemy aircraft" are complete subjects.

The verb is the action bit in any sentence. They are the central part of the predicate, the word or words naming what happens. In the two previous examples, the actions are "neared" and "exploded." They are the verbs.

If we write:

The girls was late for the school bus.

We have a disparity between subject and verb. "The girls" is plural and "was" is singular. We can rewrite the full sentence as singular or plural, depending on the writer's need:

The girl was late for the school bus.

The girls were late for the school bus.

In simple sentences, subject-verb agreement is not often a problem, but when we have several nouns in the same sentence, attributing the verb can be a problem.

The main problem for the soldiers were how to capture the fortress.

Here, the writer noticed that the closest noun was "soldiers" and crafted the verb accordingly. But the subject is "The main problem," a singular entity. Therefore, the sentence's verb must agree:

The main problem for the soldiers was how to capture the fortress.

Let's try another example.

The pattern of meteoroids are monitored by our navigators to determine when to blast off.

Same problem. "Meteoroids" is plural, but the subject in the sentence is "the pattern," which is singular.

The pattern of meteoroids is monitored by our navigators to determine when to blast off.

 **4.5.3.9 APOSTROPHE ERRORS**

We use apostrophes to indicate possession for nouns

This is Renée's llama, and this is Carlos's rhino.

We never use apostrophes with personal pronouns, such as "its," "your," "their," and "whose." We do use apostrophes to signal that letters are missing, such as in contractions.

We've endured much hardship.

In this weather, it's unlikely we can sail.

Problems arise when writers dust apostrophes like confetti over their prose.

I wonder who's cars are these.

John marbles' are all over the place.

We found it's tracks.

These three sentences should be rewritten like this:

I wonder whose cars are these.

John's marbles are all over the place.

We found its tracks.

And now for the bad news. The only way we can be sure our apostrophes are where they should be is to place the cursor at the beginning of the manuscript, use the search feature of the word processor to find ', and ask each and every one, "Do you belong here?"

 **4.5.3.10 WORDS EASILY CONFUSED**

In the rush of creating a wonderful tale, we often mistake one word for another. There are hundreds of instances when our fingers don't cooperate, and we type "layed" instead of "laid" or "lay"— which is what we meant to write. Is it "pig out" or "pigout?" "Further" or "farther?" "Trope" or "troupe?" "A while" or "awhile?" "Unhuman" or "inhuman?" "Irregardless?"

We've compiled a list of words that confuse some writers and others, or whose usage is often mistaken. The compilation is on pages 322 to 369.

4.5.3.11 PASSIVE VOICE

We discuss the problems associated with passive constructions on pages 147, 186 and 551. When revising a manuscript, it pays to use the word processor's search feature to isolate "was," and while we are at it, check "were," and any verb that can take an object in a passive construction such as:

Present Simple: Books are written.

Present Continuous: Books are being written.

Past Simple: The book was written.

Past Continuous: The book was being written.

Present Perfect: The books have been written.

Future Simple: It will be finished tomorrow.

If the usage is correct we can proceed to the next instance. Using the passive voice is not wrong, but when the sentence explains what is done to the subject, instead of what the subject did too often, we run into trouble. Careless use of the passive voice usually renders sentences vague. For example:

The judge's verdict was thought unfair by us.

The pillbox was rushed by the infantry.

These short stories have been written by Thomas.

Whether or not these sentences read better in active voice is up to the writer, but we think they do.

We thought the judge's verdict was unfair.

The infantry rushed the pillbox.

Thomas wrote these short stories.

 ### 4.5.3.12 SHIFTS IN TENSE

This is a difficult issue to address on one's own. A long time ago, as we read a loose chapter from a colleague at a writer's haunt, we came across this sentence:

Will she have felt the same protuberance under the wall covering?

In our review, we suggested that the writer should check his tenses. He wrote back demanding to know "where exactly."

After we replied something like "second paragraph, last sentence," he blew a fuse and stated that the sentence was grammatically correct. We didn't argue.

A couple of weeks later, we fielded an abject apology. The man had read and re-read the sentence many times, until the day his twelve-year-old daughter glanced over his shoulder and declared: "that's wrong."

He planned to rewrite as "Would she have felt the same protuberance under the wall covering?" but then he thought it over and rendered it more palatable as: "Had she felt the same protuberance under the wall covering?"

We've chosen this example because spotting tense shifts requires snapping off the writer's frame of mind and slipping into that of a reader. This is often impossible, because we're too close to our work. We have memorized many passages and often we read what's in our mind, without noticing that it doesn't match the words on the paper or the screen.

To spot these and similar errors, nothing beats our trusted beta readers.

 **4.5.3.13 SPLIT INFINITIVES**

An infinitive is a construction formed by "to" and a verb. For example, "to write," "to shoot," "to love," and "to cry" are infinitives.

Sometimes, we omit the "to" as in, "Help me baste the turkey."

Whenever we omit "to," the resulting form is termed "bare infinitive."

We must point out that an infinitive is not a verb, but a construction functioning as a noun, adjective, or adverb. Since an infinitive is not a verb, we cannot add any endings to it.

To read is all Renée wants to do when she's not tending her orchids.

Here, "to read" works as a noun.

Whenever Carlos stands in line at the soup kitchen, he brings a book to read while he waits.

Here, "to read" works as an adjective.

Renée trudged through a snowstorm to read from one of her books to a blind man.

Here, "to read" works as an adverb.

There are other forms of infinitive, such as the perfect infinitive formed with "to have" + past participle.

For example: to have read or to have written

The continuous infinitive formed with "to be" + present participle.

For example: to be reading or to be writing

The perfect continuous infinitive formed with "to have been" + present participle.

For example: to have been reading or to have been writing

The passive infinitive formed with "to be" + past participle

For example: to be read or to be written

A split infinitive occurs when we insert a modifier between "to" and the verb.

For example: to quickly read, to smoothly write, to really love, to suddenly cease

Despite the cries of old-school grammarians, splitting an infinitive is not a style or syntax error, but rather a construction. Writers should split infinitives when the alternative would be awkward. For example:

"I intend to really enjoy reading Kate's latest novel."

Here, "to really enjoy" is a split infinitive. What are the alternatives?

"I intend really to enjoy reading Kate's latest novel."

"I intend to enjoy really reading Kate's latest novel."

"I really intend to enjoy reading Kate's latest novel."

In all instances, the meaning has changed, and rendered the sentence ugly.

Remember that splitting infinitives is not wrong, and sometimes it is the only reasonable option. But... there's always a "but." Split infinitives draw attention to themselves; they are powerful constructions. Unless the writer uses them for a particular effect or as a tool, we recommend using this construction sparingly.

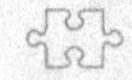 **4.5.3.14 STRINGY SENTENCES**

We better open this one with an example:

> She never buys ice cream because she doesn't know what's gone into it, and she doesn't like fresh cheese either, so she never buys it, but she doesn't mind tofu, so yesterday she tried the new tofu ice cream with fresh cheese, and she loved it!

The sentence might be mind numbing, but there's nothing wrong with it. As long as full sentences are correctly punctuated with commas and conjunctions, we can string as many as we want. But sentence-stringing is not creative writing. It is more akin to babbling.

> Donna never buys ice cream because she doesn't know what's gone into it. She doesn't like fresh cheese either, so she never buys it. But she doesn't mind tofu. Only yesterday, Donna tried the new tofu ice cream with fresh cheese, and she loved it!

We won't be short listed for the Pulitzer with that one, but it conveys the idea. (Of course, we gave Donna quite a belly ache).

Powerful sentences should convey a single idea. There's nothing wrong with short and focused sentences.

The important issue to keep in mind is variety in composition, structure, opening, and length. Section 3.1.7 on pages 172 to 177 touches the mechanics of sentence variety.

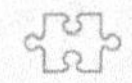 **4.5.3.15 PARTICIPIAL PHRASES**

Participial phrases are fine; there's nothing wrong with them. As usual, the trick is to understand the effect that some constructions have on the reader.

A participial phrase is one containing a participle (a verb form ended in "–ing.") Naturally, not every phrase containing an "–ing" verb is a participial phrase, else English would be predictable and boring.

> Drawing her two-foot machete, Grandma opened the kitchen's back door and ran toward the front of the house where the bandits tried to pick the lock.

"Drawing her two-foot machete" is a participial phrase. The problem is that we don't discover who is doing what until we've cleared the comma (a comma always separates a participial phrase from the rest of the sentence). This can be confusing to the reader.

On rewrite, it pays to check sentences starting with a participle to determine if it's clear. The easy way to address possible confusion is to ensure the previous sentence paves the way for the use of a participle:

This time Grandma was sure; the scratching at the front door had nothing to do with Tibbs. She searched in the drawer where she keeps the candles and other emergency supplies. Drawing her two-foot machete, etc.

The next issue has to do with participial phrases either following or preceding the main clause. It's a common error plaguing many otherwise excellent manuscripts. Sometimes, in the rush to get scenes out of the way, we insert phrases where the action of the participle and that of the main verb in the sentence take place simultaneously.

Kurt closed the door, running to his car in the thick of the blizzard.

In the previous sentence, "running to his car" is the participial phrase. The main clause is "Kurt closed the door." Kurt cannot close a door and run at the same time.

Here's another example:

Bolting to his feet, Jeremiah strutted toward the verandah, one hand on his yarmulke.

Here, the participial phrase is "Bolting to his feet." Regardless of Jeremiah's prowess, he couldn't bolt and strut at the same time.

We recommend using the search feature on the word processor to highlight "–ing" terminations and check for unlikely coincident actions.

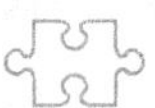 **4.5.4 PARAGRAPH DOUBTS**

Paragraphing is exceedingly difficult to master, since it not only involves syntax rules but a measure of stylistic and aesthetic values. Most writers, in particular those just starting, study elements of technique such as POV and dialogue. Later, after a few rebukes from fellow writers or beta readers, they dust up their grammar and sentence construction, often forgotten from distant school days. Yet, the mechanics of paragraphs is often neglected, as if it didn't matter as much as other elements of good writing.

Just like scenes and chapters have definite parts (beginning, middle, and end) so do paragraphs, both in fiction and non-fiction writing. Dialogue is an exception, in particular when made of short paragraphs.

Pace, action, style, and readability are intimately associated with good paragraphing. Many stories would improve greatly with careful paragraph structure.

If we imagine a bowl of baked beans as a book, and the individual beans as sentences, then each spoonful is a paragraph. Tackling a hearty bean soup with a tiny spoon would be trying. This is often the effect on readers when writers string short paragraphs like beads on a necklace. A huge spoon wouldn't be of much help either, since we wouldn't be able to eat its contents in one go unless we're pigging out. A reasonably sized spoon and a little variety, a little bread dunking, or a foray to dig for bits of sausage, can greatly improve our bean-eating experience.

On rewriting and polishing a manuscript, the usual routine is to first address story issues, such as plot, characterization, continuity, etc. The second step is to line edit, addressing each sentence for construction, integrity, variety, and content. A third step—one that many writers neglect—is to start at chapter one and read, looking exclusively at paragraph structure.

Breaking the narrative into well-structured paragraphs guides readers through the story by setting the text into focused blocks.

So far we've discussed theory, but what is a paragraph? A paragraph is a sentence or a group of sentences with a particular physical appearance, structure, length, and content.

On the following pages we've listed the principal aspects of paragraphing, highlighting not errors but usage; it follows that departing from these would either constitute an error or most likely render the narrative or dialogue harder for a reader to follow.

 ### 4.5.4.1 PHYSICAL APPEARANCE

In published works, paragraphs are easily recognized by their physical appearance: a block of text opening with an indented line and closing with a period, followed by trailing spaces at its end.

> Having positioned his brigantine—under the cloak of witty conversation—he would fire his broadside: what about dinner?
> She would open her eyes wide, blush a little and nod before smiling. Dimples would take over her face and the sparkle in her irises would put the stars to shame.[127]

Formatting cues readers by bridging between the shape of a paragraph and its contents.

Often, non fiction work, correspondence, and a few publishing houses don't indent paragraphs. Instead, they separate paragraphs by increasing the space between them by a few points.

> Before Susan's arms encircled his waist he sensed a soft crunch of sand. Paul turned to kiss salt and sea from her neck. He leaned on her breast, to the sound of life compressed into a beat. Then they had rolled on the sand, mixing laughter with grit and kisses; she ran and he chased her to the water.
>
> Paul pushed the embers aside with a stick, and dug to pry small lobsters, bright red and steaming after cooking in the shell. More races to the water, shouts after scalding their fingers to wash the shellfish before hoarding their treasure into their tent of palm leaves.
>
> Tipsy from wine and skin, he'd dropped a stone in the crook of her hand, a piece of fire he'd pried from the earth's entrails. He asked her to walk with him the rest of his summers and she cried, and pledged to keep the stone forever; without cutting it, without stealing the beauty of that shard of moon. The same moon that peeped and blushed till the sun chased it away.[128]

It's worth noting that in printed works—such as The Companion—the opening paragraph of each chapter is often left without indent to improve the text's aesthetic appearance.

 ### 4.5.4.2 STRUCTURE

Paragraphs, other than dialogue—which we will review separately—should contain a group of related sentences dealing with a single topic, situation, or event.

---

127 Carlos J Cortes, Spring Sprung.

128 Carlos J Cortes, Bad Water.

As to formal structure, or the order of sentences within a paragraph, fiction is different from non-fiction.

In technical writing, essays, and general non-fiction works, paragraph structure is formal. We will explore the classic layout in the section "Paragraph Contents" on pages XXX.

In fiction, besides adding information, the paragraphs must move the story along. This we attempt with two paragraph forms:

Leading

A paragraph opening with a leading sentence, followed by one or more sentences supporting the first:

> Maura caught a glint in Hogan's eye that wasn't there before. *Fear!* Hogan McLamroch was scared! What kind of sorcery ran through Fernando's arm? A stray light caught in the steel like a wink from the devil as the men whirled in a pagan ballet to the swish of foils slicing through the air and the reedy twang of polished steel.[129]

Developing

A paragraph developing an action, item or thought, designed to move the story along:

> How could it be? After years of harrowing physical abuse Fernando matched one of Scotland's finest blades. She spied his feet, nimble and springy as a cat's, dancing on the rough hewn boards, pacing on tiptoe to sidestep effortlessly like a ballerina turned predator. She flinched with each fresh lunge. A dozen times it seemed as though Fernando must be run through, but each time, by some miraculous means, he regained his opposition, and Hogan's blade met steel. Once, indeed, thrusting in *quarte,* Hogan's point, aimed too high, flashed above Fernando's guard and ripped his coarse shirt at the sleeve. Fernando retired his foot nimbly, parried, and riposted with a straight thrust, wrist held high, before Hogan could recover his opposition. The blades clashed as forte met foible.[130]

There are other ways to organize paragraphs, and writers should stick to forms that encapsulate focused and related ideas. We have found the two preceding structures particularly useful.

4.5.4.3 PARAGRAPH LENGTH

Size matters. Paragraphs may contain anything from one word to thousands. Long paragraphs, in particular pages and pages without breaks, may intimidate readers when they browse novels at a library or bookshop. On the other hand, many short paragraphs give prose a choppy feel.

Sentence length, composition, and variety are important in creative writing, and paragraphs deserve a similar treatment.

> Something covered his mouth. Sam drew a breath, sucking in something soft and squishy. For a moment, panic crept into his chest and he raised a hand to remove whatever suffocated him. Fine hairs, a ring… *Rita.*

---

[129] Carlos J Cortes, The Spaniard's Woman

[130] Carlos J Cortés, The Spaniard's Woman

"Jesus." He removed his wife's arm from his face. She rolled, mumbling, away from the dark blotch left on the pillow by her drool.

Turning on his back, Sam pushed his irritation away. Rita couldn't help the way she slept. Hell, he used to find her flailing arms funny, even a little cute. If only he didn't have to wake up with one of them either thwacking his nose or smothering the air from his lungs every damn morning.[131]

Paragraph extension, like sentence length, governs the rhythm of prose. Longer paragraphs usually signal exposition, complex or profound description or backstory. Naturally, the action slows down through these passages. However, short descriptive paragraphs and dialogue (which often consists of small paragraphs) accelerate the pace and ratchet up the action.

Creative writing, regardless of its norms and drudgery, is an art form. And like other expressions of art, the aesthetic makeup and sensitivity of the writer contribute to create unique styles. Short paragraphs are wonderful devices to pep up flagging prose, but many in a row read staccato and disjointed—because ideas conveyed in short paragraphs must be necessarily shallow.

 4.5.4.4 PARAGRAPH CONTENTS

In creative writing, whether fiction or non-fiction, the first rule is to keep one idea to one paragraph. This implies that as soon as we begin to transition into a new idea we should consider a new paragraph.

Paragraphs may contain the idea and supporting sentences or a number of related points as long as they relate to the overall topic of the paragraph. In fiction, if a single idea is too long, it pays to elaborate each point separately and place them in their own paragraphs.

The classic list of overlapping elements within a paragraph is:

Unity

Coherence

Topic Sentence

Development

Since these elements are flexible, each writer should strive to adapt them to his individual style and the manuscript demands in terms of pace.

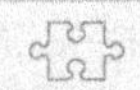 4.5.4.5 PARAGRAPH UNITY

A paragraph should contain a single focus, and its development (if necessary). Writers should refrain from opening a paragraph with an idea and wander off on tangents.

Love clouds perception, they say. Defects shrink, virtues expand out of all proportion and the loved one's icon plunges the lover's brain into a travesty of reality. Jung delved deeper than Freud on the tricks we play when we idealize images and shape them into a construct having little resemblance to the original. Of course, both of these masters lived in a different

---

131 Renée Miller, Sam and Rita

society, which in turn shaped the way people experienced reality. Jung was Swiss and Freud Austrian, but these societies shared...

Excuse me but, didn't we open the paragraph with love? How did we end up discussing a psychiatrist and a neurologist's social background?

The paragraph, focusing on love, belongs to a section that originally read:

> Love clouds perception, they say. Defects shrink, virtues expand out of all proportion and the loved one's icon—contorted into an idealized image having little resemblance to the original—plunges the lover's brain into a travesty of reality.[132]

4.5.4.6 PARAGRAPH COHERENCE

Coherence is the trait shaping a paragraph so the reader follows the development of an idea. To structure coherence, we create both logical and verbal bridges.

Logical bridges

These contain the same idea or topic carried over from sentence to sentence.

> Our innermost desires are so improbable that, instead of sizing them down to reason, our mind chooses the path of lesser resistance and warps the target of our yearns to accommodate our irrational construct. The lover's distorted senses—blind to snores and rancid sweat—feast on musical words and the magic of uncharted skin; each newly discovered dimple, valley and mound, a treasure-trove of sensation and fragrance.[133]

In the previous paragraph, "Our innermost desires" and "The lover's distorted senses" carry the theme of surreal idealization from sentence to sentence.

Verbal bridges

These consist of keywords, synonymous words and transitions to link the points from different sentences to the main focus of the paragraph.

> I understand bewildered onlookers; *whatever does she see in him? What does he have that I haven't?* I also understand the forecast of disgruntled oracles: Won't last long, mind my words, it always fizzles down. I understand when the lover hides a rueful smile as he or she thinks that others are not privy to the wonder they've discovered, and wrong to boot because he or she *is* different. Yes, I understand the logic behind the prophet's augur: Soaring spirits must eventually land in the mire where ordinary mortals struggle predictable existences. Yes, I understand, of course I do. But Nathalie *is* different. Nathalie is home, my home, and she waits for *me*.[134]

---

[132] Carlos J Cortés, Nathalie

[133] Carlos J Cortés, Nathalie

[134] Carlos J Cortés, Nathalie

"I understand," repeated like a mantra is the bridge this writer used to link the sentences in the paragraph, also focused on the theme of idealized love.

🧩 4.5.4.7 TOPIC SENTENCES

A topic sentence, although much more appropriate to non-fiction than fiction writing, is a sentence that conveys the idea or concept the paragraph will deal with.

Often, the topic sentence opens the paragraph. But regardless of its location within a paragraph, the task of the remaining sentences is to support, explain, justify, or expand upon the matter outlined on the topic sentence. Think of a topic sentence or clause as the controlling idea, a blurb or résumé of a paragraph contents.

> The chair faced my host, but was positioned closer to the hearth, forcing Mr. Nousel to turn ever so slightly. The effect was off-putting. The brass eyepiece gleamed, and ruddy shadows flowed from his waxen face as if they didn't belong there. Eyes that had only a moment ago appeared as large cobalt fish had been replaced by two tiny red flickers, simulacra of the low burning fire.[135]

In the preceding paragraph the writer uses a topic sentence to describe the exact positioning of a chair, and the strain that such position places on Mr. Nousel. The remaining sentences enlarge on the consequences.

● Development

Developing the topic sentence is a technique borrowed from non-fiction writing that is adequate for fiction work. To ensure a paragraph is well developed, a writer has at his disposal several tools:

<u>Analysis:</u> Analyze and describe the topic; define the paragraph's terms

<u>Narrative:</u> include elements or parts of the story or their origins

<u>Description:</u> paint verbal pictures of the topic

<u>Comparison and contrast:</u> how things, issues, or ideas share similarities or differences

<u>Evaluating cause and effect:</u> causes, reasons, the causal relationship between things, the effects of actions and their consequences

> A woven band on my wrist carried my name, Anya. Mother made it two nights before as a parting gift even though we both knew no slave would be allowed to keep such a trinket. I slipped it into the pocket of my breeches and smoothed the fabric over the lump—an insignificant tangle of yarn that represented my mother's love.[136]

In this paragraph, the writer offers a topic: "a woven band." She then goes on to naming its origins, (mother made it) its reason (a parting gift) and its consequences (a lump in her breeches). She then compares "woven band" to "tangle of yarn."

---

[135] Michael Keyton, *Mr. Nousel's Mirror*

[136] Wendy Swore, *Colorless*

 4.5.5 PARAGRAPHING

And here we come to the crux of the matter. How do we decide when to start a new paragraph or to keep writing in the one we're in?

Every paragraph implies a switch in the focus of a story. As writers become more confident, they sense natural places to end a paragraph or begin new ones. But some writers—like us—never become confident enough and must think hard. Here are some situations when we should end one paragraph and start another:

To shift between the actions of different characters.

If we're writing about the actions of Jon, a fearless dwarf hopelessly in love with Chanelle, a water nymph, we should change paragraphs to describe her actions. There's a golden rule in fiction: one player, one paragraph.

To signal new ideas.

This should be easy, but it isn't. In a nutshell; if we're writing about something and decide to write about something else, the change merits a paragraph break. The problem is not to determine which sentences deal with one topic and which with another, but the transition sentences. These are the no man's land between ideas.

It's up to the writer to determine which ideas he wants the reader to closely associate with. Since this issue touches the realm of individual style and aesthetic considerations, we can offer no further help.

To denote a shift in time or place.

Whenever moving from one place to the next or when shifting in time, even if it's only a few minutes, it's a good idea to signal the event with a paragraph break.

> An ambulance pulled up to the door and people swarmed out of the hospital on cue. Now or never. I walked into the side door.
> The smell of death, medicine, and stale antiseptic stung my nose. Ignored by nurses and doctors bustling about, people waited in the lobby, their faces blank and tired as if the world had chewed them up until there was nothing left. I hated hospitals.[137]

In the previous example the writers signal the change in place with a paragraph break. It's worth noting that in the second paragraph Rita and Wendy have set the topic sentence last. The central descriptive sentence is hemmed by two related ones to round off a coherent paragraph.

To emphasize points.

If an item, concept, or idea is important enough, the writer may want to emphasize it, in particular if the distinction is a subtle one. In the example, Michael Keyton insists on the binomial

---

[137] Wendy Swore & Rita Webb, *Strike*

"return/returned." He could have joined both paragraphs, but the emphasis on a keyword is a signpost for the reader. "Returning" has a meaning that transcends the word.

> She had returned to find Andrew in ferment, engaged to a vain empty-headed creature and oblivious to advice. She hadn't offered any. She knew Andrew too well. Instead she had quietly resumed her role as Mistress of the house, arranging in minute detail every aspect of the wedding, and in all essentials but one, the honeymoon itself.
> On their return, Celia had remained in the shadows, an invisible force, lost in the backwash of nuptial bliss. Marianne, like her husband, had soon found Celia a vital part of her life, as did Eleanor when she eventually took up residence at Pemberley Lodge.[138]

 **To change speakers, characters or narrators.**

Here, we must repeat: one player, one paragraph.

> Wilkes hadn't left by the back door. He waited, clinging to the kitchen ceiling.
> As I charged in, he dropped on me, swinging a tremendous punch to my mouth. I felt the acid flare of agony as teeth shattered. He gripped me by the throat but I wasn't a dentist. I rammed a finger in his eye and head-butted him on the nose. Blood sprayed in my face as if from a hose.
> Wilkes, or whatever was in Wilkes, howled, letting go of my throat and punching me in the ribs as I tried to wipe his blood from my eyes.[139]

In the previous passage, Wilkes (or whatever is in him/it) has separate paragraphs from that of the POV, even though all three share the same narrator.

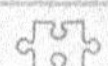 **To mark a POV shift**

The correct and sensible way of denoting POV shifts is through a section change, since we believe that scenes should be shown through a single POV. Many writers don't agree and change POV mid-scene. There's nothing wrong with this practice, if done seamlessly. In these instances, the reader deserves a little warning, at least with a paragraph break.

 **To break up long paragraphs**

Many readers have a pet peeve about long paragraphs and often return a book to the bookshop shelf after spotting pages of solid text. Savvy writers, rather than risking a sale, prefer to break long paragraphs—even those syntactically above board. To do so, they insert a line of exposition, description, a dialogue line, or a gesture from a listener, even if it doesn't amount to more than nose scratching. It's a sign of the times that blocks of text, and the ideas they attempt to develop, shrink rapidly to a point where we will soon be asked to limit paragraph extension to a single line. But we count ourselves lucky. Perhaps, paragraphs longer than five words might be enough reason to reject the manuscripts of the future.

---

138 Michael Keyton, Neut

139 Paul Mitton, Yellowfang, Ménage à 20, Tales With a Hook

 **4.5.5.1 PARAGRAPHING DIALOGUE**

In creative writing, whether fiction or non-fiction, the first rule is to keep one idea to one paragraph.

Following the golden rule, paragraphing dialogue is easy: one player, one paragraph.

And now for a snippet of trivia: The word "paragraph" has its root in "paragraphos," the Greek word describing a line marking a change in the speakers of dialogue.

As usual with the English language, in general, and creative writing in particular, rules are not cast in stone. Sometimes, separating attributions can alter the flow of dialogue, and it's up to the writer to choose how to break paragraphs.

The following example is from a conversation between a thirteen-year-old girl and a Gypsy soothsayer. There are two speakers, and the writer doesn't want to use tags.

> "My name is Maria—"
> "No, no." The gypsy didn't let go of my hand. "Your name is Cordova. Maria is for nuns and holy women. Cordova will darken your shadow."
> "What's the matter with my shadow?"
> "Some people's shadows are dark and strong. Others are gray, their edges hazy, uncertain, feeble. Shadows have more to do with the soul than the body."
> I relaxed, my hand engulfed in the gypsy's warm fingers.
> "A faint shadow and a strong character, a strange combination." She peered into my eyes, her earrings dancing, stealing golden sparkles from the strong sun seeping through the netting. "What made you come here?"
> "I needed to know."
> "With the last of your money?"
> I nodded.
> Creases in the gypsy's face rearranged like disturbed waters in a pool and her eyes closed. "You must strengthen your shadow."
> "How can I do that?"
> "Listen and learn from everyone, even the dull and ignorant, and never speak to hear your own voice. Above all, don't let anyone see the person that gazes at you from the mirror or show them the pictures that comfort you at night."[140]

Strictly speaking, in the previous dialogue there are two paragraphs (numbers two and six) with attributes from the POV on the Gypsy's lines. To give their own paragraph to "The gypsy didn't let go of my hand." and "She peered into my eyes, her earrings dancing, stealing golden sparkles from the strong sun seeping through the netting." would interfere with the rhythm of the conversation.

---

[140] Carlos J Cortés, *Cordova*

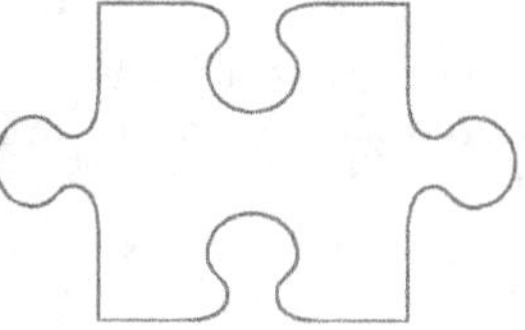

5 THE PRESENTATION

Presentation is important. Before a date, an important meeting, or an engagement where we want to present our best image, we lavish copious amounts of time and attention on our appearance. We know there's a difference between turning up at our appointment wearing jeans, a T-shirt, our prize baseball cap, and flip-flops and arriving draped in a dove-gray Armani suit.

When we write a first draft (here "we" stands for Renée and Carlos), our routine already takes into account from page one that we will have to set our chapters and scenes in order. We open files for notes, loose thoughts, bits of information connected with our plot however tenuously, and an assortment of sentences, odd lines and items we might use in blurbs or bullets.

As we write, we never forget that sooner or later we'll need a synopsis, an outline, a proposal, and a format for our manuscript to look its best. In a way, we keep in mind that our manuscript has a future date. Rather than leaving everything for a mighty last-minute rush and risk arriving late to the party, we prepare clothes and accessories to dress our work as we go along.

The present chapter covers the aspects of writing, structuring and formatting a writer will need to present his work to prospective buyers, or to compose and format his polished manuscript for beta readers or reviewers.

New writers often ask what's the most important aspect to consider once a first draft is over, and we always answer: "the presentation you make before your first readers."

It's impossible to gather valuable feedback from our beta readers and reviewers if we feed them a jumble of pages, because every time something doesn't fit they'll stop reading and loose the story thread.

This section examines the steps and techniques to organize a manuscript for presentation in society.

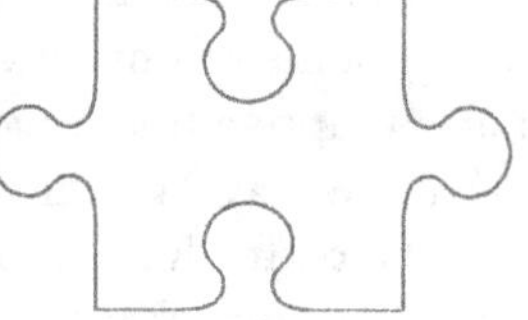

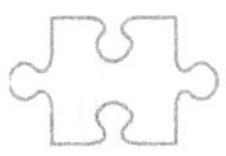 # 5.1 DRAFTING

There's an old parable about a rich man who wanted to learn the history of Humanity. He summoned a historian and commissioned him to write it. When the historian returned one year later with a tome, the rich man complained that he didn't have the time to read such a voluminous book and wanted it condensed.

The historian set to work and produced, one month later, a much streamlined book. But the rich man wasn't satisfied. Could he abbreviate it further? Make it concise and linear? The next day, the historian returned with a single sheet of paper. On it he had condensed the linear history of Humanity: "After birth, people love, suffer, and die."

Linearity is a trait of all animate and most inanimate processes. Writing is no different. We write, carry on writing, and stop when we've committed our thoughts to text. Writing a letter, a list, an essay, or a novel are linear processes: we start at one point and finish at the other.

For writers, the process starts at draft then goes through editing, formatting, and submission to end at publication.

The particulars of each step are as individual and idiosyncratic as the writer. There are guidelines, and even strict rules dictated by custom, grammar, agents, publishing houses, critics, and editors. Still, many aspects of writing are flexible. What matters is to start and finish with having achieved what we set out to do.

Perhaps some will complain that the process is different for a new writer as compared with a household name, but that would be a myopic view.

A consecrated writer—one of the industry's sacred cows—follows *exactly* the same process: he writes, polishes, formats, submits, and publishes. Of course, after the writing is done, he could leave the drudgery of the following steps in the hands of indentured scribes. The submission would probably be done even before he set to write the book and its publication is assured.

Yet, if our imaginary famous writer didn't want to rewrite, polish, or format, he would need to pass onto his ghost writer, book doctor, or editor, a physical item termed a draft. It couldn't consist of a pile of papers or loose computer files without order or sequence, or the workers wouldn't know where to start. The item or file must be structured to be read linearly.

The following pages don't explain how to write a draft. After all, most of this book is dedicated to that. Rather, we want to share our experience with the different processes to turn blocks of text into manuscript, outline, synopsis, blurb, and bullet drafts.

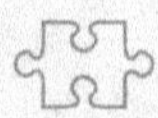 **5.1.1 FIRST DRAFT**

The form of the actual page we face when hammering away at our keyboard is one of the pet peeves of every writer we know.[141] Some writers use a pre-formatted template (there's a link to one on page 432) others use a word processor blank template with little or no formatting, others still use software programs, or write away in the throes of inspiration until they reach the end and pack it up in a single file.

There's nothing wrong with either approach to writing, but some practices waste precious time and often turn what could be a straightforward process into a nightmare.

Word processors are wonderful instruments for writers, even though most of us use a small percentage of their capacity and features.

To start writing a novel on the first white space that flashes upon our screen is not easier than preparing our work space to do many things automatically for us, instead of leaving everything for the formatting stage.

For example: Imagine a writer colleague confessed that he doesn't capitalize or use punctuation when drafting. Again, there's nothing wrong in such a practice, but we shudder to think about the harrowing job of navigating through such a manuscript inserting capital letters and commas. Most of us would consider such a manner of working wasteful. The same is true of indents, italics, centering, as well as chapter and section breaks. Why leave everything for the end? A few minutes spent preparing the workspace can save many hours of thankless misery. The instructions to prepare a manuscript template are on pages 432 and 433.

Though the area where we work is a personal element, we recommend using the same manuscript template we would use for submission. Why? Because the conversion to manuscript format later on may cause the loss of whatever formatting we've used in the draft. For example: italics.

In addition, working always with the same document format soon becomes a routine, every line is more focused and there's no physical difference from draft to finished manuscript.

There's another bonus. Most editors worth their salt never edit on-screen documents. On paper, errors leap from the page, and penning annotations is easier and more focused. In our opinion, editing, polishing, and appending notes for rewrite should be done on a physical copy.

If we've worked in manuscript format, printing it is a question of striking a key and the product is ready for the next stage.

Filing

Most writers use one of two mechanics to produce a draft:

1. Write away, inserting scene breaks until they reach THE END.

2. Write away, inserting scene breaks until they reach the end of a chapter.

Each procedure has advantages and disadvantages.

---

[141] We assume that most writers reading this book use a computer and a word processor.

In 1, the advantage is that on rewrite we can insert chapter breaks after having addressed major flaws, additions, and deletions. The disadvantage is that working with a long document and revising details previously written can be difficult and time-consuming.

In 2, the advantages and disadvantages of 1 are reversed. On rewrite, we might find that the original chapter breaks are no longer adequate, though locating particular blocks of text, errors, weak verbs, or plot holes is easier.

Our working routine varies; one of us works with the full document while the other works with chapters. But both of us keep track of scene first lines and their locations.

When we finish a scene, we open a file named "Scene Lines" copy-paste the first line and append a page number.

Later, on reaching page 340, we may draw a blank. The restaurant porter who opened the door for Tatiana at the beginning of the book... what was his name? A quick glance over scene first lines will identify the text where Igor Voinovich planted the listening device in Tatiana's purse.

Once the draft is finished, we recommend compiling it into a single document [142] and numbering the pages sequentially. When we work on several manuscripts at the time, we append the manuscript's title to the top of each page. Disaster strikes proportional to Murphy's Law. Trying to match the scattered pages Fido left in his wake is for masochists.

 ### 5.1.2 SECOND DRAFT

After we have compiled the first draft, we print it, grab a few pages, and move over to a different setting, perhaps the living room, or the garage where we hide from the moles or whatever the dogs bring in, or the back yard if there are no icicles dangling from the roof edges. We do this to change our mindset: from creator to inquisitor.

Prose's best friend is a little hostility. By changing the format (from screen to paper) and the environment (from our den or corner of the garage to another setting) we change the perspective from which we view our work.

The sheets with lines of words look different, even a little alien, as if produced by someone else. Now we only need to concentrate, and repeat several times: "This was written by the guy who ran away with my baseball cards (or my Barbie, take your pick)." Suitably primed, we grab our red pen and attack the pages until they bleed.

 ### 5.1.3 FINAL DRAFT

After tearing through the pages written by our worst enemy, we settle back at our computer to change, replace, rewrite, add a little, and delete vast quantities of useless dribble. While we do this, we try to straighten sentences, get rid of typos and spelling mistakes. This is the document we'll forward to our priceless Beta Readers.

---

[142] We assume that at draft stage most writers work on small documents containing a single chapter or a part, since the full manuscript may be cumbersome.

Why so much work before we send out the draft to be read? After all, we may have to change many things. This is a legitimate comment, but one that doesn't take into account the way we read. It's difficult to concentrate when plodding through a manuscript riddled with errors, and we don't want our readers to stumble at every other line.

The distance between the final draft and the polished manuscript will depend on the speed with which our Beta Readers return their comments. The interim is a time to start another project, take a vacation, or—more likely—tend to the chores we've neglected during our writing stint. A couple of weeks or longer should afford us distance to change our perspective yet again in preparation for the last hurdle. Our readers will deliver their opinions, rants, praises, and caveats, which we must address with a cool head. We must mull and digest each comment before doing anything about it. When we're ready, we add our final changes, apply a strict manuscript format to our document and print on our home printer for the last time (the next will be on high-speed machines working triple shifts to keep up with demand).

5.1.4 POLISHED MANUSCRIPT

This is the document we must address as technicians, not as writers. The plot, sub-plots, pace, continuity, POV, characterization, and many other story issues are behind us. Those who can afford a good copy-editor will entrust the document to his or her tender mercies. The rest of us will struggle to do our best. This is the time to line edit and scour the manuscript for syntax flaws, repetitions, poor grammar, typos, vocabulary, usage, and other unaddressed horrors.

A good editor—one that has been professionally scrounging a living out of copy-editing all his life—will proofread three-thousand words in one hour and copy-edit about half that. Naturally, if the work entails substantial fact-checking, continuity and syntax errors galore, the sky is the limit.

For us, editing more than four or five pages in one hour is beyond our reach. Consequently, polishing a full-sized novel will take about one-hundred hours. Not surprisingly, that's about the time that a professional editor will invest, at an average hourly rate of $20 to $30+. The difference is that a professional editor will do a much better job than we can ever hope for.

How can a writer, turned inexperienced editor, proofread a novel in a day or two is beyond comprehension; in-house editors roll their eyes in dismay when they hear such things. Our advice is to dedicate many hours to polish a manuscript, unless we can afford an editor, or seduce one to do it for free.

Once we transfer our findings to the master document in our computer, we will own a polished manuscript.

5.1.5 OUTLINE DRAFT

When an agent or publisher asks a writer to prepare an outline, also termed a "chapter-by-chapter synopsis" it's time for jubilation, soon followed by a sober feeling of despair. On the one hand, the request means that his work has cleared several hurdles and it is being seriously considered for representation or publication. On the other, an outline represents preparing one synopsis for each chapter; in a full-sized novel with forty chapters, this means forty synopses. If this is not enough to merit despair, we don't know what qualifies.

But condensing chapters has a positive side; it forces the writer to learn how to pack the gist of several pages into a paragraph or two. This is a priceless exercise, a boon when crafting manuscript synopses.

The draft of an outline can take many shapes, but in our experience, one of the most effective is to include excerpts of the actual text. Later, when rewriting, polishing, and editing, the mini-blurbs in each chapter outline can help focus the contents.

The example that follows is from the outline of The Damn Book, one of Carlos's follies, a thriller romp about the search for a book purportedly written by Fulcanelli, the last of the great alchemists.

The underscored passages are the fragments of text to accompany the chapter synopsis.

 **5.1.5.1 CHAPTER ONE**

<u>"Eighty pounds? Do I hear one hundred?" He didn't, but on the third row the little guy with the goatee nodded once.</u>

Zvi gets a Bible when a judge auctions the estate of an eccentric and ruined noble, the Earl of Chiswick, to pay his many debts.

The library is auctioned as one lot but is far too expensive. Zvi buys two boxes of assorted books gathered from other rooms of the house an auctioneer's assistant will later deliver on a trolley to his car.

When he's about to leave, Zvi is accosted by a tall man who introduces himself as Lionheart Flimsbender and offers to buy the lot for one thousand, twice what he's paid for the books. Zvi refuses. Then, two police officers stroll in their direction. Zvi jumps into his car and drives away.

5.1.5.2 CHAPTER TWO

Zvi goes home. As he unloads the boxes off his car, helped by his five-year-old daughter and Elle, a local constable, he spots a car with darkened windows cruising past his house.

Unnerved, he rushes into his house. Elle writes down the car number. He fields a phone call from the same man who offered to buy the bible. But he refuses to sell.

In a country house, Lionheart debates what to do next. Over many months, he's traced the whereabouts of Fulcanelli's Bible. Now the Jew has the Bible. Waterfind Inc. is Lionheart's business, a corporation dedicated to locating mineral and water resources. With a little electronic device of his invention—to amplify telluric currents—his trained dowsers can pinpoint the position of mineral or water deposits.

At a gathering with his seven most trusted lieutenants, he proposes how to recover the Bible.

<u>"We must convince the little Jew."</u>

<u>The orange burst with a soft slosh. Juice spurted in all directions and trickled along his arm, soaking his shirtsleeve.</u>

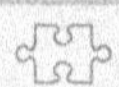 **5.1.5.3 CHAPTER THREE**

"Go back inside the house."
Zvi pushed Adah roughly.
The little girl opened her eyes wide and stared uncomprehendingly as Zvi debated what to do next.
"Mum is doing the dishes; go help her while I get the car out."
Adah hesitated.
"Please, darling, do as I say."
She made an I'll-never-understand-adults face, turned on her heel, and carted her satchel back to the kitchen.
Zvi let his breath out. Mercifully, she hadn't spotted Manuel, the house cat, nailed to the door.
Then Zvi hears a meow. He turns to see Manuel. He peers back at the door to discover it's a moth-eaten rabbit pelt and some red paint, but the meaning is obvious.
Lionheart calls in person. He seems shocked to see the cat. He offers to buy the Bible Zvi has bought at the sale. Zvi refuses, and threatens to go to the police.
They take the girl to school. When they return, the house has been ransacked and the walls painted with strange symbols. Lionheart phones. Zvi hangs up on him and goes to the police station. When they return, his car has been torched. Zvi blows a fuse. The police offer excuses, but no one seems to have seen who threw the Molotov cocktail. Lionheart rings again to tell him his daughter is next. "You have my number." The couple races to the school to find the little girl crying. A tall man very pale and thin has thrown a dead big black bird (a crow) at her feet. When they return home, Zvi has lost the will to fight.
"What are we going to do?"
Zvi squeezed Mahola's hand. "Do? There's only one thing we can do. Give the swine what he wants."
As he reaches for the phone to call his tormentor and sell him the Bible, it dawns on him Lionheart Flimsbender is an anagram for "hell fire and brimstone."

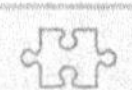 **5.1.5.4 CHAPTER FOUR**

"Will you stop fidgeting and start again at the beginning?"
Scared stiff, Zvi takes the Bible to his old friend Tyler, who tells him all that's happened and sells him the Bible for five-hundred pounds; five times what he paid for it. Then he calls Lionheart and tells him he doesn't own the Bible anymore.
In the evening, the family goes to a takeout and then the cinema. When the family returns home, flames lick the top deck.
Framed against the reddish glare of leaping flames, Zvi gapes at a silhouette he'd only seen before on films: someone attired in KKK garb moved on the first floor, a flaming torch in his hand.

 **5.1.5.5 CHAPTER FIVE**

Gordon stared at the telephone handset where an insect, seemingly trapped inside the earpiece, droned away. What is in that Bible? He stood, ambled to the bookcase housing religious works and reached for the one he'd bought from Zvi. He hefted it in his hand, checked an upper shelf, and picked a second one identical to the first; same type, edition, and binding.

Gordon Tyler hears of the fire and inspects the Bible. He owns a copy of the same Bible, and after comparing them, he fails to spot any difference. Then he fields a threatening phone call from Lionheart. Tyler calls the police and hands to them *his* Bible. He calls Zvi, tells him that he's swapped Bibles but not that he's sent the original to Claire, a book restorer.

When Lionheart rings again, Gordon tells him the police have the Bible. Although the police are listening, Lionheart hangs up before they can track the call. The same evening, a violent fire breaks out close to the local police constabulary. In the confusion, a band of hooded men attack the station, knock out the only cop not helping with the fire and ransack the evidence room, making off with the bogus Bible.

"Check outside. We're taking our baby home were she belongs."

"She?"

"Fickle, mysterious, and hard to get. Definitely a she."

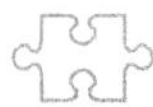

These excerpts are as rough as they come, laden with extraneous information, redundant in a synopsis or outline. When we get around to polishing the outline, the order of the day will be to cut every irrelevant detail, to pare down the résumé to a fraction. Let's examine the contents of chapter one:

 **5.1.5.6 CHAPTER ONE FIRST REVISION**

"Eighty pounds? Do I hear one hundred?" He didn't, but on the third row the little guy with the goatee nodded once.

Zvi gets a Bible when a judge auctions the estate of **an eccentric and** ruined noble, **the Earl of Chiswick, to pay his many debts**.

The library is **auctioned as one lot but** far too expensive. Zvi buys two boxes of assorted books gathered from other rooms of the house **an auctioneer's assistant will later deliver on a trolley to his car**.

When **he's** about to leave, Zvi **is accosted by** a **tall** man who introduces himself as Lionheart Flimsbender **and** offers to buy the lot for one thousand, twice what he's paid for the books. Zvi refuses. **Then, two police officers stroll in their direction. Zvi jumps into his car and drives away.**

The sections in bold are chaff, irrelevant in a synopsis. Though the details might be important enough for micro-managing the narrative line, they don't add to the storyline.

After a first pass, the chapter outline would read something like:

5.1.5.7 CHAPTER ONE SECOND REVISION

"Eighty pounds? Do I hear one hundred?" He didn't, but on the third row the little guy with the goatee nodded once.

Zvi gets a Bible when a judge auctions the state of a ruined noble. The library is far too expensive, so he buys two boxes of assorted books gathered from other rooms of the house.

When Zvi is about to leave, a man who introduces himself as Lionheart Flimsbender offers to buy the lot for one thousand, twice the knock down value of the books. Zvi refuses.

After reducing the text—except the quoted passage—to about half its original length, it's ready for polishing. The original chapter is over three-thousand words long, which we have condensed to its plot points.

5.1.6 SYNOPSIS DRAFT

When we outline a plot for a novel, the first thing we prepare is a rough synopsis draft, often just a few lines with the main plot points. This example is the original draft synopsis from Mahdi, a thriller by Carlos J Cortes.

Mahdi
Synopsis

Mahdi: The Guided One; an eschatological figure; the prophesied redeemer of Islam.

Like scores before him over the last five hundred years, Jameel Muhammad Ibn Rushd is a self-proclaimed Mahdi but, unlike his predecessors, he's using Jihad to cripple the West. Yet, Jameel knows that he needs a miracle to win.

Out of London, an aircraft explodes in midair. A mine sinks a cruise liner at Haifa. In Tel-Aviv, a suicide bomber blows up a school bus, and a devastated Prime Minister swears to avenge the children regardless of political cost. Then, a team of British-Israeli archaeologists excavating in Qumran unearths clues to an impossible document. The first century AD Ben Sanbatis Chronicle, with a different account of the New Testament, could be the Mahdi's miracle.

Hounded by Mahdi fanatics, the archaeologists follow a two-thousand-year-old trail across three continents, when a giant awakens. The Vatican will place the Mahdi within Israel's reach in exchange for the Chronicle.

Later, as the writing progresses and the storyline gathers focus, the synopsis grows to incorporate details and elements that flesh the finished product. On finishing the manuscript's draft, this was the state of the draft full synopsis:

Mahdi
Synopsis

The Mahdi or Rightly-guided One is an Islamic eschatological figure. Mahdi is a title: redeemer or savior, as the Christ or Messiah of Christian tradition.

Over the past five-hundred years, many have professed to be the Mahdi and had varying degrees of success in convincing fellow Muslims of their station. This work of fiction touches the struggle for recognition of a self-proclaimed Mahdi, his gestation, trajectory and eventual clash with the living realities of our society.

The Middle East and Europe have endured an unprecedented wave of terror. Governments know little but the name behind the bombings: Jameel Mohammad Ibn Rushd, the Mahdi. Jameel uses doubles and lives simply, cared for by his followers in villages or the desert. He shares his tent with a thirteen-year-old boy. A hacker known as "ghost," his neural system. Like his charge, Jameel is little more than a shadow to security agencies and the intelligence community. He shuns public appearances and has never been photographed. Some even doubt the Mahdi is a single man, but an organization using such a name. But Jameel knows his time is running out and that only a miracle can make reality his dream of a universal Islam.

By the Dead Sea, a British-Israeli archeological team digs under Qumran. Professors Aurelio Hawkins and Nell Keating discover a fiendishly hidden library of scrolls. But the Israelis don't share the British scholars' enthusiasm. Since Essenian writings wouldn't merit such an elaborate hiding place, the repository could be a prop to hide Temple relics. Unwilling to risk having to share sacred artifacts, the Israelis expel the British archeologists. Nell returns to England bewildered by Aurelio's studied indifference; unknown to her, he's stolen a codex from the dig.

In the codex Aurelio finds four diagrams hidden in its wooden covers. The pages are those of a Pinakes, a catalogue listing The Royal Library of Alexandria's contents. On the last page there's a list of documents, including an exchange of letters between Roman and Judean authorities and the chronicle of Ben Sanbatis, a Temple scribe. If found, these documents would portray a vastly different account of the Christian New Testament.

When the Mahdi learns of the theft, he has a vision. The codex could unlock his elusive miracle. The faithful must have these documents at any cost.

After spotting strangers at a house across the street, Aurelio realizes he's a marked man. To flee his home, he packs the dismantled codex and his notes in an envelope with his clinical history, stages a heart attack, and summons an ambulance. The paramedics call Nell.

The Mahdi followers murder Aurelio, and Nell calls Yehudi Ben Shahar, a colleague from the Israel Ministry of Antiquities. The Israelis spirit Nell and the codex back to Jerusalem where she joins Yehudi and a team of experts to search for the texts.

Israel has been suffering more than any other country the Mahdi's terror, and its Government is in disarray. Their intelligence services fight internecine wars and blame one another for their inability to apprehend the Mahdi. Then a suicide bomber blows up a school bus in downtown Tel Aviv, killing the Minister of the Interior's grandsons.

Nell enters a parallel world of intrigue, a shady war with lopsided ethics and morals, where armies swap flags in mid-battle. There she finds love with Yehudi. The couple, hounded by the Mahdi fanatics, follows the diagram's thread through Yumbulagang in Tibet to another Essenian settlement by Lake Mareotis in Egypt.

In Israel, the Prime Minister realizes the Mahdi issue is no longer a security or political concern but—as their millennia-long struggle—a fight for survival. He asks his ministers to name the best mind in Israel. Then he gives Colonel Yitzhak Maccobi authority over Israel's forces and carte blanche to find and destroy the Mahdi.

Maccobi knows the Mahdi wants the documents to attempt proving his prophet is the only one, and spread Islam. He also knows the Vatican would dearly like to secure the manuscripts and strikes a deal: Israel will swap the documents for the Mahdi.

The archeologists discover the Library's hiding place but are caught in the crossfire of the different groups vying for the document's possession. Yehudi is shot and abandoned in the desert. Then, after a virtuoso display of high-tech and old-fashioned Machiavellian maneuvering, the Mossad and the Vatican succeed in springing a trap to lure the Mahdi. The deed done, the unlikely allies spirit the Mahdi's corpse to Israel, leaving Nell alone to meet Father Kiral, the brain behind the Vatican plan. Kiral patches Nell's tortured soul as she mourns Yehudi. She must deliver the documents to Rome.

At the Vatican, a frail Pope explains why the manuscripts should be buried and humanity's need to be nurtured regardless of books, names, or interpretations. Before she leaves, His Holiness ponders the nature of small miracles: Yehudi is alive.

The writer has split the draft synopsis into three sections. The first paragraph explains the meaning of the term "Mahdi," since non-Muslims wouldn't be familiar with the title.

The manuscript opens with a prologue. The second paragraph is its synopsis, a necessary item to better understand the Mahdi's role.

Finally, the following blocks of text are the body of the draft synopsis.

The draft synopsis contains over eight-hundred words, or a little over three pages of double-spaced text—a tad long. This needs to be addressed on rewrite. Most of the adjectives are redundant, as are descriptive items and the bits the writer inserted because he loved them and not out of necessity. For example:

Then, <u>after a virtuoso display of high-tech and old-fashioned Machiavellian maneuvering,</u> the Mossad and the Vatican <u>succeed in</u> springing a trap to lure the Mahdi.

The underlined items might add color, but these have no room in a synopsis. The paragraph needs to be much leaner:

Then, the Mossad and the Vatican spring a trap to lure the Mahdi.

When this rough project of a synopsis is polished and whittled down to essentials, it should occupy two pages of double-spaced text.

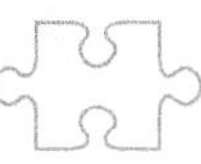

5.2 OTHER MANUSCRIPT ITEMS

5.2.1 THE BLURB

Blurbs, in fiction work, are the teasers on the back of paperbacks or the inside flap of hardcover books. They are brief pieces of writing used in the advertising of a creative work. Here, the capital word is "advertising." Whenever we observe prospective buyers at bookstores or airports, they are busy reading blurbs.

Most blurbs strive to convey the idea that the work is unique, breathtaking, leading people to conclude that *they need* to read the book at once, before anybody else. Alternatively, blurbs can stress the work's shock value and wet the prospective reader's appetite with phrases emphasizing its bizarre or unexpected themes.

Structurally, blurbs are blocks of text containing anything from 50 to 250 words.

Writing a blurb is not easy. The text cannot be a synopsis, since we don't want to give away the plot, but a carefully constructed hook to entice the reader to buy the book. Style wise, a blurb owes more to the craft of reporting and media headlines than fiction writing.

To learn effective blurb writing, nothing can beat reading, copying, and painstakingly studying the blurbs in successful books. We recommend that writers analyze style, structure, voice, length, and vocabulary. Another issue to examine in depth is the relationship (plot wise) between the blurb and the actual plot of the novel. In this sense, it's better to work with the blurbs in books we've actually read.

The material for blurbs should be gathered in a separate file, as soon as we start writing. This is the place to collect lines, details, and items with which to craft page-long pieces.

Once the blocks of text are about five-hundred words long it's time to start whittling down the prose and reduce the contents to its bare minimum.

A blurb should be succinct, active, and filled with strong verbs, adjectives, and nouns. In a word: powerful.

Formatting the blurb should be the same as the manuscript: double-spaced and all-round inch margins. This arrangement helps on-paper editing.

We recommend including blurbs, bullets, and other material suitable for promotion separate from the manuscript, since the final text of the blurbs is normally agreed in conjunction with the publisher's marketing department.

5.2.2 BULLET

What is a bullet? Everybody makes lists, and word processors have handy little dots, symbols or dingbats to enhance the list's items:

Grab pen.

Steal paper.

These are bullet points. We can imagine readers scratching their heads in puzzlement. What has this to do with fiction? The bullet point is not the symbol, but the text.

A bullet point is a short summation of a key point, the gist of an idea, and these can add much value to the cover or front matter if used well. In other words, bullets are snippets of marketing designed to whet the appetite of onlookers.

We're writing our novel about hermaphrodite aliens (pages 51 to 57) and would love to compile a list of bullets we might use as teasers.

Is ~~him,~~ ~~her,~~ it. It?

There's a breeder…

But these feel incomplete, no? And that's the idea, because a bullet point is not necessarily a sentence, but the fragment of a teaser. Too many times, writers put complete sentences as bullet points. This defeats the object of a bullet point, which is to convey the germ of a key point, a tantalizing set of words.

We format these in single lines on a separate document, a spare file we title "Bullets" where we add the weirdest of concepts and lines as we write the body of our book. Later, when the manuscript is ready for publication, we reach for our bullet file to tweak, rearrange, and play with our disconnected ideas until the gold nuggets shine through.

In a world made of lies, the truth is about to break free…[143]

A bloody secret that someone will kill to keep…[144]

Finally, there are other bullets, exchanged from fellow writers or collected from reviews after the first edition:

Astounding… awesomely crafted… desperately readable…[145]

Stunning… A novel that is both literary and a page-turner…[146]

---

[143] Carlos J Cortes, *The Prisoner*

[144] Joseph Geary, *Mirror*

[145] Twenty Writers, *Ménageà 20, Tales With a Hook*

[146] Kate Quinn, *Mistress of Rome*

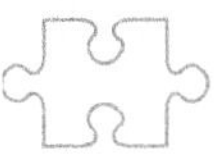

5.3 FORMATTING

When submitting a query to agents or publishers, their instructions always include a word count and specific formatting requirements. Unknown to many, this is overkill, since traditional formatting will provide a rough page count, reinforced by the word count from the word processor.

Accurate word count is essential in the translation industry, since translations are often billed by words on the final document. Naturally, a translation contract involves a fixed price, which in turn requires accurate word-counting. To make matters more complicated, some languages require more words than others to express a similar idea.

Take Spanish, for example. When translating from English into Spanish, the number of words increases by about seven percent.

In fiction manuscripts, we don't need such accurate counting mechanisms because publishers only need to know page count and not word count.

In the bygone times of typewriters, page count gave an estimated word count. With the advent of computers, the industry dictated formatting norms to determine page count, by specifying a monospace typeface of a certain size and a standard page format. Unfortunately, Microsoft, and other word-processor producers, soon replaced their traditional monospace typeface with Times New Roman, a proportional typeface.

This seemingly small change resulted in much confusion. While a few die-hard advocates of tradition doggedly stuck to the old ways, others moved with the times, while writers struggled to comply with scores of different requirements from as many agents or publishers.

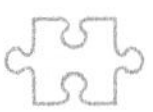

5.3.1 TYPEFACES AND FONTS

Most members of the public use the word "font" to describe types such as Courier or Times New Roman. This is wrong. Courier is a typeface.

Imagine "typeface" as a family, much like the Miller family. The family has several members that include husband and wife, children, relatives, and pets. These are the "fonts." Hence, in the Courier typeface we have Courier Bold, Courier Cursive, Courier Condensed, etc., the fonts of the Courier typeface.

Another detail to broaden our knowledge of the tools of the trade, resides in the word "serif."

In a typeface, a "serif" is the "feet" on a letter. This book is set in a serif font. Note how the base of the letter "i" broadens and splays. That little platform the "i" rests on is the letter's serif. In a sans-serif typeface, such as Arial, the "feet" are absent.

And now let's explain the differences between typefaces.

On a screen, san-serif typefaces, such as Arial or Verdana, are easier to read. Yet, the industry standards are serif typefaces, such as Times New Roman, Courier or Garamond as in The Companion.

We can write in any typeface we choose, without forgetting that sooner or later we will have to adopt an industry standard. If this is so, why not use a serif typeface to begin with?

Most publishers and agents like Times New Roman, though some old-school adherents still favor Courier. Why?

The reason is proportionality. For example:

I seem to have loved you in numberless forms

I seem to have loved you in numberless forms

The first line of this Rabindranath Tagore poem is set in Times New Roman 12 pt, the one below in Courier New 12 pt. Check the space occupied by the letters "m" and "i." In the first line, the space occupied by each letter varies. In the one below, each space is the same.

The line of verse contains thirty-six characters and eight spaces, altogether forty-four spaces are occupied. If the letters "m" and "i" are really the same size as every other letter and share the same space, we should be able to write forty-four of them under the Courier New line:

I seem to have loved you in numberless forms

mmmmmmmmmmmmmmmmmmmmmmmmmmmmmmmmmmmmmmmmmmmm

iiiiiiiiiiiiiiiiiiiiiiiiiiiiiiiiiiiiiiiiiiii

There. Forty-four. Do you still doubt? Then let's remove the ones occupying empty spaces so you can see that the number of "m's" match the number of letters on the word above.

I seem to have loved you in numberless forms

m mmmmm mm mmmmm mmmmmm mmmm mm mmmmmmmmmmmm mmmmmm

i iiii ii iiii iiiii iii ii iiiiiiiii iiiii

But if we try the same experiment with the Times New Roman line, the results are different:

I seem to have loved you in numberless forms

mmmmmmmmmmmmmmmmmmmmmmmm

iiiiiiiiiiiiiiiiiiiiiiiiiiiiiiiiiiiiiiiiiiiiiiiiiiiiiiiiiiiiiiiiiiii

Here, we could fit only twenty-four "m's" and sixty-six "i's." There's no way we can remove the letters from the empty spaces because these don't match. Courier[147] is a non-proportional, or monospace typeface where all letters occupy identical space. This means, that the number of letters and spaces in each full line written with this font is the same.

---

[147] Other non-proportional fonts besides Courier are: Brougham, Letter Gothic, Orator and Lucida Sans Typewriter.

 **5.3.1.1 REASONS BEYOND STANDARD INDUSTRY FORMATTING**

By formatting a page with 1" margins and 12 pt Courier typeface double spaced, we obtain twenty-five lines per page with exactly sixty characters on each line. The estimate is that on average, five characters + one white space = one word. So there would be, on average, ten words on each line, or on average, 250 words on a page.

By giving a word count and dividing into 250 we obtain a rough number of pages. Why rough? Because a story with many blocks of dialogue will occupy more pages with the same number of words than another with more narrative.

Naturally, when Times New Roman became the default typeface of most word processors, the 250-word page didn't work anymore: A page set in Times New Roman houses many more words due to its proportional nature.

At present, digital composition, typesetting, and processing have rendered obsolete the traditional ways of estimating page count based on formatting alone. This is the reason why agents and publishers still demand a semi-traditional formatting to ease reading and physical editing and a word count to estimate page contents.

 **5.3.1.2 WORD COUNT**

Every processor has this feature. In MS Word, the tab is on the "Tools" menu, aptly named "Word Count." The user opens the manuscript, clicks on "Tools," selects "Word Count," and a panel displays the document's statistics, including not only the number of words in the document but also lines, paragraphs, characters, and spaces.

Of course, like the 250-word page of non-proportional typefaces, word count is not exact, but a reasonable estimate, which is what agents and publishers need.

Why is word count not exact? There are many reasons. The "word count" routine houses an algorithm programmed to look at blocks of letters followed by a space and count them as words. The algorithm doesn't distinguish between letters and punctuation but excludes numbers.

Imagine we have the sentence:

Oh to be in England!

The algorithm counts "Oh to be in" as four words; groups of letters followed by a space, and "England!" as another word followed by a line break. Total five words, sixteen characters, and twenty spaces.

But if we add a space between the last word and the punctuation mark the count changes:

Oh to be in England !

Here, the algorithm counts "Oh to be in England" as five groups of letters followed by a corresponding space, and another "letter" (the exclamation point) followed by a line break. Total: six words, sixteen characters and twenty-one spaces. This is a twenty-percent increase.

This is the reason why empty spaces can throw off the word count.

The algorithm treats numbers differently and doesn't take into account footnotes and sundry other matter.

Should we worry about these discrepancies?

If the manuscript is correctly formatted, the word count provided by word processors is all we need, without entering into technical disquisitions about its accuracy. Please, don't forget that publishers want to know the number of words in a manuscript to establish page count.

What happens if my word processor doesn't have a word count? What if it has one but it doesn't work or I can't find it?

Fear not. Typing this link: http://www.wordcounttool.com/ into any browser, will access a page with a large window. Paste your text into the window and the program will deliver a word count, sufficiently accurate to pass muster with any agent or publisher.

On pages 423 to 429 we have included the mechanical data to format a manuscript to the industry standards.

5.3.2 STYLES

Paying hard-earned money for this book has been a good deed. The huge—colossal or elephantine, take your pick—royalties from sales will keep these writers away from the soup kitchen lines for a day or two. We would be ungrateful if we didn't attempt to repay your boundless generosity. Therefore, we'll share one of the most closely-guarded secrets in the publishing industry. Please hoard it, like a miser would his treasure, and divulge it to no one. If the word spreads, agents and editors won't be able to spot even before reading the first paragraph if a manuscript has been done by a professional or a dilettante. Dilettante is a nice word, it beats newbie or rookie anytime.

When agents and editors receive a proposal, synopsis, partial or manuscript, from an unknown (and often unwanted) writer, they look around to ensure they're alone and click on a tab on the uppermost toolbar of their MS Word screen. A magic tab with a funny shape and a dreadful name "reveal format":

This symbol spells doom for a careless writer. Once clicked upon, the document on the screen will instantly show if the document is properly formatted or not.

Why should that make a difference?

It goes like this: Any craftsman that doesn't take the time and effort to understand, and handle with mastery, the tools of his chosen trade, cannot be considered a professional.

Whatever we do in a document leaves behind telltale marks. Some things, like how many times a document has been used, altered, mauled, rewritten, (and by whom) are very well hidden as "metadata" and need a special application to view or remove. On the other hand, everything we add, besides letters and punctuation marks, show on the manuscript if we click on the fatidic "reveal formatting" tab.

There are two ways of using word processors. The first is casual, on whatever blank page that pops up on our screen. We use such a page to write letters, recipes with photos and drawings, cards, and leaflets and generally mess about with fancy fonts on fancier backgrounds. When facing the blank page, we start writing away. If we reach a point where italics are needed we highlight the word and click on the "italics" tab. If we want to indent the first line of a paragraph, we place the mouse cursor there and hit the indent key or five times the space bar. Do we need something centered? No problem: we hit the space bar until the thing is more or less in the middle of the page. Those more sophisticated might click on the "center" tab. Does the "Chapter" need to be lowered down the page seven spaces? Piece of cake; we hit "enter" seven times. No?

Yes, of course, that's the way to do it for a leaflet to advertise a yard sale, a note to the postman or a reminder to stick on the fridge door. But a manuscript is a serious document, perhaps the most serious document in a writer's life, and serious documents are formatted with styles, not manually-entered tabs, indents, formats or typefaces.

And the difference is?

Vast.

On a style-formatted document, the only formatting marks on view are the hard returns at the end of a paragraph and the dots signaling the interspaces between letters.

Using a word processor like a typewriter is for amateurs, not writers. It takes all of two minutes to prepare a template with styles, and save it so we can use it in the next hundred manuscripts without having to do anything else to it. Agents and editors know, and resent, that someone who has the effrontery to call himself a writer doesn't bother to learn how to use the tools of his trade.

In addition, and this is terribly time-wasting, manual format doesn't follow from one page to the other. As soon as the writer removes one block of text or adds a few lines, chances are that the formatting on the following pages will go haywire.

But there's more. If accepted, the manuscript will eventually go to a professional, who will dump the text into a composing program, such as QuarkX or InDesign. There, he will spend time removing the thousands of formatting items from the pages. And time is expensive.

So, what is a style?

A style is a set of parameters we apply to an item of text. Take "CHAPTER." It looks a bit chunky, so we'll use smallcaps instead. "CHAPTER." This is better. Then we determine where we want the word "CHAPTER" to be. We choose halfway down the page and centered. These parameters we enter in the style box and finally we name the style "Chapter."

Whenever we start a new chapter, we write Chapter 24, select it, click on the "Chapter" style and Chapter 24 will, as if by magic, format with smallcaps and position itself halfway down the page, centered, and devoid of formatting marks.

But the beauty of styles goes much further. Imagine that once the manuscript is fully formatted, we don't like the smallcaps, and would prefer capitals and bold. Easy. We open the "Chapter" style, change smallcaps to capitals, add bold, and close. Every chapter heading in the manuscript will have adopted the new format.The same is true of every other parameter in the document.

We have inserted two images of the same document; the opening page from the first chapter of Carlos's *The Prisoner*. Both show how the first page looked with "reveal format on":

Image one is the page of *The Prisoner* original manuscript formatted with styles, as delivered in 2009 to Bantam, an imprint of Random House. The page shows the unavoidable paragraph breaks the writer hit to change paragraph. Altogether there are eight signs in as many paragraphs and one after the last line to signify the text was cut there. The rest, including chapter, indents, centering, italics, and format are done with styles embedded in the template. The writer didn't need to indent paragraph or center or space anything, as the template did these things automatically. Once finished, the writer removed all extra spaces and the page was perfectly formatted.

CHAPTER 1

"Remain calm and then follow instructions"

Calm? How can anyone about to die remain calm?

Laurel Cole sniffed. The truck's enclosure had a subtle smell ingrained into its polished steel surfaces and expanded metal grilles; a smell no amount of steam and disinfectant could remove, the odor of fear: sweat tinged with a whiff of feces and vomit.

A shudder, a hollow thud and the hiss of hydraulic bolts locking. The overhead speaker continued its monotonous mantra.

"Remain calm"

The rear of the truck had coupled against the building. Laurel blinked. Although it was outside her field of vision, she knew every step of the docking procedure.

Do people scream? In retrospect, it had been a stupid question, but Laurel had asked her trainer anyway. "No. If you open your mouth before you're told to, or depart from instructions in any way, it will cost you another year."

She pushed her fingers through the wire mesh fronting her pen and narrowed her eyes as a panel behind the truck inched upwards, blinding light pouring through

Image One

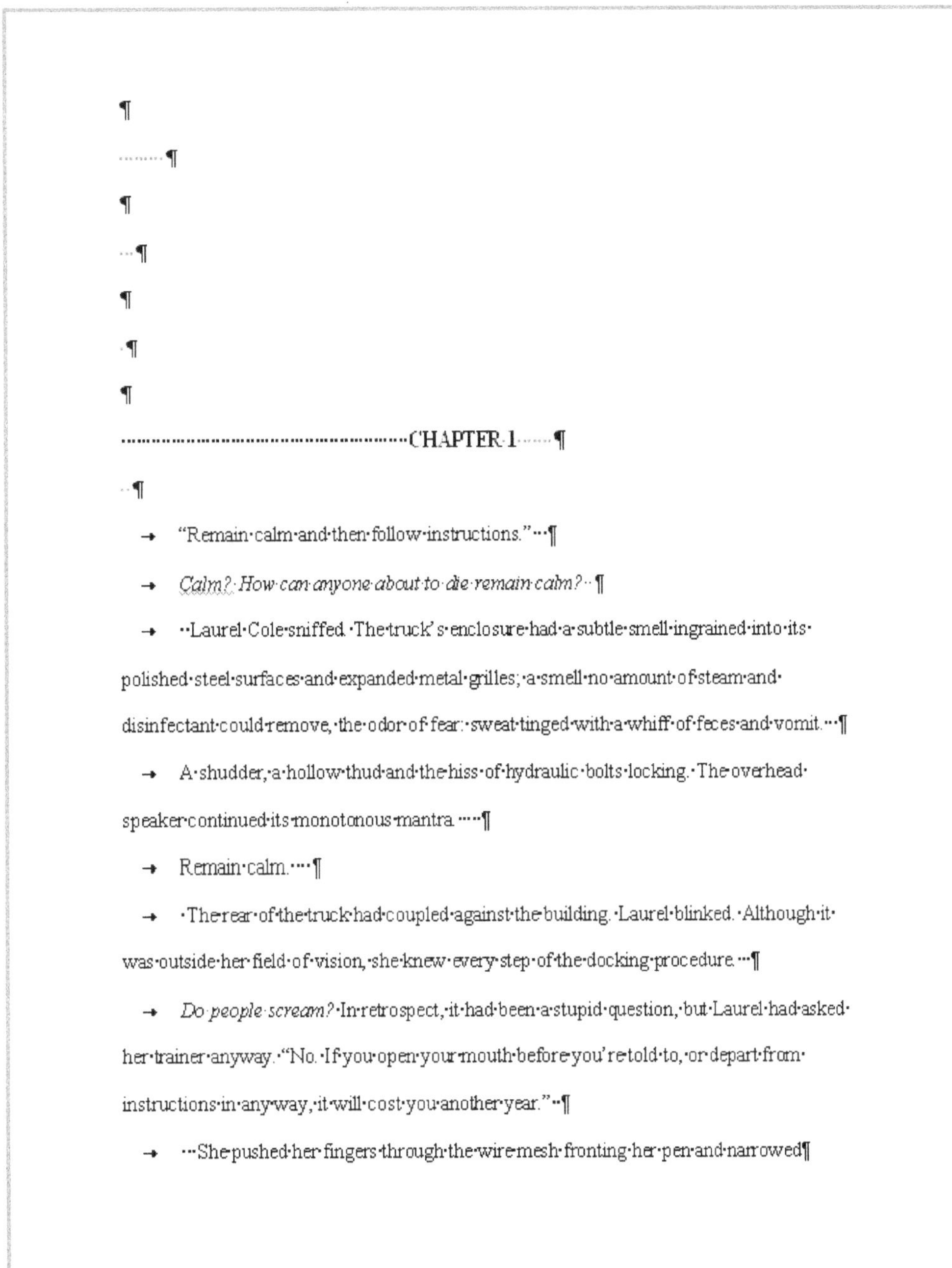

Image Two

Image two shows the same document where the writer has used the word processor as an old typewriter's keyboard, to position the chapter, add indents, etc. Unfortunately 95% of all submitted manuscripts are in the same disgraceful shape. Here we have seven manual line breaks at the top of the page to lower "Chapter 1," a string of dots centering the word, little arrows from manual indents, and a flurry of tiny dots trailing after every paragraph. These are the empty spaces the writer didn't bother to remove. In an average manuscript, there can be thousands of formatting marks and extra spaces.

A quick comparison between both pages shows a formatted and clean document against a strikingly different one full of formatting marks.

Those writers who want to carry on struggling are welcome to do so. But if they want to learn how to format with flair *and styles*, Microsoft has a number of tutorials.

> http://office.microsoft.com/en-gb/word-help/format-your-document-with-styles-RZ001103924.aspx

The above link opens a one-hour tutorial, with downloadable exercises, tests, tips, and all the information needed to format a page with styles.

At http://onfictionwriting.com, in the downloads section, there are several ready-made manuscript templates, each with its own set of parameters embedded. After downloading one and following the step-by-step instructions, the new styles in the template become resident in any computer. Once installed, anything written using the manuscript template will be perfectly formatted.

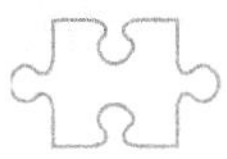# 5.4 SUBMISSION

### 5.4.1 QUERY LETTERS

The document every writer knows as a "query" or "query letter" is a standard business communication between a party trying to sell a product—or service—and a buyer. Every day, on every continent and in all walks of industry, millions of people settle down to craft millions of these instruments.

As anyone working in an office knows—it doesn't matter whether the company manufactures paper clips or rocket engines—in-boxes are chockablock with scores, even hundreds of spam pieces, which most of us highlight and delete without even opening.

Spam is the Internet bane and most users hate it; it wastes precious time and is mostly useless. Above all, it's unwanted. Yes, there are many definitions of Spam but "unsolicited mail" and "junk mail" are perhaps two of the most accurate.

"But agents welcome queries."

Yes, and that would get rid of the "unsolicited" bit, which leaves the "junk."

"What is junk mail?"

Defining junk is dicey. The Merriam Webster has, among others, these two definitions of junk:

A. Something of poor quality: trash.

B. Something of little meaning, worth, or significance.

Most agents we know would concur that these two descriptions sum up the great majority of queries.

Earlier we pointed out that to define "junk" is difficult. And yet we've listed two definitions above. Problem is that "junk" as a concept is subjective. Examples:

Wonderbra clearance.

Be a real man.

The first example may be intriguing to Renée, and thus not junk, but it's unlikely she would entertain opening the second. Carlos is flat-chested; he wouldn't be tempted by the clearance and after scratching an itchy nose and experiencing relief, would conclude he's real enough. Delete.

Whenever we receive e-mail from someone not already in our contact list, the first thing we do is to check the subject line. "Trip to Paradise" or "Four in a Row" might be interpreted as attempts to peddle magic mushrooms or wishful thinking. Such careless titles can spell doom and promote instant deletion of the message. Please notice that it would matter little that the writer has sent queries for two instant bestsellers, the first about a new Shangri-la hidden in the Virunga Mountains and the second about innocent people waiting for their last supper and early-morning needle. Chances are these queries would be deleted. Unread.

Why risk it?

Subject lines on query letters demand a five-letter word, followed by the title of the work offered. Naturally, the five-letter word is "query."

Query. Trip to Paradise

Query. Four in a Row

Of course, the title matters, sort of opens the door a crack. Why? Because on a long list of subject matters with insipid titles, a killer one will stand out and *might* be opened first, before the agent's patience wears thin. And we want our agents happy and receptive.

Query. The Fierce Pirates of Malayssia

Query. My Really Big Boyfriend

After glancing at the first title, the agent would determine that if the writer uses a stupid adjective (to qualify a noun where ruthlessness is already implied) and can't spell "Malaysia," chances are the work on offer is crap. On reading the second, he or she would throw both hands up in despair and reach for a tranquilizer (after deleting the wretched thing).

Details matter, after all a query is an important document. Our book might still be dribble, but a proper subject line might tempt the agent to go for broke and open it. Please, don't forget that the object of the exercise is to tempt agents. Think of it as fly fishing. It's all about finesse. A little tug here, a flicker there, easy does it. We want the sturgeon wild enough to swallow the lure whole.

Query. Scavengers

Query. The Bulge

We're not suggesting the above two titles would guarantee success, but at least would improve our chances.

New writers have one chance, and one chance only to create a favorable impression with an agent. That chance typically resides in the query letter.

We assume that the writer has done his homework and studied the particular likes, dislikes, specialties, and talents of the agent in question. We recommend checking the agent's background before sending off a query.

How do we make a good impression?

We're eternally baffled about the lengths to which people will go to prepare for a new date:

"What should I wear? Ohmygod! Look at my legs! The organza bustier or a horsehair passion killer?"

Yet, to attempt seducing the most important person in their writing career, most new writers don't mind dirty nails or spinach between their teeth.

Agents and editors are professionals dying to spot new concepts and writers who can write them well. To clue them, a first impression is capital: make or break.

Whether we're sending our query by snail mail or e-mail, the requirements are the same: a business letter.

Appearances sell, and we want to sell our book. Our first concern, therefore, should be the aesthetic layout of our document:

 **5.4.1.1 SNAIL MAIL**

Business letter format[148]

Typed, never hand-written

On clean, white stationery (If you own stationery with letterhead, use it)

Large type (12pt Times New Roman)

Single page

Inch all-round margins, and preferably much wider top and bottom

Refrain from spraying Chanel onto the page, or adding glitter, or confetti

Ensure you've affixed sufficient postage stamps to reach its destination

Include a self-addressed envelope with enough postage stamps for the reply

Seal the envelope before posting

Cross your fingers

 **5.4.1.2 E-MAIL**

Business letter format

On a white screen background, without fancy colors, animations, or other childish silliness

Large type (12pt Arial or Verdana) [149]

Refrain from adding emoticons (♥v♥) or silly bits such as smiley faces

Format it with paragraph breaks, as you would a format letter

Hit "send."

Cross your fingers.

---

[148] There are many Internet sites offering free Business Letter formatted templates, and excellent advice on composition and structure.

[149] Refrain from ever using fancy typefaces. If the intended query recipient doesn't have such a typeface installed, chances are format will be lost and your guess is as good as ours what your e-mail will look like when opened.

● Regardless of the delivery method:

The letter should be addressed to a particular sentient being by name, such as "Dear Ms. Spencer," or "Dear Mr. Williams," and never to a generic "Dear Sir or Madam," or "To whom it may concern." By targeting a particular agent we "show" that we've done our groundwork researching the most appropriate professional to make our pitch.

The letter should be flawless. This means without typos as well as syntactic and grammatical errors. Besides running the word processor's spell check, we recommend having friends or colleagues (who are reasonably competent on the intricacies of the English language) give it a read.

Once we've dressed our letter in our finest livery for the sake of appearances, we come to the substance: the contents and its structure. We can drape ourselves in Dior or Armani, but if we stand before our buyer with nothing worthwhile to say, chances are our pitch will flounder.

There are reams of advice everywhere about the structure of a query, even sound advice, often mixed with a rehash of pet peeves and outdated concepts. We don't claim to be in possession of the truth, or even know if truth exists, but the sensible approach to structure a product pitch lends itself to four sections:

One: A *short* product introduction (hook)

Two: A *short* account of the product's content

Three: A *short* description of the product's physical characteristics (mechanics)

Four: A *short* closing, outlining the virtues (if any) of the company or individual making the pitch

Our thesaurus could have yielded a bagful of synonyms, but we couldn't find anything with the rotundity of "short." Queries must be short, succinct, and to the point. More than ever, the prose must be focused and lean, each word set to convey meaning as opposed to just looking pretty.

The order of these four sections, however, is not set in stone. Think of them as the ingredients of a decent Manhattan: Rye whiskey, sweet vermouth, and bitters, garnished with a maraschino cherry on a stick. The cherry is our closing and it's there to add the finishing touch to our letter. The main ingredients go into the shaker in no particular order; it doesn't make a difference if we add the whiskey last because the order of factors doesn't alter the product. Later we'll approach the issue of sequence in more detail.

● One: Product introduction

Many books don't explain the purpose of a query letter. A query is a marketing device to sell a book to a reader (the agent or publisher). Using a term borrowed from the advertising business, we aim to sell the sizzle, not the steak. And "sizzle" means hook. In the same fashion that we create hooks and cliffhangers to cajole readers into turning the page, the first paragraph in a query letter should do just that: nudge our precious reader to carry on reading.

Our first paragraph can be a bullet destined for the front page of our novel.

Susan Cunnigham-Smith is a gorgeous model, tall, with never-ending legs, and beguiling beauty. But there's a dark side to her loveliness. When a virus mutates in her body, she decides to make men pay and spread the disease, infecting as many as she can.

As far as bullets go, the paragraph above is dismal. Do we need her full name? Would it make any difference if we named her Sue? More important, does it matter if we omit her name altogether?

Then there's the plethora of adjectives and nouns when "gorgeous" says it all.

We close with a brushstroke of the plot, at odds with the "sizzle" we need in an opening paragraph. Everything is wrong with the paragraph above, everything but the message. This is what we must to synthesise it into a hook.

> She's gorgeous, diseased, hates men…, and breeds.

Though we hope you can do better, the preceding line has everything:

It poses implied questions one could formulate by adding "why?" to each of its four clauses, it ends with a hook, and by virtue of its construction paves the way for the second paragraph where we'll elaborate the questions. We mean to grab the reader's interest, so we don't need to answer those questions in the query letter but in the synopsis and the manuscript.

Two: Product's content

Here, we give a brief appetizer of what the story is about in a few lines, five or six, in a single paragraph if possible. For fiction, this paragraph should identify the central character, establish the dilemma or goal, and preview the obstacles facing the protagonist. For non-fiction, the extension caveats are the same, only the paragraph should state the central thesis, the approaches to prove it, and the conclusions. In all instances cut, cut, cut, and remove the chaff.

This section is the most important item on the query; it contains our prose.

Our opening hook was:

> She's gorgeous, diseased, hates men… and breeds.

Which we can break down into its constituent phrases:

> She's gorgeous.

> She's diseased.

> She hates men.

> She breeds.

Next we add a little meat to the sizzle:

> <u>She's gorgeous.</u> Sue is a top model.

> <u>She's diseased.</u> On a photo session in Australia, she contracts a viral disease; nothing to be concerned about since the virus is inoffensive for humans. But in Sue, it mutates.

> <u>She hates men.</u> Soon, she discovers the horror she harbors and the precise mechanism to infect others. Her cheating fiancée dies in excruciating agony.

> <u>She breeds.</u> Sue embarks on a crusade to punish men, hounded across the nation while humanity's countdown ticks away.

Those snippets we can contort into a second paragraph:

> Sue is a top model. After a photo session in Australia, she contracts a viral disease; nothing to be concerned about since the virus is inoffensive for humans. But in Sue, it mutates. Soon,

she discovers the horror she harbors and the precise mechanism to infect others. Her cheating fiancée dies in excruciating agony, and Sue embarks on a crusade to punish men, hounded across the nation while humanity's countdown ticks away.

After reading this, the agent or editor will have made up his mind. Does the product merit spending a little time? Does it fit the current market? Is there room for such a tale? If affirmative, he will ask for a synopsis, a partial, or the manuscript. As simple as that, and only on the strength of a hook and a single paragraph. Because a great piece of work, a great idea, or a great plot (please, read a great "product") doesn't need any more. If a writer needs greater extension to sell his concept, he should think again. Perhaps the idea is not so great, or the query needs trimming down to essentials.

The remaining paragraphs can be condensed into one, as a function of the writer's career to date.

●   Mechanics:

This should consist of the length and other relevant characteristics of the product, such as genre, and whether it's a stand-alone novel or part of a series.

●   Closing:

The concluding paragraph or lines common in every business letter with the writer's relevant credits (if any).

We imagine that the cognoscenti out there will scream murder at the query layout we've outlined. Before you despair, please, follow our reasoning. We often read queries and submissions galore, so many our eyes bleed.

> "But I've read that queries must open with a paragraph describing the extension, genre, and the reasons why the writer chose such a theme."

Yes, we've read such advice before. Our question is: If the product's premise is uninteresting, or doesn't fit the agenda of a particular agent or editor, what use is knowing its extension or that the novel in question is a part of a saga stretching over twenty tomes?

Writers should keep in mind two important aspects of the querying process:

A) Agents and editors field thousands of queries over the course of a year.

B) A query is a marketing device tailored to offer a particular product to a particular buyer.

From A we should infer that the harassed professionals wading through countless queries must be sickened of formulaic, stiff, and unimaginative queries. The corollary is that any query displaying sensible creativity would stand out from the others.

Naturally, by "sensible creativity" we don't mean confetti and pink stationery but a letter showing that the writer can handle words and composition. After all—and this is an often-overlooked issue—if a writer can't compose a business letter, why should an agent assume he could pen a full-length novel?

From B we must draw a lesson and a warning: no two queries can ever be formatted the same way. Why? Because agents are highly specialized individuals, often focused in a particular genre or type of product. In addition, they have sets of guidelines they expect writers to follow.

The sections of our letter will always be the same: hook, prose, product description, and closing. The closing is static. We must append it to the end of our letter, but the rest, like the ingredients in a Manhattan, can go in any order dictated by the requirements of a particular agent and the writer's creativity.

Next, we need a title for our subject line. We toyed with "Praying Mantis," but since the novel has no religious undertones it might have lead to confusion, so we settled on "Missionary Mantis." After all, she's on a mission. Most men are unimaginative and predictable in their fun and games and she eats them alive (sort of).

The description of our product is straightforward. Our manuscript is as polished as we can make it, and it's a standalone title and a little on the long side for a first novel. We have a title for it (which we set as "Query; Missionary Mantis" on the subject line), and we want this particular agent or editor to accept us as clients. This we can set on a single sentence:

> I'm seeking representation for MISSIONARY MANTIS, a mainstream thriller complete at 120,000 words.

Then we work out a suitable closing, outlining who we are, what we do, publishing credits if any, and finally, a dab of humanity.

> Though I'm a freelance technical writer and scrounge a living of sorts from a daily article output, my fiction publishing credits are scarce: four short stories in paying markets. With your help, I hope to further my career.

> Please, let me know if you need additional material. Thank you for your time.

> Best regards,

Experts advise to set a closing line with "a synopsis and a partial or the complete manuscript are available on request." If we include such a sentence in our query, we've done nothing wrong, except "telling" when we should be "showing."

IF we draft a professional query, the wording should convey that we offer a complete product. Therefore "manuscript" is redundant. We have everything in the next sentence:

> ...a mainstream thriller complete at 120,000 words.

IF we draft a professional query, the wording should convey that we offer a complete product. Therefore, "synopsis, partial, chapters, or the complete manuscript" is telling and redundant. From a full manuscript, anyone should be able to excise a section or chapters at a click of the mouse. The following sentence covers it:

> Please let me know if you need additional material.

This leaves the reference to "synopsis." "Material" implies anything the agent or editor might request to peruse the details of the product on offer. Of course, the writer must have prepared short and long synopses, a chapter-by-chapter outline, and formatted the manuscript correctly to select any part of it. Why? Because otherwise he's not done his homework, and shouldn't be querying any agent until he does.

If we lay down the contents of our imaginary query, we have:

> <u>Hook:</u> She's gorgeous, diseased, hates men…, and breeds.

> <u>Description:</u> Sue is a top model. After a photo session in Australia, she contracts a viral disease; nothing to be concerned about since the virus is inoffensive for humans. But in Sue, it mutates. Soon, she discovers the horror she harbors and the precise mechanism to infect others. Her cheating fiancée dies in excruciating agony and Sue embarks on a crusade to punish men, hounded across the nation while humanity's countdown ticks away.

<u>Mechanics:</u> I'm seeking representation for MISSIONARY MANTIS, a mainstream thriller complete at 120,000 words.

<u>Closing:</u> Though I'm a freelance technical writer and scrounge a living of sorts from a daily article output, my fiction publishing credits are scarce: four short stories in paying markets. With your help, I hope to further my career.

Please, let me know if you need additional material or information. Thank you for your time.

Best regards,

These sections, or blocks of text, we can arrange in many different ways to address different agents or editors. In some instances, we will set the mechanics uppermost and perhaps add a different comment, reference, or detail.

The concept we seek to transmit is the nature and role of each item of the contents within a query letter and not a formulaic layout to copy. However, this brings to mind a parable:

"Give a man a fish and he will eat for a day. Teach him how to fish and he will eat for a lifetime."

We don't want to feed new writers but rather show ways to gather food. How to compose and structure each individual query letter must reflect the individual writer's creativity.

 **5.4.2 FOLLOW-UP TO A QUERY LETTER**

We are in business! We've contacted our prospective customer and now we must prepare to monitor the operation in a professional manner.

Though there are Internet services to help writers process and keep track of queries, we suggest crafting a spreadsheet to keep tabs on the status of our dealings with the industry.

The templates are simple documents with one book per sheet and columns to enter the names of those queried, addresses, links, specific requirements, dates, and other information every writer should have at his fingertips.

Some writers might wonder if it's worthwhile to spend time entering data on a spreadsheet. If those writers plan to limit their work to a single item, be it a book, a short story, or an article, the concern may be valid. But for the great majority of us who write all the time, professionally or otherwise, our manuscripts soon multiply. After a few years, monitoring scores, or even hundreds of manuscripts, can be a nightmare-- unless we have the means to keep an eye on our work.

We've seldom heard of an agent or editor replying to a standard query with an emphatic YES! Therefore, the possible outcomes of our queries are three:

Our prospective client doesn't reply.

Our prospective client passes.

Our prospective client wants to know more about our product.

Each of these replies merits particular actions, which we must be prepared to address.

> ### Our prospective client doesn't reply

Iffy news. In our experience, queries are read at once, or in any case within the day they're received. It wouldn't make business sense to leave messages unopened on the in-tray when one could contain a pile of revenue.

There are several reasons why an agent or editor doesn't answer a query.

A. He's a bad-mannered ignoramus who missed urbanity lessons at school and believes that business ethics is a rock band. Well, there are a fair number of these constructs in all lifestyles, and the publishing industry is no exception.

B. He's glanced at our query and decided that, although it has merit, replying to it can wait a few days. Agents and editors have very full agendas with well-defined priorities. Many take bagfuls of work to sort out on weekends. But urgent issues can crop up; one of their clients may need help with a manuscript the editors are clamouring for, another might face a libel or plagiarism lawsuit, a third could have had an offer for film rights. These issues take precedence because they mean revenue for their business, which is the principal reason for their existence.

C. He's glanced at our query and decided that he will pass, but replying to it can wait a few days. The reasons for the delay are the same as those offered in B.

In all cases, the correct procedure is to follow up the original inquiry. Of course, this raises a flurry of questions we'll endeavor to answer:

How soon should I follow up on a query?

Four weeks, or one calendar month, is a reasonable interval. Naturally, if the agent's instructions specify that replies may take two or three months, professionalism dictates that we wait. Why would any writer query an agent who warns that a season might pass before he gets around to answering queries is beyond us. It may be worthwhile to check the Writer's Market current report time for the agent or editor in question.

Should I phone?

Our emphatic advice would be, NO. When we field a phone call from a stranger (that's the status of the new writer who has addressed an unsolicited query to any agent), we're often at a loss to find any supporting document to buttress a meaningful conversation. Besides, unlike a written query the agent can read at his convenience, a phone call demands immediate attention. The agent may be preparing a meeting, talking to clients, discussing a deal, or simply having a coffee break to gather a little fortitude with which to rough the hours ahead.

What should I write?

This one is easy: a business letter follow-up.

Our note should succinctly ask if the agent or editor has had time to consider our proposal. As with the query, everything counts and the first item we must take care of is the subject line:

Follow-up, Missionary Mantis

<u>Follow-up, Missionary Mantis</u>

Dear Ms. Muffet,

Further to my query of September 22, I am writing to inquire if you have had the time to consider it.

I look forward to your reply and take this opportunity to thank you once more for your valuable time.

Best regards,

Joe Bloggs

P.S. Please, find pasted below the body of the original query.

Perfect. The above is equally valid for a snail-mail follow-up or an e-mail. We preface the title of our work with "Follow-up," so the agent, as soon as he opens the letter or even without opening the e-mail, can have an idea of the matter at hand.

The important elements to include are:

<u>The date of the original query.</u>

Many agents and editors offices file incoming queries by date of arrival. By ensuring that the date of previous correspondence is stated, the recovery of the original is much easier.

A word of warning to writers addressing queries to agents in a different time zone: It's important to log in our spreadsheet the actual date the agent *received* the query, and not necessarily the date it was sent from a different continent. To give an example: Anything e-mailed in the Unites States' West Coast after 15:00 local time, will log in the computer of a London agent with the following day's date. The same is true (in reverse) for European writers querying American agents.

<u>A copy of the original query.</u>

This is not overkill because in busy offices it is sometimes one hell of a job to track a single mail item. Simply paste the original query below the e-mail. If sending the follow-up letter via snail mail, include a photocopy—or scanned copy.

A follow-up letter or e-mail, correctly formatted and including the relevant information, seldom fails to elicit a response. If the agent doesn't reply to a well-timed follow-up the writer can be certain said agent is a type A, and he's definitely much better off without the agent.

Our prospective client passes

Hum… we're sorry. It happens to the best writers and it makes sense it would happen to us too. Rather than throwing a tantrum, hitting the bottle, or sinking into a depressed stupor[150], we must study the rejection note, even if it's a formulaic one.

---

[150] In one of her rare moments of lucid and serene contemplation, Renée described the syndrome as the "Unbearable Pains and Yearnings of Outraged Underdogs and Rejected Scribes." The acronym is most refreshing if shouted at the top of your lungs.

If the query was reasonably drafted, the reasons for the rejection can be legion, almost certainly having to do with having sent the wrong product at the wrong time and to the wrong agent.

Rather than agonizing over the query letter, what a writer must do is to enter the rejection on his spreadsheet, carefully noting the date and any relevant information, and prepare another query—or a bunch of them—following the procedure of research, personalization, and mailing.

 **Our prospective client wants to know more about our product**

Smile but don't break out the bubbly, not yet anyway. We are in business, and this calls for a sober assessment. The agent or editor is intrigued by the lure we've dangled before their beady eyes. This can only mean that the concept is good and timely. There's a market for it.

Calm and collected, with the overwhelming certainty of winners (even if onlookers ignore that we're about to break down any minute), we must prepare the appropriate material to quench our client's zest for knowledge. And we must do it in our everyday, detached, and professional manner.

5.4.3 THE MANUSCRIPT

Before sending off the first query letter or e-mail, do a quick check:

We have short and long synopses, outline, and manuscript prepared and polished.

We have correctly formatted our material following the guidelines on pages 423 to 429.

We have checked the formatting, removed extraneous spaces, odd indents, and dangling bits.

We have ensured that each page is set as it should be, with chapter headings, section breaks, and italics formatting nicely in place.

We have checked that the page numbers run concurrently, that we have no blank pages anywhere, etc.

The next step means additional work, which may be a waste of time after all, but we need to be prepared to react when an agent or editor asks to see the goods.

Let's imagine our manuscript is on one document named "MyBook.doc" We save it in a folder also named "MyBook." Next, we open the document and save it on the same folder as "MyBook_Bare.doc" Therefore, we now have two documents with different names but the same contents.

From the second document, we remove the heading (title of the work, writer's name, and the numbering of the pages). Then we save.

This "bare" document we will format differently to comply with the demands of particular agents or editors as necessary.

This process we repeat with short synopsis, long synopsis, and outline. Each we save with standard format and in separate documents without header.

Nowadays, the standard manuscript formatting (see pages 432 and 433) entails inch all round margins, double-spaced 12pt Times New Roman with a ragged right-hand margin and indented paragraphs. The heading contains the title of the work, a slash, and the surname of the writer on the left, with the page numbers on the top right.

Yet, some agents and editors prefer the page numbers aligned right on the bottom of the page and Courier or Courier New typefaces. When querying or sending material to people requesting different formatting from the standard, our "bare" document is the template we use to change styles and conform to the recipient's specification.

The process of selecting blocks of text to compile partials is the same, regardless of the template we use.

Our manuscript is as ready as we can get it. This is it.

We have researched the marketplace to determine which agents or publishers are most suitable, tailored our queries to the requirements (or whims) of each individual, and plunged into another project while the cogs slowly grind and The Fates mess about with their threads.

We don't know why, but one morning we awake to an in-box brimming with requests for material. The documents agents or editors request are:

Synopsis

Partial

Full

Or a combination of those. Piece of cake, since we have "My Book" folder decked with material files and templates.

The first item to consider is a cover letter to accompany the material. This, like any other business communication, should be succinct and to the point.

The subject has changed. Now, instead of "query" we must preface the title of our book with "Requested Material." This will ensure that our letter or e-mail will be given priority. We cannot overemphasize the importance of using the "correct" subject matter in our communications: "Query" or "Requested Material."

Our immediate concern is formatting, which will depend on the form in which we are supposed to submit the material:

Pasted into the body of an e-mail

As an e-mail attachment

Via snail mail

Pasted into the body of an e-mail

Not surprisingly, this is more complicated than the other means of conveying material. The reasons are two: format and typeface.

Documents formatted with double spacing and the standard manuscript typefaces look awful if pasted directly onto the body of an e-mail.

We suggest formatting to single space and changing the typeface to a 10pt Arial or Verdana.

The suggested layout is:

Subject

Cover letter

Material

After the closing of the letter, we leave three or four blank spaces, open with a line detailing what comes below, such as "Gone with the Wind / Synopsis," and paste the material.

⚫ As an e-mail attachment

Our e-mail should contain the subject and cover letter with an attached, a file containing the material formatted according to the specification of each particular agent or editor. If there are no specific requirements, our standard formatting is perfect.

On the line naming the document attached, it is customary to mention the type of file and program used to create it. A simple:

> … please find attached the <u>Gone with the Wind synopsis</u> as a MS Word 2004 file.

Unless specifically requested, or agreed beforehand, we discourage writers from compressing files or using PDF format, as the recipient may not own the programs to handle these files.

⚫ Via snail mail

In this instance, our cover letter should accompany the pages containing the material and a self-addressed and stamped envelope for the reply. Many agents and editors who have moved with the times will dispense with the self-addressed and stamped envelope requirement, preferring that the writer includes an e-mail address for a speedier reply. As detailed on the templates, e-mail address and telephone should always be included on the cover letter heading.

5.4.3.1 SYNOPSIS

We have a single page synopsis, and a more detailed document occupying anything up to four or five pages. We also have a chapter-by chapter synopsis.

With these, we can prepare three sets of documents:

Short synopsis, plus a cover letter.

Long synopsis, plus a cover letter.

Long synopsis, plus a chapter-by-chapter synopsis plus a cover letter.

In this last set of documents, the long synopsis acts as a brief summary of the manuscript, followed by the chapter-by-chapter outline, which shows the development of the plot, secondary plots and storyline as a whole.

Like other documents, these sets must be formatted to allow for different means of transmission:

With a first page showing the writer's full address and the title of the book, a header, and numbered pages if appending as an attachment to an electronic submission.

Without first page or header and formatted in Arial or Verdana to paste on to the body of an e-mail.

With a first page showing the writer's full address and the title of the book, a header, numbered pages, and a self-addressed and stamped envelope if sending by snail mail.

5.4.3.2 PARTIAL

A document with sample chapters is like a reduced manuscript; it should always be prefaced with the first page, which includes the writer's address, title of the work and the name if its author. If the partial is for an editor and the writer has representation, the name and address of the agent should be centered at the bottom of the first page.

Common requests from agents or editors are:

The first (number) pages

The first (number) chapters

A sample

These documents are seldom if ever pasted onto the body of an e-mail, but appended as an attachment or sent via snail mail.

When sending via snail mail, we recommend securing the pages—including the one with the writer's address and the title of the work—with a rubber band. The cover letter should be loose. In addition, we must back the block of pages with a piece of stiff cardboard, place inside of an envelope of the correct size to hold the pages flat, and enclose a self-addressed and stamped envelope for the reply. If the writer wants the pages back, then another large-size self-addressed envelope with enough postage must be also included.

The idea behind the envelope, the cardboard, and the rubber band is to ensure our precious pages land on our editor's desk in pristine condition.

First pages

Prefaced with the front page with a header containing the title of the work, the name of the writer, and numbered.

The first page doesn't count.

If the request is for the first ten pages, we don't recommend to stick to the ten-page specification, but to select a number of pages ending on a section or chapter break, as close as possible to the number requested. Say your "Chapter one" has a section break on page twelve. Then, send up to page twelve. This is common sense. And if the section break is on page eight, these are the pages to send.

A similar concept applies when our client requests the first twenty, thirty, or fifty pages. We recommend you send complete chapters if possible, keeping the partial's extension close to the number of pages required.

First chapters

In this instance, common sense doesn't come into play. If we're asked for several chapters, we prepare a manuscript with those—following the routine outlined before—and send them off.

A sample

As they say in posh places, this is a different kettle of fish.

Agents and editors sometimes request so see "sample chapters." The idea behind the request is to explore the writer's style and his writing ability. Unless our client indicates that he wishes to read consecutive chapters, we recommend that you don't send a chunk from the front end of the manuscript. Instead, include the first chapter, the best chapter from the center of the book—the one showing killer prose, a plot point or climax—and the concluding chapter.

The idea is to present a mini arc proving that the writer has planned the novel and concluded it.

Chapter one. "Can I help you, sir?" Brenda batted her eyelashes and the dust from the counter shrouded the dishy lieutenant in misty splendor.

Chapter thirty-four. "Die, you bastard!" The lieutenant fired his revolver until he ran out of ammunition. The villain jerked in the dust and did as prompted.

Chapter fifty. "Please… let go of me." *I'll kill you if you do.* Brenda's knees buckled when the searing mouth of the lieutenant found the nape of her neck.

5.4.3.3 FULL

A request for the full manuscript is serious business. It's unusual for agents or editors to ask for a full manuscript after a simple query. Likely, such a momentous event would have been preceded by a request for a synopsis and proof of writing (first pages, chapters or any chunk of our manuscript).

If our prospective client wants the kit and caboodle, it can only mean that he liked the premise of our book AND the way we wrote it.

There are no special preparations or added caveats. A full needs the same attention to detail we'd lavish on any other presentation of our work. In reality, a full is another sample of our writing, only larger and complete.

E-mail

After composing our cover letter as usual, it's advisable to append the manuscript as a compressed attachment; sometimes, servers and the gremlins manning the tortuous routes of cyberspace take a dislike to voluminous text files, MS Word ones in particular. Of course, this is easier said than done unless the writer is conversant with the process.

Windows XP, Vista, and Windows 7 have the facility to create a basic Zip file using Windows Explorer. For more advanced options and better compression, you may wish to use a WinZip alternative such as JZip instead, a free compression program and easy to use. The links are available from the resources section at OFW. JZip is versatile and compatible with other compression programs.

Snail mail

Follow the instructions for a partial regarding the compilation and arrangement of pages. In this instance, however, it's a better idea to use a box instead of an envelope.

Once we have the body of our manuscript backed with a piece of stiff cardboard and secured with rubber bands we need the customary cover letter placed loosely on top of the stack of pages. Then, a trip to our local post office should solve the box issue.

A few reminders (do's and don'ts) when complying with a request for additional material.

 **E-mail Do's** 

1. Format anything sent in the body of an e-mail with a suitable typeface (Arial or Verdana).

2. Don't append any attachments unless specifically suggested by the agent or editor.

3. Preface the title of the manuscript with "Requested Material," on the subject line.

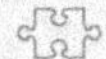 **E-mail Don'ts** 

1. We know that the e-mail looks bare and uninteresting, but refrain from adding colored backgrounds, smiley faces, smacking lips, and silly add-ons. These have no room in professional correspondence.

2. Don't use the confirmation of reception feature available in most mail programs. Doing so necessitates extra work from the recipient (he or she will have to OK the confirmation request).

 **Snail-mail Do's** 

1. Always include a cover letter.

2. Print everything in good-quality bond paper using one side only.

3. Preface the address with a "Requested Material" line.

4. If possible, use a typewritten label for the address instead of using a marker or a pen.

 **Snail-mail Don'ts** 

1. Don't staple or glue the pages together.

2. Don't use padded envelopes. Some types have a nasty filling prone to litter anything coming out of the envelope.

3. Don't include "gifts," such as confetti, dried flowers, crocheted coasters, underwear, or sweets.

4. Don't use couriers or registered mail, or any means of delivery requiring the recipient's signature.

6 THE TOOLBOX

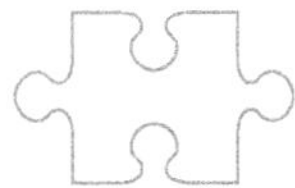

From templates, chapter, scene and character files, editing macros, Internet resources, genre classification, a glossary, tables and proofreading symbols, to a prosaic examination of the Publishing Industry, the reference items in this chapter should be a treasure trove for any writer.

Though the different sections or "tools" are prefaced with suitable introductions, the section on Genre and Subgenre needs a more comprehensive introduction.

Since genre is a pivotal aspect of manuscript categorization, we encourage writers to peruse pages 463 to 502 to determine the taxonomy of their work. With agents and publishers demanding works targeting specific reader segments, a precise classification is a necessity.

The publishing industry classes fiction according to similarities. For example, a reader looking for a story with mythical characters, such as elves or dragons—or where the protagonist lives in a fictional world and magic is commonplace—will wander over to the fantasy section of the bookstore. Others, looking to have the pants scared right off them, will search for horror.

Genre formulas separate fiction types and help define story categories, signaling to readers what they can expect when choosing a book. For these formulas to work, writers need to know what they must include or leave out to appeal to their chosen group of readers.

Of course, not every story fits a routine formula, which is why subgenres have taken on lives of their own. In the works of a subgenre, any given piece will have a dominant genre convention, such as a romance between two protagonists. Then, a theme, trope or setting, such as a specific time in history, can be woven in to cross two or more genres. Publishers classify works of this genre combination as historical romance, which is traditionally a subgenre of romance.

Now, a little disclaimer: Fiction genres evolve rapidly. Writers continually push the boundaries of what separates one genre from another, making it impossible to list every possible subgenre and its definition without repetition and overlap. Our goal in defining genre is to give you, the writer, a broad overview of common fiction divisions and their definitions. A work classed in one category may also fit into several others. The intent of this section is to elucidate why, for example, a reader finds one book on a science fiction shelf and another in mystery, and how a historical fantasy differs from a medieval fantasy.

To compile the genre section, we have pored over publishers' guidelines and examined definitions of each element then, in the interest of brevity and clarity, selected the most commonly recognized genres and subgenres. Of course, far more subgenre categories will appear as new writers challenge conventions and explore expanding possibilities.

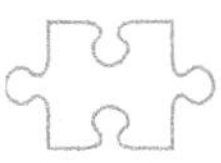 # 6.1 TEMPLATES

A document template is the set of instructions that can be used to produce new documents sharing the same pattern. A manuscript template stores the layout, typefaces, fonts, margins, paragraph indentation, interlines (or vertical kerning) and other features.

Whenever we open a word processing application, a blank document appears on screen; a rectangular white field where to start writing.

This is the program's default template the calls and it contains set values for typeface, margins and spacing between the interlines. The default template is useful to format text for informal communications, notes and other documents that don't require specific parameters.

The default template in MS Word is called the "Normal Template." To redesign the normal template or add a new template, perhaps named "Manuscript," it's necessary to format a blank document with the correct details and styles.

Microsoft has excellent guides to help users altering the normal template as needed or create and store new ones at:

http://office.microsoft.com

The appropriate help files are:

Change the normal template

About templates in Word

Modify a template

How to change the default settings for Word documents.

The exact procedure depends on the particular version of the program in use.

6.1.1 MANUSCRIPT

To format a manuscript for submission, the parameters come dictated by the industry standards, and sometimes by the preferences of particular literary agents or publishers.

Industry standards

Margins: Inch all round (top, bottom, left and right).

Typeface: 12pt Times New Roman

Paragraph indent: 1/2"

Line spacing: double

Widow and orphan control: No

Additional formatting

Italics

Section break: centering without indent

Chapter: centering without indent[151]

These are the parameters and styles to format a manuscript document. Manuscripts shouldn't have any bold or underlined words or passages.

In addition, a manuscript template should have a header with the work's title, the writer's surname and page numbers.[152]

Manuscript templates can be downloaded for different versions of MS Word from OFW.

---

[151] The correct form to define a chapter heading is by setting the paragraph format spacing at 260pt before and 12pt after. The templates lodged at OFW have these parameters defined.

[152] The usual location for the page number is the upper right corner, but some literary agents and editors prefer the lower right corner. These details should be checked, and the formatting altered to comply before submission.

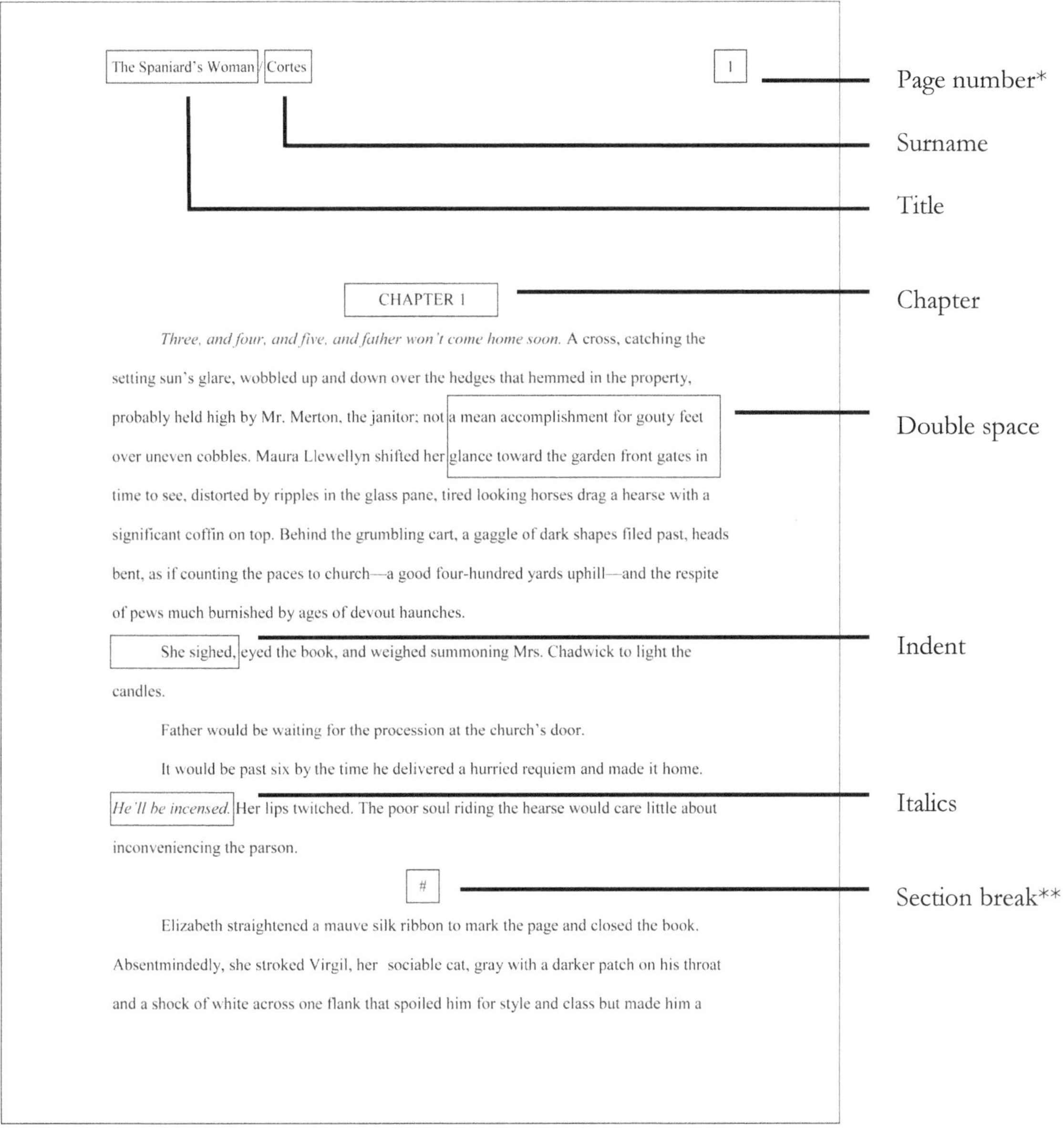

* Editors may request page numbers on the page's footer

** Editors may want paragraph breaks defined with other signs, such as a single asterisk (*) or three asterisks (***) but always centered on the page.

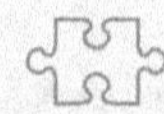 **6.1.2 CHARACTER FILE**

This is the basic file we use with all characters. Each classification requires a different level of detail. Principal and secondary characters may need this file and the Inner Character File. Other characters, in particular accidental and milieu, don't need all the details—perhaps only name and a few physical traits.

A. Principal and B. Secondary: Character File + Inner Character File
C. Minor or subplot, D. Accidental, and E. Milieu: Character File only
Manuscript:: Title of the manuscript, whether provisional or definitive
Update: Date of last entry or revision
Number: Reference number for character list

General

Name: Character name, whether provisional or definitive
Importance: According to the character's role within the story
Goal: Principal purpose of the character within the plot

Physical characteristics

Gender: Male, female, or other if needed in fantasy or SF genres
Age: Age at the beginning of present-day storyline
Height: Overall height in cm or inches
Hair color: Specify color and whether natural of dyed
Body type: Ectomortph, Mesomorph; Endomorph
Eye color: Include different colors if they change as a function of ambiance light
Mannerisms: Distinctive repetitive or stereotyped motor movement or vocalization

Personality

Speech pattern: Use of contractions, swear words, slang, regional accents, etc.
Likeability: How the character is viewed by others
Competence: Level of role proficiency
Courage: Ability to confront and respond to fear, pain, danger, uncertainty, or intimidation
Ethics / Virtue: Character's standards of right and wrong. Include religious affiliation

Background

Geography: Country or region of origin
Family: Extraction and current family situation.
Education: School, college, and university details, with degrees if applicable
Occupation: Profession or current work relative to the storyline
Culture: Level of cultural status, irrespective of studies
Abilities: Areas where the character is particularly able
Other Traits: Items not already covered but relevant to the story.

OFW	**CHARACTER FILE**		
	Manuscript		
	Updated		Number

GENERAL

Name	
Importance	
Goal	

PHYSICAL CHARACTERISTICS

Gender		Age	
Height		Hair color	
Body type		Eye color	
Mannerisms			

PERSONALITY

Speech pattern	
Likeability	
Competence	
Courage	
Ethics / Virtue	

BACKGROUND

Geography	
Family	
Education	
Occupation	
Culture	
Abilities	
Other traits	
Notes	

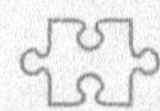 **6.1.3 INNER CHARACTER FILE**

This file is an extension to the previous one. Here the writer can draft the personality and character makeup of the players whose psychological analysis is necessary to the story. Only main characters need this level of description.

>   Manuscript:: Title of the manuscript, whether provisional or definitive
>   Update: Date of last entry or revision
>   Number: Reference number for character list

Personal life

Here we lay down the hobbies, activities, and social life of the player; the occupations with which the player fills his life when away from work. Family life, friends, habits, customs, affiliation to groups or clubs, etc. This section can also be used to outline the character's public life, as opposed to his inner persona, which is analyzed elsewhere.

Private life

This is perhaps the most important item in the file.

Work life

How the character interacts with his work.

Strenght and weakness

These sections have a capital importance when drawing the deep and hidden aspects of a player's character. It's important to list every quirk and feature in the character's inner makeup. In particular, it pays to specify if the strengths and weaknesses are real or imagined and separate how others understand these character traits, as opposed to how the player views them.

Other special issues and traits

This is the section to house notes, issues, and details not covered in other sections.

<table>
<tr><td rowspan="3">OFW</td><td colspan="3">INNER CHARACTER FILE</td></tr>
<tr><td>Manuscript</td><td></td><td></td></tr>
<tr><td>Updated</td><td></td><td>Number</td></tr>
</table>

PERSONAL LIFE (when not working)

PRIVATE LIFE (when alone)

WORK LIFE

STRENGTH

WEAKNESS

OTHER SPECIAL ISSUES AND TRAITS

 **6.1.4 SCENE FILE**

We use this form for our work; a simple scene file we print, collate in a ring binder, and carry about. We check and recheck openings, middles, and ends, always with an eye on the type of scene and its grade. It also serves as a reminder for the factual details and outstanding research.

> Manuscript:: Title of the manuscript, whether provisional or definitive
> Update: Date of last entry or revision
> Scene: Reference number for scene list
> Type: Resolved, Unresolved or Reactive
> Grade: We've separated scenes into five categories prefixed with a capital letter to later help the draft of a tension graphs: A Payoff. B Critical. C Important. D Detail, active. E Information, passive.

Characters

Here we list the characters involved in the scene, prefixed with a capital letter indicating the importance of each player. A. Principal. B. Secondary. C. Minor or subplot. D. Accidental. E. Milieu

POV

This entry can be useful later to determine how many scenes share the same POV.

Setting

Here we outline the environment where the scene takes place.

Opening

Statement of conflict.

Middle

Heightening of conflict or critical point of the scene.

End

Resolution of conflict or reactive ending.

Key information / research

Key information / Research (80 words): Here we list ideas, concepts, and details needing corroboration or research. This is also an excellent place to write down Internet links where such information can be found.

<table>
<tr><td rowspan="3">OFW</td><td colspan="5">SCENE FILE</td></tr>
<tr><td>Manuscript</td><td></td><td></td><td>Updated</td><td></td></tr>
<tr><td>Scene</td><td></td><td>Type</td><td>Grade</td><td></td></tr>
</table>

CHARACTERS

POV(S)

SETTING

OPENING

MIDDLE

END

KEY INFORMATION / RESEARCH

NOTES

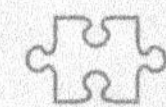 **6.1.5 CHAPTER FILE**

We've found this form to be especially useful. Even writers who don't structure a novel, the collated printed forms with chapter outlines lays a wealth of information at the writer's fingertips.

> Manuscript:: Title of the manuscript, whether provisional or definitive
> Update: Date of last entry or revision
> Number: Reference number for chapter list

Scene first lines

Having a list of scene first lines helps identifying locations within the manuscript, without having to search through the document. In addition, this is an excellent tool to tweak and improve these all-important first lines.

Opening

First paragraph or chapter opening lines

Plot

Chapter outline. Having the outlines already prepared can save much time and effort when being requested a chapter-by-chapter outline.

Closing

Last paragraph or chapter closing lines

Notes

Items not covered in other sections

OFW

CHAPTER FILE

Manuscript		
Updated		Number

SCENE FIRST LINES

OPENING

PLOT

CLOSING

NOTES

442

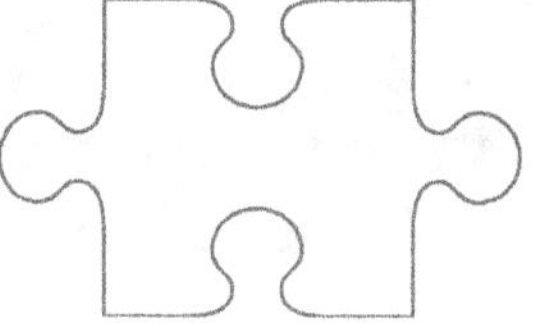

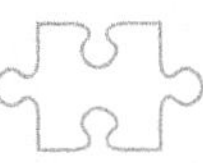

6.2 RESOURCES

6.2.1 MACROS

Macros are a type of sophisticated shortcut. To apply format to individual words or sentences, say italics, bold or underline, we select the item and click on a toolbar button. But everything we do with the menu buttons can be done with the keyboard. Take italics. If we want to set a word in italics, we need to highlight it and then press CTRL and the letter "i" at the same time. Therefore, for bold we need CTRL and the letter "b" and for underline CTRL and the letter "u." These are shortcuts.

Similar to the way a keyboard shortcut can do the same thing as pressing a button on a toolbar or menu, a macro can do a sequence of actions.

Suppose we wanted to find and highlight in a chapter or manuscript every "was." We could use the "find and replace" option,[153] its mechanics we have already explained on page 201. Then, if we wanted to do the same with "were," we would have to repeat the process.

The problem with this approach would become apparent if we needed to find and highlight twenty or thirty words we need to remove from our writing, such as "almost, seem, seemed, just, really, nearly, etc," we would have to repeat the process each time.

We could make a macro to scan the manuscript, detect every instance of the words in our list and highlight every one at the same time. Microsoft has an excellent help file detailing how to record a macro here:

http://office.microsoft.com/en-us/word-help/create-a-macro-HP005189420.aspx

We have created a series of macros containing every item writers might need to edit a manuscript, and nested them on a toolbar.

6.2.2 CARE

CARE is a collection of macros built by Luis Cano, our computer wizard extraordinaire. It searches a page, a chapter, or the full manuscript, highlighting in colors according to the part of speech words that may constitute a problem or merit close examination.

---

[153] Throughout this book, unless specifically stated, all word processing notes and examples refer to MS Word.

The program is embedded in a MS Word document and the installation is simple: after downloading the document from WWW.ofwcompanion.com follow the instructions printed in the document.

Once installed, in the "View" menu, there should be another toolbar named CARE. Check the box next to it and a new set of buttons will integrate with existing toolbars:

The "check" tab on the left will open a window with a text field. After entering a word on the field and clicking "ok" the macro will scan the document and highlight in gray every occurrence of the word.

The other tabs highlight different items or lists of words for revision. Finally, the "clear" tab on the right hand side will remove all highlight marks and return the cursor to the beginning of the document.

6.2.3 SOFTWARE

The explosive development of computer hardware taxes even a creative writer's imagination. Only a few years ago, we messed about with Sinclair and Commodore 64 machines, concocting our own programs with low-level languages and using floppy disks as storage support. A few lucky souls managed to upgrade to 3½" diskettes, each storing a stupendous 1.44Mb of data. The other day we bought a 2Tb portable drive for the cost of a decent meal and soberly pondered that we held in our grubby hands a device capable of storing the contents of 1,400,000 diskettes, 2,000 copies of the Encyclopedia Britannica, or 500 hours of good-quality video.

Unfortunately, software development hasn't followed suit and word processors are as clumsy as they were twenty years ago. The same is true of editing software. There isn't a program capable of copyediting a single page of text with any degree of accuracy.

This is good news for editors, but not so great for writers. Fact is that the best editing software is no match for a mediocre human editor. (Some will contend that editors are not human, but that's another matter).

6.2.3.1 EDITING SOFTWARE

In our opinion, the first "pass" of a manuscript must involve a spellchecker, as long as the writer weighs every change, since spell check programs seldom catch homophone[154] errors, and users also can generate these by accident if they are not proficient with the language.

---

[154] A homophone is a word pronounced the same as another word but differing in meaning. The words may be spelled the same, such as "bear" (the animal) and "bear" (to carry), or differently, such as borough, burro, burrow, or lightening, lightning. (We've come across "lightening" in several manuscripts, when the writer obviously meant "lightning." As you know, "lightening" means to become lighter or brighten, though Carlos always chuckles because it also means a drop in the level of the womb during the last weeks of pregnancy, as the head of the fetus engages in the pelvis.

Some companies have attempted to remedy the homophone problem with more sophisticated programming to read words in context, instead of just looking for typos. These programs can catch some homophone errors and learn from use. This implies that each generation will be better than the previous one. At least that's the theory. In practice, spell checkers must be used with care.

The next level of editing software is a group of programs checking style, repetitions, passive, some usage, jargon, unusual words, and limited syntax, such as subject-verb agreement, dangling modifiers, run-on sentences, and comma splices.

Though these programs cannot replace an eagle-eyed editor, they can be an excellent addition to a writer's toolbox to tighten the prose and eliminate gross errors <u>before entrusting the manuscript to a human editor.</u>

The programs and software suites listed below are the most popular add-ons to word processors, and most writers we know own and use one or the other.

Style Writer

http://www.editorsoftware.com/

StyleWriter works by trimming and replacing words from the text, in a bid to make it clean, tight writing.

The main problem with StyleWriter is its broad range; it lacks fiction-specific suggestions. The publishers pull no punches and warn that StyleWriter is most useful for the typical office worker. Carlos owns an early version of the program and uses it regularly to control issues such as sentence length. The program produces a graph showing how many sentences of each length are found in the text and average sentence length. This can be priceless to spot choppy passages.

StyleWriter integrates with Word. After it analyzes the text, it highlights problem words or sentences to direct the writer into evaluating each suggestion. On a bar located at the bottom of the screen there are readability, style, and passive construction statistics. The figures change real time as the writer addresses each suggestion.

StyleWriter does not offer a trial version of the software. Current price is $150.00

White Smoke

http://www.whitesmoke.com/

We approached the task of finding out the usefulness of this software with some trepidation. You see, we're naturally wary of bizarre declarations such as: "WhiteSmoke is the most comprehensive English writing software tool in the world today. With advanced technology at your fingertips you can be sure your writing will be no less than perfect."

Er... no. Carlos tried it, pasted 300 words of his latest manuscript, and clicked "Check." After applying the program's suggestion, the prose turned farcical, to say the least, and far from perfect. We've never seen a "perfect" piece of writing and remain wary of outlandish claims.

After our test, we checked several independent review sites, including http://reviewandjudge.org/.

We found good reviews—in sites advertising the program or offering direct links—and a few horror stories[155] worth reading before buying this product.

WhiteSmoke does have a free trial but it can be hard to find on their website. Current price for the Creative Writing version is $82.88.

● Auto Crit

http://www.autocrit.com/

The AutoCrit Editing Wizard is probably the best editing software available in the market today. It identifies slow pacing, overused words, clichés, and other problems typical of early drafts. Altogether, the "service" (more about this later) is excellent. One feature that impressed us was the program's capacity to detect repeated words up to 100 characters apart. This can be very useful, and it's a routine lacking in other editing programs (although you can download a free tiny application from a French site to exclusively perform such a task).[156]

We were impressed at the level of usefulness of this program but…

Yes, there's a "but." AutoCrit is not really editing software a writer can own, but a recurring yearly membership to a website. The version adequate for a fiction writer costs $117 each year. Carlos worked out that in the ten years he's owned StyleWriter he would have had to fork out $1,117, a sizeable chunk of cash.

Autocrit offers a free trial online. The trial version will only accept 800 words at a time and there's a limit to submissions, but it's sufficient to get a good idea of how the program works.

● Master Edit

http://masteredit.net/

This is probably the simplest editing tool we've come across. Its engine is similar to that of our own CARE macro routine (which you can download free from www.onfictionwriting.com). In reality this program is a collection of macros; routines to compare the words in the text against a database of weak words, passive constructions, "ing" and "ly" terminations, conjunctions, word proximity, etc.

The program will highlight words with different colors to warn the writer.

Altogether it's a straightforward tool.

There's no trial version (that we could find) but there're several videos of the program in use at the Master Edit website. Current price is $30.00.

6.2.3.2 STRUCTURING SOFTWARE

A structuring program is a combination of word processor, database, and spreadsheet with additional tools, features, and applications—often a function of the program's price.

---

[155] www.ripoffreport.com

http://www.complaintsboard.com/

http://www.consumerreports.org/cro/index.htm

http://www.bbb.org/us/Find-Business-Reviews/

[156] http://www.gaddy.fr/repetitiondetector/index.php?l=en

With a good program, the writer can produce chapters and scenes, place them in order, shuffle them about, and append attributes to each block of text. "Attributes" is a magical word. In each scene, the writer can highlight the different characters taking part, POV, give the overall scene a tension value, classify the scene as narrative, informative, dialogue, etc., and so on to the level of complexity the writer requires.

Obviously, once these details have been attached to each scene, the program will compute the values and display graphs. This might seem a little silly, but nothing can be farther from the truth. Different graphs will display the tension peaks and valleys, the regularity of POVs, and the levels and occurrence of narrative, color, description, and dialogue. Concisely, the graphs show the story beat, highlighting areas where rewriting may be in order. Coupled with character sheets, databases for names, places, details, word processing, and editing features, a structuring program can integrate every tool a writer needs.

Whether or not the writer structures or "wings it" is a personal decision and a matter of working habits. In our opinion, there's nothing wrong with either approach, as long as the writer feels comfortable.

As we explained on pages 17 to 73—in the section dealing with structuring methods—a level of structuring can save many hours of work and a few heartaches, but we insist: it's a personal matter.

In the market, there are software packages to help writers design and implement structural schemes. Some programs we own, for others we've downloaded free trial versions from the publisher's websites.

We have listed and outlined below the most salient features of each program, but nothing can match a visit to the program's website to ascertain the full features, operating requirements, and other details. Before purchasing any software, writers should scour the Internet for comments, tips, and complaints from other users of the chosen program to determine issues such as after-sales help, refund policies, bugs, and other details impossible to isolate otherwise.

Power Structure

http://www.write-brain.com/

Of all the programs we've tested, this is the most versatile and useful. Carlos regularly uses it for his fiction work and has owned a copy for the past ten years. Unlike other programs, Power Structure allows the writer to structure his story in several different ways and choose his own terminology. The program is user friendly and powerful.

One of the best features of Power Structure is that it is very easy to modify. Take the character sheets—a template with a set number of windows—each with a question or detail to fill. If you don't like the labels, deleting the program's labels and replacing them with your own is easy. Almost every aspect of the program can be modified to suit different methods of story planning.

We love Power Structure because it offers different alternatives for planning and structuring to suit individual working schemes. The program can adjust to suit personal preferences of plotting and planning.

A trial version is available at the Write-Brain website. Although you won't be able to save, print or export, every other feature is functional. Current price is $99.95, or $149.95 if bundled with Power Writer, probably the best word processor for writers. (Check the features of Power Writer on page 449).

WriteItNow

http://www.ravensheadservices.com/

This is a much simpler program, specially designed for outlining. There are a few tabs to create an overview and outline chapters, develop characters, and keep track of ideas and concepts.

An interesting feature of WriteItNow is a submission tracker for tracking your manuscript after submission and a clever routine to follow the age of characters through the story and create an event timeline. Other charts follow the characters' relationships and personality traits.

A trial version is available at the WriteItNow website. Current price is $59.95

Newnovelist

http://www.newnovelist.com/

Version 3 of this popular software for writers, launched November 2010, has many more features than its predecessors. It's an excellent buy. Although loosely based on Campbell's Hero's Journey (see pages 20 to 33), its story-development engine has a clean interface with a free-form environment that can be adapted to several styles of story structuring. It's a well-designed program with options to add and rename steps and customize many aspects of story development.

A trial version is available at the Newnovelist website. Current price is $49.99

Writer's Cafe

http://www.writerscafe.co.uk/

This program incorporates a neat set of applications for writers with different levels of accomplishment. It includes StoryLines, a powerful but easy to use story development tool, a notebook, writing tips, journal, research organizer, pinboard, inspirational quotations, writing exercises, name generation, etc.

One of its most salient features is portability; the program can be housed and run from a USB memory stick.

A trial version is available at the Writer's Cafe website. Current price is $40

Storyblue

http://storyblue.com/index.shtml

An interesting structuring program, Storyblue integrates the planning and writing processes into a simple, user-friendly interface. This is a modern-looking program with scores of attractive features, to incorporate in a single screen chapters, scenes, characters, notes, etc.

Some features will suit most writers, while others won't be of much use. An example is the charts for daily word count (a boon to NaNoWriMo writers) and setting daily writing goals.

A trial version is available at the Storyblue website. Current price is $29.99

Just like cars and T-shirts, no software will suit every writer. If you're contemplating using a structuring program, we recommend you download a trial version from the publisher's website and put it through its paces before considering its purchase.

6.2.3.3 MISCELLANEOUS SOFTWARE

With the increasing popularity of e-books and self-publishing, many writers face having to write, edit, typeset, format, and publish their own work. Once upon a time, disenfranchised musicians managed to stave off famine by piling upon their bodies scores of instruments before hitting the streets.

> "The one-man band exists, in all its uniqueness and independence, as a most elusive yet persistent musical tradition. As a category of musicianship, it transcends cultural and geographic boundaries, spans stylistic limits, and defies conventional notions of technique and instrumentation. Defined simply as a single musician playing more than one instrument at the same time, it is an ensemble limited only by the mechanical capabilities and imaginative inventiveness of its creator, and despite its generally accepted status as an isolated novelty, it is a phenomenon with some identifiable historical continuity."[157]

We could have sworn the author had writers in mind when he wrote the previous words.

To write and edit a manuscript, a writer needs a word processor. In an ideal world, to typeset the text, the writer would resort to specialized software, such as QuarkX or InDesign. Alas, these programs are too expensive for the average scribe; therefore, most of us have to make do with the limited features of MS Word and similar products and hope the formatting holds.

But to produce an e-book, the writer-editor-typesetter-publisher-printer-salesman needs a compiler, which is a program capable of transforming a formatted manuscript into a file suitable to be read in different devices with different protocols.

The two programs we've selected below cover everything a writer needs, from plotting and writing to publishing his manuscript as an e-book.

Power Writer

http://www.write-brain.com

In our opinion, Power Writer is the best word processor for writers, since its integrated Story Development & Outline Tools allow writing to proceed as one continuous act of creation, from concept through to final manuscript. This is a writer's dream writing software. A writer who structures before writing no longer needs separate software for each process. Power Writer is versatile, allowing the writer to design and write the story, structure first and then write, structure as he writes, or jump right in and start writing.

As a program developed for novels, Power Writer consists of three frames, the outline, the notes section, and the word processor.

The outline and notes sections can be minimized off the screen. This allows the writer to just write while going back to check notes or outline as needed.

The outline section of Power Writer mimics the outlines taught in grade school. But instead of 1, 1a, 1b, etc., the writer can give each section a name. The subsections then become chapters and plot points.

---

[157] Hal Rammel -Article MT098 - from Musical Traditions No 8, 1990.

The notes section will hold the back story, pitch, premise, synopsis, and theme. Other sections include acts, with opening and ending hooks, ticking clock, conflict, chapters, plot points, character files—to define physical details, goals, strengths, weaknesses, roles in the story, attitudes, character arcs, etc.—a name bank, and a research section to store personal notes, links to web pages, or background information.

The word processor works like any market leader's and includes a spell checker and a thesaurus. In addition, a bar at the bottom of the screen displays chapter and page numbers and a running word count.

A trial version is available at the Write-Brain website. Current price is $99.95 from the publisher's website, but it's worth trying other outlets, and even eBay for bargains.

Jutoh

http://www.jutoh.com/

Jutoh is an e-book compiler to convert standard manuscripts to popular formats such as Epub, Mobipocket, ODT, single-page HTML, and text; suitable for Amazon's Kindle and Apple's iBooks.

Any project can be created in minutes from existing files using the New Project Wizard and selecting a book-cover design from the included templates, or creating your own with the built-in cover designer. Fully portable—can run from a USB drive—the program works on all major desktop platforms: Windows, Mac, Linux, FreeBSD, and Solaris x86.

A trial version is available at the Jutoh website. Current price is $39

6.2.3 LINKS

In this book, we've attempted to cover basic aspects of grammar and syntax for writers. For those wishing or needing to attain broader knowledge, there are scores of excellent websites dealing with grammar, syntax, style, and composition.

One of the advantages of sites solely dedicated to English grammar is the quality and quantity of their examples and exercises. By practicing interactive exercises, concepts are much easier to assimilate and understand.

The websites referenced below constitute, in our opinion, a priceless collection of tools to understand the intricacies of the English language or simply to freshen up forgotten rules of usage.

6.2.3.1 GRAMMAR AND SYNTAX

The Owl at Purdue University

http://owl.english.purdue.edu/owl

This is one of the finest Internet resources for grammar. Award-winning and frequently linked, it is packed with excellent articles on grammar and style. There are scores of worksheets and MS PowerPoint downloads. Both The OWL and The Writing Lab are run by Purdue University.

◉ Grammarian.com

http://www.grammarian.com/1_style.php

Grammarian is a veritable clearinghouse. There are several divisions, such as:

Grammar

References, Dictionaries, Thesauri (sic)

Composition, Editorial and Miscellany

Courses and Exercises

Texts, Reviews and Mythology

Each section contains scores of links to sites covering all aspects of grammar, syntax, style and technique, along with many others.

◉ Capital Community College

http://www.ccc.commnet.edu/grammar

Created by Professor Charles Darling of Capital Community College (Hartford, Connecticut), Guide to Grammar and Writing is one of the best grammar sites on the web, with hundreds of pages devoted to grammatical constructions.

Besides 150 computer-graded grammar quizzes, letter templates in PDF format and a huge FAQ file with hyperlinked answers, the site boasts dozens of pages for correct sentence and paragraph construction and Principles of Composition: An entire website for writers. It should be on any list of grammar reference sites.

◉ University of Ottawa

http://www.uottawa.ca/academic/arts/writcent/hypergrammar

The University of Ottawa has an excellent Writing Centre. For writers wishing to polish their grammar, there's a great online resource called HyperGrammar, covering topics from parts of speech to punctuation and paragraphing.

◉ Bartelby

http://www.bartleby.com/141/index.html

Here you can find free the full text of The Elements of Style in its first edition, 1918 (in the public domain). Naturally, if you want to buy a hard copy you can ask at your bookstore for a newer edition.

🧩 6.2.3.2 DICTIONARIES

A good dictionary is an essential item in the writer's toolbox. Words have different meanings as a function of the sentence's context. Often it pays to use a synonym or a word with a closely related meaning to avoid confusion. Besides a dictionary, a thesaurus is even more valuable in those instances where we must repeat a word at close quarters. This is particularly important when the word is unusual or used infrequently, since it will call attention to itself. We've listed next the addresses of sites offering good dictionaries and/or thesauruses, along with other tools and features to ease the task of substituting or finding the right word.

Merriam Webster

http://www.merriam-webster.com
This is one of the best dictionary resources on the web and mandatory for American-English writers. In addition to the wonderful dictionary and thesaurus, this site has many other goodies, such as the vocabulary quiz, (Note that scores below the 3,000 mark are unworthy of a decent scribe).

Dictionary Reference

http://dictionary.reference.com
Besides a superb dictionary, this site offers additional tools for writers. The thesaurus is also excellent but the crown jewel is the "Reference Dictionary." Here the seeker will find articles containing or devoted to the item of your search. The site offers, for free, downloads for several interesting applications for writers. We liked CleverKeys. This is a software to install in your computer to look up words in most word processors, including MSWord. You will find the link to download this and other software packs by clicking the "Tools" tab.

Onelook

http://www.onelook.com
Onelook is not a dictionary but a search engine indexing hundreds of online dictionaries, encyclopedias, and other reference sites. After entering a word, expression, phrase, or concept, the engine delivers links to the correct definition in several online dictionaries. This is useful when seeking contrasting explanations. In addition, the site offers a great "reverse dictionary," a magical tool for writers. The reverse dictionary lets you describe a concept with one or a few words, a sentence, or question. After hitting the "Find words" tab, a list of words and phrases *related* to that concept is returned. The relationships offered are often surprising and open new avenues to describe an event or plot point. This is a must-have in the bookmark bar of any writer.

6.2.3.3 ENCYCLOPEDIAS

Regardless of the genre, it's unusual that a writer can complete a manuscript without having to check details in an encyclopedia. Of course, certain genres demand more fact checking than others. SF, thrillers, historical, and mainstream often demand careful research because the science, geography, timeline and color details must be accurate.

Fantasy and certain romance subgenres require less precision but it's a fallacy to assume anything goes. Take a vampire story, for instance. As long as the shenanigans happen between folkloric vampires, werewolves, or other legendary demons, there's no problem. The writer can give his creatures whichever properties he chooses. But as soon as a human enters the equation, anatomy and physiology must be taken into account. Since a human body contains ten to twelve pints of blood, it's farcical to depict a ten-second bite to empty a victim. Yes, we know it's fantasy, but to extract such a volume of liquid through two tiny holes in a *human* neck needs time.

Many will disagree and contend that fantasy doesn't need factual details, and they would be committing a dreadful mistake. Good fantasy, like any other genre, benefits from the attention to detail the writer invests in the manuscript.

Wikipedia

http://en.wikipedia.org/wiki/Main_Page

In the XXI century, encyclopedias and the Internet conjure a household name: Wikipedia.

Wikipedia is a priceless resource for writers. In our opinion, it is the best and broadest compendium of articles—almost three million—ranging from the sublime to the ridiculous. Writers should have no problems using Wikipedia, <u>as long as they adopt standard research procedures.</u> As a collaborative writing project, which allows virtually anyone to edit entries, Wikipedia can never be regarded as an authoritative source. Errors are rife and many articles suffer substantial lacunae.

Anything gathered from Wikipedia must be checked and contrasted against reliable sources. Below each entry, there's a list of works the author of the article used to substantiate his claims. It's up to the writer to check these sources to determine their trustworthiness.

Wikipedia Online Encyclopedias

http://en.wikipedia.org/wiki/List_of_online_encyclopedias

Still in Wikipedia, this is an excellent list of the available online encyclopedias. The right-hand columns show the language and whether the resource is free or subscription only.

Infoplease

http://www.infoplease.com

Although not an encyclopedia in the strictest of senses, this site offers a wealth of authoritative information on diverse topics. In addition, it boasts links to good dictionaries and other reference sources.

6.2.3.4 LIBRARIES

Serious scribes must check details, descriptions, dates, and events to ensure their data is accurate. Failing to do so will harm sales and the writer's reputation. Our particular routine on rewrite consists of highlighting items needing corroboration and later pasting the lines onto a spreadsheet. Once we have a list of items, it's relatively easy to check the veracity of our assertions using Internet resources.

Naturally, practice makes perfect and there's a knack to fact-finding (and to spot whether a detail needs checking or not). Consider the following line:

> "The truck, carrying the slaves to the cotton plantations, rumbled down the uneven road shrouded in a cloud of dust."

We don't know where the action takes place or the date, but the line paints an impossible scenario. Great Britain abolished slavery in 1833 and the United States in1865. So far so good. Problem is that Gottlieb Daimler didn't build the first motor truck until 1896. And if you think readers won't spot the gaffe, you're wrong. Somehow, somewhere, a buff collector of miniature trucks will cry foul.

Even the most mundane and innocent details can spell doom for a careless writer:

> "She sliced the vegetables: lettuce, celery, tomatoes, and watercress and dressed the lot with a sultry vinaigrette. In no time, she produced a bowl of scrumptious salad."

Yum. Er... tomatoes are fruits, not vegetables.

Yes, writing—good and accurate writing—is not as easy as it seems.
Below we've listed a few free excellent research libraries we use.

● Refdesk

http://www.refdesk.com

Though not a library the desk is a "fact checker," and our resource of choice to research details, sources, and data on any subject. Most Internet libraries and repositories of specialized information can be accessed from here, to a point where it makes sense using this site as the departure point to any research project. But beware; this site is addictive. Unless the user exercises restraint and discipline it's easy to become engrossed opening tabs here and there to check trivia and scores of tantalizing snippets (quickly forgetting why we went there in the first place).

● The Internet Public Library

http://www.ipl.org

The Internet Public Library is an excellent research resource sponsored by Intel and Sun Microsystems and hosted by The iSchool at the College of Information Science and Technology from Drexel University.

Besides a splendid "Resources by Subject" section, the site has other goodies tucked away under the "Special Collections" tab, such as the A+ Research / Writing guide and extensive material on literary criticism.

● The Free Library

http://www.thefreelibrary.com

The Free Library is a superb research tool, fast and easy to use. Although the homepage has a cluttered feel, locating information on virtually any topic is straightforward. For complex or involved projects there's a facility to create a personal homepage where to store contents, add bookmarks and RSS feeds from other websites.

6.2.4 EDUCATION

There are scores of creative writing courses and workshops available for those wishing to further their general knowledge of writing techniques.

As usual, we'll start with a caveat: writing courses and workshops are not for every writer. We know that writing is a highly subjective endeavor, to a point where valid descriptions of many terms or what constitutes good prose don't exist. Take "literary fiction." What does it mean? "Serious" fiction? And what does "serious" mean? Most editors of literary magazines will eschew genre work. Apparently, genre novels cannot be "serious." Pulitzer Prize-winning novelist John Updike once deadpanned: "All my works are literary simply because they are written in words."

Of course, the subjective nature of prose quality implies that those who attempt teaching, evaluating, reviewing, or criticizing creative writing must be subjective in their appreciations. Writers' workshops can help greatly a budding writer, but they can also steal his soul. We've heard from writers who attended creative writing courses and workshops and found them not only worth the money but worth a king's ransom. Others came out thinking their work was substandard and unworthy, despite being excellent writers. As a result, priceless scribes quit, and thus made the world a poorer place. To lose a writer is a tragedy for humanity.

6.2.4.1 WRITING GROUPS

Writer Magazine

http://www.writermag.com/groups.aspx?page=list
This site has a comprehensive listing of writers groups in the US.

OWW

http://sff.onlinewritingworkshop.com
In our opinion, for beginning, intermediate, and advanced writers in the genres of SF, fantasy, and horror, this is the finest working community. Both writers and the editor responsible for The Companion are alumni of this superb workshop. Fees have been kept at under $50 a year and the insights gleaned are worth every penny.

National Association of Writers' Groups

http://www.nawg.co.uk
For those writing in British English, the NAWG lists the most salient associations, workshops and groups in the UK.

Greatwriting

http://www.greatwriting.co.uk
In particular, we recommend this writer's community. The site is classified according to genres and has a great atmosphere.

6.2.4.2 COURSES

Clarion Writers Workshop

http://clarion.ucsd.edu/index.html
Clarion is a six-week residential workshop focusing on writing technique, in particular geared to the science fiction, fantasy, and horror genres.

Located on the beachside campus of the University of California, San Diego, the workshop runs through the summer months with an application and candidate evaluation period on the first quarter of the year.

The Clarion Writers Workshop website is clear and informative, detailing the application process, the background and focus of the workshop and a comprehensive Q&A section.

There's a non-refundable $50 application fee and a $5,000 tuition fee. Scholarships, usually in the range of $500-$1,500 may be available to qualifying applicants.

Clarion West in Seattle, Washington, is another Clarion Workshop. Though following the Clarion model with similar schedules, it is run independently.

Since the number of students is limited to eighteen, prospective students are encouraged to apply concurrently to both venues.

For those interested in learning more about Clarion, its style and goals, we recommend reading Storyteller: Writing Lessons and More from 27 Years of the Clarion Writers' Workshop by Kate Wilhelm, Small Beer Press, 2005.

Oddyssey

http://www.sff.net/odyssey
This is another six-week workshop running through the summer at Saint Anselm College in Manchester, New Hampshire. This course also specializes in fantasy, science fiction, and horror. Odyssey is run by Jeanne Cavelos a former senior editor at Bantam Doubleday Dell.

Their website is excellent and offers extensive details on all aspects of the workshop.

Anyone interested in applying should read "Workshopping at Odyssey" by David J.Schwartz. You can read the full text here: http://www.sff.net/odyssey/schwartz.htm

The application fee is $35. Tuition, food at the Coffee Shop and lodgings at the Saint Anselm College apartments runs between $3,300 and $4,100, depending on whether the accommodation is in a shared bedroom or your own bedroom in an apartment.

The Tongue Untied

http://grammar.uoregon.edu/toc.html
Subtitled "A Guide to Grammar, Punctuation and Style for Journalists," this is an entire semester's course, with weekly lessons and quizzes. It is designed as a "book" online for the course. Although it is for students taking specific courses at the University of Oregon, anyone can profit from working through the lessons.

6.2.4.3 CONVENTIONS

We are often asked if it's worth the cost, both in terms of time and money, to attend conventions.

On one hand, writers conferences are a chance to get together with friends, socialize, network, talk about the business, learn more about the craft, etc. In particular, one can meet or hear agents, editors, publishers, and other professionals talk about the industry, which can be a revelation for most writers starting up. Thus, conferences can be a valuable social activity. Note, however, that too many writers don't realize most conventions are a direct financial loss. Attendees can easily spend $1000 for a 3- to 4-day long conference, and that's bargain basement price. Some conferences, such as ThrillerFest can cost twice as much.

Our advice would depend on the writer's expectations. If you're attending to improve yourself as a writer, pick one major convention a year and spend the rest of your money on books, paper, and ink. If you want to buddy up to and hang around the heavyweights of the industry, go to as many major conventions as you can afford.

We have stressed "major conventions" because the hundreds of smaller venues are really workshops, courses or a medley of talks delivered by mediocre panels often made from the same people rehashing the same stuff. This is a serious problem with minor writer's conferences. The panels are often lousy.

Major events depend on the writer's particular genre. In our opinion some of the best are:

AWP Annual Conference & Bookfair

ThrillerFest

World Horror Convention

Norwescon

Worldcon

World Fantasy Convention

Smaller conferences and other events are listed on several websites, with often-extensive information and links to the organizers' homepages. The two links below offer a fair selection of these venues, although it's interesting in a wicked sort of way that neither list gives information about the major events.

Writers' Conferences & Centers

http://writersconf.org/
The Writers' Conferences & Centers (WC&C) has references to 550 writers' conferences, festivals, residencies, and retreats in the U.S. and abroad.

Shawguides

http://www.shawguides.com
Shawguides profiles more than 400 writers' conferences in the U.S. and abroad.

 ## 6.2.5 PROFESSIONAL EDITING

Any serious and intelligent writer, even the most brilliant, needs an editor. For a new or upcoming writer, a professional editor is a necessity and often the critical factor between rejection and acceptance for publication. While every novel needs an editor, that editor cannot be the writer, because he cannot be impartial.

Why do I need an editor?

A writer's reputation hinges on producing good material, which is, by definition, prose that has been revised several times to a point where the writer thinks it's perfect. This is the stage when we must submit our work to an editor because we don't have the ability to step back and evaluate our work objectively. Trust us: it's not perfect! As the writers, we are simply too close to our work.

Our writer's perspective is the view of a garden from the ground. We've planted the bushes one by one, trimmed plants, added rocks, a lake, a bridge, a labyrinth, paths, and clearings. The editor's perspective is the view from above looking down at the garden, taking it all in at once.

Each writer has a unique set of limitations when approaching the craft. An editor can identify problems with a manuscript or copy, such as issues of consistency, tension, continuity, and structure, all the weak points in the writer's approach.

It follows that if a professional editor finds flaws in any of these elements the writer should listen and work with him to make the necessary changes. Pride has no place in writing.

Often, writers think of editors as proofreaders—someone who checks grammar, syntax, and typos. Though editors perform many such housekeeping tasks to make the written work structurally sound, their key role is to remove the chaff so the story shines and holds true from beginning to end.

In the countless manuscripts and partials we peruse every year, we've never seen a piece of writing longer than a sentence that couldn't benefit from editing.

I'm self-publishing, so I don't need an editor

The opposite is usually true. When skipping the gatekeepers and self-publishing, the writer's competition is mindboggling. Besides fighting the flood of self-published titles struggling for recognition in a ruthless market, he must compete against the edited books from traditional publishers. No amount of self-promotion and backslapping from family, friends, and well-wishers can overcome the bad reviews a book will receive if it has glaring errors, typos, or common structural flaws. Unedited books stand out, and readers will seldom forgive being conned to spend money on it. This means fewer still will take the bait twice.

Any writer on the road to self-publishing should consider professional editing. Which brings us to an unpalatable conundrum, but then life is only easy for those who choose delusion. The average self-published book sells fewer than one hundred copies. (Yes, we've also heard about the few who have made it, just like we've heard of folks winning the lottery or taking a casino to the cleaners. These are exceptions). If the writer manages a royalty of ten bucks a copy, that's one-thousand dollars. Naturally, we're being generous here by skipping over even more unpalatable facts: ten dollars is a huge royalty and many copies will be given away to family, beta-readers, reviewers, etc.

No competent editor will look at a manuscript for one thousand dollars, or twice that amount. The alternative is to print the product of many hours of work unedited—regardless of the efforts of our collaborators, writing friends, and workshop colleagues. This, in turn, will make the chances of success even more remote.

What kind of editing do I need?

Answering this question requires insight. It's somewhat akin to asking what kind of work your house needs before placing it in the market, if you hope to sell it in these rarefied times when nothing moves. Should you give the façade a lick of paint? Trim the lawn? What about the dry rot? And the leaking faucets? Considering there are thousands of similar—perhaps better, nicer, and cheaper— properties for sale in your neighborhood. How far are you prepared to go to improve your chances? Correct: it will depend on how dilapidated your property is to start with.

There are different types of editing, and each writer needs something a little different, depending on his skills, experience, goals, and the status of his manuscript.

In general terms, a typical manuscript undergoes three editing stages: substantive editing, copyediting, and proofreading.

Substantive editing

In substantive editing, (sometimes called content editing or structural editing) manuscript editors assess the work as a whole for style, characterization, tone, core substance, story structure, and accuracy. While retaining the author's intent and voice, the editor seeks to eliminate the manuscript's weaknesses and enhance its strengths, perhaps suggesting organizational changes and large revisions. The editor may counsel reshaping paragraphs, scenes, and chapters. He could suggest rewriting portions of text to eliminate wordiness or promote structural changes to resolve inconsistencies or clarify confusing passages.

Copyediting

This is known in writing parlance as "line editing" or "line-by-line editing." The editor disregards structure, story, flow, POV, or any technical issue other than grammar and syntax, in a bid to obtain overall correctness and consistency.

Copyeditors revise the manuscripts line by line, often starting from the end and working one sentence at a time in reverse order. The reason is focus. When reading front to back it's easy to have one part of the mind following the story, and this can cause distraction.

There's no standard copyediting. The process can be light, medium, or heavy, depending on the quality and complexity of the manuscript. This will reflect on the editor's fee because a shoddy manuscript demands much more work than a polished one.

It bears repeating that no manuscript should go to an editor before it's been polished to the best level a writer and his colleagues can achieve. Failing to do so is throwing away hard-earned money.

Proofreading

 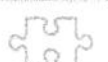

Many novices assume that proofreading is editing. This is a common misunderstanding. Once the substantive edit is over; inclusive of all rewrites, changes, additions, and deletions, the copyeditor takes over for his line editing. Then, the manuscript should be proofread to catch typos and minor editorial oversights that may have hitched a ride into the work with each revision.

Rather, proofreading is the last read before the manuscript is typeset and sent to printers.

The rule is to get as much editing as the writer can afford, if he wants his manuscript to stand out as a viable product among the thousands that agents and acquiring editors receive each month.

Why do I need to pay someone?

If you're lucky enough to count a manuscript editor, a copyeditor, and a proofreader among your friends, *and* they're willing to invest many hours in your project in exchange for a smile, you don't.

A friendly reader might confess to being bored after page fifteen or being lost before reaching chapter six. A professional editor will explain why, and suggest how to rewrite the story to avoid reader's blues.

It's true that traditional publishers will offer these three editorial services—if they believe in the book— but before the choice of two equally interesting projects (and there are millions out there), they will always choose the one requiring fewer editorial hours.

Fellow workshop writers and beta readers can help greatly to polish a manuscript, but they never replace a professional editor. An unedited manuscript will always be a sub-standard product when compared to a professionally edited one.

How much will this cost?

A good editor can do five to ten pages of substantive edits in one hour, ten to fifteen pages of copyediting, and twenty to thirty of proofreading. A standard-length novel has four-hundred pages. This might mean eighty hours for the main edit, forty for the second, and twenty for the last, totaling one hundred and thirty hours, give or take a few, or three solid working weeks. But the main edit requires reshuffling, rewriting, adding much text, and deleting large chunks of prose. This, in turn, requires more editing hours to assess the new material.

An editor worth his salt will charge $40-100 an hour on average, and $20-35 an hour for copyediting and proofreading.

How do we determine the cost for each page or word?

Substantive editing from 2.5c to 8c each word ($2,500 to $8,000 for a typical manuscript).

Copyediting from 0.7c to 2c each word ($700 to $2,000 for a typical manuscript).

Proofreading from 0.5c to 1.25c each word ($500 to $1,250 for a typical manuscript).

Some editors charge a flat fee for copyediting/proofreading, ranging from $1.25 to $6 each page, or $500 to $2,400 for a typical manuscript.

No doubt, writers have scoured the Internet and found editorial services with prices ranging from basement bargain to princely. In every instance, the prospective client must determine what the service offered includes, taking into account that:

Most editorial services advertised on the Internet offer copyediting and proofreading, seldom substantive editing. When they do, their fees are similar to these suggested above.

Copyediting and proofreading will *not* improve a story, detect POV slips, or analyze the structure, characterization, continuity, and the myriad technical flaws usually plaguing a manuscript.

No professional editor will venture a quotation without having first perused a sample of the manuscript, usually gathered from the middle part.

How do I find an editor?

Nothing can be simpler: enter "manuscript editing" or "editorial services" in your web browser. (This assumes you don't have a writer friend, who having published with a traditional house, can recommend his editor).

We can't name our favorite editors, but we can suggest a few personal considerations, which might help a fellow writer.

Beware of:

Editors who flaunt a Master or a Ph.D. in English. While proficiency with the language is capital, having a degree doesn't guarantee good editorial services.

Editors who are reluctant to provide references or lack published feedback from clients.

Editors whose clients are not published in magazines, professional or academic journals, or by major publishing houses.

Editors who offer a free edit. No serious professional works *gratis*. A fine editor may offer a sample edit for a flat fee, deductible from the full work if later entrusted to his tender mercies.

Editors who state a price for each word, page, or manuscript, without first having studied a substantial sample of prose.

Editors who offer to return a fully edited (not just copyedited or proofread) manuscript within a week or two. Please, check the hours involved and do the math.

Editors who will start working at once on your project. This needs further explaining, but we're sure you've spotted the logic behind it. Good editors are in demand and must schedule their work accordingly. While there's a possibility of cancellation or a slow month, any editor who can take an assignment at a moment's notice would have been twiddling his thumbs but for your project. The same holds true of groups. A company offering editorial services usually farms out the work to freelancers, who may be the salt of the earth... or simply mediocre. Any writer should reconsider entrusting the fruit of his wretched labor to an unknown entity, regardless of the company's stature.

Editors who offer a two-, six-, ten-, or one hundred-page critique, evaluation, commentary, or whatever. That's not an editor's job, but a reviewer's. An editor will append well-reasoned and objective comments and recommendations in the body of the manuscript he's editing, not a lump of verbiage at the end.

Editors who promise a foot in the door of publishing houses, a publishing contract, a recommendation, or a promise of publication. (Unless the offer happens after he's finished his job to the writer's satisfaction, has no additional cost, or is backed by a five-figure advance).

A parting thought: Publishing a book, any book, costs money. Somebody's money. A literary agent will have to read the book, make phone calls, send off copies of the manuscript, and perhaps buy lunch for an acquisitions editor to make a pitch on the writer's behalf. A publisher will have to pay editors, composers, typesetters, printers, and salespeople to place a physical book on sale.

If a writer believes his work to be worthy of publication by a major house, knows that his story will enthrall readers, and feels it can proudly share the library shelves with the best in his chosen genre, then going without new shoes, or beer, or having to live off peanut butter sandwiches and tap water while he saves up the fee for a professional editor should be natural. But if the writer doesn't believe in his work to the extent of enduring hardship and risking his money, why should agents or publishers? The choice is clear: pay for professional editing. Remember, only serious and intelligent writers will sooner or later see their work on bookshelves.

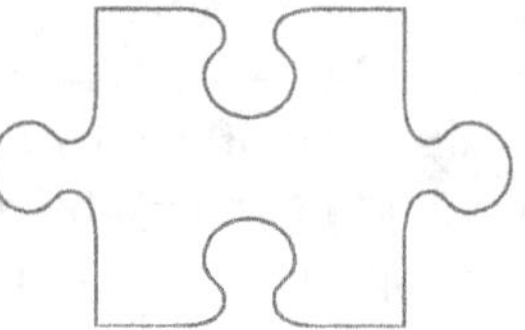

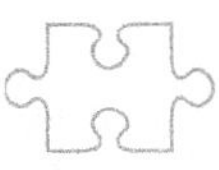

6.3 REFERENCE

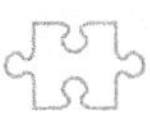

6.3.1 GENRE / SUBGENRE

All fiction is essentially genre fiction, also known as popular, commercial, contemporary, or category fiction.

Genre fiction tells a story with greater emphasis on plot than literary fiction or mainstream fiction. The plots have a beginning, middle, and end with less emphasis on characterization, the exploration of theme, and literary writing. This isn't to say genre fiction can't contain theme development, good characterization, and quality prose. Rather its readers seek first and foremost a good, entertaining read meaning a story trimmed with everything else.

Most genre fiction involves protagonist and antagonist characters enduring a setting and the challenges of the story to emerge triumphant from the ashes or perishing there.

Though there are scores of genres and hundreds of sub-genres most fiction can be slotted into five main categories:

Fantasy

Horror

Mystery/ Crime

Romance

Thriller/ Adventure

Science Fiction, Historical Fiction and other genres can be grouped with one or several of the above categories, although they are labeled under their own genre heading.

Excellent writers (some would say every writer) have authored great genre works. Examples include Edgar Rice Burroughs, John Le Carre, Stephen King, H.P. Lovecraft, Thomas Harris, Raymond Chandler, Ray Bradbury, and Ursula K. LeGuin.

6.3.1.1 CHILDREN'S FICTION

The children's-fiction genre likes to defy categorization. The guidelines listed include age ranges and key elements within each category, but these are not hard and fast rules. Why? Each child is unique. The stage-one six year old is at a cognitively different level from a stage-three six year old. A kindergartner may be reading at the same level as her fourth-grade sister, while her classmates struggle to decipher the letters in their names.

Examples cited are books used in school curricula or in daycare environments. These include classics passed down over the generations, books generally accepted to be timeless. Agreement is not at issue here. While one person might feel *Anne of Green Gables* is not an appropriate transition book, another might say Dr. Seuss's *The Grinch Who Stole Christmas* advances beyond a typical picture book. These examples are only guides, used because they contain key elements to the children's-fiction genre. A reader may feel one example fits better with another category because she or her child read that book at a much younger age. Here, the focus is on the elements defining these categories.

Why the explanation? Educational expectations and guidelines change like the seasons. With the significant amount of resources available to them, children are changing and growing more rapidly than ever before. Publishers struggle to keep up and try to select age ranges that accommodate these changes. One just has to pick up a couple of banned books lists to see how subjective the age classifications can be. This is why you'll see a category listed as 10 to 14 years old, when we all know the cognitive and emotional maturity of a fourth grader is much different than that of a ninth grader.

What never changes are the basic elements of the children's-fiction genre. Intended for parents to read aloud, picture books are always about capturing a toddler's imagination. Words and ideas used in pre-readers are simple and clear. Transition books add characters and use plots that are more complex. Writers design such works to move children from the basic concepts of pre-readers into the more involved plots of chapter books. Focusing on these stable concepts is a must when writing stories for children.

Children's fiction comprises books written for children, or readers up to their early teens. Writing children's fiction is a challenge. The writer strives to reach a complex target audience with different comprehension and focus levels. This entails composing stories with enthralling characters, but must consider the intellectual capacity and reading abilities of young readers. To add to that challenge, a child is the toughest audience a writer can have. The writing should never underestimate them.

Plots are simple in this genre, meaning there are no subplots or fancy twists, except for middle grade books. In children's fiction, there is usually one main character (protagonist) that represents the child's emotions, anxiety, and point of view (how they see their world). When writing children's fiction, authors must answer hard questions: Is this word too hard? Is this sentence too complicated? Will my readers be able to understand a metaphor? Am I talking down to them? Will this bore them?

As a child grows and learns more about the world, his intellectual capacity also expands. One style of writing will not fit every child at every age. No author can target one book to all audiences of this genre. This is one reason why publishers classify subgenres by age. Although some overlap, the distinctions are logical.

Children ages one to three cannot read. Parents and caregivers read the stories aloud. Often, the children relate more to illustrations than words since they are still building their vocabularies. In comparison, children ages four to eight are well on their way to reading independently. Four year olds are learning to identify letters and sounds and eight year olds can understand a simple story with basic words and plot.

In deciding which subgenre best describes a book, publishers use a specific list of guidelines. We examine these in detail in the Children's Fiction Subgenres section.

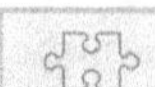 **6.3.1.1.1 CHILDREN'S FICTION SUBGENRES**

Pre-Readers

This genre addresses the youngest audience in children's fiction, which is usually the preschool years. Pre-readers—commonly called "baby and toddler books"—are simple stories. These books often contain lullabies, nursery rhymes, or just illustrations. The length and format varies with the content but, as a rule, if these stories contain words, they span no more than three hundred words. The plot either reflects a child's everyday life, or teaches ideas such as colors, numbers, or shapes. Formats for these vary from hardback and paperback to board books, pop-up, or novelty books that produce sounds or have different textures. Books that target this age group are generally read aloud to a child.

The writing in this category should be short and simple, but not without meaning. Children as young as three can understand a metaphor. They use it to bridge the gap between words they know and ones they don't. Metaphors for pre-readers need to be tangible, using sensory objects. For example:

Clouds are pillows.

The wind is a kiss.

However, pre-readers would not understand riddles and puns, as they are not yet able to grasp that words can have several meanings.

Brown Bear, Brown Bear, What do You See? By Eric Carle is an example of the use of rhyme, alliteration, and humor to encourage the child to join in and try to predict what marvelous animal will come along next.

"Blue Horse, Blue Horse, What do you see? I see a green frog looking at me."[158]

The simple words Carle uses in this book ensure the child will follow along. Each page has only one sentence, making memorization easy, but this doesn't imply that a writer should limit word variety when writing for this age group. While complex writing and sentences are beyond their understanding, children between the ages of one and three learn words rapidly. By their third year, they'll have picked up more than two thousand words. Pre-reader books should challenge them, introducing new words, sounds, and ideas to meet the voracious appetite for learning children have at this age.

Picture Books

Standard formatted picture books contain about thirty-two pages or around one-thousand words (may be slightly more or less) and are intended for ages four to eight. Don't let the simplicity and low word count of a picture book fool you. A writer must strike the perfect balance between illustrations and text to tell the story, allowing the art to act as adverbs and adjectives, while keeping the writing crisp. Writers need not describe characters in detail, since the illustrator does this with artwork. The story should unfold so each illustration is different to keep the child's interest. Action brings the pictures to life. The key to remember when writing a picture book is that the artist needs variety in either scenery or action (preferably both) to create vivid and dynamic illustrations.

By age four, children are learning the letters of the alphabet, and they understand that a story has a beginning and an end. They often recite their favorite stories from memory, and use pictures to both see these story elements and predict what will happen next. Writers for this reading level should use concrete words in short sentences. One idea in each sentence is enough. The challenge is to do this in a voice that is authentic, never contrived. Catchy rhymes, complex sounds, and ideas are the best ways to engage children at this age.

The Very Hungry Caterpillar by Eric Carle is a good example of a picture book.

---

[158] Brown Bear, Brown Bear, What do You See, Bill Martin Jr. and Eric Carle, 2nd edition, revised edition (Sep 22 1996) Henry Holt and Co.

Early Readers

Written for children from kindergarten to grade three who are beginning to read on their own, early readers, or easy-to-read books, have illustrations like picture books, but their format is more grown up. The length varies from thirty-two to sixty-four pages, depending on the publisher. Stories and sentences are grammatically simple, using only one idea in each sentence. *Little Bear* by Else Holmelund is a classic early reader series. There are several sentences on each page, but they are easy to understand. *The Cat in the Hat* and *Oh the Things You Can Think* by Dr. Seuss are among the best-known early readers and a great example of the format for this genre. Dr. Seuss uses rhyming and verse to engage children while they read. Hidden in the fun words and silly phrases resides an inspiring moral for kids to learn.

In early readers, the sentences are more complex than in pre-readers and picture books, and writers express more than one thought on each page.

Transition and Chapter Books

Publishers aim transition books, or early chapter books, at children ages six to nine to bridge the gap between easy readers and chapter books. Written like easy readers in style, transition books are longer and divided into short chapters. Writers for this subgenre favor illustrations in black and white, and only every few pages. The industry often classes transition with chapter books, since the age group and format are similar. Chapter books are typically forty-five to sixty pages long and divided into short chapters. The sentences in chapter books are more complex, although writers strive for short paragraphs. Both of these types of books will still include a lot of action. To keep the reader turning the pages—young children are easily distracted and bored—writers of chapter books will often end the chapters in the middle of the scene, pausing the action to keep the young person interested.

Beverly Cleary's *Ramona* series books are classic examples of transition books. They deal with one primary character and follow her through a series of life lessons. The classic *Chronicles of Narnia* by C.S. Lewis are chapter books, although geared to the older end of the age range and using more complex ideas and sentences.

Middle Grade

In elementary school, children enter their golden age of reading. This is the audience for middle-grade books. Children between the ages of eight and twelve (although they may be younger) begin to understand and recognize subtle character traits such as motivation. This time in a child's life marks many changes in their physical, cognitive, and emotional make-up. They have a heightened awareness of gender roles and identities. As their reasoning capacity matures, so does their interest in social and cultural issues. The writer must keep this in mind when developing their plot and create characters around the same age or slightly older to appeal to this age group. In other words, a child of ten usually prefers to read about protagonists between the ages of ten and twelve rather than a protagonist who is eight. Also, boys make the best protagonists because a girl is more likely to read a story about a male protagonist than a boy is about a female in this age range.

These books are usually about 100-150 pages, which is longer than chapter books, although the two subgenres are often confused. The difference is that middle-grade stories are just starting to include subplots involving secondary characters woven through the story. A strong main character, or protagonist, is important when writing these books. Readers at this level will cheer for a hero/heroine to succeed and overcome the obstacles a writer places in front of them, so an active protagonist is important. Like the target audience, these characters will care for people and issues. They will take risks, such as standing up to bullies.

Another issue to consider while writing for this genre is that middle graders are perceptive. They notice subtleties and know when something is off. The writer must research and figure out how children this age think, feel, speak, and act. Memories of childhood are not enough; each generation is different. However, there are similarities—or constants—that remain unchanged no matter what the decade. Smart writers will seek this middle ground so their books aren't dated before they are published. If children do not identify with the character, their interest will wane with surprising speed.

Setting begins to become important at this level as well, but ninety percent of the story will still consist of dialogue and action. Genres in middle grade books range from present day to science fiction and fantasy. *Anne of Green Gables* by L.M. Montgomery (literature) and *The Nancy Drew Series* by Carolyn Keene (mystery) are classic examples of middle-grade books. *Artemis Fowl* by Eoin Colfer is another good example that targets ages ten to twelve years.

6.3.1.2 FANTASY FICTION

Fantasy uses magic or other supernatural forces as a primary ingredient in plot, setting, and theme. According to experts, "supernatural" means beyond what is unexplainable by natural law. Most societies consider miracles, magic, curses, and the afterlife supernatural happenings, whether individual members of these societies believe in them or not. These extraordinary occurrences are mostly lacking in proof by nature beyond the norm.

Many fantasy stories take place in fictional settings where magic is commonplace. Publishers distinguish fantasy from other speculative fiction (science fiction and horror) by its avoidance of scientific and macabre themes, although there are overlaps of the three genres that have created subgenres. Therefore, fantasy, science fiction, and horror—separately and in combination within their subgenres—comprise the category of speculative fiction.

Inspiration from real-world history, sociology, culture, mythology, and folklore provide consistent themes in fantasy. Writers may hide the fantastical ingredient, or weave it into a real-world setting. They may draw the characters into an alternate reality, or set the story in an imagined setting, where magic is an accepted part of that world. Some fantasy worlds are set in medieval or futuristic times. Others are parallel worlds connected to Earth through magical portals or objects.

While the events of a story may be implausible or even impossible, they bind together with internal logic, following a pre-determined set of laws or strictures, such as those of magic, and take place in a setting that is internally consistent. For example, in J.R.R. Tolkien's *Lord of the Rings*, the author-created world has a unique set of rules: Middle Earth is a living, breathing world brimming with mythical creatures. This world has its own languages, and its people have their own unique laws, beliefs, and prejudices. These elements must combine in ways that make sense in order to create an illusion that allows the reader to suspend disbelief. Put simply, if a character insists one must say "hocus-pocus" for a certain spell to work, then every spell caster must intone "hocus-pocus" each time that particular spell is used. If a wizard cannot use magic without waving a wand while standing on one foot and crossing his eyes, then he had better stand on one foot, cross his eyes, and wave that wand every time he casts a spell.

Fantasy has several subgenres defined in the following pages. When these subgenres overlap, the strongest influence in the story elements decides their classification.

 **6.3.1.2.1 FANTASY FICTION SUBGENRES**

Arthurian Fantasy

The legend of Merlin, the powerful wizard mentor of King Arthur, fascinates writers and readers alike. Arthurian fantasy novels include some facet of King Arthur's legend. They are often retellings of the old legend, focusing on The Knights of the Round Table, Excalibur, Merlin, Morgaine, or King Arthur, either individually or together, and may be based in historical settings, fantastical settings, or adapted to modern times.

The Mists of Avalon by Marion Zimmer Bradley is an example of this Fantasy subgenre.

Comic Fantasy

Poking fun at other serious fantasies or adding doses of humor to lighthearted magical tales is a key ingredient to comic fantasies. This subgenre is humorous in intent and tone. Set in imaginary worlds, it often includes puns and parodies of other works. Editors sometimes refer to it as 'low fantasy' but many examples of this subgenre have serious undertones.

Practical Demonkeeping by Christopher Moore is an excellent exponent of comic fantasy.

Dark Fantasy

Black magic, demons, evil, mystical creatures, nightmares: Dark fantasies encompass the darker side of the fantasy genre. Stories in this subgenre contain elements of horror. Oftentimes, editors slot tales of dark fantasy as horror fiction because of their darkness, but the fantasy ingredient is also strong. The publishing house decides where each story fits based on its own needs.

The publishing industry has split dark fantasy into two types, depending on whether horror or fantasy is the main theme. Dark fantasy diverges from horror when supernatural beings and monsters, such as vampires, are more sympathetic to the human viewpoint. Anne Rice is perhaps the most popular writer of this subgenre, although the industry classifies her *Vampire Chronicles* as horror. Many of her series have for more fantastical elements than horror elements.

Books in the second category (leaning toward fantasy) focus on features common in the horror genre as well, but happen in settings closer to sword and sorcery and works of high fantasy. They are set in an author-created imaginary world. *Beowulf* falls within this category.

Epic Fantasy

A young nobody, who is often a hopeless case, gets thrown into a mammoth "Good vs. Evil" struggle where he must reach deep inside to uncover his own inner hero to save the day. Epic fantasy favors an underdog hero, often coming into powers or an inheritance and/or engaged in a grail-finding quest. The grail may be an icon, a person, a talisman or some other form of symbolic token. These stories involve a large cast of characters and take place in vast fantastical worlds.

J.R.R. Tolkien is, perhaps, the best-known example of this subgenre, with his *Lord of the Rings* trilogy set in Middle Earth—a wonderful place full of elves, magical rings, men, dwarves, and kings.

Fairytales and Mythology

The original versions of many fairytales and myths were often violent stories with strange creatures, mythical lands and unlikely heroes. Fairytales and mythological fantasies involve moral tales and beastlike creatures. They include characters drawn from folklore or myths, such as fairies, goblins, elves, and giants who have magical qualities. They are tales with a happy ending, hence the term "fairytale ending." A fairytale fantasy can be any far-fetched story or tall tale taken from traditional fairytales, myth, or legend.

In this subgenre, writers expand stories and characters and add plot twists to create novels around widely known tales. Although they are fiction, readers sense historical truths in the account, as if demons, witches, and all that they entail once existed. References to real places and religions are superficial, and they seldom comprise the focus of these stories. Fairytale fantasies exist in once-upon-a-time settings rather than in the present.

Lilith by George MacDonald is a fairytale fantasy that draws from myth to carry its message and portray the battle of Good vs. Evil, all telling features of a fairytale/mythical fantasy.

Heroic Fantasy/Sword and Sorcery

Ingredients crucial to heroic fantasy, as well as its offspring sword and sorcery fantasy, include: characters battling wizards and sorcerers; dragons and pet unicorns; battalions of goblins or other monsters; a muscle-bound hero, a god—except for the immortal part—determined to rescue his damsel in distress. Magic in these stories is a part of life, although the workings or explanation for how it works and why is often left untold in this subgenre.

Plots in both heroic and sword and sorcery fantasies are often intricate, involving many characters and lands. When emphasizing Good vs. Evil, monumental battles with the world's fate hanging in the balance is a common theme.

The protagonist in both subgenres is generally of low birth or humble origin and reluctant to take the hero's journey. Often he will be unaware of his royal ancestry. Thrust into a hero's role, spiritual and mental challenges will test both his courage and intellect. Heroic tales share traits with themes of sword and sorcery, but the blurry defining line between these subgenres is that heroic fantasy focuses on the hero and sword and sorcery focuses on the battle and magic that may surround him.

Robert E. Howard's *Conan the Barbarian* series is one of the best-known examples of heroic/sword and sorcery fantasy, because it shares focus on both magic and the hero.

High Fantasy

Perhaps the most popular of the fantasy genre, or at least the most widely known among those unfamiliar with fantasy, is high fantasy. This subgenre includes a cast of lords and ladies, dragons and knights. Writers often invent settings in medieval parallel worlds, with great kingdoms and castles grounded in classical mythology and European legends. Other characteristics include fantastical races, magic, and invented languages. As with other fantasy subgenres, high fantasy focuses on Good vs. Evil. Sometimes this subgenre crosses over into epic fantasy, as many stories span three or more books.

Terry Brooks' *Shannara* series are high fantasy novels.

Magic/Magical Realism

This subgenre has often been the center of writer's debates. They argue that magic realism is not fantasy because nothing in the stories is fantastical. By that, we mean readers of magic realism are not required to suspend belief or escape into other fictional worlds during the story. In magic realism, writers strive to show the reader our world in a different way, but it is still our modern world. Put a different way, writers tell stories from the perspective of people who live in our world and experience a different reality from the one we would call objective. Magic realism leaves the reader feeling that the world the character lives in, a world of witches for example, is one that real people truly inhabit.

Magic realism can be read as fantasy, just as it's possible to dismiss people who believe in witches as fools. However, the subgenre at its best invites the reader to experience the world as many of our fellow humans see it.

Magic realism suggests a different worldview through three main components:

1. Time is not linear.

2. Causality (relation of an event to a second event, the second being the consequence) is subjective.

3. The magical and the ordinary are the same.

Writers of this subgenre will set causally connected events together—so they don't violate reality—while convincing the reader that more than mere coincidence links the events.

In magic realism, a writer must portray the ordinary as miraculous and the miraculous as ordinary. This means that a view of the world including angels, demons, and the like walking among us can be normal and expected. An appreciation of the possibility or belief in the presence of these beings makes the world seem enchanted. Rain, sunshine, and ice can be as astonishing as seeing angels. Ice, to a group of people who have never seen it, seems amazing. Magical. How does this cold solid object disappears into a puddle of water? What makes it so cold? Look at how it catches the sunlight, reflecting the colors from within. This stuff called "ice" is incredible!

On the other hand, the tribe that considers worshipping the bringer-of-ice as a god and speaks regularly to spirits wouldn't find a ghost interrupting their ice inspection surprising. In fact, it wouldn't faze them at all. Spirits are commonplace, a daily event, but this ice…well, it's truly an amazing sight.

Magic is a part of culture in magic realism tales, and the realism surfaces in the outcomes, during which the magic carries a heavy consequence. It is also likely that the user must utilize a prop to make it work, such as a potion, amulet, or spell. Realism is an attempt to depict modern life. While characters in these novels accept magic as real, the outcomes, or the rules under which the characters must use magic, are the writer's tools to keep the fantasy rooted in realism.

Midnight's Children by Salman Rushdie is one of the better-known examples of the subgenre for its use of magic realism, although a few sources have classified it as historical since it depicts real events.

Modern Fantasy

Fantasies set in modern or contemporary times are often confused with horror fiction, as both genres set alternate worlds and magic in modern times. The distinction lies in the feeling that modern fantasy inspires in the reader. Horrific events may happen in both genres but, while the protagonist of a horror novel is horrified, in a modern fantasy, she is filled with a sense of joy and wonder, not fright.

Many modern fantasy authors set their stories in familiar places, filling the stories with local color and atmosphere, which lends an extra sense of magic to those settings.

Neil Gaiman's *Neverwhere* is a popular example of modern fantasy.

Romantic Fantasy

Critics have described romantic fantasy as the intersection between the genres of fantasy and romance. Plots focus on developing a romantic relationship between the protagonists in a setting comprised of fantastic elements. However, to rate as fantasy rather than romance, the fantasy aspect must be crucial to the plot.

So how do you know if a story is a romance or a fantasy? Fantasy publishers prefer that the emphasis be on the fantastic ingredients of the storyline, while romance would put that emphasis on developing the romantic relations of the protagonists. Still, some authors move between romance and fantasy publishers. This is not always obvious because writers use different pseudonyms (pen names) for each genre.

There are three common plots in romantic fantasy.

> 1. A teenager from a rough background (strict or abusive parent or a village razed by monsters or armies) runs away and finds he has magical or psychic powers. Therefore, his destiny involves saving a kingdom from harm by a dangerous villain or monster.

> 2. An older person, typically a minor noble or someone in search of a new life (a magician or psychic), either saves his kingdom from an invasion or overthrows a usurper from the throne. These protagonists are not warriors—or at least they seldom are. They uncover the dastardly plots through intrigue, luck, and the use of their mystical powers. In this type of romantic fantasy, the protagonist falls in love over the course of his journey. This plot focuses on the complexities of the romance between protagonist and love interest.

> 3. Circumstance or destiny draws together a motley group of orphaned teens or outcast adults. Some group members possess special powers, which complement those of the other members. For example, four group members are able to control the four elements: Earth, Water, Air/Wind, and Fire. Although reluctant, and with much conflict among some members, the group finds friendship and love with others in their group. They often end by overcoming some threat that no one else seems aware of—or can conquer—or by overthrowing the current (usually oppressive) ruling power.

Tamora Pierce's *The Immortals* series is an example of romantic fantasy.

Historical Fantasy

A mage trying to stop Hitler in Nazi Germany? An elfin plot to overthrow the Queen of England? *My, the events are accurate, but magic used in World War II and mythical creatures plotting against England's monarchy didn't happen.* This would be a historical fantasy: A story that is either set in a specific historical period—with fantasy items added to the world (magic or creatures)—or in a fictional world that resembles a historical period. Historical fantasy uses one of three common approaches:

> 1. Magic, mythical creatures or other supernatural beings coexist with the real world. Most are not aware of its existence. This overlaps with contemporary or modern fantasies, but the difference is in the historical features.

2. An alternative history with distinct differences from our own real history.

3. A secondary world that parallels a known place and a specific historical period.

Publishers have classified historical fantasies into several subgenres.

Celtic Fantasy

From Dark Ages Celtic cultures. Writers have used the folklore of Ireland, Wales, and Scotland either separately or together. A great example is the four-part series by Evangeline Walton *The Island of the Mighty, The Children of Llyr, The Song of Rhiannon,* and *Prince of Annwn,* focusing on the *Mabinogion,* the title given to a collection of eleven tales taken from medieval Welsh manuscripts.

Steampunk

This subgenre is set in the Victorian or Edwardian eras. Steam power mixed with Victorian or Gothic-style architecture or technology is the most popular formula for this subgenre. Some sources classify steampunk as science fiction. The difference between sci-fi and fantasy novels in this subgenre is focus. Adding fantastical elements, such as magic or other worlds, sets the story as a steampunk fantasy. Without those details, it is science fiction.

YA author Arthur Slade's *The Hunchback Assignments* series follows the criteria for steampunk fantasy and is a good example.

Wuxia

A strange word which means "martial arts heroes," names a subgenre of historical fantasy. It is prominent in Chinese popular culture and has a devoted following. Wuxia is a combination of the philosophy of *xia* or the honor code, and China's history in kung fu and martial arts.

A typical Wuxia plot features a young male protagonist who experiences a tragedy (losing his family or a dear friend). He endures trials throughout his adventures and learns many forms of martial arts from various teachers. At the end of the story, the protagonist emerges as a powerful fighter whom few can equal. He follows the Code of Xia—the hero's code of honor, common to all heroes whether warrior, knight, or other, and offers his powers to mend the ills of the community or world. (*Jianghu* in Wuxia stories often translates as underworld, world of vagrants, or world of martial arts.)

Medieval Fantasy

This subgenre focuses on the Middle Ages and sometimes shows fictitious versions of historical events. Its followers use it in role-playing games and high fantasy literature. While the setting is medieval, writers don't set these stories in any real world medieval setting.

What also sets these novels apart as fantasy, rather than historical fiction, is the tropes: the fantasy races (elves and dwarves), magic, fantastic creatures (dragons, ogres, werewolves, unicorns and monsters), royalty, castles, heroes, and great tragedy.

A popular example of this subgenre is *The Princess Bride* by William Goldman.

Prehistoric Fantasy

A story set in prehistoric times, which describes the lives of that era's people. Fictional, of course, these books include prehistoric creatures such as saber-toothed tigers, woolly mammoths, or Mastodons.

The writer ventures into anthropological guesswork to compose these tales. They're often a blend of fiction peppered with a dash of scientific fact. The writer creates a world that no one has visited and makes it believable enough so the reader considers the details to be facts. To do this, writers often include fictional languages, beliefs, and cultures.

Perhaps the best example of this genre is Jean M. Auel's *Earth's Children* series.

Urban Fantasy

Urban fantasy can take place in history, modern times, or the future. The defining characteristic of urban fantasy is place. The story has to take place primarily in a city and have supernatural or paranormal elements. Because of this, urban fantasy is sometimes combined with the paranormal or modern fantasy subgenres. The difference is that paranormal fantasy might not have an urban setting and modern fantasy is set in present day, while the urban fantasy writer is free to choose any period.

Charlaine Harris's Sookie Stackhouse novels are considered urban fantasies by some, although they also fit into the paranormal romance and modern fantasy subgenres.

How can a writer guess where their work fits? Typically, publishers place books according to their internal guidelines. Some common elements in urban fantasy, other than the main elements of supernatural and urban settings, include characters often having some personal issues or a tragic past. Conflicts such as these blend into the plot and play a key role in the protagonist's development. As we mentioned, although urban fantasies may be set in modern times, this isn't necessary.

Cassandra Clare's YA urban fantasy *Clockwork Angel* is set in Victorian London.

Laurell K. Hamilton's Anita Blake urban fantasy novels have also been classified as paranormal romances. Urban fantasy is a subgenre that tends to combine many other genres, which makes it difficult to define on its own. In fact, we considered leaving it out of our subgenre list because it's so hard to pin down to a simple definition. Often urban fantasy authors blend mystery, romance, and science fiction into the fantasy elements, which confuses the matter further. We define urban fantasy as a novel that uses supernatural elements like vampires, werewolves, magic and such, with urban settings like New York, London, or another major city. The period does not have to be contemporary to make it an urban fantasy novel.

Sherrilyn Kenyon's novels are excellent examples of urban fantasies.

6.3.1.3 HORROR FICTION

Horror fiction seeks to induce feelings of terror and dread in the reader. Supernatural horror—the most popular subgenre—has its roots in folklore and religious myth that focuses on death, the afterlife, the demonic, and the principle of evil embodied in the devil. These traits manifest in stories of witches, vampires, werewolves, and ghosts as well as demonic pacts, selling your soul for beauty or love or, the most popular desire: power. However, not all horror is supernatural. Some subgenres deal with truly possible horrors within our world, capturing them from the headlines or far worse: from their readers' nightmares.

Whether you write supernatural or psychological, splatter, or black comedy horror, all subgenres are similar in that they use overwhelmingly dark, evil forces, either human or supernatural. They provoke feelings of unease and dread as well as psychological and physical responses within readers. A cornerstone of horror fiction is evoking terror with the unexpected or the unknown. H.P. Lovecraft once remarked, "The oldest and strongest emotion of humankind is fear, and the oldest and strongest fear is fear of the unknown."

Horror stories aren't always filled with ghosts, ghouls, or blood, and gore. The only requirement is that the writing elicits an intense emotional reaction that includes some aspect of fear or dread. Setting in horror novels is dark, the atmosphere intense, and the pace fast. Often, the writer may slip in calm interludes, then shatter them with sudden intense jolts of action (or terror) and create a menacing effect, setting the reader on edge.

Unlike other fiction genres, there isn't always a happy ending. Rather, the resolution may be vague and leave the reader with a sense that the menace still lurks in the shadows.

Horror fiction has many subgenres, ranging from subtle dread to in-your-face, gut-wrenching terror. In the following pages, we define and discuss the most popular or well known.

6.3.1.3.1 HORROR FICTION SUBGENRES

Slipstream/Cross-Genre

When speculative fiction (horror, fantasy, science fiction) slips into mainstream fiction it's called slipstream or cross-genre fiction. Some authors classify slipstream as "weird" fiction. A slipstream or cross-genre horror novel hinges on the writer's theme focus. Physical laws may be broken, but the science is not questioned. In slipstream or cross-genre horror, the strange characters of speculative fiction (wizards, zombies, and vampires) are not present, so the reader can't blame the weirdness on them. Human characters lend creepiness to these tales, but not by being bizarre. They are average people, and their normalcy in the face of strange circumstances typifies a slipstream story.

This subgenre usually has a literary feel to it. Writers of cross-genre stories take risks with style, and the stories have a message or a lesson, some even making outright political or social statements.

In slipstream, structure, theme, and emotion rise above character and plot. Although there is a plot, what the writer says, or *how* he says it, is more important than the sequence of events. Often the characters are symbolic and are not as significant to the story as the writing.

Shirley Jackson's short story, "The Lottery," is an excellent example of slipstream fiction.

Cutting Edge

Cutting-edge horror purposely goes against the accepted rules of the genre. This subgenre can be hard, soft, psychological, surreal, literary, erotic, or other. While it has traits of horror fiction, the departure from the norm is likely to be stylistic or thematic.

Definitions of cutting-edge horror shift but, in general, it is fiction that refuses conventional and supernatural traits, unless they're used in a manner where they stand in opposition to traditional horror.

Writers of cutting edge worry less about the big scare and more about style and tone. A writer may stretch the standard three-act plot (although it's important to understand the three-act plot before doing so), using the first two hundred pages to set the mood of the story and the last hundred or so to bring out the intricacies of the plot. This is cutting edge, or fiction that goes against conventional rules. Often with cutting-edge horror, the writer plays with atmosphere, slipping the sensation of unease and terror into the reader before anything horrific occurs.

Douglas Clegg's *Purity* is a pioneer story of this subgenre.

Dark Fantasy

This subgenre is "interstitial," meaning it bleeds or crosses into other genres, sharing a similar definition that makes them hard to separate. Dark fantasy is also a subgenre of fantasy, and many writers become confused about whether they've written a horror novel or a fantasy novel. The difference between horror and fantasy stories remains in the focus given to the story details.

A dark-fantasy horror plot combines traits of fantasy, such as supernatural beings like vampires and werewolves, and themes from myths and fairytales, with horrific concepts to inspire fear in the reader. These stories may focus on human evil and strife rather than on monsters.

A dark-fantasy story is often about a tremendous struggle in a bleak setting threatened by overwhelming forces. It is most often marked with a pessimistic tone and moral ambiguity. The story may even offer hope as characters grow and change.

Parasite by Ramsey Campbell includes many elements of a great dark-fantasy horror tale.

Erotic Horror

The word erotic brings to mind sex, pleasure, romance, and titillating prose that leaves the reader stimulated. However, erotic horror is usually far from pleasant or arousing. "Erotic" is sometimes assumed to mean graphic, intentionally explicit sex in a story meant for a pornographic market. That isn't always the intent. Erotic horror can contain explicit sex, but it shouldn't cross the line into porn. Naturally, as among readers and writers, there is disagreement in the publishing industry about the difference between explicit sex and porn.

Erotic horror must have sex woven into the plot so the horror is still the main drive of the story. The sex scenes must grow from the storyline—not be added in for the sake of it—and blended in such a way that the reader can't decide whether to be aroused or afraid.

Writers must hold the reader in the erotic scene with description, but avoid coarse language. Vulgarity leads to pornography. Erotic horror keeps readers in the scene long enough to distract them from the horror (or to arouse them...just a little) before throwing the terror in when they least expect it. Good erotic horror takes the reader from arousal to repulsion in a heartbeat, before dragging him back.

Graham Masterson's erotic horror tale *Epiphany* successfully combines sex with horror to create a story that disturbs, arouses, and then horrifies the reader.

Extreme

Stories that go straight for the gross-out and involve loads of blood and gore are extreme horror. The writer heaps explicit violence and gore from beginning to end in stories as raw as fiction can get. This subgenre is further split into splatterpunk and visceral.

Splatterpunk

A term coined by David J. Schow in the mid 1980s, splatterpunk is characterized by its graphic depiction of violence, sex, and gore. Although the term was popular through the following decade, and the genre has maintained a cult-like following, editors class splatterpunk as extreme horror.

Visceral

This horror genre falls in between regular horror and splatterpunk. It is not gross enough for the latter but is too graphic for other subgenres.

Exquisite Corpse by Poppy Z. Brite is a good example of extreme horror fiction.

Fabulist

Stories that bridge the gap between literary and genre fiction are called fabulist horror. Writers of these stories explore genre conventions within a literary framework, experiment with form, and use dense or uncommon language. The works are intended for savoring in small sips. Because the term "fabulist" is subjective, what one publisher classifies as suitable, another may reject or slot into straight horror. Since it is difficult to place, writers who wish to publish quickly would be wisely advised to stick to the more marketable subgenres.

Something Wicked This Way Comes by Ray Bradbury bills as fabulist horror.

Gothic

At one time, Gothic and horror were identical, but in recent decades they have diverged. Gothic literature has pointed toward a certain tone and setting—in horror as well as other genres—making it unique. Written in a literary style, many Gothic horror novels focus on evil from the past, such as haunted mansions or buildings and/or an outside forces influencing sanity. Most of Edgar Allen Poe's work fits this category.

Major ingredients of a Gothic-horror novel include terror (psychological and physical), mystery, the supernatural, ghosts, Gothic architecture, castles, death, decay, madness and curses.

Common characters found in this subgenre include all those found in horror or fantasy novels. Themes often define Gothic literature; for example, a character trapped by something, such as family, location, or destiny. These stories combine features of horror and romance to achieve the effect of a pleasing terror. Melodrama and parody are also components that make the genre distinctive.

Although often mistaken as related, Gothic fiction and the Goth subculture are not the same.

There are two 'styles' or subgenres of Gothic horror: English and American (Southern) Gothic.

Salutation

Writers of this genre often use medieval buildings and settings. They associate these settings with dark and terrifying times, with harsh laws enforced by torture and mysterious, superstitious rituals. For example, anti-Catholicism literature features European Roman Catholic excesses like the Inquisition.

An important theme throughout English Gothic fiction intrudes the past on the present. The writer uses haunted settings, such as crypts, castles, and convents, creating images of ruin and decay, imprisonment, cruelty, and persecution to show this oppression of the past on the "enlightened" present.

An American setting and more of a psychological interest in abnormal mindset defines **American Gothic.** Mental breakdown plays a larger role than the gloomy atmosphere of English Gothic. Specific themes include the rational vs. irrational, Puritanism, guilt, ghosts, and monsters. The basis of these ideas comes from a past riddled with slavery, racism, hostile Native American relations (and their eventual genocide), and the intimidating wilderness of the American frontier. American Gothic fiction rarely includes castles or objects which allude to a civilized history.

The Mysteries of Udolpho by Ann Radcliffe is a standard Gothic novel.

Lovecraftian

If a writer considers horror her genre of choice, we would urge her to read H.P. Lovecraft's works. His brand of horror is cerebral, mostly about letting the reader's mind take planted hints and run with them in his own time.

Inspired by the pioneering fiction of H.P. Lovecraft, Lovecraftian works (old and new) have a distinct style with florid prose and buckets of pessimism.

Anti-anthropocentrism (the idea that humans view themselves as the central and most significant entities in the universe) and misanthropy (a generalized disgust, dislike, and distrust of humans, society, and human nature in general) are key traits of Lovecraftian horror. His works don't focus on human characterization, which reflects the view of humanity's inconsequential place in the universe and the general Modernist (questioning accepted truths of a previous age) trend of literature at the time.

Another ingredient that dominates this subgenre is preoccupation with visceral secretions, from innards, intestines, and inner organs. Lovecraft's stories usually involve semi-gelatinous substances and slime, rather than standard horror elements such as blood, bones, or corpses.

Language use is a key identifier of Lovecraft's style. Old-fashioned words and anachronisms, such as "shew" for show and "men of science" for scientists give his work a distinctive flavor. He does the same when dealing with modern technology.

Characterization is another element. Heroes in Lovecraftian works are usually intelligent loners with academic backgrounds. Driven by an outside force to their end, the heroes are unable to escape. They sometimes deal a blow to the forces working against them, but their victories are temporary. Often, the hero must pay a steep price.

Unanswered questions are another common denominator. While most fiction resolves questions by the end, Lovecraftian characters often go insane if they dare try to understand what happens to them. Characters in many Lovecraft stories can't cope with the extraordinary and unreasonable truths they bear witness to. The strain of trying to cope, as Lovecraft illustrates, is impossible to bear unscathed.

Stephen King's work shows Lovecraftian influence and some name his novel *Duma Key* a good example of Lovecraftian horror.

Noir

Noir horror is dark and cynical, rife with paranoid themes of corruption, alienation, lust, obsession, revenge, and the difficulty of finding redemption in an imperfect world. Set in gritty urban environments, with cynical and weary characters, this subgenre steeps in an atmosphere of menace, pessimism, and anxiety. Realism dominates it.

A modern example of noir horror is *Life Expectancy* by Dean Koontz.

Psychological Horror

Just as the term suggests, this subgenre focuses on the human psyche, written from a tight point of view. In fact, the viewpoint must be so firmly entrenched in the character's head that the reader knows every thought, feeling, smell, taste, sound, touch, reaction, facial expression, and motivation. In short, intimate. Consider how a loose POV (point of view) would show the reader emotions and senses, but he would never become part of the character's psyche.

This subgenre can alter the readers' perceptions by exposing them to an insane perspective, or offer a confusing reality verging on the supernatural: Does the protagonist see these terrible things, is he really battling against demonic possession, or is he going insane? Alternately, the POV might be a tormented serial killer. The reader already knows the protagonist is insane and gets a rare peek into a terrifying mind.

When compared with traditional horror, this subgenre is subtle in many ways. Typically, it contains less physical harm and focuses on mentally shifting its readership rather than relying on the graphic imagery of the slash and splatter subgenres. Psychological horror discomfits the reader by baring what humans fear in themselves: the darker parts of the psyche we often repress or deny.

A writer of psychological horror strives to expose evil hiding behind normalcy, while splatter fiction focuses on bizarre evil the average reader can't relate to.

Another common theme of psychological horror is its use of body horror, to provoke uneasiness by exploiting fears of disease, suffering, and human experimentation.

Psychological horror is not to be confused with the psychological thriller, which has a subtle but important difference. In horror, the goal is to frighten the audience. Writers delve for fear. Thrillers rely on tension and action plots, stimulating adrenaline.

Heart Shaped Box by Joe Hill is an excellent psychological horror story.

Quiet (or Soft) Horror

Quiet horror is a mild subgenre, subtle, never visceral or too shocking, using atmosphere and mood to create a cloud of fear but lacking in graphic description. Understated but strong emotion, rather than in-your-face violence, makes these stories work.

'48 by James Herbert is a good example of quiet horror.

Supernatural

In supernatural horror, the rules of the normal world no longer apply. The reader is treated to tales of ghosts, demons, vampires, zombies, the occult, and more. This subgenre has an ever-expanding list of categories, most of which include vampires. However, in horror fiction, supernatural stories focus on monsters from beyond, who rather persistently insist on ruining the lives of a tormented humanity. The protagonist often gets stranded in an isolated village or other remote setting. Anne Rice's *Vampire Chronicles* novels brim with powerful mystical and mysterious beings.

The popularity of supernatural horror has spawned a branch subgenre called paranormal horror. Sporting mortal heroes, these tales play out a battle against supernatural invasion, whether by a saintly exorcist, high-tech vampire hunters, or ghost busters. Unlike most horror fiction, there's a good chance the good guys will prevail.

Suspense (or Dark Suspense) and Thriller

No vampires or ghosts, evil demons, or werewolves reside in suspense/dark suspense and thriller horror. Instead of supernatural elements, these stories include a hovering threat from an external menace. Care must be taken, however. Add too much of an investigative angle, and the story becomes more mystery than horror. Underline action and adventure with that suspense and a thriller emerges. The difference again is in the writer's intent to frighten readers, rather than excite them.

Though thriller horror adds action and mystery to the story, the overriding theme is terror. The hero may run, but he can't hide. His desperation is palpable, but the reader isn't as sure of a happy ending as he would be in other genres.

David Morrell's *Black Evening*, a short story collection, is a good example of this subgenre.

⊛ Body Horror, Biological Horror, or Organic Horror

Imagine a body decaying, infected with some parasite. When the body is about to dissolve, or at least it looks like it might—muscles cave in, crushing the bones until there is nothing but tissue and blood left on the cold metal table before you—the stomach moves.

Terror rises.

Out pops a small, but disgusting little head. Over a beaked nose, its beady eyes take in its surroundings, slowly, as though digesting each item, every shadow, and storing it for future use. Then the head turns and the eyes, so dead yet so… intelligent... focus *on you.*

This is body or biological horror. Graphic destruction or degeneration of the body marks this subgenre. These tales deal with disease, decay, parasitism, mutilation, and mutation. They may include unnatural movements, wrong placement of limbs to create monsters out of human body parts, and other such niceties.

Sometimes these stories find themselves in the extreme subgenre, but that placement is often wrong. The narrative is not always in your face and might focus on real, possible horrors, not extreme in any way.

Clive Barker's *The Hellbound Heart*, is an excellent example of the genre.

⊛ Monster

Think *Frankenstein.* Monster horror begs the question: How does science affect the creation and destruction of supernatural beings? In *Frankenstein* by Mary Shelley, the protagonist, Dr. Frankenstein, grows up in the eighteenth century, the Age of Enlightenment. This philosophy or new thinking inspires him to give up his love for science. He creates a monster that soon threatens the lives of many.

In *I Am Legend* by Richard Matheson, the protagonist uses scientific advances to search for a medicine. The antidote he creates will fight the bacteria that have turned the world population into vampires.

A key element to monster horror is isolation. In *Frankenstein*, both the doctor and his monster are alone. Doctor Frankenstein obsesses over his experiments and neglects love and family. His creation complete, he leaves the monster to fend for itself. The monster then retaliates, killing friends and relatives until Doctor Frankenstein and his wife are isolated.

Because of the helplessness it implies, loneliness is another crucial component of monster horror. Again, in *I Am Legend*, Robert Neville is the last human on Earth (or so he believes.)

Monster horror must also have duality. The most obvious example would be *The Strange Case of Dr. Jekyll and Mr. Hyde* by Robert Louis Stevenson. At night, Dr. Jekyll turns into Mr. Hyde, his evil and monstrous side. By day, he returns to his real identity as the docile doctor. In time, this duality blends, and he changes identity.

Another common example of duality is a vampire resting through the day only to become a bloodthirsty monster by night.

Holocaust

Although not often tagged as a subgenre, tales that involve mass deaths, whether during the horrific holocausts of the 20th century, or similar tragedies, past or future, are termed holocaust horror because they are unique from other horror subgenres.

The deaths might be due to human slaughter, but they can also be from a plague or monsters (think zombies). In a few bizarre versions, everyone has already died, and today's humanity is the replacement—but doesn't know it. Stephen King's novel *The Stand* paints a picture of a near-future apocalyptic plague that echoes these elements.

Black Comedy

Black comedy understates the macabre or exaggerates it into parody. Here, the writer treats disturbing or sinister subjects like death, disease, or warfare with bitter amusement, usually in a manner calculated to shock and offend.

Using grotesque or morbid humor, the writer shows the absurdity, insensitivity, and cruelty of the modern world. He exaggerates characters and situations beyond the limits of satire. The black humor writer uses devices often associated with tragedy, and his work is sometime termed a tragic farce.

Kurt Vonnegut's *Slaughterhouse Five* is a superb example of the genre.

6.3.1.4 MYSTERY / CRIME FICTION

In mystery/crime fiction, plot is everything. It's about solving a puzzle, and it should be a tingling challenge. Because of this, each plot point must be logical, believable, and fast-paced. Getting mired in backstory or wandering off on tangents ruins the reader's experience.

Some critics classify mystery and crime novels separately, but the framework is the same, with the difference being mysteries focus on the detective and crime novels focus on the evidence or the puzzle. However, the structure, or formula, is the same for both, which qualifies them as one genre.

First, the writer should introduce the detective (protagonist) and villain/criminal (antagonist) early on to plant a suspect in the reader's mind. Don't identify him as the culprit though, or risk giving the game away. Instead, introduce him as one possible suspect among others. If he appears too late, readers will feel cheated; they didn't get the whole story to puzzle out ahead of time—which puts them at a disadvantage for trying to figure out whodunit. This is like delaying a runner's start by tying his shoelaces together. As a result, he loses.

Next in the recipe is the crime, which is best introduced within the first three chapters. An early crime starts the puzzle and hooks readers at once, the goal of fiction writing.

The genre masters recommend that the crime be violent, yet believable. Murder is the most enthralling candidate for a three hundred-page book. However, the how, where, and why (means, opportunity, and motive) and the crime's discovery, must be plausible. How the pieces fit together is what makes the puzzle unique, just remember to keep the logical part in mind. The reader works to solve the crime using reason, and she will feel cheated if she learns the crime could never logically happen in the real world.

Another must in mystery/crime fiction is that the protagonist solves the mystery using only the skills given him on-stage. Divine revelation, intuition, coincidence or acts of god are not realistic or logical, and unsuitable to solve a crime.

In the same vein, the villain must be able to commit the offense within physical, psychological, and emotional constraints. A shy, one hundred-pound, pro-life, antiviolence spinster maid with a bum leg and a heart condition could not strangle her landlord with panty hose. She's not strong enough, healthy enough, or big enough to overpower a full-grown man with her bare hands.

In addition, the motivation must be believable. It can't be because that the urge took her one night. Her personality needs to harbor homicidal tendencies somewhere in the story for any sudden urge to make sense. What stakes could make this woman deny everything she has stood for to commit murder? She would certainly seem like a sympathetic villain. What action could she take against a large man whose one-room efficiency unit is the only thing standing between her and living on the street? Now, there's a mystery!

The mystery writer's goal is to challenge, not fool, the reader. While red herrings (deliberate diversions) are welcome, disguises, evil twins, coincidental, or supernatural solutions dilute the reader's fun. Clues revealed to the reader as the detective receives them build suspense toward the climactic exposure of the culprit. Timing is everything. If the writer answers the question of whodunit too early, there is no reason for the reader to stick around. In addition, if the answer can never be deduced logically from the information revealed, the reader is likely lost for the next adventure.

Last, as with all fiction, the writer should be a careful researcher. Legal procedure, scientific evidence, human nature, and other elements that go into mystery/crime fiction must be authentic. The reader will know when a writer doesn't have a good grasp on what he's writing about. Vague, glossed-over details won't win reader interest. The writer must know his stuff, from the crime to the punishment.

6.3.1.4.1 MYSTERY/CRIME SUBGENRES

Whodunit

Stories that comprise the whodunit subgenre show the protagonist working through well hidden clues to solve a crime, which is often a murder. Most whodunits are either first person POV (I frowned, I ran, etc.) or third person limited (he frowned, he ran), focusing on one character's point of view (usually the detective's). This allows an intimate connection between the reader and the detective and creates a sense of fair play in revealing clues.

Often whodunits include characteristics of other mystery/crime subgenres. As in all fiction, a little crossing over is common. The defining difference between a whodunit and other mysteries is the puzzle. Puzzles are the key ingredient, which allow the clever reader the opportunity to solve the mystery before the detective, but not too far in advance. The detective is sometimes eccentric and if not an amateur, no more than a beginner or novice in investigative work.

Of course, there are exceptions and the detective can be a hardened professional. Agatha Christie's *Hercule Poirot* novels are classic whodunits.

Medical Mystery

As science evolves, this genre grows more popular. Medical mysteries, as the title implies, take place in a hospital setting and often involve illegal deeds by medical personnel or bureaucrats. Most writers in this genre have vast knowledge and understanding of medical procedures and laws. Robin Cook (an M.D.) and Patricia Cornwell are among the most popular today.

Outbreak by Robin Cook has every feature for a medical mystery in place: disease, bureaucrats, murder, corruption, and one detective—not a criminal investigator—who must expose the culprit.

Courtroom Drama

The legal process that brings criminals to justice fascinates people. Courtroom dramas satisfy this curiosity. In these stories, an attorney is the protagonist, generally the defense attorney representing a client that may be falsely accused. Of course, it's up to him or her to prove their client's innocence.

In a courtroom drama, the main character must endanger his or her career, relationships, or life in pursuit of justice. In many of these books, the justice system becomes a character as well, almost an antagonist to the attorney seeking justice, adding obstacles at every turn.

John Grisham's *The Firm*, *A Time to Kill,* and *The Client*, are good examples of Courtroom Dramas.

Detective Fiction

Detective fiction is a story in which the detective solves a crime, or a series of crimes. The bad news is writing detective fiction is much harder than defining it. Detective stories always rely on sound logic. Supernatural elements rarely come into play, so these stories must make sense. This means the plots must be have rational conclusions—even if the Butler did it. The writer must hide clues in the story so that when the reader adds two and two, four is the only possible answer.

The detective character can be a professional, such as a private investigator or a cop, or can be an amateur sleuth like an unemployed spy or a soccer mom. The key detail is that he or she will have nothing to gain by solving the crime or crimes. The motivation for these protagonists is to see justice served.

As in other genres, detective stories follow a set of guidelines. Readers want a particular experience and choose genre books with such an expectation. In detective stories, readers demand the intellectual challenge of solving the crime and the payoff of knowing everything will come together in the end. The baddies are revealed, and the detective gets his or her man…or woman.

Detective fiction divides further into two subgenres: **Cozies and Hard-boiled.**

Cozies

Novels belonging to this subgenre contain little violence, apart from the murder, and no detailed blood and gore. They're called cozies because of their settings, which are often genteel and benign. They use an "average Joe" or amateur sleuth as a protagonist, and every story finishes with the loose ends tied up and sees the bad guy punished for his or her crimes. Think Agatha Christie's *Miss Marple* novels for an example of this kind of novel. The protagonist, Jane Marple, is a grandmotherly type who spends her leisure time knitting and tending her garden. Often she comes across to other characters as confused or flighty, but when a mystery presents itself, she displays a sharp mind and a keen understanding of human nature. Invariably, she embarrasses the professionals in the story by solving the crime before they do.

Hard-boiled

These mysteries are gritty, with a professional investigator as the protagonist. They're more realistic than cozies and often full of corruption, sex, and violence. The protagonist is generally tough and street smart, therefore the term hard-boiled. *The Maltese Falcon* by Dashiell Hammett is a classic hard-boiled detective novel. Its protagonist, Sam Spade is also typical for such a novel. He is detached, with an eye for detail. He shows determination to see justice done, and although he has seen the darker side of life, he still keeps his tarnished idealism.

Locked Room

A crime has been committed and the criminal vanished. Impossible! Not in a locked-room mystery. After a murder under far-fetched circumstances where the culprit has disappeared, all will be revealed in the end, and—this is the writer's challenge—it will make sense.

This subgenre shares many likenesses with whodunits. However, the circumstances make it different. The crime scene is one that no intruder or culprit could have either entered or exited, hence, "locked room." The investigator or detective in these stories faces evidence that the perpetrator has vanished into thin air, leaving only what appear, at the time, to be minor clues. The need for a rational explanation, and a solution to the crime, drives the protagonist to look beyond first appearances and solve the puzzle.

With the detective, the reader confronts the puzzle and the clues in the first few chapters. He tries to solve the mystery before the solution surfaces through a series of events told after the climax. This is called a denouement (final resolution), an important ingredient in locked room mysteries. Denouements untie or unravel the twists or complexities of the plot.

Arthur Conan Doyle's *Sherlock Holmes* novels are classic examples of locked room mysteries.

Police Procedural

These plots flip the traditional mystery/crime guidelines on their ear. Rather than focusing on one crime, they depict investigations by a police force into several crimes. They often reveal the perpetrator at the outset.

Research for this subgenre is critical. The writer must draw on the activities of the police as they investigate crimes, and must be knowledgeable in related topics like forensics, autopsies, evidence gathering, securing search warrants, and interrogation techniques. The writer must know whether fingerprints can be obtained from a gun (they can but it's difficult), how and where a man would have to be stabbed to die in a short time, procedure when entering or discovering a crime scene, how to interrogate witnesses as opposed to suspects, etc. The list is long and complex.

As if this weren't challenging enough, police procedural writers must also keep the reader interested in a story where they already know whodunit. Excitement, danger, intrigue, and corruption are good ways to do this, but the writer must know how much and where to place detail, and how to dose out information to the reader so she will stick around to see how the story develops. Readers have to learn something, such as howdunit.

Michael Connelly is one of the leading authors of police procedural novels.

Caper

Theft, swindling, the occasional kidnapping are all perpetrated in full view of the reader. Gasp!

These caper stories often involve one or more of such crimes at a time. Although they portray the police trying to prevent or solve the crimes, solution is not the focus of the story. If the criminal or culprit is the main character or the protagonist, the reader follows him as he attempt to get away with it, through one, often humorous, event after another.

Cleverness and daring are key traits for the main character of this type of crime story.

Donald Westlake creates the perfect caper in *What's the Worst that Can Happen?*

6.3.1.5 ROMANCE FICTION

The romance genre relies on one of the strictest formulas in fiction. Some believe the genre has added too many limitations, from plot essentials, such as the guaranteed happy ending, to excluding taboo themes like adultery. While most romance novels comply, some do deviate from traditional rules. The basic definition—as given by the Romance Writers of America and romance publishers—only requires that writers include two components in a romance story:

1) A romance must contain a central love story, with the plot conflict focusing primarily on two people falling in love and then struggling to preserve that love.

2) These stories must include an emotionally satisfying, i.e. "happy" ending. Romance fans want to escape reality and to "feel good." After the intense emotional battle of trying to set up a bond, readers want the good guys to come together in the end.

As long as the work meets these standards, it can be set in any time period or location. Beyond the taboo topics, there are no limits on what can or cannot be included in a romance novel—although individual publishers may list their own preferences and pet peeves in the guidelines. Romance plots often include controversial topics like date rape, domestic violence, and addiction. The ingredients of time, location, and other plot essentials contribute to ground a novel into one of several romance subgenres.

Those who have never read romance fiction sometimes think of it as erotica, which is not the case. Although the main themes are relationships and love, these do not always center on sexuality. Romance focuses on the love story between two people rather than on physical intimacy. Writers may integrate sex scenes into the plot for payoff, but the main goal is to develop the romantic relationship.

Romance has generated much ridicule and criticism. Some reviewers call the stories "predictable and boring," citing the inevitability that the hero and heroine will get together in the end. These critics often disparage the mental capacity of romance fans, wondering about the motivation to read books with such predictable endings. In this case, the draw to the genre mirrors the critics' skepticism. Romance fiction postulates a certainty in something essential to our psyche that is uncertain in the real world: Perfect love is out there somewhere.

Romance novels divide into two groups: category romances—also known as series romances—and single-title romances. Most writers publish within a single format, but some, like Jayne Ann Krentz, have been successful in both.

Category romances are short, around two hundred pages (about fifty thousand words). Publishers release defined "lines," with a specific number of books published in each line every month. Often, they number the books in sequence within the line. These novels remain on the shelves until they sell out or until the next month's releases take their places.

To write a novel of this limited length, the author must trim the story down to essentials and tighten it, removing subplots and minor characters or pushing them into the backstory.

Each category romance line has a unique set of characteristics, which may use similar settings, characters, conflict types, or time periods. Publishers of category romances will issue guidelines for each line, specifying the ingredients that must be present for a novel to qualify. This fuels the misconception that *all* romance novels are alike and must share specific elements.

Romance novels that are not part of publisher-defined lines are called single-title romances. These stories average between 350 and 400 pages. Single-title romances can remain on the shelves for a long time, at the discretion of the store.

Single titles are not always stand-alone novels. Some authors write sets of unified books—from trilogies to longer running series—revisiting characters or settings. However, publishers don't consider these to be series romances because they are not part of a particular line.

Because the definition of romance fiction does not limit plot devices, time periods, or locations, the genre encompasses multiple subgenres. The following section will explore these.

6.3.1.5.1 ROMANCE SUBGENRES

Contemporary Romance

Contemporary romance, the most popular subgenre of romance, may contain suspense, humor, and/or drama. Set in the time during which they are written (or close to it), they reflect the views and values of that time period. For example, female protagonists in contemporary romances written before 1970 will understand "happily ever after" as marrying, having children, and leaving work to care for their new family. In novels written after 1970, the heroines think that having a career *and* a family is the ideal happy ending.

Contemporary romance novels touch issues that date the stories, and most will end their print run as values change for modern readers. Plots that transcend time usually fall under other subgenres, like the works of Jane Austen as historical romances.

Nora Roberts, Jennifer Crusie, and Linda Howard are among the most popular contemporary romance novelists.

Fantasy Romance

Although still centered on a relationship, fantasy romances include elements of magic and often are set in imaginary worlds. They can incorporate supernatural creatures, like fairies and dragons, or frightening ones, like vampires and werewolves. Although, in fantasy romance, vampires and werewolves are more sexy or intriguing than horrific. Some fantasy romance writers blend myth into these romances as well.

Both fantasy and romance publishers have produced fantasy romances. The distinguishing invisible line between the two genres is drawn where the writer points the plot's focus. Fantasy romance (in the romance genre) addresses the relationship between the protagonists, both social and romantic, while romantic fantasy (in the fantasy genre) focuses on the fantasy components.

Writers handle magic in fantasy romance differently than they would in romantic fantasy. It usually spotlights innate abilities sensed as natural, like empathy or precognition, or is oriented toward controlling a natural element. Romance presents magic in the story as a positive part of someone's nature. In fantasy romance, writers depict fear of these abilities as an attitude born of ignorance or evil.

The market recognizes Jennifer Blake as a pioneer in the romance genre and many of her novels fall into the fantasy romance subgenre.

Historical Romance

Romance stories set in the past (before World War II) are historical romances. A historical romance story demands excellent research; writers must include events or characters from history and portray them accurately. Clothing, language, architecture, attitudes, beliefs, and social caste must be detailed and authentic. In general, the story is set within the United States or Europe, although some authors depict other countries and settings—sometimes fictional—in their stories. The historical setting may become a character in itself, adding romance and drama to the story line. The main characters are brave, often challenging the norms of the times.

Historical romances have several subcategories, usually classed by period.

Paranormal Romance

Romantic tales mixed with supernatural ingredients, such as ghosts, vampires, demons, or angels, fall in the paranormal romance category.

This subgenre blends the real world with either fantastic or science fiction details. Writers may weave fantastic elements like vampires, demons, or werewolves into a fictional version of our own world. Instead, the story may contain what readers see as normal expressions of the paranormal, such as humans with psychic abilities, witches, or ghosts.

Paranormal romances can be set in any time period as long as they contain the requisite paranormal element. Many writers blend elements of modern life with the existence of supernatural or magical beings. Sometimes the community around the protagonist is aware of the magic in its midst and sometimes it isn't. Paranormal romances focus less on the specifics of their alternate worlds than traditional science fiction or fantasy stories, keeping the focus on the underlying romance.

Sherilyn Kenyon is one of the most popular paranormal romance authors today. Her novels are thick with legend, myth, and of course, vampires, werewolves, and magic.

Inspirational/Christian Romance

Inspirational romances contain clear Christian themes within the romantic relationship of its protagonists. These stories seldom include uncalled-for violence or swearing and the courtship between the hero and heroine is chaste. Sex, if the author includes it, occurs after marriage and is not explicit. Another focus is the hero or heroine's faith, which turns the love angle into a triangle: the man, the woman, and their relationship with God.

This genre often bleeds into other subgenres of romance. Set in the past or the present, the writer can use themes of any subgenre as long as the element of Christianity and/or faith is present.

A good example of inspirational/Christian fiction would be novels by Lyn Cote or Diana Palmer, although some of Diana's romance work is mainstream.

Erotic Romance

Strong sexual content and "raw" language that avoids the euphemisms used in other subgenres (such as loin, orbs, or love cave) characterize erotic romance novels. Sex scenes dominate, although the romance ingredient must be strong, or else reputable publishers might class the manuscript as porn rather than romance.

While a good part of the story focus is on sexuality, erotic romance should not be confused with pornography. Pornography concentrates only on the mechanics of sex, whereas erotic romance writers must include developed characters and a plot that could exist without the sex. It is a common misconception that these stories focus on orgies, incest, bestiality, and more. Rather, the sex in erotic romances is always between two consenting adults, with focus on the growing romantic attraction between the protagonists. A novel with little romance and many sexual encounters would cross the line to pornography.

A popular author in this genre is Lora Leigh, who has several novels ranging from mild erotic romance to explicit.

❖ Romantic Suspense

Espionage, homicide, drug dealers, kidnappers, or ransom are elements of a romantic suspense novel. These works rely heavily on drama and often take place in a modern setting. As a rule, the female protagonist is the victim of a crime. She works with the hero, who is usually a police officer, FBI agent, or bodyguard, an occupation from which he can serve as her protector and see the perpetrator brought to justice. Although packed with action and edge-of-your-seat situations, the heart of the story develops a relationship between the two protagonists. By the end of the novel, the mystery is solved, the bad guy put away, and the attraction between the hero and heroine matures.

Their relationship should affect every decision they make, increasing the tension and suspense as it moves the story forward. In turn, the suspense and action must also affect the connection between the hero and heroine. Because the mystery and suspense is a crucial part of this subgenre, these stories are plot driven, and sexual content is clean when compared to other romance novels—which are character driven and more inclined to emotional intimacy.

Many of Nora Roberts' "J.D. Robb" novels are romantic suspense. Her *In Death* series is one of the most popular.

❖ Science Fiction/Time Travel Romance

A woman in modern day America leads a team researching time and space. Her colleagues think they've created a device that would allow them to see through portals in time. Before the team presents it to their supervisors, she takes the device home to tinker with last minute glitches. Why? Perhaps in the hope of getting more funding to continue a project other researchers sneer at, calling it silly and fantastical. She catches a cab, cradling her invention in its special indestructible case. A beep. She opens the case and....

Is that a bus barreling down the road at them?

Everything fades to black, and our protagonist opens her eyes to a tall, dark, and handsome man frowning down at her. He wears tights with a chainmail suit, and he has the sexiest green eyes she's ever seen. She sits up, aided by the strange man who stares at her low-cut, close-fitting suit with its tiny pencil skirt, his face reddening. Our heroine looks around her. More men stare back. They sit atop horses with their long swords and hairy faces. Is it possible she's in the middle of medieval England?

A science fiction romance includes elements found in science fiction. Often these are romances set across two different time periods with one or more characters time traveling.

Other plots may include scientific elements, such as aliens, biological experimentation, or new technologies. The dominant theme, however, is romance and the bond development between the hero and the heroine.

Writers of this subgenre must endeavor to keep the science believable and its use or misuse logical, or as logical as traveling through time, cavorting with aliens, or battling a monster virus can be. Everything that happens must have a logical hypothesis or theory behind it. The characters should react according to their experience and examine the differences, both physical and mental, between the worlds where the characters live and the one in which they have landed. Some writers choose to end their stories with the protagonists trapped in different time periods and unable to be together, an outcome not recommended for attaining the necessary "happily ever after."

Diana Gabaldon's *Drums of Autumn* is romantic science fiction, a time-travel romance set, in part, in 1760s North Carolina.

Multicultural Romance

Although romances of the past have focused on interrelations between two characters of Caucasian descent, multicultural romance features protagonists who are African-American, Asian, or Hispanic. The subgenre even encourages interracial pairing.

The themes have much in common with other romance subgenres, with the focus on race and culture and the issues that these raise in a romantic relationship. Sometimes writers of multicultural romances minimize their focus on the characters' cultural origins—letting it remain in the background—and use the romantic aspects of the story to drive the plot forward.

Popular multicultural romance author Brenda Jackson writes primarily African-American romance

6.3.1.6 SCIENCE FICTION

Science fiction answers the all-important question: what if? It explores moral, philosophical, and technological possibilities by creating new realities. Sci-fi stories focus on themes that include science, space travel, aliens, and worlds or life forms (not in any way magical) that resemble Earth and the creatures found here. Time travel is also a common theme in many science fiction novels.

Science fiction is part of the larger speculative fiction category, along with horror and fantasy. Writers of science fiction use settings outside of everyday reality to inspire discussion of new and controversial ideas.

Characterization doesn't play a huge role in most science fiction novels, and is usually secondary to the questions raised through the action of the plot. The literary end of the genre places heavier focus on characters.

Based on alternative possibilities, settings, and plots science fiction often relies on the reader's suspension of disbelief and achieves it by providing scientific explanations for fictional elements.

Fictional settings in a science fiction tale include development of a future setting, alternative timelines, or historical pasts that contradict known facts of history. Outer space or other imaginary worlds make good settings. Some tales include aliens, while others involve technology or principles that contradict the laws of nature. These exploit the discovery of new scientific principles as varied as time travel and artificial intelligence.

Science fiction often overlaps with other genres. Even within its subgenres, crossovers are common, making pinning its definition down as difficult as fleshing out the details of a new world. In addition, a plethora of innovative writers enjoys redefining genre lines and experimenting with variations of the original science fiction tropes and characteristics. The resulting list of subgenres is a long one. In the next section, we'll discuss the most popular subgenres of science fiction as publishers use them when listing their guidelines.

6.3.1.6.1 SCIENCE FICTION SUBGENRES

Hard Science Fiction

For a story to be hard science fiction, it must incorporate hard sciences (accurately) into the elements of fiction. Hard sciences are the natural or physical sciences with a strong mathematical basis, such as astronomy, biology, chemistry, and physics. In these sciences, the universe is explored with experiments or plausible theories. In short, a hard science fiction story wouldn't have spaceships powered by cooking oil and cheese strings traveling faster than light to parallel worlds.

Hard science fiction is practical and intentional. In other words, the story must be accurate, logical, and precise in its use of scientific and technical knowledge. Of course, there is flexibility in how far a story can stray from "real science" before it leaves the sphere of hard science fiction.

The terms hard or soft science fiction are markers of how strictly the writer has applied the scientific method to the sciences used in the story. Physics has a strong mathematical base, and because of that, it's generally harder to use than psychology or anthropology.

Writers of hard science fiction must have a solid knowledge base in their chosen field of science. Many writers of this genre are scientists (Gregory Benford and Geoffrey A. Landis) or mathematicians (Rudy Rucker and Vernor Vinge).

A good way to find out whether or not a novel is hard science fiction is to isolate its scientific ingredients. Now, take them away. Is there still a story? If so, it isn't hard science fiction. If there is not a story without the science, then it is. Science is crucial to hard science fiction plots.

Eon by Greg Bear is a good example of this genre.

Soft/Social Science Fiction

Soft science fiction focuses on the soft or social sciences, such as psychology, political science, anthropology, and sociology. This subgenre still uses science as a part of the plot, but the writer pays less attention to the science issues and focuses on the social or political facets of the story. Our spaceship running on cooking oil might exist in one of these novels because it is a possibility, even if there is no "hard science" to support it yet. The science fiction writer must ensure there is a possibility of using cooking oil as the key to time travel before including it. She must then shift the story focus onto character development, rather than worrying about moving faster than light or how hot the oil has to be to achieve this speed. In other words, the science doesn't have to be detailed and accurate as it does in hard science fiction, but it does have to be logical and possible.

Fahrenheit 451 by Ray Bradbury is a good example of this genre.

Cyberpunk

Stories set in the near future, often in dystopian societies where corporations have more control and power than governments, are called cyberpunk. Sometimes they depict humanity annihilating itself with its own technology. Other themes in cyberpunk include advances in technology, such as the Internet, artificial intelligence, and prosthetics. Nihilism, the belief that existence is senseless or that conditions are so bad that destroying the existing structure is preferable, and postmodernism are common themes.

The protagonists tend to be reluctant anti-heroes. Cyberpunk serves as a warning about what could happen if technology falls into the wrong hands.

Neuromancer by William Gibson (the grandfather of cyberpunk) is a perfect example of this subgenre.

Time Travel

The most famous time travel novel of all time is, perhaps, *The Time Machine*, by H. G. Wells. He also coined the term "time machine."

Writers planning to write a time-machine novel must be careful, as stories in this subgenre are plagued with logistics problems. Many critics point to the grandfather paradox, which suggests the impossibility of time travel. This paradox says that one can travel back in time and kill one's own grandfather to prevent something catastrophic in the future. Critics argue that if a character does this, he should cease to exist. Without a grandfather, the character has no parents, and without parents, the time traveler wouldn't exist—and therefore he would have prevented nothing because the grandfather would have to exist if his killer doesn't because he couldn't come back and kill his grandfather if he never existed in the first place. It's a dizzying idea.

Writers of time-travel novels can avoid this paradox by suggesting within the story the notion that the traveler moves through time in a parallel world, therefore altering nothing as he goes and respecting time's unchangeable nature.

Alternate History/Reality/Humanity

What if Napoleon invaded Canada? Perhaps Hitler won World War II and ruled the world. Maybe a race of dogs from the planet Pluto landed on Earth and demoted humans to house pets.

Alternate (or alternative) history stories follow the premise that historical events could have been different. Writers may use time travel to change the past, or set a story in a universe with a different history from our own. *The Man in the High Castle* by Philip K. Dick, in which Germany and Japan win World War II, is a great example of alternate history or alternate reality science fiction.

In alternate humanity stories, animals might speak, think, or act as humans. These novels portray humans as appalling or evil, in comparison to the animals, and make a political or social statement. The most notable alternate humanity story is George Orwell's *Animal Farm*.

Military

Wars between national or interplanetary armies feature in military science fiction, where the POV characters are often soldiers. These stories include military technology, procedure, and history and often parallel historical conflicts. Heinlein's *Starship Troopers* is a good example of this subgenre, as well as Joe Haldeman's *The Forever War*.

Superhuman/Hero

Consider the possibility that scientists built bionic men and women or created a superhuman gene the government has injected into a select group of children, raising them to be X-men-like soldiers. What if Robocop exists? With scientific advancements, he doesn't look anything like a robot (he looks human) and hunts down terrorists. Could there be races beyond Earth that look and act like humans but who have superhero skills like Superman? If pondering these or similar questions as he sets about plotting his story, chances are the writer will write superhuman or superhero science fiction.

Superhuman stories focus on beings with abilities beyond the average human. Either these abilities come from natural causes, such as in Olaf Stapledon's *Odd John*, or they are the result of intentional augmentation such as in A.E. van Vogt's novel *Slan*.

Alienation plays an important part in these stories as the characters come to terms both with how they feel and how society reacts to them. Such stories have played a role in the real life debate over the pros and cons of human enhancement.

Apocalyptic/Post-apocalyptic

Imagine a giant tsunami wipes out all but a small group of people and Earth, as we know it, is no more. Maybe a virus, the product of genetic engineering, has wiped out all but a select few.

Apocalyptic and post-apocalyptic science fiction focuses on the end of civilization through war, pandemic, astronomic impact, ecological disaster, or humanity self-destructing.

Apocalyptic fiction focuses on the disaster and its immediate aftermath, such as in Pat Frank's novel *Alas, Babylon*. Post-apocalyptic stories, look at anything from the near aftermath to several years into the future. Stephen King's *The Stand* is a good example of post-apocalyptic fiction.

Space Opera/Space Western

Perhaps the most significant trait of space opera or space westerns is that settings, characters, battles, and themes are large-scale. These stories are adventure science fiction set in outer space or on distant planets, where the focus is on action rather than science or characterization. Space opera's detractors criticize the subgenre for its use of questionable plots, illogical science, and flat characters.

Space Western is a subgenre of Space Opera that moves themes of the American West onto a backdrop of futuristic space. These stories are set in frontier worlds, colonies that have been recently settled, as the backdrop of chaos and lawlessness that characterized the American frontier.

Critics dub *Ender's Game* by Orson Scott Card and *Dune* by Frank Herbert classic space opera novels.

New Wave

Typified by a high degree of experimentation and written with literary intent, new wave science fiction goes against science fiction convention—and what its proponents denounce as "the genre's preoccupation with science and technology over structure and content."

Although the subgenre lost its popularity in the early 1980s, a few science fiction writers strive to create novels within this concept's framework and broaden the range of themes and styles in science fiction. This subgenre often tackles taboo issues and uses techniques like stream-of-consciousness and unreliable narrators.

John Brunner's novels *Stand on Zanzibar* and *The Sheep Look Up* are good examples of new wave science fiction.

Steampunk

Steampunk stories are set in the 19th century—often in Victorian England—where steam power is still used. These works include elements of science fiction, such as fictional inventions like those found in the works of H. G. Wells and Jules Verne, or real developments in technology, like the Internet, but invented earlier in time.

The Difference Engine by William Gibson is a good example of steampunk science fiction.

Dystopian/Utopian

Utopian and dystopian tales explore opposing views as well as differing political and social structures. Utopian science fiction involves creating an ideal world as its setting. Dystopian is its opposite, or the creation of a nightmare world. Set in a society distinguished by poverty or oppression, the point of a dystopian story is to make the reader think about the world he lives in and how the concept of happiness can be distorted if the members of that society know nothing else. Aldous Huxley's *Brave New World* is a dystopian novel.

Many writers combine both, and use as a metaphor the different directions humanity could go, depending on the choices made. Utopias and dystopias are found in science fiction and other speculative fiction genres like fantasy.

In a typical dystopian-utopian science fiction story, an onlooker from our world, as we know it, travels to another place or time. There, he experiences an ideal society and then sees another that symbolizes the worst possible outcome. Often that worst possible outcome reflects our own world. Ursula K. Le Guin's *Always Coming Home* is a good example of this structure.

The Giver, by Lois Lowry begins by portraying the world as a utopia, but as the story progresses she exposes its dystopian facets.

Religious Science Fiction

Some readers believe science fiction is anti-religious, as it explores and often sidelines theological beliefs through scientific theory and method. But other branches of science fiction are actively Christian or convey a clear moral message. (Few are actually "anti-religious.") Religious or theological science fiction comprises futuristic stories containing a clear religious theme or message. John Wyndham's *The Chrysalids* is a good example of this subgenre. Religious beliefs rule the protagonists in this story, and they are often scorned for them. Another good example of religious science fiction is *Children of God* by Mary Doria Russell.

6.3.1.7 THRILLER / SUSPENSE FICTION

Excitement, suspense, exhilaration, nail biting, edge-of-your-seat reading.... Although there's no simple definition for the thriller suspense genre, a good thriller has definite traits. The emotions listed previously, which should drive the narrative forward, characterize this genre. Sometimes the writer achieves this goal with subtle peaks and lulls, and at other times by keeping a constant fast pace. This requires meticulous and skillful plotting. Cover-ups are a common plot device in thrillers, often showing society as dark and dangerous. They typically have a successful conclusion where the villains are exposed and either brought to justice or killed. Strategic appearances of red herrings, cliffhangers, confusion, and anxiety heighten the suspense or thrill of this genre.

The setting is usually urban, although, sometimes writers will take the suspense to exotic locations like foreign cities, deserts, or even the high seas.

Heroes in thriller novels are ordinary guys or girls with extraordinary resourcefulness and inner strength. These find themselves working against villains out to destroy them, their country, or even the stability of the world. Thrillers come packed with adrenaline and gritty, fast-paced scenes, which take the protagonist through the wringer and back before he can get to the bottom of the plot to root out and stop the culprits. Heroes can be lawyers, journalists, or soldiers—often cut off from the resources they might have used in their occupations. Character development takes a backseat to the plot in these novels.

The best advice? Keep the action nonstop and include plot twists that both surprise and excite the reader. An excellent device is to put the hero on the run. Combine these ideas with an intense pace that leaves the reader breathless—right up to the climax of the story—and produce a classic thriller.

This genre is popular, although it often merges well into other genres. The basic difference between the other genres and a thriller is the life-and-death situation the protagonists face. Thriller writers focus on atmosphere and characterize their stories with menace, violence, and crime.

Thrillers overlap most often with mysteries. The two genres get confused, but their plot structures are different. In a thriller, the hero thwarts the enemy's plans rather than trying to uncover a crime. In other words, in a thriller story the crime hasn't necessarily happened yet. Therefore, the hero isn't trying to uncover "whodunit" but to stop "he who plans to do it." Another difference is the villains' identity is usually known from the outset, while in a mystery, early knowledge of the culprit's identity often ruins the story.

Large-scale thriller plots thrive on higher stakes. Typical crimes include mass murder (rather than a single murder), terrorism, assassination, and the overthrow of governments. Danger and violence typify the plot elements. Thrillers focus on the hero defeating the villain and saving his own life as well as the world, whereas mystery focuses on a single crime or handful of crimes and a criminal being brought to justice.

There are many subgenres of thriller/suspense fiction. In the next section we'll explore the most popular.

6.3.1.7.1 THRILLER/SUSPENSE SUBGENRES

Conspiracy

In a well done conspiracy thriller, rumors, lies, propaganda, and counterpropaganda layer until it's impossible to tell where the coincidence stops and the conspiracy begins.

Common plots include the protagonists discovering a conspiracy where they are unable to separate truth from reality. The writer uses the layers to confuse the reader and the characters until they find themselves following one small thread that will lead to the answers.

Usually, the protagonists of conspiracy thrillers are journalists or amateur investigators.

Because of their potential for drama, and the subtle complexities of morality and fact, writers plot conspiracies as "man-in-peril" stories. Bad people wreak havoc, but the good guys reveal their crimes and defeat them. The key: The writer must layer lies and rumors in such a way that the "big reveal" is exciting and makes sense. Each thread should have a reason for its inclusion, other than to confuse the reader.

Sam Bourne and Steve Berry have written excellent conspiracy thrillers.

Crime

Love, danger, and death, the most important characteristics of crime thrillers, are present in many genres, making it difficult to decide whether a story is a crime thriller or another subgenre. But there are some characteristics that every crime thriller must have, no matter what other genre it bleeds into.

Crime thrillers often focus on the criminals rather than the police. They stress action over psychological elements and have several reoccurring themes. Serial killers and murderers are the most popular, but other themes include robberies, shootouts, double-crosses, high-speed chases, and heists. Writers of crime thrillers should have extensive knowledge of crime, the justice system, and police procedure. Factual information is essential to portraying the crime, the good guy's pursuit, and eventual capture of the criminal accurately.

Jeffery Deaver's *Lincoln Rhyme* series, which includes the bestseller *The Bone Collector*, are crime thrillers.

Disaster

On the edge of a metaphorical seat, biting nails, turning pages, desperate to know how the protagonists will ever survive a flood that has sent the United States into turmoil. What caused it? Was it natural? Was something more sinister at work? This is a disaster thriller.

In this subgenre, natural or man-made disasters are the sources of conflict. Natural disasters include floods, earthquakes, hurricanes, and volcanoes. Manufactured disasters might be nuclear bombs and biologically engineered plagues, among others. The protagonists must first survive the disaster then figure out what to do in the aftermath.

Stormy Weather by Carl Hiaasen is a good example of a disaster thriller.

Legal

In legal thrillers, the protagonists are lawyers who face the bad guy both inside and outside the courtroom. Often it's not only the case at stake, but also their lives. They fight to see that justice is served and face many life-threatening situations along the way.

Sometimes, the lawyer is a young defense attorney trying to make his mark. He gets a client, believes his innocence, and embarks on a mission to prove it.

John Grisham's novels are well known legal thrillers, the most popular being *The Client, A Time to Kill,* and *The Juror.*

Medical Thriller

Doctor or medical personnel protagonists working to resolve a medical disaster is the benchmark of medical thrillers. Writers of this subgenre must do their research and know the different jobs around and scientific terms for illnesses, medication, and procedures.

Robin Cook, Tess Gerritsen, and Gary Braver are well-known authors of this subgenre.

⚙ Political

Set against a backdrop of political power struggle, political thrillers may involve plots intended to give political power to someone, or to take it away. Often they involve national or international scenarios, like American presidential elections or terrorist plots intent on taking down a power that interferes with their own agendas.

The most important plot element in political thrillers is an average-Joe protagonist stumbling over a trip line of political corruption. The protagonist must unravel a tangled mess of corruption and lies to figure out who pulls the larger strings and often risks his life in doing so.

Popular authors of political thrillers include Jeffrey Archer and Daniel Silva.

⚙ Psychological

The most frightening monster in any fiction is of the human variety, which is what psychological thrillers focus on. This subgenre blends mystery and dramatic elements into its plots. It borders on horror, but the intent of the psychological thriller is to give readers the feeling of discomfort and chills rather than to scare them outright.

Most thrillers focus on plot rather than characters. Psychological thrillers are different from other thriller subgenres in that characters are often given more focus than plot. The suspense in this subgenre comes from the games the characters play as they prey on each other's minds. Consequently, the psychological ingredient is strong.

Put more simply, the protagonists suffer mental danger, but that does not mean they won't be physical hurt. However, physical strength matters less than mental prowess, opposite what it would in thrillers where action and overcoming physically intimidating villains is important.

Misery, by Stephen King, although often considered horror fiction, is a good example of a book with the components of a psychological thriller.

⚙ Religious

The words "religious fiction" may conjure certain expectations. Perhaps a story where religion is the basis for all decisions made, or where the protagonist is a priest, a devout Christian, or someone defending or protecting their faith, congregation, or place of worship? While these are possible, most religious thriller plots simply include a form of religion as a major theme. It's more of a questioning or an investigation surrounding a conspiracy or corruption within a religious sect.

Dan Brown's *Da Vinci Code* gives a good example of the subgenre. Or perhaps the *Templar Legacy* by Steve Berry, where a secret church cult called The Templars spurs a search for buried gold, assassination attempts, and gunfights.

In a religious thriller, the writer must weave religious objects, institutions, and investigation into a plot filled with action, suspense, and intrigue.

⚙ Supernatural

Vampires, ghosts, demons, psychic abilities, and paranormal phenomena combined with intrigue, action, and suspense make up a supernatural thriller. Often this kind of story has a protagonist with psychic ability. The protagonist might use such a gift to unravel a crime, conspiracy, or corruption. She may or may not know about her abilities from the outset, or she might gain them through an otherworldly event. Ghosts are a common theme as well, but as long as the plot includes an ingredient without logical or natural explanation, it is a supernatural thriller.

Sometimes, supernatural thrillers get confused with horror fiction, but there is a definite, if sometimes thin, line between the two. As stated before, horror intends to scare its reader, where supernatural thrillers seek to drag the reader to the edge of his seat, or to immerse him in tension and suspense.

Dean Koontz's *Odd Thomas* series are supernatural thrillers.

Techno

Techno thrillers draw plot elements from many genres, like spy thrillers and science fiction. Compared to other genres, they include much technical detail, often focusing on military technology. Sometimes publishers slip these in the science fiction category, but they differ from straight sci-fi because the plot includes politics or espionage.

This subgenre focuses on the inner workings of modern or near-future technology with a tendency to incorporate war and political unrest into the plots. Although once popular, since many thrillers incorporate technology into their plots and because of its blending into the category of hard science fiction, this subgenre is seldom used to define novels anymore.

An excellent classic example of a techno thriller is Tom Clancy's *The Hunt for Red October*. Clancy uses the plot elements of submarine technology and espionage to keep readers on the edge of their seats to the very last page.

6.3.1.8 CHRISTIAN/INSPIRATIONAL FICTION

Literature that celebrates God's presence in the individual's life or that portrays a Christian worldview in its plot or characters--dealing with Christian themes in a positive way--is called Christian or religious fiction. In a broader sense, inspirational fiction uses faith but keeps it in the background of the story.

Because readers seek a compelling, yet wholesome read, the characters' relationship with God is the primary focus in many of these stories. Another common definition of this genre is that stories focus on "the journey of the soul."

In this genre, readers seek characters like themselves in some important way. They want God or religion to play a significant role in the plot and the protagonists' lives. Although God is an important element of plot and the outcome of the stories, the characters are ordinary people. The difference between religious fiction and mainstream protagonists is clear: the former is challenged to live by Christian principles.

Publishers often bundle the genre with inspirational fiction, but there are fundamental differences in the two categories. Inspirational fiction doesn't always have a religion present. As long as the message or the moral uplifts the reader, it could be considered inspirational, whereas religious fiction must have the faith ingredient. Inspirational fiction covers broader issues. Rather than focusing on the religious aspects of faith, they stress morals, values, and life lessons.

Janette Oke's novels are an example of both Christian and inspirational fiction. Her stories are usually set in the early West and depict pioneers who must draw upon their faith to overcome misfortune.

Readers sometimes refer to Christian and inspirational stories as gentle fiction. Although they share many traits, gentle fiction may not have the Christian element. These stories contain no profanity or sex, and the plot doesn't intend to shock the reader. Instead, gentle fiction aims to provide a calm, thoughtful read, as the term "gentle" implies. However, the link to religious fiction is that most examples of this subgenre move around a small community, such as a town, church, or group of friends where the realities of sex, violence, and other passions are downplayed in favor of a feel-good read.

This genre crosses most other fiction genres. Fantasy, historical, romance and so on, can touch a Christian element, which can also make the story part of this genre.

6.3.1.9 YOUNG ADULT FICTION (YA)

The publishing industry labels fiction written for and marketed to readers ages twelve years and up as young adult fiction. YA books have distinct characteristics that set them apart from adult and children's fiction. These traits have helped YA establish itself as its own genre in recent years.

YA spans the entire range of fiction already discussed. The only difference being that writers gear the contents toward a younger audience, with themes related to their age group and experiences. Certain elements, like sex, profanity, and graphicness are scaled back to be appropriate for a younger audience. YA fiction still shares the basic elements of character, plot, setting, theme, and style that all stories must have.

How does a writer define what is suitable content and what is not? Although YA novels were once conservative in confronting situations and social issues, the genre has fast become known for authors who push the envelope in terms of acceptable content for younger readers. YA literature filling bookstore shelves includes themes of peer pressure, drugs, divorce, crime, sexuality, incest, rape, and violence. Critics argue that these themes encourage youth toward destructive or immoral behavior. Writers and publishers of these books—and many readers, both parents and teens—contend that the fictional characters in these stories confronting difficult issues and making the right decisions helps young readers cope with challenges in life.

The truth is what we today consider groundbreaking or crossing the line may not be a big deal tomorrow. Most YA writers want their books to reach a wide market, young and old, so they write accordingly. For example, many critics questioned the appropriateness of content that dealt with sexual abuse and incest in the works of YA author VC Andrews. Yet current opinion now hails the same books as young adult classics. Both teens and adults love and despise *The Twilight Series* by Stephenie Meyer. On the other hand, JK Rowlings's Harry Potter novels span the age categories from middle grade to YA to adult, with fans in every category.

The distinctions between YA literature and adult literature have always been loosely defined, fueling a never-ending debate. It's up to the writer to know and test the limits of appropriateness, although many publishers have already drawn a clear line. Adults often enforce this invisible boundary because they feel strongly about them. Setting aside the debate over appropriate content, there are some basic elements that YA authors must include in their works.

Most YA fiction depicts an adolescent protagonist. Often YA stories are told from a first person POV, but third person is becoming more common. Length ranges from 125 pages and up, the average being around 250 pages. Adult characters, such as parents and teachers, blend in the background and are not major players in the story.

YA stories have a limited number of characters and subplots (if any) and the time span is short. Writers of YA must also be familiar with the way young adults speak, while being wary of using too much slang to avoid dating the story. The setting should be familiar to teens, such as the often used school settings.

Also important to YA novels is a detailed description of appearance and dress, reflecting adolescents' tendency to focus on these things. Of course, every story should have a positive resolution if not a happy conclusion.

As mentioned earlier, subgenres for YA encompass the same range of genres reviewed in adult fiction. YA authors looking to write a fantasy story, for example, would follow the guidelines for fantasy as any adult writer would, while keeping in mind the younger audience and the characteristics that make the story YA, such as the age of the protagonist and keeping subplots to a minimum.

6.3.1.10 COMMERCIAL FICTION

This genre of fiction encompasses all other genres, except literary fiction. In commercial fiction, the focus is on narrative and plot, where action affects the conflict. The characters are not realistic but rather have exaggerated and unreal traits to make them seem larger than life.

Commercial fiction depicts social issues, similar to the ones portrayed in movies and television shows, and can be read easily and often quickly, creating an escapist experience for the reader. Writers embrace this genre to entertain a wide audience and to distract readers from life for a short time. It works, which is why it's popular.

In novels rated as commercial, the protagonists move through a world where experiences and challenges arise and the character is either victorious or defeated. They center on how a character navigates his world to achieve a certain goal. Writers focus on outside environments and influences—and how these affect the journey—rather than the character's inner struggle. The plot is active.

Although the wok may blend action, love scenes, dialogue, etc., with inner thoughts and character struggles, the story is about how that character interacts with the outside world. Things happen on the surface so the reader can watch it unfold, making these works appeal to such a wide audience.

Dean Koontz and Tom Clancy are commercial fiction writers.

6.3.1.11 HISTORICAL FICTION

Historical fiction tells a story that is set in the past. The writer may depict real events drawn from history or historical figures, but the story and main characters are often fictitious. While writing in this genre, it is important to capture the spirit, speech, fashion, and social conditions of the chosen time period. Therefore, research and attention to detail are crucial. The goal of a historical novel is to bring history to life for the reader.

There are several ways to write historical fiction. A viewpoint not show in history books experiencing events subjectively is one. Another is to use the historical ingredient to complement a story's narrative. This means the history would happen in the background, while the protagonists flesh out a story unrelated to historical events or figures.

Writers take "artistic license" with historical fiction, in terms of how they present history and historical figures. As long as this doesn't negate history, it's fine to do so. If the writer shows changed events, like Hitler winning WWII or being alive and well in eighteenth century England, then the book will fall under the alternate history subgenre. Events happening in historical fiction must also adhere to the laws of physics. A novel where Wyatt Earp was a wizard and his famed gunfight was really a battle for supremacy between opposing supernatural forces would make the story historical fantasy.

Historical fiction overlaps with most other genres, like mystery, romance, and fantasy. Susanna Clarke's *Jonathan Strange & Mr. Norrell*, an alternative history novel within the fantasy genre, uses historical details to create a world of historical fantasy.

Another example of genre crossing is Elizabeth Kostova's *The Historian*, which blends the horrific element of vampires with historical fact. This blending of historical fiction with other genres is becoming popular. But the basic historical novel is a story (no matter what genre it touches) that is set in the past and that depicts an actual historical event or time period. These periods often form subgenres. Regency, for example, is a period and a subgenre of romance. The frontier of the American Old West is a real period and a subgenre of both romance and historical fiction. Most historical fiction is set in Britain, the US, or France although this is not a rule. Historical novels have been set in Australia, Spain, and Canada as well. The former are the most popular settings.

Historical fiction often focuses on times of political upheaval—like the American Civil War—as a backdrop for the story. This adds drama while giving the reader a familiar setting. Most readers will have knowledge about major historical events, and a story set against these times gives readers a sense of familiarity.

Apart from American and European histories, many writers have opted for Roman times, ancient Greece, the Stone Age, and the Viking and Bronze Ages for different types of setting*. Writers should research meticulously when writing any historical fiction. Details are critical, in particular when writing about periods that people remember or that have been widely studied.

Many class historical fiction by time periods. Civil War novels portray characters and stories related to the war. Georgian novels depict life in England's Georgian period, and Roman novels describe ancient Rome. We have discussed these divisions in other genre sections, however a few subgenres of historical fiction are unique. The following pages list and define these subgenres.

6.3.1.11.1 HISTORICAL FICTION SUBGENRES

Non-historical historical

Non-historical novels are still set in the past, but they do not fit the other guidelines of historical fiction. They are set in a fictional or mythological time rather than a real one.

Works can include Arthurian fiction, but the story must be non-fantasy, such as based on the legend of King Arthur and Camelot without the magical spin.

Events and places in these books are factual or based on fact, but the writer uses myth and legend to blur reality. Though the description of castles, maidens, warriors, and Vikings are accurate, as they would be in a historical novel, the story is steeped in well-known myth and legend. Camelot, the legends associated with the Greek gods, and so forth, fall into this category.

Writers of this subgenre must research the accepted facts of the period they're writing rather than the accepted solid facts of a time period.

Western

Western fiction is set in the American Old West, on the frontier. Experts often ground the genre somewhere west of the Mississippi River in the nineteenth century.

These stories depict cowboys, mountain men, outlaws, settlers, and the lawmen who tamed the western wilderness. Although fictional, many western novels are based in fact, often weaving the plot around events or people from that time, such as Buffalo Bill, Jesse James, Belle Starr, and Wyatt Earp.

These stories reflect that, in reality, only a small fraction of the population actually became outlaws, gunfighters, or lawmen and not many widows defied convention to ride the range. Westerns and cowboy novels have lost some of their popularity, but they are still written and published.

Historical Sagas

Stories that span years and follow the fortunes (or misfortunes) of one or more families over more than one generation are called historical sagas. They can take place in any historical period and might depict real historical figures or characters created and placed into an existing time.

Historical Romance

Although a discussion on historical romance can be found in the romance section, we did not touch on what makes a novel more historical than romantic. Both can subgenres show a relationship. In an historical romance, it is common for the woman to say goodbye to her hero as he leaves for battle or sets sail for the new world. Then, the reader follows him on his journey before he returns, near the end of the story. For romance, such long partings are unacceptable, because the relationship is central to the story. The woman would have to find new love or the man gone to war would do so at some point, and they might not meet up at the end.

In a historical novel, the relationship plays an important part, but it will not affect the action or the outcome. In addition, a historical novel doesn't need a happily ever after. Some historical romances have a common ground with non-historical works: the mythical quality of its heroes. Nowadays, we wouldn't consider it romantic to show a medieval affair as it really happened. A relationship portrayed as it would have happened—say an adulterous husband in ancient Rome and a wife who is okay with that—would be historical fiction rather than historical romance.

Historical Adventure

Once a favorite subgenre of young adult and children's fiction, because of lacking laws and the ability to send younger characters off on grand adventures without having to be concerned about the proper authorities chasing them down, historical adventures are about an adventure set in a particular historical period. The story often features a fictional protagonist and leans toward alternate history in that some historical events are changed to fit the adventure.

6.3.1.12 LITERARY FICTION

It can be argued that literary fiction is not a genre, but the fact remains that books considered to be "literary" have definite characteristics that set them apart from other fiction, which is the hallmark of genre.

Literary fiction focuses on style, depth, and character, while the plot may or may not be of minor importance. However, the plot does exist. Literary fiction is not about rambling on about a character's ponderings in fancy prose with nothing happening in between and no real purpose besides showing how deep or profound the character is. Good literary fiction has a plot. It starts at point A and ends at point B. Characters in literary fiction face challenges and conflict, and they evolve as a result. The writer does not, however, focus on the journey or the action, at least not as much as on developing that character and the imagery used to describe what he faces.

The plot happens beneath the surface, usually in the minds of the characters. Action may be taken, issues arise, and obstacles crop in the path of the protagonist, but the thoughts and motivations of the character—and the social and cultural threads woven within them—are what matters.

Even when the writing is clear, literary fiction is challenging because it demands much from the reader. Rather than sitting back and watching the story unfold, much of the plot is implied. Literary fiction seeks to provoke empathy from the reader so she can relate to the characters and understand motivations hidden beneath their actions. Readers must also pick out turning points based on what they know of human nature. So what happens outside isn't as important in literary novels as what happens inside the characters. The climax and resolution may be little more than a decision made or a new outlook or belief rather than a grand shootout, or even the exciting discovery of who killed the butler after the butler killed the guest who came to extort millions from the banker who was sleeping with the heiress. Done right, it can be as entertaining and rewarding for the reader.

Literary stories confront life as we know it, and the action makes no difference to the conflict, which isn't always resolved by the end. Literary fiction has endings; the story is always resolved, but perhaps not the conflict the protagonist faces. For example, an alcoholic would battle his addiction for the rest of his life. Though alcoholism is the conflict that motivates the story and its evolution throughout, it does not mean the conflict will have a resolution. The story will close, questions will be answered, and the characters will change for good or ill, but the protagonist's battle with himself does not end.

As we mentioned, the writing plays an important role in this genre. In literary novels, the beauty of the prose is often noted as the writer focuses on description, psychological insight, and character.

The distinction between literary fiction and other genres is subjective, however. As with all other genres, overlaps are common. Perhaps the easiest way to define literary fiction is by what it is not. Literary fiction is not romance, mystery, science fiction, or horror. The intent is not to use narrative and plot to make readers feel good, terrified, or to help them solve a crime. These genres may be incorporated into literary stories, but the purpose behind literary writing is to use characterization and prose to leave a deeper impression on the reader. The language can be heavy, with rich imagery and detailed characters written in such a way that the storyline is provokes thought, forcing the reader to question and reflect on the human situation or issues related to society.

John Irving, James Joyce, F. Scott Fitzgerald, and Ernest Hemingway are among the literary greats.

 ### 6.3.1.13 MAINSTREAM FICTION

Stories that can't be slotted into a particular genre or combination of genre comprise mainstream fiction. The manuscripts may cover any topic or period and be of any length. Like commercial genre fiction, mainstream stories focus on plot but include deeper characterization than genre fiction—but not as deep as literary fiction. The main goal of mainstream fiction is to entertain the reader, though the writer may decide to touch on philosophical issues.

Writers of mainstream fiction typically start out wanting to write a specific genre but end up not sticking to the rules or conventions of that genre. So, for example, a writer who composes a love story where the hero and heroine don't get together would be writing mainstream fiction.

Mainstream stories are straightforward and linear, where the writer resolves problems and leaves no loose ends dangling. The ending is at least satisfying, if not happy, and readers of mainstream fiction should never need to struggle to understand the story.

This genre is harder to market than commercial fiction because there's no niche audience. Most mainstream novels sell on author recognition. That said, publishers don't look on mainstream as a hard sell since it has the potential to reach a wider audience than genre fiction. When a writer reaches beyond the traditional audience for a certain genre, publishers consider them mainstream.

Stephen King is a fine example, as his work often moves over the edge of horror and into other areas. With novels like *Hearts in Atlantis, Shawshank Redemption,* and *The Green Mile,* King moved beyond the boundaries of horror fiction and into mainstream. Readers who would never pick up a horror novel were attracted to these stories because King downplayed the horror element. He focused instead on plot and characterization to shape his novels (while still horrific and appealing to his usual readership) with something for other readers as well.

Two successful mainstream fiction writers are Maeve Binchy and John Irving.

 **6.3.2 GLOSSARY**

In our frequent exchanges at writer's haunts we're often confronted with questions about the meaning of literary terms. Creative writing has its own lexicon of more or less specialized terms, not unlike other professions. On the following pages we have compiled some of the most common words in the vocabulary of writing, style and literature. There are hundreds more, but far too specialized to be useful to the average writer.

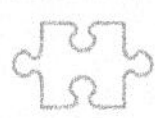

- A -

ABBREVIATION
A shortened form of a word or a phrase.

ABSTRACT
A short summary of the main ideas of a piece of writing, such as an article, proposal, or report. It is typically placed at the beginning of a manuscript.

ABSTRACT NOUN
A noun that defines ideas, events, or qualities that one can't physically interact with. "Her <u>courage</u> will see her through to <u>freedom</u>."

ABSURD, THEATER OF THE
A form of drama that defies logic, in which characters attempt to find order and reason in irrational or implausible situations using repetitious and nonsensical dialogue, confusing situations, and plots that lack logical progression.

ACCENT
Marks placed on vowels to indicate where the pronunciation stress should fall. Accents do not change how the vowel sounds, but do change where the emphasis falls when pronouncing the word. "My fiancé would like a word with you, Renée."

ACRONYM
Words formed from the first letters of a name or by combining the first letters of several words. They are intended to make a longer title or phrase easier to remember. SCUBA, for example, is the acronym for "Self Contained Underwater Breathing Apparatus" and MADD is the acronym for the organization "Mothers Against Drunk Driving."

ACROSTIC
A series of lines or verses in which the first, last, or other particular letters form a word or a message when read in sequence.

ACT
The sections or primary divisions of a structure, such as a novel or a play. In fiction writing, acts are often divided into chapters or scenes.

ACTION
Method by which writers show the reader what is happening, or the internal and external activities the characters use to achieve their goals.

ACTIVE VOICE
The voice in which the subject of the sentence performs or causes the action described with the verb. "Charlie caught the ball." is active voice. "The ball was caught by Charlie" is passive voice.

AD HOMINEM
An argument attacking an opponent's character rather than basing said argument on the facts of the case; appealing to emotions or biases rather than producing evidence against claims made.

ADAPTATION
A piece of work that is based upon another work. For example, scripts are often adapted from novels and short fiction.

ADJECTIVE
A word that modifies or describes a noun or a pronoun. "The red car sped past."

ADVENTURE STORY
A type of story in which the primary focus is action, danger, and a happy ending for the hero, often resulting in a lack of dynamic characterization.

ADVERB
A word or part of speech used to modify a verb, adjective, or another adverb. "She stood, boldly defying the order to sit quietly. It would be a very cold day before she obeyed her stepmother."

AESTHETIC DISTANCE
Separating oneself from a work to view it as a reader; recognizing a work as art and not reality.

AESTHETICISM
1. The philosophy that beauty is a basic principle and all other principles (moral in particular) are derived from it.

2. Nineteenth century movement in art and literature in which beauty held the most value, with morality being irrelevant to art.

AESTHETICS
The study of the origins or nature of beauty, art, and discrimination in all art forms, along with the creation and appreciation of beauty.

AFFECTIVE FALLACY
Evaluating a piece of literature based on the emotional response it evokes from the reader.

AFFIX
A morpheme, or the smallest meaningful word element possible that is attached to a base, stem, or root to form a new word. "He tried to undo the rope, but the damage was already done."

AFTERWORD
A literary device, typically at the end of a piece of literature, that explains or tells the story of how the book came into being.

AGE OF SENSIBILITY
Period of history from around 1744 to 1800 in English literature.

AGRAMMATISM
The pathological inability to speak or use words in a grammatically correct way.

AGREEMENT
The correspondence of a verb with its subject in number, gender, and person, or of a pronoun with its antecedent. "The dogs is chewing the couch" is incorrect. "Dogs" is plural, so the verb should be "are." "The dogs are chewing on the couch."

ALITERACY
Having the ability to read but not being interested in doing so.

ALLEGORY
Stories that have a hidden or figurative meaning, often told to teach theoretical morals. In most allegories, plants or animals are used in the place of human characters.

ALLITERATION
Repetition of a certain sound in the first syllables of two or more words. "The frog slogged through the murky muck" and "He pulled his languishing lazy lady along the lane toward home."

ALLUSION
An implied or indirect reference to a person, place, or event that may be real or fictional. For example, writers may say a character has "met his Waterloo," meaning the character is meeting his doom (referencing Napoleon's defeat at Waterloo).

ALPHABET
The standardized set of letters or characters of a language arranged in a particular order to form words, as determined by custom.

ALTERNATE REALITY
Stories that take a real or fictional time, character, or event and create a new story around it. This is a common type of story in fan fiction, where writers take existing characters, such as those in Harry Potter, and place them in a different setting, like World War I.

AMBIGUITY
The state of a word, phrase, or sentence having more than one meaning. "Frank loves his wife and so does Jack." This is ambiguous. It could mean that Jack loves Frank's wife too, or his own wife. It's unclear as the sentence is written because it can be interpreted both ways.

AMERICAN GOTHIC
Subgenre of gothic fiction that focuses on differentiating between horror and terror. Often these works include concepts such as rational versus irrational, puritanism and guilt, and are characterized by ghosts and monsters and the American history of slavery. These works do not include objects like castles, which suggest a civilized history.

AMERICANISM
An English word or phrase, spelling, or pronunciation that originates in the United States and/or is used primarily by Americans. "I <u>reckon</u> <u>y'all</u> better <u>keep your eyes peeled</u> for the burglar." This

regionalized sentence in many states and in other English-speaking countries might read "I think you should watch out for the burglar."

AMPERSAND
The character (&) representing the word "and."

AMPHIBOLY
An ambiguous word or grammatical structure in a sentence that deliberately or accidentally misleads the reader. "The music languished in the halls." This sentence is deliberately ambiguous, using an action that is physically impossible to make a subconscious suggestion to the reader.

AMPLIFICATION
A term that refers to the ways in which an argument, statement or description can be expanded or enriched.

ANACHRONISM
An error or inconsistency in chronological order; something that is out of its correct order in time.

ANACOLUTHON
A syntactical inconsistency within a sentence, such as when a writer changes from one grammatical structure to another within the same sentence. Frequently used by Shakespeare as an ironic device. "I came over here to—what is that?"

ANADIPLOSIS
The repetition of the last word or phrase of clause or sentence at the beginning the next sentence. "He is a loser—a loser and a jerk."

ANAGRAM
A type of word play in which a word or phrase is formed by rearranging the letters of another word or phrase. "My name is only an anagram of toilets." (T.S. Eliot)

ANALOGY
A comparison of two concepts based on their similarity; using one concept to explain another. "The heart works like a pump."

ANALYSIS
A form of expository writing in which the writer separates a subject into its elements or parts.

ANALYTICAL CRITICISM
An objective criticism of a work that is intended to clarify the author's meaning; detailed analysis of a work's elements and their relationship.

ANAPHORA
The intentional repetition of the same word or phrase at the beginning of several successive clauses, paragraphs, or verses. "To die, to sleep; To sleep: perchance to dream: ay, there's the rub." *Hamlet* by William Shakespeare

ANASTROPHE
Rhetorical term referring to the inversion of the usual syntactical order of words, used to emphasize an idea or a word or to accommodate a rhyme, rhythm, or sound. "Blessed are the meek" and "Tripping the light fantastic" are examples of anastrophe.

ANECDOTE
A brief amusing or interesting account of a real incident that is often intended to demonstrate or support a point.

ANTAGONIST
The character who opposes the protagonist or main character in the plot. Although the antagonist is in opposition to the protagonist's goal, he is not always evil or villainous.

ANTECEDENT
In grammar, the phrase, word, or clause to which a pronoun refers. In fiction, an antecedent is the event or circumstance that leads up to a new scene.

ANTICLIMAX
1. An effect that ruins the climax of the story.

2. A stylistic device used to move from something solemn or serious to something trivial.

ANTIHERO
The opposite of the typical hero. A protagonist who has none of the virtues—such as bravery, good looks, or morality—of the traditional hero.

ANTIPHRASIS
A word used in the opposite sense, contrary to its usual meaning, for humorous or ironic effect. "He was a young lad of eighty-seven."

ANTITHESIS
The contrast of ideas or thoughts using a parallel arrangement of words, phrases or sentences. "Joe was a lover, not a fighter."

ANTONOMASIA
The substitution of a title or phrase for a name to label a member of a group or class. For example, "The King" for Elvis Presley or "The Man of Steel" for Superman.

ANTONYM
A word that is opposite in meaning to another word. Fast is the antonym of slow.

APHORISM
A short statement of principle or truth; a maxim. "The difference between stupidity and genius is that genius has its limits." Albert Einstein

APOCALYPTIC
A subgenre of science fiction focused on the end of civilization as the result of a major catastrophe like nuclear war, pandemics, alien invasions, or natural disasters.

APOLOGUE
A brief allegory tale. Although similar to a fable, with an apologue, the focus is more on the moral than the narrative.

APOLOGY
A defense or justification that provides a framework for discussion of the author's personal beliefs or ideas, without acceptance of blame or wrong-doing.

APOPHASIS
Mentioning something by claiming it will not be mentioned. "I'd never speak ill of the dead, especially when the decedent in question was such a vile creature while he lived."

APOSIOPESIS
An abrupt break in the middle of a sentence that is typically conveyed using a dash or ellipses. The ending is usually left to the reader's imagination and gives the impression of a character's inability or unwillingness to finish the thought. "If I had to lay eyes on him again…"

APOSTROPHE
A mark of punctuation used to identify a noun in the possessive case or indicate the omission of one or more letters in a contraction. "You <u>couldn't</u> have known she was <u>Joe's</u> wife."

APPENDIX
A collection of additional materials typically included at the end of a book.

APPLIED CRITICISM
The analysis and appraisal of certain works of literature.

APPOSITION
Two words, clauses, or phrases placed close together that share the same part of a sentence. The second word, clause, or phrase usually acts as an explanation or modification of the first. "My daughter the doctor is getting married." "My daughter" and "the doctor" are in apposition, sharing "is getting married."

APPOSITIVE
A noun, noun phrase, or series of nouns that renames a noun next to it. "The man, <u>a god</u>, offered me a ride in his chariot, <u>a black pickup truck</u>."

ARCHAISM
A word or phrase that is considered extremely old fashioned and long out of common use. For example, "thou" and "thee" are archaisms for "you." "Hinder" is sometimes considered an archaism for "prevent."

ARCHETYPE
A pattern, character type, model, or image that recurs consistently enough to be considered universal.

ARGOT
A secret vocabulary or set of idioms used by a particular social class or group, particularly criminals or outlaws, to prevent others from understanding their conversation.

ARGUMENT
1. Dialogue meant to influence through appeals to logic or emotion, the goal being to sway belief or to prompt action.

2. A summary of the plot or the main idea of a work.

ARGUMENTATION
A type of writing designed to prove a point or to convince the reader to accept an idea or proposal.

ARGUMENTATIVE ESSAY
A type of essay, sometimes referred to as rhetorical, written with the intention to change attitudes, beliefs, or opinions.

ARRANGEMENT
The parts of a speech or the structure of a text.

ARTHURIAN FANTASY
Fantasy subgenre that uses the legend of King Arthur and Camelot as an inspiration or theme.

ARTICLE
1. A word that comes before a noun indicating the type of reference being made by the noun: "a," "an," and "the" are articles.

2. A work of nonfiction that contains fewer than 1500 words.

ASCENDER
The part of a letter that is positioned above the top of a lowercase letter x. The letters b, d, f, h, k, l, and t have ascenders.

ASIDE
Dramatic device in which the character or narrator speaks briefly to the reader to reveal a character's thoughts, feelings, or interpretations of the action. Typically this is a brief comment, not a monologue or a speech.

ASTERISK
A star-shaped symbol or mark (*) primarily used to indicate an omission or call attention to a footnote.

ASYNDETON
The practice of omitting conjunctions between sentence elements, typically intended to speed up the rhythm of a passage or to give an idea more impact. "...and that government of the people, by the people, for the people shall not perish from the earth." Abraham Lincoln (from the Gettysburg Address)

ATMOSPHERE
The general mood or tone of a literary work such as gloom, foreboding, or expectation. Atmosphere is often created and sustained by the author's use of setting and symbolism.

ATTITUDE
Refers to the author, narrator, or the character's outlook on a subject.

AUTHOR'S NOTE
Story-related information that the author wants the reader to know but isn't included in the body of the work.

AUTOBIOGRAPHY
The author's account of his or her own life.

AUTOTELIC
Literature that is meaningful in and of itself, with purpose and meaning that are self-justified.

AUXILIARY VERB
A verb form that determines the mood or tense of another verb in a verb phrase. The words to, be, and have are commonly used auxiliary verbs. Other auxiliary verbs include: could, can, may, might, must, should, ought, will, and would.

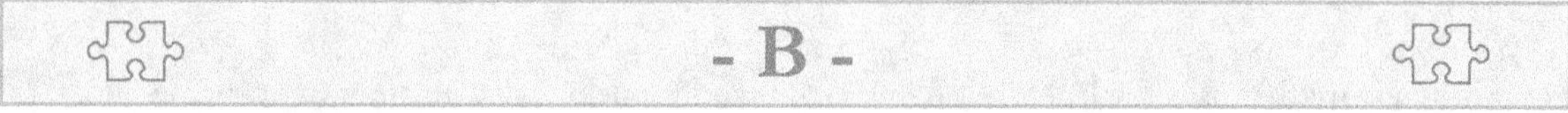

- B -

BABY TALK
Simplified language forms used by adults when speaking to young children, characterized by a high pitched tone of voice, shortened or mispronounced words and nicknames. Also often used when speaking to pets or as a form of affection or condescension to another adult. "Who's your daddy, baby?" "You are, Sugar-Lips."

BACK SLANG
A form of slang where words are spoken or spelled backward.

BACK-FORMATION
The process of forming a new word by extracting actual or supposed affixes from another word; creating shortened words from longer words. "Edit" is the back-formation of "editor" and "one-up" is the back-formation of "one-upmanship".

BACKSTORY
Events that occurred before the main plot of a story.

BALLADE
Derived from the old French word "balade," meaning "a dancing song." A song or poem that tells a story of adventure and love. A basic ballade consists of three stanzas of eight lines.

BANDWAGON
A fallacy based on the notion that the opinion of the majority is always valid. "Everyone else believes it/is doing it, so I should too."

BARBARISM
Basically a barbarism is an incorrect use of language. More specifically, it is a word that is considered "improper" because it combines elements from different languages.

BAROQUE
An artistic style that was prevalent in late 16th to early 18th century Europe, characterized by a striking and wildly ornate style.

BASELINE
An imaginary line on which type is set. Descenders fall below this line.

BATHOS
Bathos is created by a failed attempt to bring about pity or grief from the reader, using unnecessary sentimentality or absurdity.

BEAT GENERATION

Refers to a group of writers from the 1950s and early 1960s who spoke out against their isolation from society by defying both social and literary conventions.

BELIEF, PROBLEM OF

The problem of to what extent a reader's reaction to a literary work is influenced by that reader's belief or disbelief in the version of "truth" given in the work.

BETA READER

Readers who read the almost finished version of a manuscript with a critical eye to improve spelling, grammar, and other elements like plot and characterization. Similar to beta testers in software, a beta reader is used to weed out issues with a work that may have been overlooked.

BIBLIOGRAPHY

A list of works on a specific subject or by a particular author.

BILDUNGSROMAN

A German word meaning "development novel," which is a novel that follows the early experiences and education of the protagonist.

BIOGRAPHICAL FALLACY

The mistake of basing the interpretation or evaluation of a work on an understanding of the author's life.

BIOGRAPHY

A person's life story that is written by another.

BIOLOGICAL HORROR

See "Body horror"

BLACK COMEDY

A genre of fiction that focuses on disturbing subjects, such as death, war, disease, or social injustice with a tone of bitter amusement. Often black comedy is intended to offend or shock its audience.

BLACK HUMOR

Humor that is derived from grotesque, morbid, or macabre situations.

BLEND

A word formed by combining two or more words. For example, "brunch" is a blend of breakfast and lunch.

BLOCK

The assignment of physical locations to actors on a stage. Blocks are commonly referred to as "marks."

BLOCK LANGUAGE

Language structures made of only words that are necessary to convey a message. Block language is commonly used in headlines, slogans, lists, and text messages.

BLOCK QUOTATION

A direct quotation that is set off from the rest of a text by starting it on a new line and indenting it from the left margin. A block quotation does not have quotation marks.

BLUESTOCKING
A term given to scholarly, well-read women in eighteenth-century English society, particularly those who socialized with literary men rather than the typical card playing.

BLURB
A short summary of a work that is intended to spark interest. Typically blurbs are brief and do not give away much of the plot.

BODY HORROR
A subgenre of horror fiction in which the horror is derived from the destruction or degeneration of the body. Disease, decay, mutilation, and creating monsters out of body parts are examples of body horror. Also called biological horror, organic horror, and venereal horror.

BOILERPLATE
A unit of writing or part of a text that can be used over and over without change; standardized text. Mission statements, form letters, copyright statements, and disclaimers are common examples of boilerplates.

BOLD / BOLDFACE
Applying a heavier stroke to a typeface without altering the measure in points.

BOOK REPORT
A written or oral report that describes and evaluates a fiction or nonfiction book.

BOURGEOIS TRAGEDY
Also called a domestic tragedy; a dramatic work featuring a tragedy concerning a middle- or lower-class protagonist who suffers a personal disaster.

BOWDLERIZE
To remove perceived immoral or offensive passages from a piece of writing.

BRACES / BRACKETS
Punctuation marks {} or [] used to signify omitted words or to add a clarification within text.

BRAINSTORMING
Listing random thoughts or ideas before beginning to write of a work of fiction or nonfiction.

BRITICISM
A word or phrase that is used in or unique to Britain. "Banger" for example, is unique to Britain, meaning "sausage."

BROADSIDE
A large sheet of paper that is printed on one side and then distributed or posted.

BROGUE
A strong dialectal accent, typically referring to an Irish or Scottish accent.

BULLET
A type of dingbat [o] often used to indicate items in a list.

BURLESQUE
A literary, dramatic, or musical work that is a humorous or satirical imitation or a caricature of a serious work.

BUZZWORD
Refers to a fashionable word or phrase that is more often used to impress than to inform.

BYLINE
A short line of text before or after an article that gives the author's name.

CACOPHONY
Harsh, conflicting or jarring sounds; words that contain several voiced or unvoiced plosive consonants, such as "b," "d," "g," "k," "p," and "t." "With throats unslaked, with black lips baked, Agape they heard me call." Samuel Taylor Coleridge ("Rime of the Ancient Mariner")

CANADIAN ENGLISH
A variety of the English language that is used in Canada.

CANON
A list of honest works by one or more authors.

CANT
See "argot."

CAPER
A subgenre of crime fiction distinguished from other crime fiction by elements of humor, adventure, and unusual cleverness or audacity in the criminal, who is often the protagonist. In Huckleberry Finn, Tom Sawyer's plan to "steal" Jim to rescue him from slavery is a classic example of a caper.

CAPITAL LETTER
Uppercase letter typically used to begin a sentence or proper noun.

CARDINAL NUMBER
A number used to indicate quantity but not order.

CARICATURE
A literary or pictorial representation of a subject that exaggerates certain features of personality or appearance usually done for comic effect.

CASE
An inflectional form of nouns and some pronouns that expresses their function within a sentence, phrase, or clause. A pronoun, for example, may play the role of the subject (I kissed Julie), the direct object (Julie kissed me), or the possessor (Julie accepted my kiss).

CATACHRESIS
The incorrect use of a word due to a misunderstanding of its meaning.

CATASTROPHE
The event that brings a plot—often a tragedy—to its conclusion.

CATCHPHRASE

A popular expression, often media-inspired, that is usually short-lived. "Whatchu talkin' 'bout, Willis?" was a popular catch phrase in the 1980's originating from Gary Coleman's character "Arnold" on the television show *Different Strokes*.

CATHARSIS

The emotional release and sense of satisfaction that the reader feels first at the intensity of the conflict, and then at the hero's acknowledgement of tragic waste and the eventual return to order.

CAUSE AND EFFECT

Though typically used in essays, this is also a method of paragraph development in which a writer analyzes the reasons for and/or the consequences of an action or decision.

CAVALIER

Refers to soldiers and courtiers who celebrated love, loyalty, chivalry, and bravery by writing lyrical poetry using those same themes.

CELTIC FANTASY

A subgenre of fantasy that focuses on Celtic mythology as a theme. Elements of Celtic fantasy novels include powerful Celtic themes such as mystery, magic, the Sidhe, pagan religions, tragic endings, and druids.

CENSORSHIP

Destroying or omitting portions of art, media, and other communications such as books, films, newspapers, and television programs because they are believed to be nonreligious, immoral, or politically incorrect.

CHAPTER

A main division of a book that is typically numbered and/or titled.

CHAPTER END

The last sentence or sentences that close a chapter. Typically these resolve the main conflict that opened the chapter and present a new conflict for the following chapter.

CHAPTER OPENING

The first sentence or sentences that begin a new chapter.

CHARACTER

A person or "actor" in a narrative or story.

CHARACTER SKETCH

A theatrical portrayal of a highly individualized character. A list of traits associated with an individual.

CHARACTERIZATION

The method by which an author creates a character. Characterization varies in its depth from one author to another. Some create realistic characters, while others prefer larger-than-life characters.

CHARACTONYM

A name that suggests the personality traits of a fictional character.

CHEKHOV'S GUN
A literary technique where an element introduced early in the story must become significant later on. For example, if you're placing something in a scene, like a gun, it should be used in a subsequent scene.

CHIASMUS
A figure of speech in which two parallel statements are inverted. Example: "Ask not what <u>your country can do for you</u>, but what <u>you can do for your country</u>." John F. Kennedy

CHICANO ENGLISH
An imprecise term for a nonstandard variety of English that is influenced by the Spanish language.

CHILDREN'S FICTION
Fiction written for children up to 12 years of age.

CHIVALRY
The code of conduct of the medieval court, often referring to knights, which includes traits such as valor, courtesy, and generosity.

CHORAL CHARACTER
A character in a play who participates in the action to some degree, but whose primary role is to comment on the actions of the main characters.

CHRISTIAN ROMANCE
A subgenre of romance fiction in which the themes of God and faith influence the actions and decisions of its characters.

CHRONOLOGICAL PRIMITIVISM
A belief system that values the past over the present.

CHRONOLOGICAL TIME
The natural passage of time.

CINEMATIC POV
Literary term for point of view where the story is told as though viewed through a camera lens. The story is told through no particular POV, but rather as an outsider looking in.

CIRCULAR ARGUMENT
An argument that restates rather than proves by stating the conclusion in another form. Instead of offering proof, it assumes the listener will accept the argument as settled.

CIRCUMLOCUTION
Using wordy or indirect language to avoid reaching the point.

CITATION
A source quoted in a written work to clarify, illustrate, or substantiate a point.

CLASSICISM (IN CRITICISM)
Evaluating a literary work based on principles derived from qualities admired in the classic works of Greek and Roman literature.

CLAUSE
A group of words that contains a subject and a predicate. "She didn't know her hair was on fire." The clause in this sentence is "her hair was on fire."

CLICHÉ
An expression that has been used so often it lacks freshness; an overused expression.

CLIFFHANGER
An ending that does not resolve the main conflict of the plot. Many writers use cliffhangers as chapter or scene breaks to keep the reader's interest. Not advisable to use at the end of the story.

CLIMAX
The moment of highest intensity and interest in a novel or dramatic work.

CLIMAX ORDER
Ordering a story from the least important event to the most dramatic event.

CLIPPING
A process in which a word is formed by removing one or more syllables from a multisyllabic word. For example, "lab" is clipped from "laboratory" and "gym" is clipped from "gymnasium".

CLUSTERING
A type of prewriting in which the writer groups ideas in a nonlinear fashion, using lines and circles to indicate relationships; similar to brainstorming but doesn't require the writer to begin without clear ideas.

COHERENCE
Gives a piece of writing a natural flow and gives the reader a clear idea of what to expect, making the work easy to follow. Ideas are presented in a logical way so that the reader is not confused.

COLLABORATION
Two or more people working together to write a script, novel, or other work.

COLLECTIVE NOUN
A noun that refers to a collection of individuals, such as "team," "clan" or "family."

COLLOGUE
Private scheming or conspiring between two characters.

COLLOQUIAL
Characteristic of writing that is informal or conversational rather than formal or literary.

COLLOQUIALISM
A word or phrase that is more often used in casual conversation than in formal speech or writing. "Y'all," for example, is a colloquialism.

COLON
A mark of punctuation (:) used after a statement that introduces a quotation, an explanation, an example, or a series. "You have three choices: Go away, get lost, or drop dead."

COMEDY
Stories featuring a light and humorous tone.

COMEDY OF HUMORS
A type of comedy in which the character's actions are dictated by some exaggerated trait or absurdity.

COMEDY OF INTRIGUE
A type of comedy in which the importance is placed more on plot than characterization.

COMEDY OF MANNERS
A comedy set in sophisticated society where wit and polite behavior are valued over ethics or morality.

COMIC FANTASY
Subgenre of fantasy fiction that is humorous in tone and intent. Comic fantasy often includes puns or parodies of other fantasy works.

COMING-OF-AGE STORY
A plot which emphasizes the emotional growth of the protagonists.

COMMA
A punctuation mark (,) used to indicate a separation of ideas or of elements within a sentence.

COMMA SPLICE
Two independent clauses separated by a comma instead of a period or semicolon, often called a run-on sentence.

COMMERCIAL FICTION
Fiction that appeals to a broad audience. Commercial fiction may fall into any subgenre, such as crime thriller, romance, or speculative fiction.

COMMON NOUN
A noun that names general items. Common nouns are not capitalized unless they begin a sentence. "Please tell Julie to bring me the phone." Phone is the common noun, referring to a general item.

COMMONPLACE
A statement or piece of information that is well-known or commonly shared among an audience or group.

COMPARATIVE LITERATURE
A study that compares the relationships between the literary works of different cultures or languages.

COMPLEMENT
A word or phrase that completes the predicate in a sentence. For example, "I want" needs a complement to be complete "I want to go home."

COMPLEX PREPOSITION
A word group, such as "in order to" that acts as a single preposition.

COMPLEX SENTENCE
A sentence consisting of at least one independent clause and one dependent clause. "After I closed the door, I let him have it." The dependent clause is "After I closed the door," and the independent clause is "I let him have it."

COMPLICATION
A tangling of relationships or events that occurs early in the plot and that must be undone by the end of the story.

COMPOUND ADJECTIVE
A combination of words that serves as a single adjective. "She held the much-loved bear to her chest."

COMPOUND NOUN
Two or more nouns combined to form a single noun. "He wrote his name on the <u>blackboard</u>, using <u>toothpaste</u> and a paint brush."

COMPOUND SENTENCE
A sentence that contains at least two independent clauses joined by a coordinator such as "for," "so," or "and." "Maggie was a cheerleader, so Mike learned to play football."

COMPOUND SUBJECT
A verb that consists of two or more simple subjects joined by a coordinating conjunction, such as "and." "<u>Monica</u> and <u>Denise</u> gasped at the decayed nightmare that was their teacher." Monica and Denise are the compound subject and "gasped" is the verb.

COMPOUNDING
The process of combining two words to create a new word, often a noun, verb, or adjective.

COMPRESSION
The altering of time for dramatic effect.

COMPUTATIONAL STYLISTICS
The analysis of measurable traits of an author's style, such as word usage and repetition or sentence length and structure.

CONCEIT
Literary or rhetorical term for a witty expression; often a stressed or bizarre figure of speech in the form of a metaphor. "See! How she leans her cheek upon her hand: O! That I were a glove upon that hand, That I might touch that cheek." William Shakespeare from *Romeo and Juliet*

CONCISENESS
A characteristic of writing in which a great deal is conveyed using only the most necessary words.

CONCRETE NOUN
A noun that names a tangible object, material, or phenomenon; something recognizable through the senses. "Which came first, the <u>chicken</u> or the <u>egg</u>?"

CONDITIONAL CLAUSE
A clause that expresses a hypothesis or condition, whether it is real or imagined.

CONFESSIONAL LITERATURE
A type of autobiographical writing in which the author discusses personal or private experiences.

CONFIDANT/CONFIDANTE
Someone that the protagonist confides in, thus allowing the reader to know the protagonist's motivation.

CONFLICT
An emotional or physical struggle within a plot.

CONJUNCTION
The part of speech that connects two or more words, phrases, clauses, or sentences together. For example "and," "but," and "so" are conjunctions.

CONNOTATION
The inferred meaning of a word or phrase, as opposed to its denotation (dictionary meaning). For example "squat," "petite," and "stubby" have a similar denotative meaning (short or small), but each carries a different connotative meaning, "petite" carrying a more positive connotation than "squat" or "stubby."

CONSONANCE
The close repetition of consonant sounds before and after different vowel sounds: leave / love, short / shirt.

CONSONANT
A letter of the alphabet that represents a speech sound produced by a partial or complete obstruction of the air stream by a partial or complete closure of the vocal tract.

CONTEMPORARY ROMANCE
Subgenre of romance fiction set after World War II that typically reflects the traditions or mores of the time in which it is written.

CONTENT
What is represented within a work; how characters interact with other characters and/or the setting.

CONTEXT
The parts of a text that precede or follow a specific word, phrase, or passage. Context is important in illustrating, extending, and changing meaning.

CONTRACTION
A shortened form of a word or group of words. For example, "do not" makes the contraction "don't" and "cannot" makes the contraction "can't".

CONVENTION
A literary device used enough to become established with readers. Doomed love and the corruption of power are examples of literary conventions.

COORDINATING CONJUNCTION
A conjunction that joins two similarly constructed and/or syntactically equal words, phrases, or clauses For example, "and," "but," or "so."

CONSPIRACY
A subgenre of thriller fiction in which the protagonist's main conflict is to find the truth amid an endless succession of deceptions, including rumors, lies, propaganda. Often the deceptions build and tangle with the truth so that what is real and what is coincidence is unclear.

COUNTERPLOT
A subplot that provides a contrast to the main plot.

COURTLY LOVE
In medieval fiction, refers to the emotion that a knight was expected to demonstrate toward a lady.

COURTROOM DRAMA
A subgenre of crime fiction that is set primarily in a courtroom. Protagonists in courtroom dramas are usually lawyers or young law students striving to right a wrong or prove their client's innocence.

COVER LETTER
Formal letter intended to introduce a person, object, or idea. In terms of writing, a cover letter is often sent to an agent or publisher to introduce the author and the book he or she wishes to publish.

COZIES
A subgenre of crime fiction in which sex and violence are downplayed or given a humorous angle. Violent crime, such as murder, typically take place "off-stage" and sexual interaction is only implied, never directly addressed. Often cozies use a clever and endearing amateur detective to solve the crime.

CREATIVE DRAMA
A creative exercise during which scenes are improvised to develop a story.

CRIME FICTION
A genre of fiction in which the theme is one of crime. Detectives, lawyers, murder, and "whodunit" are common elements of crime fiction.

CRISIS
The point at which the action turns and the fortune of the protagonist changes for better or worse.

CRITICISM
The classification, interpretation, analysis, and evaluation of literary works.

CROSS-GENRE
Blending the main elements of two or more fiction genres to create a new subgenre that may be slotted into either category. This is often how subgenres, such as dark fantasy or romantic comedy, are created.

CULTURAL PRIMITIVISM
The belief that the natural and the spontaneous are better than the artificial, crafted, and controlled; any changes to the "natural conditions" of mankind are believed to be harmful.

CUPERTINO EFFECT
The tendency of spellcheckers to replace a word considered to be incorrect with a wholly inappropriate word.

CUTTING EDGE
Genre of fiction in which the boundaries of conventional fiction are pushed or changed. Typically cutting edge fiction does not fit neatly into one existing genre or subgenre.

CYBERPUNK
A subgenre of science fiction with plots that often center on conflicts such as the protagonist against artificial intelligence or mega-corporations, set in near-future post-industrial dystopias.

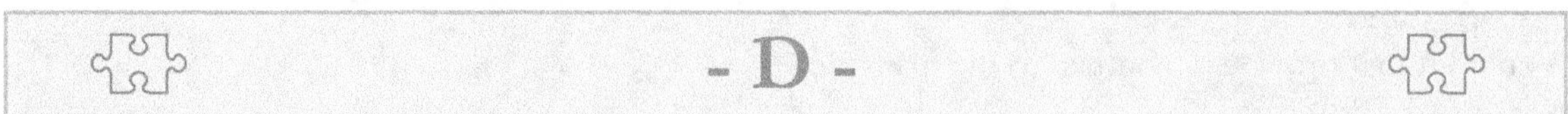

DANGLING MODIFIER
A word or phrase that modifies a word that does not appear in the sentence. "Turning the corner, a dog appeared." "Turning the corner" appears to either modify the dog or nothing at all, when it is intended to refer to the narrator.

DARK FANTASY
Subgenre of fantasy fiction with a strong horror element.

DASH
A punctuation (—) mark known as an "em dash," that is used to set off a word or phrase after an independent clause or to set off words, phrases, or clauses that interrupt a sentence. "He practiced daily at the piano—a beautiful black monster given to him by his grandmother—for most of his childhood."

DEAD METAPHOR
A figure of speech that has diminished in its effectiveness through overuse.

DEATHTRAP
A location, situation or structure where there is a threat of imminent death. A car careening over a cliff, for example, is a deathtrap.

DECADENCE
A term used in literary criticism referring to a decrease in values, moral tone, and rhythmical control, often following the end of a great period of literature or art.

DECLARATIVE SENTENCE
A sentence that makes a statement. "The sky is blue."

DECONSTRUCTION
A type of analytical reading based on the extremely cynical theory that the language of written speech is inherently unreliable, or more simply, that total context is impossible.

DECONSTRUCTIVE CRITICISM
Uses reader-based theories of meaning within a work that ignore mentions of the author's intention and deny the possibility of a "correct" interpretation for any text.

DECORUM
The principle of matching a writing style to character, situation, subject, or genre, thus making the elements in a work applicable to each other.

DEFAMILIARIZATION
A literary technique in which a writer takes a common, everyday object and forces the reader to see it in an unfamiliar or strange perspective.

DEFINITE ARTICLE
A definite article refers to something that both the speaker and the listener know. The definite article "the" refers to particular nouns.

DEFINITION
In terms of fiction writing definition means to provide an example or explanation to clarify a character or plot element.

DELETED AFFAIR
Refers to literary works in which a relationship occurs at some point prior to the time depicted in the story but is not revealed in that work. Often these affairs are revealed in subsequent novels, or sequels.

DEMONSTRATIVE
An adjective or pronoun that indicates a particular noun or the noun it replaces in relation to ourselves. "Do you want <u>this</u> sweater?" "No, I want <u>that</u> one over there."

DEMONYM
A name for the people who live in a particular place. For example, people living in the United States are called "Americans," while those living in Canada are "Canadians."

DENOTATION
The dictionary meaning of a word.

DÉNOUEMENT
The outcome or resolution of a plot.

DEPENDENT CLAUSE
A phrase or group of words that begins with a relative pronoun or a subordinating conjunction. "<u>When the dogs bark</u>, our cat hides under the bed."

DESCENDER
The portion of a letter printed below the baseline. Letters with descenders include g, j, p, q, and y.

DESCRIPTION
Prose that presents details of any kind to readers, such as setting, past events, character appearance, or emotions.

DETAILS
Words or facts that are important to the meaning of a passage.

DETECTIVE FICTION
A genre of fiction in which a mystery or crime (often featuring a theft or murder) is solved by a detective, amateur or professional, who gathers evidence and interprets clues.

DETECTIVE STORY
A story in which a mystery or crime must be solved.

DETERMINER
Adjectives that are grammatically alike, including "the," "an," "my," and "some" that are used at the beginning of noun phrases. Typically only one Determiner is used in a single noun phrase.

DETERMINISM
The belief that people's actions and all other life events are pre-determined or caused by forces over which they have no control.

DEUS EX MACHINE
Forced or artificial plot devices that are introduced by an author to solve a problem with the resolution of a plot.

DIACRITICAL MARK
A mark placed above or below a letter that changes its phonetic sound. For example, Renée has a diacritic mark above the second "e" in her name to change the sound from "ee" to a long "a" sound.

DIALECT
Localized characteristics of speech that deviate from any standard language. For example, writers sometimes use modified spellings to express dialects. "Y'all give 'em hell for me too. Git 'er done."

DIALOGUE
Conversation between characters.

DIARY
A record of personal experiences and thoughts.

DICTION
Selection and use of words in speech or writing.

DIDACTIC
Words or phrases chosen to educate rather than entertain; tendency to lecture. "He was a didactic speaker. I was bored to tears."

DIGRESSION
In literature, the use of information that appears to have no bearing on the main theme or subject but that is relevant later in the work.

DILEMMA
Situations in which a character must choose between two or more equally unpleasant alternatives.

DIMINUTIVE
A word form or suffix that indicates smallness. "Let" in the words "booklet" and "piglet" is a diminutive suffix.

DINGBAT
A special character such as a star, bullet, or another type of symbol.

DIPHTHONG
1. A sound formed by the combination of two vowels in a single syllable in which the sound of one vowel moves toward the other, such as "coin," "cloud," and "eon."

2. A digraph (two characters combined to make a distinct sound) representing the sound of a single vowel, as in "beat."

3. A compound vowel character such as æ.

DIRECT ADDRESS
A construction in which a speaker or writer directly talks to another individual or speaks the name of the individual who is being addressed.

DIRECT OBJECT
A noun or pronoun in a sentence that follows a transitive verb. "Charles fired the gun." "Fired" is the transitive active verb, so "gun" is the direct object.

DIRECT QUOTATION
A report of the exact words of an author or speaker.

DIRECTNESS
In speech and writing, the quality of being straightforward and concise; stating a main idea or point early and without embellishments or digressions.

DIRGE
A song of lamentation appropriate for a funeral to express grief and mourning. "In the Sweet By-and-By" is a dirge.

DISCOURSE
Spoken or written language.

DISCOVERY
The moment near the end of a story, when the protagonist finally realizes a truth or gains an insight previously unknown or ignored.

DISTANCE
The ability to "stand apart" from a work of art, aware that it is a work of art and not real life.

DOCUMENTARY FICTION
Fiction constructed around current events, such as memorable trials, disasters, and other real events or people. True Crime novels may be considered a form of documentary fiction.

DOMESTIC TRAGEDY
A tragedy depicting a middle or lower-class protagonist who suffers disaster.

DONNÉE
The main premise or set of assumptions used as the basis for plot development in fiction.

DOPPELGANGER
The double of a living person. In fiction, a technique used to show a character's introspection. Dr. Jekyll and Mr. Hyde is an example of a doppelganger in fiction.

DOUBLE COMPARATIVE
The use of both "more" and the suffix "-er" to indicate the comparative form of an adjective or adverb. This is a no-no in writing unless done for comedic effect or as part of character development through dialogue. "You're more braver than me," said the boy.

DOUBLE ENTENDRE
A figure of speech in which a word or phrase can be understood in two ways, especially when one meaning is suggestive.

DOUBLE NEGATIVE
A nonstandard form of language that uses two negative words where only one is necessary, sometimes in an effort to express a positive. "I don't not want you to go, so you can't stay."

DOUBLESPEAK
Language intended to hide, distort, or obscure its actual meaning.

DRAFT
An early version of a piece of writing; a "rough draft" that is in need of revision and editing.

DRAFTING
A stage of the writing process during which a writer organizes information and ideas into sentences and paragraphs.

DRAMA
In fiction, the tension created by events and conflict within the plot of the story.

DRAMATIC IRONY
A device used to provide the reader with more knowledge than the characters where the words or actions of the characters in a work of fiction hold a different meaning for the reader than they do for the characters.

DRAMATIC QUESTION
The main conflict within a plot in the form of a question which requires a "yes" or "no" answer and that is resolved by the end of the story.

DRAMATIC VISUALIZATION
In narrative, this refers to representing an object or character with a significant amount of descriptive detail. In dialogue, this refers to detailing realistic gestures and speech to make a scene more visual to the reader.

DRAMATIS PERSONAE
A list of characters printed at the beginning of a published play or in a program, often including brief descriptions of the characters and their relationships.

DRAMATISM
A system for analyzing literature that is based on the idea that all works of literature are made up of five elements: act, scene, agent, agency, and purpose.

DRAMATURGY
The study of the composition and the performance of dramatic works.

DYNAMIC CHARACTER
Characters that are critical to the plot. A dynamic character drives events within the plot and tends to change as the plot progresses.

DYSPHEMISM
Substituting an offensive word or phrase for one that is considered to be less offensive. Usually used to shock, offend, or amuse. For example, when referring to people, animal words like "bitch," "pig," or "snake" are dysphemisms.

DYSTOPIA
A fictional place or situation in which conditions and life are awful, horrific, or depressing. Frequently used in Gothic fiction, fantasy, and dark drama.

DYSTOPIAN
Often categorized as a subgenre of science fiction, but may be a subgenre of any speculative fiction. Themes typically include a futuristic setting with technological innovations not existing in present times and feature conflicts such as war, revolution, uprisings, or shifts of government or societal norms.

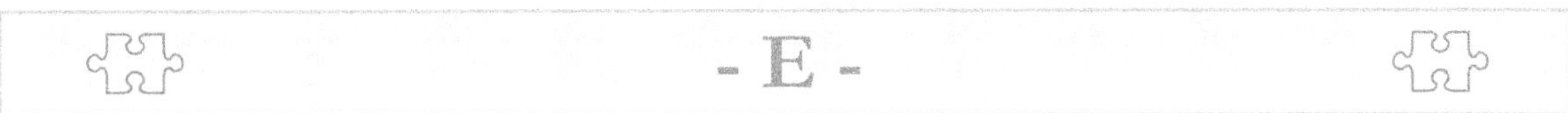

- E -

EARLY READERS
Category of children's fiction typically written for those around kindergarten age who are just learning to read.

EDITING
A stage of the writing process in which the writer polishes a draft by correcting errors and clarifying words and sentences, making them more precise and effective.

EDITING TERM
In conversation analysis, a filler word like "um" or a cue phrase such as "let's see" used to mark a hesitation in speech.

EDITOR
An individual who is in charge of the final content published in any text, such as newspapers, magazines, and books. In fiction, an editor assists the author in copyediting a manuscript before publication.

EDITORIAL STYLE
See "House style."

EFFECT
The impression left on a reader by a work of literature.

ELLIPSIS
Punctuation mark of three equally spaced points (. . .) used in fiction to indicate an unfinished thought or a pause or in nonfiction to indicate the omission of words in a quotation.

EM DASH
A long dash [—], approximately the width of the capital letter M. (See "Dash")

EMPHASIS
The stress or importance placed on specific words or passages by emphasizing their importance in some way. Repetition and word placement are two ways an author might add emphasis to a word or passage.

EN DASH
A short dash [–], approximately the width of the capital letter N.

ENCOMIUM
Warm, glowing praise of a person or thing; a tribute.

ENDNOTE
A reference, explanation, or comment placed at the end of an article, chapter, or book.

ENGLISH GOTHIC
A subgenre of horror fiction that features elements of horror, such as darkness, decay, romance, mystery, and the supernatural. Settings include medieval castles with paranormal creatures, such as ghosts and vampires.

ENTHYMEME
An argument based on probability in which the conclusion is not stated but implied.

EPIC
A long narrative depicting the adventures of a traditional hero.

EPIC FANTASY
See "High Fantasy."

EPIC SIMILE
Also referred to as "Homeric simile," epic similes are long, elaborate comparisons.

EPIGRAM
A brief, clever, and often contradictory statement or verse. "Always forgive your enemies; nothing annoys them so much." Oscar Wilde

EPIGRAPH
A quotation at the beginning of a book or chapter that is relevant to the content of the work.

EPILOGUE
A concluding scene or chapter added to the ending of a work.

EPIPHANY
A moment of revelation or profound insight.

EPISODE
An incident or event that is presented as a single act but that is also part of a longer story.

EPISTOLARY
A letter or collection of letters presented as a book.

EPITAPH
A short caption engraved on a tombstone or monument, or a statement or speech honoring someone who has died.

EPITHET
An adjective, noun, or phrase given to characterize a person or thing. Although they are intended to give specific information about a person, as in "President Lincoln" or "His Highness," epithets are often used in a derogatory manner.

EPONYM
A real or fictional person from whom a nation, group, organization, etc., is said to take its name. For example, H.P. Lovecraft is an eponym from which the fiction genre Lovecraftian horror gets its name.

EQUALITY BY ASSOCIATION
When a character is perceived as equal to another character.

EQUIVOQUE
A type of pun in which a word has double meaning or ambiguity.

EROTIC HORROR
Subgenre of horror fiction which combines horror and erotica. The goal of the writer in erotic horror is to arouse the reader while also terrifying or disgusting her.

EROTIC ROMANCE
Subgenre of romance fiction that features sex as an integral part of the relationship between the protagonists. Designed to arouse the reader, but does not contain blatant pornography.

EROTICA
Genre of fiction in which the goal is to arouse sexual desire in the reader.

ESSAY
A short work of nonfiction written as an article that addresses a concept.

ETHOS
Persuasive appeal based on the credibility of the speaker or narrator.

ETYMOLOGY
1. The study of word origins.

2. The origins of a word.

EULOGY
A formal composition that pays tribute to something or someone that can be either living or dead.

EUPHEMISM
Substitution of an inoffensive term for one considered offensively explicit. Romance writers often use euphemisms such as manhood when referring to the character's penis, to avoid offending the reader.

EUPHONY
A succession of melodious sounds; a term often applied to prose or poetry that flows smoothly.

EUPHUISM
A mild, inoffensive word, either real or created, used to refer to something unpleasant, embarrassing, or offensive.

EXAGGERATION
Overstating or stretching the truth. "I laughed my head off" is an exaggeration, as laughing one's head off is impossible. "Fish stories" and tall tales are examples of exaggeration as well.

EXCLAMATION POINT
A punctuation mark (!) used after a sentence that expresses strong emotion.

EXEGESIS
Originally the critical analysis and interpretation of religious text, but now may refer to the same evaluation of any literary or intellectual text.

EXEMPLUM
A moralized story used to illustrate a point, often included in a sermon.

EXISTENTIAL CRITICISM
A form of literary criticism that discards traditional critical questions and instead analyzes literature with emphasis on the struggle to define identity and meaning amidst feelings of loneliness and alienation.

EXISTENTIALIST NOVEL
A novel that focuses a character's sense of isolation and his exploration of personal responsibility.

EXPLETIVE
A profane or distasteful word, usually an exclamation.

EXPLICATION DE TEXTE
The detailed analysis of a passage of verse or prose.

EXPOSITION
A statement or type of written composition intended to give information about an issue, subject, method, or idea. In fiction, the purpose of exposition is to give the reader background information about the plot, character, setting, and theme.

EXPOSITORY ESSAY
An essay meant to explain conditions or concepts.

EXPRESSIVE CRITICISM
A form of literary criticism that is based on viewing the work as an expression of the originality of the writer instead of focusing on its effect on the reader.

EXTENDED METAPHOR
Comparing two unlike things over several sentences or paragraphs, typically using multiple techniques. Sometimes referred to as a "conceit."

EXTERNAL CONFLICT
A character's struggle against something in his environment, such as nature or another character.

- F -

FABLE
A short narrative told to teach a moral lesson.

FABULIST
A subgenre of speculative fiction that focuses heavily on magic realism and stretches past the boundaries of science fiction, fantasy, or horror.

FACE
A typeface in a given style and weight in all point sizes. Computer programs sometimes use font to mean face. (Times New Roman, Bold, Italic)

FAIRY TALES
A subgenre of children's fiction that features short stories using folkloric characters like fairies and goblins, often including magical elements.

FALLACY
Arguments that sound logical, but are not, rendering them invalid. For example, "Two wrongs make a right."

FALLING ACTION
That part of the plot that follows the climax and leads to the resolution of the story.

FALSE DOCUMENTS
A literary technique in which the author invents documents that appear to be authentic in order to fool the reader into thinking what is being presented is actually fact and not fiction.

FAMILIAR ESSAY
An essay characterized by an informal and conversational tone that deals with personal subjects such as opinions, observations, and/or prejudices.

FANCY
Wishful thinking, imagination, or whim.

FANTASY
A genre of fiction featuring mythical characters, creatures, settings, and societies.

FANTASY ROMANCE
A subgenre of romance in which elements of fantasy are included in the story. In this subgenre, romance is the dominant element, with the focus on the romantic relationship between the protagonists.

FARCE
A Greek play that features humor or satire and relies heavily on stereotypes.

FICTION
Writing that tells a story that is imaginary or "made up." Fiction may also be a story based on real historical events where the writer has taken great liberties with characters and events.

FIGURATIVE LANGUAGE
The use of figures of speech, such as metaphors and similes.

FIGURES OF SPEECH
Words or phrases that deviate from their original meaning used to construct figurative language.

FIRST-PERSON POINT OF VIEW
A form of fiction or nonfiction narrative in which the use of "I," "me," and "we" (first-person pronouns) are used to relate the thoughts, experiences, and observations of a narrator.

FLASHBACK
A shift in a narrative to an earlier event that interrupts the normal chronological development of a story.

FLASHFORWARD
A shift in narrative to a future event that interrupts the normal chronological development of a story.

FLAT CHARACTER
Two dimensional characters that lack the depth or complexity of a real person that are most often static.

FLY-ON-THE-WALL TECHNIQUE
A method of narration in which the narrator reports events in the story objectively, outside of the characters and events. Also called the "scenic method."

FOIL
A character created and used to contrast with another, more primary character to highlight specific traits of the primary character.

FOLK EPIC
An epic or long narrative that consists of shared knowledge or facts of unknown origin.

FOLKLORE
The traditional songs, legends, beliefs, and customs of a people or a group that are passed on from one generation to the next.

FONT
A typeface at a given size, weight, and style. For example: 10-point Times New Roman Bold Italic.

FOOTER
The space between the bottom primary margin and the bottom of the page. Page numbers and other information, such as sources, can be placed in the footer.

FOOTNOTE
A reference, explanation, or comment placed below the main text on a page.

FOREGROUNDING
Making something, such as a word, a rhythm, a character, an idea, a viewpoint, or a trait more prominent by placing it in the front or foreground.

FORESHADOWING
Presenting details, characters, or events in narrative so that later events or actions make sense or are prepared for.

FOREWORD
A brief introduction to a book that is typically written by someone other than the author.

FORM
A method of conveying a plot that is similar to genre. For example, a romance novel takes a particular form: man meets woman, is attracted to woman, and is rejected by woman. A major event brings them together, and they fall in love. Forms like this often lead to conventions.

FORMAL CRITICISM
A type of literary criticism that doesn't analyze the content of the work against truth or morality, but instead attempts to explain or evaluate the way the content of the work is structured.

FORMAL ESSAY
An objective and logically developed composition that is written to inform or to persuade.

FORMAL PATTERNING
A type of foreshadowing where plot elements or events that might occur later in the story are suggested.

FORMAL SATIRE
Also called direct satire, formal satire is a type of written satire where the author or the narrator speaks in first person to the reader or to another character.

FORMAL STRUCTURE
In poetry, the way the poem is put together in terms of its elemental parts, such as stanzas or paragraphs. A relationship typically exists between the parts. For example, the first paragraph takes place in the past, the second in the present, and the third in the future.

FORMATTING
Preparing a document for submission in accordance with the house style.

FRAGMENT
A type of sentence that contains a capital letter and a period, question mark, or exclamation point to end it, but is grammatically incomplete; a part of a sentence that is not technically a sentence because of subordinating words or missing words. For example: I knew he wouldn't show and still I waited. <u>As I did every time</u>.

FRAME
To put an event within a plot into context or to put a thought or idea into words.

FRAME STORY
A short story contained within a larger story.

FREEWRITING
A writing exercise in which the writer simply writes what "comes to her" and does not worry about grammar, spelling, or organization.

FREYTAG'S PYRAMID
The stages of a five-act drama: introduction, complication, rising action, climax, falling action, and denouement.

FUTURE PERFECT TENSE
A verb tense that expresses action that will be completed in the future, using "will have" or "won't have." For example, "I will have cleaned this mess by the time my parents return on Sunday."

FUTURE TENSE
A verb tense indicating action that has not yet occurred, using "will" or "will not." For example "I will not have a cookie."

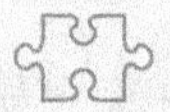 - G - 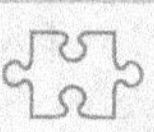

GENDER
A grammatical classification in which a noun, pronoun, article or adjective is masculine, feminine, or neutral. "Mary is your new teacher." "Mary" is a feminine noun. "She is your teacher." "She" is a feminine pronoun.

GENERIC PRONOUN
A personal pronoun that refers to both masculine and feminine nouns. "Cal and I tried to outrun our pursuers, but we didn't have to worry. They drove their car off the cliff."

GENRE
A category of artistic composition that is distinguished by style, form, and/or content. For example, fiction genres include romance, horror, and mystery. Music genres include rock, classical, and country.

GERUND
A verb ending in "-ing" that functions in a sentence as a noun. "Sara's passion is singing." In this sentence, "singing" is a gerund because the verb is acting as a noun. If we were to write "Sara is singing in the shower," it is not a gerund because it is functioning as a verb rather than a noun.

GESTALT
A unified whole is greater than the sum of its parts; seeing something as a whole.

GLOSS
A brief explanation of a foreign word or a technical term within a text. Glosses may be placed between lines, in margins, or at the foot of a page.

GLOSSARY
An alphabetized list of specialized terms with their definitions.

GOBBLEDYGOOK
Inflated, jargon-cluttered prose that fails to communicate the ideas within it clearly.

GOTHIC
From the Middle Ages.

GOTHIC NOVEL
A novel set between the 12th and 16th centuries with a medieval setting that is used to suggest horror or mystery.

GRAMMAR
The systematic study and description of a language.

GRAMMARIAN
A specialist in the grammar of one or more languages.

GRAPHEME
A written symbol such as a letter or a group of letters used to represent a phoneme (sound). For example, "cat" is the grapheme for the phoneme's k, a, and t.

GRAPHOLOGY
The study of handwriting as a means of analyzing character.

GROTESQUE
A work characterized by distortions and inconsistencies, often an element in gothic novels.

GUTTER
1. The distance between two columns of text.

2. A margin between two pages, used to make binding easier. The inside gutter of the pages of a book is often greater than the outside margin, to compensate for binding.

 - H - 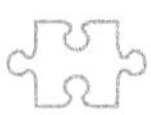

HAMARTIA
The mistake, weakness, or flaw that leads to the demise of a tragic hero.

HARD SCIENCE FICTION
A subgenre of science fiction that focuses on scientific and/or technical accuracy and details.

HARD-BOILED
Subgenre of crime fiction which is characterized by graphic sex and violence and fast-paced dialogue and action.

HEADER
1. A space between the main margin and the top of the page, where numbers and other information are printed.

2. A label for any regularly appearing section in a publication.

HEADLINESE
The abbreviated style of newspaper headlines; often characterized by short words, clichés, and ellipses.

HERMENEUTICS
The theory and practice of interpreting sacred and literary texts.

HERO / HEROINE
A primary character that shows strength and courage and is admired for other positive virtues.

HEROIC FANTASY
Subgenre of fantasy characterized by epic battles and themes of good and evil, typically chronicling the tales of heroic characters in fictitious settings.

HETERONYMS
Words with the same spelling but different pronunciations and meanings. "The wind blew the flag, causing it to wind around the pole."

HIGH FANTASY
Subgenre of fantasy fiction in which stories are set in fictional or parallel worlds with their own languages, laws, and creatures.

HISTORICAL FANTASY
A subgenre of fantasy that uses real historical events as a backdrop or basis for the plot.

HISTORICAL FICTION
Fiction that uses past events and re-creates them around a fictional framework.

HISTORICAL PRESENT TENSE
The use of a verb phrase in the present tense to refer to an event that took place in the past.

HISTORICAL ROMANCE
A subgenre of romance set in past time periods, typically before World War II.

HOLOCAUST
Subgenre of speculative fiction that includes in the theme great destruction, which results in a significant loss of life. Often the destruction is related to a nuclear devastation like that created by an atomic bomb.

HOLOPHRASE
A single word that is used to express a complete thought. "Thanks" is a holophrase.

HOMERIC EPITHET
A hyphenated adjective used frequently in combination with the same noun. For example "god-like man" is a Homeric epithet.

HOMERIC SIMILE
A long and elaborate simile; another term for epic simile.

HOMOGRAPHS
Words that have the same spelling but different origin, meaning, and sometimes pronunciation. For example, bear can refer to the animal or to carrying a heavy load. One may also close the door or stand close to someone.

HOMONYMS
Words that sound alike but have different meanings and/or spellings. "Their," "They're," and "There" are homonyms, as are "two," "to," and "too."

HOMOPHONES
Two or more words (such as "knew" and "new") that are pronounced the same but differ in meaning, origin, and sometimes spelling.

HOOK
The opening lines of a novel, chapter, or scene; place in the text where the action should begin. The hook must grab the reader's attention.

HORATIAN SATIRE
Horatian satire is temperate, humorous, witty, and gently corrective.

HORROR FICTION
Genre of fiction with themes that are intended to frighten, unnerve, and /or horrify readers.

HOUSE STYLE
The set of standards, punctuation, and usage styles set by an editorial /publishing house to guarantee consistency of its product.

HUBRIS
The Greek word for pride or insolence.

HUMORS
A term that originates from the belief that four fluids were responsible for one's disposition: phlegm, blood, choler, and melancholy. It refers to a character's disposition or temperament or the quality that makes a scene comical or absurd.

HYPERBOLE
A figure of speech used for emphasis or effect. An exaggeration not intended to be taken literally. For example, "I'm so hungry, I could eat a horse."

HYPHEN
A punctuation mark [-] that is used to join compound words or to indicate the break of a typed word across two lines on a page.

HYPHENATION
Splitting words across lines of text, whether manually or by allowing software to determine hyphen breaks. In fiction writing, it is not recommended to have more than three hyphens end consecutive lines of text.

HYPOTAXIS
The relationship between clauses.

- I -

IDIOM
An expression that means something other than the literal definition of its individual words. For example, "On a roll" means you're having a lucky streak or doing well, not standing on a piece of bread.

ILLITERACY
The inability to read or write.

ILLUMINATION
In fiction writing, illumination means to reveal a previously unidentified character trait.

ILLUSTRATION
Using examples to explain, clarify, or justify.

IMAGE / IMAGERY
Describing something that can be observed through one or more of the senses. The metaphorical language of a written work or the sensory details (sight, smell, taste, touch, sound) given to readers to enhance a scene.

IMAGINATION
The source of creative thought; creative power of the human mind.

IMITATION
A copy or representation.

IMPERATIVE MOOD
The mood of a verb that makes direct commands or requests; indicates the writer's attitude toward a particular statement as it is made. For example, "Stop that nonsense!" or "Please, forgive his stupidity."

IMPLIED AUTHOR
A persona created by the author used to represent a literary work to the reader; an artificial voice through which the author speaks. For example, Charlaine Harris writes as Sookie Stackhouse to speak to the readers in the *True Blood* novels.

IMPRESSIONISM
Symbolic poetry or language meant to capture a moment in time or the sensory image of a scene.

IMPRESSIONISTIC CRITICISM
A type of literary criticism that is restricted to the critic's personal subjective response to the work.

IN MEDIAS RES
A Latin expression meaning "in the middle of things," which is used to describe the narrative method of beginning a story in the middle of the action to hook the reader into the story, and then using flashbacks to fill in what led up to the beginning.

INCITING INCIDENT / MOMENT
The first event in a plotline.

INCONGRUITY
The quality of being inconsistent.

INCREMENTAL REPETITION
The repetition of a previous line or lines, when writing poetry, with a slight variation that adds to the story incrementally.

INDEFINITE ARTICLE
Indefinite articles refer to generalized nouns. For example "a" and "an" are indefinite articles.

INDENT
Any part of a text column set narrower or wider than the majority of the text.

INDENTATION
The blank space between a margin and the beginning of a line of text.

INDEPENDENT CLAUSE
A group of words consisting of a subject and a verb that expresses a complete thought; a sentence.

INDICATIVE MOOD
The mood of the verb used in ordinary objective statements when stating a fact, asking a question, or expressing an opinion; used to make factual statements.

INDIRECT OBJECT
A noun or pronoun that is indirectly affected by the action of a verb; the indirect object comes immediately after the verb and before the direct object. For example, "Give her the doll." "Her" in this sentence comes after the verb (give) and is the indirect object. "Doll" follows it, and as the object "given," is the direct object.

INDIRECT QUESTION
A sentence that is formed as a question but ends with a period rather than a question mark. "Why don't I fix that for you."

INDIRECT SATIRE
A type of satire in which the author does not speak to the reader directly.

INFERENCE
The process of forming logical conclusions from premises that are either known or assumed to be true.

INFINITIVE
The base form of a verb preceded by "to," which functions as a noun, an adjective, or an adverb. "You'll have to ask your mother."

INFLECTION
The process of adding morphemes (smallest units of meaning) to the base form of a word to express grammatical meanings.

INFODUMPING
Using large blocks of narrative or exposition to clarify, explain, or inform the reader. This may be to explain things omitted in the prose, such as past events or motivations. Often in fiction writing, infodumping bores the reader and turns him away. Such information should be distributed in small amounts throughout the text or written as action or dialogue to hold the reader's interest.

INFORMAL ESSAY
A written composition, usually brief and without formal structure, intended to amuse or to entertain.

INITIAL
The first letter of a word or name.

INNUENDO
An allusive, indirect, or subtle, usually derogatory remark; an insinuation.

INSPIRATIONAL ROMANCE
Subgenre of romance fiction featuring themes of honesty, forgiveness, and fidelity that does not include love triangles or graphic sex.

INTERJECTION
A short utterance that usually expresses emotion and is capable of standing alone. In fiction writing, interjections are often followed by an exclamation point. "Well!" "Wow!"

INTERNAL CONFLICT
A character's struggle against himself or herself.

INTERPRETATION
The attempt to understand the intended meaning of a literary work.

INTERROGATIVE
A word that asks a question that can't be simply answered with yes or no. "Why" and "How" are interrogative words.

INTERRUPTING PHRASE
A group of words that interrupts the flow of a sentence. The phrase may be a statement, question, or exclamation and is usually set off by commas, dashes, or parentheses. "He came by the house—late as usual—and expected me to be eager to see him."

INTRANSITIVE VERB
A verb that has no direct object. "The train from Montreal _arrived_ too late." "Arrived" is intransitive because it does not transmit action to a direct object (a noun in the predicate).

INTRODUCTION
A passage before the main text of a book that is written by someone other than the author.

INVECTIVE
A verbal attack; verbal abuse.

INVENTION
In literature invention refers to originality in creating style, plot, language, or form.

INVERSION
Reversing the usual order of sentence parts to ask a question. "Again, I ask you, why walk all the way to the river?"

INVOCATION
An appeal to a god or goddess, or some other "higher power," for inspiration; a device typically used at the beginning of an epic.

IRONY
1. The use of words to convey the opposite of their literal meaning.

2. A situation where the meaning is directly contradicted by the appearance of the idea.

IRREGULAR VERB
A verb that does not follow the patterns of regular verb forms. When making an irregular verb past tense (adding –ed) or past participle (adding –ing) the root form of the verb doesn't remain the same. For example, "see" is an irregular form because you can't simply add "-ed" to create the past tense. The word becomes "saw."

ISOCOLON
A succession of phrases of similar length and structure. "I opened the door. John stepped into the hall. I raised the gun. John held up his hands. I squeezed the trigger."

ITALICS
A style of printing or typeface in which letters are *slanted to the right*.

JARGON
The specialized language of a group that is often meaningless to outsiders. For example, doctors use medical jargon and lawyers use legal jargon that most people without the same training would not understand.

JEREMIAD
A prophecy that states transgression or sin will bring on destruction; a lament.

JOURNAL
A written or otherwise recorded account of incidents, experiences, and ideas.

JOURNALESE
An informal, often derogatory term for a style of writing and word choice that is characteristic of many newspapers and magazines.

JUDICIAL CRITICISM
A type of literary criticism in which the content, structure, and style of a work is evaluated against some standard of excellence.

JUSTIFICATION
The position of text in relation to a column. Text may be justified right, left, centered, or full (both right and left).

JUVENALIAN SATIRE
A type of satire that mimics the writing of a child that is actually written by adult. Typically juvenalian satire is written in this voice so that the writer can criticize or parody with impunity.

JUXTAPOSITION
A literary technique in which two words, phrases, ideas, settings, actions, or characters are arranged side-by-side or in similar narrative moments to create contrast, comparison, or suspense or for the purpose of rhetorical effect or character development.

KAIROS
The right time or place to say or do the right thing.

KENNING
A symbolic compound word or phrase used as a synonym for a common noun. For example, in *Beowulf*, blood is referred to using the kenning "battle-sweat."

KERNING
Typography term that refers to adjusting the space between characters.

KÜNSTLERROMAN
Term meaning "Artist-novel;" a type of developmental novel that tells the story of an artist's development.

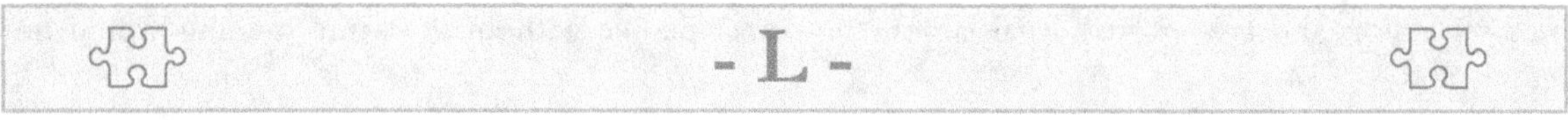

LAMPOON
A piece of extremely sarcastic or satirical writing that is usually intended to ridicule someone.

LANGUAGE
A human system of communication that uses random signals, such as voice sounds, gestures, or written symbols.

LEGEND
A story about the life of a saint, hero, or historical figure that may be a blend of fact and fiction and is handed down from generation to generation.

LEITMOTIF/LEITMOTIV
Refers to a recurring theme associated with a particular person, place, or idea that functions as a unifying element.

LEITWORTSTIL
The intentional speaking of particular words or phrases throughout a literary work to express a theme or motif that is important to the plot.

LETTER
An alphabetic symbol.

LEXICAL AMBIGUITY
The presence of two or more possible meanings within a single word. For example, "Rose rose to put rose roes on her rows of roses." (Robert J. Baran) Rose (a girl) rose (stood) to put rose (pink) roes (fish eggs) on her rows (lines) of roses (flowers).

LIMITED OMNISCIENCE
The point of view that presents all characters externally but only reveals the thoughts of a single character.

LINGO
An informal term for the unique vocabulary of a particular group, often perceived as strange or unintelligible by those outside the group.

LINGUA FRANCA
A language adopted as a common language used between people whose native languages are different.

LINGUISTICS
The study of languages as systems.

LINKING VERB
A verb that joins the subject of a sentence to a subject complement. "Charlie thought the play <u>became</u> predictable after the first act." "Became" links the subject (play) to the subject complement (predictable).

LIPOGRAM
A text that purposefully excludes a particular letter of the alphabet. For example, *Lost and Found*, by Andy West, does not contain words using the letter "e."

LITERACY
The ability to read and write.

LITERAL
The most obvious or nonfigurative sense of a word or phrase; language that is not perceived as metaphorical.

LITERAL LANGUAGE
Words or phrases that are accurate or concise beyond question or doubt.

LITERAL TRANSLATION
A translation of a work from one language to another that renders the text word for word.

LITERARY CRITICISM
The process of analyzing, describing, and interpreting literature.

LITERARY EPIC
A long narrative that utilizes the style, structure, themes, and other conventions of an epic. *Beowulf*, for example, is considered a literary epic.

LITERARY FICTION
A genre of fiction in which the focus of the prose is more on style, psychological depth, and characterization and less on narrative or plot.

LITERATURE
Writing that is of accepted excellence and valued for its intense, personal, and imaginative expression of life.

LITOTES
Understatement for effect. Something expressed by a negation. Example: He had not a few qualms about lending his car to his son.

LOCAL COLOR
In fiction writing, the use of the physical setting, dialect, customs, and attitudes common to a particular region.

LOCKED ROOM
A subgenre of detective fiction in which a crime is committed under seemingly impossible circumstances.

LOGIC
The study of the principles of reasoning.

LOGICAL FALLACY
An error in reasoning that makes an argument invalid.

LOOSE SENTENCE
A sentence structure in which a main idea (clause) of the sentence comes first and is followed by subordinate phrases and clauses. "She drove to work, stopping for gas along the way."

LOOSE TRANSLATION
Translating text from one language to another while preserving the tone, essence, and effect of the original, rather than attempting to make an exact version.

LOVECRAFTIAN
Subgenre of horror fiction that focuses on fear of the unknown rather than other horror elements like gore or monsters, although these may still be included.

Low comedy

Unsophisticated, unruly comedy characterized by burlesque humor and jokes that is more physical than intellectual.

LOWERCASE
In the printed alphabet, small letters (a,b,c . . .) as distinguished from upper case or capital letters (A,B,C . . .).

LYRICAL
Written in a song-like manner.

– M –

MACARONIC
A term applied to text written using more than one language, typically in the form of foreign words that are inserted, often for comedic effect.

MACGUFFIN
An element of plot that catches the reader's attention or drives the plot. Characters are typically willing to do anything initially to obtain this element. It may be ambiguous, undefined, generic or left open to interpretation. For example, money, victory, survival, and power are common types of MacGuffins.

MACRO
1. One instruction that expands into several.

2. Large in scale; overall.

MAGIC REALISM
A subgenre of fantasy fiction characterized by magical elements combined with a realistic atmosphere. For example, all magic has rules, such as uttering a word when using a wand. If these rules are not observed, the magic cannot be performed.

MAIN CHARACTER
The character through whom the story is told. This is often, but not always the protagonist.

MAIN CLAUSE
A group of words consisting of a subject and a predicate that can stand alone as a sentence.

MAINSTREAM
A genre of fiction characterized by the elements of multiple genres that is appealing to a broad audience. Typically novels that do not fit into a particular genre are called "mainstream."

MAJUSCULE
The technical term for uppercase letters.

MALAPROPISM
The substitution of one word for another that is similar in sound but different in meaning. For example, using "illiterate" when meaning "obliterate".

MANUSCRIPT
The original copy of a written composition, typically a novel or a play, before it has been published / performed.

MARGIN
The section of a page that is outside the main body of text.

MARXIST CRITICISM
A type of historical criticism of literature that perceives a literary work as both a reflection and a result of economic conflict between social classes.

MASS NOUN
A noun that names things that cannot be counted and is used only in the singular. For example, air, food, furniture, garbage, and traffic are mass nouns.

MAXIM
A short statement that expresses a common truth or a rule of conduct. For example, "Birds of a feather flock together" is a maxim.

MEANING
The message conveyed by words, sentences, and symbols in a particular context.

MEDICAL MYSTERY
A subgenre of mystery and crime fiction that features a medical setting or characters within the medical profession

MEDICAL THRILLER
Subgenre of thriller fiction in which the theme is related to medicine. Characters are typically doctors or researchers and settings are often a hospital or other medical environment.

MEDIEVAL
Of or relating to the middle ages; European historical period from roughly C.E. 500 to 1500.

MEDIEVAL FANTASY
A subgenre of fantasy fiction where the story takes place in the middle ages from C.E. 500 to 1500, often characterized by knights, epic battles, castles, and sorcery.

MEIOSIS
The use of understatement to emphasize a point, such as understated descriptions of, or responses to, a situation or event in order to heighten the impact of the scene or moment. For example, showing a brooding, quiet protagonist against boisterous and loud peers is a type of meiosis that makes the protagonist stand out.

MEMOIR
A form of autobiography that covers a specific time period.

MEMORANDUM
A short message or record used for internal communication in a business.

MENIPPEAN SATIRE
A form of satire that ridicules such things as pretentiousness, intolerance, and arrogant professionalism.

METAPHOR
A figure of speech that uses an image, story or some tangible thing to describe an intangible quality or idea. "It's raining cats and dogs" and "Her eyes were brilliant sapphires" are metaphors.

METER
The pattern of accented and unaccented syllables in the lines of a poem that produces its general rhythm.

METONYMY
A word or group of words used as a substitute for another in which an object is not addressed by its name but by something closely related. For example, using "the crown" when referring to royalty or "the press" when referring to reporters.

MIDDLE GRADE
A subgenre of children's fiction in which the content, plot, and characters are targeted to children between the ages of 10 and 12 years.

MIDDLE AGES
The period in European history from roughly A.D. 500 to 1500.

MIDDLE ENGLISH
The language spoken in England from about 1100 to 1500.

MIMESIS
Greek word meaning "imitation."

MIMETIC CRITICISM
A type of literary criticism that views an individual work in terms of the "truth" of its depiction of humanity, character, and the "real" world.

MINOR / SECONDARY CHARACTER
A character used to either contrast the main character or to advance the plot.

MINUSCULE
The technical term for lowercase letters.

MISPLACED MODIFIER
Words, phrases, or clauses that are improperly separated from the word they're supposed to modify, resulting in awkward or confusing sentences.

MIXED METAPHOR
A metaphor that combines two contradictory images in a single expression. For example, "Let's burn that bridge when we come to it," is a mixed metaphor, combining the metaphors "don't burn your bridges" (meaning don't do something you'll regret later) and "cross that bridge when we come to it" (meaning deal with one problem at a time).

MOCK EPIC
A literary work that parodies or satirically mimics the form and style of traditional epics.

MODE
The choosing and arranging of words to convey an attitude and may refer to an element of writing style. Types of modes include satire, realism, romanticism, impressionism, expressionism, naturalism, and neo-classicism.

MODERN ENGLISH
The English language since about 1500.

MODERN FANTASY
A subgenre of fantasy fiction that is set in modern times, while featuring the elements of typical fantasy.

MODIFIER
A word, phrase, or clause that acts as an adjective or adverb to affect the meaning of another word or phrase, usually to describe it, or restrict its meaning. "The <u>illegal</u> activities of your father will soon be made known to the <u>proper</u> authorities."

MONODY
A lament over the death of a loved one, usually in the form of soliloquy.

MONOLOGUE
An extended speech that is presented by one character.

MONSTER
Subgenre of horror fiction that features creatures, either manmade or "freaks of nature," that are grotesque, evil, hideous, or strange. "Frankenstein" is an example of monster fiction.

MOOD
1. The encompassing feeling within a story.

2. The characteristic of verbs that indicate a speaker's attitude toward an action.

MORAL CRITICISM
A type of literary criticism that evaluates a work on the basis of the moral elements it contains.

MORPHEME
A combination of sounds that have meaning; the smallest meaningful word or word element.

MORPHOLOGY
A branch of linguistics that studies the forms of words and word parts, such as prefixes and suffixes.

MOTHER TONGUE
The language a person learns from birth; native language.

MOTIF
A recurring theme or pattern in a single text or over many separate texts.

MOTIVATION
The psychological and moral urges and the environmental conditions that cause a character to act, think, or feel a certain way.

MOTTO
A brief sentence or phrase used to summarize the beliefs or morals that guide an individual, family, or institution.

MULTICULTURAL ROMANCE
A subgenre of romance fiction traditionally characterized by African-American protagonists, although some multicultural romances frequently include Asian or Hispanic protagonists or interracial relationships.

MULTIPLE PLOTS
Presenting more than one major and minor story line simultaneously.

MYSTERY FICTION
Genre of fiction that encompasses cozies, police procedurals, detective, crime fiction, and noir, in which a professional or amateur detective solves a crime.

MYTH
1. A narrative, usually anonymous in origin, derived from the folklore of a culture or a nation.

2. Any unproven or unsupported belief that is accepted as truth.

MYTHIC CRITICISM
A type of literary criticism that views literary genres and plot patterns of individual works as repetitions of recurring patterns, such as life and death, youthful rebellion, and the change of the seasons.

MYTHOLOGY
The study of myths.

NAIVE NARRATOR
A narrator that is unreliable due to innocence, inexperience, or lack of understanding of the story and its true consequences.

NAME
A word or phrase that defines or labels a person, place, or thing.

NARRATION
The way a story is told. Refers to any story told in chronological order that builds to a climax and a conclusion.

NARRATIVE
A spoken or written recounting of a sequence of events, usually in chronological order.

NARRATIVE ESSAY
A brief nonfiction work that recounts an event.

NARRATIVE HOOK
See "Hook."

NARRATIVE PERSPECTIVE
The viewpoint or position from which a story is told; a synonym for point of view.

NARRATIVE TECHNIQUE
The method or devices used by an author to tell a story. For example, a flashback is a narrative technique used to share with the reader past events not included in the story.

NARRATOR
The person or character telling a story.

NATURALISM
The manner or technique of adopting an objective view to tell a story that is without preconceived ideas, biases, etc. and focusing on accurate details.

NATURE WRITING
A type of creative nonfiction in which the natural environment is the focus or main subject.

NEGATIVE PARTICLE
The word "not" or "-n't" is used to indicate negation, denial, or refusal. "<u>Don't</u> ask me again. I'm <u>not</u> <u>going</u>."

NEOCLASSIC DRAMA
Refers to a period during which Renaissance writers attempted to imitate the styles of ancient Greece.

NEO-CLASSICISM
The revival of a classical style in literature, art, architecture, and music; popular in England from 1660 to 1740.

NEOLOGISM
A newly created word or expression, or new usage for existing words and expressions that is not yet common.

NEW AGE
Genre of fiction that is characterized by alternative approaches to culture, often emphasizing themes such as spirituality, mysticism, and environmentalism.

NEW WAVE
A fashion in literature, art, music, film, or politics that is intentionally different from traditional ideas or conventions.

NICKNAME
A descriptive or affectionate name given to a person or a thing that is added to or that replaces a real name. Often humorous in intent, but sometimes used to simplify a longer or complicated proper name. For example, a tall, thin man might be named George, but his friends nickname him "Slim."

NOIR
Genre of fiction characterized by an overwhelming feeling of doom and darkness.

NOM DE PLUME
A fictitious name assumed by a writer. See also "pseudonym."

NONFICTION
An essay, biography, autobiography, article, or text that details real people and events.

NOUN
The part of speech used to name a person, place, thing, quality, or action.

NOVEL
A fictional story, typically exceeding 200 pages, or 80,000 words, with a complex plot and several subplots.

NOVEL OF MANNERS
A literary genre that focuses on the behavior, language and morals of a specific class of people in a specific historical context. Typically comical and satirical, the characters and plot are restricted by the characteristics of their particular social class in the time period depicted.

NOVEL OF SENSIBILITY
Refers to a literary genre that reflects the cult of sensibility that was predominant during the last part of the eighteenth century.

NOVEL OF THE SOIL
A literary genre that that focuses on the sociological aspects and hardships of those who struggle to earn a living off the land.

NOVELETTE
A short work of prose, typically between 7, 500 and 17,000 words, that is shorter than a novel, built often on one incident or event, but longer and more developed than a short story.

NOVELLA
A short novel that is typically between 17,000 and 40,000 words, although some publishers classify any story between 17,000 and 70,000 words a novella.

NUMBER
Grammatical category of nouns, pronouns, and adjectives that distinguish count agreement with the verb. For example, "One bear" not "One bears."

- O -

OBJECT
A noun, pronoun, or noun phrase that is affected by the action of a verb within a sentence. "Billy kicked the ball." "Billy" is the subject, or the noun that acts, "ball" is the object, and "kicked" is the action given to it.

OBJECT POINT OF VIEW
A method of narration in which a story is told in an objective manner with the author avoiding any expression of personal opinions, attitudes, biases, or emotions.

OBJECTIVE CORRELATIVE
Creating a specific emotional reaction by placing a particular word or words next to each other; using the image of an object, circumstance, or event to communicate emotion without an explanation.

.OBJECTIVE CRITICISM
A type of literary criticism that focuses on the basic merits of a work rather than relating the work to the life of its author, the time in which it was written, or its effect on the reader.

OBJECTIVE THEORY OF ART
In literature, a term given to the idea that a work is significant as an object in itself.

OBJECTIVITY
The impersonal depiction of events and characters, their thoughts, and their feelings in a literary work.

OEUVRE
The collective works of a particular writer.

OLD ENGLISH
The language spoken in England from around 450 to 1100 CE.

OMNISCIENT
A form of narration, or point of view, used in novels where the narrator is "all seeing or all knowing," typically written in third person point of view, as in "she said" and "he walked."

ONOMATOPOEIA
The formation or use of words that mimic the sounds associated with the objects or actions they refer to. The words "ding dong," for example, imitate a doorbell, and "bang" mimics the sound of a gunshot.

ORAL LITERATURE
The ballads, tales, and proverbs of preliterate or non-literate cultures that are verbally passed down through generations from memory rather than recorded.

ORDINAL NUMBER
A number that identifies position or order in relation to other numbers. "First," "second," and "third" are ordinal numbers.

ORGANIC HORROR
See "Body Horror"

ORPHAN
A word or short phrase at the top of a column that is often the last part of a sentence from a previous column. Orphans should be avoided in fiction writing.

ORTHOGRAPHY
1. The conventional spelling system of a language.

2. The study of how letters are used to express sounds and form words.

OUTLINE
A technique used to arrange the elements of a particular plot, typically in point form or in brief summaries of scenes and/or chapters, before the actual writing of the story. The Snowflake Method is a type of outline.

OUTLINE (CHAPTER)
A brief summary of a chapter prepared prior to writing the story.

OVERWRITING
A longwinded writing style characterized by too much detail, needless repetition, strange figures of speech, and/or convoluted sentence structures.

OXYMORON
A figure of speech that combines incongruous or contradictory terms. "Sweet sorrow" and "bitter sweet" are examples of oxymorons.

- P -

PALINDROME
A word, phrase, or sentence that reads the same backward or forward. For example, "madam" is a palindrome, as is "race car" and "level."

PARABLE
Short metaphorical stories used to illustrate a moral point.

PARADOX
A statement that appears to contradict itself, but may in fact be true. "Each person is completely unique, just like everyone else."

PARAGRAPH
A group of closely related sentences that develop a main idea.

PARALLEL STRUCTURE
Two or more words, phrases, or clauses that are similar in length and grammatical form.

PARALLELISM
Similarity of structure in two or more related words, phrases, or clauses.

PARANORMAL ROMANCE
Subgenre of romance characterized by supernatural or paranormal elements such as immortality, vampires, or witchcraft.

PARAPHRASE
Restating a piece of text or a passage in different words, typically to clarify meaning or for brevity.

PARATAXIS
Placing associated clauses in a series without using coordinating conjunctions like "and," "but," or "so."

PARENTHESIS
Punctuation marks ( ) used to isolate clarifying or qualifying remarks in writing or to insert text that interrupts the normal flow of the sentence.

PARODY
A literary or artistic work that imitates the style of an author or a work for comic effect.

PARONOMASIA
Punning or playing with words by exploiting multiple meanings of a single word.

PARSING
A grammatical exercise in which a text is broken down into its component parts of speech with an explanation of the form, function, and syntactical relationship of each part.

PARTIAL
A manuscript fragment, excerpt, or section.

PARTICIPLE
A verbal that functions as an adjective. For example, "I walk" is changed to the present participle by adding "-ing" to make "I am walking."

PASSIVE VOICE
In grammar, a sentence in which the object of an action precedes the verb phrase. "The beer was drunk by Charlie." This sentence is passive because the direct object "beer" is placed before the action "drunk." To be active, the action must come before the object. "Charlie drank the beer."

PAST PARTICIPLE
The third principal part of a verb, which is created by adding "-ed", "-d", or" –t" to the root form of regular verbs.

PAST PERFECT
A verb tense used to describe an action already completed in the past, typically relying on the use of "had" or "had been" combined with the verb. "I had finished…"

PAST PROGRESSIVE
A verb construction that conveys a sense of ongoing action in the past. Typically made up of a past form of the verb, such as "was" or "were" and a present participle. "He was supposed to be doing his homework."

PAST TENSE
A verb tense that indicates past action that does not extend into the present. "We walked home."

PASTICHE
An artistic work done in a style that imitates another work or style.

PATHETIC FALLACY
A term coined to criticize the use of personification, in which inanimate objects or nature are treated as though they had human emotions and thought.

PATHOS
The quality in an artistic work that evokes feelings of sympathy, pity, or grief.

PATOIS
Slang or jargon used by a particular social group; usually considered low in status to standard language.

PEN NAME
A fictitious name assumed by an author.

PERIOD
A single dot punctuation mark (.) used to indicate a full stop that is placed at the end of sentences and complete statements and after abbreviations.

PERIODIC SENTENCE
Long and usually involved sentence that is not grammatically complete until the readers reaches the final part of the sentence.

PERSON
The relationship between a subject and its verb that shows whether the subject is speaking in first person ("I" or "we"), second person ("you") or in third person ("he," "she," "it," or "they").

PERSONA
The characters in a work of fiction.

PERSONAL ESSAY
A brief written composition that expresses personal opinions and thoughts in a conversational, informal, or humorous tone.

PERSONAL PRONOUN
A pronoun that refers to a particular person, group, or thing, such as "I," "he," "she," "it," "we," or "they."

PERSONIFICATION
Giving human characteristics such as emotion or thought to other creatures or inanimate objects.

PERSUASION
A form of essay intended to change opinions.

PHILOLOGY
The study of the changes in structure, historical development, and relationships of language.

PHONEME
The smallest unit of sound in a language that is able to convey meaning. English has 44 phonemes. For example the sounds "k," "a," and "t" are phonemes, that when blended make the word "cat."

PHONOLOGY
The study of rudimentary speech sounds.

PHRASE
Any small group of words within a sentence or clause.

PICA
A printer's unit of type size; equal to or slightly less than 1/6th of an inch.

PICARESQUE NOVEL
A kind of fiction which originated in Spain that features the adventures of a scoundrel, rogue, or quick-thinking vagabond.

PICTURE BOOKS
A type of children's fiction in which the story is told using words and illustrations.

PIDGIN
A simplified form of language that is formed out of one or more local languages and used for communication between people who do not share a common language.

PLAGIARISM / PLAGIARIZE
The act of using the work of another and passing it off as your own. Taking or using the words of another as your own.

PLATONIC CRITICISM
A type of criticism that focuses on the non-essential rather than the fundamental ideas of a work.

PLAY
A literary work that is meant to be performed by actors before an audience.

PLEONASM
The use of unnecessary words to express what is clear without them; redundancy.

PLOT
The events or incidents that make up the story in a narrative.

PLOT DEVICES
Objects, events, or characters in a story whose sole purpose is to move the plot forward or overcome some conflict in the story.

PLOT STRUCTURE
The sequence of events within a literary work.

PLOT TWIST
An unexpected change or development in the expected outcome or direction of a fictional work.

PLOT VOUCHER
An object presented to the protagonist at the beginning of a story that is crucial later in resolving conflict.

PLURAL
The form of a noun that typically signifies more than one person or thing.

POETIC JUSTICE
A literary device in which virtue is ultimately rewarded, and evil or badness is punished.

POETIC LICENSE
The freedom taken by poets and other artists to depart from conventional rules of language, such as proper word order or pronunciation, to achieve certain effects.

POETRY
A form of literary art in which words are selected for their expressive qualities, traditionally featuring rhythm and rhyme. Modern forms tend to lack this structure.

POINT
In typography, a measure of 1/12th of a pica, and the smallest unit of measure. There are 72.27 points in one inch.

POINT OF VIEW
The vantage point or the lens through which a story is told. First, second, third, cinematic, and omniscient are the points of view used in fiction writing.

POLICE PROCEDURAL
A subgenre of crime fiction which focuses on the police and the procedures used to catch a criminal or to solve a crime.

POLYSYNDETON
Using several conjunctions in a series. "We make buns _and_ cakes _and_ pastries _and_ donuts."

POPULAR ROMANCE
A subgenre of modern romance fiction characterized by exotic settings, mystery, and love.

PORNOGRAPHY
Writing intended solely for the purpose of sexual arousal or excitement that lacks any social value or literary quality.

PORTMANTEAU WORDS
Words created by combining two or more words in such a way that their meanings are also combined. "Smog," for example, was coined to describe a climatic condition by blending the words "smoke" and "fog."

POSSESSIVE DETERMINER
A Determiner used before a noun to express possession. "My," "your," "his," "her" and "their" are possessive Determiners.

POSSESSIVE PRONOUN
Used in place of a noun to show ownership. "<u>Mine</u> is red and <u>yours</u> is blue."

POST-APOCALYPTIC
A subgenre of science fiction in which the story takes place after a major disaster or catastrophe that has resulted in the end of civilization.

POV
See "Point Of View"

PRACTICAL CRITICISM
An objective style of literary criticism that analyzes works utilizing the principles of art and hypothetical observations.

PRAGMATIC CRITICISM
A type of literary criticism that evaluates a work based on the perception that it is something intended to produce certain emotional and moral responses in the reader and that analyzes how those effects are created.

PREDESTINATION PARADOX
Refers to a paradox in time travel where a traveler from the future unwittingly affects events that already happened in the past.

PREDICATE
One of the two main parts of a sentence or clause, the other part being the subject, that modifies the subject and includes the verb, objects, and phrases that are ruled by the verb. For example, "The car is black." The car acts as the subject, and "is black" is the predicate.

PREFACE
A statement written by the author intended to place the story in context, or to give it perspective. Appears before the main text of the work.

PREFIX
A letter or group of letters attached to the beginning of a word that partly indicates its meaning. In the word "review" for example, the prefix "re-" means again, making the word mean "to view again."

PREHISTORIC FANTASY
A subgenre of fantasy fiction and/or science fiction that attempts to recreate or imagine prehistoric worlds.

PREMISE
The basis of an argument or the information from which a conclusion is drawn.

PREPOSITION
A word that specifies the relationship between a noun or pronoun and other words in a sentence. "He traveled to England <u>by</u> boat."

PREPOSITIONAL PHRASE
A group of words made up of a preposition, its object, and any of the object's modifiers. "They went <u>to the movies</u>."

PRE-READERS
Subgenre of children's fiction targeted to children in elementary grades who are beginning to identify letters and sounds but not yet reading independently.

PRESENT PARTICIPLE
A verb form made by adding "-ing" to the root form of the verb that functions as an adjective. "The blinking light drew her attention."

PRESENT PERFECT
A verb tense utilizing the present tense form of "to have" that expresses an action begun in the past that either has been completed or continues into the present. "I _have studied_ all night, but I can't remember it all."

PRESENT PROGRESSIVE TENSE
A verb tense that is made up of a present participle (-ing) with a form of the infinitive "to be" that conveys ongoing action, or action that is happening right now. "He _is taking_ the lead."

PRESENT TENSE
A verb tense that expresses action in the present time or indicates regular actions. For example, "I work," "He says," and "Joe drives."

PREWRITING
Thinking about writing, or what you will write, before actually doing any of the work.

PROBLEM NOVEL
Subgenre of young adult fiction in which a social problem is presented as the central conflict.

PROCESS ANALYSIS
Written compositions that explain how to accomplish a task or how a device works. Technical manuals are a type of process analysis document.

PROLETARIAN NOVEL
A novel that focuses on the sociological problems of the working class, typically written in the period between 1930 and 1945.

PROLOGUE
An introduction or preface to a work.

PRONOUN
A word that takes the place of a noun, such as "we," "he," "she," "I," "they," and "you" are used in place of nouns to make sentences less repetitive.

PROOF (EDITING)
A draft or trial sheet of printed material created to be checked and corrected.

PROOFREADING
The process of reviewing the final draft of a text, such as a manuscript, to ensure that all obvious errors have been corrected.

PROPAGANDA LITERATURE
Literature meant to influence opinions on a social or a political issue, often by appealing to fear and prejudice.

PROPER NOUN
A noun that is used to identify, such as individual, event, or place names, usually capitalized. John drove to the lake, hoping to see Carrie before she left for Toronto. "John", "Carrie," and "Toronto" are examples of proper nouns, but "lake" is a common noun.

PROSE
Any written composition that is not classified as poetry, drama, or song.

PROTAGONIST
The person or character around whom the action occurs. The primary character in a work of fiction.

PROTEST LITERATURE
Prose written in objection to a social or political policy or action.

PROVERB
A short statement that expresses a common truth or folk wisdom. "A leopard can't change his spots" or "If you lie with dogs, you'll wake up with fleas."

PSEUDONYM
A fictitious name assumed by a writer.

PSYCHIC DISTANCE
Standing apart from a work as a reader or a viewer, aware that it is a work of art and not real life.

PSYCHOLOGICAL HORROR
Subgenre of horror fiction that relies on irrational fears, guilt, or beliefs to horrify or scare the reader.

PSYCHOLOGICAL NOVEL
A type of novel written in any genre that focuses on the mental state and emotions of its characters, emphasizing the psychological motivation behind their actions rather than on the actions themselves.

PULP FICTION
A term that originally referred to books printed on low-grade paper and sold at a low price.

PUN
A form of wit that involves a play on a word with more than one meaning.

PUNCTUATION
Set of marks used to standardize texts and clarify their meanings, primarily by separating or linking words, phrases, and clauses.

PURPLE PROSE
Writing that is characterized by ornate or flowery language and words.

PURPOSE
An author's intent or reason for writing a work. The purpose might be entertainment, instruction, or persuasion.

- Q -

QUALIFIER
A word or phrase that precedes an adjective or adverb, increasing or decreasing the quality signified by the word they modify. For example "very" and "only" are qualifiers.

QUERY LETTER
A cover letter written to a publisher or an agent that summarizes a specific work and requests permission to send the full manuscript for their evaluation in the hopes of eventual publication of the work.

QUESTION MARK
A punctuation symbol (?) written at the end of a sentence or phrase to indicate a direct question.

QUIBBLE
A minor objection or criticism.

QUIET HORROR
Subgenre of horror fiction, sometimes called suspense, in which little blood or violence is used to achieve terror. Typically the writer takes a normal situation and makes it scary by using elements like everyday locations and Freudian psychology as a central part of the fear.

QUOTATION
The restating of words already written or spoken by another.

QUOTATION MARKS
Either of a pair of punctuation marks (" ") used in fiction to separate dialogue from narration and in other text to mark the beginning and end of a quote attributed to another source.

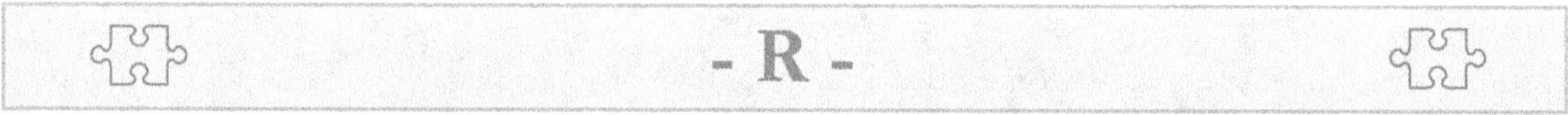

- R -

READER-RESPONSE CRITICISM
A collective term used to describe various critical theories that focus on the responses of the reader to a literary work rather than on the text itself as the source of meaning.

REALISM
A style of writing that depicts the people and events in a story as if they are real.

RECOGNITION
The moment when a character gains vital knowledge, insight, or understanding that he or she previously lacked.

RED HERRING
Rhetorical or literary device used to draw attention away from an item or issue of significance.

REDUNDANCY
Repeating the same idea or information within a phrase, clause or sentence, the meaning or idea of which is clear without the repetition.

REFLEXIVE PRONOUN
A pronoun formed by adding "-self" or "-selves" to a personal pronoun; used as an object to refer to a previously named noun or pronoun. "Mom said she'd rather make the cake <u>herself</u>."

REGIONALISM
Literature or poetry that focuses on specific features, such as setting, dialect, customs, manners, people, beliefs, and history of a particular region.

REGULAR VERB
A verb that forms its past tense and past participle by adding "-d", "-ed", or "-t" to its base form. "Skate" for example becomes "skated."

RELATIVE CLAUSE
Subordinate clauses attached to a noun that add information to the noun. They are introduced by a relative pronoun like "which," "that," "who," "whom," or "whose" or a relative adverb like "where," "when," or "why." "The men <u>who built the structure</u> died when it collapsed."

RELATIVE PRONOUN
A pronoun that introduces an adjective clause. It is called a relative pronoun because it relates to the word it modifies. "The car <u>that</u> we bought is a lemon."

RELIGIOUS SCIENCE FICTION
A subgenre of science fiction that integrates religious or theological themes into the plot to explore, prove, or disprove their accuracy.

REPETITIVE DESIGNATION
A foreshadowing technique that uses repeated references to a character, object or event that at first seems insignificant, but later is proven to be significant to the plot.

REPORT
A document that provides information in an organized format intended for a specific audience and purpose.

REPORTED SPEECH
Retelling in the writer's own words what a speaker said or writer stated.

REQUIEM
The final resolution of the conflicts and complications in a plot.

RESEARCH
The process of collecting and evaluating information about a particular subject.

RESOLUTION
Near the end of a story, the moment when all remaining facts are revealed and the conflict is resolved.

RESTORATION COMEDY
Theatre or fiction that is characteristic of the English Restoration period (1660-1700), featuring scandalous plots and debauchery.

REVENGE TRAGEDY
A predictable type of tragedy, popular during Elizabethan times, which featured murder and revenge as primary elements.

REVERSAL
A sudden change of fortune for the protagonist in a work of fiction.

REVIEW
An article or written composition that provides a critical evaluation of a work of fiction such as a novel or a play.

REVISION
The process of rereading a text and improving it by making changes in content, sentence structure, organization, and word choice.

REWRITING
The process of changing a text, making corrections or alterations to content, sentences, characters, and elements of plot with a goal to improve the work.

RHETORICAL
A question or statement not usually intended to be answered or evaluated, but instead posed to inspire thought.

RHETORICAL CRITICISM
A type of literary criticism in which the author's use of language in communicating with the reader is emphasized and evaluated.

RHETORICAL QUESTION
See "Rhetorical"

RHETORICAL TECHNIQUES
Techniques such as comparisons, repetitions, and paradoxes used in constructing rhetorical or persuasive essays.

RHYME
Similarity of sound between accented syllables.

RHYTHM
The flow of the elements within a story.

RIDDLE
A question intentionally phrased in a confusing manner and presented as a problem to be solved.

RISING ACTION
An element of plot in which the events become increasingly exciting or intense. Rising action is used in all genres and forms of literature.

ROMAN À CLEF
A French term meaning "novel with a key" that refers to novels in which real people are depicted under fictitious names.

ROMANCE
A genre of fiction in which the story is shaped around the romantic relationship between two characters, typically both acting as protagonists.

ROMANTIC FANTASY
A subgenre of fantasy fiction that combines fantasy elements with a romantic relationship between two characters. The main focus is on the fantasy elements, however, and not the romance.

ROMANTIC MOVEMENT
An early 19th-century movement against classical literature and art that focused on originality, primitive emotions like passion, and the natural world.

ROMANTIC NOVEL
A type of novel focusing more on action and emotion than on characterization; often involving adventure, love, and battle.

ROMANTIC SUSPENSE
A subgenre of suspense fiction in which the romantic relationship between two characters is included in the plot alongside the mystery and suspense.

ROOT
A word from which other words are formed, typically through the addition of prefixes and/or suffixes.

ROUGH
Draft manuscript.

ROUND CHARACTER
Also referred to as dynamic, a character in fiction depicted in detail as a complex, multi-faceted personality; the opposite of a flat character.

RUN-ON SENTENCE
Two independent clauses that have been strung together without an appropriate conjunction and/or mark of punctuation between them. "She pulled the gun from her purse aiming it directly at the masked man running across the vacant lot." Correct structure, "She pulled the gun from her purse, and aimed it directly at the masked man."

- S -

SANS SERIF
Refers to any typeface without added strokes for effect. Also referred to as sans and swiss forms, typically smooth in appearance. Arial, Avante Garde, and Helvetica are sans serif fonts.

SARCASM
Writing characterized by a caustic tone and the use of irony to mock or convey contempt.

SATIRE
Literature in which absurdities and abuses are ridiculed.

SCENE
A series of events contained within a single setting and uninterrupted period of time.

SCENE END
The resolution of a scene that occurs before moving to a new series of events or time period.

SCENE OPENING
The beginning of a series of events in a single setting or a different period of time within a work of fiction.

SCENIC METHOD
A narrative technique that presents a work of fiction in scenes as though it were a play.

SCIENCE FICTION
Genre of fiction featuring science and technology as a basis for plot development.

SCOPE
The items of events revealed within the text of a work of fiction.

SCRIPT
Refers to plays or film scripts.

SECOND-PERSON POINT OF VIEW
A method of storytelling that uses the imperative mood (commanding, authoritative) and the pronouns "you," "your," and "yours" to address the reader.

SELF-EFFACING AUTHOR
A style of writing in which the writer presents the actions, thoughts, and dialogue of the characters within the work without personal or subjective commentary. The author becomes an impersonal medium through which the story is witnessed.

SEMANTICS
The field of linguistics focused on the study of meaning in language.

SEMICOLON
A mark of punctuation (;) used to connect independent clauses, indicating a closer relationship between the clauses than a period would.

SEMIOTICS
The study of signs or signals of communication such as words, Morse code, music, gestures, facial expressions, or anything that is thought to communicate meaning.

SENSIBILITY
The capacity for feeling and responding emotionally; relying on emotion rather than intellect as a guide.

SENSORY DETAIL
Describing something, such as a person or a place, using at least one of the five senses (sight, sound, taste, touch and smell) to give the reader a clear picture.

SENTENCE
The largest independent unit of grammar, beginning with a capital letter and ending with a period, question mark, or exclamation point.

SENTENCE COMBINING
The process of joining two or more simple sentences to make one long sentence, typically using a comma or semi-colon to connect them.

SENTENTIOUS
Given to using maxims or morals in a way that is trite or laborious; pithy, terse.

SENTIMENTAL NOVEL
A novel reflecting the cult of sensibility which was popular during the latter eighteenth century, relying on emotional responses in the characters and the reader.

SENTIMENTALISM
Demonstrating or evoking an exaggerated emotional response that is disproportionate to the situation that prompted it.

SEQUEL
A work of fiction that is a continuation of events in a previous work.

SERIAL COMMA
The comma that precedes the conjunction before the final item in a series.

SERIES
A collection of fictional works that share common characters, settings, and/or themes.

SERIF
A decorative stroke used to add flair to a typeface, also known as Roman and book forms. Times, Palatino, and Century Schoolbook are examples of serif fonts.

SESQUIPEDALIAN
The tendency to use long words.

SETTING
The place and time in which a story takes place.

SHORT STORY
A work of fiction that is typically less than 50 pages in length.

SHOWING
Technique used to illustrate what is happening in a work of fiction for the reader instead of telling him as if after the fact. This is to make the story more vivid and engage the senses.

SIGN
Any event, gesture, image, motion, pattern, or sound that conveys meaning.

SIMILE
A figure of speech in which two unlike things are compared, usually in a phrase introduced by "like" or "as." For example, "The motor roared like a lion."

SIMPLE SENTENCE
A sentence with only one independent clause, which includes a subject and a verb and is a complete thought. "I love chocolate."

SINGULAR
The simplest form of a noun: a classification of number signifying one person, thing, or instance.

SITUATIONAL IRONY
The contrast that exists between what is intended to happen and what actually occurs.

SLANG
An informal nonstandard variety of speech that is characterized by newly created and rapidly changing words and phrases.

SLASH
A forward sloping line (/) used as a mark of punctuation in writing.

SLICE OF LIFE
A phrase depicting the detailed, unselective, and realistic presentation of everyday aspects of life that is without comment or evaluation by the author.

SLIP OF THE TONGUE
An accidental error in speaking that is often inconsequential and sometimes amusing.

SLIPSTREAM
A genre of fiction that blurs the boundaries between such genres as science fiction and fantasy or mainstream and literary fiction.

SLOGAN
A brief, attention-getting expression or phrase used to promote a product, candidate, or cause.

SOCRATIC IRONY
The technique of feigning ignorance in order to draw out another's true opinions or arguments.

SOFT HORROR
See "quiet horror"

SOLECISM
A nonstandard usage or grammatical construction often perceived as a grammatical mistake. "This is between you and I." (Should be "you and me")

SOLILOQUY
Dialogue delivered aloud by a character that is alone on stage.

SPACE OPERA
Subgenre of speculative fiction emphasizing the romance and melodrama of adventure, often set in outer space. Elements such as characters, setting, and battles tend to be large-scale.

SPACE WESTERN
Subgenre of science fiction in which themes of American Western fiction are set in futuristic landscapes, such as space frontiers.

SPECULATIVE ESSAY
A brief nonfiction work that presents a theory and proposes evidence or proof.

SPELLCHECKER
A computer application that identifies possible misspellings in a text by referring to the accepted spellings in a pre-existing database.

SPELLING
The selection and arrangement of letters that form words.

SPLIT INFINITIVE
A construction in which a modifier interrupts an infinitive. "I don't want <u>to ever go</u> to Mars."

SPOONERISM
A transposition of sounds of two or more words that is usually accidental. For example saying "miss the can" instead of "kiss the man". Also referred to as a slip of the tongue.

STACKING
The use of several modifiers before a noun.

STATIC CHARACTER
A character that does not change significantly over the course of the story or that does not influence the plot.

STEAMPUNK
A subgenre of science fiction that may include elements of the alternate history and fantasy genres. Typically features futuristic technology and innovations as those living in the Victorian era may have envisioned them and may use alternative history themes.

STEREOTYPE
Characters or plots that are frequently used so that they are easily recognized by readers and considered overused.

STOCK CHARACTER
A character created because the plot requires it for consistency. Stock characters do not mean stereotypical characters, however. For example, a wedding requires various nameless guests.

STOCK EPITHET
An epithet that is used frequently.

STORY
How characters respond to the events within a plot, which forms the basis for a story, giving characters a context for action.

STORY WITHIN A STORY
A literary device in which one story is told during the action of another story.

STRATEGY
Also called "rhetorical strategy." The organization of words and phrases for a specific effect; often involves manipulative dialogue.

STRAW MAN
A fallacy in which an opponent's argument is exaggerated or misrepresented in order to be criticized or rebutted without having addressed the actual argument.

STREAM OF CONSCIOUSNESS
A literary style or method in which thoughts are presented in a continuous and uninterrupted flow.

STRUCTURALISM
A method of analyzing literature characterized by interpreting and analyzing works in terms of contrasts and ordered structures, particularly as they might reflect common psychological characteristics or unifying principles.

STRUCTURE
The formal or traditional manner of presenting a work of fiction.

STYLE
The way that a writer writes. This includes the devices, techniques, and words choices used to create a work.

STYLISTICS
A term that refers to several types of analytical studies of literature that relate to the techniques and concepts of modern linguistics.

SUBJECT
The topic or thing described in a work of literature.

SUBJECTIVITY
The expression of the writer's person feelings, thoughts, and opinions.

SUBJUNCTIVE MOOD
The mood of a verb used in statements that are hypothetical or that express wishes, suggestions that stipulate demands, or make statements contrary to fact. Typically requires a modal auxiliary or subjunctive verb form. For example, "I wish I'd known this before." (wish) "You must return by midnight." (demand)

SUBORDINATE CLAUSE
A group of words that is typically introduced by a relative pronoun or a subordinating conjunction and that contains a subject and a verb but cannot stand alone as a sentence. "I didn't go before we left because you said we were late."

SUBPLOT
Secondary action in a work of fiction that is complete and interesting apart from the main plot, often used to intensify the main plot or to illustrate a character's nature.

SUBSTANTIVE
In grammar, a word or phrase that functions as a noun.

SUFFIX
A letter or group of letters, such as "-ly" or "-ful," added to the end of a word to form a new word or functioning as an inflectional ending.

SUMMARY
A condensed version of a text that highlights the main points or ideas.

SUPERHUMAN
Subgenre of science fiction featuring "improved humans" engineered through genetic modification or cybernetics, or humans with unusual talents like superior strength, psychic ability or anything considered outside normal human ability.

SUPERLATIVE
The form of an adjective that implies the most or the least of something, often using the suffix "-est" or preceded by "most" or "least." "You must be the biggest fool I've ever met."

SUPERNATURAL
A subgenre of fantasy fiction that features elements considered outside of the natural world. May also be considered horror fiction if the intent to scare or disturb is present. Often includes themes such as vampires, witches, superpowers, or magic.

SUSPENSE
Tension or anticipation created through the use of unpredictable plot twists.

SWEAR WORD
A word or phrase that is commonly considered obscene, vulgar, or otherwise offensive.

SWORD AND SORCERY
A subgenre of fantasy fiction characterized by magic, unchanging heroes, and heroic battles.

SYLLABLE
A unit of spoken language consisting of one vowel sound that may or may not be surrounded by consonants. Each syllable in a word consists of a single continuous sound. "Water," for example, has two syllables: wa-ter.

SYLLOGISM
A form of logic or deductive reasoning that consists of a major premise, a minor premise, and a conclusion.

SYMBOL
A person, place, action, or thing that represents something other than itself.

SYMBOLISM
The use of an object as a symbol, which represents or suggests something else.

SYNECDOCHE
A figure of speech in which a part is used for a whole or a whole is used to represent a part. For example, referring to the Bible as "the Book" or using "bug" to refer to any "insect," even if it is not a true insect.

SYNONYM
Words that share the same or approximately the same meaning.

SYNOPSIS
A summary of key events in a plot, including beginning, middle, and end.

SYNTAX
The arrangement and grammatical relation of words, phrases, and clauses that make up well-formed sentences.

TABOO LANGUAGE
Words and phrases that are considered inappropriate or offensive in certain contexts.

TAFF TALE
A comedic story of the impossible adventures of a hero possessing superhuman abilities.

TAG
A clause consisting of two or more words that attributes dialogue to a specific speaker. "I hate Mondays," Chloe said.

TAUTOLOGY
Unnecessarily repeating an idea using different words.

TECHNICAL WRITING
Written communications completed on the job, typically in fields with specialized vocabularies or jargon, such as science, technology, and medicine.

TECHNO-THRILLER
Subgenre of thriller fiction that borrows elements from the science fiction and fantasy genres.

TELLING
Description, in narrative, that "tells" the reader what she is seeing, rather than creating an image for her to visualize.

TEMPLATE
Blank document pre-formatted with styles and/ or sections.

TEMPO
The pace at which a plot moves from event to event.

TENSE
The time of a verb's action: past, present or future.

TENSION
The interaction of conflicting elements in a work of fiction, such as literal versus metaphorical, serious versus ironic, or intense versus low-key.

TEXT
The main body of a manuscript or an intelligible section of written language that may be viewed as an object of critical analysis.

TEXTUAL CRITICISM
A form of literary criticism in which the original manuscript or most authoritative text of a literary work is reconstructed.

THEMATIC PATTERNING
The distribution of repeating thematic concepts and moralistic ideas throughout the action of a plot. May be arranged to emphasize a unifying idea or argument.

THEME
The main idea of a text, which may be expressed directly or indirectly.

THESAURUS
A book consisting of synonyms, which often includes related words and antonyms.

THESIS
The position or statement a writer wishes to prove or support.

THIRD-PERSON POINT OF VIEW
A method of presenting a work of fiction or nonfiction which uses "he," "she," "they" and other third-person pronouns to recount events.

THOUGHT
The idea an author intends to leave with readers.

THRENODY
A song of death; a dirge.

THRILLER
Genre of fiction that features suspense, tension, and action as its main elements.

TICKING CLOCK SCENARIO
A literary device often used in thrillers where there is a time-sensitive threat of impending disaster.

TIME TRAVEL
A subgenre of science fiction that features time travel as a main element. For example, futuristic characters traveling to the past, or modern-day characters traveling to the future.

TITLE
A word or phrase applied to a written work such as a novel, article, or report that identifies the subject of the work and attracts the reader's attention.

TONE
A writer's attitude toward the subject of the work and its audience. Tone is typically conveyed through language, point of view, syntax, and level of formality.

TOPIC
The main issue or idea that serves as the subject of a work.

TOPIC SENTENCE
A term used in the traditional study of writing that identifies the sentence that either directly or indirectly states the topic to be developed in subsequent paragraphs.

TOPONYM
A named or a word derived from a geographical place or region.

TRADEMARK
A distinguishing word, phrase, symbol, or design that identifies a specific product that is legally owned by its manufacturer or inventor.

TRADITION
Anything passed through generations; the inherited past.

TRAGEDY
1. A serious story or play dealing with the problems of a central character that ends unhappily or disastrous due to the flaws of this character.

2. Any work with an unhappy ending.

TRAGIC FLAW
Those flaws that lead to a character's downfall in a work of fiction.

TRANSFERRED EPITHET
An adjective that is linked to a noun that it would not normally modify but that makes sense figuratively. Often done intentionally for effect. For example, "diluted electricity" instead of "low voltage" or "deafening silence" instead of just "silence."

TRANSITION
A word, phrase, sentence, paragraph, or longer passage of writing that blends one paragraph, subject, scene, or chapter to the next.

TRANSITION BOOKS
Children's fiction intended for children between the ages of about 10 and 14 years. Targeted to children who are interested in but not quite ready to read YA fiction.

TRANSITIVE VERB
An action or linking verb.

TRANSLATION
The process of changing the language in which a work is written to different language.

TRAVEL WRITING
A form of creative nonfiction in which the author's experiences in foreign places is the main subject.

TRAVESTY
An absurd, false or farcical imitation of something. In writing, a literary composition so lacking in quality that it is a grotesque imitation of its model.

TROPE
1. A figure of speech.

2. A common or conventional theme, motif, or style.

TURNING POINT
Refers to the point in a narrative when the protagonist's life or situation changes, whether for better or for worse.

TURN-TAKING
The way in which logical conversation ordinarily takes place. One person speaks, the other replies, and then the first person speaks and so on.

TYPE
Fictional characters that represent a typical group of people or a type of behavior, instead of being a fully recognized individual.

TYPEFACE
In typography, the characters in one family, across all sizes, weights, and styles. For example, New Brunswick, Times, and Helvetica are typefaces. Computer software now uses font as a synonym for typeface.

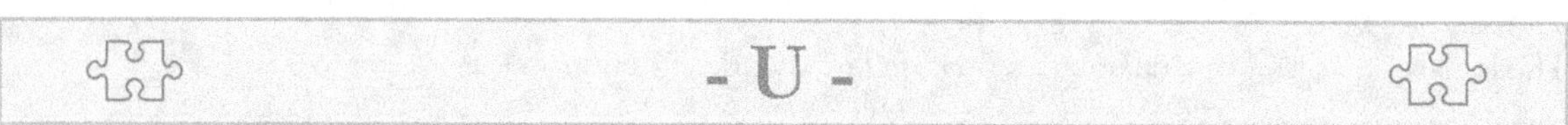

- U -

UNDERSTATEMENT
A figure of speech in which a situation is deliberately downplayed or made to seem less important or serious than it is.

UNITIES
Refers to the three unities of dramatic literature: unity of action, unity of time, and unity of place. This means that a play or a dramatic work has a single action occurring in a single place over the course of a single unit of time.

UNITY
That quality of cohesion or "oneness" in a literary work in which all parts are connected by some principle of organization, creating a whole that is complete in itself.

UPPERCASE
The traditional large alphabetical characters, known as "capitals."

USAGE
The standard ways in which words or phrases are spoken or written in a language group.

UTOPIA
A fictional "ideal" society or political state.

UTOPIAN
Subgenre of fantasy fiction featuring a setting that depicts an "ideal" world or system of government. May also be a subgenre of science fiction.

 - V - 

VERB
The part of speech that describes an action or event or that specifies a state of being.

VERBAL
A type of verb that functions as a noun or a modifier instead of as a true verb. Often the suffix "-ing" is added to these verb forms.

VERBAL IRONY
A figure of speech in which there is a significant contrast between what is said and what is actually meant. "My house is on fire. This is just great."

VERBOSITY
Wordiness.

VERFREMDUNGSEFFEKT
A German term meaning "the distancing effect"; refers to a dramatic concept in which the audience is prevented from losing itself entirely in the character created by the actor, and as a result becomes a deliberately critical observer.

VERISIMILITUDE
The appearance of being true or real.

VERNACULAR
The language of a particular group, profession, or country, particularly as spoken rather than written.

VERSE
Originally a "verse" referred to a single line of poetry, but in common usage it refers to a complete poem.

VERSIFICATION
The art of poetic composition.

VIEWPOINT
The position or vantage point from which the setting and the action of a work are viewed and remarked upon by the narrator.

VILLAIN
An antagonist that has no redeeming qualities; the bad guy. Not all antagonists are villains, although the two terms are often mistakenly assumed to be the same.

VOCABULARY
The collective words of a language, or all of the words used by a particular person or group.

VOICE
The unique style or mode of expression of an author or of a narrator in a text.

VOWEL
A letter of the alphabet that signifies a speech sound created by the free passage of breath through the larynx and the mouth. A, E, I, O, U and sometimes Y are vowels.

- W -

WEASEL WORD
Also called "anonymous authority", words or phrases that re intended to create the impression that something specific has been said, when in reality what has been communicated is vague or ambiguous. Words like "many," "somewhat," "often" or "up to" are weasel words.

WEIGHT
The thickness of a typeface.

WESTERN
Genre of fiction set in the American Old West, typically featuring the "American Frontier" around the late eighteenth to the late nineteenth century.

WHODUNIT
A subgenre of crime fiction in which the puzzle of who committed the crime is the main feature. The reader plays along with the detective as an amateur sleuth attempting to figure out "whodunit" before the end of the story.

WILLING SUSPENSION OF DISBELIEF
Refers to the reader of fiction temporarily withholding doubt about the truth or believability of the plot and accepts the fictional world created by the author.

WIT
The ability to make intelligent, imaginative, or clever connections between ideas quickly.

WORD
A sound or a combination of sounds, either spoken or represented in writing, which symbolizes and communicates meaning that may consist of one or more morphemes.

WORD COUNT
In fiction writing, the number of words contained in a manuscript. For example, a novel typically contains a word count of around 80,000 to 100,000 words.

WORD PLAY
1. Literary device in which the use of rhetorical figures of speech and verbal wit are used to enhance the prose.

2. Witty or clever verbal exchange.

WRITERISM
Figures of speech or informal rules related to writing fiction and nonfiction. For example, "Write what you know."

WRITER'S BLOCK
A state in which a writer who has the necessary skills to write is unable to do so due to a "block" that may be psychological or emotional.

WRITER'S VOICE
A literary term used to describe the individual or unique writing style of an author. A combination of the author's use of syntax, punctuation, and diction as well as the use of fictional elements like character development and plot in a given text or over several texts.

WRITING
The process of composing a text.

WRITING PROCESS
The series of steps that writers typically follow in creating a work of fiction or nonfiction.

WUXIA
Genre of fiction originating in Chinese literature that typically features martial arts and chivalrous heroes and may include themes of honor and/or vengeance.

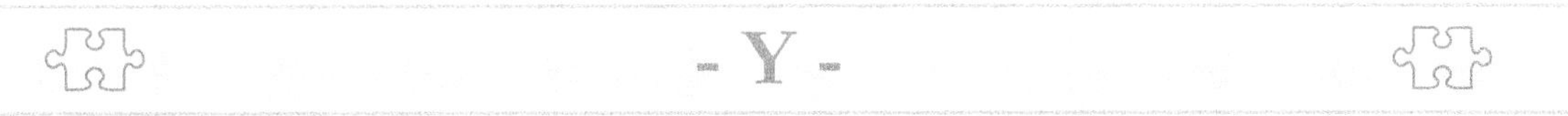

YA (YOUNG ADULT)
Genre of fiction targeted to ages 12 and up. May be classified in any genres of adult fiction except for erotica.

YELLING
Type set in all caps. Considered rude and annoying.

- Z -

ZEITGEIST

From German, the "spirit of the age"; the ethical, cultural, spiritual, emotional, or intellectual climate within a nation or group, or the general mood that is characteristic of a period or era.

ZEUGMA

A figure of speech in which a word is used to modify or govern two or more words when it is appropriate to only one word or to each in a different way. For example: "She stole my heart and my wallet."

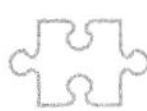 **6.3.3 EXTENSION / FORMAT**

In creative writing, be it genre, literary, YA, middle grade or children's fiction, word count is important, and often the only yardstick a writer has to classify his work according to extension.

Over the years, the industry has adopted word count guidelines to categorize works of fiction.

But like everything else in writing, word count is fluid and subjective; the boundaries between one format and the next are flexible to the point of being meaningless.

Word count is a tool publishers use to determine the number of pages a finished book will have. So far so good. Naturally, the number of words in each page is a function of page dimension, interline kerning, type size, margins, and a plethora of other physical parameters.

To give you an example, The Companion is formatted in 650-word pages. Its 250,000 words would fit in 385 pages. Had we packed these pages with dense text it would have been unreadable, therefore we "thinned" the prose with extra vertical kerning, examples, headers, titles, dingbats and blank matter. In doing so, we almost doubled the page count.

Another example? Certainly. J. K. Rowling's last delivery, Harry Potter and the Deathly Hallows contains approximately 200,000 words. On the UK edition, the book has 607 pages, although for the U.S version the tome has miraculously fattened to 759 pages.

Therefore, when a book hits the shelves, word count doesn't translate into a set number of pages. Not that it matters much, really. Unforgettable prose doesn't depend on quantity, but quality. Kurt Vonnegut's *Slaughterhouse-Five* had only 49,459 words and George Orwell's *Nineteen Eighty-Four* a modest 88,942. Emily Bronte's *Wuthering Heights* contains a respectable 107,945 words and Leo Tolstoy's *War and Peace* a whopping 587,287. We doubt anyone would place any of these four masterpieces above the others because of their extension.

Of course, word count is more important for new writers than for bestselling authors. This is another paradox of the publishing industry. Once a writer becomes a household name, publishers might insist on thicker manuscripts to extract a heftier price from readers. An illustrative example is J.K. Rowling's saga. Her first three books were of reasonable size—probably completed before the first one was released:

Harry Potter and the Philosopher's Stone - 76,944 words

Harry Potter and the Chamber of Secrets - 85,141 words

Harry Potter and the Prisoner of Azkaban - 107,253 words

By then she was a sales phenomenon and resorted to tomes:

Harry Potter and the Goblet of Fire - 190,637 words

Harry Potter and the Order of the Phoenix - 257,045 words

Harry Potter and the Half-Blood Prince - 168,923

Harry Potter and the Deathly Hallows - About 200,000

As detailed on pages 407 and 408 there are several ways to determine word count. The exact number of words is of little consequence if we except micro fiction, since most other formats allow leeway and rounding up figures to the nearest 100. This is good news for writers. We might calculate rocket trajectories or predict the behavior of subatomic particles, but obtaining the exact word count of a printed book seems to be beyond our reach.

	FORMAT	EXACT WORD COUNT	WORD COUNT RANGE
Micro	55 Fiction	55	
	69er	69	
	Drabble	100	
	Other Micro Fiction		6 to 100
Basic Formats	Flash		100 to 1,000
	Short Story		1,000 to 7,500
	Novelette		7,500 to 17,500
	Novella		17,500 to 50,000
	Novel		50,000 to 150,000
	Epics and Sequels		50,000 to ∞
Children and YA	Board Book		Up to 100
	Early Picture Book		Up to 500
	Picture Book		Up to 1,000
	Non-fiction Picture Book		Up to 2,000
	Early Reader		Up to 3,500
	Chapter Book		Up to 10,000
	Middle Grade		Up to 45,000
	YA		Up to 90,000

The Bible is the best selling book of all time. Yet, we haven't found a conclusive word count anywhere. When perusing data for the King James Version, one source cites 783,137[159] words a second source 788,258[160] and a third 789,626.[161]

Resume: Unless a writer toils in the devilishly difficult micro-fiction formats, approximate word counts are sufficient for most publishers.

On this table, we have listed the word counts of different formats according to industry standards.

---

159 http://agards-bible-timeline.com/q10_bible-facts.html

160 http://www.biblebelievers.com/believers-org/kjv-stats.html

161 http://www.artbible.info/concordance

Remember, these word counts are subjective and different sources have different ideas about word count. Writers should check the guidelines of agents, editors, or publications before submitting any work. Regardless of the genre and format, manuscripts are judged on the strength of the story itself and not on extension.

 ### 6.3.4 PROOFREADING SYMBOLS

Once a manuscript has been edited, rewritten, revised and line-edited—and before the text goes to a designer or typesetter—manuscripts undergo copyediting. At this stage, the editor uses a clean printout of the double-spaced manuscript to input symbols and suggest alterations or replacements between the lines.

Later, when the designer finishes laying out the text, the writer is often given "galleys." These are quarto-sized sheets with a single page of the book set in its center.

Naturally, on single-spaced text, there's no room in the interlines to write anything. In this instance, most of the symbols and instructions must be set in the margins, next to the line of text to be altered.

To do so, carets (these funny-looking marks resembling an inverted "vee" (^)), strikeouts, circles, and other marks on the text itself show where each change is supposed to go.

Writers must never forget (it would be an expensive exercise if they do), that the final proofreading stage is not for rewriting or making revisions, but catching typos and errors. The pages are set and numbered. Though typesetters won't grumble too much if the writer adds the odd line or sentence here or there, they will blow a fuse if any addition causes page numbers to jump, since this will entail resetting a chunk of the book. If the pagination alters, the writer, not the publisher, must foot the bill. A caveat warning about the consequences of disturbing the pagination is made in a letter containing instructions and other directions usually appended to the galleys.

On the following pages, we have illustrated the most common symbols used by editors, proofreaders, and typesetters to mark up the galleys, which are also known as "copy."

Professional writers append these proofreading symbols with a red pencil, never ink, ball point, or marker, to allow for erasure. Using these symbols ensures that everyone involved in the process follows the same procedure and uses the same method of communication to minimize the possibility of error or misunderstanding.

We recommend that writers practice on physical copy, perhaps printing a chapter or two, to become familiar with proofreading mechanics.

MARK	MEANING	HOW TO USE IT
	Delete a word or letter	Renéee loves poutine poutine.
	Insert word(s) or letter(s)	She is love moles. (in, with)
	Insert space	Courtney is verypretty.
	Insert hyphen	Kurt's twin-barreled shotgun.
	Delete space: close	Some where over the rainbow.
	Delete and close	Somewwhere over the rainbow.
	Start a new paragraph	"Come here," Mom said. "Me?"
	No paragraph.	"Come here," Mom said. And bring the Listerine.
	Transpose: switch order.	Is where it?
	Insert underscore	I need a receipt.
	Make lowercase	Rich, my Uncle is Rich.

Mark	Meaning	How to use it
☰	Make uppercase	ken loves the internet.
◯	Spell	Only 20%
⊙	Insert period	I'm cold You're cold
∧	Insert comma	Hello Carlos,
∨	Insert apostrophe	Its just my luck the moles are back.
∨	Insert quotation mark	She asked where's my suitcase?
M dash	Insert M dash	Enters Carlos the very debonair.
N dash	Insert N dash	The Tweed Ontario bus stops here.
?	Check the data	Renée was born in 1685 ?
(rom)	Set in Roman	(rom) *Where am I,* she thought.
(ital)	Set in Italics	(ital) The Writer's Companion

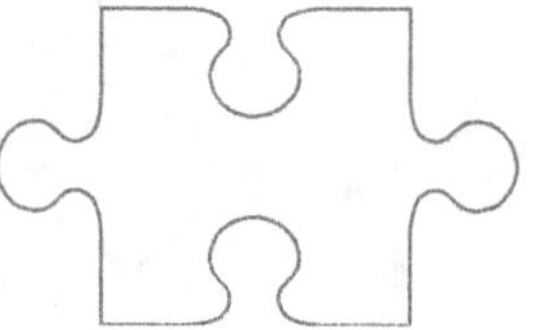

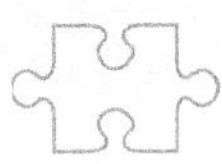 # 6.4 THE PUBLISHING INDUSTRY

To publish is to produce and distribute, or attempt to distribute information.

Production: Create information in a format suitable for distribution

Distribution: Make available the production to its viewers or readers.

Information: Text, images or a combination of both.

It is intentional that we have outlined publication and its components in telegraphic fashion to avoid leaving out any format of information dissemination. You see, the label on your aspirin bottle, a newspaper, a video game, a film, the operating instructions for your new microwave oven, a novel, and an SMS are all publications.

Logically, it follows that each time we write a list of groceries and give it to John, so he picks the bits and pieces on his way back from work, we are publishing. When we print out a college essay, or paint with black marker on a wall "Writers are cool," we are publishing. However, when we write in our dairy about our heartbreak because our date cancelled five minutes before the movie started we're not publishing.

The difference is that with our list, essay, and graffiti we meant to pass on information to others. Pouring our wretchedness into a personal dairy that nobody else will read doesn't qualify. Of course, a cynic would contend that dairies are meant for others to read eventually. If so, publication would happen when the writer removed the diary from its hiding place and left it on the breakfast table for Susan to find.

For a writer, it's important to understand that the concept of publishing (and therefore, copyrighting) is much broader than penning a short story or a novel and posting it in the Internet, or having it printed and offered for sale at every bookshop in the land. Only a few days ago Carlos visited a friend—a wine producer in Tarragona, a province in Spain's Catalonia. The man was devastated after having had to recall thousands of bottles from stores and restaurants. Was the wine bad? No. It was a small masterpiece and reasonably priced. The problem was the label.

A few months earlier, he entrusted a freelance designer with the craft of his label: a white rectangle, perhaps three inches by four inches, with the wine's name topped with a small golden crown, a quote in Latin beneath it and a line or two of tiny text under that. The typography was excellent and the overall design broadcasted good taste.

Unfortunately, the designer had sought inspiration (copied, plagiarized or stolen, which in this instance are synonyms) the typography, font, color, and overall design from a bottle belonging to another grower in Northern Spain. Enters a polite lawyer and threatens hellfire and brimstone if the offending labels are not removed from the market.

Please, don't lose sight of the fact that the name of the wine was different as was the remaining text on the label. It didn't matter, because any judge couldn't miss the gross copyright infringement. The first label had been published when the original wine hit the store. Side-by-side with this friend, both bottles looked identical when viewed from a distance.

Some of the examples we've given relate to the publishing industry, while others don't.

The difference?

When publication creates income (or losses) for any of the parties involved, it falls within the publishing industry realm. From the examples above, labels, SMS's, and operating instructions would relate but notes and graffiti wouldn't.

Though this manual should be useful to contents providers, regardless of the target market, its focus is fiction writers. Our analysis and comments about the Publishing Industry, therefore, refer to these companies or entities who publish works of fiction with profit in mind.

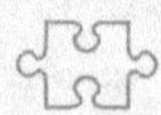 ## 6.4.1 PUBLISHING INDUSTRY PLAYERS

The traditional players or terms in the equation of bringing a work of fiction to its consumers are:

Writers

Agents

Publishers

Printers

Distributors

Retailers

Some methods of publication involve all six players while others need fewer. Reduced to its minimum expression, only the first is obligatory: the writer.

To avoid needless explanations and repetition, a writer is anyone who writes, a publisher anyone who publishes, and so on.

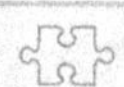 ### 6.4.1.1 WRITERS

Writers produce content and to be included in the Publishing Industry they must sell, or offer to sell their product. The term "professional writer" is vague, as many things are in our chosen profession, but it implies that the scribe derives his livelihood in part or in full from selling his work. The IRS, to put an example, won't accept "writer" as a profession if after two years the subject doesn't file an income of $50,000. Otherwise, and for their reckoning, they class writing as a hobby.

In this book, we have eschewed using "Author" or "Published Author" because anyone who is responsible for a deed is its author and "published," being such a hazy term, has become essentially meaningless.

 ### 6.4.1.2 AGENTS

Agents are handlers who take care of a writer's business much as they would arrange fights for boxers or gigs for musicians. A literary agent represents a writer, seeks venues to sell his work, and negotiates contracts with the intent of securing the most profitable deal. Since agents work on commission, they strive to maximize their client's income and thus their own.

Whether a writer needs intermediaries or not is a discussion that would fall outside the scope of this manual; the Internet is rife with articles extolling the virtues of both avenues. In our opinion, some writers and their chosen publishing path could benefit from the figure of a literary agent.

Traditional publishers are difficult to approach by a writer without references or an introduction. In addition, if the writer has created a product appropriate for broad distribution, perhaps in different languages, or formats such as film, play, or syndication, professional help would be mandatory.

A typical agent derives his income from a share of the writer's income. Leaving aside special deals with household names, a writer can expect to pay an agent ten to twenty percent (fifteen percent being the norm) of his earnings or 20 to 25% for publication in other countries. In this last instance, a local agent would share the commission.

6.4.1.3 PUBLISHERS

Publishers manage the production of books in a format for being sold to readers. As we write these lines, there are three paths to publication available to writers:

Traditional Publishers

e-Publishers

Self-Publishing

Traditional Publishers

This group consists of companies, more or less sizeable, whose business model is to bring books to market in physical formats. The world's largest conglomerates are:

1. Pearson

2. Reed Elsevier

3. Thomson Reuters

4. Wolters Kluwer

5. Bertelsmann

6. Lagardère Publishing/ Hachette

7. Grupo Planeta

8. McGraw-Hill Education

9. De Agostini Editore

10. Holtzbrinck[162]

And the top ten trade (books sold in shops as opposed to school books) publishers in the U.S. are:

1. Random House

2. Pearson

---

[162] http://www.publishersweekly.com

3. Hachette

4. HarperCollins

5. Simon & Schuster

6. Holtzbrinck

7. Thomas Nelson

8. Scholastic

9. John Wiley

10. Workman[163]

Most of these are foreign owned.

These companies are usually inaccessible to unagented writers and have an operating procedure that has shown little change in the last one-hundred years.

A traditional publisher's business model involves an acquisitions editor meeting with an agent and agreeing on the terms to purchase the right to publish a particular work of a writer. In exchange for these rights, the publisher pays an advance on future royalties and undertakes to provide items and/or services:

Editing

Copyediting

Proofreading

Cover art

Illustrations

Book design

ISBN

Galley copies sent out to garner bullets from successful writers

Pre-production copies sent out to reviewers

Media and press releases

A century ago, the process to turn an acquired manuscript into a finished book was the same.

The business model of traditional publishers is not only obsolete, but verging on lunacy and destined to change, or follow the tracks of dinosaurs on their way to extinction.

The venture capital investment model goes like this: For every ten projects they back, they recover their investment on two and lose money on seven. The remaining one is a success, pays for the failures, and makes them money.

The traditional publishing industry follows this model. On acquisition, new writers get an advance on royalties, averaging from $5,000 to $10,000. Every book published is a non-trivial investment of time and money and writers get to keep the advance even for failed books. Since most books are not

---

[163] http://michaelhyatt.com

successful, and publishers do not earn back the advance (not to mention other costs of publishing them), their business is in shambles.

Extrapolating all kinds of figures from scores of sources, we come to the unpalatable discovery that the average sales for a new writer's first novel is about 2,000 copies, with 5,000 copies being rated as a success.[164] Since a larger publisher must sell 10,000 books to break even,[165] it doesn't make any sense.

Traditional publishers are top heavy and cumbersome, ill prepared to compete in a market changing at lighting speed. By paying writers a royalty on books actually sold, and trimming the plethora of industry managers and executives to a fraction of its present size, they might manage to keep the Jeff Bezos's of this new world at bay.

Although the big players monopolize the vast majority of publications, they're not alone. Thousands of smaller publishers are doggedly nipping away at the edges to gain a little market share. Figures are hard to come by, but extrapolating ISBN blocks yields a figure of over 80,000 publishers in the U.S. alone.[166]

E-publishers

E-publishers are companies (or sometimes individuals) whose business model is to bring books to market in digital formats. All large traditional publishers offer their titles in e-book format. Consequently, they could also be listed as e-publishers.

E-publishing is a method for delivering literary, educational, and informational works to consumers via digital screens of all sizes and platforms, including pads and phones.

An e-publisher's business model usually involves a direct submission by the writer, often without the agent's third-party involvement. The publisher's acquisitions editor evaluates the submissions, and if interested offers a contractual agreement for the right to e-publish a particular manuscript. In exchange for these rights, the e-publisher pays royalties and (sometimes) undertakes to provide items and/or services:

Editing

Copyediting

Proofreading

Cover art

Illustrations

Book design

ISBN

Galley e-copies sent out to garner bullets from successful writers

E-copies sent out to reviewers

---

[164] Authors Guild. http://www.authorsguild.org/

[165] Brian DeFiore, Maui Writers Conference. http://www.defioreandco.com/

[166] http://BookStatistics.com

Media and press releases

Placement in e-book retailers such as Amazon

At first glance, there's no variation for a writer between the services given by traditional and e-publishers. This is so because printing only counts for 10% or so of an offset-printed book in reasonable (5,000+) quantities.

When a traditional publisher prepares a book for market, everything is committed to digital format until it reaches the printer's shop. From this point onward, the only differences reside in the costs relative to handling a physical object against a digital one. In the "Business Models" section on pages 589 to 593 there's a breakdown of production costs.

Therefore, since we're commenting on the different publishing methods but with the interest of writers at heart, we must repeat that there's no intrinsic difference beyond the format: paper or bits.

We couldn't compile a list of e-publishers beyond repeating that of the traditional houses with any certainty of permanence. On revisiting the list we prepared two years before the Companion's publishing date—revised twelve months ago—we discovered that more than half had disappeared. Others had changed their business model and demanded money from writers, thus setting them on the other side of the fence that separates honest publishers from crooks.

As long as the e-publishing company provides the same services and quality controls as a traditional house, e-publishing is a legitimate option for any writer, and chances are that within a not-so-distant future it will be the only one.

Self-Publishers

These are writers who use available technology to produce a paper or e-book with total control of all stages, from writing to retailing.

Throughout this manual, we have expressed our misgivings about self-publishing. But our dislike has nothing to do with the practice, but rather the malpractice. There's a legend about the vast sums that everybody—but the writer—earns from each published book.

Fact is that sixty percent of the cover price of a mass-market paperback goes to distributors and retailers, leaving forty percent for the publisher. From his share, a publisher must cover ten percent printing costs and another ten percent for the writer's royalties. This leaves a grand twenty percent gross margin, from where the house must pay staff, offices, utilities and a myriad additional expenses, besides taking care of unsold goods.

	Writer	Agent	Publisher	Printer	Distributor
Traditional Publishing	$1.28	22c	$3	$1.5	$9
Self-Publishing			$7.55	$7.45	
Self-Publishing + site distribution			$4.55	$7.45	$3.00
Self-Publishing + Amazon distribution			$4.55	$4.45	$6.00
Self-Publishing + expanded distribution			$1.55	$4.45	$9.00

Let's examine the typical cost breakdown of a 300-page five-by-eight inch trade paperback priced at $14.95 (we'll round it up to $15 to ease the arithmetic).[167]

At first glance, the figures from the table on the previous page don't look too bad. In all instances, the publisher (the writer) takes a larger share of revenues if he chooses self-publishing. But it's an illusion. Without distribution channels, the chances of selling a decent number of copies is as hard as winning the lottery. Then, as soon as distribution enters the equation, profits dwindle to almost nothing.

Of course, some will contend that distributing through Amazon is enough. $4.55 is an excellent profit. But such a line of thought would be shortsighted. We expect more from a publisher than just publishing, like providing a cover, editing, copyediting, and proofreading. And this forms the core of our misgivings. A self-published work can be a good product, providing the writer applies the same quality controls a reader expects in a book signed by traditional publishers. Otherwise, he's attempting to sell a sub-standard product, and that's dishonest.

We have perused scores of self-published books and only a tiny fraction passed muster; these were found where the writer/publisher lavished the kind of services a traditional publisher would.

Naturally, there are other options to self-publish, like e-book, Kindle and others, but the same caveat applies. But for the writer being a wizard editor or getting editorial and artistic work free from friends and acquaintances, the cost of setting up a book with high standards of excellence would offset any possible profits and probably create huge losses for the writer, unless he happens to have an instant bestseller. If he does, agents and traditional publishers would snatch the manuscript as soon as it was offered.

Self-published writers often quote the success stories of self-publishing, but forget to investigate what lies behind their success. Take the Eragon series of Christopher Paolini.

Paolini spent one month drafting the saga, wrote Eragon in one year and spent another year revising it. Then, he passed it over to his parents, *who happened to be editors*. The whole family spent another year (that's three) revising the book, designing the cover, the manuscript's composition, and the marketing material before sending it off to printers. Some writers also forget that the Paolini family owned Paolini International LLC, a publishing company that had already produced three other books before tackling the first edition of Eragon in early 2002.

It follows that if a writer spends three years working on a manuscript helped by a couple of competent editors, has the money to professionally publish the book, owns a publishing company, *and has a potential bestseller in his hands*, self-publishing is the way to go.

 **6.4.1.4 PRINTERS**

Printers are responsible for transforming digital files into physical entities with shape, weight, and pages. Trade books are produced in offset printing machines capable of churning out 100 sheets—each containing sixteen book pages—per minute. Thus, a single machine can produce 2,000 books in a single shift.

Out of the many thousands of printing companies in the U. S. only about one-hundred are specialized in producing books. These companies usually offer digital and offset printing.

---

[167] Printing and distribution costs from Create Space, https://www.createspace.com

Digital printers are similar to an office laser printer but much faster and adequate for small runs as they require little setup time.

Offset printing is different in that it involves large sheets running through a traditional printing press. The sheets are then cut to size, folded, or further processed to achieve the desired finish. This printing method involves setup time to make printing plates, setting up printing inks, etc.

With traditional offset printing, much of the cost is in the set-up and plate-making process. Once the press is running, the incremental cost of each additional copy is low. These economic differences generally suggest that it is more cost effective to print 500 or fewer copies using digital printing and 1000 or more copies with offset printing equipment. In between 500 and 1000 copies, it's usually best to get quotes from both digital and offset printers.

 **6.4.1.5 DISTRIBUTORS**

These are large companies, such as Baker and Taylor, Ingram, Quality Books and Bookpeople.

These companies have books on consignment. This means that the publisher ships the books from the printer to the distributor who then processes and fulfils the orders of retailers. A point to watch is that after a set time distributors will return unsold books. An order of 10,000 books from Barnes &Noble can sound like a dream come true for a writer, unless 9,900 are returned two months later. This can be a catastrophe for a self-publisher and would tax his garage capacity to hold the boxes. (Not to mention a second mortgage to pay the print run).

Distribution is important, but relies on large numbers of books. Biblio.com is one of a few traditional book distributors who could be of use to self-publishers, as long as the marketing plan and budget contemplates several thousand copies per year. Traditional book distribution is something that independent publishers grow into, not start with.

 **6.4.1.6 RETAILERS**

Retailers are the shops with shelves where we hope to see our books one day. Some of the largest are Barnes & Noble, Book Off USA, Books-A-Million and Follett's. (We were about to type "Borders" before we remembered it recently filed for bankruptcy). In addition, there are tens of thousands independent retailers in the U.S. alone.[168]

While writers can approach Indie retailers, they have been deluged by queries and most are reluctant to deal directly with self-publishers. After experiencing complaints and the returns of poorly produced work, most independent bookshop owners are reticent to deal directly with writers. They will trade with distributors, but since these will only entertain large quantities (5,000+ books) writers face a devilish conundrum.

---

[168] Manta lists 29,738 bookstores in the U.S. http://www.manta.com/

 **6.4.2 PUBLISHING INDUSTRY BUSINESS MODELS**

We're often asked the same questions over and again: Why are books so expensive? Where does the money go? Why do writers get such tiny royalties?

Perhaps the figures will come as a surprise to those unfamiliar with the business models of publishing, in particular the huge chunk distributors and retailers demand and how little money publishers make out of books. Of course, this is an oversimplification. Publishing is a complex business. Most publishers survive by walking a tightrope of spiraling costs while scraping income from book rights to which an individual has no access without professionals and connections.

If publishing was such a profitable business, publishers would be filing large year end profits, when the opposite is true; most large houses are breaking even or losing money.

The following lists and graphs attempt to answer these questions. The figures are averaged and vary in small percentages depending on format and many factors impossible to set or explain without dedicating scores of pages to the subject. Royalties are lower for a new writer than for an established house name, and retailers reduce their margins for surefire bestsellers. Printing costs can be tweaked depending on the size of runs and other considerations, etc.

 **6.4.2.1 TRADITIONAL PUBLISHERS**

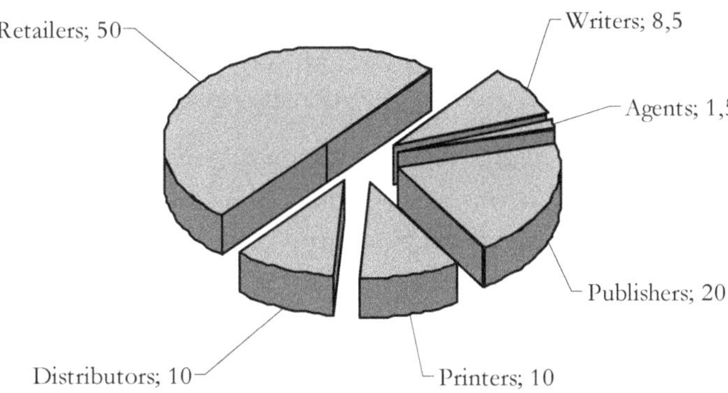

This is the standard breakdown of book costs in traditional paper publications for agented writers:

Writers. 8.5% is the writer's royalty, after having deducted the agent's 15% commission.

Agents. 1.5% is the agent's commission.

Publishers. 20% is the publisher's gross margin.

Printers. 10% is the average cost of offset printing a paperback in sufficient quantities with a full color cover.

Distributors. 10% is the typical percentage of the retail price allocated to warehousing and distribution.

Retailers. 50% is the margin for retailers.

Notes

1. Even though this may come as a surprise for some, a writer has expenses: paper, ink, electricity, a place to work, reference books and subscriptions, sustenance, and other necessities we take for granted. A professional writer (one whose main source of income stems from his pen) must factor these expenses to determine his income. Income? (Here we cried so hard we couldn't continue without 40-proof refreshment).

2. As sentient beings (some of them are), agents also have expenses: offices, staff, lunch tabs, and a plethora of bits and pieces. Like any other legitimate business.

3. From their princely twenty percent publishers must pay an army of editors, artists, accountants, lawyers, salespeople, and publicists before a manuscript is ready to sell. In addition, they have to fork out advances, in the knowledge that they will never recoup their investment.

4. Printers are the forgotten underdogs of the industry. Their investment in state-of-the-art machinery, industrial premises, and highly trained and experienced professionals is astronomical. That they manage to produce a book for $0.85, including paper, ink, glue, and overheads is not a small miracle, and one marvels at their accountant's wizardry.

5. Without distribution, goods cannot reach distant markets. A distributor is a logistics enterprise who must have considerable warehousing premises, means of transport, and comprehensive office staff to operate the mind-boggling software to keep the system in operation.

6. The large chunk of book costs that retailers need is also misleading. Most books, hardbacks in particular, are often sold at a discount. Although it should be obvious, twenty percent off the cover price of a book doesn't represent twenty percent off the retailer's income but double that. From a book priced at $10 (which the retailer bought for $5), twenty percent off the cover price is $2. These two dollars come off the retailer's margin, leaving $3, or thirty percent of sales. From this margin, a retailer must pay staff, utilities, and very expensive premises. Most book retailers barely manage to cover costs, and some can't keep their doors open (Borders is a good example).

 **6.4.2.2 E-PUBLISHERS**

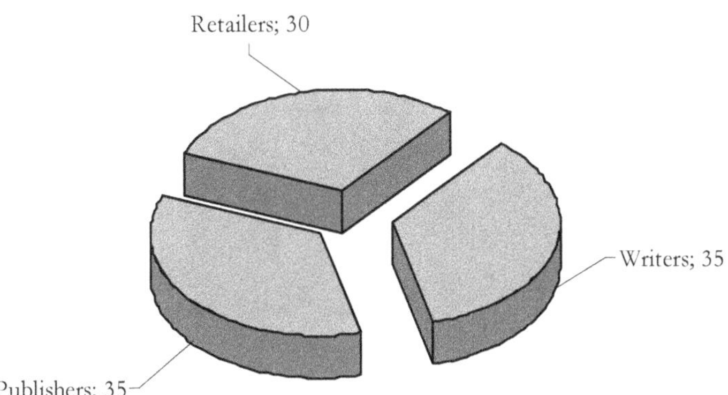

This is the standard breakdown of e-book costs:

> **Writers.** 35% is a regular percentage of the retail sales a writer earns.
>
> **Agents.** Often, e-book sales don't involve an agent. If he does, his commission is deducted from the writer's percentage.
>
> **Publishers.** 35%
>
> **Printers.** 0% because there's no hard copy.
>
> **Distributors.** 0%
>
> **Retailers.** 30%

  **Notes**

1. There's a lively argument about the royalties a writer should receive from an e-publication, after all, it costs nothing to produce a book since there's nothing to print. We hope that the explanations elsewhere in this section have dispelled the legend. The costs of a professionally produced e-book are the same as those of a paper one, save for the paper, ink, and distribution. At best, these items account for twenty percent of the retail price. Since readers don't understand why they should pay a similar price for a digital book, they clamor for much lower prices: $4.95; $2.95, or even as low as $.99.

These basement-bargain figures can only be attained by removing most production costs, including editing, copyediting, proofreading, and cover design.

2. Retailers are willing to take much lower margins on e-books because moving digital products is considerably easier than physical ones. But there's a limit to how far they can reduce margins. Selling an item has many other costs besides warehousing. The logistics are similar and require complex systems and expensive staff to run them.

3. In addition, there's a factor often forgotten when comparing the cost of an e-book to that of a paper one. Purchasing a physical book has additional costs for the reader: time and gas if buying from a bookshop and shipping charges if purchased through the Internet. With a few odd exceptions, a reader will always benefit economically from buying an e-book.

 **6.4.2.3 SELF-PUBLISHERS**

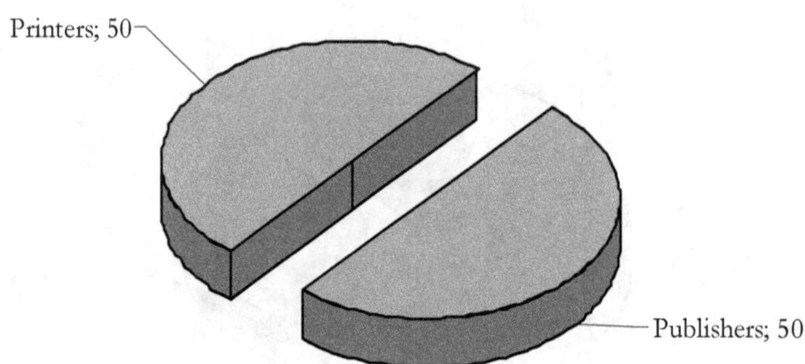

This is the standard breakdown of self-publishing without distribution costs:

Writers. 0% since their royalty, if any, is already accounted for in their role as publishers.

Agents. 0% because they don't intervene.

Publishers. 50%, as long as they don't engage external professionals to prepare the work for release and are willing to do the distribution themselves.

Printers. 50% is the average percentage of the retail price for a POD book.

Distributors. 0% because they don't intervene. If they do, the printer usually will take care of the logistics with charge to the customer.

Retailers. 0% because they don't intervene.

 **Notes** 

1. The diagram above shows the business model we flatly reject and oppose. It fills us with professional and aesthetic horror. On one hand, it implies that the writer (and publisher) is a maverick with inhuman abilities, capable of revising, reviewing, editing, copyediting, proofreading, composing, formatting, publishing, marketing, and selling his product, without external paid help and often burdened with scant knowledge of the language or the publishing industry. Also, it implies that the writer/publisher will release the rough draft of a book.

2. A raw manuscript is akin to the ingredients for a cake. We all know that a sponge cake uses flour, leavening, water, eggs, butter, sugar, and heat. Writers following the business plan in the above diagram pile the ingredients in a container without measuring, mixing or even removing the wrappers, and stuff the lot into an oven without thermostat. The ingredients are there, but what comes out of the oven is not cake.

3. POD printers charge high prices to produce a single book. This is sensible on account of the logistics, the costs of setting up, the paper and the handling of a unique item. Their prices drop somehow when the numbers of a single run brings in economies of scale. As mentioned elsewhere, digital printing is a sensible service for one to five-hundred copies. In excess of these quantities, offset printing may be a better proposition.

 **6.4.2.4 SELF-PUBLISHERS WITH DISTRIBUTION**

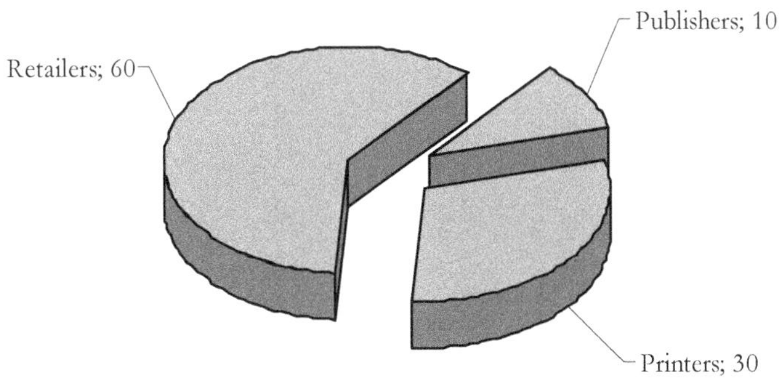

This is the standard breakdown of self-publishing with distribution costs:

Writers. 0% since their royalty, if any, is already accounted for in their role as publishers.

Agents. 0% because they don't intervene.

Publishers. 10%

Printers. 30%

Distributors. 0% because they don't intervene.

Retailers. 60%

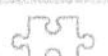 **Notes** 

1. With extended distribution through Amazon and independent bookshops, the "cut" for the publisher is paltry. Naturally, this implies that the publisher will not use external paid professionals to improve his product. If he does, he will lose money on each book sold.

2. POD printers will lower their costs if they are somehow involved in the product's retail, as is the case in the example from Create Space, in our opinion the most economic POD service available at this time.

3. Retailers can't operate with lower margins, since they offer discounts (often deep discounts and other promotions) to entice customers.

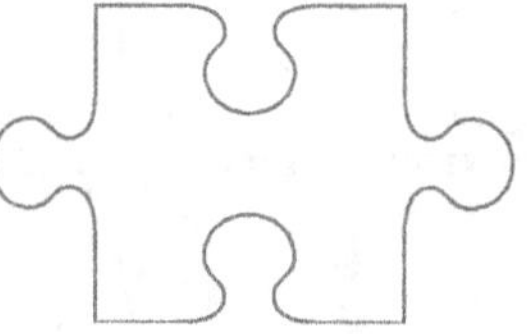

7 THE ORACLE

As an afterword, and closing brooch for the Companion, we want to be reckless and play the game of prophesy.[169]

What's the future of the publishing industry?

Prophets engage in a risky business, in particular if they survive their prophecies. Most prophets we know of would have had to eat their words if they were still around, though it strikes us as crafty that most weighty prophecies entailed such a long time lapse that the prophet was safe from having to face the hordes of his peeved followers. Others—doomsday prophets in particular—weren't so lucky and had to swallow a bitter pill (and often run for dear life) when the event didn't pan out.

In our opinion, there's a difference between a forecast that contravenes physics and scientific observation and a prediction founded on logic. Most of the conjectures in Huxley's *Brave New World* and Orwell's *1984* stem from logic. Naturally, with so many variables and unknowns, a logical prophecy doesn't have more weight than an educated guess.

Our oracle, firmly grounded on state-of-the art resources (crystal ball, tealeaves, Ouija, I-ching and a deck of funny-looking cards) predicts that within the next ten years:

1. E-publishing will overtake traditional publishing.

2. E-publishing with reputable publishers will be as hard to access for new writers as traditional publishing is at present times.

3. E-publishers will only accept submissions through literary agents.

4. e-books will be rated by an agency, as to their literary and editorial merits.

5. POD will shrink down to a tenth of its present size.

---

[169] Not "prophesize". "Prophecy" is the noun and "prophesy" the verb. "Prophesize" is iffy English. Though listed in the Merriam Webster, its use is frowned upon by almost every other dictionary and language authority.

6. Two-thirds of traditional book retailers will have disappeared.

7. The number of readers will remain unchanged.

8. A large percentage of successful writers will issue from the East.

9. Most of the Internet free services to writers will be subscription only.

10. Traditional writers will be on the road to extinction.

We suppose that our readers might agree with some of these predictions and disagree with the rest, perhaps all. In our defense, we'll attempt to justify the logic behind each forecast.

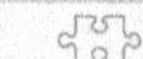 **1. E-publishing will overtake traditional publishing.**

In our experience, there are four kinds of books:

A. Reference

B. Leisure

C. Keepsakes

D. Educational

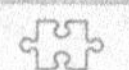 **Reference books**

Reference books comprise encyclopedias, dictionaries, and other volumes listing facts. To date, almost every paper encyclopedia has disappeared. The reason must be found in the implicit obsolescence of these publications. Take the Spanish Enciclopedia Espasa, the world's largest. In its origins, the work consisted of seventy-two volumes published from 1908 to 1930 and enlarged by a further ten-volume appendix and updates from 1930 to1933. The encyclopedia was enlarged with biannual volumes until 2005, when the publishers gave up. It ended as a 118-volume unwieldy monstrosity occupying a full wall and containing 165,000 pages and 200 million words. The problem for its owner was to find anything, without having a good idea of the item's background. Trying to find Burkina Faso (an African country surrounded by Mali, Niger, Benin, Togo, Ghana, and Côte d'Ivoire) was a nightmare, unless the researcher knew that the country changed its name in 1984. Before that date, the country was named Republic of Upper Volta.

The same is true of other reference works touching every area of human knowledge or endeavor. Theories are proven or ditched, phenomena are understood (often highlighting our supine ignorance), technology advances, societies change, and there's no way we can keep track unless we continuously update our references.

Reference e-books are not only a logical development but, in our opinion, unavoidable. Of course, newspapers can also be classified as reference publications. These may last a little longer, suffering a more protracted agony, but their days in paper format are numbered because they make no sense in a technological society.

 **Leisure books**

Leisure books are novels, comics, and the printed matter we use, store, and finally discard when we run out of space. With a few exceptions, novels are read once (bad ones in particular) before setting them in shelves to gather dust. Though we agree that the feeling of a book in our hands is unique, we're biased. After growing up surrounded by books it's only normal we are in love with them. But the young generations don't miss a telephone dial or having to produce technical drawings with pen and ink. Washing the dishes without detergent would be alien to them—they didn't have to feed the meager slops to the pig—as would be terry-cotton diapers that had to be washed by the cartload. We can't miss what we haven't experienced.

Buying a paperback is not only wasteful but silly. Once read we have no further use for it. If prices level at half the cost of a paper edition, most readers would rather read two e-books than one paperback for the same price.

The remaining obstacle is a versatile and cheap e-reader. These are around the corner. Five years ago, most people had a clumsy monitor sitting before their eyes and occupying most of the table. Now we can buy a many-inch flat panel for a fraction of the cost.

Keepsakes

These will remain, as their name indicates. In our libraries we have books, some useless, others dear, and others still in daily use—religious, poetry, inspirational, etc. These books will survive because their intrinsic value goes further than their cost or usefulness; they are objects with emotional attachments.

Educational books

Educational books are also undergoing a dramatic change. Things in the U.S. may be different, but in Europe several countries are providing young children with discounted laptops. The study books are then downloaded into their machines (previous payment, of course). This way, the students can move from home to the school carrying their laptop and lunch box, instead of a carry-all on wheels piled high with a ton of books. Once more, this seems an unstoppable trend.

2. E-publishing with reputable publishers will be as hard to access for new writers as traditional publishing is on present times.

We think it's inevitable. The market is awash with manuscripts, a few sublime, some good, and most of them unreadable. Traditional publishers will embrace e-publishing with a vengeance and other publishers, those whose livelihood will depend exclusively on e-book sales, will have to be selective and offer good products to stay afloat. This will entail a ruthless selection, not unlike the harrowing gauntlet new writers have to negotiate nowadays. Of course, there will be outlets for writers to post rough manuscripts, but we're referring to the publishing industry not the hobbies of the delusional.

3. E-publishers will only accept submissions through literary agents.

This follows from the previous prediction. Traditional publishers passed onto agents the onus of sifting through the trash because it made economic sense to make the writer pay for the selection. Publishers eliminated a sizeable chunk of their staff by compelling writers to submit their work through an agent—and foot his wages.

Professional e-publishers will follow suit because it doesn't cost them anything and removes a considerable burden from their shoulders. Besides, literary agents have to live. Their role as critics and reviewers doesn't change because the format of the final buyer's product. changes

4. E-books will be rated by an agency, as to their literary and editorial merits.

Again, this is logical and sensible. Through the argument about other forms of publishing, we have taken into consideration the writer, the publisher and other forces involved in the merchandising of books. But there is a most important and forgotten player: the reader. As a consumer, the reader will demand protection, and we wouldn't be surprised if our predicted rating agency comes imposed by circumstances. In the U.S., a country with such a zest for litigation, we're surprised no writer has been dragged through the courts and made to pay damages. A book is a product and a reader its consumer. There comes a point when a book is so badly written as to be unreadable. An unreadable book is not a book. Extracting money for an object that doesn't fulfill its natural usability is fraud, misrepresentation or whatever the correct legal term is. We have spoken with many readers who bought a book and felt cheated because they couldn't read it.

Imagine buying a Whopper from Burger King, only to discover there's no meat in the bun. Most people would demand to receive the paddy or have their money returned. Others would sue.

Just as most products have a stamp of approval certifying its usefulness to fulfill a given task, we think that something along these lines will be mandatory in self-published books. We don't mean a label rating the story, voice, style, plot, or characterization but a stamp certifying the book is written in accordance with current standards of grammar, syntax, and a limit on typo contents. This will be good news for all writers: the professional ones will see their work certified, and the others (without quality stamp) will have a level of protection against litigation since the reader will have purchased a product without guarantee.

5. POD will shrink down to a tenth of its present size.

Independent (self) and vanity publishing has existed since Guttenberg. There's a difference between these two terms.

Independent or self-publishing has been the only recourse open to those writers who, by the nature of their work and its intended audience, couldn't use the services of a traditional publisher. On page 585 we've pointed out that 10,000 copies is the minimum break-even figure for a traditional publisher. Therefore, any book with a total audience of fewer than 10,000 readers is almost impossible to publish, unless the book retails for a small fortune. Writers who create books for small groups, or touch specialized subjects (such as how to care for your suit of armor) have known this unpalatable fact from time immemorial. Poetry and family histories are often published independently, as they have a limited market.[170] These books will continue to be printed on demand or published in small runs because there's no other option.

Vanity publishing is another matter, and we recommend the unforgettable *Foucault's Pendulum* by Umberto Eco, for an insight in the world of vanity presses. One of the best descriptions of the practice we've ever read is from an anonymous contributor to Wikipedia:

---

[170] *Gadsby*, by Ernest Vincent Wright, is a good example. The book is a masterpiece, a triumph of circumlocution, a glory to man's spirit and an example of virtuosity for any writer. It's a 50,000-word novel in English, but written without the letter "e". Mr. Wright couldn't find a publisher, so he self-published.

While a commercial publisher's intended market is the general public, a vanity publisher's intended market is the author.[171]

We think the quote is self-explanatory. When the millions of writers out there learn that self-publishing without the backing of good editors and better distributors is a chimera, POD will dwindle to pre-Internet-era values.

6. Two-thirds of traditional book retailers will have disappeared.

The trend is unstoppable. Some Indie book retailers will scrounge a living from keepsakes, but the bulk of leisure and impulse books will be digital. A few will survive by diversifying their offer, much as bookshops at airports where one can find luggage straps, aspirin, diapers, drinks, and snacks among the books.

The big chains will fare worse and will be forced to drastically change their business model, to a point where books contribute only a fraction of their turnover. This doesn't mean that their book division will vanish. Rather than they will regroup it in the Internet to fight another day.

7. The number of readers will increase.

People read fewer books, this might be true, but the time dedicated to absorb information has increased dramatically in the last decades. While people may spend less time reading books, they use phenomenal chunks of time to text, blog, hang about social networks, play games, and watch TV (all of which need content).

With more free time and so much information floating about, people soak up information and are greedy for content. This is great news for writers.

In addition, though the number of readers is decreasing in the West, it's exploding elsewhere. In the East and Africa there's a trifle of over three billion potential readers.

8. A large percentage of successful writers will issue from the East.

This is another logical outcome of the development of Eastern countries. English is the Esperanto of the XXI century. In almost every country, millions are learning English as a vehicle to communicate with a wider segment of the world's population. This will promote generations of contents and creative writers using the English language as their vehicle of choice, which in turn will overflow to Western countries. The East is taking over, however surreptitiously, scores of niches in the global market and it's naïve to assume they won't try their hand at all levels of publishing and writing.

9. Most of the Internet free services to writers will be subscription only.

We meant to write that most of the *valuable* or *relevant* Internet content will be subscription only but we exercised restraint. The digital bubble has burst once or twice and it will do it again because the business models (or the lack of one) are untenable. Some people will maintain informative sites without expecting any income, as a hobby or for the hell of it, take your pick.

Other commercial ventures will have to rely on heavier advertising practices to survive; after all, to go by the name of "business" an enterprise is supposed to attempt making money.

---

[171] http://en.wikipedia.org/wiki/Vanity_press

Services to writers, such as promotion, retail, edition, and review will have to be paid for one way or another, to provide income to whoever has built a website and staffed it. The dream of an Internet where everything is free is... well, a dream, a beautiful dream, but one that shatters before the shrill of an alarm clock.

 ●   **10. Traditional writers will be on the road to extinction.**

By this we mean the scribes of old (such as Carlos) who would hammer away at keyboards and typewriters sixteen hours each day to complete a manuscript and rejoice when typing THE END. These writers still linger, but they'll soon be a memory like the Dodo. The writer of the future will be a hybrid of politician, speaker, pimp, blogger, publicist, hustler, diplomat, and writer—almost as an afterthought.

This has been the easiest prediction to make, because the signs are already upon us. Nowadays, many publishers and literary agents demand that submissions include a sample of the writing *and* a detailed marketing plan or "platform." Without a platform, we doubt Conrad reincarnate would manage to publish anything.

We leave you with this heartfelt counsel: Build a marketing platform concurrently with your fiction writing; create a presence, a following, and expectations. Without it, your chances in the flux of the New Publishing Industry are close to nil.

QUOTED WORKS

Throughout this volume we have quoted works from the writers listed below in descending alphabetical order:

Atwood, Margaret

        The Blind Assassin

Austen, Jane

        Pride and Prejudice

Bryson, Bill

        Troublesome Words

Campbell, Joseph

        The Hero with a Thousand Faces

Carle, Eric

        Brown Bear, Brown Bear, What do You See (With Bill Martin Jr.)

Carter, Ally

        Don't Judge a girl by Her Cover

Cortés, Carlos J.

        Bad Water

        Cordova

        Light Bondage

        Mahdi

        My Valentine

        Nathalie

        Oiran

        Perfect Circle

        Rent-a-Friend

        Spring Sprung

        The Damn Book

        The Gathering

        The Hive

        The Prisoner

        The Spaniard's Woman

        Where's me man?

Forsyth, Frederick

    Avenger

Garner, Bryan

    Garner's American Usage

Geary, Joseph

    Mirror

Greene, Graham

    Our Man in Havana

Harris, Charlaine

    Dead in the Family

    From Dead to Worse

Harris, Thomas

    Black Sunday

    Hannibal Rising

    Hannibal

Johnson, Donna

    Alien Dead: Dogean Fellows Say News to Blame

    All about Snarflagoging

    Drowning of Worms

    True Daughter

    Spider's Web: Ties that Bind

Joyce, James

    Ulysses

Kerouac, Jack

    On the Road

Keyton, Michael

    Elizabeth's Head

    Mr. Nousel's Mirror

    Neut

King, Stephen

    On Writing

Kolln, Martha

>Understanding English Grammar

Lara, Henry

>Por Amor (With Renée Miller)

>The Knight and the Demon

Larsson, Stieg

>The Girl with the Dragon Tattoo

Le Carre, John

>A Most Wanted Man

LeHane, Dennis

>Shutter Island

Ludlum, Robert

>The Sigma Protocol

Martin Jr., Bill

>Brown Bear, Brown Bear, What do You See (With Eric Carle)

Melville, Herman

>Moby-Dick

Meyer, George A.

>The Two-Word Verbs

Meyer, Stephenie

>Twilight

Miller, Renée

>Ancient Blood

>Bayou Baby

>Dirty Truths

>False Prophet

>I Do… and other Lies we Tell

>In the Bones

>Por Amor (With Henry Lara)

>Sam and Rita

>The Auction

>The Chosen

>The Legend of Jackson Murphy

Mitton, Paul

  Yellowfang

Nin, Anaïs

  Little Birds

Orwell, George

  1984

Quinn, Kate

  Mistress of Rome

Remic, Andy

  Spiral

Rowling, J. K.

  Harry Potter and the Chamber of Secrets

Stein, Sol

  Stein on Writing

Swore, Wendy

  Strike (With Rita Webb)

  Colorless

  Coyote Dreams

  Crop Circles

  Firebug

Tagore, Rabindranath

  Nationalism

Truss, Lynne

  Eats, Shoots & Leaves: The Zero Tolerance Approach to Punctuation

Twenty Writers

  Ménage à 20; Tales with a Hook

Voelker, Jeanne

  Unlocking William

Walker, Alice

  The Color Purple

Webb, Rita

  Strike (With Wendy Swore)

Wilson, Kenneth G.

Columbia Guide to Standard American English; Descriptive Genitive

Wright, Ernest Vincent

Gadsby

Zilahy, Lajos

Century in Scarlet

BIBLIOGRAPHY

Barnet, Sylvan, Pat Bellanca, and Marcia Stubbs. A Short Guide to College Writing. N.Y.: Pearson/Longman, 2005.

Bickham, Jack M. The 38 Most Common Fiction Writing Mistakes. Cincinnati, Ohio: Writer's Digest Books, 1992.

Burchfield, R. W., ed. The New Fowler's Modern English Usage. N.Y.: Oxford University Press, 1996.

Card, Orson Scott. Characters and Viewpoint. Cincinnati, Ohio: Writer's Digest Books, 1988.

Christ, Henry I. Modern English in Action, Ten. Boston: D. C. Heath and Co, 1965.

Cooper, Bruce M. Writing Technical Reports. Harmondsworth, Middlesex: Penguin Books Ltd, 1987.

Eastwood, John. Oxford Guide to English Grammar. N.Y.: Oxford University Press, 2002.

Ellsworth, Blanche and Higgens, John A. English Simplified. N.Y.: Pearson Education, 2004.

Gordon, Karen Elizabeth. The New Well-Tempered Sentence. N.Y.: Mariner Books, 1993.

Grambs, David. Dimboxes, Epopts, and other Quidams. N.Y.: Workman Publishing Company, 1986.

Hacker, Diana. A Writer's Reference. Boston: Bedford/St. Martin's, 2003.

Hacker, Diana. Bedford Handbook, The. Boston: Bedford, 1998.

Hacker, Diana. Pocket Style Manual. Boston: Bedford, 2004.

Hale, Constance. Sin and Syntax. N.Y.: Broadway Books, 2001.

Kane, Thomas S. The New Oxford Guide to Writing. N.Y.: Oxford University Press, 1988.

King, Stephen. On Writing. London: Hodder and Stoughton, 2001.

Lamott, Anne. Bird by Bird. N.Y.: Anchor Books, 1995.

Lederer, Richard and Dowis, Richard. The Write Way. N.Y.: Pocket Books, 1995.

Lukeman, Noah. The First Five Pages. N.Y.: Simon & Schuster, 2000.

Madden, David. Revising Fiction. N.Y.: Barnes & Noble Books, 2002.

Marshall, Evan. Novel Writing. Cincinnati, Ohio: Writer's Digest Books, 2001.

McCollister, John. Writing for Dollars. N.Y.: Barnes & Noble Books, 1999.

McMahan, Elizabeth. Here's How to Write Well. N.Y.: Longman, 2002.

Meyers, Alan. Writing With Confidence: Writing Effective Sentences and Paragraphs. N.Y.: Longman, 2000.

Mulvey, Dan. Grammar the Easy Way. N.Y: Hauppauge, Barron's, 2002.

O'Conner, Patricia T. Words Fail Me. Orlando, Florida: Harcourt,Inc., 2000.

O'Conner, Patricia. Woe Is I: The Grammarphobe's Guide to Better English in Plain English. N.Y.: Riverhead Books, 2003.

Ramage, John D., John C. Bean, and June Johnson. The Allyn & Bacon Guide to Writing. N.Y: Pearson/Longman, 2006.

Rozakis, Laurie E. Grammar and Style. Complete Idiot's Guide to. N.Y. Simon & Schuster, Alpha Books, 1997.

Scholastic Writer's Desk Reference. N.Y.: Scholastic, 2000.

Shertzer, Margaret. Elements of Grammar, The. N.Y.: MacMillian Publishing, 1986.

Strumpf, Michael and Douglas, Auriel, The Grammar Bible. N.Y.: Henry Holt and Company, LLC, 2004

Strunk, William and White, E. B. Elements of Style, The. N.Y.: MacMillan Publishing, 1979.

Swain, Dwight V. Creating Characters. Cincinnati, Ohio: Writer's Digest Books, 1990.

Swain, Dwight V. Techniques of the Selling Writer. University of Oklahoma Press, 1973.

Wallraff, Barbara. Word Court. Orlando, Florida: Harcourt, Inc., 2001.

Wallraff, Barbara. Your Own Words. N.Y.: Counterpoint, 2004.

INDEX

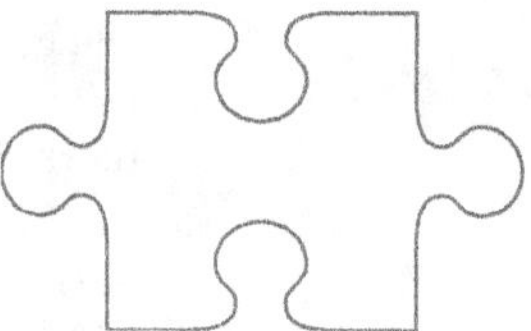

ABOUT THE AUTHORS

Renée Miller

Growing up in Tweed, Ontario—the summer home of Elvis's ghost—Renée Miller learned early that in a small town, only dreams escape the neighbors' inquest. So, she dreamed, tasted adventure through books, and created wonderful hidden worlds in her childhood stories. One day, she discovered a little book titled "IT" by Stephen King and writing became her passion.

Before losing whatever little common sense she had left, Renée worked as a bartender, waitress, convenience store clerk, gas station attendant, office administrator, lumber yard inventory control something-or-other, coffee-slugging drive-thru grunt, and day-care provider.

When the excitement of that daily grind proved too much, she opted out of one asylum and jumped into another: she became a professional writer. Renee now freelances to pay the bills and has published short fiction and hundreds of articles including, but not limited to, how to install vinyl tile and the seven taxonomies of the kingdom of roses.

Still residing in Tweed, she lives the glamorous life of a Canadian housewife and underpaid scribe with her three children and a man who has stopped pretending to know what's going on.

Carlos J Cortes

Born in Madrid, Spain, Carlos J Cortes grew up on the streets. Over the years he's worked as an altar boy, musician, waiter, lightning rod installer, site engineer, salesman, dishwasher, night porter, and sundry other high-level executive jobs.

Eventually, he settled down as a design engineer specialized in high-level lighting and remote sourcing. But the fun didn't stop there. His hearing is impaired from being near a bomb at too close quarters; he spent a stretch in an African jail, crossed the Israeli-Egyptian border inside the trunk of a car, and in lean times drove a taxi in Rio de Janeiro. As a consultant on civil and military installations, he has traveled the five continents and written seven texts on lighting, light physics and fiber optics systems.

At present, as Chief Technical Officer, he leads the R&D division of a Norwegian group of hi-tech companies, and lives in Barcelona, Spain.

A competition bridge player, Carlos has co-authored three books on different aspects of the game. His published fiction includes "Perfect Circle," now in its second printing, "The Prisoner," nominated in 2010 for the Philip K. Dick award—both with Random House—and "Ménage à 20," with Renée Miller and a bunch of talented mongrel writers.

His favorite book is Don Quixote by Miguel de Cervantes, which taught him that a life without dreams is only existence.

CARLOS J CORTÉS & RENÉE MILLER